COOKIES

COOKIES

Over 600 Great Recipes

Zak
BOOKS

This 2008 edition published by Zak Books,
an imprint of McRae Books.

© 2008 McRae Books Srl

ISBN 978-88-6098-075-5
This book was conceived, edited and designed by McRae Books Srl
Via del Salviatino 1 - 50016 Fiesole (Florence), Italy
info@mcraebooks.com
www.mcraebooks.com

Publishers: Anne McRae, Marco Nardi
Project Director: Anne McRae
Art Director: Marco Nardi
Texts: McRae Books archive
Photography: Marco Lanza, Walter Mericchi, Cristina Canepari, Keeho Casati,
Gil Gallo, Sandra Preussinger
Home Economist: Benedetto Rillo
Prepress: Filippo delle Monache

Printed in Thailand (KNP) supervised by Kyodo Printing Co. (S) Pte Ltd

CONTENTS

Introduction 11

Butter Cookies 12

Sugar Cookies 44

Chocolate Cookies 60

Coffee & Cream Cookies 94

Nut & Spice Cookies 106

Fresh Fruit Cookies 146

Dried Fruit Cookies 162

Cereal & Seed Cookies 192

Bars & Brownies 212

Meringues & Macaroons 244

No Bake Cookies 272

Tea Cakes, Tartlets, & Muffins 292

Fritters 338

Party Cookies 366

Basic Recipes 412

Index 418

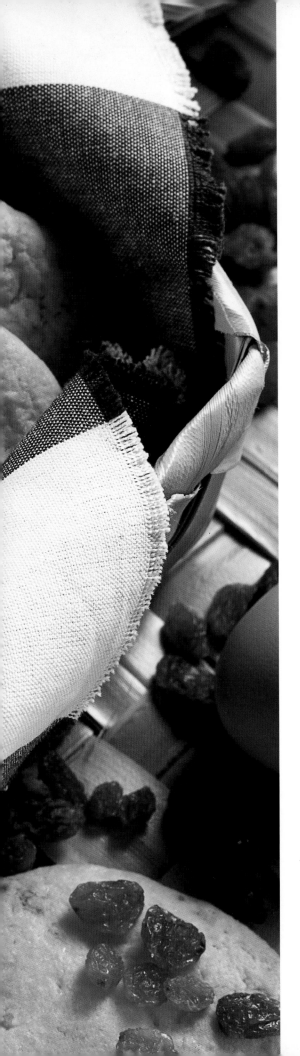

INTRODUCTION

E asy to prepare and delicious to eat, homemade cookies are one of life's simple pleasures. The word itself is a hold-all term that covers a huge range of sweet, bite-sized, baked goods—from crisp wafers, crumbly meringues and macaroons, and light-as-air madeleines, to buttery shortbread, chewy chocolate chip super-cookies, and rich gooey bars and brownies. In this book we have included recipes for all these different types of cookies, plus we have added two extra chapters—one featuring a host of cupcakes, tartlets, and muffins, and another which is packed full with recipes for mouth-watering fritters!

But the pleasure in cookies is not all in the eating; making cookies is a satisfying pastime that the whole family can enjoy. Children can learn baking basics with ease, since most cookie recipes are not complicated. Our recipes are all graded for difficulty at three levels: 1 (easy); 2 (fairly easy); and 3 (complicated). Over 90 percent of our recipes fall into the first two categories. Here you will find more than 600 great recipes, carefully selected from baking traditions all over the world—Enjoy!

BUTTER COOKIES

Rich and creamy, sweet and nourishing, butter cookies are perfect for cold winter days. Serve them with a steaming cup of freshly brewed tea or coffee, or a glass of milk. Shortbread—of Scottish origin—is the classic butter cookie and we have included a good selection of shortbread recipes in this chapter. For special occasions, try the mouth-watering Butter cookies with chocolate (see page 20), the Passionfruit butter diamonds (see page 24), or the Strawberry pinwheels (see page 32). If you want to taste a classic shortbread, bake the Vanilla shortbread (see page 31); if you are looking for more exotic flavors, prepare the Provence shortbread (see page 40) or the Sicilian butter crisps (see page 43).

Buttercream kisses (see page 14)

Butter Cookies

MARZIPAN CUTOUT COOKIES

- 2²/₃ cups (400 g) all-purpose (plain) flour
- ²/₃ cup (100 g) cornstarch (cornflour)
- ¹/₄ teaspoon salt
- ³/₄ cup (150 g) sugar
- 1 teaspoon vanilla extract (essence)
- 3 oz (90 g) marzipan, cut up and softened
- 1 cup (250 g) cold butter, cut up
- 1 large egg, lightly beaten + 1 large egg yolk, mixed with ¹/₂ cup (125 ml) water

Mix the flour, cornstarch, and salt in a bowl. Stir in the sugar and vanilla. • Dot the butter and marzipan evenly over the dry ingredients. Use a pastry blender to cut them in until the mixture resembles coarse crumbs. • Make a well in the center and add the beaten egg. Stir until combined then knead briefly on a lightly floured surface into a smooth dough. • Wrap in plastic wrap (cling film) and refrigerate for 30 minutes. • Preheat the oven to 350°F (180°C/gas 4). • Butter three cookie sheets. • Roll out the dough on a lightly floured surface to ¹/₈ inch (3 mm) thick. Use small cookie cutters to stamp out different shapes. • Gather the dough scraps, re-roll, and continue cutting out cookies until all the dough is used. • Arrange on the prepared cookie sheets, spacing 1 inch (2.5 cm) apart. • Brush with the egg yolk glaze. • Bake for 10–15 minutes, or until golden brown. • Cool on the cookie sheets for 5 minutes. Transfer to racks to cool.

Makes: about 70 cookies • Prep: 30 min + 30 min to chill
Cooking: 10–15 min • Level : 1

VANILLA KNOTS

Mix the flour, baking powder, allspice, and salt in a large bowl. • Beat the butter and sugar in a large bowl with an electric mixer on medium speed until creamy. • Add the vanilla, egg, and egg yolk, beating until just blended. • Stir in the milk and lemon zest. • Mix in the dry ingredients to form a smooth dough. Press the dough into a disk, wrap in plastic wrap (cling film), and refrigerate for 30 minutes. • Preheat the oven to 350°F (180°C/gas 4). • Butter two cookie sheets. • Roll out the dough on a lightly floured surface to ¹/₈ inch (3 mm) thick. Cut into 12 x ¹/₂-inch (30 x 1-cm) long strips. • Carefully tie the dough strips into knots. • Place the cookies ¹/₂ inch (1 cm) apart on the prepared cookie sheets. • Bake for 15–20 minutes, or until lightly browned. • Transfer to racks and let cool completely. • Dust with the confectioners' sugar.

Makes: about 20 cookies • Prep: 40 min + 30 min to chill
Cooking: 15–20 min • Level: 2

- 2 cups (300 g) all-purpose (plain) flour
- 1 teaspoon baking powder
- ¹/₄ teaspoon ground allspice
- ¹/₄ teaspoon salt
- ¹/₂ cup (125 g) butter, softened
- ¹/₃ cup (70 g) sugar
- ¹/₂ teaspoon vanilla extract (essence)
- 1 large egg + 1 large egg yolk
- ¹/₄ cup (60 ml) milk
- finely grated zest of ¹/₂ lemon
- 1 tablespoon confectioners' (icing) sugar, to dust

VANILLA BUTTERCREAM KISSES

- 1²/₃ cups (250 g) all-purpose (plain) flour
- ¹/₄ teaspoon salt
- ³/₄ cup (180 g) butter, softened
- 1 cup (200 g) sugar
- 2 tablespoons milk
- 1 teaspoon vanilla extract (essence)
- 2 large egg yolks, lightly beaten

Mix the flour and salt in a medium bowl. • Beat the butter and sugar in a large bowl with an electric mixer on medium speed until creamy. • Add the milk, vanilla, and egg yolks, beating until just blended. • Mix in the dry ingredients to form a smooth dough. • Press the dough into a disk, wrap in plastic wrap (cling film), and refrigerate for 30 minutes. • Preheat the oven to 375°F (190°C/gas 5). • Butter three cookie sheets. • Roll out the dough on a lightly floured surface to ¹/₈ inch (3 mm) thick. • Use a 2¹/₂-inch (6-cm) cookie cutter to cut out the cookies. Cut out the centers from half the cookies using a ¹/₂-inch (1-cm) cutter.

Gather the dough scraps, re-roll, and continue cutting out cookies until all the dough is used. • Transfer the cookies to the cookie sheets, placing them ¹/₂ inch (1 cm) apart. • Bake until lightly browned, 8–10 minutes. • Transfer to racks and let cool completely. • Filling: Beat the butter in a medium bowl until creamy. • Beat in the confectioners' sugar and milk. • Divide the filling among three small bowls and add a different color of food coloring to each one. • Spread the fillings over the whole cookies and place a ring cookie on top.

Makes: about 20 cookies • Prep: 45 min + 30 min to chill
Cooking: 35–40 min • Level: 2

Filling
- ¹/₄ cup (60 g) butter, softened
- 1²/₃ cups (250 g) confectioners' (icing) sugar
- 2 tablespoons milk
- 3 drops each red, green, and yellow food coloring

Butter Cookies

MINT FROSTED BUTTER COOKIES

- 1²/₃ cups (250 g) all-purpose (plain) flour
- ²/₃ cup (100 g) confectioners' (icing) sugar
- 1 tablespoon unsweetened cocoa powder
- 1 teaspoon baking powder
- ¹/₈ teaspoon salt
- ²/₃ cup (150 g) butter, softened
- 1 large egg
- 1 tablespoon vanilla sugar (see page 414)

Frosting
- 1²/₃ cups (250 g) confectioners' (icing) sugar
- 3 tablespoons light corn (golden) syrup
- 1 tablespoon freshly squeezed lemon juice
- ¹/₂ teaspoon peppermint extract (essence)
- 2–3 drops green food coloring
- 2 oz (60 g) semisweet (dark) chocolate, chopped

Mix the flour, confectioners' sugar, cocoa, baking powder, and salt in a large bowl. • Mix in the butter, egg, and vanilla sugar to form a smooth dough. • Divide the dough in half. • Press the dough into disks, wrap in plastic wrap (cling film), and refrigerate for 30 minutes. • Preheat the oven to 350°F (180°C/gas 4). • Butter four cookie sheets. • Roll out the dough on a lightly floured surface to ¹/₈ inch (3 mm) thick. • Use a 1¹/₂-inch (4-cm) cookie cutter to cut out the cookies. Gather the dough scraps, re-roll, and continue cutting out cookies until all the dough is used. • Use a spatula to transfer the cookies to the prepared cookie sheets, placing them 1 inch (2.5 cm) apart. • Bake until the edges are firm and the bottoms are lightly browned, 10–15 minutes. • Transfer —on the parchment paper—to racks and let cool completely. • Frosting: Mix the confectioners' sugar, corn syrup, lemon juice, peppermint extract, and green food coloring in a medium bowl until it forms a smooth paste. • Roll the mint paste out on a surface lightly dusted with confectioners' sugar to ¹/₈ inch (3 mm) thick. • Use 1¹/₂-inch (4-cm) petit four cutters to cut out green shapes. • Melt the chocolate in a double boiler over barely simmering water. • Spoon the melted chocolate into a small freezer bag and cut off a tiny corner. • Pipe chocolate dots on top of the cookies and top with the mint shapes.

Makes: about 60 cookies • Prep: 1 hr + 30 min to set
Cooking: 10–15 min • Level: 3

LEMON CORNMEAL COOKIES

Preheat the oven to 375°F (190°C/gas 5). • Butter two cookie sheets. • Place the cornmeal, flour, confectioners' sugar, baking powder, and salt in a mound on a work surface and make a well in the center. • Add the egg and egg yolk, butter, lard, and lemon zest. • Use your hands to knead the mixture into a smooth dough. • Roll out the dough on a lightly floured surface to ¹/₈ inch (3 mm) thick. • Use a 2-inch (5-cm) fluted cookie cutter to cut out the cookies. Gather the dough scraps, re-roll, and continue cutting out cookies until all the dough is used. • Use a spatula to transfer the cookies to the prepared cookie sheets. • Bake until just golden, 12–15 minutes. • Transfer to racks and let cool completely.

Makes: about 25 cookies • Prep: 40 min • Cooking: 12–15 min
• Level: 2

- 2 cups (300 g) finely ground yellow cornmeal
- 1 cup (150 g) all-purpose (plain) flour
- 1 cup (150 g) confectioners' (icing) sugar
- 1 teaspoon baking powder
- ¹/₈ teaspoon salt
- 1 large egg + 1 egg yolk
- ²/₃ cup (150 g) butter, cut up
- ¹/₄ cup (60 g) lard or vegetable shortening
- finely grated zest of 1 lemon

PEANUT SHORTBREAD

Preheat the oven to 350°F (180°C/gas 4). • Line a 9-inch (23-cm) round cake pan with parchment paper. • Shortbread Base: Mix the flour and salt in a medium bowl. • Beat the butter and sugar in a large bowl with an electric mixer on medium speed until creamy. • Mix in the dry ingredients. • Firmly press the dough into the prepared pan to form a smooth even layer, pressing back the edges to make them thick. • Peanut Topping: With mixer on medium speed, beat the butter and sugar in a medium bowl until creamy. • Mix in the ground peanuts and flour. • Spread the topping over the shortbread base and sprinkle with the chopped peanuts. • Press the peanuts in a little and score the round into 16 wedges. • Bake until pale gold, 25–30 minutes. • Let cool before cutting along the scored lines.

Makes: 16 cookies • Prep: 30 min • Cooking: 25–30 min
Level: 1

Shortbread Base
- 2¹/₃ cups (350 g) all-purpose (plain) flour
- ¹/₄ teaspoon salt
- 1 cup (250 g) butter, softened
- ¹/₂ cup (100 g) sugar

Peanut Topping
- ¹/₃ cup (90 g) butter, softened
- ¹/₃ cup (70 g) sugar
- 1 cup (150 g) finely ground peanuts
- ¹/₂ cup (75 g) all-purpose (plain) flour
- 3 tablespoons coarsely chopped peanuts

Butter Cookies

GINGER SHORTBREAD

- 2½ cups (375 g) all-purpose (plain) flour
- ½ teaspoon baking powder
- ¼ teaspoon salt
- 1 cup (250 g) butter, softened
- ⅔ cup (140 g) + 2 tablespoons sugar
- 2 large egg yolks
- 1 tablespoon light corn (golden) syrup
- 1 tablespoon brandy
- ½ cup (50 g) finely chopped crystallized ginger

Preheat the oven to 325°F (170°C/gas 3). • Butter an 11 x 7-inch (28 x 18-cm) baking pan. • Mix the flour, baking powder, and salt in a medium bowl. • Beat the butter and ⅔ cup (140 g) of sugar in a large bowl with an electric mixer on medium speed until creamy. • Add the egg yolks, beating until just blended. • Beat in the corn syrup and brandy. • Mix in the dry ingredients to form a stiff dough. • Divide the dough in half. Firmly press one half into the prepared pan to form a smooth, even layer. Sprinkle with the ginger. • Roll out the remaining dough on a lightly floured surface into an 11 x 7-inch (28 x 18-cm) rectangle. Place the dough on top of the ginger. • Sprinkle with the remaining sugar. • Bake for 35–40 minutes, or until pale gold. • Cool completely before cutting into squares.

Makes: about 20 cookies • Prep: 30 min • Cooking: 35–40 min • Level: 1

LEMON BUTTER COOKIES

Preheat the oven to 350°F (180°C/gas 4). • Butter two cookie sheets. • Mix the flour and salt in a large bowl. Stir in the brown sugar. • Use a pastry blender to cut in the butter until the mixture resembles fine crumbs. • Turn out onto a lightly floured surface, add the lemon zest and extract, and knead into a smooth dough. • Roll out the dough into ¼-inch (5-mm) thick rectangle. Use a sharp knife to cut the dough into three ¾ x 1-inch (2 x 2.5-cm) bars. • Transfer the bars to the prepared cookie sheets, spacing them ½ inch (1 cm) apart. • Prick all over with a fork. • Bake for 15–20 minutes, or until golden. • Cool the shortbread completely on the cookie sheets.

Makes: about 25–30 cookies • Prep: 30 min • Cooking: 15–20 min • Level: 1

- 1¼ cups (180 g) all-purpose (plain) flour
- ⅛ teaspoon salt
- ¼ cup (50 g) firmly packed light brown sugar
- ½ cup (125 g) cold butter, cut up
- 2 teaspoons finely grated lemon zest
- ½ teaspoon lemon extract (essence)

Ginger shortbread

Citrus shortbread

CITRUS SHORTBREAD

- 1 cup (150 g) all-purpose (plain) flour
- 1 tablespoon semolina flour
- ⅛ teaspoon salt
- ½ cup (125 g) butter, softened
- ¼ cup (50 g) granulated sugar
- 1 teaspoon finely grated lemon zest
- 1 teaspoon finely grated orange zest
- ¼ cup (50 g) superfine (caster) sugar, to dust

Preheat the oven to 325°F (170°C/gas 3). • Butter an 8-inch (20-cm) springform pan. • Mix both flours and salt in a medium bowl. • Beat the butter and granulated sugar in a large bowl with an electric mixer on medium speed until creamy. • Mix in the dry ingredients and lemon and orange zests. • Firmly press the mixture into the prepared pan, pinching the edges to make a decorative pattern. Use a sharp knife to score the shortbread into 16 wedges. • Bake for 35–40 minutes, or until firm to the touch. • Dust with the superfine sugar. Use a sharp knife to cut into 16 wedges along the scored lines. • Loosen and remove the pan sides and bottom. Transfer to racks and let cool completely.

Makes: 16 cookies • Prep: 20 min • Cooking: 35–40 min Level: 1

RICH BUTTER COOKIES

Preheat the oven to 375°F (190°C/gas 5). • Butter two cookie sheets. • Mix both flours and the salt in a medium bowl. • Beat the butter and ¼ cup (50 g) of sugar in a large bowl with an electric mixer on medium speed until creamy. • Mix in the dry ingredients to form a soft dough. • Turn the dough out onto a lightly floured surface and knead until smooth. • Roll out to ¼ inch (5 mm) thick. • Use a 2-inch (5-cm) cookie cutter to cut out the cookies. Gather the dough scraps, re-roll, and continue cutting out cookies until all the dough is used. Transfer the cookies to the prepared cookie sheets, placing them 1 inch (2.5 cm) apart. • Bake for 15–20 minutes, or until just golden. • Sprinkle with the remaining sugar. • Cool the cookies completely on the sheets.

Makes: about 24 cookies • Prep: 40 min • Cooking: 12–15 min • Level: 1

- 1 cup (150 g) all-purpose (plain) flour
- ⅓ cup (50 g) semolina flour
- ⅛ teaspoon salt
- ½ cup (125 g) butter, softened
- ⅓ cup (70 g) sugar

Butter Cookies

BUTTER COOKIES WITH CHOCOLATE

- 2²/₃ cups (400 g) all-purpose (plain) flour
- ⅛ teaspoon salt
- 1¼ cups (250 g) sugar
- ¾ cup (180 g) butter, softened
- 1 large egg + 2 large egg yolks
- 3 oz (90 g) semisweet (dark) chocolate, coarsely grated

Mix the flour and salt in a large bowl. • Use a wooden spoon to mix in the sugar, butter, egg, egg yolks, and chocolate to form a smooth dough. Press the dough into a disk, wrap in plastic wrap (cling film), and refrigerate for 30 minutes. • Preheat the oven to 350°F (180°C/gas 4). • Butter two cookie sheets. • Roll out the dough on a lightly floured surface to ¼-inch (5-mm) thick. • Use a 2-inch (5-cm) cookie cutter to cut out the cookies. Gather the dough scraps, re-roll, and continue cutting out cookies until all the dough is used. • Use a spatula to transfer the cookies to the prepared cookie sheets, placing them 1 inch (2.5 cm) apart. • Bake for 10–15 minutes, or until just golden. • Transfer the cookies to racks to cool.

Makes: about 30 cookies • Prep: 40 min + 30 min to chill Cooking: 10–15 min Level: 1

BUTTER WREATHS

Preheat the oven to 375°F (190°C/gas 5). • Set out two cookie sheets. • Mix the flour, baking powder, and salt in a medium bowl. • Beat the butter and sugar in a large bowl with an electric mixer on medium speed until creamy. • Add the vanilla and egg, beating until just blended. • Mix in the dry ingredients. • Fit a pastry bag with a ¾-inch (2-cm) plain tip. Fill the pastry bag, twist the opening tightly closed, and squeeze out 1½-inch (4-cm) wreaths, spacing 1 inch (2.5 cm) apart on the prepared cookie sheets. • Press the sugar strands and balls in a decorative manner into the tops of the cookies. • Bake for 8–10 minutes, or until the edges are just golden. • Transfer to racks to cool.

Makes: about 35 cookies • Prep: 25 min • Cooking: 8–10 min • Level: 1

- 1¼ cups (180 g) all-purpose (plain) flour
- ½ teaspoon baking powder
- ⅛ teaspoon salt
- ½ cup (125 g) butter, softened
- ¾ cup (150 g) sugar
- ½ teaspoon vanilla extract (essence)
- 1 large egg
- silver and colored balls, to decorate
- 2 tablespoons sugar strands, to decorate

CHERRY SHORTBREAD

- 2½ cups (375 g) all-purpose (plain) flour
- ½ teaspoon baking powder
- ¼ teaspoon salt
- 1 cup (250 g) butter, softened
- ⅔ cup (140 g) sugar + 2 extra tablespoons, to sprinkle
- 2 large egg yolks
- 1 tablespoon light corn (golden) syrup
- 1 tablespoon dark rum
- ½ cup (50 g) finely chopped candied cherries

Preheat the oven to 325°F (170°C/gas 3). • Butter an 11 x 7-inch (28 x 18-cm) baking pan. • Mix the flour, baking powder, and salt in a bowl. • Beat the butter and sugar with an electric mixer on medium speed until creamy. • Add the egg yolks, beating until just blended. • Beat in the corn syrup and rum. • Mix in the dry ingredients to form a stiff dough. • Divide the dough in half. Press one half into the pan. Sprinkle with the cherries. • Roll out the remaining dough to fit the pan. Place on top of the cherries. Sprinkle with the remaining sugar. • Bake until pale gold, 35–40 minutes. • Let cool before cutting into squares.

Makes: about 25 cookies • Prep: 30 min • Cooking: 30–35 min • Level: 1

CHERRY-TOPPED SHORTBREAD

Preheat the oven to 325°F (170°C/gas 3). • Set out twelve mini paper liners on a baking sheet. • Mix the flour and salt in a medium bowl. • Beat the butter, sugar, and vanilla in a large bowl with an electric mixer on medium speed until creamy. • Mix in the dry ingredients and milk. • Fit a pastry bag with a ½-inch (1-cm) star tip. Fill the pastry bag, twist the opening tightly closed, and squeeze rosettes into the paper liners. Press a piece of cherry into the top of each cookie. • Bake until firm to the touch, 20–25 minutes. • Transfer the cookies still in the liners to racks to cool.

Makes: about 12 cookies • Prep: 25 min • Cooking: 20–25 min • Level: 1

- 1¼ cups (180 g) all-purpose (plain) flour
- ⅛ teaspoon salt
- ¾ cup (180 g) butter, softened
- ¼ cup (50 g) sugar
- ½ teaspoons vanilla extract (essence)
- 1 tablespoon milk
- 2 tablespoons finely chopped candied cherries

Butter Cookies

WALNUT SHORTBREAD

- 2 cups (300 g) all-purpose (plain) flour
- ¼ teaspoon salt
- 1 cup (250 g) butter, softened
- 1 cup (200 g) firmly packed dark brown sugar
- 1 large egg yolk
- ½ cup (50 g) candied cherries, cut in half
- ½ cup (50 g) finely chopped walnuts

Mix the flour and salt in a medium bowl. • Beat the butter and brown sugar in a large bowl with an electric mixer on medium speed until creamy. • Add the egg yolk, beating until just blended. • Mix in the dry ingredients, cherries, and walnuts to form a smooth dough. • Divide the dough in half. Form into two 4-inch (10-cm) logs, wrap in plastic wrap (cling film), and refrigerate for 30 minutes. • Preheat the oven to 375°F (190°C/gas 5). • Butter two cookie sheets. • Slice the dough ¼ inch (5 mm) thick and place 1 inch (2.5 cm) apart on the prepared cookie sheets. • Bake for 10–12 minutes, or until just golden at the edges. • Transfer to racks to cool.

Makes: about 30 cookies • Prep: 25 min + 30 min to chill
Cooking: 10–12 min • Level: 1

CHOCOLATE CHIP WEDGES

Preheat the oven to 325°F (170°C/gas 3). • Butter two 9-inch (23-cm) springform pans. • Mix the flour, confectioners' sugar, cornstarch, and salt in a large bowl. • Use a pastry blender to cut in the butter until the mixture resembles coarse crumbs. • Stir in the chocolate chips. • Firmly press the mixture evenly into the prepared pans to form smooth, even layers. • Bake for 15–20 minutes, or until just golden. • Cool for 5 minutes in the pan. • Loosen and remove the springform sides. Let cool completely. • Cut each round into sixteen wedges.

Makes: 32 cookies • Prep: 20 min • Cooking: 15–20 min
Level: 1

- 1¾ cups (275 g) all-purpose (plain) flour
- 1/2 cup (75 g) confectioners' (icing) sugar
- 2 tablespoons cornstarch (cornflour)
- ¼ teaspoon salt
- 1 cup (250 g) butter, cut up
- 2 cups (260 g) semisweet (dark) chocolate chips

Walnut shortbread

Sugar shortbread

SUGAR SHORTBREAD

- 1½ cups (225 g) all-purpose (plain) flour
- ⅛ teaspoon salt
- ½ cup (125 g) butter, softened
- ¼ cup (50 g) granulated sugar
- ¼ cup (50 g) superfine (caster) sugar, to dust

Mix the flour and salt in a medium bowl. • Beat the butter and granulated sugar in a large bowl with an electric mixer on medium speed until creamy. • Mix in the dry ingredients to form a smooth dough. • Press the dough into a disk, wrap in plastic wrap (cling film), and refrigerate for 30 minutes. • Preheat the oven to 300°F (150°C/gas 2). • Butter a cookie sheet. • Roll out the dough on a lightly floured surface to ¼-inch (5-mm) thick. • Use a 3-inch (8-cm) fluted cookie cutter to cut out the cookies. Gather the dough scraps, re-roll, and continue cutting out cookies until all the dough is used. • Use a spatula to transfer the cookies to the prepared cookie sheet, placing them 1 inch (2.5 cm) apart. • Bake for 25–35 minutes, or until just golden at the edges. • Transfer to racks to cool and dust with the superfine sugar.

Makes: about 15 cookies • Prep: 40 min + 30 min to chill
Cooking: 25–30 min • Level: 1

CRISP BUTTER COOKIES

Beat the egg yolk and milk in a small bowl until frothy. • Stir together the flour, sugar, butter, and salt in a medium bowl. • Use a wooden spoon to stir in the beaten egg mixture until well blended. Press the dough into a disk, wrap in plastic wrap (cling film), and refrigerate for 30 minutes. • Preheat the oven to 400°F (200°C/gas 6). • Butter a cookie sheet. • Roll out the dough on a lightly floured surface to ⅛-inch (3-mm) thick. • Use a 2-inch (5-cm) cookie cutter to cut out the cookies. Gather the dough scraps, re-roll, and continue cutting out cookies until all the dough is used. • Use a spatula to transfer the cookies to the prepared cookie sheet, placing them 1 inch (2.5 cm) apart. • Bake for 5–8 minutes, or until lightly browned. • Cool on the sheet until the cookies firm slightly. • Transfer to a rack and let cool completely.

Makes: about 12–16 cookies • Prep: 40 min + 30 min to chill
Cooking: 5–8 min • Level: 1

- 1 large egg yolk
- 2 tablespoons milk
- 1¼ cups (180 g) all-purpose (plain) flour
- ⅓ cup (70 g) sugar
- 2 tablespoons butter, melted
- ⅛ teaspoon salt

Butter Cookies

PASSIONFRUIT BUTTER DIAMONDS

Butter Cookie Base
- 2¼ cups (330 g) all-purpose (plain) flour
- 2 tablespoons rice flour
- ½ teaspoon salt
- 1 cup (250 g) butter, softened
- ⅓ cup (70 g) sugar

Passionfruit Drizzle
- 1 cup (150 g) confectioners' (icing) sugar
- 2 tablespoons passionfruit pulp
- 1 tablespoon butter, softened
- 1 tablespoon cold water
- 2 oz (60 g) white chocolate, coarsely chopped

Butter Cookie Base: Mix both flours and the salt in a medium bowl. • Beat the butter and sugar in a large bowl with an electric mixer on medium speed until creamy. • Mix in the dry ingredients to form a soft dough. • Turn the dough out onto a lightly floured surface and knead until smooth. • Press into a disk, wrap in plastic wrap (cling film), and refrigerate for 30 minutes. • Preheat the oven to 300°F (150°C/gas 2). • Line two cookie sheets with parchment paper. • Roll out the dough on a lightly floured surface to ¼ inch (5 mm) thick. • Cut into 1½-inch (4-cm) diamonds. • Transfer to the prepared cookie sheets, placing them 1 inch (2.5 cm) apart. • Bake until just golden at the edges, 12–15 minutes. • Transfer to racks to cool. Passionfruit Drizzle: Mix the confectioners' sugar, passionfruit pulp, butter, and water in a double boiler over barely simmering water until smooth. • Drizzle the tops of the cookies with the icing. • Let stand for 30 minutes until set. • Melt the white chocolate in a double boiler over barely simmering water and drizzle over the cookies. Let stand for 30 minutes.

Makes: about 35 cookies • Prep: 40 min + 90 min to chill and set • Cooking: 12–15 min • Level: 2

COCONUT AND WALNUT SHORTBREAD

Preheat the oven to 325°F (170°C/gas 2). • Set out a 9-inch (23-cm) springform pan. • Process the walnuts and sugar in a food processor or blender until very finely ground. • Mix the flour, baking powder, and salt in a medium bowl. • Beat the butter and confectioners' sugar in a large bowl with an electric mixer on medium speed until creamy. • Mix in the dry ingredients and half the coconut to form a stiff dough. • Firmly press the dough into the pan to form a smooth, even layer. Sprinkle with the remaining coconut. Use a sharp knife to score the shortbread into 16 wedges. • Bake until golden brown, 25–30 minutes. • Cool in the pan for 15 minutes. • Use a sharp knife to cut into wedges along the scored lines. • Loosen and remove the pan sides and let cool completely.

Makes: 16 cookies • Prep: 25 min • Cooking: 25–30 min Level: 1

- ½ cup (75 g) walnuts
- 2 tablespoons sugar
- 1 cup (150 g) all-purpose (plain) flour
- ½ teaspoon baking powder
- ¼ teaspoon salt
- ⅓ cup (90 g) butter, softened
- 2 tablespoons confectioners' (icing) sugar
- ½ cup (60 g) shredded (desiccated) coconut

DUTCH SHORTBREAD

- 1⅔ cups (250 g) all-purpose (plain) flour
- 2 tablespoons unsweetened cocoa powder
- ½ teaspoon salt
- 1 cup (250 g) butter, softened
- 1 cup (150 g) confectioners' (icing) sugar

Mix the flour, cocoa, and salt in a medium bowl. • Beat the butter, confectioners' sugar, vanilla sugar, and vanilla in a large bowl until creamy. • Gradually beat in the dry ingredients. • Spread out a large sheet of plastic wrap (cling film) and turn the dough onto it. • Place a sheet of plastic wrap on top and roll out the dough to ⅔-inch (1.5-cm) thick. • Refrigerate for 2 hours. • Preheat the oven to 325°F (170°C/gas 3). • Butter two cookie sheets and line with

parchment paper. • Remove the dough from the refrigerator and peel off the top sheet of plastic wrap. • Use a 2-inch (5-cm) cookie cutter to cut out cookies. • Transfer to the prepared baking sheets, spacing ½ inch (1 cm) apart. • Bake for 10–15 minutes, or until firm to the touch. • Let cool completely. • Dust with the confectioners' sugar.

Makes: about 30 cookies • Prep: 40 min + 2 hr to chill Cooking: 15–20 min • Level: 2

- 1 teaspoon vanilla sugar (see page 414)
- ½ teaspoon vanilla extract (essence)
- 1 tablespoon confectioners' (icing) sugar, to dust

Scottish shortbread

SCOTTISH SHORTBREAD

- 1⅓ cups (200 g) all-purpose (plain) flour
- ⅛ teaspoon salt
- ½ cup (70 g) sugar
- ½ cup (125 g) butter, softened

Mix the flour and salt in a medium bowl. • Beat the butter and sugar in a large bowl with an electric mixer on medium speed until creamy. • Mix in the dry ingredients until well blended. • Press the dough into a disk, wrap in plastic wrap (cling film), and refrigerate for 30 minutes. • Preheat the oven to 350°F (180°C/gas 4). • Butter a cookie sheet. • Roll out the dough on a lightly floured surface to ⅛-inch (5-mm) thick. • Use a 2-inch (5-cm) cookie cutter to cut out the cookies. Gather the dough scraps, re-roll, and continue cutting out cookies until all the dough is used. • Use a skewer to prick each cookie with three rows of three dots. • Use a spatula to transfer the cookies to the prepared cookie sheets, placing them 1 inch (2.5 cm) apart. • Bake until pale golden, 12–15 minutes. • Transfer to racks to cool.

Makes: about 16 cookies • Prep: 30 min + 30 min to chill
Cooking: 12–15 min • Level: 1

ALMOND BUTTER WEDGES

Preheat the oven to 325°F (170°C/gas 3). • Butter a 9-inch (23-cm) round cake pan. • Mix the all-purpose and rice flours and salt in a medium bowl. Use a pastry blender to cut in the butter until the mixture resembles coarse crumbs. • Stir in the granulated sugar. • Mix in the candied peel and almonds. • Firmly press the dough into the prepared pan to form a smooth, even layer, using your thumb to make a raised, decorative edge. • Prick all over with a fork and sprinkle with the superfine sugar. Use a sharp knife to score the shortbread into 16 wedges. • Bake until pale gold, 35–40 minutes. • Cool completely before cutting along the scored lines.

Makes: 16 cookies • Prep: 30 min + 30 min to chill
Cooking: 35–40 min • Level: 1

- 1½ cups (225 g) all-purpose (plain) flour
- 2 tablespoons rice flour
- ⅛ teaspoon salt
- ¾ cup (180 g) butter, cut up
- ⅓ cup (70 g) granulated sugar
- 2 tablespoons finely chopped mixed candied peel
- 1 tablespoon coarsely chopped almonds
- 2 tablespoons superfine (caster) sugar, to sprinkle

BRANDY WEDGES

- ¾ cup (125 g) all-purpose (plain) flour
- ½ cup (75 g) rice flour
- ⅛ teaspoon salt
- ½ cup (125 g) butter, softened
- ¾ cup (150 g) sugar + 2 tablespoons extra, to sprinkle
- 1 tablespoon brandy

Preheat the oven to 350°F (180°C/gas 4). • Set out a 9-inch (23-cm) springform pan. • Mix both flours with the salt in a medium bowl. • Beat the butter and sugar in a large bowl with an electric mixer on medium speed until creamy. • Mix in the dry ingredients and brandy. • Press the mixture into the pan in an even layer. Prick all over with a fork. Sprinkle with the extra sugar. • Use a sharp knife to score the shortbread into 16 wedges. • Bake until pale gold, 20–25 minutes. • Use a sharp knife to cut into wedges. • Loosen and remove the pan sides and bottom. Transfer to racks to cool.

Makes: 16 cookies • Prep: 20 min • Cooking: 20–25 min
Level: 1

PINE NUT SHORTBREAD

Preheat the oven to 350°F (180°C/gas 4). • Butter and flour two cookie sheets. • Stir the pine nuts and granulated sugar in a small bowl. • Beat the butter and confectioners' sugar in a large bowl with an electric mixer on medium speed until creamy. • With mixer at low speed, gradually beat in the flour and salt. • Scoop out tablespoons of dough and shape into balls. • Place on the prepared cookie sheets, spacing them 1 inch (2.5 cm) apart. • Sprinkle with the pine nut mixture. • Bake until golden brown, 15–20 minutes. • Cool the cookies completely on the cookie sheets.

Makes: about 30 cookies • Prep: 20 min • Cooking: 15–20 min • Level: 1

- ¾ cup (75 g) finely chopped pine nuts
- 2 tablespoons granulated sugar
- 1 cup (250 g) butter, softened
- 1⅓ cups (200 g) confectioners' (icing) sugar
- 2⅔ cups (400 g) all-purpose (plain) flour
- ¼ teaspoon salt

Butter Cookies

HAZELNUT SHORTBREAD

VANILLA-LEMON SHORTBREAD

- ½ cup (100 g) raw sugar (Demerara or Barbados)
- 1⅔ cups (250 g) finely ground hazelnuts
- 1½ cups (225 g) all-purpose (plain) flour
- ¼ teaspoon salt
- ⅔ cup (150 g) butter, cut up
- 1 large egg yolk, lightly beaten

Process the raw sugar, hazelnuts, flour, and salt in a food processor until well blended. • Add the butter and process briefly until the mixture resembles fine crumbs. • Add the egg and process briefly to mix. • Gather the dough together and press into a disk. Wrap in plastic wrap (cling film) and refrigerate for 30 minutes. • Preheat the oven to 350°F (180°C/gas 4). • Line two cookie sheets with parchment paper. • Roll out the dough on a lightly floured surface to ⅛ inch (3 mm) thick. • Use a 2½-inch (6-cm) cookie cutter to cut out the cookies. Gather the dough scraps, re-roll, and continue cutting out cookies until all the dough is used. • Transfer the cookies to the prepared cookie sheets, spacing them 1 inch (2.5 cm) apart. • Bake until lightly browned, 12–15 minutes. • Transfer to racks to cool.

Makes: about 32 cookies • Prep: 30 min + 30 min to chill
Cooking: 12–15 min • Level: 1

Preheat the oven to 350°F (180°C/gas 4).
• Line a cookie sheet with parchment paper.
• Mix the flour and salt in a large bowl.
• Use a pastry blender to cut in the butter until the mixture resembles coarse crumbs.
• Mix in the sugar, egg yolk, vanilla, and grated lemon zest to form a smooth dough.
• Form the dough into 1½ x ½-inch (4 x 1-cm) logs and place 1 inch (2.5 cm) apart on the prepared cookie sheet, flattening them slightly. • Bake for 10–12 minutes, or until just golden. • Transfer to racks to cool. • Dust with the confectioners' sugar.

Makes: about 16 cookies • Prep: 25 min • Cooking: 10–12 min • Level: 1

- 1⅓ cups (200 g) all-purpose (plain) flour
- ⅛ teaspoon salt
- ⅔ cup (150 g) butter, cut up
- ⅓ cup (70 g) sugar
- 1 large egg yolk, lightly beaten
- ½ teaspoon vanilla extract (essence)
- finely grated zest of 1 lemon
- ⅓ cup (50 g) confectioners' (icing) sugar

Hazelnut shortbread

Gold dust butter cookies

GOLD DUST BUTTER COOKIES

- 2¼ cups (330 g) all-purpose (plain) flour
- ½ cup (75 g) unsweetened cocoa powder
- ¼ teaspoon salt
- 1 cup (250 g) butter, softened
- ¾ cup (125 g) confectioners' (icing) sugar
- ½ teaspoon vanilla extract (essence)
- 2 tablespoons 24-carat gold dust or metallic luster dust

Mix the flour, cocoa, and salt in a medium bowl. • Beat the butter, confectioners' sugar, and vanilla in a large bowl with an electric mixer on medium speed until creamy. • Mix in the dry ingredients to form a smooth dough. • Press the dough into a disk, wrap in plastic wrap (cling film), and refrigerate for 30 minutes. • Preheat the oven to 300°F (150°C/gas 2. • Set out a cookie sheet. • Lightly dust a work surface with confectioners' sugar and roll out the dough to ¼ inch (5 mm) thick. • Use a 3-inch (8-cm) cookie cutter to cut out the cookies. Gather the dough scraps, re-roll, and continue cutting out cookies until all the dough is used. • Use a spatula to transfer the cookies to the cookie sheet. • Dust the tops with the gold dust. • Bake until firm to the touch, 12–15 minutes. • Transfer to racks to cool.

Makes: about 15 cookies • Prep: 30 min + 30 min to chill
Cooking: 12–15 min • Level: 1

BUTTER RINGS

Stir the yeast, 1 tablespoon of sugar, and the water in a small bowl. Set aside for 10 minutes. • Mix the flour and salt in a large bowl. • Stir in the yeast mixture to make a smooth dough. • Cover the bowl with a clean cloth and let rise in a warm place for 1 hour, or until doubled in bulk. • Punch down the dough and let rise for 30 minutes more. • Preheat the oven to 350°F (180°C/gas 4). • Butter three cookie sheets. • Break off small pieces of dough and form into 2½-inch (6-cm) long ropes, about ⅛ inch (3 mm) in diameter. Bend into rings, pressing the ends together, and sprinkle with the remaining sugar. • Transfer to the prepared cookie sheets, placing 1 inch (2.5 cm) apart. • Cover with a kitchen towel and let rest for 15 minutes. • Bake until crisp and golden brown, 12–15 minutes. • Transfer to racks to cool.

Makes: about 36 cookies • Prep: 30 min + 1 hr 45 min to rise
Cooking: 12–15 min • Level: 2

- 1½ teaspoons active dry yeast
- 2 tablespoons sugar
- ¼ cup (60 ml) warm water
- 1⅔ cups (250 g) all-purpose (plain) flour
- ¼ teaspoon salt
- ⅓ cup (90 g) butter, softened

Vanilla shortbread

Vanilla shortbread

- 1²/₃ cups (250 g) all-purpose (plain) flour
- ³/₄ cup (125 g) cornstarch (cornflour)
- 1 teaspoon baking powder
- ½ cup (125 g) butter, cut up
- ¼ teaspoon salt
- ³/₄ cup (150 g) sugar
- 2 large eggs, lightly beaten
- 1 teaspoon vanilla extract (essence)

Mix the flour, cornstarch, baking powder, and salt in a large bowl. • Use a pastry blender to cut in the butter until the mixture resembles fine crumbs. • Mix in the sugar, eggs, and vanilla to form a smooth dough. • Wrap in plastic wrap (cling film) and refrigerate for 30 minutes. • Preheat the oven to 375°F (190°C/gas 5). • Butter three cookie sheets. • Roll out the dough on a lightly floured surface to ¼-inch (5-mm) thick. • Use a 2-inch (5-cm) cookie cutter to cut out the cookies. Gather the dough scraps, re-roll, and continue cutting out cookies until all the dough is used. • Use a spatula to transfer the cookies to the cookie sheets, placing them 1 inch (2.5 cm) apart. • Prick the cookies all over with a fork. • Bake for 10–15 minutes, or until just golden at the edges. • Transfer to racks and let cool completely.

Makes: about 40 cookies • Prep: 40 min + 30 min to chill
Cooking: 10–15 min • Level: 1

Butter esses

Mix the flour and salt in a large bowl. • Beat the butter and sugar in a large bowl with an electric mixer on medium speed until creamy. • Add the eggs and lemon zest, beating until just blended. • Mix in the dry ingredients and hazelnuts to form a smooth, not sticky, dough. • Refrigerate for 30 minutes. • Set out four cookie sheets. • Fit a pastry bag with a ½-inch (1-cm) round or star tip, twist the opening tightly closed, and squeeze out long strips of dough onto a sheet of parchment paper. • Cut into 3-inch (8-cm) lengths and press into S-shapes with your fingers . Use a spatula to transfer to the prepared cookie sheets, spacing 2 inches (5 cm) apart. • Refrigerate for 1 hour. • Preheat the oven to 375°F (190°C/gas 5). • Bake for 7–10 minutes, or until golden and the edges are firm. • Cool on the sheets for 2 minutes until slightly firm. Dip in the vanilla sugar while still warm. • Transfer to racks and let cool completely.

Makes: about 60 cookies • Prep: 40 min + 90 min to chill
Cooking: 7–10 min • Level: 2

- 2²/₃ cups (400 g) all-purpose (plain) flour
- ½ teaspoon salt
- 1 cup (250 g) butter, softened
- 1¼ cups (250 g) sugar
- 3 large eggs
- finely grated zest of ½ lemon
- 1¼ cups (125 g) finely ground hazelnuts or almonds
- 1 cup (200 g) vanilla sugar (see page 414)

Sweet butter cookies with syrup

Cookies
- ³/₄ cup (180 g) butter
- 1 cup (200 g) sugar
- 2 large egg yolks
- 1¼ cups (180 g) all-purpose (plain) flour
- ¼ teaspoon baking soda (bicarbonate of soda)

Syrup
- 1 cup (200 g) sugar
- 1 tablespoon water
- 1 vanilla bean
- 3 cloves

Cookies: Preheat the oven to 325°F (170°C/gas 3). • Line a cookie sheet with parchment paper. • Beat the butter and sugar in a large bowl with an electric mixer on high speed until creamy. • Add the egg yolks, one at a time, beating until just blended after each addition. • With mixer at low speed, gradually beat in the the flour and baking soda. • Roll to ¼-inch (5-mm) thick on parchment paper. Refrigerate for 15 minutes. • Use a pastry cutter to cut out 1-inch (2.5-cm) disks. Place on the prepared cookie sheet. • Bake until golden brown,

15–20 minutes. • Cool the cookies on the sheet. • Syrup: Bring the sugar, water, vanilla bean, and cloves to a boil. Simmer for 15 minutes. • Wash down the pan sides with a pastry brush dipped in cold water to prevent sugar crystals from forming. Cook, without stirring, until the mixture reaches 238°F (114°C) or the soft-ball stage. Set aside. • Serve the cookies in the warm syrup.

Makes: about 35 cookies • Prep: 45 min • Cooking: 15–20 min • Level: 2

Butter Cookies

STRAWBERRY PINWHEELS

- 2 cups (300 g) all-purpose (plain) flour
- 1/4 teaspoon salt
- 1/2 cup (75 g) finely ground almonds
- 1/2 cup (100 g) sugar
- 1/3 cup (90 g) butter, cut up
- 1 large egg, lightly beaten with 2 tablespoons cold water
- 1/4 cup (90 g) raspberry preserves (jam)

Mix the flour and salt in a large bowl. Stir in the almonds and sugar. • Use a pastry blender to cut in the butter until the mixture resembles fine crumbs. • Mix in the egg mixture to form a firm dough. • Turn the dough out onto a lightly floured surface and knead until smooth. • Transfer to a large sheet of parchment paper and roll into a 10 x 14-inch (25 x 35-cm) rectangle. Spread evenly with the preserves and tightly roll up the dough from the long side. • Wrap in plastic wrap (cling film) and refrigerate for at least 30 minutes. • Preheat the oven to 350°F (180°C/gas 4). • Line two cookie sheets with parchment paper. • Slice the dough 1/2 inch (1-cm) thick and place 1/2 inch (1-cm) apart on the prepared cookie sheets. • Bake for 12–15 minutes, or until just golden at the edges. • Transfer to racks to cool.

Makes: about 28 cookies • Prep: 30 min + 30 min to chill Cooking: 12–15 min • Level: 2

ORANGE BUTTER COOKIES

Beat the butter and sugar in a large bowl with an electric mixer on medium speed until creamy. • Add the egg yolk, beating until just blended. • Mix in the flour, salt, and orange juice until well blended. • Refrigerate for 1 hour. • Preheat the oven to 375°F (190°C/gas 5). • Butter two cookie sheets. • Fit a pastry bag with a 1-inch (2.5-cm) star tip. Fill the pastry bag, twist the opening tightly closed, and squeeze out four long strips on each sheet, spacing them at least 1 inch (2.5 cm) apart on the prepared cookie sheets. • Use a sharp knife to score each strip at 2½-inch (6-cm) intervals. • Bake for 8–10 minutes, or until just golden. • Cut up the cookies along the scored lines. • Cool on the sheet until the cookies firm slightly. • Transfer to racks to finish cooling.

Makes: about 36 cookies • Prep: 40 min + 1 hr to chill Cooking: 30 min • Level: 2

- 2/3 cup (150 g) butter, softened
- 1/2 cup (100 g) sugar
- 1 large egg yolk
- 1 2/3 cups (400 g) all-purpose (plain) flour
- 1/8 teaspoon salt
- 2 tablespoons freshly squeezed orange juice

CHOCOLATE AND VANILLA PIPED COOKIES

- 1 1/3 cups (200 g) all-purpose (plain) flour
- 1/3 cup (50 g) cornstarch (cornflour)
- 1 cup (250 g) butter, softened
- 2/3 cup (100 g) confectioners' (icing) sugar + extra, to dust
- 1 large egg
- 1/4 teaspoon vanilla extract (essence)
- 1/4 teaspoon lemon extract (essence)

Preheat the oven to 350°F (180°C/gas 4). • Butter two cookie sheets. • Mix the flour and cornstarch in a medium bowl. • Beat the butter and confectioners' sugar in a large bowl with an electric mixer on medium speed until creamy. • Add the egg, beating until just blended. Stir in the vanilla and lemon extracts. Continue beating until pale and fluffy. • Mix in the dry ingredients. • Divide the dough evenly between two bowls. • Mix the cocoa and oil in a small bowl. Stir the cocoa mixture into one bowl of dough. • Fit a pastry bag with a 1/4-inch

(5-mm) star tip. Fill the pastry bag with the plain batter, twist the opening tightly closed, and pipe out small rings, hearts, circles, and swirls spacing 1½ inches (4 cm) apart on the prepared cookie sheets. • Repeat with the chocolate batter. • Bake, one sheet at a time, for 10–15 minutes, or until the plain cookies are golden brown. • Cool the cookies on the cookie sheets for 2 minutes. • Transfer to racks to cool. • Dust some of the dark cookies with the confectioners' sugar.

Makes: about 30 cookies • Prep: 25 min • Cooking: 10–15 min • Level: 2

- 2 tablespoons unsweetened cocoa powder
- 1 teaspoon vegetable oil

Butter Cookies

GLAZED BUTTER ESSES

Cookies
- 1²/₃ cups (400 g) all-purpose (plain) flour
- 3 large egg yolks
- ½ cup (125 g) butter, softened
- ²/₃ cup (140 g) granulated sugar
- ⅛ teaspoon salt

Lemon Glaze
- 1 cup (150 g) confectioners' (icing) sugar
- 4–5 tablespoons freshly squeezed lemon juice
- 1½ teaspoons finely grated lemon zest

These S-shaped cookies are fun to serve at children's birthday parties.

Cookies: Use a wooden spoon to mix the flour, egg yolks, butter, sugar, and salt in a large bowl to form a smooth dough. • Press the dough into a disk, wrap in plastic wrap (cling film), and refrigerate for 30 minutes. • Preheat the oven to 350°F (180°C/gas 4). • Butter two cookie sheets. • Form the dough into 1-inch (2.5-cm) long logs and place 1 inch (2.5 cm) apart on the prepared cookie sheets. • Shape the logs into S-shapes. • Bake for 8–10 minutes, or until just golden. • Lemon Glaze: Put the confectioners' sugar in a medium bowl. Beat in 4 tablespoons of lemon juice and the zest until smooth, adding the additional tablespoon of lemon juice as needed to make a good spreading consistency. • Drizzle the glaze over the cookies.
Makes: about 25 cookies • Prep: 35 min + 30 min to chill Cooking: 8–10 min • Level: 1

ORANGE GLAZED COOKIES

You will need a cookie press to prepare these cookies. Choose the design plate you wish to use according to the occasion, spoon in the dough, and press it out directly onto the prepared cookie sheets. If you do not own a cookie press, roll the dough out on a floured surface and cut into squares or diamonds.

Butter Cookies: Preheat the oven to 375°F (190°C/gas 5). • Set out two cookie sheets. • Mix the flour and salt in a medium bowl. • Beat the butter and sugar in a large bowl with an electric mixer on medium speed until creamy. • Add the egg yolk, beating until just blended. • Beat in the sour cream and almond extract. • Mix in the dry ingredients to form a smooth dough. • Insert a design plate into a cookie press by sliding it into the head and locking in place. Press out the cookies, spacing about ½ inch (1 cm) apart on the cookie sheets. • Bake for 8–10 minutes, or until lightly browned. • Orange Glaze: Mix the confectioners' sugar and orange juice in a small bowl. • Warm the apricot preserves in a small saucepan over low heat until liquid. • Brush the cookies with the preserves, followed by the orange glaze. • Bake for 5 minutes more, or until the glaze begins to crystallize. • Cool on the sheets until the cookies firm slightly. • Transfer to racks to finish cooling.
Makes: about 25 cookies • Prep: 45 min • Cooking: 13–15 min • Level: 2

Butter Cookies
- 1 cup (150 g) all-purpose (plain) flour
- ⅛ teaspoon salt
- ⅓ cup (90 g) butter, softened
- ¼ cup (50 g) sugar
- 1 large egg yolk
- 2 tablespoons sour cream
- ¼ teaspoon almond extract (essence)

Orange Glaze
- 6 tablespoons confectioners' (icing) sugar
- 2 tablespoons freshly squeezed orange juice
- ¼ cup (90 g) apricot preserves (jam)

Butter Cookies

PRESSED VANILLA COOKIES

- 1 cup (250 g) butter, softened
- ½ cup (100 g) + 2 tablespoons sugar
- 1½ teaspoons vanilla extract (essence)
- 1 large egg
- 2 cups (300 g) all-purpose (plain) flour
- ¼ teaspoon salt

Preheat the oven to 375°F (190°C/gas 5). • Set out four cookie sheets. • Beat the butter and ½ cup (100 g) sugar in a large bowl with an electric mixer on medium speed until creamy. • Add the vanilla and egg, beating until just blended. • Mix in the flour and salt to form a soft dough. • Insert the chosen design plate into a cookie press by sliding it into the head and locking it in place. Press out the cookies, spacing 1 inch (2.5 cm) apart on the cookie sheets. • Sprinkle with the remaining sugar. • Bake for 5–8 minutes, or until just golden at the edges. • Transfer to racks and let cool completely.

Makes: about 48 cookies • Prep: 40 min • Cooking: 5–8 min Level: 2

BROWN SUGAR DROPS

Preheat the oven to 375°F (190°C/gas 5). • Butter three cookie sheets. • Mix the flour, baking soda, and salt in a medium bowl. • Beat the butter and brown and granulated sugars in a large bowl with an electric mixer on medium speed until creamy. • Add the egg and vanilla extract, beating until just blended. • Mix in the dry ingredients. • Drop teaspoons of the dough 2 inches (5 cm) apart onto the prepared cookie sheets. • Bake for 7–10 minutes, or until golden. • Transfer to racks to cool.

Makes: about 40 cookies • Prep: 20 min • Cooking: 7–10 min • Level: 1

- 1¼ cups (180 g) all-purpose (plain) flour
- ½ teaspoon baking soda (bicarbonate of soda)
- ⅛ teaspoon salt
- ½ cup (125 g) butter, softened
- 3 tablespoons firmly packed light brown sugar
- 3 tablespoons granulated sugar
- 1 large egg, lightly beaten
- ½ teaspoon vanilla extract (essence)

SPICY CHOCOLATE SHORTBREAD

- ½ cup (75 g) all-purpose (plain) flour
- ½ cup (75 g) cornstarch (cornflour)
- 2 tablespoons unsweetened cocoa powder
- ½ teaspoon ground cinnamon
- ⅛ teaspoon salt
- ½ cup (125 g) butter, softened
- ¼ cup (30 g) confectioners' (icing) sugar

Preheat the oven to 325°F (170°C/gas 3). • Butter two cookie sheets. • Mix the flour, cornstarch, cocoa, cinnamon, and salt in a medium bowl. • Beat the butter and confectioners' sugar in a large bowl with an electric mixer on medium speed until creamy. • With mixer at low speed, gradually add the dry ingredients. • Knead the mixture briefly on a lightly floured surface. • Form into an 11 x 1½-inch (28 x 4-cm) log and slice ½ inch (5 mm) thick. • Use a spatula to transfer the cookies to the prepared cookie sheets, placing them 1 inch apart. • Bake for 15–20 minutes, or until firm. • Transfer to racks to cool.

Makes: about 22 cookies • Prep: 20 min • Cooking: 15–20 min • Level: 1

GINGER AND BRANDY SHORTBREAD

Preheat the oven to 325°F (170°C/gas 3). • Butter an 11 x 7-inch (28 x 18-cm) baking pan. • Mix the flour, baking powder, and salt in a medium bowl. • Beat the butter and sugar in a large bowl with an electric mixer on medium speed until creamy. • Add the egg yolks, beating until just blended. • Beat in the corn syrup and brandy. • Mix in the dry ingredients to form a stiff dough. • Divide the dough in half. Firmly press one half into the pan in a smooth, even layer. Sprinkle with the ginger. • Roll out the remaining dough to fit the pan. Place on top of the ginger. • Sprinkle with the remaining sugar. • Bake for 35–40 minutes, or until pale gold. • Cool completely before cutting into bars.

Makes: about 20 cookies • Prep: 30 min • Cooking: 35–40 min • Level: 1

- 2½ cups (375 g) all-purpose (plain) flour
- ½ teaspoon baking powder
- ⅛ teaspoon salt
- 1 cup (250 g) butter, softened
- ⅔ cup sugar + 2 tablespoons extra, to sprinkle
- 2 large egg yolks
- 1 tablespoon light corn (golden) syrup
- 1 tablespoon brandy
- ½ cup (75 g) finely chopped crystallized ginger

Butter Cookies

SWEET SUMMER KISSES

- 3/4 cup (180 g) butter, softened
- 1/2 cup (75 g) confectioners' (icing) sugar
- 1 teaspoon vanilla extract (essence)
- 2 cups (300 g) all-purpose (plain) flour
- 1/4 teaspoon salt
- 1/2 cup (160 g) apricot preserves (jam)

Preheat the oven to 350°F (180°C/gas 4). • Butter two cookie sheets. • Beat the butter, confectioners' sugar, and vanilla in a large bowl with an electric mixer on medium speed until creamy. • Mix in the flour and salt. • Drop tablespoons of the dough 2 inches (5 cm) apart onto the prepared cookie sheets, flattening them slightly with a fork. • Bake for 15–20 minutes, or until just golden at the edges. • Transfer to racks to cool. • Warm the preserves in a small saucepan over low heat until liquid. • Stick the cookies together in pairs with the preserves.

Makes: about 18–20 cookies • Prep: 20 min • Cooking: 15–20 min • Level: 1

GLAZED RASPBERRY KISSES

Place the flour in a medium bowl. • Beat the butter and sugar in a large bowl until creamy. • Mix in the flour, almonds, and lemon zest and juice. • Wrap in plastic wrap (cling film) and refrigerate for 30 minutes. • Roll out half the dough to 1/8-inch (3-mm) thick. • Use a 1½-inch (4-cm) cookie cutter to cut out the cookies. • Place 1 inch (2.5 cm) apart on the sheets. • Use a 3/4-inch (2-cm) fluted cutter to cut the centers out of half the cookies. • Refrigerate for 30 minutes. • Preheat the oven to 375°F (190°C/gas 5). • Bake for 6–8 minutes, or until just golden and the edges are firm. Let cool. • Glaze: Mix the confectioners' sugar with enough lemon juice to make a smooth glaze. • Drizzle the cookies with cut-out centers with the glaze. • Set aside until the glaze has dried. • Stick the cookies together in pairs with the preserves.

Makes: about 16 cookies • Prep: 45 min + 1 hr to chill Cooking: 6–8 min • Level: 2

- 1 cup (150 g) all-purpose (plain) flour
- 2/3 cup (150 g) butter, softened
- 1/2 cup (100 g) sugar
- 1 cup (150 g) finely ground almonds
- 1 teaspoon finely grated lemon zest
- 1 teaspoon freshly squeezed lemon juice

Glaze
- 2/3 cup (100 g) confectioners' (icing) sugar
- 1 teaspoon freshly squeezed lemon juice, + more as needed
- 1/2 cup (120 g) seedless red currant or raspberry preserves (jam)

PASSIONFRUIT SHORTBREAD

- 1¼ cups (180 g) all-purpose (plain) flour
- 1/3 cup (50 g) cornstarch (cornflour)
- 1/4 teaspoon salt
- 3/4 cup (180 g) butter, softened
- 1/4 cup (50 g) sugar
- 2 passionfruit

Mix the flour, cornstarch, and salt in a medium bowl. • Beat the butter and sugar in a large bowl with an electric mixer on medium speed until creamy. • Mix in the dry ingredients. • Use a teaspoon to scoop the pulp from the passionfruit and stir into the mixture. • Press the dough into a 5-inch (12-cm) log, wrap in plastic wrap (cling film), and refrigerate for 30 minutes. • Preheat the oven to 350°F (180°C/gas 4). • Butter two cookie sheets. • Slice the dough 1/4-inch (5-mm) thick and place 1 inch (2.5 cm) apart on the prepared cookie sheets. • Bake for 15–20 minutes, or until pale gold. • Transfer to racks to cool.

Makes: about 48 cookies • Prep: 40 min + 30 min to chill Cooking: 15–20 min • Level: 1

BROWN PECAN SHORTBREAD

Preheat the oven to 325°F (170°C/gas 3). • Butter two 9-inch (23-cm) springform pans. • Mix the flour, confectioners' sugar, cornstarch, and salt in a large bowl. • Use a pastry blender to cut in the butter until the mixture resembles coarse crumbs. • Stir in the chocolate chips and pecans. • Firmly press the mixture into the prepared pans to form smooth, even layers. • Bake for 15–20 minutes, or until just golden. • Cool for 5 minutes in the pan. • Loosen and remove the springform sides. Let cool completely. • Cut each round into sixteen wedges. • Melt the chocolate in a double boiler over barely simmering water. • Drizzle over the cookies and let stand for 30 minutes until set.

Makes: 32 cookies • Prep: 20 min + 30 min to set • Cooking: 15–20 min • Level: 1

- 13/4 cups (270 g) all-purpose (plain) flour
- 1/2 cup (75 g) confectioners' (icing) sugar
- 1/4 cup (30 g) cornstarch (cornflour)
- 1/4 teaspoon salt
- 1 cup (250 g) butter, cut up
- 1 cup (180 g) semisweet chocolate chips
- 1 cup (120 g) finely chopped pecans
- 2 oz (60 g) semisweet (dark) chocolate, coarsely chopped

Butter Cookies

CHERRY-TOPPED WHIRLS

- 1¼ cups (180 g) all-purpose (plain) flour
- ½ teaspoon baking powder
- ⅛ teaspoon salt
- ¾ cup (180 g) butter, softened
- ⅓ cup (50 g) confectioners' (icing) sugar
- ½ teaspoon vanilla extract (essence)
- 8 candied cherries, cut in half

Preheat the oven to 325°F (170°C/gas 3). • Butter a cookie sheet. • Mix the flour, baking powder, and salt in a medium bowl. • Beat the butter, confectioners' sugar, and vanilla in a large bowl with an electric mixer on medium speed until creamy. • Mix in the dry ingredients until well blended. • Fit a pastry bag with a ½-inch (1-cm) star tip. Fill the pastry bag, twist the opening tightly closed, and squeeze out flat whirls, spacing 1 inch (2.5 cm) apart on the prepared cookie sheet. • Place a half cherry on top of each whirl. • Bake for 15–20 minutes, or until lightly browned. • Cool on the sheet until the cookies firm slightly. • Transfer to racks and let cool completely.

Makes: about 16 cookies • Prep: 25 min • Cooking: 15–20 min • Level: 2

PROVENCE SHORTBREAD

Preheat the oven to 325°F (170°C/gas 3). • Set out a 9-inch (23-cm) springform pan. • Mix the flour, cornstarch, and salt in a medium bowl. Stir in the lavender. • Beat the butter, sugar, and vanilla in a large bowl with an electric mixer on medium speed until creamy. • Mix in the dry ingredients. • Firmly press the dough into the pan to form a smooth, even layer. Use a sharp knife to score the shortbread into 16 wedges. • Bake for 25–30 minutes, or until lightly browned. • Use a sharp knife to cut the shortbread into wedges along the scored lines. • Loosen and remove the pan sides and bottom. Transfer to racks to cool.

Makes: 16 cookies • Prep: 25 min • Cooking: 25–30 min • Level: 1

- 1 cup (150 g) all-purpose (plain) flour
- 2 tablespoons cornstarch (cornflour)
- ⅛ teaspoon salt
- 1 teaspoon lavender flowers (heads only), rinsed and dried
- ½ cup (125 g) butter, softened
- ¼ cup (50 g) sugar
- ½ teaspoon vanilla extract (essence)

MANTECADOS

- 3⅓ cups (500 g) all-purpose (plain) flour
- 1 teaspoon ground cinnamon
- ½ teaspoon salt
- 1 cup (250 g) lard (or butter), softened
- 1¼ cups (250 g) sugar
- 3 large egg yolks
- finely grated zest and juice of 1 lemon
- 1 cup (120 g) finely ground almonds

These lard cookies are a traditional Spanish treat served at Epiphany, on January 6.

Preheat the oven to 325°F (170°F/gas 3). • Grease four cookie sheets with lard. • Mix the flour, cinnamon, and salt in a large bowl. • Beat the lard and sugar in a large bowl with an electric mixer on medium speed until creamy. • Add the egg yolks, beating until just blended. • Mix in the dry ingredients and lemon zest. • Stir in the almonds and lemon juice until well blended. • Turn out onto a lightly floured surface and knead to form a smooth, firm dough. If the dough is too crumbly, knead in a little cold water. Cover with a large piece of parchment paper. Roll out the dough to ½-inch (1-cm) thick. Remove the paper.

• Use a 2½-inch (6-cm) cookie cutter to cut out the cookies. • Use a spatula to transfer the cookies to the prepared cookie sheets, placing them 1 inch apart. • Bake for 20 minutes. • Lower the oven temperature to 300°F (150°C/gas 1) and bake for 5–10 minutes more, or until lightly golden. • Cool on the cookie sheets for 1 minute. Use a thin metal spatula to transfer the cookies to racks and let cool completely. • Wrap the cookies separately in colored tissue paper to serve.

Makes: about 50 cookies • Prep: 30 min • Cooking: 25–30 min • Level: 2

Sicilian butter crisps

SICILIAN BUTTER CRISPS

- 1 cup (150 g) all-purpose (plain) flour
- 1 cup (150 g) finely ground cornmeal
- 1/8 teaspoon salt
- 2/3 cup (150 g) butter, cut up
- 3/4 cup (150 g) sugar
- 3 large egg yolks
- 1 tablespoon Marsala
- finely grated zest of 1 orange

Mix the flour, cornmeal, and salt in a large bowl. • Use a pastry blender to cut in the butter until the mixture resembles fine crumbs. • Stir in the sugar, egg yolks, Marsala, and orange zest. • Press the dough into a disk, wrap in plastic wrap (cling film), and refrigerate for 30 minutes. • Preheat the oven to 350°F (180°C/gas 4). • Butter two cookie sheets. • Roll out the dough on a lightly floured surface to 1/4-inch (5-mm) thick. • Use a fluted 2-inch (5-cm) cookie cutter to cut out the cookies. Gather the dough scraps, re-roll, and continue cutting out cookies until all the dough is used. • Transfer the cookies to the prepared cookie sheets, placing them 1 inch (2.5 cm) apart. • Bake for 15–20 minutes, or until just golden. • Transfer to racks to cool.

Makes: about 25 cookies • Prep: 40 min + 30 min to chill Cooking: 25–30 min Level: 1

ALMOND WEDGIES

- 2/3 cup (100 g) all-purpose (plain) flour
- 2/3 cup (100 g) finely ground yellow cornmeal
- 1/8 teaspoon salt
- 1/2 cup (125 g) butter, cut up
- 1 cup (150 g) finely ground almonds
- 1/2 cup (100 g) granulated sugar
- 2 large egg yolks, lightly beaten
- finely grated zest and juice of 1 lemon
- 1/2 teaspoon almond extract (essence)
- 2 tablespoons finely chopped almonds
- 2 tablespoons raw sugar (Barbados or Demerara)

Preheat the oven to 350°F (180°C/gas 4). • Butter a 9-inch (23-cm) springform pan. • Mix the flour, cornmeal, and salt in a medium bowl. • Cut in the butter until the mixture resembles coarse crumbs. • Stir in the ground almonds and granulated sugar. • Mix in the egg yolks, lemon zest and juice, and almond extract to form a stiff dough. • Firmly press the dough into the prepared pan in an even layer. Sprinkle with the chopped almonds and raw sugar. • Use a sharp knife to score the cookie into 16 wedges. • Bake for 20 minutes. • Reduce the oven temperature to 300°F (150°C/gas 2). • Bake for 20–25 minutes more, or until pale gold and firm to the touch. • Use a sharp knife to cut along the scored lines. • Remove the pan sides and bottom. Transfer to racks and let cool.

Makes: 16 cookies • Prep: 35 min • Cooking: 40–45 min Level: 1

HONEY AND NUT SHORTBREAD

Preheat the oven to 325°F (170°C/gas 3). • Butter a 9-inch (23-cm) springform pan. • Mix the flour and salt in a large bowl. • Cut in 3/4 cup (180 g) of the butter until the mixture resembles fine crumbs. • Mix in the ground hazelnuts, sugar, and egg yolks to form a stiff dough. • Firmly press the mixture into the prepared pan in an even layer. • Melt the remaining butter with the honey in a small saucepan over low heat. • Stir in the chopped hazelnuts and simmer until the hazelnuts are well coated. • Spread evenly over the shortbread base. • Use a sharp knife to score the shortbread into 16 wedges. • Bake for 40–45 minutes, or until golden brown. • Use a sharp knife to cut along the scored lines. • Remove the pan sides and bottom. Transfer to racks to cool.

Makes: 16 cookies • Prep: 30 min • Cooking: 40–45 min Level: 1

- 1 1/2 cups (225 g) all-purpose (plain) flour
- 1/4 teaspoon salt
- 1 cup (250 g) butter, cut up
- 1 cup (150 g) finely ground hazelnuts
- 1/3 cup (70 g) sugar
- 2 large egg yolks, lightly beaten
- 3/4 cup (180 ml) honey
- 2 1/4 cups (225 g) finely chopped hazelnuts

LEMON DROPS

Mix the flour, cornstarch, and salt in a medium bowl. • Beat the butter and sugar in a large bowl with an electric mixer on medium speed until creamy. • Add the lemon juice and egg yolk, beating until just blended. • Mix in the dry ingredients to make a soft, sticky dough. • Cover the bowl with plastic wrap (cling film) and refrigerate for 30 minutes. • Preheat the oven to 350°F (180°C/gas 4). • Line three cookie sheets with parchment paper. • Form the dough into balls the size of walnuts and place 1 inch (2.5 cm) apart on the cookie sheets. Make a slight hollow in each center and fill with a small amount of lemon curd • Bake for 20–25 minutes, or until just golden. • Transfer to racks to cool. • Dust with the confectioners' sugar.

Makes: about 35 cookies • Prep: 20 min + 30 min to chill Cooking: 20–25 min Level: 1

- 1 3/4 cups (275 g) all-purpose (plain) flour
- 1/3 cup (50 g) cornstarch (cornflour)
- 1/8 teaspoon salt
- 1 cup (250 g) butter, softened
- 1/4 cup (50 g) sugar
- 1 tablespoon freshly squeezed lemon juice
- 1 large egg yolk
- 1/3 cup (90 ml) lemon curd (see page 414)
- confectioners' (icing) sugar, to dust

SUGAR COOKIES

S ugar cookies can be soft or crisp, chewy or smooth, creamy or golden brown, glazed or plain; but whatever their texture and color, they are always sweet and comforting. In this chapter we have selected twenty-six scrumptious recipes for sugar cookies of every kind. For special coffee mornings or afternoon teas, try the eye-catching Glazed sugar cookies shown here (left; see recipe page 46), the Sugar kisses (see page 46), or the Brown sugar kisses (see page 52). If you prefer more exotic flavors, then try the Caraway crisps or Caraway rose cookies (for both, see page 46).

Sugar Cookies

CARAWAY CRISPS

- ½ cup (125 g) butter, cut up
- 1 tablespoon heavy (double) cream
- 1²/₃ cups (250 g) all-purpose (plain) flour
- ²/₃ cup (140 g) sugar
- 1½ teaspoons caraway seeds
- ½ teaspoon freshly grated nutmeg
- ⅛ teaspoon salt
- 1 large egg yolk
- 1 tablespoon sweet sherry

Melt the butter with the cream in a small saucepan over low heat. • Transfer to a large bowl. • Mix in the flour, sugar, caraway seeds, nutmeg, and salt. • Beat the egg yolk and sherry in a small bowl until frothy. • Stir the egg mixture into the dry ingredients to form a stiff dough. • Press the dough into a disk, wrap in plastic wrap (cling film), and refrigerate for 1 hour. • Preheat the oven to 325°F (170°C/gas 3). • Butter two cookie sheets. • Roll out the dough on a lightly floured surface to ¼ inch (5 mm) thick. • Use a 2-inch (5-cm) cookie cutter to cut out the cookies. • Gather the dough scraps, re-roll, and continue cutting out cookies until all the dough is used. • Use a spatula to transfer the cookies to the cookie sheets, placing them 1 inch (2.5 cm) apart. • Bake until just golden, 10–15 minutes. • Transfer to racks to cool.

Makes: about 20 cookies • Prep: 40 min + 1 hr to chill
Cooking: 10–15 min • Level : 1

GLAZED SUGAR KISSES

Mix the flour, baking powder, and salt in a large bowl. • Beat the butter and sugar in a large bowl with an electric mixer on medium speed until creamy. • Add the egg and vanilla, beating until just blended. • Turn out onto a lightly floured surface and knead until smooth. • Press into a disk, wrap in plastic wrap (cling film), and refrigerate for 30 minutes. • Preheat the oven to 350°F (180°C/gas 4). • Butter two cookie sheets. • Roll out the dough to ¼ inch (5 mm) thick. • Use a 1½-inch (4-cm) cookie cutter to cut out the cookies. • Gather the dough scraps, re-roll, and cut out cookies until all the dough is used. • Transfer the cookies to the cookie sheets, spacing well. • Bake until lightly browned, 8–10 minutes. • Cool on the sheets for 2–3 minutes. Transfer to racks to finish cooling. • Warm the preserves in a small saucepan over low heat. • Stick the cookies together with the preserves. • Mix the confectioners' sugar with enough water to make a soft glaze. • Spread the cookies with the frosting and top with a half cherry.

Makes: about 20 cookies • Prep: 40 min • Cooking: 8–10 min • Level: 1

- 2 cups (300 g) all-purpose (plain) flour
- 1½ teaspoons baking powder
- ¼ teaspoon salt
- 1 cup (250 g) butter, softened
- 1½ cups (300 g) sugar
- 1 large egg
- 1 teaspoon vanilla extract (essence)
- ½ cup (160 ml) raspberry preserves (jam)
- 1 cup (150 g) confectioners' (icing) sugar
- 1 tablespoon boiling water, + more as needed
- 10 candied cherries, cut in half

CARAWAY ROSE COOKIES

- 1½ cups (225 g) all-purpose (plain) flour
- ¼ teaspoon salt
- 1 cup (200 g) sugar
- 1 teaspoon caraway seeds
- 1 large egg yolk + 3 large egg whites
- 1 tablespoon (15 ml) rose water

Mix the flour, salt, sugar, and caraway seeds in a medium bowl. • Beat in the egg yolk, egg whites, and rose water to form a stiff dough. • Press the dough into a disk, wrap in plastic wrap (cling film), and refrigerate for 30 minutes. • Preheat the oven to 325°F (170°C/gas 3). • Butter two cookie sheets. • Roll out the dough on a lightly floured surface to ⅛ inch (3 mm) thick. • Use a 2-inch (5-cm) cookie cutter to cut out the cookies. • Place on the sheets, spacing well. • Bake until golden brown, 10–15 minutes.

Makes: about 24 cookies • Prep: 30 min + 30 min to chill
Cooking: 10–15 min • Level : 1

ALMOND CRISPS

Stir the almonds, sugar, flour, cornstarch, and salt in a large bowl. • Add the butter, almond extract, and cinnamon. • Stir in the egg whites. • Refrigerate for 30 minutes. • Preheat the oven to 400°F (200°C/gas 6). • Line two cookie sheets with aluminum foil. • Drop half tablespoons of the dough 2 inches (5 cm) apart onto the prepared cookie sheets. • Bake until golden brown, 5–7 minutes. • Transfer to racks to cool.

Makes: about 25 cookies • Prep: 20 min • Cooking: 5–7 min Level : 1

- 1⅓ cups (150 g) coarsely chopped almonds
- ³/₄ cup (150 g) sugar
- 5 tablespoons all-purpose (plain) flour
- 1 tablespoon cornstarch (cornflour)
- ¼ teaspoon salt
- 3 tablespoons butter, melted
- ½ teaspoon almond extract (essence)
- 1 teaspoon ground cinnamon
- 3 large egg whites, lightly beaten

Sugar Cookies

SUGAR KISSES

Cookies
- 1 cup (150 g) all-purpose (plain) flour
- 1/8 teaspoon salt
- 1/3 cup (90 g) butter, cut up
- 1/4 cup (60 ml) light (single) cream
- 1/3 cup (50 g) confectioners' (icing) sugar, to dust

Pink Filling
- 1 cup (150 g) confectioners' (icing) sugar
- 1 tablespoon butter, softened
- 1 tablespoon light (single) cream
- 1/2 teaspoon vanilla extract (essence)
- few drops red food coloring

Mix the flour and salt in a large bowl. • Use a pastry blender to cut in the butter until the mixture resembles coarse crumbs. • Mix in the cream. • Press the dough into a disk, wrap in plastic wrap (cling film), and refrigerate for 30 minutes. • Preheat the oven to 375°F (190°C/gas 3). • Line two cookie sheets with parchment paper. • Roll out the dough on a lightly floured surface to 1/8 inch (3 mm) thick. • Use a 1 1/2-inch (4-cm) cookie cutter to cut out the cookies. Gather the dough scraps, re-roll, and continue cutting out cookies until all the dough is used. • Transfer the cookies to the cookie sheets, spacing them 1 1/2 inches (4 cm) apart. • Bake until just golden at the edges, 8–10 minutes. • Transfer to racks to cool. • Pink Filling: Mix the confectioners' sugar, butter, cream, vanilla, and red food coloring in a small bowl. • Stick the cookies together in pairs with the filling. • Dust with the confectioners' sugar.

Makes: about 12 cookies • Prep: 30 min + 30 min to chill Cooking: 8–10 min • Level: 2

THREE-SUGAR COOKIES

Mix the flour, baking powder, baking soda, and salt in a medium bowl. • Beat the butter, granulated sugar, brown sugar, and vanilla sugar in a large bowl with an electric mixer on medium speed until creamy. • Add the eggs, beating until just blended. • Stir in the vanilla and lemon zest and juice. • Mix in the dry ingredients until well blended. • Add enough milk to form a soft, but not sticky dough. • Turn the dough out onto a lightly floured surface and knead until smooth. • Divide the dough in half. Form each half into a 12-inch (30-cm) log, wrap in plastic wrap (cling film), and refrigerate for 30 minutes. • Preheat the oven to 400°F (200°C/gas 6). • Butter four cookie sheets. • Slice the dough 1/4 inch (5 mm) thick and place 1 inch (2.5 cm) apart on the prepared cookie sheets. • Bake, one batch at a time, until lightly browned and firm around the edges, 8–10 minutes. • Transfer to racks to cool.

Makes: about 80 cookies • Prep: 30 min + 30 min to chill Cooking: 8–10 min • Level: 1

- 3 cups (450 g) all-purpose (plain) flour
- 1 teaspoon baking powder
- 1/2 teaspoon baking soda (bicarbonate of soda)
- 1/2 teaspoon salt
- 1 cup (250 g) butter, softened
- 3/4 cup (150 g) granulated sugar
- 2/3 cup (140 g) firmly packed light brown sugar
- 2 tablespoons vanilla sugar (see page 414)
- 2 large eggs, lightly beaten
- 1 teaspoon vanilla extract (essence)
- 1 teaspoon finely grated lemon zest
- 1 teaspoon freshly squeezed lemon juice
- 2 tablespoons milk, or more, as needed

BUTTERMILK COOKIES

- 1 1/2 cups (225 g) all-purpose (plain) flour
- 1 teaspoon baking powder
- 1/2 teaspoon baking soda (bicarbonate of soda)
- 1/8 teaspoon salt
- 1/3 cup (90 g) butter, cut up
- 1/4 cup (60 g) sugar
- 1/2 cup (125 ml) buttermilk

Preheat the oven to 350°F (180°C/gas 4). • Butter a cookie sheet. • Mix the flour, baking powder, baking soda, and salt in a large bowl. Stir in the sugar. • Use a pastry blender to cut in the butter until the mixture resembles fine crumbs. • Stir in the buttermilk to form a smooth dough. • Roll out the dough on a lightly floured surface to 1/2 inch (1 cm) thick. • Use a 2-inch (5-cm) cookie cutter to cut out the cookies. • Gather the dough scraps, re-roll, and cut out cookies until all the dough is used. • Transfer the cookies to the cookie sheet, spacing well. • Bake until lightly browned, 10–15 minutes. • Transfer to racks to cool.

Makes: about 20 cookies • Prep: 40 min • Cooking: 10–15 min • Level: 1

VANILLA HONEY COOKIES

Mix the flour, sugar, egg, butter, water, baking soda, honey, vanilla, and salt in a large bowl to form a smooth dough. Press the dough into a disk, wrap in plastic wrap (cling film), and refrigerate for 30 minutes. • Preheat the oven to 350°F (180°C/gas 4). • Butter two cookie sheets. • Roll out the dough on a lightly floured surface to 1/4 inch (5 mm) thick. • Use a knife to cut out squares. • Transfer the cookies to the prepared cookie sheets, placing them 1 inch (2.5 cm) apart. • Brush with the milk. • Bake until just golden at the edges, 10–15 minutes. • Transfer to racks to cool.

Makes: about 25 cookies • Prep: 15 min + 30 min to chill Cooking: 10–15 min • Level: 1

- 2 1/3 cups (350 g) all-purpose (plain) flour
- 1/2 cup (100 g) sugar
- 1 large egg
- 1/3 cup (90 g) butter, softened
- 2 tablespoons water
- 1 teaspoon baking soda (bicarbonate of soda)
- 2 tablespoons honey
- 1 teaspoon vanilla extract (essence)
- 1/4 teaspoon salt
- 1 tablespoon milk

Sugar Cookies

PECAN VANILLA CRISPS

- 2⅓ cups (350 g) all-purpose (plain) flour
- ¼ teaspoon salt
- 1 cup (250 g) butter, softened
- 1¼ cups (250 g) sugar
- ½ teaspoon vanilla extract (essence)
- 1 large egg + 1 large egg white, lightly beaten
- 1 cup (100 g) finely chopped pecans

Mix the flour and salt in a medium bowl. • Beat the butter and sugar in a large bowl with an electric mixer on medium speed until creamy. • Add the whole egg, beating until just blended. • Mix in the dry ingredients. • Press the dough into four disks, wrap in plastic wrap (cling film), and refrigerate for 30 minutes. • Preheat the oven to 350°F (180°C/gas 4). • Butter three cookie sheets. • Roll out the dough on a lightly floured surface to ¼ inch (5 mm) thick. • Use a 2-inch (5-cm) cookie cutter to cut out the cookies. Gather the dough scraps, re-roll, and cut out cookies until all the dough is used. • Transfer the cookies to the prepared cookie sheets, placing them 1 inch (2.5 cm) apart. • Brush with the beaten egg white and sprinkle with the pecans. • Bake until just golden, 8–10 minutes. • Cool on the sheets until slightly firm. Transfer to racks to cool completely.

Makes: about 35 cookies • Prep: 30 min + 30 min to chill Cooking: 8–10 min • Level: 1

ROSE WATER LADYFINGERS

Preheat the oven to 350°F (180°C/gas 4). • Line two cookie sheets with parchment paper. • Mix the flour and salt in a large bowl. • Beat the egg whites with an electric mixer at high speed until soft peaks form. Gradually add the confectioners' sugar, beating until stiff, glossy peaks form. • With mixer at medium speed, beat the egg yolks and rose water in a medium bowl until well blended. • Fold the beaten yolks into the beaten whites. • Fold in the dry ingredients. • Fit a pastry bag with a ½-inch (1-cm) plain tip. Fill the pastry bag, twist the opening tightly closed, and squeeze out 3-inch (8-cm) fingers, spacing well. • Bake until just golden, 8–10 minutes. • Cool on racks.

Makes: about 30 cookies • Prep: 25 min • Cooking: 8–10 min • Level: 2

- 1 cup (150 g) all-purpose (plain) flour
- ⅛ teaspoon salt
- 3 large eggs, separated
- ½ cup (75 g) confectioners' (icing) sugar
- 1 teaspoon rose water

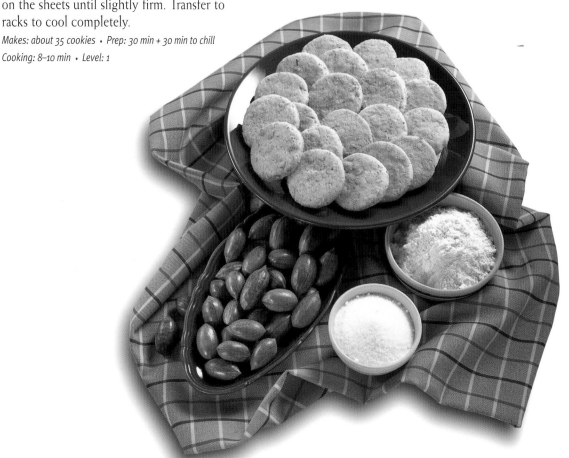

Pecan vanilla crisps

Frosted mace cookies

FROSTED MACE COOKIES

- 1³/₄ cups (275 g) all-purpose (plain) flour
- 2 teaspoons baking powder
- ½ teaspoon ground mace
- ½ cup (125 g) butter
- 1 cup (200 g) sugar
- 1 teaspoon vanilla extract (essence)
- 2 large eggs
- 1 cup (150 g) confectioners' (icing) sugar
- 1–2 tablespoons hot water

Stir the flour, baking powder, and mace in a medium bowl. • Beat the butter, sugar, and vanilla in a large bowl with an electric mixer on medium speed until pale and creamy. • Add the eggs, one at a time, and beat until just combined. • With mixer at low speed, gradually beat in the mixed dry ingredients. • Wrap in plastic wrap (cling film) and refrigerate for at least 2 hours. • Preheat oven to 350°F (180°C/gas 4). • Butter and lightly flour two cookie sheets. • Roll out the dough on a lightly floured work surface to ⅛ inch (3-mm) thick. Cut out heart and star shapes. Transfer to the prepared sheets. • Bake until golden, 10–12 minutes. Transfer to racks to cool. • Mix the confectioners' sugar and water and spread over the cookies.

Makes: about 36 cookies • Prep: 30 min + 2 hr to chill
Cooking: 10–12 min • Level: 1

SAVOY LADYFINGERS

Preheat the oven to 325°F (170°C/gas 3). • Line two cookie sheets with parchment paper. • Mix the flour and salt in a medium bowl. • Beat the eggs, ½ cup (100 g) of superfine sugar, and vanilla in a double boiler over barely simmering water. Beat until the batter falls off the beaters in ribbons. • Fold in the dry ingredients. • Fit a pastry bag with a ½-inch (1-cm) star tip. Fill the pastry bag, twist the opening tightly closed, and squeeze out 3 x ¾-inch (8 x 2-cm) lengths, spacing them 1 inch (2.5 cm) apart on the prepared cookie sheets. • Sprinkle with the remaining sugar. • Bake until crisp and dry to the touch, 10–15 minutes. • Cool on the sheets until slightly firm. Transfer to racks to finish cooling.

Makes: about 30 cookies • Prep: 20 min • Cooking: 10–15 min • Level: 2

- ²/₃ cup (100 g) all-purpose (plain) flour
- ⅛ teaspoon salt
- 3 large eggs
- ²/₃ cup (140 g) superfine (caster) sugar
- ½ teaspoon vanilla extract (essence)

Sugar Cookies

BROWN SUGAR KISSES

Cookies
- 1 cup (150 g) all-purpose (plain) flour
- 4 tablespoons unsweetened cocoa powder
- 1/8 teaspoon salt
- 1/3 cup (90 g) butter, cut up
- 5 tablespoons light (single) cream
- 1/3 cup (70 g) sugar, to sprinkle

Filling
- 2 oz (60 g) semisweet (dark) chocolate, coarsely chopped
- 1 cup (150 g) confectioners' (icing) sugar
- 1 tablespoon light (single) cream

Mix the flour, cocoa, and salt in a large bowl. • Use a pastry blender to cut in the butter until the mixture resembles coarse crumbs. • Mix in the cream. • Press the dough into a disk, wrap in plastic wrap (cling film), and refrigerate for 30 minutes. • Preheat the oven to 375°F (190°C/gas 5). • Line two cookie sheets with parchment paper. • Roll out the dough on a lightly floured surface to 1/8 inch (3 mm) thick. • Use a 1 1/2-inch (4-cm) cookie cutter to cut out the cookies. Gather the dough scraps, re-roll, and continue cutting out cookies until all the dough is used. • Use a spatula to transfer the cookies to the cookie sheet, spacing them 1 1/2 inches (4-cm) apart. • Sprinkle with the sugar. • Bake until just firm to the touch, 8–10 minutes. • Transfer to racks to cool. • Filling: Melt the chocolate in a double boiler over barely simmering water. Remove from the heat and mix in the confectioners' sugar and cream. • Stick the cookies together in pairs with the filling. • Let the cookies stand for 30 minutes to set.

Makes: about 12 cookies • Prep: 40 min + 1 hr to chill and set • Cooking: 8–10 min Level: 2

SUGAR HEARTS WITH CHOCOLATE

Mix the flour, baking powder, and salt in a medium bowl. • Beat the butter and sugar in a large bowl with an electric mixer on medium speed until creamy. • Add the vanilla and almond extracts and half-and-half. • Add the egg and egg yolk, beating until just blended. • Mix in the dry ingredients. • Divide the dough in half. Press into disks, wrap in plastic wrap (cling film), and refrigerate for 30 minutes. • Preheat the oven to 350°F (180°C/gas 4). • Line three cookie sheets with parchment paper. • Roll out one of the disks of dough on a lightly floured surface to 1/4 inch (5 mm) thick. • Use a 2 1/2-inch (6-cm) heart-shaped cookie cutter to cut out the cookies. • Transfer the cookies to the prepared cookie sheets, placing them 2 inches (5 cm) apart. • Repeat with the remaining dough. • Bake until just golden, 12–15 minutes. • Transfer to racks and let cool completely. • Melt the chocolate in a double boiler over barely simmering water. • Dip the hearts halfway into the chocolate and let stand for 30 minutes until set.

Makes: about 40 cookies • Prep: 40 min + 1 hr to chill and set • Cooking: 12–15 min Level: 1

- 3 cups (450 g) all-purpose (plain) flour
- 1/2 teaspoon baking powder
- 1/2 teaspoon salt
- 1 cup (250 g) butter, softened
- 1 cup (200 g) sugar
- 1 teaspoon vanilla extract (essence)
- 1/4 teaspoon almond extract (essence)
- 1/4 cup (60 ml) half-and-half
- 1 large egg + 1 large egg yolk
- 6 oz (180 g) semisweet (dark) chocolate, coarsely chopped

LAVENDER HEARTS

- 1 1/4 cups (180 g) all-purpose (plain) flour
- 1 teaspoon baking powder
- 1/8 teaspoon salt
- 1/3 cup (90 g) butter
- 1/4 cup (50 g) sugar
- 1 large egg yolk
- 1 tablespoon lavender flowers (heads only), rinsed and dried

Preheat the oven to 450°F (230°C/gas 8). • Line two cookie sheets with parchment paper. • Mix the flour, baking powder, and salt in a large bowl. • Beat the butter and sugar in a large bowl with an electric mixer on medium speed until creamy. • Add the egg yolk, beating until just blended. • Mix in the dry ingredients. • Turn the dough out onto a lightly floured surface and knead to form a soft dough. • Roll out the dough to 1/4 inch (5 mm) thick. • Sprinkle the dough with the lavender flowers, pressing them in with a rolling pin. • Use a heart-shaped cookie cutter to cut out the cookies. Gather the dough scraps, re-roll, and continue cutting out cookies until all the dough is used. • Transfer the cookies to the cookie sheets. • Bake until lightly browned, 10–12 minutes. • Transfer to racks to cool.

Makes: about 20 cookies • Prep: 30 min • Cooking: 10–12 min • Level: 1

Sugar Cookies

CINNAMON CRISPS WITH STRAWBERRY

- 2⅓ cups (350 g) all-purpose (plain) flour
- 1 teaspoon baking powder
- 1 teaspoon ground cinnamon
- ½ teaspoon salt
- ⅓ cup (90 g) butter, softened
- ½ cup (100 g) sugar
- 2 large eggs
- ½ teaspoon vanilla extract (essence)
- ½ cup (160 g) strawberry preserves (jam)

Preheat the oven to 400°F (200°C/gas 6). • Butter three cookie sheets. • Mix the flour, baking powder, cinnamon, and salt in a large bowl. • Beat the butter and sugar in a large bowl with an electric mixer on medium speed until creamy. • Add the eggs and vanilla, beating until just blended. • Mix in the dry ingredients. • Fit a pastry bag with a ½-inch (1-cm) plain tip. Fill the pastry bag, twist the opening tightly closed, and squeeze out 2-inch (5-cm) rounds, spacing 1 inch (2.5 cm) apart on the prepared cookie sheets. • Press your thumb into each cookie to make a small hollow. • Bake until just golden, for 8–10 minutes. • Transfer to racks to cool. • Heat the preserves in a small saucepan over low heat until liquid. • Fill each hollow with preserves and let stand for 20 minutes until set.

Makes: about 50 cookies • Prep: 25 min + 20 min to set
Cooking: 8–10 min • Level: 2

DUSTED SUGAR COOKIES

Mix the flour, cinnamon, and salt in a medium bowl. • Beat the butter and sugar in a medium bowl with an electric mixer on medium speed until creamy. • Mix in the dry ingredients to form a smooth dough. Press the dough into a disk, wrap in plastic wrap (cling film), and refrigerate for 30 minutes. • Preheat the oven to 400°F (200°C/gas 6). • Butter a cookie sheet. • Roll out the dough on a lightly floured surface to ¼ inch (5 mm) thick. • Use a 3-inch (8-cm) cookie cutter to cut out the cookies. Gather the dough scraps, re-roll, and continue cutting out cookies until all the dough is used. Use a spatula to transfer the cookies to the prepared cookie sheet, placing them 2 inches (5 cm) apart. • Bake until just golden, 15–20 minutes. • Transfer to racks to cool. Dust with the confectioners' sugar.

Makes: about 18 cookies • Prep: 30 min + 30 min to chill
Cooking: 15–20 min • Level: 1

- 1½ cups (225 g) all-purpose (plain) flour
- ½ teaspoon ground cinnamon
- ⅛ teaspoon salt
- ½ cup (125 g) butter, softened
- ½ cup (100 g) sugar
- 4 tablespoons confectioners' (icing) sugar

GOLDEN CRISPS

- 1⅓ cups (200 g) all-purpose (plain) flour
- ¾ cup (150 g) sugar + 2 tablespoons, to sprinkle
- 2 tablespoons arrowroot starch
- ½ cup (125 g) butter, softened
- 1 large egg + 1 large egg yolk, lightly beaten

Mix the flour, sugar, and arrowroot in a large bowl. • Use a pastry blender to cut in the butter until the mixture resembles coarse crumbs. • Add the egg and egg yolk to form a stiff dough. • Press the dough into a disk, wrap in plastic wrap (cling film), and refrigerate for 30 minutes. • Preheat the oven to 425°F (220°C/gas 7). • Butter two cookie sheets. • Roll out the dough on a lightly floured surface to ¼ inch (5 mm) thick. • Use a 2-inch (5-cm) cookie cutter to cut out the cookies. • Transfer to the cookie sheets, spacing well. • Bake until pale golden brown, 10–15 minutes. • Transfer to racks to cool. Sprinkle with the extra sugar.

Makes: about 20 cookies • Prep: 30 min + 30 min to chill
Cooking: 10–15 min • Level: 1

GINGER MOLASSES COOKIES

Mix the flour, ginger, baking powder, and salt in a medium bowl. • Melt the butter with the brown sugar and molasses in a medium saucepan over low heat. • Remove from the heat and mix in the dry ingredients to form a stiff dough. • Press the dough into a disk, wrap in plastic wrap (cling film), and refrigerate for 1 hour. • Preheat the oven to 325°F (170°C/gas 3). • Butter two cookie sheets. • Roll out the dough on a lightly floured surface to ¼ inch (5 mm) thick. • Use a 2-inch (5-cm) cookie cutter to cut out the cookies. • Transfer the cookies to the cookie sheets, spacing well. • Bake until just golden, 10–15 minutes. • Transfer to racks to cool.

Makes: about 24 cookies • Prep: 30 min + 1 hr to chill
Cooking: 10–15 min • Level: 1

- 1¼ cups (180 g) all-purpose (plain) flour
- 1 teaspoon ground ginger
- ½ teaspoon baking powder
- ¼ teaspoon salt
- ¼ cup (60 g) butter, cut up
- ¼ cup (50 g) firmly packed light brown sugar
- 4 tablespoons light molasses

Orange sesame wafers

BROWN SUGAR PECAN SNAPS

- ½ cup (75 g) all-purpose (plain) flour
- ¼ teaspoon baking powder
- ⅛ teaspoon salt
- ¼ cup (60 g) butter, cut up
- ⅓ cup (90 ml) light corn (golden) syrup
- ¼ cup (50 g) firmly packed dark brown sugar
- ½ cup (50 g) finely chopped pecans
- ½ cup (125 ml) heavy (double) cream
- ¼ teaspoon vanilla extract (essence)
- 2 tablespoons confectioners' (icing) sugar

Preheat the oven to 375°F (190°C/gas 5). • Line three cookie sheets with parchment paper. Butter two rolling pins. • Mix the flour, baking powder, and salt in a medium bowl. • Melt the butter with the corn syrup and brown sugar in a medium saucepan. Remove from the heat. • Mix in the dry ingredients and pecans. • Drop teaspoons of the dough 3 inches (8 cm) apart onto the sheets. Do not drop more than six cookies onto each sheet. • Bake until lightly browned, 5–7 minutes. • Lift each cookie from the sheet and drape it over a rolling pin. Slide each cookie off the pin and onto racks to finish cooling. • Butter the cookie sheets again and continue to bake until all the batter has been used. • Beat the cream with the vanilla and confectioners' sugar until stiff. Fit a pastry bag with a 1½-inch (4-cm) star tip. Fill the pastry bag, twist the opening tightly closed, and squeeze out cream rosettes into the cookies.

Makes: about 20 cookies • Prep: 30 min • Cooking: 5–7 min Level: 3

ORANGE SESAME WAFERS

Toast the sesame seeds in a frying pan over medium heat until lightly browned, 5–7 minutes. • Mix the flour and salt in a medium bowl. • Beat the butter, confectioners' sugar, and orange zest in a large bowl with an electric mixer on medium speed until creamy. • Gradually beat in the egg whites. • Mix in the dry ingredients and sesame seeds. Refrigerate for 1 hour. • Preheat the oven to 350°F (180°C/gas 4). • Butter four cookie sheets. • Butter two rolling pins. • Drop teaspoons of the mixture 2 inches (5 cm) apart onto the cookie sheets. Use a thin spatula to spread out to 3 inches (8 cm) in diameter. • Bake until the edges are lightly golden, 5–6 minutes. • Working quickly, use a spatula to place the cookies over a rolling pin. Slide each cookie off the pin onto a rack to finish cooling. • Butter the cookie sheets again and continue until all the batter has been used.

Makes: about 25 cookies • Prep: 40 min + 1 hr to chill Cooking: 5–6 min • Level: 3

- 1 cup (100 g) sesame seeds
- ⅔ cup (100 g) all-purpose (plain) flour
- ⅛ teaspoon salt
- ⅓ cup (90 g) butter, softened
- ⅔ cup (100 g) confectioners' (icing) sugar
- 2 tablespoons vanilla sugar (see page 414)
- finely grated zest of 1 orange
- 3 large egg whites, lightly beaten

PECAN WAFERS

- ½ cup (50 g) finely chopped pecans
- ½ cup (100 g) sugar
- 2 tablespoons all-purpose (plain) flour
- ¼ cup (60 g) butter, melted
- 2 large egg whites, lightly beaten
- ½ teaspoon vanilla extract (essence)
- ⅛ teaspoon salt

Preheat the oven to 350°F (180°C/gas 4). • Butter four cookie sheets. • Butter two rolling pins. • Process the pecans and sugar in a food processor until finely ground. • Transfer to a large bowl and stir in the flour, butter, egg whites, vanilla, and salt. • Drop teaspoons of the batter 3 inches (8 cm) apart onto the prepared cookie sheets. Spread the mixture out into thin circles. • Bake until just golden at the edges, for 8–10 minutes. • Use a spatula to lift each cookie off the sheet. Working quickly, drape it over a rolling pin to give it a rounded finish. • Let cool completely.

Makes: about 20 cookies • Prep: 30 min • Cooking: 8–10 min • Level: 3

HONEY COOKIES

Mix the flour and salt in a medium bowl. • Use a pastry blender to cut in the butter until the mixture resembles fine crumbs. • Mix in the cream and honey to form a stiff dough. • Press the dough into a disk, wrap in plastic wrap (cling film), and refrigerate for 30 minutes. • Preheat the oven to 300°F (150°C/gas 2). • Butter two cookie sheets. • Roll out the dough on a lightly floured surface to ⅛ inch (3 mm) thick. Use a 2-inch (5-cm) cookie cutter to cut out the cookies. • Transfer to the cookie sheets, spacing well. • Bake until golden, 15–20 minutes. • Transfer to racks to cool.

Makes: about 20 cookies • Prep: 30 min + 30 min to chill Cooking: 15–20 min • Level: 1

- 1⅔ cups (250 g) all-purpose (plain) flour
- ⅛ teaspoon salt
- ½ cup (125 g) butter, cut up
- 2 tablespoons heavy (double) cream
- 2 tablespoons honey

Sugar Cookies

GLAZED CRIMSON COOKIES

Cookies
- 3/4 cup (180 ml) pure maple syrup
- 2/3 cup (150 g) butter, cut up
- 1 cup (150 g) all-purpose (plain) flour
- 1/4 teaspoon baking soda (bicarbonate of soda)
- 1/8 teaspoon salt
- 1/4 cup (50 g) sugar
- 1 teaspoon vanilla extract (essence)
- 1 large egg

Frosting
- 1 cup (150 g) confectioners' (icing) sugar
- 2–3 tablespoons water
- few drops red food coloring

Cookies: Preheat the oven to 375°F (190°C/gas 5). • Butter three cookie sheets. • Bring the maple syrup to a boil in a small saucepan over medium heat and simmer for 5 minutes. • Add the butter and simmer for 2 minutes. • Let cool for 10 minutes. • Mix the flour, baking soda, and salt in a large bowl. Stir in the sugar. • Add the vanilla and egg to the maple syrup mixture, beating until just blended. • Pour into the dry ingredients and mix well. • Drop teaspoons of the batter 3 inches (8 cm) apart onto the prepared cookie sheets. • Bake until lightly browned, 10–12 minutes. • Cool on the sheets until the cookies firm slightly. • Transfer to racks to finish cooling. • Frosting: Mix the confectioners' sugar, water, and food coloring in a small bowl to make a thin glaze. Drizzle over the tops of the cookies in a decorative manner.
Makes: about 35 cookies • Prep: 30 min • Cooking: 10–12 min • Level: 1

SIMPLE RICE COOKIES

Beat the butter and sugar in a large bowl with an electric mixer on medium speed until creamy. • Mix in the rice flour. • Add the eggs, beating to form a smooth dough. • Press the dough into a disk, wrap in plastic wrap (cling film), and refrigerate for 30 minutes. • Preheat the oven to 300°F (150°C/gas 2). • Butter two cookie sheets. • Roll out the dough on a surface lightly dusted with rice flour to 1/4 inch (5 mm) thick. • Use a 2-inch (5-cm) cookie cutter to cut out the cookies. • Gather the dough scraps, re-roll, and continue cutting out cookies until all the dough is used. • Use a spatula to transfer the cookies to the cookie sheets, placing them 1 inch (2.5 cm) apart. • Bake until just golden, 15–20 minutes. • Transfer to racks to cool.
Makes: about 18 cookies • Prep: 30 min + 30 min to chill Cooking: 10–15 min • Level: 1

- 1/2 cup (125 g) butter, softened
- 2/3 cup (140 g) sugar
- 1 1/2 cups (225 g) rice flour
- 2 large eggs

NORTHERN LIGHTS COOKIES

- 2/3 cup (100 g) all-purpose (plain) flour
- 1 teaspoon baking powder
- 1/2 teaspoon ground ginger
- 1/4 teaspoon ground cinnamon
- 1/8 teaspoon salt
- 1/4 teaspoon baking soda (bicarbonate of soda)
- 1 tablespoon warm water

Mix the flour, baking powder, ginger, cinnamon, and salt in a large bowl. • Dissolve the baking soda in the water. • Melt the butter with the corn syrup and sugar in a small saucepan over medium heat. • Mix in the baking soda mixture. • Mix the butter mixture into the dry ingredients. • Cover with plastic wrap (cling film) and refrigerate for 12 hours. • Preheat the oven to 300°F (150°C/gas 2). • Butter two cookie sheets. • Roll out the dough on a lightly floured surface to 1/4 inch (5 mm) thick. • Use 1-inch (2.5-cm) cookie cutters to cut out the cookies. • Gather the dough scraps, re-roll, and continue cutting out the cookies until all the dough is used. • Use a spatula to transfer the cookies to the prepared cookie sheets, placing them 1 inch (2.5 cm) apart. • Bake until lightly browned, 15–20 minutes. • Transfer to racks to cool.
Makes: about 20 cookies • Prep: 30 min + 12 hr to chill Cooking: 15–20 min • Level: 1

- 3 tablespoons butter
- 1/4 cup (60 ml) light corn (golden) syrup
- 2 tablespoons sugar

CHOCOLATE COOKIES

Chocolate is always a winner and chocolate-flavored cookies are no exception. In this chapter we have selected more than fifty great-tasting chocolate cookie recipes, most of which can be prepared in record time. And that's not including brownie recipes, which can all be found in the Bars & Brownies chapter beginning on page 212. Among the superb offerings here, we suggest you try the Mint chocolate kisses (see page 62), the Chocolate chip wedges (see page 75), the Chocolate hazelnut hearts (see page 79), and the Double chocolate nut cookies (see page 92)—to start with!

Chocolate cream kisses (see page 62)

Chocolate Cookies

CHOCOLATE CREAM KISSES

- 1½ cups (225 g) all-purpose (plain) flour
- 2 tablespoons unsweetened cocoa powder
- ½ teaspoon baking powder
- ⅛ teaspoon salt
- ½ cup (125 g) butter, softened
- ½ cup (125 g) lard or vegetable shortening, softened
- ½ cup (100 g) sugar
- 1 cup (150 g) old-fashioned rolled oats
- ¼ cup (60 ml) light corn (golden) syrup dissolved in 1 tablespoon boiling water

Filling
- ¼ cup (60 g) butter, melted
- 1 cup (150 g) confectioners' (icing) sugar
- 2 tablespoons unsweetened cocoa powder
- ½ teaspoon vanilla extract (essence)

For a deeper, nuttier taste in this recipe, substitute the granulated sugar with the same quantity of firmly packed dark brown sugar.
Preheat the oven to 350°F (180°C/gas 4). • Butter two cookie sheets. • Mix the flour, cocoa, baking powder, and salt in a medium bowl. • Beat the butter, lard, and sugar in a large bowl with an electric mixer on medium speed until creamy. • Mix in the dry ingredients, followed by the oats and corn syrup mixture to form a smooth dough. • Form the dough into balls the size of walnuts, and place 1 inch (2.5 cm) apart on the prepared cookie sheets, flattening them slightly. • Bake for 20–25 minutes, or until firm to the touch. • Transfer to racks to cool. • Filling: Beat the butter, confectioners' sugar, cocoa, and vanilla in a small bowl until creamy. • Stick the cookies together in pairs with the chocolate filling.
Makes: about 16 cookies • Prep: 25 minutes • Cooking: 20–25 minutes • Level: 1

MINT CHOCOLATE KISSES

Mix the flour, cocoa, and salt into a medium bowl. • Beat the butter and sugar in a large bowl with an electric mixer on medium speed until creamy. • Add the mint extract and egg, beating until just blended. • Mix in the dry ingredients. • Press the dough into a disk, wrap in plastic wrap (cling film), and refrigerate for 30 minutes. • Preheat the oven to 350°F (180°C/gas 4). • Butter two cookie sheets. • Roll out the dough on a lightly floured surface to ⅛ inch (3 mm) thick. • Use a 2-inch (5-cm) cookie cutter to cut out the cookies. Gather the dough scraps, re-roll, and continue cutting out cookies until all the dough is used. • Transfer the cookies to the cookie sheets, placing them 1 inch (2.5 cm) apart. • Bake for 6–8 minutes, or until just firm. • Transfer to racks and let cool completely. • Filling: Bring the cream to a boil in a small saucepan over low heat. • Remove from the heat and stir in the white chocolate until melted. Add the mint extract and transfer to a medium bowl. • Cool for 30 minutes, or until firm but not set. • Stick the cookies together in pairs with filling. • Glaze: Melt the chocolate and butter in a double boiler over barely simmering water. • Spread on top of the cookies and refrigerate for 30 minutes.
Makes: about 16 cookies • Prep: 40 min + 90 min to chill Cooking: 6–8 min • Level : 2

- 1 cup (150 g) all-purpose (plain) flour
- 2 tablespoons unsweetened cocoa powder
- ⅛ teaspoon salt
- ½ cup (125 g) butter, softened
- ¼ cup (50 g) sugar
- 1 teaspoon mint extract (essence)
- 1 large egg

Filling
- ½ cup (125 ml) heavy (double) cream
- 7 oz (200 g) white chocolate, coarsely chopped
- 1 teaspoon mint extract (essence)

Glaze
- 5 oz (150 g) bittersweet (plain) chocolate, coarsely chopped
- ⅓ cup (90 g) butter

CHOCOLATE CHIP AND CANDIED CHERRY COOKIES

- ¾ cup (125 g) all-purpose (plain) flour
- ½ teaspoon baking powder
- ⅛ teaspoon salt
- ½ cup (125 g) butter, softened
- ¼ cup (50 g) sugar
- ½ teaspoon vanilla extract (essence)

Preheat the oven to 375°F (190°C/gas 5). • Butter two cookie sheets. • Mix the flour, baking powder, and salt into a large bowl. • Beat the butter, sugar, and vanilla in a large bowl with an electric mixer on medium speed until creamy. • Mix in the dry ingredients, cherries, and chocolate. • Drop rounded teaspoons of the dough 1 inch (2.5 cm) apart onto the prepared

cookie sheets. • Bake for 15–20 minutes, or until just golden. • Cool on the sheets until the cookies firm slightly. • Transfer to racks to finish cooling.
Makes: 18–20 cookies • Prep: 20 min • Cooking: 15–20 min Level: 1

- ½ cup (50 g) coarsely chopped candied cherries
- 2 oz (60 g) semisweet (dark) chocolate, coarsely chopped

Chocolate Cookies

PEANUT BUTTER COOKIES

- 2 cups (300 g) all-purpose (plain) flour
- 2/3 cup (100 g) rice flour
- 1 1/2 teaspoons baking powder
- 1/8 teaspoon salt
- 3/4 cup (180 g) butter, softened
- 1 cup (200 g) firmly packed light brown sugar
- 6 tablespoons crunchy peanut butter
- 1 oz (30 g) semisweet (dark) chocolate, coarsely chopped
- 2 tablespoons milk
- 2 cups (500 ml) chocolate frosting, made with milk chocolate (see page 414)

Mix both flours, the baking powder, and salt in a large bowl. • Beat the butter, brown sugar, and peanut butter in a medium bowl until creamy. • Mix in the dry ingredients and milk until well combined. • Melt the chocolate in a double boiler over barely simmering water. Mix the chocolate into the dough. • Form the dough into two 8-inch (20-cm) logs. Refrigerate for 2 hours. • Preheat the oven to 350°F (180°C/gas 4). • Line two cookie sheets with parchment paper. • Slice the dough 1/4 inch (5 mm) thick and place 2 inches (5 cm) apart on the prepared cookie sheets. • Bake for 8–10 minutes, until golden brown and firm around the edges. • Transfer to racks to cool. Spread the frosting over the cookies.

Makes: 64 cookies • Prep: 1 hr + 2 hr to chill • Cooking: 8–10 min • Level: 2

CHOCOLATE SANDWICHES

Mix the flour, custard powder, cocoa, and salt in a medium bowl. • Beat the butter and sugar in a large bowl with an electric mixer on medium speed until creamy. • Add the egg, beating until just blended. • Mix in the dry ingredients. Press the dough into a disk, wrap in plastic wrap (cling film), and refrigerate for 30 minutes. • Preheat the oven to 350°F (180°C/gas 4). • Butter two cookie sheets. • Roll out to 1/4 inch (5 mm) thick. Cut into rectangles. • Arrange the cookies 1 inch (2.5 cm) apart on the sheets. • Bake for 10–12 minutes, or until lightly browned. • Cool completely on the sheets. • Stick together with the buttercream.

Makes: about 15 cookies • Prep: 45 min • Cooking: 10–12 min • Level: 1

- 1 cup (150 g) all-purpose (plain) flour
- 1/3 cup (50 g) custard powder
- 2 tablespoons unsweetened cocoa powder
- 1/8 teaspoon salt
- 1/2 cup (125 g) butter, softened
- 1 cup (200 g) sugar
- 1 large egg
- 1/2 cup (125 g) chocolate buttercream (see page 416)

Peanut butter cookies

Chocolate tipped arches

CHOCOLATE TIPPED ARCHES

- 3/4 cup (125 g) all-purpose (plain) flour
- 3/4 cup (125 g) finely ground yellow cornmeal
- 1/4 teaspoon salt
- 1/3 cup (70 g) sugar
- 1/2 teaspoon vanilla extract (essence)
- 2 large eggs
- 2/3 cup (150 g) butter, melted
- 8 oz (250 g) semisweet (dark) chocolate, coarsely chopped

Mix the flour, cornmeal, and salt in a large bowl. Stir in the sugar and vanilla. • Add the eggs, beating until just blended. • Stir in the butter to form a stiff dough. • Cover with a clean kitchen towel and let stand for 30 minutes. • Preheat the oven to 400°F (200°C/gas 6). • Line two cookie sheets with parchment paper. • Fit a pastry bag with a 1/2-inch (1-cm) star tip. Fill the pastry bag and squeeze out 4-inch (10-cm) tall arches (horseshoes) spacing them 2 inches (5 cm) apart on the cookie sheets. • Bake for 10–15 minutes, or until just golden. • Cool the cookies on the cookie sheets. • Melt the chocolate in a double boiler over barely simmering water. • Dip the cookies halfway into the chocolate and let stand until set, about 30 minutes.

Makes: 20–25 cookies • Prep: 30 min + 30 min to set
Cooking: 10–15 min • Level: 2

CHOCOLATE MUNCHIES

Mix the flour, cocoa, baking powder, baking soda, and salt in a medium bowl. • Beat the butter and sugar in a large bowl until creamy. • Add the egg, beating until just blended. • Beat in half of the semisweet chocolate and vanilla. • Mix in the dry ingredients. • Divide the dough in half. Form into two long logs 2 inches (5 cm) in diameter, wrap in waxed paper, and freeze for at least 4 hours. • Preheat the oven to 350°F (180°C/gas 4). • Line two cookie sheets with foil. • Slice the dough 1/4 inch (5 mm) thick and place 1 inch (2.5 cm) apart on the sheets. • Bake for 10–12 minutes, or until lightly browned. • Transfer the cookies to racks to cool. • Drizzle the remaining semisweet and white chocolate over the cookies.

Makes: about 45 cookies • Prep: 40 min + 4 hr to freeze
Cooking: 10–12 min • Level: 1

- 2 1/4 cups (330 g) all-purpose (plain) flour
- 1/3 cup (50 g) unsweetened cocoa powder
- 1/2 teaspoon baking powder
- 1/2 teaspoon baking soda (bicarbonate of soda)
- 1/4 teaspoon salt
- 3/4 cup (180 g) butter, softened
- 1 cup (200 g) sugar
- 1 large egg
- 8 oz (250 g) semisweet (dark) chocolate, melted
- 1 teaspoon vanilla extract (essence)
- 3 oz (90 g) white chocolate, melted

Chocolate Cookies

PRESSED CHOCOLATE COOKIES

- 1²/₃ cups (250 g) self-rising flour
- 2 tablespoons unsweetened cocoa powder
- ²/₃ cup (150 g) butter, softened
- ³/₄ cup (150 g) sugar
- 1 large egg yolk
- 20 chocolate drops (buttons) or small squares of semisweet (dark) chocolate

Preheat the oven to 375°F (190°C/gas 5). • Butter two cookie sheets. • Mix the flour and cocoa in a medium bowl. • Beat the butter and sugar in a large bowl with an electric mixer at medium speed until creamy. • Add the egg yolk, beating until just blended. • Mix in the dry ingredients. • Form the dough into three equal-size disks, wrap in plastic wrap (cling film), and refrigerate for 30 minutes. • Roll out on a lightly floured surface to ¼ inch (5 mm) thick. • Use a 2-inch (5-cm) cutter to cut out 20 larger disks and use a 1½-inch (4-cm) cutter to cut out 20 smaller disks. • Place the larger disks on the prepared cookie sheets. Place a piece of chocolate in the center. Cover with one of the smaller disks. Mold the smaller disk over the chocolate and turn the edges of the larger disk up. Press around the edges with a fork to seal. • Bake for 8–10 minutes, or until the cookies have spread slightly. • Cool on the sheet for 5 minutes. • Transfer to racks to cool.

Makes: 20 cookies • Prep: 20 min + 30 min to chill • Cooking: 8–10 min • Level: 2

CHOCOLATE ALMOND BITES

Preheat the oven to 325°F (170°C/gas 3). • Line two cookie sheets with rice paper. • Sprinkle half the almonds on a large baking sheet. Toast for 7 minutes, or until lightly golden. Lower the oven temperature to 300°F (150°C/gas 2). • Place the almonds on a clean kitchen towel and rub off the skins. • Coarsely chop half the peeled almonds. • Process the remaining almonds in a food processor until finely chopped. Set aside. • Beat the egg whites in a medium bowl until frothy. • Beat in the superfine sugar, vanilla sugar, cream of tartar, and salt. • Fold in all the almonds and the chocolate. • Form domes the size of apricots. • Place 2 inches (5 cm) apart on the prepared baking sheets. • Bake for 20–30 minutes, or until firm to the touch. • Cool on the cookie sheets.

Makes: 20 cookies • Prep: 40 min • Cooking: 20–30 min Level: 1

- ³/₄ cup (125 g) almonds
- 2 large egg whites
- ½ cup (100 g) superfine (caster) sugar
- 2 tablespoons vanilla sugar (see page 414)
- ⅛ teaspoon cream of tartar
- ⅛ teaspoon salt
- 2 oz (60 g) bittersweet (dark) chocolate, grated

CHOCOLATE VANILLA COOKIES

- 1¹/₃ cups (200 g) all-purpose (plain) flour
- 1 teaspoon baking powder
- ⅛ teaspoon salt
- ½ cup (125 g) butter, softened
- ½ cup (100 g) sugar
- 1 teaspoon vanilla extract (essence)
- 1 large egg yolk, lightly beaten

Line a 9 x 5-inch (22 x 11-cm) loaf pan with waxed paper. • Mix the flour, baking powder, and salt in a medium bowl. • Beat the butter and sugar in a large bowl with an electric mixer on high speed until creamy. • Add the vanilla, egg yolk, and dry ingredients. • Divide the dough among three bowls. • Melt the chocolate in a double boiler over barely simmering water. • Add the almond extract to the first bowl, the chocolate to the second bowl, and the walnuts to the third bowl. • Spread the

almond mixture in the pan, followed by the walnut mixture. Finish with the chocolate mixture. • Refrigerate for 4 hours. • Preheat the oven to 350°F (180°C/gas 4). • Butter four cookie sheets. • Cut the dough into ¼-inch (5-mm) thick slices. • Place 1 inch (2.5 cm) apart on the sheets. • Bake for 10–12 minutes, or until browned. • Cool on racks.

Makes: 30–35 cookies • Prep: 30 min + 4 hr to chill Cooking: 10–12 min • Level: 2

- 1 oz (30 g) semisweet (dark) chocolate, coarsely chopped
- ½ teaspoon almond extract (essence)
- ²/₃ cup (70 g) chopped walnuts

Chocolate Cookies

WHITE CHOCOLATE REFRIGERATOR COOKIES

- 1²/₃ cups (250 g) all-purpose (plain) flour
- 1½ teaspoons baking powder
- ¼ teaspoon salt
- ½ cup (125 g) butter, softened
- ¼ cup (60 ml) sunflower or peanut oil
- ¾ cup (150 g) firmly packed light brown sugar
- 1 large egg, lightly beaten
- ½ teaspoon vanilla extract (essence)
- 6 oz (180 g) white chocolate
- 1 cup (100 g) chopped walnuts

Mix the flour, baking powder, and salt in a medium bowl. • Beat the butter, oil, and brown sugar in a large bowl with an electric mixer on medium speed until creamy. • Add the egg and vanilla, beating until just blended. • Mix in the dry ingredients, chocolate chips, and walnuts. • Form the dough into a 7-inch (18-cm) log, wrap in plastic wrap (cling film), and refrigerate for 30 minutes. • Preheat the oven to 375°F (190°C/gas 5). • Butter two cookie sheets. • Slice the dough ¼ inch (5 mm) thick and place 2 inches (5 cm) apart on the prepared cookie sheets. • Bake for 8–10 minutes, or until just golden at the edges. • Transfer to racks to cool.

Makes: 28 cookies • Prep: 40 min + 30 min to chill
Cooking: 8–10 min • Level: 1

PIQUANT MOCHA COOKIES

Preheat the oven to 350°F (180°C/gas 4). • Butter two cookie sheets. • Mix the flour, baking powder, pepper, and salt in a small bowl. • Heat the raisins with the coffee liqueur in a small saucepan over low heat. • Melt the chocolate with the butter in a double boiler over barely simmering water. Set aside to cool. • Beat the eggs and sugar in a large bowl until creamy. • Beat in the melted chocolate and vanilla. • Beat in the dry ingredients, followed by the raisin mixture and the chocolate chips. • Drop tablespoons of the dough 2 inches (5 cm) apart onto the prepared cookie sheets. • Bake for 10–12 minutes, or until set but still slightly soft. • Cool until the cookies firm slightly. Transfer to racks to finish cooling.

Makes: 25–30 cookies • Prep: 20 min • Cooking: 10–12 min
Level: 1

- 2 cups (300 g) all-purpose (plain) flour
- ½ teaspoon baking powder
- ½ teaspoon freshly ground black pepper
- ¼ teaspoon salt
- ½ cup (90 g) raisins
- 2 tablespoons coffee liqueur
- 8 oz (250 g) bittersweet (dark) chocolate, coarsely chopped
- ¼ cup (60 g) butter
- 2 large eggs
- ¾ cup (150 g) sugar
- 2 teaspoons vanilla extract (essence)
- 1 cup (180 g) semisweet (dark) chocolate chips

White chocolate refrigerator cookies

Chocolate wheel cookies

CHOCOLATE WHEEL COOKIES

- 1²/₃ cups (250 g) all-purpose (plain) flour
- 1 teaspoon baking powder
- ⅛ teaspoon salt
- ²/₃ cup (150 g) butter
- ¾ cup (150 g) firmly packed light brown sugar
- 1 large egg, lightly beaten
- 2 teaspoons rum extract (essence)
- 1 teaspoon vanilla extract (essence)
- 2 oz (60 g) semisweet (dark) chocolate, coarsely chopped
- 2 tablespoons vanilla sugar (see page 414)
- 2 tablespoons unsweetened cocoa powder
- 1 tablespoon milk

Mix the flour, baking powder, and salt in a large bowl. • Cut in the butter until the mixture resembles fine crumbs. • Mix in the brown sugar, egg, and rum and vanilla extracts. Form the dough into two equal-size disks, wrap in plastic wrap (cling film), and refrigerate for 30 minutes. • Melt the chocolate in a double boiler over simmering water. Add the vanilla sugar, cocoa, and milk. • Knead the chocolate mixture into half the dough. • Form the chocolate dough into a 9-inch (23-cm) log. Refrigerate for 30 minutes. • Roll out the plain dough to fit around the chocolate roll. Wrap the plain dough around the chilled chocolate dough. • Refrigerate for 20 minutes. • Preheat the oven to 350°F (180°C/gas 4). • Line two cookie sheets with parchment paper. • Slice the dough ¼ inch (5 mm) thick and place on the sheets. • Bake for 12–15 minutes, or until lightly browned.

Makes: 36 cookies • Prep: 45 min + 80 min to chill • Cooking: 12–15 min • Level: 2

CHOC-TOP DROPS

Preheat the oven to 400°F (200°C/gas 6). • Butter three cookie sheets. • Mix the flour, baking soda, and salt in a large bowl. • Melt the chocolate in a double boiler over barely simmering water. • Beat the butter, sugar, and melted chocolate in a large bowl with an electric mixer on medium speed until creamy. • Add the vanilla and egg, beating until just blended. • Mix in the dry ingredients and milk until well blended. • Drop teaspoons of the dough 1 inch (2.5 cm) apart onto the prepared cookie sheets. • Bake for 8–10 minutes, or until slightly risen. • Cool on the sheets until the cookies firm slightly. Transfer to racks to finish cooling. • Spread the frosting over the tops of the cookies and decorate with the pecans.

Makes: 36 cookies • Prep: 25 min • Cooking: 8–10 min Level: 1

- 1¹/₃ cups (200 g) all-purpose (plain) flour
- ½ teaspoon baking soda (bicarbonate of soda)
- ⅛ teaspoon salt
- 2 oz (60 g) semisweet (dark) chocolate, coarsely chopped
- ½ cup (125 g) butter, softened
- 1 cup (200 g) sugar
- 1 teaspoon vanilla extract (essence)
- 1 large egg, lightly beaten
- 2 tablespoons milk

- 1 cup (250 ml) chocolate frosting (see page 414)
- ½ cup (50 g) pecans, halved

Chocolate Cookies

CHOCOLATE HAZELNUT COOKIES

- 3/4 cup (90 g) hazelnuts
- 1 cup (200 g) granulated sugar
- 2 cups (300 g) all-purpose (plain) flour
- 1 teaspoon baking powder
- 1/4 teaspoon salt
- 1 cup (250 g) butter, softened
- 1/2 cup (100 g) firmly packed light brown sugar
- 2 large eggs
- 1 teaspoon vanilla extract (essence)
- 1–2 tablespoons freshly squeezed orange juice
- 7 oz (200 g) semisweet (dark) chocolate, coarsely chopped

Preheat the oven to 325°F (170°C/gas 3). • Set out three cookie sheets. • Spread the hazelnuts on a baking sheet. Toast for 7 minutes, or until lightly golden. • Let cool completely. Transfer to a food processor, add 1/2 cup (100 g) of the granulated sugar and process until the nuts are coarsely chopped. • Mix the flour, baking powder, and salt in a medium bowl. • Beat the butter and remaining granulated sugar and brown sugar in a large bowl with an electric mixer on medium speed until creamy. • Add the eggs, beating until just blended. Add the vanilla. • Mix in the dry ingredients and enough orange juice to make a smooth dough. • Stir in the chocolate and hazelnuts. • Drop teaspoons of the dough 1 inch (2.5 cm) apart onto the cookie sheets. • Bake for 10–12 minutes, or until golden brown. • Cool on the cookie sheets for 3 minutes. • Transfer to racks to finish cooling.

Makes: about 45 cookies • Prep: 40 min • Cooking: 10–12 min • Level: 1

DRIZZLED CHOCOLATE FINGERS

Preheat the oven to 350°F (180°C/gas 4). • Line two cookie sheets with parchment paper. • Mix the flour, cornstarch, and salt in a medium bowl. • Beat the butter, confectioners' sugar, and vanilla in a large bowl with an electric mixer on medium speed until creamy. • Mix in the dry ingredients. • Fit a pastry bag with a 1/2-inch (1-cm) tip. Fill the pastry bag, twist the opening tightly closed, and squeeze out 3-inch (8-cm) lines, spacing them 2 inches (5 cm) apart on the prepared cookie sheets. • Bake for 12–15 minutes, or until just golden at the edges. • Transfer to racks to cool. • Melt the semisweet and white chocolate separately in double boilers over barely simmering water. • Spoon the chocolates into separate small freezer bags and cut off tiny corners. • Drizzle over the cookies in a decorative manner. • Let stand for 30 minutes until set.

Makes: 18–20 cookies • Prep: 30 min + 30 min to chill Cooking: 12–15 min Level: 2

- 1 cup (150 g) all-purpose (plain) flour
- 1/2 cup (75 g) cornstarch (cornflour)
- 1/8 teaspoon salt
- 3/4 cup (180 g) butter, softened
- 1/3 cup (50 g) confectioners' (icing) sugar
- 1/2 teaspoon vanilla extract (essence)
- 2 oz (60 g) semisweet (dark) chocolate, coarsely chopped
- 2 oz (60 g) white chocolate, coarsely chopped

FILLED MARZIPAN COOKIES

Cookies
- 2 1/3 cups (350 g) all-purpose (plain) flour
- 1 tablespoon ground ginger
- 2 teaspoons baking soda (bicarbonate of soda)
- 1/8 teaspoon salt
- 1 cup (250 g) honey
- 2/3 cup (140 g) sugar
- 2 cups (200 g) finely ground almonds
- 3/4 cup (75 g) chopped candied peel

Mix the flour, ginger, baking soda, and salt in a medium bowl. • Heat the honey and sugar in a small saucepan over low heat until the sugar has dissolved. • Let cool for 5 minutes. • Use a wooden spoon to work in the dry ingredients, almonds, and candied peel to form a smooth dough. • Cover with a clean kitchen towel and let rest for 2 days. • Preheat the oven to 375°F (190°C/gas 3). • Line four cookie sheets with parchment paper. • Marzipan Filling: Knead the marzipan and preserves in a medium bowl until smooth. Work in the almonds and candied lemon peel. • Roll out the cookie dough on a lightly floured surface to a 1/4 inch (5 mm) thick. Cut into two 12 x 6-inch (30 x 15-cm) rectangles. • Cover the dough with the marzipan and sprinkle with currants. • Roll the dough up tightly to form logs about 2 inches (5 cm) in diameter. Slice 1/2 inch (1 cm) thick. Use a spatula to transfer the slices to the prepared cookie sheets, placing them 1 inch (2.5 cm) apart. • Bake, one sheet at a time, for 15–20 minutes, or until just golden. • Let cool completely. • Drizzle the frosting over the cookies. • Decorate with the pistachios and candied fruit.

Makes: 30–35 cookies • Prep: 1 hr + 2 days to rest Cooking: 15–20 min • Level: 2

Marzipan Filling
- 7 oz (200 g) marzipan, softened
- 3/4 cup (240 g) white currant preserves (jam)
- 1 cup (100 g) chopped almonds
- 1/2 cup (50 g) chopped lemon peel
- 1/2 cup (90 g) dried currants
- 1 cup (250 ml) chocolate frosting (see page 414)
- 3–4 tablespoons chopped pistachios
- 2 tablespoons finely chopped candied fruit

Chocolate Cookies

GLAZED CHOCOLATE COFFEE COOKIES

- 3 oz (90 g) semisweet (dark) chocolate, coarsely chopped
- 1 cup (150 g) all-purpose (plain) flour
- 2 tablespoons unsweetened cocoa powder
- 1 teaspoon instant coffee powder
- 1 teaspoon baking soda (bicarbonate of soda)
- 1/4 teaspoon salt
- 2/3 cup (150 g) butter
- 1/2 cup (100 g) firmly packed brown sugar
- 1 large egg
- 1 teaspoon vanilla extract (essence)

Frosting
- 1 1/3 cups (200 g) confectioners' (icing) sugar
- 1 teaspoon instant coffee powder
- 1–2 tablespoons warm water

Melt the chocolate in a bowl set over simmering water. • Mix the flour, cocoa, coffee, baking soda, and salt in a medium bowl. • Beat the butter and brown sugar in a large bowl with an electric mixer on medium speed until creamy. • Add the egg and vanilla and beat for 1 minute. • Stir in the melted chocolate. • Mix in the dry ingredients. • Divide the dough in half. Form into two 9 x 2-inch (23 x 5-cm) logs, wrap in plastic wrap (cling film), and refrigerate for 2 hours. • Preheat the oven to 350°F (180°C/gas 4). • Butter two cookie sheets. • Slice the dough 2/3 inch (1.5 cm) thick and place on the cookie sheets. • Bake for 12–15 minutes, or until just firm. • Cool on the sheets for 5 minutes. • Transfer to racks to cool. • Frosting: Mix the sugar and coffee in a small bowl. Stir in enough warm water to make a drizzling consistency. • Drizzle over the cookies and let set.

Makes: about 20–25 cookies • Prep: 45 min + 2 hr to chill Cooking: 12–15 min • Level: 1

DOUBLE CHOCOLATE COOKIES

Preheat the oven to 325°F (170°C/gas 3). • Set out two cookie sheets. • Mix the flour, baking powder, and salt in a large bowl. • Melt the semisweet and white chocolates and butter in a double boiler over barely simmering water. • Beat the eggs and sugar in a large bowl with an electric mixer on medium speed until pale and thick. • Beat in the chocolate mixture, coffee granules, and almond extract. • Mix in the dry ingredients, almonds, and white chocolate chips. • Drop tablespoons of the dough 3 inches (8 cm) apart onto the cookie sheets. • Bake for 20–25 minutes, or until lightly cracked on top. • Transfer to racks and let cool.

Makes: about 35 cookies • Prep: 20 min • Cooking: 20–25 min • Level: 1

- 2/3 cup (100 g) all-purpose (plain) flour
- 1/2 teaspoon baking powder
- 1/8 teaspoon salt
- 6 oz (180 g) semisweet (dark) chocolate, coarsely chopped
- 6 oz (180 g) white chocolate, coarsely chopped
- 1/2 cup (125 g) butter, cut up
- 3 large eggs
- 1 cup (200 g) sugar
- 1 tablespoon instant coffee granules
- 1 teaspoon almond extract (essence)
- 3 cups (300 g) coarsely chopped almonds
- 1 cup (180 g) white chocolate chips

CHOCOLATE PEANUT BITES

- 1 cup (150 g) all-purpose (plain) flour
- 2 tablespoons cocoa unsweetened powder
- 1 teaspoon baking powder
- 1/8 teaspoon salt
- 1/2 cup (125 g) butter, softened
- 1/2 cup (100 g) sugar
- 1 large egg
- 1 cup (100 g) coarsely chopped salted peanuts

Preheat the oven to 325°F (170°C/gas 3). • Butter two cookie sheets. • Mix the flour, cocoa, baking powder, and salt in a medium bowl. • Beat the butter and sugar in a large bowl with an electric mixer on medium speed until creamy. • Add the egg, beating until just blended. • Mix in the dry ingredients, followed by the peanuts. • Drop teaspoons of the dough 1 inch (2.5 cm) apart onto the prepared cookie sheets. • Bake for 20–25 minutes, or until crisp and golden brown. • Cool on the sheets until the cookies firm slightly. • Transfer to racks to cool.

Makes: 20–25 cookies • Prep: 20 min • Cooking: 20–25 min Level: 1

CHOCOLATE HAZELNUT TRUFFLES

Preheat the oven to 350°F (180°C/gas 4). • Butter two cookie sheets. • Mix the flour and salt in a large bowl. • Beat the butter and sugar in a large bowl with an electric mixer on medium speed until creamy. • Add the vanilla. • Stir the ground hazelnuts and dry ingredients into the mixture. • Form the dough into balls the size of marbles and place 1 inch (2.5 cm) apart on the prepared cookie sheets. • Bake for 12–15 minutes, or until firm. • Transfer to racks to cool. • Roll in the cocoa until well coated.

Makes: about 24 cookies • Prep: 20 min • Cooking: 12–15 min • Level: 1

- 2/3 cup (100 g) all-purpose (plain) flour
- 1/8 teaspoon salt
- 1/2 cup (125 g) butter, softened
- 1/4 cup (50 g) sugar
- 1 teaspoon vanilla extract (essence)
- 1 cup (150 g) finely ground hazelnuts
- 1/3 cup (50 g) unsweetened cocoa powder

Chocolate chip wedges

CHOCOLATE CHIP WEDGES

- 2¼ cups (330 g) all-purpose (plain) flour
- 1 teaspoon baking soda (bicarbonate of soda)
- ½ teaspoon salt
- 1 cup (250 g) butter, softened
- ¾ cup (150 g) granulated sugar
- ¾ cup (150 g) firmly packed light brown sugar
- ½ teaspoon vanilla extract (essence)
- 2 large eggs
- 1 cup (180 g) semisweet (dark) chocolate chips

These crisp cookies are packed with chocolate and energy. Serve still warm with coffee.
Preheat the oven to 375°F (190°C/gas 5). • Set out a 14-inch (35-cm) pizza pan. • Mix the flour, baking soda, and salt in a medium bowl. • Beat the butter and granulated and brown sugars in a large bowl with an electric mixer on medium speed until creamy. • Add the vanilla and eggs, beating until just blended. • Mix in the dry ingredients and chocolate chips. • Spread the mixture in the pan. • Bake for 20–25 minutes, or until lightly browned. • Cool completely in the pan. • Cut into wedges.
Makes: 16 cookies • Prep: 20 min • Cooking: 20–25 min Level: 2

TWO-TONED COOKIES

Mix the flour, baking powder, and salt in a large bowl. • Cut in the butter until it resembles fine crumbs. • Mix in the sugar, egg, and vanilla. • Divide the dough in half. • Mix the cocoa and milk in a small bowl. • Knead the cocoa mixture into one piece of dough. • Form the plain dough into a 12-inch (30-cm) log. Brush with cold water. • Roll out the cocoa dough into a 12 x 6-inch (30 x 15-cm) rectangle. • Wrap the cocoa dough around the plain dough. • Wrap in plastic wrap (cling film) and refrigerate for 30 minutes. • Preheat the oven to 375°F (180°C/gas 4). • Butter three cookie sheets. • Slice the dough ¼ inch (5 mm) thick and place 2 inches (5 cm) apart on the sheets. • Bake for 8–10 minutes, or until lightly browned.
Makes: about 48 cookies • Prep: 40 min + 30 min to chill Cooking: 8–10 min • Level: 2

- 1⅔ cups (250 g) all-purpose (plain) flour
- 1 teaspoon baking powder
- ⅛ teaspoon salt
- ½ cup (125 g) butter, cut up
- ¾ cup (150 g) sugar
- 1 large egg, lightly beaten
- 1 teaspoon vanilla extract (essence)
- 4 tablespoons unsweetened cocoa powder
- 1 tablespoon milk

BANANA CHOCOLATE CHIP COOKIES

- 2⅓ cups (350 g) all-purpose (plain) flour
- 1 teaspoon baking soda (bicarbonate of soda)
- ¼ teaspoon salt
- 1 cup (250 g) butter
- ¾ cup (150 g) firmly packed dark brown sugar
- ½ cup (100 g) granulated sugar
- 1 teaspoon vanilla extract (essence)
- 2 large eggs
- 1 large banana, peeled and lightly mashed
- ½ cup (125 g) semisweet (dark) chocolate chips
- ½ cup (50 g) coarsely chopped dried banana chips

Preheat the oven to 375°F (190°C/gas 5). • Butter three cookie sheets. • Mix the flour, baking soda, and salt in a medium bowl. • Beat the butter and both sugars in a large bowl with an electric mixer on medium speed until creamy. • Add the vanilla and eggs, beating until just blended. • Mix in the banana and dry ingredients, followed by the chocolate and banana chips. • Drop teaspoons of the dough 1 inch (2.5 cm) apart onto the prepared cookie sheets. • Bake, one sheet at a time, for 15–20 minutes, or until just golden. • Cool on the sheets until the cookies firm slightly. • Transfer to racks to finish cooling.
Makes: about 36 cookies • Prep: 20 min • Cooking: 15–20 min • Level: 1

CHERRY AND WHITE CHOCOLATE COOKIES

Preheat the oven to 375°F (190°C/gas 5). • Butter two cookie sheets. • Mix the flour, baking powder, and salt in a large bowl. • Beat the butter, sugar, and vanilla in a large bowl with an electric mixer on medium speed until creamy. • Mix in the dry ingredients, cherries, and white chocolate. • Drop rounded teaspoons of the dough 1 inch (2.5 cm) apart onto the prepared cookie sheets. • Bake for 15–20 minutes, or until just golden. • Cool on the sheets until the cookies firm slightly. Transfer to racks to finish cooling.
Makes: 18–20 cookies • Prep: 20 min • Cooking: 15–20 min Level: 1

- 1 cup (150 g) all-purpose (plain) flour
- ½ teaspoon baking powder
- ⅛ teaspoon salt
- ½ cup (125 g) butter, softened
- ¼ cup (50 g) sugar
- ½ teaspoon vanilla extract (essence)
- ⅓ cup (40 g) finely chopped candied cherries
- 1 oz (30 g) white chocolate, finely chopped

Chocolate Cookies

Chocolate vanilla drop cookies

- 1 cup (150 g) all-purpose (plain) flour
- 2 tablespoons unsweetened cocoa powder
- 1 teaspoon baking powder
- 1/8 teaspoon salt
- 2/3 cup (175 g) butter, softened
- 1/2 cup (100 g) sugar
- 1/2 teaspoon vanilla extract (essence)

Preheat the oven to 375°F (190°C/gas 5). • Butter a cookie sheet. • Mix the flour, cocoa, baking powder, and salt in a medium bowl. • Beat the butter and sugar in a large bowl with an electric mixer on medium speed until creamy. • Mix in the vanilla and dry ingredients. • Drop tablespoons of the dough 2 inches (5 cm) apart onto the prepared cookie sheet. • Bake for 15–18 minutes, or until firm to the touch. • Cool on the sheets until the cookies firm slightly. • Transfer to racks to finish cooling.

Makes: 15–20 cookies • Prep: 20 min • Cooking: 15–18 min Level: 1

Chocolate chip cookie cakes

Butter and flour two 12-cup muffin pans, or line with foil or paper baking cups. • Mix the flour and salt in a medium bowl. • Beat the butter and both sugars in a large bowl with an electric mixer on medium speed until creamy. • Add the vanilla and egg and egg yolk, beating until just blended. • Mix in the baking soda mixture, followed by the dry ingredients. • Stir in the chocolate chips. • Spoon the cookie dough evenly into the prepared cups and refrigerate for 30 minutes. • Preheat the oven to 350°F (180°C/gas 4). • Bake for 15–18 minutes, or until set. • Cool completely in the pans.

Makes: 20–24 cookies • Prep: 20 min + 30 min to chill Cooking: 15–18 min Level: 1

- 2 cups (300 g) all-purpose (plain) flour
- 1/4 teaspoon salt
- 1 cup (250 g) butter, softened
- 1 1/2 cups (300 g) firmly packed dark brown sugar
- 1/4 cup (50 g) granulated sugar
- 1 teaspoon vanilla extract (essence)
- 1 large egg + 1 large egg yolk
- 1 teaspoon baking soda (bicarbonate of soda) dissolved in 1 tablespoon hot water
- 1 1/4 cups (230 g) semisweet (dark) chocolate chips

Chocolate vanilla drop cookies

Chocolate cinnamon munchies

CHOCOLATE CINNAMON MUNCHIES

- 1 cup (150 g) all-purpose (plain) flour
- 2 tablespoons unsweetened cocoa powder
- 1 teaspoon baking powder
- ¼ teaspoon ground cinnamon
- ⅛ teaspoon salt
- ½ cup (125 g) butter, softened
- ½ cup (100 g) sugar
- 1 large egg yolk
- 2 oz (60 g) semisweet (dark) chocolate, coarsely chopped

Preheat the oven to 350°F (180°C/gas 4). • Butter two cookie sheets. • Mix the flour, cocoa, baking powder, cinnamon, and salt in a medium bowl. • Beat the butter and sugar in a large bowl with an electric mixer on medium speed until creamy. • Add the egg yolk, beating until just blended. • Mix in the dry ingredients. • Drop teaspoons of the dough 1 inch (2.5 cm) apart onto the prepared cookie sheets. • Bake for 12–15 minutes, or until firm around the edges. • Transfer to racks to cool. • Melt the chocolate in a double boiler over barely simmering water. Drizzle the tops with the melted chocolate.

Makes: 25–30 cookies • Prep: 20 min • Cooking: 12–15 min Level: 1

COCOA BALLS

Preheat the oven to 325°F (170°C/gas 3). • Line three cookie sheets with parchment paper. • Mix the flour, cornstarch, cocoa, and salt in a medium bowl. • Beat the butter and granulated sugar in a large bowl with an electric mixer on medium speed until creamy. • Mix in the dry ingredients to make a smooth dough. • Form heaping teaspoons of the dough into balls the size of walnuts and place 2 inches (5 cm) apart on the prepared cookie sheets. • Bake, one sheet at a time, for 35–40 minutes, or until pale gold. • Cool on the sheets until the cookies firm slightly. Transfer to racks to finish cooling. • Place the confectioners' sugar in a small bowl and dip the cookies until well coated.

Makes: about 40 cookies • Prep: 20 min • Cooking: 35–40 min • Level: 1

- 1½ cups (225 g) all-purpose (plain) flour
- ⅔ cup (100 g) cornstarch (cornflour)
- 2 tablespoons unsweetened cocoa powder
- ⅛ teaspoon salt
- 1 cup (250 g) butter, softened
- ¼ cup (50 g) sugar
- ⅔ cup (100 g) confectioners' (icing) sugar, to dust

Chocolate hazelnut hearts

CHOCOLATE HAZELNUT HEARTS

- 1⅓ cups (200 g) all-purpose (plain) flour
- ⅓ cup (50 g) unsweetened cocoa powder
- ⅛ teaspoon salt
- ½ cup (125 g) butter, softened
- ⅔ cup (140 g) firmly packed light brown sugar
- 2 large eggs, 1 separated
- ½ cup (75 g) finely ground hazelnuts
- ½ cup (50 g) finely chopped hazelnuts

Mix the flour, cocoa, and salt in a medium bowl. • Beat the butter and brown sugar in a large bowl with an electric mixer on medium speed until creamy. • Add 1 whole egg and 1 egg yolk, beating until just blended. • Mix in the dry ingredients and ground hazelnuts to form a smooth dough. • Press the dough into a disk, wrap in plastic wrap (cling film), and refrigerate for 30 minutes. • Preheat the oven to 350°F (180°C/gas 4). • Line two cookie sheets with parchment paper. • Roll out the dough on a lightly floured surface to ¼ inch (5 mm) thick. • Use a 1½-inch (4-cm) heart-shaped cookie cutter to cut out the cookies. Gather the dough scraps, re-roll, and continue cutting out cookies until all the dough is used. • Use a spatula to transfer the cookies to the prepared cookie sheets, placing them 1 inch (2.5 cm) apart. • Use a wire whisk to beat the remaining egg white in a small bowl until frothy and brush over the tops of the cookies. Sprinkle with the chopped hazelnuts. • Bake for 10–15 minutes, or until golden brown. • Transfer to racks to cool.

Makes: about 25 cookies • Prep: 40 min + 30 min to chill Cooking: 10–15 min • Level: 1

DOUBLE CHOCOLATE CHERRY COOKIES

Preheat the oven to 350°F (180°C/gas 4). • Line three cookie sheets with parchment paper. • Soak the cherries in the kirsch in a medium bowl for 15 minutes. Drain well. • Mix the flour, baking soda, and salt in a medium bowl. • Beat the butter and granulated and raw sugars in a large bowl with an electric mixer on medium speed until creamy. • Add the vanilla and almond extracts and egg, beating until just blended. • Mix in the dry ingredients, followed by the cherries, white and semisweet chocolates, and macadamia nuts. • Drop heaped tablespoons of the dough 2 inches (5 cm) apart onto the prepared cookie sheets. • Bake for 12–15 minutes, or until lightly browned. • Cool the cookies on the sheets for 15 minutes. • Transfer to racks and let cool completely.

Makes: about 32 cookies • Prep: 20 min + 15 min to soak the cherries • Cooking: 12–15 min • Level: 1

- 1 can (7 oz/200 g) pitted sour cherries, drained
- ½ cup (125 ml) kirsch
- 1½ cups (225 g) all-purpose (plain) flour
- ½ teaspoon baking soda (bicarbonate of soda)
- ¼ teaspoon salt
- ½ cup (125 g) butter, softened
- ½ cup (100 g) granulated sugar
- ½ cup (100 g) raw sugar (Demerara or Barbados)
- 1½ teaspoons vanilla extract (essence)
- ¼ teaspoon almond extract (essence)
- 1 large egg
- 5 oz (150 g) white chocolate, coarsely chopped
- 5 oz (150 g) semisweet (dark) chocolate, coarsely chopped
- ½ cup (50 g) finely chopped macadamia nuts

PEANUT BUTTER WEDGES

- 1¾ cups (275 g) all-purpose (plain) flour
- ½ teaspoon baking soda (bicarbonate of soda)
- ½ teaspoon salt
- ½ cup (125 g) butter, softened
- 1¼ cups (250 g) firmly packed light brown sugar
- ¾ cup (180 g) smooth peanut butter

Preheat the oven to 375°F (190°C/gas 5). • Set out two 12-inch (30-cm) pizza pans. • Mix the flour, baking soda, and salt in a medium bowl. • Beat the butter, brown sugar, peanut butter, milk, and vanilla in a large bowl with an electric mixer on medium speed until creamy. • Add the egg, beating until just blended. • Mix in the dry ingredients. • Divide the dough in half. • Spread the dough in the pans. • Bake for 10–12 minutes, or until lightly browned.

• Cool completely in the pans. • Melt the white and semisweet chocolates in separate double boilers over barely simmering water. • Drizzle the chocolate over the cookies and let stand for 30 minutes to set. • Cut each pan into 16 wedges.

Makes: 32 cookies • Prep: 20 min + 30 min to stand Cooking: 10–12 min • Level: 1

- ¼ cup (60 ml) milk
- ½ teaspoon vanilla extract (essence)
- 1 large egg
- 4 oz (125 g) white chocolate, coarsely chopped
- 4 oz (125 g) semisweet (dark) chocolate, coarsely chopped

Chocolate Cookies

CHOCOLATE DIED FRUIT WAFERS

- 3/4 cup (125 g) all-purpose (plain) flour
- 1/8 teaspoon salt
- 1/2 cup (125 g) butter, cut up
- 3/4 cup (150 g) sugar
- 2 teaspoons honey
- 1/2 cup (50 g) flaked almonds, toasted
- 2/3 cup (70 g) finely chopped dried cranberries
- 2/3 cup (70 g) finely chopped dried pineapple
- 2/3 cup (70 g) finely chopped dried apricots
- 4 oz (125 g) semisweet (dark) chocolate, coarsely chopped

Preheat the oven to 350°F (180°C/gas 4).
• Line four cookie sheets with parchment paper. • Mix the flour and salt in a medium bowl. • Melt the butter with the sugar and honey in a medium saucepan over low heat until the sugar has dissolved. • Increase the heat and bring the mixture almost to a boil.
• Remove from the heat and mix in the almonds and dried fruit. • Add the dry ingredients all at once and stir until well blended. • Drop teaspoons of the dough 3 inches (8 cm) apart on the prepared cookie sheets, flattening them slightly. • Bake for 8–10 minutes, or until golden brown on top.
• Cool on the sheets until the cookies firm slightly. Transfer to racks to finish cooling. •
Melt the chocolate in a double boiler over barely simmering water. Arrange the cookies flat-side up on a sheet of waxed paper. •
Brush with the melted chocolate and let stand for 30 minutes until set.

Makes: about 45 cookies • Prep: 25 min + 30 min to set Cooking: 8–10 min • Level: 2

CHOCOLATE APRICOT PRETZELS

Preheat the oven to 350°F (180°C/gas 4).
• Line three cookie sheets with parchment paper. • Mix the apricots, orange juice, and 1 tablespoon butter in a small saucepan. Simmer over low heat for 5 minutes, or until the apricots have softened. • Let cool completely. • Mix the flour, baking powder, and salt in a large bowl. Stir in the sugar.
• Use a pastry blender to cut in the remaining butter until the mixture resembles fine crumbs. • Add the egg yolks, chocolate, and apricot mixture to make a stiff dough.
• Form tablespoons of the dough into 6-inch (15-cm) ropes. • Make each rope into a pretzel shape by twisting the two ends around each other, then bringing both back near to the center of the strip, about 1 inch apart. • Use a spatula to transfer the cookies to the cookie sheet, spacing 1 inch (2.5 cm) apart. • Bake for 12–15 minutes, or until just golden. • Transfer to racks to cool.

Makes: about 35 cookies • Prep: 45 min • Cooking: 12–15 min • Level: 2

- 1 cup (100 g) finely chopped dried apricots
- 1/3 cup (90 ml) freshly squeezed orange juice
- 5 tablespoons butter
- 1 1/3 cups (180 g) all-purpose (plain) flour
- 1 teaspoon baking powder
- 1/4 teaspoon salt
- 1/4 cup (50 g) sugar
- 2 large egg yolks, lightly beaten
- 2 oz (60 g) semisweet (dark) chocolate, finely grated

COCOA CORN FLAKE COOKIES

- 3/4 cup (180 g) butter, softened
- 1/2 cup (100 g) sugar
- 2 cups (300 g) all-purpose (plain) flour
- 2 tablespoons unsweetened cocoa powder
- 1/4 cup (50 g) corn flakes, lightly crushed
- 1 cup (250 g) chocolate frosting (see page 414)
- 30 walnut halves, to decorate

Preheat the oven to 350°F (180°C/gas 4).
• Butter two cookie sheets. • Beat the butter and sugar in a large bowl with an electric mixer on medium speed until creamy. • Mix in the flour and cocoa. Stir in the corn flakes until well mixed. • Drop teaspoons of the dough 1 inch (2.5 cm) apart onto the prepared cookie sheets. • Bake for 10–15 minutes, or until firm to the touch. •
Transfer to racks to cool. • Spread the frosting over the tops of the cooled cookies. Decorate with the walnut halves.

Makes: about 30 cookies • Prep: 15 min • Cooking: 10–15 min • Level: 1

DUSTED COOKIES

Preheat the oven to 350°F (180°C/gas 4).
• Butter two cookie sheets. • Mix the flour, baking powder, and salt in a large bowl and make a well in the center. • Add the butter, sugar, eggs, and milk. • Use your hands to knead the mixture into a smooth dough.
• Form the dough into balls the size of walnuts and place 1 inch (2.5 cm) apart on the prepared cookie sheets. • Bake for 15–20 minutes, or until just golden.
• Transfer to racks and let cool completely.
• Dip half of each cookie in the confectioners' sugar and the other half in the cocoa.

Makes: about 25 cookies • Prep: 35 min • Cooking: 15–20 min • Level: 1

- 1 2/3 cups (250 g) all-purpose (plain) flour
- 1 teaspoon baking powder
- 1/8 teaspoon salt
- 1/3 cup (90 g) butter, softened
- 1/4 cup (50 g) sugar
- 2 large eggs
- 1 tablespoon milk
- 4 tablespoons confectioners' (icing) sugar
- 2 tablespoons unsweetened cocoa powder

Chocolate Cookies

WHITE CHOCOLATE FLORENTINES

M• ½ cup (125 ml) heavy (double) cream
• ¼ vanilla pod
• 2 tablespoons butter
• ½ cup (100 g) sugar
• ½ cup (50 g) coarsely chopped almonds
• ¼ cup (30 g) coarsely chopped hazelnuts
• 1 cup (100 g) finely chopped mixed candied peel
• ¼ cup (25 g) finely sliced red candied cherries
• 1 tablespoon finely chopped candied angelica
• 2 tablespoons all-purpose (plain) flour
• 7 oz (200 g) white chocolate, coarsely chopped

Preheat the oven to 325°F (170°C/gas 3).
• Line four cookie sheets with parchment paper. • Heat the cream with the vanilla pod, butter, and sugar in a medium saucepan over medium heat, stirring constantly, until the sugar has dissolved. Bring to a boil and remove from the heat immediately. Let cool then discard the vanilla pod. • Mix the almonds, hazelnuts, candied peel, cherries, angelica, and flour in a large bowl. • Stir in the cooled cream mixture and mix well.
• Drop heaped teaspoons of the mixture 4 inches (10 cm) apart onto the prepared cookie sheets, flattening them to make 2-inch (5 cm) circles. Do not place more than five cookies on one sheet. • Bake for 10–12 minutes, or until golden around the edges. • Cool on the sheets until the cookies firm slightly. Transfer to racks and let cool completely. • Melt the white chocolate in a double boiler over barely simmering water. • Lay the cold florentines flat-side upward on a sheet of waxed paper, and spread the chocolate over them with a pastry brush. For a thick coating, paint the cookies several times. • When they are nearly set, make swirly patterns with a fork on the white chocolate base.

Makes: about 20 cookies • Prep: 45 min • Cooking: 10–12 min • Level: 3

HAZELNUT FLORENTINES

Preheat the oven to 325°F (170°C/gas 3).
• Spread the hazelnuts on a large baking sheet. Toast for 7 minutes, or until lightly golden. • Transfer to a food processor with ¼ cup (50 g) of sugar and process until very finely chopped. • Increase the oven temperature to 375°F (170°C/gas 3). • Set out three cookie sheets. • Melt the butter with the honey, cream, and remaining sugar in a small saucepan over low heat until the sugar has dissolved completely. • Bring to a boil and boil for 2 minutes. • Remove from the heat and stir in the nut mixture and salt.
• Drop teaspoons of the mixture 3 inches (8 cm) apart onto the cookie sheets. • Bake for 8–10 minutes, or until golden brown.
• Cool on the sheets until the cookies firm slightly. • Transfer to racks to cool completely. • Melt both types of chocolate separately in a double boiler over barely simmering water. Lay the cold florentines flat-side upward on a sheet of waxed paper, and spread the white chocolate over them with a pastry brush. Drizzle with the semisweet chocolate. Let stand for 30 minutes until set.

Makes: about 40 cookies • Prep: 40 min + 30 min to chill Cooking: 8–10 min • Level: 3

• 1 lb (500 g) hazelnuts
• 1 cup (200 g) sugar
• 1 cup (250 g) butter, softened
• ½ cup (125 g) honey
• ½ cup (125 ml) heavy (double) cream
• ⅛ teaspoon salt
• 6 oz (180 g) white chocolate, coarsely chopped
• 4 oz (125 g) semisweet (dark) chocolate, coarsely chopped

Chocolate Cookies

CHOCOLATE NUT BISCOTTI

- 1/3 cup (50 g) shelled hazelnuts
- 2 cups (300 g) all-purpose (plain) flour
- 2 tablespoons unsweetened cocoa powder
- 1 teaspoon baking powder
- 1/2 teaspoon ground cinnamon
- 1/4 teaspoon ground cloves
- 1/4 teaspoon salt
- 3/4 cup (150 g) sugar
- 3 large eggs + 1 large egg white
- 1 teaspoon vanilla extract (essence)
- 2 teaspoons instant coffee granules dissolved in 1 tablespoon hot water
- 1–2 tablespoons slivered almonds
- 2 tablespoons semisweet (dark) chocolate chips

Glaze
- 1 large egg yolk
- 1–2 tablespoons milk

Preheat the oven to 350°F (180°C/gas 4). • Spread the hazelnuts on a large baking sheet. • Toast for 7 minutes, or until lightly golden. Transfer the nuts to a clean kitchen towel. Gently rub to remove the skins. Pick out the nuts. • Butter two cookie sheets. • Mix the flour, cocoa, baking powder, cinnamon, cloves, and salt in a large bowl. Stir in the sugar. • Beat the eggs, egg white, and vanilla in a large bowl with an electric mixer at high speed until frothy. • Mix in the dry ingredients, coffee, hazelnuts, almonds, and chocolate chips to form a stiff dough. • Divide the dough in four. • Form into four logs about 1 inch (2.5 cm) in diameter and place 4 inches (10 cm) apart on the prepared cookie sheets, flattening slightly. • Glaze: Beat the yolk and milk in a small bowl and brush it over the logs. • Bake for 25–30 minutes, or until firm to the touch. Transfer to a cutting board to cool for 15 minutes. • Turn the oven down to 300°F (150°C/gas 2). • Cut on the diagonal into 1-inch (2.5 cm) slices. • Arrange the slices cut-side up on the cookie sheets and bake for 10 minutes, or until golden brown. • Transfer to racks to cool.

Makes: about 35 biscotti • Prep: 40 min • Cooking: 35–40 min • Level: 2

CHOCOLATE CITRUS TWISTS

Preheat the oven to 350°F (180°C/gas 4). • Line four cookie sheets with parchment paper. • Mix the flour, baking powder, and salt in a medium bowl. • Beat the butter and sugar in a large bowl with an electric mixer on medium speed until creamy. • Add the egg, beating until just blended. • Finely grate 2 oz (60 g) of the chocolate and beat into the mixture. • Beat in the orange zest. • Mix in the dry ingredients to form a soft dough. • Turn the dough out onto a lightly floured surface and knead until smooth. • Form tablespoons of the dough into 8-inch (20-cm) ropes. • Fold in half and twist, pressing the ends of the rope together. • Transfer to the prepared cookie sheets, placing them 2 inches (5 cm) apart. • Bake for 10–12 minutes, or until just firm. • Transfer to racks to cool. • Melt the remaining chocolate in a double boiler over barely simmering water. • Dip in the tops of cookies and let set for 30 minutes.

Makes: about 40 cookies • Prep: 40 min + 30 min to set Cooking: 10–12 min • Level: 2

- 3 cups (450 g) all-purpose (plain) flour
- 2 teaspoons baking powder
- 1/4 teaspoon salt
- 3/4 cup (180 g) butter, softened
- 1/2 cup (100 g) sugar
- 1 large egg
- 5 oz (150 g) semisweet (dark) chocolate
- 1 tablespoon finely shredded orange zest

CHOCOLATE PAPRIKA COOKIES

- 3/4 cup (125 g) all-purpose (plain) flour
- 1 teaspoon hot paprika
- 1/2 teaspoon baking powder
- 1/8 teaspoon salt
- 1/2 cup (125 g) butter, softened
- 2 tablespoons granulated sugar

Preheat the oven to 350°F (180°C/gas 4). • Butter two cookie sheets. • Mix the flour, paprika, baking powder, and salt in a medium bowl. • Beat the butter and granulated and brown sugars in a large bowl with an electric mixer on medium speed until creamy. • Add the egg and vanilla, beating until just blended. • With mixer on low speed, beat in the dry ingredients and chopped chocolate until well blended.

• Drop teaspoons of the cookie dough 1 inch (2.5 cm) apart onto the prepared cookie sheets. • Bake for 12–15 minutes, or until firm to the touch. • Transfer to racks to cool.

Makes: about 25 cookies • Prep: 20 min • Cooking: 12–15 min • Level: 1

- 1/4 cup (50 g) firmly packed dark brown sugar
- 1 large egg
- 1/2 teaspoon vanilla extract (essence)
- 3 oz (90 g) semisweet (dark) chocolate, finely chopped

Chocolate Cookies

Chocolate orange cookies

CHOCOLATE ORANGE COOKIES

- 1 cup (150 g) all-purpose (plain) flour
- ⅛ teaspoon salt
- ⅓ cup (90 g) butter, cut up
- ⅓ cup (50 g) finely ground almonds
- ¼ cup (50 g) sugar
- 1 tablespoon finely grated orange zest
- 1 large egg yolk, lightly beaten
- 2 tablespoons freshly squeezed orange juice
- 4 oz (125 g) semisweet (dark) chocolate, coarsely chopped

Mix the flour and salt in a large bowl. • Cut in the butter until the mixture resembles fine crumbs. • Mix in the ground almonds, sugar, and orange zest. Add the egg yolk and orange juice. • Refrigerate for 30 minutes. • Preheat the oven to 350°F (180°C/gas 4). • Line two cookie sheets with parchment paper. • Roll out the dough to ¼ inch (5 mm) thick. • Use a 2-inch (5-cm) cookie cutter to cut out the cookies. • Transfer the cookies to the prepared cookie sheets, spacing well. • Bake for 10–15 minutes, or until golden. • Transfer to racks to cool. • Melt the chocolate in a double boiler over barely simmering water. Dip the cookies halfway into the chocolate and let stand for 30 minutes until set.

Makes: about 25 cookies • Prep: 45 min + 1 hr to chill and set • Cooking: 10–15 min • Level: 1

ORANGE CHOCOLATE CHIP COOKIES

Preheat the oven to 350°F (180°C/gas 4). • Butter two cookie sheets. • Mix the all-purpose and whole-wheat flours, baking soda, and salt in a medium bowl. • Beat the granulated and brown sugars, butter, and orange zest in a large bowl with an electric mixer on medium speed until creamy. • Add the eggs, beating until just blended. • With mixer at low speed, gradually beat in the dry ingredients, followed by the walnuts and the chocolate chips. • Drop tablespoons of the dough 2 inches (5 cm) apart onto the prepared cookie sheets. • Bake for 10–12 minutes, or until lightly browned. • Cool on the sheets until the cookies firm slightly. • Transfer to racks to finish cooling.

Makes: about 40 cookies • Prep: 20 min • Cooking: 10–12 min • Level: 1

- 2 cups (300 g) all-purpose (plain) flour
- ½ cup (75 g) whole-wheat (wholemeal) flour
- 1 teaspoon baking soda (bicarbonate of soda)
- ½ teaspoon salt
- 1 cup (200 g) granulated sugar
- ½ cup (100 g) firmly packed dark brown sugar
- ¾ cup (180 g) butter, softened
- 2 tablespoons finely grated orange zest
- 2 large eggs
- 1 cup (100 g) chopped walnuts
- 1 cup (180 g) semisweet (dark) chocolate chips

DOUBLE CHOCOLATE NUT BISCOTTI

- 2½ cups (375 g) all-purpose (plain) flour
- ¾ cup (125 g) unsweetened cocoa powder
- 2 teaspoons baking powder
- ¼ teaspoon salt
- ½ cup (125 g) butter, softened
- 1¼ cups (250 g) sugar
- ½ teaspoon vanilla extract (essence)
- 3 large eggs
- 1 cup (100 g) coarsely chopped walnuts
- 4 oz (125 g) semisweet (dark) chocolate, coarsely chopped

Preheat the oven to 325°F (170°C/gas 3).
• Line a cookie sheet with parchment paper.
• Mix the flour, cocoa, baking powder, and salt in a medium bowl. • Beat the butter and sugar in a large bowl with an electric mixer on medium speed until creamy. • Add the vanilla and eggs, beating until just blended.
• Mix in the dry ingredients, walnuts, and chocolate to form a stiff dough. • Divide the dough in half. Form into two 12-inch (30-cm) logs and place 3 inches (8 cm) apart on the prepared cookie sheet, flattening slightly. •
Bake for 25–35 minutes, or until firm to the touch. • Transfer to a cutting board to cool for 15 minutes. • Cut on the diagonal into 1-inch (2.5-cm) slices. • Arrange the slices cut-side up on two cookie sheets and bake for 10–15 minutes more. • Cool on racks.

Makes: about 48 biscotti • Prep: 40 min • Cooking: 35–40 min • Level: 2

OVER THE TOP CHOCOLATE COOKIES

Preheat the oven to 325°F (170°C/gas 3). Butter two cookie sheets. • Mix the flour, cocoa, baking powder, and salt in a large bowl. • Melt the semisweet chocolate and butter in a double boiler over barely simmering water. • Beat the eggs and both sugars in a large bowl until creamy. • Beat in the chocolate mixture and vanilla. • Mix in the dry ingredients, chocolate chips, pecans, and white chocolate. • Drop tablespoons of the dough 3 inches (8 cm) apart onto the prepared cookie sheets. Flatten slightly. • Bake, one sheet at a time, for 8–10 minutes, or until cracked on top. • Transfer to racks to cool.

Makes: about 25 cookies • Prep: 20 min • Cooking: 8–10 min • Level: 1

- 1 cup (150 g) all-purpose (plain) flour
- ⅔ cup (100 g) unsweetened cocoa powder
- 1½ teaspoons baking powder
- ¼ teaspoon salt
- 8 oz (250 g) semisweet (dark) chocolate, coarsely chopped
- ¾ cup (180 g) butter, cut up
- 3 large eggs
- 1 cup (200 g) granulated sugar
- ⅓ cup (50 g) firmly packed light brown sugar
- 1 teaspoon vanilla extract (essence)
- 1⅓ cups (240 g) semisweet (dark) chocolate chips
- 1½ cups (150 g) coarsely chopped pecans
- 6 oz (180 g) white chocolate, coarsely chopped

Double chocolate nut biscotti

Chocolate Cookies

CHOCOLATE WAFERS

- 1 cup (100 g) flaked almonds
- 2 teaspoons all-purpose (plain) flour
- 2 tablespoons unsweetened cocoa powder
- 1/8 teaspoon salt
- 1 large egg + 1 large egg white, lightly beaten
- 1/2 cup (100 g) sugar
- 2 tablespoons butter, softened

These deliciously crisp wafers are so good that it is well worth the effort of learning how to make them.
Preheat the oven to 325°F (170°C/gas 3).
• Spread the almonds on a large baking sheet.
• Toast for 7 minutes, or until lightly golden.
• Butter four cookie sheets. • Set out two rolling pins. • Mix the flour, cocoa, and salt in a medium bowl. • Use a wooden spoon to mix the egg and egg white and sugar in a large bowl. • Mix in the dry ingredients and butter. • Drop tablespoons of the mixture 2 inches (5 cm) apart onto the prepared cookie sheets. Do not place more than five cookies on one sheet. Spread the mixture out into thin circles. Sprinkle with the almonds. • Bake, one sheet at a time, for 8–10 minutes, or until firm at the edges. • Working quickly, use a spatula to lift each cookie from the sheet and drape it over a rolling pin. • Let cool slightly on the pin then slip off and let cool completely on racks.

Makes: about 20 cookies • Prep: 30 min • Cooking: 8–10 min Level: 3

CHOCOLATE PECAN WEDGES

Preheat the oven to 350°F (180°C/gas 4).
• Set out a 12-inch (30-cm) pizza pan. • Mix the flour, baking soda, and salt in a medium bowl. • Beat the butter and both sugars in a large bowl with an electric mixer on medium speed until creamy. • Add the vanilla and egg, beating until just blended. • Mix in the dry ingredients, chocolate chips, pecans, and M&Ms. • Spread the mixture in the pan. • Bake for 12–15 minutes, or until lightly browned. • Cool completely in the pan. • Cut into 16 wedges.

Makes: 16 cookies • Prep: 20 min • Cooking: 12–15 min Level: 1

- 2 cups (300 g) all-purpose (plain) flour
- 1 teaspoon baking soda (bicarbonate of soda)
- 1/2 teaspoon salt
- 1/2 cup (125 g) butter, softened
- 1/3 cup (70 g) granulated sugar
- 1/2 cup (100 g) firmly packed light brown sugar
- 1/2 teaspoon vanilla extract (essence)
- 1 large egg
- 3/4 cup (125 g) semisweet (dark) chocolate chips
- 1/2 cup (50 g) finely chopped pecans
- 1/2 cup (50 g) M&Ms

CHOCOLATE FLECK COOKIES

- 1 cup (150 g) all-purpose (plain) flour
- 1 1/2 teaspoons baking powder
- 1/2 teaspoon salt
- 1/2 cup (125 g) butter, softened
- 1/4 cup (50 g) sugar
- 1 large egg
- 6 oz (180 g) semisweet (dark) chocolate, coarsely chopped

Preheat the oven to 350°F (180°C/gas 4).
• Butter two cookie sheets. • Mix the flour, baking powder, and salt in a large bowl.
• Beat the butter and sugar in a large bowl with an electric mixer on medium speed until creamy. • Add the egg, beating until just blended. • Mix in the dry ingredients and chocolate. • Drop teaspoons of the mixture 1 inch (2.5 cm) apart onto the prepared cookie sheets. • Bake for 15–20 minutes, or until golden brown. • Cool on the sheets for 15 minutes. • Transfer to racks to cool.

Makes: about 30 cookies • Prep: 15 min • Cooking: 15–20 min • Level: 1

CHOCOLATE SPICE COOKIES

Preheat the oven to 350°F (180°C/gas 4).
• Butter two cookie sheets. • Mix the flour, cocoa, baking powder, nutmeg, and salt in a medium bowl. • Beat the butter and sugar in a large bowl with an electric mixer on medium speed until creamy. • Add the egg yolk, beating until just blended. • Mix in the dry ingredients. • Drop teaspoons of the dough 1 inch (2.5 cm) apart onto the prepared cookie sheets. • Bake for 12–15 minutes, or until firm around the edges.
• Transfer to racks to cool.

Makes: 25–30 cookies • Prep: 20 min • Cooking: 12–15 min Level: 1

- 1 cup (150 g) all-purpose (plain) flour
- 4 tablespoons unsweetened cocoa powder
- 1 teaspoon baking powder
- 1/8 teaspoon freshly grated nutmeg
- 1/8 teaspoon salt
- 1/2 cup (125 g) butter, softened
- 1/2 cup (100 g) sugar
- 1 large egg yolk

Chocolate Cookies

WHITE CHOCOLATE AND PECAN COOKIES

- 1⅓ cups (200 g) all-purpose (plain) flour
- ½ teaspoon baking soda (bicarbonate of soda)
- ⅛ teaspoon salt
- ½ cup (125 g) butter, softened
- ⅔ cup (140 g) raw sugar (Demerara or Barbados)
- 1 teaspoon vanilla extract (essence)
- 1 large egg
- 4 oz (125 g) white chocolate, coarsely chopped
- ½ cup (50 g) finely chopped pecans

Preheat the oven to 350°F (180°C/gas 4). • Butter a cookie sheet. • Mix the flour, baking soda, and salt in a medium bowl. • Beat the butter and raw sugar in a large bowl with an electric mixer on medium speed until creamy. • Add the vanilla and egg, beating until just blended. • Mix in the dry ingredients, white chocolate, and pecans. • Form the dough into balls the size of walnuts and place 2 inches (5 cm) apart on the prepared cookie sheet. • Bake for 10–12 minutes, or until just golden. • Cool on the sheet until the cookies firm slightly. • Transfer to racks and let cool completely.

Makes: about 20 cookies • Prep: 20 min • Cooking: 10–12 min • Level: 1

ALMOND CHOCOLATE CHIP COOKIES

Preheat the oven to 325°F (170°C/gas 3). • Butter two cookie sheets. • Mix the flour and confectioners' sugar in a large bowl. • With an electric mixer on medium speed, beat in the butter and egg yolk until well blended. • Mix in the almond extract, almonds, and chocolate chips. • Form the dough into balls the size of walnuts and place 1 inch (2.5 cm) apart on the prepared cookie sheets. • Bake for 20–25 minutes, or until just golden. • Cool on the sheets until the cookies firm slightly. • Transfer to racks to finish cooling.

Makes: about 30 cookies • Prep: 12 min • Cooking: 20–25 min • Level: 1

- 1⅔ cups (250 g) all-purpose (plain) flour
- ¾ cup (125 g) confectioners' (icing) sugar
- 1 cup (250 g) butter, softened
- 1 large egg yolk, lightly beaten
- 1 teaspoon almond extract (essence)
- 1 cup (100 g) finely chopped almonds
- ½ cup (90 g) semisweet (dark) chocolate chips

PEANUT BUTTER CHOCOLATE CHIP COOKIES

- 1¼ cups (180 g) all-purpose (plain) flour
- ½ teaspoon baking soda (bicarbonate of soda)
- ¼ teaspoon salt
- ½ cup (125 g) butter, softened
- ½ cup (100 g) raw sugar (Demerara or Barbados)
- ½ cup (125 g) smooth peanut butter
- 1 teaspoon vanilla extract (essence)
- 1 large egg
- 4 oz (125 g) semisweet (dark) chocolate, coarsely chopped

Preheat the oven to 375°F (190°C/gas 5). • Butter a cookie sheet. • Mix the flour, baking soda, and salt in a large bowl. • Beat the butter and sugar in a large bowl with an electric mixer on medium speed until creamy. • Beat in the peanut butter. • Add the vanilla and egg, beating until just blended. • Mix in the dry ingredients, followed by the chocolate. • Drop tablespoons of the dough 2 inches (5 cm) apart onto the prepared cookie sheet. • Bake for 10–12 minutes, or until just golden at the edges. • Transfer to racks and let cool completely.

Makes: about 16 cookies • Prep: 20 min • Cooking: 10–12 min • Level: 1

DUSKY CHOCOLATE COOKIES

Mix the flour, semolina, cocoa, and salt in a medium bowl. • Beat the butter and sugar in a large bowl until creamy. • Add the egg, beating until just blended. • Mix in the dry ingredients. • Press the dough into a disk, wrap in plastic wrap (cling film), and refrigerate for 30 minutes. • Preheat the oven to 375°F (190°C/gas 5). • Set out two cookie sheets. • Roll out the dough on a lightly floured surface to ¼ inch (5 mm) thick. • Use a 2-inch (5-cm) cookie cutter to cut out the cookies. Gather the dough scraps, re-roll, and continue cutting out cookies until all the dough is used. Use a spatula to transfer the cookies to the cookie sheets. • Bake for 12–15 minutes, or until lightly browned. • Transfer to racks to cool.

Makes: about 25 cookies • Prep: 40 min + 30 min to chill Cooking: 12–15 min Level: 1

- ⅔ cup (100 g) all-purpose (plain) flour
- ½ cup (75 g) semolina flour
- 2 tablespoons unsweetened cocoa powder
- ⅛ teaspoon salt
- ⅓ cup (90 g) butter, softened
- ½ cup (100 g) sugar
- 1 large egg

Chocolate Cookies

DOUBLE CHOCOLATE NUT COOKIES

- ½ cup (125 g) butter, softened
- ⅔ cup (140 g) firmly packed dark brown sugar
- 1 large egg
- ⅔ cup (100 g) all-purpose (plain) flour
- ⅓ cup (50 g) old-fashioned rolled oats
- 1½ tablespoons unsweetened cocoa powder
- ½ teaspoon baking powder
- ⅛ teaspoon salt
- 3 oz (90 g) white chocolate, coarsely chopped
- 3 oz (90 g) milk chocolate, coarsely chopped
- 1 cup (100 g) coarsely chopped hazelnuts

Preheat the oven to 350°F (180°C/gas 4). • Butter a cookie sheet. • Beat the butter and brown sugar in a large bowl with an electric mixer on medium speed until creamy. • Add the egg, beating until just blended. • Mix in the flour, oats, cocoa, baking powder, and salt. • Stir in the white and milk chocolates and hazelnuts. • Drop teaspoons of the mixture ½ inch (1 cm) apart on the prepared baking sheet. • Bake for 10–15 minutes, or until risen and craggy. • Cool on the sheet until the cookies firm slightly. Transfer to racks and let cool completely.

Makes: about 20 cookies • Prep: 30 min • Cooking: 10–15 min • Level: 1

CHOCOLATE PRETZELS

Mix the flour, cocoa, baking powder, and salt in a medium bowl. • Beat the butter and sugar in a large bowl until creamy. • Add the egg and almond extract, beating until just blended. • Mix in the dry ingredients and almonds. • Divide the dough in half. Press into disks, wrap each in plastic wrap (cling film), and refrigerate for 30 minutes. Preheat the oven to 350°F (180°C/gas 4). Butter two cookie sheets. • Form the dough into 1½-inch (4-cm) balls and roll each into a 12-inch (30-cm) rope. • Make each rope into a pretzel shape by twisting the two ends around each other, then bringing both back near to the center of the strip, about 1 inch (2.5 cm) apart. • Bake for 10–12 minutes, or until golden. • Transfer to racks to cool. • Melt the white chocolate in a double boiler over barely simmering water. Dip the cookies halfway into the chocolate and let stand for 30 minutes until set.

Makes: about 25 cookies • Prep: 40 min + 1 hr to chill and set Cooking: 10–12 min • Level: 3

- 2 cups (300 g) all-purpose (plain) flour
- 2 tablespoons unsweetened cocoa powder
- 1 teaspoon baking powder
- ½ teaspoon salt
- ¾ cup (180 g) butter, softened
- 1 cup (200 g) sugar
- 1 large egg
- ½ teaspoon almond extract (essence)
- ½ cup (50 g) finely ground almonds
- 8 oz (250 g) white chocolate, coarsely chopped

FROSTED CHOCOLATE LOGS

- ¾ cup (125 g) all-purpose (plain) flour
- ⅓ cup (50 g) unsweetened cocoa powder
- ⅛ teaspoon salt
- ⅓ cup (90 g) butter
- ¼ cup (50 g) sugar
- ½ teaspoon vanilla extract (essence)
- 2 tablespoons milk

Frosting
- 1 tablespoon unsweetened cocoa powder

Mix the flour, cocoa, and salt in a large bowl. • Use a pastry blender to cut in the butter until the mixture resembles fine crumbs. • Stir in the sugar and vanilla. • Add the milk to form a stiff dough. • Form the dough into a log 1 inch (2.5 cm) in diameter, wrap in plastic wrap (cling film), and refrigerate for 30 minutes. • Preheat the oven to 400°F (200°C/gas 6). • Butter a cookie sheet. • Slice the dough into 2-inch (5-cm) lengths and place 1 inch (2.5 cm) apart on the prepared cookie sheet. • Bake for 20–25 minutes, or until lightly browned and firm to the touch. • Transfer to racks to

cool. • Frosting: Mix the cocoa with the water until smooth. • Beat the butter, confectioners' sugar, and the cocoa mixture in a medium bowl until smooth. • Use a thin metal spatula to spread the tops of the cookies with the frosting. • Draw the tines of a fork across the frosting to resemble the bark of a log.

Makes: about 15 cookies • Prep: 30 min + 30 min to chill Cooking: 20–25 min Level: 1

- 2 teaspoons cold water
- ¼ cup (60 g) butter, melted
- 1 cup (150 g) confectioners' (icing) sugar

COFFEE & CREAM COOKIES

The intoxicating aroma of freshly brewed coffee blends in beautifully with the creamy mix of butter and sugar on which most cookies are based. Cookies served with a hot cup of coffee is a classic combo, but coffee can also be used as a flavoring with spectacular results. Mocha, named for a port in Yemen on the Red Sea, is both a high quality type of coffee produced in that region and the name of a flavoring which is a mixture of coffee and chocolate. We have included two superb mocha recipes in this chapter—Mocha spirals (see page 98) and Mocha nut cookies (see page 105). Among the other recipes we recommend are the Cafe kisses, shown left (see recipe on page 96), the Coffee pinwheels (see page 96), and the Cavour biscotti (see page 102).

Café kisses (see page 96)

Coffee & Cream Cookies

COFFEE PINWHEELS

- 1²/₃ cups (250 g) all-purpose (plain) flour
- 1 teaspoon baking powder
- ⅛ teaspoon salt
- ½ cup (125 g) butter, softened
- ½ cup (100 g) sugar
- 2 teaspoons instant coffee granules
- 2 teaspoons milk

Mix the flour, baking powder, and salt in a medium bowl. • Beat ¼ cup (60 g) of butter with half the sugar in a medium bowl with an electric mixer at medium speed until creamy. • Mix in half of the dry ingredients. • Stir the coffee granules into the remaining flour mixture. • Beat the remaining butter and sugar until creamy. • Mix in the coffee mixture. • Roll out both doughs on a lightly floured surface into rectangles ¼ inch (5 mm) thick. • Brush the plain dough with the milk. • Top with the coffee dough and roll up tightly from a long side. Wrap in plastic wrap (cling film) and refrigerate for at least 30 minutes. • Preheat the oven to 350°F (180°C/gas 4). • Butter two cookie sheets. • Slice the dough ¼ inch (5 mm) thick and place 1 inch (2.5 cm) apart on the prepared cookie sheet. • Bake until just golden, 12–15 minutes. • Transfer to racks to cool.

Makes: about 30 cookies • Prep: 1 hr + 30 min to chill Cooking: 12–15 min • Level: 1

CAFÉ KISSES

Preheat the oven to 375°F (190°C/gas 5). • Butter two cookie sheets. • Mix the flour, cocoa, baking powder, and salt in a medium bowl. • Beat the butter, sugar, and vanilla in a large bowl with an electric mixer at medium speed until creamy. • Mix in the dry ingredients to form a stiff dough. • Form the dough into balls the size of walnuts and place 1 inch (2.5 cm) apart on the prepared cookie sheets. Use a fork to flatten them slightly. • Bake until firm to the touch, 10–15 minutes. • Cool on the sheets until the cookies firm slightly. • Transfer to racks to finish cooling. • Stick the cookies together in pairs with the buttercream.

Makes: about 12 cookies • Prep: 30 min • Cooking: 10–15 min • Level: 1

- ¾ cup (125 g) all-purpose (plain) flour
- 1 tablespoon unsweetened cocoa powder
- ½ teaspoon baking powder
- ⅛ teaspoon salt
- ½ cup (125 g) butter, softened
- ¼ cup (50 g) sugar
- ½ teaspoon vanilla extract (essence)
- 1 cup (250 ml) coffee buttercream (see page 416)

BUTTERCREAM KISSES

- 1²/₃ cups (250 g) all-purpose (plain) flour
- 1¼ cups (180 g) custard powder
- 1 cup (200 g) sugar
- ½ cup (75 g) rice flour
- 1 teaspoon baking powder
- ⅛ teaspoon salt
- ¾ cup (180 g) butter, cut up
- ¼ cup (60 ml) milk
- 1 cup (250 g) buttercream (see page 416)

Stir together the flour, custard powder, sugar, rice flour, baking powder, and salt in a large bowl. • Use a pastry blender to cut in the butter until the mixture resembles coarse crumbs. Pour in the milk to form a firm dough. • Press the dough into a disk, wrap in plastic wrap (cling film), and refrigerate for 30 minutes. • Preheat the oven to 350°F (180°C/gas 4). • Set out two cookie sheets. • Transfer the dough to a lightly floured surface and roll out to ¼ inch (5 mm) thick. • Use a 1½-inch (4-cm) cookie cutter to cut out the cookies.

• Gather the dough scraps, re-roll, and continue cutting out the cookies until all the dough is used. • Transfer the cookies to the cookie sheets, placing them 1 inch (2.5 cm) apart. • Bake until lightly browned, 12–15 minutes. • Transfer to racks to cool. • Stick the cookies together in pairs with the buttercream.

Makes: about 15–18 cookies • Prep: 45 min • Cooking: 12–15 min • Level : 1

Coffee & Cream Cookies

MOCHA SPIRALS

- 3⅓ cups (500 g) all-purpose (plain) flour
- ¼ teaspoon baking powder
- ⅛ teaspoon salt
- 1 cup (250 g) butter, softened
- ¾ cup (150 g) sugar
- 1 tablespoon coffee liqueur
- 1 teaspoon vanilla extract (essence)
- 2 large eggs
- ⅓ cup (90 g) chocolate hazelnut spread (Nutella), softened

Refrigerate four cookie sheets. • Mix the flour, baking powder, and salt in a medium bowl. • Beat the butter and sugar in a large bowl with an electric mixer at medium speed until creamy. Add the coffee liqueur and vanilla. • Add the eggs, beating until just blended. • Mix in the dry ingredients to form a soft dough. • Roll the dough out into a large rectangle about ½ inch (1 cm) thick. • Spread evenly with the chocolate hazelnut spread and roll up the dough from a long side. • Wrap in plastic wrap (cling film) and refrigerate for 30 minutes. • Preheat the oven to 375°F (190°C/gas 5). • Cut the dough into ½-inch (1-cm) thick slices. • Place 1 inch (2.5 cm) apart on the prepared cookie sheets. • Bake until lightly browned and firm to the touch, for 8–10 minutes. • Cool the cookies on the cookie sheets for 5 minutes. • Transfer to racks to cool completely.

Makes: about 60 cookies • Prep: 1 hr + 30 min to chill Cooking: 8–10 min • Level: 2

FROSTED CHOCOLATE HEARTS

Preheat the oven to 375°F (190°C/gas 5). • Butter two cookie sheets. • Mix the flour, sugar, cornstarch, cocoa, baking powder, and salt in a large bowl. • Use a pastry blender to cut in the butter until the mixture resembles coarse crumbs. • Add the coffee extract and enough milk to form a stiff dough. • Turn the dough out onto a lightly floured surface and knead until smooth. • Roll out the dough to ¼ inch (5 mm) thick. • Use a heart-shaped cookie cutter to cut out the cookies. Gather the dough scraps, re-roll, and continue cutting out cookies until all the dough is used. • Use a spatula to transfer the cookies onto the prepared cookie sheets, placing them 1 inch (2.5 cm) apart. • Bake for 10–15 minutes, or until lightly browned. • Cool on the sheets until the cookies firm slightly. Transfer to racks to finish cooling. • Spread with the frosting.

Makes: about 25 cookies • Prep: 40 min • Cooking: 10–15 min • Level: 1

- ⅔ cup (100 g) all-purpose (plain) flour
- ¼ cup (50 g) sugar
- 2 tablespoons cornstarch (cornflour)
- 1 tablespoon unsweetened cocoa powder
- ½ teaspoon baking powder
- ⅛ teaspoon salt
- ¼ cup (60 g) butter
- 1 teaspoon coffee extract (essence)
- 1 tablespoon milk or more as needed
- 1 cup (250 g) chocolate frosting (see page 414)

HAZELNUT COFFEE COOKIES

- 1¼ cups (180 g) all-purpose (plain) flour
- 1 teaspoon baking powder
- ⅛ teaspoon salt
- ½ cup (125 g) butter, softened
- ¾ cup (150 g) sugar
- 2 teaspoons coffee extract or 2 teaspoons instant coffee granules dissolved in 1 tablespoon boiling water
- 1 teaspoon vanilla extract (essence)
- ½ cup (75 g) toasted hazelnuts

Preheat the oven to 325°F (170°C/gas 3). • Butter two cookie sheets. • Mix the flour, baking powder, and salt in a large bowl. • Beat the butter and sugar in a large bowl with an electric mixer at medium speed until creamy. • Add the coffee extract and vanilla. • Mix in the dry ingredients to form a smooth dough. • Roll into balls the size of walnuts and place 1½ inches (4 cm) apart on the prepared cookie sheets, pressing down lightly. • Press 2–3 hazelnuts into the top of each cookie. • Bake for 15–20 minutes, or until firm to the touch. • Transfer to racks to cool.

Makes: about 30 cookies • Prep: 15 min • Cooking: 15–20 min • Level: 1

COFFEE BUTTERBALL COOKIES

Preheat the oven to 350°F (180°C/gas 4). • Butter two cookie sheets. • Mix the flour, almonds, and salt in a large bowl. • Beat the butter and sugar in a large bowl with an electric mixer at medium speed until creamy. • Dissolve the coffee and baking soda in the water and beat into the batter. • With mixer on low speed, beat in the mixed dry ingredients. • Shape the dough into small balls and place on the cookie sheets, spacing well. • Bake until almost firm to the touch, 15–18 minutes. • Cool for 5 minutes on the sheets, then roll each cookie in the extra confectioners' sugar.

Makes: about 30 cookies • Prep: 15 min • Cooking: 15–18 min • Level: 1

- 1½ cups (225 g) all-purpose (plain) flour
- 1 cup (125 g) finely ground almonds
- ⅛ teaspoon salt
- ¾ cup (200 g) butter
- ½ cup (75 g) confectioners' (icing) sugar + ½ cup (75 g) extra, to roll the cookies
- 2 tablespoons instant coffee granules
- ½ teaspoon baking soda (bicarbonate of soda)
- 1 tablespoon water

Coffee & Cream Cookies

CRUNCHY COFFEE COOKIES

- 3/4 cup (125 g) all-purpose (plain) flour
- 1/2 teaspoon baking powder
- 1/8 teaspoon salt
- 1/2 cup (125 g) butter, softened
- 1/4 cup (50 g) sugar
- 2/3 cup (70 g) finely chopped walnuts
- 2 teaspoons instant coffee granules

Preheat the oven to 375°F (190°C/gas 5). • Butter two cookie sheets. • Mix the flour, baking powder, and salt in a large bowl. • Beat the butter and sugar in a large bowl with an electric mixer at medium speed until creamy. • Mix in the dry ingredients, walnuts, and coffee granules until well blended. • Drop tablespoons of the dough 1 inch (2.5 cm) apart onto the prepared cookie sheets. • Bake until just golden, 15–20 minutes. • Cool on the sheets until the cookies firm slightly. • Transfer to racks to finish cooling.

Makes: about 25 cookies • Prep: 20 min • Cooking: 15–20 min • Level: 1

COFFEE-GLAZED HAZELNUT COOKIES

Mix the flour and salt in a large bowl. • Beat the butter and confectioners' sugar in a large bowl with an electric mixer at medium speed until creamy. • Mix in the dry ingredients, followed by the hazelnuts. • Press the dough into a disk, wrap in plastic wrap (cling film), and refrigerate for 30 minutes. • Preheat the oven to 375°F (190°C/gas 5). • Butter two cookie sheets. • Roll out the dough on a lightly floured surface to 1/4 inch (5 mm) thick. • Coffee Glaze: Beat the egg white and coffee in a small bowl. Brush over the dough. • Cut into rectangles and use a spatula to transfer to the cookie sheets, spacing well. • Bake until firm to the touch, 12–15 minutes. • Transfer to racks and let cool completely.

Makes: about 30 cookies • Prep: 30 min + 30 min to chill Cooking: 12–15 min • Level: 1

Cookies
- 1 2/3 cups (250 g) all-purpose (plain) flour
- 1/8 teaspoon salt
- 3/4 cup (180 g) butter, softened
- 3/4 cup (125 g) confectioners' (icing) sugar
- 1 1/4 cups (125 g) finely chopped hazelnuts

Coffee Glaze
- 1 large egg white, lightly beaten
- 1 tablespoon instant coffee granules dissolved in 2 teaspoons hot water

Crunchy coffee cookies

Coffee drops

COFFEE DROPS

- 1 cup (150 g) all-purpose (plain) flour
- 1 tablespoon unsweetened cocoa powder
- ¼ teaspoon salt
- ½ cup (125 g) butter, softened
- ¼ cup (50 g) sugar
- 1 teaspoon vanilla extract (essence)
- 2 teaspoons instant coffee granules
- ½ cup (50 g) finely chopped pecans
- 2 tablespoons finely chopped candied cherries
- ⅓ cup (50 g) confectioners' (icing) sugar

Preheat the oven to 325°F (170°C/gas 3). • Butter three cookie sheets. • Mix the flour, cocoa, and salt in a medium bowl. • Beat the butter, sugar, and vanilla in a large bowl with an electric mixer at medium speed until creamy. • Mix in the dry ingredients, coffee granules, pecans, and cherries until well blended. • Form the dough into balls the size of walnuts and place 1 inch (2.5 cm) apart on the prepared cookie sheets. • Bake until firm to the touch, 15–18 minutes. • Transfer to racks and let cool completely. • Dust with the confectioners' sugar.

Makes: about 30 cookies • Prep: 20 min • Cooking: 15–18 min • Level: 1

ESPRESSO COOKIES

Preheat the oven to 375°F (190°C/gas 5). • Butter two cookie sheets. • Mix the flour, baking powder, and salt in a medium bowl. • Beat the butter and sugar in a large bowl with an electric mixer at medium speed until creamy. • Mix in the dry ingredients, pecans, and coffee until well blended. • Drop tablespoons of the dough 1 inch (2.5 cm) apart onto the prepared cookie sheets. • Bake until just golden, 15–20 minutes. • Cool on the sheets until the cookies firm slightly. • Transfer to racks to finish cooling.

Makes: about 25 cookies • Prep: 20 min • Cooking: 15–20 min • Level: 1

- 1 cup (150 g) all-purpose (plain) flour
- ½ teaspoon baking powder
- ⅛ teaspoon salt
- ½ cup (125 g) butter, softened
- ¼ cup (50 g) sugar
- ⅔ cup (60 g) finely chopped pecans
- 2 tablespoons strong espresso coffee

Coffee & Cream Cookies

RISORGIMENTO COOKIES

- 1 cup (150 g) all-purpose (plain) flour
- ½ teaspoon baking powder
- ½ teaspoon ground cinnamon
- ⅛ teaspoon salt
- ½ cup (125 g) butter, softened
- 2 tablespoons vegetable shortening
- ½ cup (100 g) granulated sugar, + 2 tablespoons extra, to sprinkle
- ¼ cup (50 g) firmly packed light brown sugar
- 1 tablespoon + 1 teaspoon instant coffee granules
- 1 large egg
- 2 teaspoons hot water
- coffee beans, to decorate

Mix the flour, baking powder, cinnamon, and salt in a medium bowl. • Beat the butter, vegetable shortening, and both sugars in a large bowl with an electric mixer at medium speed until creamy. • Dissolve 1 tablespoon of the coffee granules in the hot water. • Add the coffee mixture and egg, beating until just blended. • Mix in the dry ingredients to form a stiff dough. • Divide the dough in half. Form into two 7-inch (18-cm) logs, wrap in plastic wrap (cling film), and refrigerate for 1 hour. • Preheat the oven to 375°F (190°C/gas 5). • Butter four cookie sheets. • Slice the dough ¼ inch (5 mm) thick and place 1 inch (2.5 cm) apart on the prepared cookie sheets. • Mix the remaining granulated sugar and 1 teaspoon coffee granules in a small bowl. Sprinkle over the cookies and decorate with the coffee beans. • Bake until pale gold, 8–10 minutes. • Cool on the sheets until the cookies firm slightly. • Transfer to racks to finish cooling.

Makes: about 50 cookies • Prep: 40 min + 1 hr to chill Cooking: 8–10 min • Level: 1

SOUR CREAM COOKIES

Mix the flour, baking powder, and salt in a large bowl. • Use a pastry blender to cut in the butter until the mixture resembles fine crumbs. • Stir together the sugar, sour cream, and 1 egg. Stir into the dry ingredients to form a smooth dough. • Press the dough into a disk, wrap in plastic wrap (cling film), and refrigerate for 30 minutes. • Preheat the oven to 425°F (220°C/gas 7). • Line two cookie sheets with parchment paper. • Roll out the dough on a lightly floured surface to ¼ inch (5 mm) thick. Use a 2-inch (5-cm) cookie cutter to cut out the cookies. Gather the dough scraps, re-roll, and continue cutting out until all the dough is used. • Use a spatula to transfer the cookies to the cookie sheets, spacing them 2 inches (5 cm) apart. Prick all over with a fork. • Beat the remaining egg and brush over the tops of the cookies. • Bake for 10–15 minutes, or until golden brown. • Transfer to racks to cool.

Makes: about 20 cookies • Prep: 30 min + 30 min to chill Cooking: 10–15 min • Level: 1

- 1 cup (150 g) all-purpose (plain) flour
- ½ teaspoon baking powder
- ⅛ teaspoon salt
- 2 tablespoons butter, cut up
- 3 tablespoons sugar
- 5 tablespoons sour cream
- 2 large eggs

CAVOUR BISCOTTI

- 1 cup (150 g) almonds
- ½ cup (50 g) coarsely chopped pistachios
- 5 tablespoons espresso coffee beans
- 2⅓ cups (500 g) all-purpose (plain) flour
- 2 teaspoons baking powder
- ½ teaspoon salt
- ½ cup (125 g) butter, cut up
- 1 cup (200 g) sugar
- 3 large eggs, lightly beaten
- ½ cup (125 ml) strong black coffee

Preheat the oven to 350°F (180°C/gas 4). • Line three cookie sheets with parchment paper. • Spread the almonds and pistachios on separate baking sheets. Toast until lightly golden, 7 minutes. • Transfer the almonds to a food processor and process until finely chopped. • Coarsely grind 2 tablespoons of the coffee beans in a food processor. • Grind the remaining beans in a coffee grinder until very fine. • Mix the flour, baking powder, and salt in a large bowl. • Use a pastry blender to cut in the butter until the mixture resembles coarse crumbs. • Mix in the almonds, pistachios, coarsely and finely ground espresso beans, sugar, eggs, and coffee to

form a stiff dough. • Divide the dough in three. Form into three logs about 2 inches (5 cm) in diameter and place 2 inches (5 cm) apart on the cookie sheets, flattening slightly. • Dust each log with cocoa powder and cinnamon. • Bake until firm to the touch, 25–30 minutes. • Transfer to a cutting board to cool for 15 minutes. • Lower the oven temperature to 300°F (150°C/gas 2). • Cut on the diagonal into 1-inch (2.5-cm) slices. • Arrange the slices cut-side up on the cookie sheets and bake until golden and toasted, 15–20 minutes. • Transfer to racks to cool.

Makes: about 40 cookies • Prep: 40 min • Cooking: 40–50 min • Level: 2

- 1 tablespoon unsweetened cocoa powder
- ⅛ teaspoon ground cinnamon

Mocha nut cookies

MOCHA NUT COOKIES

- ²⁄₃ cup (100 g) all-purpose (plain) flour
- ¹⁄₂ teaspoon baking powder
- ¹⁄₈ teaspoon salt
- 12 oz (350 g) bittersweet (dark) chocolate, coarsely chopped
- ¹⁄₂ cup (125 g) butter, cut up
- 3 large eggs
- 1 cup (200 g) sugar
- 1 tablespoon instant coffee granules
- 1 teaspoon vanilla extract (essence)
- 1¹⁄₂ cups (150 g) coarsely chopped pecans
- 1¹⁄₂ cups (150 g) coarsely chopped hazelnuts
- 1 cup (180 g) semisweet (dark) chocolate chips

Preheat the oven to 325°F (170°C/gas 4). • Set out three cookie sheets. • Mix the flour, baking powder, and salt in a large bowl. • Melt the chocolate and butter in a double boiler over barely simmering water. • Beat the eggs and sugar in a large bowl with an electric mixer at medium speed until pale and thick. • Beat in the chocolate mixture, coffee granules, and vanilla. • Mix in the dry ingredients, pecans, hazelnuts, and chocolate chips. • Drop tablespoons of the dough 3 inches (8 cm) apart onto the cookie sheets. • Bake until lightly cracked on top, 20–25 minutes. • Transfer to racks to cool.

Makes: about 35 cookies • Prep: 20 min • Cooking: 20–25 min • Level: 1

VANILLA CRISPS

Preheat the oven to 350°F (180°C/gas 4). • Butter three cookie sheets. • Mix the flour, cornstarch, baking powder, and salt in a large bowl. • Use a wooden spoon to mix in the sugar, butter, egg, cream, and vanilla to form a smooth dough. • Press the dough into a disk, wrap in plastic wrap (cling film), and refrigerate for 30 minutes. • Roll out the dough on a lightly floured surface to ¹⁄₄ inch (5 mm) thick. • Use a 2¹⁄₂-inch (6-cm) fluted cookie cutter to cut out the cookies. Gather the dough scraps, re-roll, and continue cutting out cookies until all the dough is used. • Use a spatula to transfer the cookies to the prepared cookie sheets, placing them 1 inch (2.5 cm) apart. • Bake until just golden at the edges, 10–15 minutes. • Transfer to racks and let cool.

Makes: about 35 cookies • Prep: 40 min + 30 min to chill Cooking: 10–15 min • Level: 1

- 3 cups (450 g) all-purpose (plain) flour
- ²⁄₃ cup (100 g) cornstarch (cornflour)
- 2 teaspoons baking powder
- ¹⁄₈ teaspoon salt
- 1 cup (200 g) sugar
- ³⁄₄ cup (180 g) butter, melted
- 1 large egg
- ¹⁄₃ cup (90 ml) light (single) cream
- ¹⁄₂ teaspoon vanilla extract (essence)

BARBADOS CREAM KISSES

Cookies
- 2 cups (300 g) all-purpose (plain) flour
- 2 teaspoons baking powder
- ¹⁄₄ teaspoon salt
- ¹⁄₃ cup (90 g) butter, softened
- 1 cup (200 g) raw sugar (Demerara or Barbados)
- 1 large egg
- 1 tablespoon freshly squeezed orange juice
- 1 teaspoon vanilla extract (essence)

Mix the flour, baking powder, and salt in a medium bowl. • Beat the butter and raw sugar in a large bowl until creamy. • Add the egg, beating until just blended. • Beat in the orange juice, vanilla, and the dry ingredients. • Form into two logs about 2 inches (5 cm) in diameter, wrap in plastic wrap (cling film), and refrigerate for 30 minutes. • Preheat the oven to 375°F (190°C/gas 5). • Butter four cookie sheets. • Slice the dough ¹⁄₈ inch (3 mm) thick. • Place the cookies on the prepared cookie sheets. • Bake until golden brown, 6–8 minutes. • Cool on the sheets for 2 minutes. Transfer to racks and let cool completely.

Filling: Process the pistachios and brown sugar in a food processor until very finely chopped. • Add the butter and process until smooth. Continue processing, adding enough orange juice to make a thick cream. • Stick the cookies together in pairs with the filling.

Makes: about 25 cookies • Prep: 45 min + 30 min to chill Cooking: 6–8 min • Level: 2

Filling
- 2 tablespoons pistachios
- ³⁄₄ cup (150 g) firmly packed light brown sugar
- ¹⁄₃ cup (90 g) butter, softened
- 2 tablespoons freshly squeezed orange juice

SPICE & NUT COOKIES

S ugar and spice and all things nice—that's definitely what these cookies are made of! Spices have been used to flavor dishes since the dawn of time; originally, in the ages before the refrigerator, they were probably used to mask the less-than-appetizing tastes of moldy, overripe food. Some spices also act as preservatives, helping food taste good for longer periods of time. Nutritious nuts have also been a staple in the human diet for eons; rich in protein and essential oils, they are one of the most concentrated foods available. In this chapter we have selected more than sixty luscious recipes. Classic spices cookies include Gingernuts (see page 116), several biscotti recipes (see pages 130–133), and Lebkuchen (see page 140).

Marzipan cookies (see page 108)

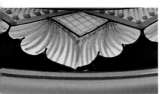

Spice & Nut Cookies

PINE NUT RINGS

- 2²⁄₃ cups (400 g) all-purpose (plain) flour
- 2 teaspoons baking powder
- ¹⁄₄ teaspoon ground cinnamon
- ¹⁄₄ teaspoon salt
- ³⁄₄ cup (150 g) sugar
- 3 large eggs
- ¹⁄₃ cup (90 g) butter, softened
- finely grated zest of ¹⁄₂ lemon
- 2–4 tablespoons milk
- 2 tablespoons pine nuts

Preheat the oven to 350°F (180°C/gas 4). • Butter two cookie sheets. • Mix the flour, baking powder, cinnamon, and salt in a medium bowl. • Stir in the sugar. • Beat the eggs in a large bowl until pale and thick. • Beat in the butter and lemon zest until well blended. • Mix in the dry ingredients and enough milk to make a stiff dough. • Break off balls of dough the size of walnuts and form into 4-inch (10-cm) ropes. Form the ropes into rings and sprinkle with the pine nuts. • Use a spatula to transfer the cookies to the prepared cookie sheets, placing 1 inch (2.5 cm) apart. • Bake for 15–20 minutes, or until just golden. • Transfer to racks to cool.

Makes: about 25 cookies • Prep: 20 min • Cooking: 15–20 min • Level: 2

MARZIPAN COOKIES

Preheat the oven to 350°F (180°C/gas 4). • Line two cookie sheets with parchment paper. • Beat the marzipan, eggs, cornstarch, superfine sugar, vanilla sugar, and almond extract in a large bowl with an electric mixer at medium speed until smooth. • Fit a pastry bag with a ³⁄₄-inch (2-cm) plain tip. Fill the pastry bag, twist the opening tightly closed, and squeeze out 1¹⁄₂-inch (4-cm) mounds, spacing them 2 inches (5 cm) apart on the prepared cookie sheets. • Crush the almonds and sprinkle over the mounds. • Bake for 12–15 minutes, or until golden brown. • Cool on the cookie sheets for 15 minutes. • Transfer to racks and let cool completely.

Makes: about 40 cookies • Prep: 25 min • Cooking: 12–15 min • Level: 2

- 8 oz (250 g) marzipan, grated
- 2 large eggs
- 2 tablespoons cornstarch (cornflour)
- 3 tablespoons superfine (caster) sugar
- 1 tablespoon vanilla sugar (see page 414)
- ¹⁄₂ teaspoon almond extract (essence)
- 5 tablespoons slivered almonds, toasted

WHOLE-WHEAT PECAN COOKIES

- 7 tablespoons butter, softened
- ¹⁄₃ cup (70 g) firmly packed light brown sugar
- 1 large egg yolk
- 1¹⁄₃ cups (200 g) whole-wheat (wholemeal) flour
- grated zest and juice of ¹⁄₂ lemon
- ¹⁄₂ cup (50 g) finely chopped dried apricots
- ¹⁄₂ cup (50 g) coarsely chopped pecans

Preheat the oven to 350°F (180°C/gas 4). • Butter two cookie sheets. • Beat the butter and brown sugar in a large bowl with an electric mixer at medium speed until creamy. • Add the egg yolk, beating until just blended. • Mix in the flour, lemon zest and juice, apricots, and pecans. • Press the dough into a disk, wrap in plastic wrap (cling film), and refrigerate for 30 minutes. • Roll out the dough on a lightly floured surface to ¹⁄₄ inch (5 mm) thick. • Use a 2-inch (5-cm) cookie cutter to cut out the cookies. Gather the dough scraps, re-roll, and continue cutting out cookies until all the dough is used. • Transfer the cookies to the prepared cookie sheets. • Bake for 15–20 minutes, or until lightly browned. • Transfer to racks to cool.

Makes: 15–20 cookies • Prep: 30 min • Cooking: 25–35 min Level: 1

CINNAMON HAZELNUT COOKIES

Stir together the hazelnuts, sugar, flour, cornstarch, and salt in a large bowl. • Add the butter, vanilla, and cinnamon. • Stir in the egg whites. • Refrigerate for 30 minutes. • Preheat the oven to 400°F (200°C/gas 6). • Line two cookie sheets with aluminum foil. • Drop half tablespoons of the dough 2 inches (5 cm) apart onto the prepared cookie sheets. • Bake for 5–7 minutes, or until golden brown. • Transfer to racks to cool.

Makes: about 25 cookies • Prep: 20 min • Cooking: 5–7 min Level : 1

- 1¹⁄₄ cups (125 g) finely chopped hazelnuts
- ²⁄₃ cup (140 g) granulated sugar
- 3 tablespoons all-purpose (plain) flour
- 1 tablespoon cornstarch (cornflour)
- ¹⁄₈ teaspoon salt
- 3 tablespoons butter, melted
- 1 teaspoon vanilla extract (essence)
- 1 teaspoon ground cinnamon
- 3 large egg whites, lightly beaten

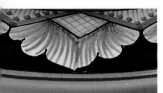

Spice & Nut Cookies

HAZELNUT COOKIES

- 2¹/₂ cups (250 g) finely chopped hazelnuts
- 1 large egg, lightly beaten
- ³/₄ cup (150 g) sugar
- ¹/₂ teaspoon orange liqueur
- ¹/₂ teaspoon freshly squeezed lemon juice
- ¹/₂ teaspoon vanilla extract (essence)
- ¹/₈ teaspoon salt
- 13 candied cherries, cut in half
- 26 chocolate-coated coffee beans

Replace the hazelnuts with the same quantity of finely chopped almonds for a delicious variation.
Preheat the oven to 350°F (180°C/gas 4). • Line two cookie sheets with parchment paper. • Use a wooden spoon to mix the hazelnuts, egg, sugar, orange liqueur, lemon juice, vanilla, and salt until a stiff dough has formed. • Form the dough into balls the size of walnuts and place 1 inch (2.5 cm) apart on the prepared cookie sheets. • Decorate with cherry halves. • Bake for 15–20 minutes, or until just golden at the edges. • Transfer to racks and let cool completely. • Decorate the cookies with the coffee beans.
Makes: about 26 cookies • Prep: 25 min • Cooking: 15–20 min • Level: 1

FROSTED NUT AND RAISIN COOKIES

Preheat the oven to 375°F (190°C/gas 5). • Butter two cookie sheets. • Mix the flour, baking powder, cinnamon, ginger, and salt in a large bowl. • Beat the butter, shortening, and brown sugar in a large bowl with an electric mixer at medium speed until creamy. • Add the eggs, beating until just blended. • Mix in the dry ingredients, raisins, and walnuts. • Drop teaspoons of the dough 1 inch (2.5 cm) apart onto the prepared cookie sheets. • Bake for 8–10 minutes, or until just lightly browned at the edges. • Transfer the cookies to racks to cool. • Spread the frosting on the cookies.
Makes: about 40 cookies • Prep: 25 min • Cooking: 8–10 min • Level: 1

- 2¹/₂ cups (375 g) all-purpose (plain) flour
- 1¹/₂ teaspoons baking powder
- ¹/₂ teaspoon cinnamon
- ¹/₄ teaspoon ginger
- ¹/₄ teaspoon salt
- ¹/₂ cup (125 g) butter, softened
- ¹/₂ cup (125 g) vegetable shortening
- 2 large eggs
- 1 cup (200 g) firmly packed brown sugar
- ¹/₂ cup (90 g) raisins
- ¹/₂ cup (50 g) coarsely chopped walnuts
- 1 quantity chocolate frosting (see page 414)

SESAME SEED ESSES

- 1¹/₃ cups (200 g) all-purpose (plain) flour
- 1 teaspoon baking powder
- ¹/₈ teaspoon salt
- ¹/₂ cup (125 g) butter, softened
- ¹/₂ cup (100 g) sugar
- 1 teaspoon ground aniseeds
- 1 teaspoon finely grated lemon zest
- 1 large egg + 1 large egg yolk + 1 large egg white
- 2 tablespoons + 1 teaspoon milk
- 4 tablespoons sesame seeds

Mix the flour, baking powder, and salt in a medium bowl. • Beat the butter and sugar in a large bowl with an electric mixer at medium speed until creamy. • Add the aniseeds and lemon zest. • Beat in the whole egg and egg yolk and 2 tablespoons of milk. • Mix in the dry ingredients. • Divide the dough in half. • Form into 8-inch (20-cm) logs, wrap in plastic wrap (cling film), and refrigerate for 30 minutes. • Preheat the oven to 375°F (190°C/gas 5). • Line two cookie sheets with parchment paper. • Slice the dough ¹/₂ inch (1 cm) thick. • Roll into 6-inch (15-cm) logs and form into S-shapes. • Place on the prepared cookie sheets. • Mix the egg white and remaining milk in a small bowl. • Brush over the cookies and sprinkle with the sesame seeds. • Bake for 8–10 minutes, or until just golden.
Makes: about 30 cookies • Prep: 40 min + 30 min to chill Cooking: 8–10 min • Level: 2

SIMPLE PEANUT COOKIES

Preheat the oven to 375°F (190°C/gas 5). • Line two cookie sheets with parchment paper. • Mix the flour and baking powder in a medium bowl. • Beat the butter, shortening, and brown sugar in a large bowl with an electric mixer at medium speed until creamy. • Add the vanilla and egg, beating until just blended. • Mix in the dry ingredients and peanuts. • Drop teaspoons of the dough 2 inches (5 cm) apart onto the prepared cookie sheets. • Bake for 8–10 minutes, or until firm to the touch. • Transfer to racks to cool.
Makes: 16–20 cookies • Prep: 20 min • Cooking: 8–10 min Level: 1

- 1 cup (150 g) all-purpose (plain) flour
- 2 teaspoons baking powder
- ¹/₂ cup (125 g) butter, softened
- ¹/₄ cup (60 g) vegetable shortening
- ¹/₃ cup (70 g) firmly packed light brown sugar
- ¹/₂ teaspoon vanilla extract (essence)
- 1 large egg
- ¹/₂ cup (75 g) salted peanuts

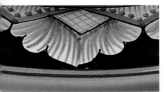

Spice & Nut Cookies

SPICY ROUGH DIAMONDS

- 1²/₃ cups (250 g) all-purpose (plain) flour
- 1 teaspoon baking soda (bicarbonate of soda)
- 1 teaspoon ground cinnamon
- ¼ teaspoon ground nutmeg
- ⅛ teaspoon ground cloves
- ⅛ teaspoon salt
- ½ cup (125 g) butter, softened
- 1 cup (200 g) sugar
- 2 teaspoon milk
- 1 large egg, lightly beaten
- ½ cup (90 g) raisins

Mix the flour, baking soda, cinnamon, nutmeg, and cloves in a medium bowl. • Beat the butter and ¾ cup (150 g) of sugar in a large bowl until creamy. • Add the milk and egg, beating until just blended. • Mix in the dry ingredients and raisins. • Press the dough into a disk, wrap in plastic wrap (cling film), and refrigerate for 30 minutes. • Preheat the oven to 375°F (190°C/gas 5). • Set out three cookie sheets. • Roll out the dough on a lightly floured surface to ⅛ inch (3 mm) thick. • Sprinkle with the remaining sugar. • Cut into diamond shapes. Transfer to the cookie sheets. • Bake for 5–8 minutes, or until lightly browned. • Transfer to racks to cool.

Makes: about 36 cookies • Prep: 40 min + 30 min to chill Cooking: 5–8 min • Level: 1

SALTED PEANUT COOKIES

Preheat the oven to 300°F (150°C/gas 2). • Butter two cookie sheets. • Mix the flour, baking powder, and baking soda in a medium bowl. • Beat the butter and sugar in a large bowl with an electric mixer at medium speed until creamy. • Add the egg, beating until just blended. • Mix in the dry ingredients, peanuts, corn flakes, and oats to make a stiff dough. • Drop teaspoons of the dough 1 inch (2.5 cm) apart onto the prepared cookie sheet. • Bake for 10–15 minutes, or until lightly browned. • Cool on the sheet until the cookies firm slightly. • Transfer to racks and let cool completely.

Makes: about 30 cookies • Prep: 20 min • Cooking: 10–15 min • Level: 1

- 1 cup (150 g) all-purpose (plain) flour
- ½ teaspoon baking powder
- ½ teaspoon baking soda (bicarbonate of soda)
- ½ cup (125 g) butter, softened
- 1 cup (200 g) sugar
- 1 large egg
- ½ cup (75 g) salted peanuts
- 1 cup (100 g) corn flakes
- 2¼ cups (330 g) old-fashioned rolled oats

Spicy rough diamonds

Ginger pecan cookies

GINGER PECAN COOKIES

- 2 cups (300 g) all-purpose (plain) flour
- 2 teaspoons baking soda (bicarbonate of soda)
- 1 tablespoon ground ginger
- 1/4 teaspoon salt
- 1 cup (200 g) firmly packed light brown sugar
- 3 tablespoons light corn syrup (golden) syrup
- 3 tablespoons water
- 1 large egg
- 1/2 cup (50 g) finely chopped candied cherries
- 1/2 cup (50 g) finely chopped walnuts

Preheat the oven to 375°F (190°C/gas 5). • Butter three cookie sheets. • Mix the flour, baking soda, ginger, and salt in a medium bowl. • Beat the brown sugar, corn syrup, water, and egg in a large bowl with an electric mixer at medium speed until well blended. • Stir in the dry ingredients, cherries, and walnuts. • Drop teaspoons of the dough 2 inches (5 cm) apart onto the prepared cookie sheets. • Bake for 10–12 minutes, or until just golden at the edges. • Transfer to racks to cool.

Makes: about 30 cookies • Prep: 20 min • Cooking: 10–12 min • Level: 1

BLACK PEPPER AND SPICE COOKIES

Mix the flour, baking powder, baking soda, cinnamon, allspice, and salt into a medium bowl. • Beat the butter and sugar in a large bowl with an electric mixer at medium speed until creamy. • Beat in the cream. • Mix in the dry ingredients and black pepper to form a smooth dough. • Form the dough into a log 2½ inches (6 cm) in diameter. Wrap in plastic wrap (cling film) and refrigerate for 30 minutes. • Preheat the oven to 375°F (190°C/gas 5). • Butter four cookie sheets. • Slice the dough ¼ inch (5 mm) thick and place the cookies 1 inch (2.5 cm) apart on the prepared cookie sheets. • Bake for 5–7 minutes, or until just golden. • Transfer to racks and let cool completely.

Makes: about 60 cookies • Prep: 40 min + 30 min to chill Cooking: 5–7 min • Level: 1

- 3 cups (450 g) all-purpose (plain) flour
- 1 teaspoon baking powder
- 1 teaspoon baking soda (bicarbonate of soda)
- 1 teaspoon ground cinnamon
- 1 teaspoon ground allspice
- 1/4 teaspoon salt
- 1 cup (250 g) butter
- 1 cup (200 g) sugar
- 1/4 cup (60 ml) heavy (double) cream
- 1 teaspoon freshly ground black pepper

Spice & Nut Cookies

GINGER AND CANDIED PEEL COOKIES

- 1²/₃ cups (250 g) all-purpose (plain) flour
- 2 teaspoons ground ginger
- ¼ teaspoon baking soda (bicarbonate of soda)
- ⅛ teaspoon salt
- ³/₄ cup (150 g) sugar
- 1 cup (100 g) finely chopped mixed candied peel
- ½ teaspoon grated lemon zest
- ½ cup (125 g) butter, cut up
- 4 tablespoons light molasses (treacle)

Mix the flour, ginger, baking soda, and salt in a large bowl. • Stir in the sugar, candied peel, and lemon zest. • Heat the butter and molasses in a small saucepan over low heat until liquid. • Mix the molasses mixture into the dry ingredients to form a stiff dough. • Press the dough into a disk, wrap in plastic wrap (cling film), and refrigerate for 30 minutes. • Preheat the oven to 350°F (180°C/gas 4). • Butter two cookie sheets. • Roll out the dough on a lightly floured surface to ⅛ inch (3 mm) thick. • Use a 2-inch (5-cm) cookie cutter to cut out the cookies. Gather the dough scraps, re-roll, and continue cutting out cookies until all the dough is used. • Use a spatula to transfer the cookies to the prepared cookie sheets, placing them 2 inches (5 cm) apart. • Bake for 8–10 minutes, or until just golden. • Cool on the sheets until the cookies firm slightly. • Transfer to racks to cool.

Makes: about 25 cookies • Prep: 40 min + 30 min to chill • Cooking: 8–10 min • Level: 1

WALNUT MAPLE SYRUP COOKIES

Beat the butter, both sugars, and maple syrup in a large bowl with an electric mixer at medium speed until creamy. • Mix in the flour, coffee, walnuts, and salt to form a soft dough. • Turn the dough out onto a lightly floured surface and knead until smooth. • Press the dough into a disk, wrap in plastic wrap (cling film), and refrigerate for 30 minutes. • Preheat the oven to 375°F (190°C/gas 5). • Butter and flour two cookie sheets. • Roll out the dough to ⅛ inch (3 mm) thick. • Use a 3-inch (8-cm) cookie cutter to cut out the cookies. • Gather the dough scraps, re-roll, and continue cutting out cookies until all the dough is used. • Use a spatula to transfer the cookies to the prepared cookie sheets, placing them 1 inch (2.5 cm) apart. • Bake for 8–10 minutes, or until barely colored. • Transfer to racks to cool.

Makes: about 30 cookies • Prep: 40 min + 30 min to chill • Cooking: 8–10 min • Level: 1

- ½ cup (125 g) butter, softened
- ½ cup (100 g) granulated sugar
- 2 tablespoons light brown sugar
- 1 tablespoon pure maple syrup
- 1¹/₃ cups (200 g) all-purpose (plain) flour
- 1 teaspoon instant coffee granules
- ²/₃ cup (60 g) finely chopped walnuts
- ⅛ teaspoon salt

GLAZED NUTTY COOKIES

Cookies
- 1 large egg white
- ⅛ teaspoon salt
- ½ cup (100 g) superfine (caster) sugar
- 1 cup (150 g) finely ground hazelnuts + more as needed
- 1 cup (150 g) finely ground almonds + more as needed
- ½ cup (50 g) coarsely chopped pistachios
- 2 teaspoons finely chopped candied peel

Cookies: Beat the egg white and salt in a large bowl with an electric mixer at medium speed until frothy. • With mixer at high speed, gradually add the superfine sugar, beating until stiff, glossy peaks form. • Use a large rubber spatula to fold in the hazelnuts, almonds, pistachios, and candied peel to form a stiff dough. Add more ground nuts if the dough is very sticky. • Press the dough into a disk, wrap in plastic wrap (cling film), and refrigerate for 30 minutes. • Preheat the oven to 300°F (150°C/gas 2). • Line three cookie sheets with parchment paper. • Roll out the dough between sheets of waxed paper dusted with confectioners' sugar to

¼ inch (5 mm) thick. • Cut into 2 x ¾-inch (5 x 4-cm) strips. • Gather the dough scraps, re-roll, and continue cutting out cookies until all the dough is used. • Transfer the cookies to the prepared cookie sheets, placing them 1 inch (2.5 cm) apart. • Bake for 12–15 minutes, or until golden brown. • Transfer to racks to cool. • Orange Glaze: Mix the confectioners' sugar, orange juice, and orange zest in a small bowl. • Dip the cookies halfway into the glaze and let stand for 30 minutes until set.

Makes: about 35 cookies • Prep: 45 min + 1 hr to chill and set • Cooking: 12–15 min • Level: 2

Orange Glaze
- 1 cup (150 g) confectioners' (icing) sugar
- 1–2 tablespoons freshly squeezed orange juice
- finely grated zest of ½ orange

Spice & Nut Cookies

GINGERNUTS

- 1¼ cups (180 g) all-purpose (plain) flour
- 2 teaspoons ground ginger
- 1 teaspoon baking powder
- ½ teaspoon baking soda (bicarbonate of soda)
- ⅛ teaspoon salt
- ⅓ cup (70 g) firmly packed light brown sugar
- ¼ cup (60 g) butter, softened
- 3 tablespoons light corn (golden) syrup
- 1 large egg

Preheat the oven to 350°F (180°C/gas 4). • Butter two cookie sheets. • Mix the flour, ginger, baking powder, baking soda, and salt in a large bowl. • Stir in the brown sugar. • Melt the butter with the corn syrup in a small saucepan over low heat. • Remove from the heat and let cool. • Stir the butter mixture into the dry ingredients. • Add the egg and mix to make a stiff dough. • Form the dough into twenty balls the size of walnuts and place 2 inches (5 cm) apart on the prepared cookie sheets. • Bake for 12–15 minutes, or until just golden and firm to the touch. • Cool the cookies on the sheets for 5 minutes. • Transfer to racks and let cool completely.

Makes: about 20 cookies • Prep: 20 min • Cooking: 12–15 min • Level: 1

CINNAMON PECAN COOKIES

Preheat the oven to 375°F (190°C/gas 5). • Butter two cookie sheets. • Mix the flour, baking powder, and salt in a medium bowl. • Beat the butter and sugar in a large bowl with an electric mixer at high speed until creamy. • Add the egg, beating until just blended. • Mix in the dry ingredients to form a smooth dough. • Mix the pecans and cinnamon in a small bowl. • Form the dough into balls the size of walnuts and roll them in the nut mixture until well coated. • Place the cookies 2 inches (5 cm) apart on the prepared cookie sheets. • Bake for 10–15 minutes, or until golden. • Transfer to racks to cool.

Makes: about 20 cookies • Prep: 30 min • Cooking: 10–15 min • Level: 1

- 1¼ cups (180 g) all-purpose (plain) flour
- 1 teaspoon baking powder
- ⅛ teaspoon salt
- ½ cup (125 g) butter, softened
- ¾ cup (150 g) sugar
- 1 large egg
- ¾ cup (75 g) finely chopped pecans
- 2 teaspoons ground cinnamon

LEMON SNACKERS

- ⅓ cup (90 g) butter, softened
- ½ cup (100 g) sugar
- 1 large egg yolk
- 1⅓ cups (200 g) all-purpose (plain) flour
- finely grated zest and juice of ½ lemon
- ½ cup (50 g) finely chopped dried apricots
- ½ cup (50 g) coarsely chopped pecans

Preheat the oven to 350°F (180°C/gas 4). • Butter two cookie sheets. • Beat the butter and sugar in a large bowl with an electric mixer at medium speed until creamy. • Add the egg yolk, beating until just blended. • Mix in the flour, lemon zest and juice, apricots, and pecans. • Press the dough into a disk, wrap in plastic wrap (cling film), and refrigerate for 30 minutes. • Roll out the dough on a lightly floured surface to ¼ inch (5 mm) thick. • Use a 2-inch (5-cm) cookie cutter to cut out the cookies. • Transfer to the prepared cookie sheets. • Bake for 15–20 minutes, or until lightly browned. • Transfer to racks and let cool completely.

Makes: 16–20 cookies • Prep: 20 min + 30 min to chill Cooking: 15–20 min • Level: 1

PEANUT AND RAISIN COOKIES

Preheat the oven to 375°F (190°C/gas 5). • Line two cookie sheets with parchment paper. • Mix the flour, baking powder, cinnamon, nutmeg, cloves, and salt in a large bowl. • Beat the oil, honey, and peanut butter in a large bowl with an electric mixer at medium speed until well blended. • Mix in the dry ingredients, oats, and raisins. • Drop tablespoons of the dough 1 inch (2.5 cm) apart onto the prepared cookie sheets. • Bake for 8–10 minutes, or until golden brown. • Cool on the sheets until the cookies firm slightly. • Transfer to racks to finish cooling.

Makes: about 30 cookies • Prep: 20 min • Cooking: 8–10 min • Level: 1

- 1⅔ cups (250 g) all-purpose (plain) flour
- 1 teaspoon baking powder
- ½ teaspoon ground cinnamon
- ½ teaspoon ground nutmeg
- ⅛ teaspoon ground cloves
- ½ teaspoon salt
- ⅓ cup (90 ml) sunflower or canola oil
- ⅓ cup (90 ml) honey
- 1 cup (250 ml) smooth peanut butter
- ½ cup (75 g) old-fashioned rolled oats
- ½ cup (90 g) raisins

Raisin and spice cookies

RAISIN AND SPICE COOKIES

- 1/3 cup (60 g) raisins
- 2 tablespoons brandy
- 1½ cups (225 g) all-purpose (plain) flour
- 1 teaspoon ground cinnamon
- ½ teaspoon freshly grated nutmeg
- ½ teaspoon baking soda (bicarbonate of soda)
- ⅛ teaspoon salt
- ¾ cup (180 g) butter, softened
- ¾ cup (150 g) granulated sugar
- ¼ cup (50 g) firmly packed dark brown sugar
- ¼ cup (60 ml) milk
- finely grated zest of 1 orange

Preheat the oven to 350°F (180°C/gas 4). • Butter two cookie sheets. • Plump the raisins in the brandy in a small bowl for 15 minutes, or until almost all the liquid has been absorbed. • Mix the flour, cinnamon, nutmeg, baking soda, and salt in a medium bowl. • Beat the butter and both sugars in a large bowl with an electric mixer at medium speed until creamy. • Mix in the milk, raisin mixture, dry ingredients, and orange zest. • Drop teaspoons of the dough 1 inch (2.5 cm) apart onto the prepared cookie sheets. • Bake for 10–15 minutes, or until just golden. • Cool on the sheets until the cookies firm slightly. • Transfer to racks to finish cooling.

Makes: about 25–30 cookies • Prep: 20 min + 15 min to plump the raisins • Cooking: 10–15 min • Level: 1

HONEY AND SPICE COOKIES

Mix the flour, baking soda, cinnamon, cardamom, nutmeg, and salt in a medium bowl. • Beat the eggs and sugar in a large bowl with an electric mixer on medium speed until pale and thick. • Heat the honey in a small saucepan over low heat until liquid. • Stir the honey and vanilla into the egg mixture. • Mix in the dry ingredients to form a stiff dough. • Cover with plastic wrap (cling film) and refrigerate for 1 hour. • Preheat the oven to 375°F (190°C/gas 5). • Butter two cookie sheets. • Roll out the dough on a lightly floured surface to ½ inch (1 cm) thick. • Use a 2-inch (5-cm) cookie cutter to cut out the cookies. • Transfer the cookies to the prepared cookie sheets, placing them 2 inches (5 cm) apart. • Bake for 15–20 minutes, or until just golden. • Cool on the sheets until the cookies firm slightly. • Transfer to racks to finish cooling. • Dust with the confectioners' sugar.

Makes: about 35–40 cookies • Prep: 30 min + 1 hr to chill Cooking: 15–20 min • Level: 1

- 3 cups (450 g) all-purpose (plain) flour
- 1 teaspoon baking soda (bicarbonate of soda)
- ½ teaspoon ground cinnamon
- ½ teaspoon ground cardamom
- ¼ teaspoon ground nutmeg
- ⅛ teaspoon salt
- 2 large eggs
- 1 cup (200 g) sugar
- 1 cup (250 ml) honey
- ½ teaspoon vanilla extract (essence)
- 1/3 cup (50 g) confectioners' (icing) sugar, to dust

LOMBARDY COOKIES

- 1 tablespoon baking soda (bicarbonate of soda)
- ½ cup (125 ml) milk
- 3⅓ cups (500 g) all-purpose (plain) flour
- 1/3 cup (90 ml) extra-virgin olive oil
- ¾ cup (150 g) sugar
- ½ cup (50 g) coarsely chopped toasted hazelnuts
- ¼ cup (60 ml) grape juice or vincotto

Preheat the oven to 350°F (180°C/gas 4). • Butter three cookie sheets. • Mix the baking soda and milk in a small bowl. • Use a wooden spoon to mix the flour, olive oil, sugar, hazelnuts, grape juice, and baking soda mixture to make a soft dough. • Form the dough into balls the size of walnuts and place 1 inch (2.5 cm) apart on the prepared cookie sheets, flattening them slightly. • Bake for 15–20 minutes, or until just golden. • Transfer to racks and let cool completely.

Makes: about 40 cookies • Prep: 25 min • Cooking: 15–20 min • Level: 1

CARDAMOM COOKIES

Butter two cookie sheets. • Mix the flour, cornstarch, cardamom, and salt in a large bowl. • Beat the eggs, sugar, and vanilla in a large bowl with an electric mixer at medium speed until pale and thick. • Mix in the dry ingredients. • Drop teaspoons of the dough 2 inches (5 cm) apart onto the prepared cookie sheets. • Cover with a clean kitchen towel and let rest for 12 hours. • Preheat the oven to 300°F (150°C/gas 2). • Bake for 25–30 minutes, or until golden brown. • Transfer to racks and let cool.

Makes: about 20 cookies • Prep: 20 min + 12 hr to rest Cooking: 25–30 min • Level: 1

- ¾ cup (125 g) all-purpose (plain) flour
- ¾ cup (125 g) cornstarch (cornflour)
- 1 tablespoons ground cardamom
- ⅛ teaspoon salt
- 3 large eggs
- 1 cup (200 g) sugar
- ½ teaspoon vanilla extract (essence)

Spice & Nut Cookies

CARAWAY DIAMONDS

- 1½ cups (225 g) all-purpose (plain) flour
- ⅛ teaspoon salt
- ¼ cup (60 g) butter, softened
- ¼ cup (50 g) sugar
- 1 large egg
- 1 teaspoon caraway seeds
- 2 tablespoons colored sugar crystals

Mix the flour and salt in a medium bowl. • Beat the butter and sugar in a large bowl until creamy. • Add the egg, beating until just blended. • Mix in the dry ingredients and caraway seeds. Refrigerate for 30 minutes. • Preheat the oven to 325°F (170°C/gas 3). • Butter three cookie sheets. • Roll out the dough to ⅛ inch (3 mm) thick. Cut into 2-inch (5-cm) diamonds. • Transfer the cookies to the prepared cookie sheets, placing them 1 inch (2.5 cm) apart. Sprinkle with the sugar crystals. • Bake for 10–12 minutes, or until pale gold. • Transfer to racks to cool.

Makes: about 30 cookies • Prep: 30 min + 30 min to chill Cooking: 10–12 min • Level: 1

CHOCOLATE DIAMONDS

Heat the milk in a small saucepan. Remove from the heat and mix in the baking soda. • Mix the flour, baking powder, and salt in a large bowl. • Stir in the sugar. • Add the vanilla and 2 eggs. • Pour in the oil and baking soda mixture and mix until smooth. Press the dough into a disk, wrap in plastic wrap (cling film), and refrigerate for 30 minutes. • Preheat the oven to 350°F (180°C/gas 4). • Butter three cookie sheets. • Roll out the dough on a lightly floured surface to a thickness of ¼ inch (5 mm). • Use a 2½-inch (6-cm) diamond-shaped cookie cutter to cut out the cookies. • Transfer to the prepared sheets, placing them 1 inch (2.5 cm) apart. • Brush with the egg white and sprinkle with chocolate. • Bake for 20 minutes, or until golden.

Makes: about 30 cookies • Prep: 30 min + 30 min to chill Cooking: 15–20 min • Level: 1

- ¼ cup (60 ml) milk
- 1 teaspoon baking soda (bicarbonate of soda)
- 3⅓ cups (500 g) all-purpose (plain) flour
- 2 teaspoons baking powder
- ⅛ teaspoon salt
- 1 cup (200 g) sugar
- 1 teaspoon vanilla extract (essence)
- 2 large eggs + 1 large egg white, lightly beaten
- ⅓ cup (90 ml) sunflower oil
- 7 oz (200 g) semisweet (dark) chocolate, finely grated

Caraway diamonds

Almond rose water balls

ALMOND ROSE WATER BALLS

- 1 cup (150 g) all-purpose (plain) flour
- ⅛ teaspoon salt
- ½ cup (125 g) butter, softened
- ¾ cup (150 g) sugar
- ½ cup (50 g) finely chopped almonds
- 1 teaspoon rose water

Preheat the oven to 350°F (180°C/gas 4).
• Butter two cookie sheets. • Mix the flour and salt in a medium bowl. • Beat the butter and sugar in a medium bowl until creamy.
• Mix in the dry ingredients, almonds, and rose water to form a stiff dough. • Drop teaspoons of dough 1 inch (2.5 cm) apart onto the prepared cookie sheets. • Bake for 12–15 minutes, or until golden. • Transfer to racks to cool.

Makes: about 20 cookies • Prep: 20 min • Cooking: 12–15 min • Level: 1

PRESSED CINNAMON ROSETTES

Preheat the oven to 350°F (180°C/gas 4).
• Set out two cookie sheets. • Mix the flour, cinnamon, and salt in a medium bowl. • Beat the butter, cream cheese, and sugar in a large bowl with an electric mixer at medium speed until creamy. • Add the vanilla and egg yolk, beating until just blended. • Mix in the dry ingredients until well blended. •
Insert the chosen design plate into a cookie press by sliding it into the head and locking in place. • Press out the cookies, spacing 1 inch (2.5 cm) apart on the cookie sheets.
• Bake for 12–15 minutes, or until just golden. • Transfer to racks to cool.

Makes: about 30 cookies • Prep: 30 min • Cooking: 12–15 min • Level: 1

- 1 cup (150 g) all-purpose (plain) flour
- ½ teaspoon ground cinnamon
- ¼ teaspoon salt
- ½ cup (125 g) butter, softened
- ¼ cup (60 g) cream cheese, softened
- ½ cup (100 g) granulated sugar
- ½ teaspoon vanilla extract (essence)
- 1 large egg yolk

Hazelnut kisses

HAZELNUT KISSES

- 3 cups (450 g) all-purpose (plain) flour
- ¼ teaspoon salt
- 1 cup (200 g) superfine (caster) sugar
- 1⅓ cups (130 g) finely ground hazelnuts
- 1 cup (250 g) cold butter, cut up
- 2 large eggs, lightly beaten
- ½ cup (160 g) strawberry or raspberry preserves (jam)
- ¼ cup (50 g) vanilla sugar (see page 414)

Refrigerate three cookie sheets. • Mix the flour and salt in a large bowl. Stir in the sugar and hazelnuts. • Use a pastry blender to cut in the butter until the mixture resembles coarse crumbs. • Add the eggs, beating until just blended. • Turn out onto a lightly floured surface and knead into a smooth dough. • Preheat the oven to 375°F (190°C/ gas 5). • Shape into a ball, wrap in plastic wrap (cling film), and refrigerate for at least 1 hour. • Roll out small portions of dough to ¼ inch (5 mm) thick. • Use a cutter to stamp into 1-inch (2.5-cm) circles. Transfer the cookies onto the chilled baking sheets, placing them 1½ inches (4 cm) apart. • Bake for 12–15 minutes, or until just golden. • Cool the cookies on the cookie sheets for 5 minutes. • Spread each cookie with a little preserves and sandwich them together. • Dust with the vanilla sugar.

Makes: about 30 cookies • Prep: 30 min + 1 hr to chill
Cooking: 12–15 min • Level: 2

ALMOND FINGERS

Cookies: Preheat the oven to 375°F (190°C/gas 5). • Butter three cookie sheets. • Mix the flour and salt in a medium bowl. • Beat the butter and sugar in a large bowl with an electric mixer at medium speed until creamy. • Mix in the dry ingredients and almond extract. The mixture should be slightly crumbly. • Refrigerate for at least 1 hour, or until the dough can be formed into a firm, smooth dough. • Roll out the dough on a lightly floured surface to a 12 x 8-inch (30 x 20-cm) rectangle. • Cut into 3 x 1-inch (8 x 2.5-cm) bars. • Transfer the cookies to the prepared cookie sheets, placing them ½ inch (1 cm) apart. • Topping: Mix the superfine sugar, cinnamon, and almonds in a small bowl. • Brush the cookies with the beaten egg white and sprinkle with the topping. • Bake for 12–15 minutes, or until just golden. • Cool on the sheet until the cookies firm slightly. Transfer to racks to cool completely.

Makes: about 35 cookies • Prep: 30 min + 1 hr to chill
Cooking: 12–15 min • Level: 1

Cookies
- 1⅔ cups (250 g) all-purpose (plain) flour
- ⅛ teaspoon salt
- ¾ cup (180 g) butter, softened
- ⅓ cup (70 g) sugar
- 1 teaspoon almond extract (essence)

Topping
- ⅓ cup (70 g) superfine (caster) sugar
- ½ teaspoon ground cinnamon
- ⅔ cup (100 g) coarsely chopped blanched almonds, toasted
- 1 large egg white, lightly beaten

GLAZED ALMOND SPECIALS

Cookies
- 1⅓ cups (200 g) all-purpose (plain) flour
- ⅓ cup (50 g) cornstarch (cornflour)
- ½ teaspoon baking powder
- ⅛ teaspoon salt
- ⅓ cup (70 g) sugar
- 1 tablespoon vanilla sugar (see page 414)
- 1 teaspoon orange zest
- ¾ cup (180 g) butter, cut up
- 1 large egg
- milk, to brush

Cookies: Mix the flour, cornstarch, baking powder, and salt in a large bowl. • Stir in the sugar and vanilla sugar and the orange zest. • Use a pastry blender to cut in the butter until the mixture resembles coarse crumbs. • Use a fork to mix in the egg to form a smooth dough. • Press the dough into a disk, wrap in plastic wrap (cling film), and refrigerate for 30 minutes. • Set out two cookie sheets. • Roll out the dough on a lightly floured surface to ⅛ inch (3 mm) thick. • Use a 2-inch (5-cm) cookie cutter to cut out the cookies. Transfer the cookies to the cookie sheets, placing them 2 inches (5 cm) apart. • Filling: Mix the almonds,

brown sugar, and orange zest and juice in a small bowl. • Drop ½ teaspoon of the filling onto one half of each cookie. • Fold half of the cookie over the filling. • Use a fork to seal the edges together and brush with a little milk. • Set aside for 30 minutes. • Preheat the oven to 350°F (180°C/gas 4). • Bake for 8–10 minutes, or until just golden at the edges. • Transfer to racks to cool. • Orange Glaze: Mix the confectioners' sugar with the orange juice. Add enough water to make a runny glaze. Drizzle over the cookies.

Makes: about 30 cookies • Prep: 30 min + 1 hr to chill and rest • Cooking: 8–10 min • Level: 2

Filling
- 1 cup (150 g) finely ground almonds
- ⅓ cup (70 g) firmly packed brown sugar
- finely grated zest and juice of 1 orange

Orange Glaze
- ⅔ cup (100 g) confectioners' (icing) sugar
- 1 tablespoon freshly squeezed orange juice
- 2–3 teaspoons hot water

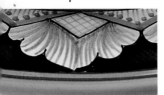

LEMON ALMOND COOKIES

- ½ cup (125 g) butter, softened
- ¾ cup (150 g) sugar
- 1½ cups (225 g) all-purpose (plain) flour
- ⅔ cup (100 g) finely ground almonds
- ⅛ teaspoon salt
- freshly squeezed juice of 1 lemon

Beat the butter and sugar in a large bowl with an electric mixer at medium speed until creamy. • Mix in the flour, almonds, and salt. • Add enough lemon juice to form a stiff dough. • Press the dough into a disk, wrap in plastic wrap (cling film), and refrigerate for 30 minutes. • Preheat the oven to 375°F (190°C/gas 5). • Butter a cookie sheet. • Roll out the dough on a lightly floured surface to ¼ inch (5 mm) thick. • Use a 2-inch (5-cm) cookie cutter to cut out the cookies. Gather the dough scraps, re-roll, and continue cutting out cookies until all the dough is used. • Use a spatula to transfer the cookies to the prepared cookie sheet, placing them 2 inches (5 cm) apart. • Bake for 12–15 minutes, or until pale golden. • Cool on the sheet until the cookies firm slightly. • Transfer to racks to cool.

Makes: about 15–20 cookies • Prep: 30 min + 30 min to chill Cooking: 12–15 min • Level: 1

GLAZED ALMOND COOKIES

Beat the whole egg and yolk, both sugars, and salt in a large bowl with an electric mixer at medium speed until creamy. • Melt the chocolate in a double boiler over barely simmering water. • Mix in the coffee. • Beat the chocolate mixture into the batter. • Mix in the almonds and baking powder to form a stiff dough, adding more almonds if needed. • Divide the dough in half. Press into two disks, wrap in plastic wrap (cling film), and refrigerate for 30 minutes. • Preheat the oven to 350°F (180°C/gas 4). • Butter three cookie sheets. • Roll out each dough disk between sheets of waxed paper into an 8 x 5-inch (20 x 13-cm) rectangle. • Cut into 2½ x ¾-inch (6 x 2-cm) strips. • Transfer to the prepared cookie sheets. • Glaze: Beat the egg white and salt in a small bowl until frothy. Add the confectioners' sugar until stiff, glossy peaks form. • Spread evenly over the cookies. • Bake for 10–12 minutes, or until golden at the edges and the bottoms are lightly browned. • Transfer to racks to cool.

Makes: about 30 cookies • Prep: 30 min + 30 min to chill Cooking: 10–12 min • Level: 1

- 1 large egg + 1 large egg yolk
- ¾ cup (150 g) granulated sugar
- 1 tablespoon vanilla sugar (see page 414)
- 1 teaspoon instant coffee granules dissolved in 1 teaspoon warm water
- ⅛ teaspoon salt
- 2 oz (60 g) semisweet (dark) chocolate, coarsely chopped
- 2 cups (300 g) finely ground almonds + more as needed
- ¼ teaspoon baking powder

Glaze
- 1 large egg white
- ⅛ teaspoon salt
- ⅓ cup (50 g) confectioners' (icing) sugar

ALMOND SQUARES

- 1 cup (150 g) whole almonds
- 1 cup (200 g) superfine (caster) sugar
- 2 large egg whites
- ⅛ teaspoon salt
- 2 cups (300 g) finely ground almonds
- ½ cup (50 g) coarsely chopped cashew nuts
- 1 teaspoon finely grated lemon zest
- 1 teaspoon finely grated orange zest
- 2–3 tablespoons raw

Toast the whole almonds in a frying pan over medium heat for 5–7 minutes, or until lightly golden. Transfer to a food processor, add 2 tablespoons of the superfine sugar, and process until finely ground. • Beat the egg whites and salt in a large bowl until frothy. • With mixer at high speed, gradually add the remaining superfine sugar, beating until stiff, glossy peaks form. • Fold in the toasted ground almond mixture, the finely ground almonds, cashews, and lemon and orange zests to form a stiff dough. • Press into a disk, wrap in plastic wrap (cling film), and refrigerate for 30 minutes. • Preheat the

oven to 300°F (150°C/gas 2). • Line four cookie sheets with parchment paper. • Roll out the dough on a surface dusted with the raw sugar to ⅛ inch (3 mm) thick. • Use a knife to cut into 1½-inch (4-cm) squares. • Transfer to the prepared cookie sheets. • Bake for 12–15 minutes, or until just golden around the edges. • Cool on the sheets until they firm slightly. Transfer to racks to finish cooling. • Mix the confectioners' sugar and water in a small bowl and spread over the cookies. Sprinkle with the sugar crystals.

Makes: about 60 cookies • Prep: 50 min + 30 min to chill Cooking: 12–15 min • Level: 1

sugar (such as Barbados or Demerara), for rolling out
- sugar crystals, to decorate
- ½ cup (75 g) confectioners' (icing) sugar
- 2 tablespoons hot water

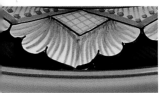

Hazelnut horseshoes

- 2 cups (300 g) all-purpose (plain) flour
- 1/8 teaspoon salt
- 1 cup (250 g) butter, softened
- 3/4 cup (150 g) sugar
- 2 tablespoons vanilla sugar (see page 414)
- 1 large egg
- 1/4 teaspoon almond extract (essence)
- 1 cup (150 g) finely ground hazelnuts or pecans
- 2 tablespoons confectioners' (icing) sugar, to dust

Preheat the oven to 375°F (190°C/gas 5). • Set out four cookie sheets. • Mix the flour and salt in a medium bowl. • Beat the butter and granulated and vanilla sugars in a large bowl with an electric mixer at medium speed until creamy. • Add the egg and almond extract, beating until just blended. • Mix in the dry ingredients and ground hazelnuts. • Fit a pastry bag with a 1/2-inch (1-cm) star tip. Fill the pastry bag, twist the opening tightly closed, and squeeze out generous 1-inch (2.5-cm) tall arches (horseshoes), spacing 1 inch (2.5 cm) apart on the cookie sheets. • Bake, one sheet at a time, for 8–10 minutes, or until golden and firm at the edges. • Transfer to racks to cool and dust with confectioners' sugar.

Makes: about 60 cookies • Prep: 30 min • Cooking: 8–10 min • Level: 2

Glazed almond crisps

Preheat the oven to 350°F (180°C/gas 4). • Butter and flour two cookie sheets. • Mix the flour, baking soda, and salt in a large bowl. • Heat the honey in a medium saucepan over low heat until liquid. Stir in the sugar, cinnamon, cloves, both almonds, and the candied lemon and orange peel. • Remove from the heat. • Mix in the dry ingredients and kirsch. • Shape the warm mixture into a ball and knead on a lightly floured surface until smooth. • If it is sticky, add more flour. • Roll out the dough to 1/4 inch (5 mm) thick. Use a sharp knife to cut into 2-inch (5-cm) rectangles. • Place the rectangles closely together on the prepared baking sheets. • Bake for 15–20 minutes, or until lightly browned. Transfer the cookies to racks and let cool to warm. • Glaze: Mix the confectioners' sugar with the lemon juice and rum in a small bowl. Add enough water to make a pouring consistency. • Brush the glaze on the hot cookies and let cool.

Makes: about 50 cookies • Prep: 45 min • Cooking: 15–20 min • Level: 2

- 4 cups (600 g) all-purpose (plain) flour
- 1 teaspoon baking soda (bicarbonate of soda)
- 1/2 teaspoon salt
- 1 cup (250 ml) honey
- 1 1/2 cups (300 g) sugar
- 1 tablespoon cinnamon
- 1/4 teaspoon cloves
- 1 1/2 cups (150 g) chopped blanched almonds
- 1 1/2 cups (150 g) chopped unblanched almonds
- 2/3 cup (70 g) chopped candied lemon peel
- 2/3 cup (70 g) chopped candied orange peel
- 1/3 cup (90 ml) kirsch

Glaze

- 1 1/3 cups (200 g) confectioners' (icing) sugar
- 1 tablespoon freshly squeezed lemon juice
- 1 tablespoon dark rum
- 1 tablespoon hot water + more as needed

Spiced honey kisses

Cookies

- 2 1/4 cups (330 g) all-purpose (plain) flour
- 2/3 cup (100 g) confectioners' (icing) sugar
- 1/4 teaspoon salt
- 1 cup (250 g) butter, softened
- 1 tablespoon warm water + more as needed

Mix the flour, confectioners' sugar, and salt in a large bowl. Use a pastry blender to cut in the butter until the mixture resembles coarse crumbs. Add enough water to form a stiff dough. • Press the dough into a disk, wrap in plastic wrap (cling film), and refrigerate for 30 minutes. • Preheat the oven to 375°F (190°C/gas 5). • Line two cookie sheets with parchment paper. • Roll out the dough on a lightly floured surface to 1/8 inch (3 mm) thick. • Use a 2 1/2-inch (6-cm) cookie cutter to cut out the cookies. Transfer to the prepared cookie sheets, spacing them 1 inch (2.5 cm)

apart. • Bake for 10–12 minutes, or until just golden. • Transfer to racks and let cool completely. • Spice Honey: Place the brown sugar, cinnamon, cloves, orange zest, and water in a medium saucepan. • Cook, without stirring, until the mixture reaches 238°F (114°C), or the soft-ball stage. • Stir in the vinegar, discard the cloves, cinnamon stick, and orange zest, and remove from the heat. • Let cool completely. • Stick the cookies together in pairs with the spice honey.

Makes: about 30 cookies • Prep: 55 min + 30 min to chill Cooking: 10–12 min • Level: 2

Spiced Honey

- 2 cups (400 g) firmly packed dark brown sugar
- 1 stick cinnamon
- 2 cloves
- zest of 1 orange, in one piece
- 1 cup (250 ml) water
- 1/4 teaspoon white vinegar

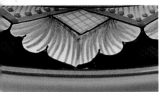

Spice & Nut Cookies

SPICED MARZIPAN SPECIALS

Sweet Honey Dough
- 1 cup (150 g) all-purpose (plain) flour
- 2/3 cup (100 g) rye flour
- 1 teaspoon baking soda (bicarbonate of soda)
- 1 teaspoon ground cinnamon
- 1 teaspoon aniseeds
- 1/2 teaspoon finely grated nutmeg
- 1/4 teaspoon ground ginger
- 1/4 teaspoon salt
- 1 cup (250 ml) honey
- 1/4 cup (50 g) sugar

Marzipan Filling
- 14 oz (400 g) marzipan, softened
- 2/3 cup (100 g) confectioners' (icing) sugar
- 1/2 teaspoon freshly squeezed lemon juice
- 1 teaspoon finely grated lemon zest

- 1 tablespoon cornstarch (cornflour)
- 1 tablespoon confectioners' (icing) sugar
- 3/4 cup (180 ml) hot water

Sweet Honey Dough: Mix the all-purpose and rye flours, the baking soda, cinnamon, aniseeds, nutmeg, ginger, and salt in a large bowl. • Heat the honey and sugar in a small saucepan over low heat until the sugar has dissolved completely. Cool for 15 minutes. • Use a wooden spoon to work the honey mixture into the dry ingredients to form a smooth dough. • Cover with a clean kitchen towel and let rest at room temperature for 3 days. • Preheat the oven to 350°F (180°C/gas 4). • Line two cookie sheets with parchment paper. • Marzipan Filling: Knead the marzipan, confectioners' sugar, and lemon juice and zest until smooth. • Roll the honey dough out on a lightly floured surface into three 12 x 4-inch (30 x 10-cm) strips. • Shape the marzipan filling into logs of the same length as the dough strips. • Place the marzipan logs on top of the dough strips and fold over the dough to seal. • Slice the filled dough 1 inch (2.5 cm) thick and place cut-side up 1 inch (2.5 cm) apart on the prepared cookie sheets. • Bake for 12–15 minutes, or until just golden at the edges. • Transfer to racks. • Toast the cornstarch in a frying pan for 3–4 minutes, or until lightly golden, shaking the pan constantly. Add the confectioners' sugar and water and bring to a boil, stirring constantly. • Remove from the heat and drizzle over the cookies while warm.

*Makes: about 35 cookies • Prep: 1 hr + 3 days to rest
Cooking: 12–15 min • Level: 3*

PRESSED ALMOND VANILLA COOKIES

Preheat the oven to 375°F (190°C/gas 5). • Butter four cookie sheets. • Mix the flour and salt in a medium bowl. • Beat the butter and granulated and vanilla sugars in a large bowl with an electric mixer at medium speed until creamy. • Gradually mix in the dry ingredients and ground almonds to form a smooth dough. • Insert a flower or star design plate into a cookie press by sliding it into the head and locking in place. Press out the cookies, spacing about 1 inch (2.5 cm) apart on the prepared cookie sheets. • Bake for 10–15 minutes, or until golden brown and firm at the edges. • Transfer to racks to cool.

Makes: about 60 cookies • Prep: 30 min • Cooking: 10–15 min • Level: 2

- 3 cups (450 g) all-purpose (plain) flour
- 1/2 teaspoon salt
- 1 1/2 cups (375 g) butter, softened
- 1 1/4 cups (250 g) granulated sugar
- 2 tablespoons vanilla sugar (see page 414)
- 1 1/2 cups (200 g) finely ground almonds

PRESSED GINGER AND LEMON CRISPS

Preheat the oven to 375°F (190°C/gas 5). • Butter four cookie sheets. • Mix the flour, ginger, cloves, and salt in a medium bowl. • Beat the butter and both sugars in a large bowl with an electric mixer at medium speed until creamy. • Add the egg and lemon zest and juice, beating until just blended. • Mix in the dry ingredients to form a stiff dough. • Insert the chosen design plate into a cookie press by sliding it into the head and locking in place. Press out the cookies, spacing about 1 inch (2.5 cm) apart on the prepared cookie sheets. • Decorate each cookie with candied ginger and sprinkle with sugar crystals. • Bake for 10–12 minutes, or until firm to the touch and golden at the edges. • Transfer to racks to cool.

Makes: about 60 cookies • Prep: 30 min • Cooking: 10–12 min • Level: 2

- 3 cups (450 g) all-purpose (plain) flour
- 2 teaspoons ground ginger
- 1/4 teaspoon ground cloves
- 1/4 teaspoon salt
- 1 1/2 cups (375 g) butter, softened
- 1 1/4 cups (250 g) granulated sugar
- 2 tablespoons vanilla sugar (see page 414)
- 1 large egg
- 1 tablespoon finely grated lemon zest
- 1 tablespoon freshly squeezed lemon juice
- 1 tablespoon chopped candied ginger
- 1 tablespoon colored sugar crystals

Spice & Nut Cookies

Coconut biscotti

COCONUT BISCOTTI

- 1²/₃ cups (250 g) all-purpose (plain) flour
- 1 teaspoon baking powder
- ¹/₈ teaspoon salt
- 2 large eggs
- 1 cup (200 g) superfine (caster) sugar
- 1 teaspoon finely grated lemon zest
- ¹/₂ cup (60 g) unsweetened shredded (desiccated) coconut
- 1 cup (150 g) blanched almonds, halved

Preheat the oven to 350°F (180°C/gas 4). • Butter two cookie sheets. • Mix the flour, baking powder, and salt in a medium bowl. • Beat the eggs, sugar, and lemon zest in a large bowl with an electric mixer at medium speed until frothy. • Mix in the dry ingredients, coconut, and almonds to form a stiff dough. • Divide the dough in two. Form into two 8-inch (20-cm) logs and place 4 inches (10-cm) apart on the prepared cookie sheet, flattening them slightly. • Bake for 30–35 minutes, or until firm to the touch. • Transfer to a chopping board and let cool for 15 minutes. • Cut on the diagonal into 1-inch (2.5-cm) slices and arrange cut-side up on two cookie sheets. • Bake for 10–15 minutes, or until golden and toasted. • Transfer to racks to cool.

Makes: about 30 cookies • Prep: 40 min • Cooking: 40–50 min • Level: 2

ALLSPICE BISCOTTI

Preheat the oven to 350°F (180°C/gas 4). • Line a cookie sheet with parchment paper. • Mix the flour, allspice, and salt in a medium bowl. • Beat the egg whites, sugar, and honey in a large bowl with an electric mixer at high speed until frothy. • Mix in the dry ingredients and almonds. • Form the mixture into a 9-inch (23-cm) log. • Bake for 25–30 minutes, or until lightly browned and firm to the touch. • Let cool completely and wrap in aluminum foil. Let stand for 12 hours. • Re-heat the oven to 300°F (150°C/gas 2). • Discard the foil. Slice the dough ¹/₂ inch (1 cm) thick and arrange on cookie sheets. • Bake for 15–20 minutes, or until golden and toasted. • Let cool completely.

Makes: about 30 cookies • Prep: 30 min + 12 hr to rest Cooking: 40–50 min • Level: 2

- 1¹/₃ cups (200 g) all-purpose (plain) flour
- ¹/₂ teaspoon allspice
- ¹/₈ teaspoon salt
- 2 large egg whites
- ¹/₄ cup (50 g) sugar
- 1 tablespoon honey
- ¹/₂ cup (75 g) blanched almonds, halved

CARDAMOM BISCOTTI

Biscotti
- 2½ cups (375 g) all-purpose (plain) flour
- 1 teaspoon baking powder
- 1 teaspoon ground cardamom
- ¼ teaspoon ground allspice
- ¼ teaspoon salt
- 1¼ cups (250 g) raw sugar (Barbados or Demerara)
- 2 large eggs + 1 large egg white
- 1 teaspoon lemon extract (essence)
- 2 tablespoons finely chopped candied mixed peel
- 1 tablespoon finely grated lemon zest
- 1 tablespoon finely grated orange zest

Glaze
- 1 large egg yolk
- 1 tablespoon milk
- 2 tablespoons sugar
- ½ teaspoon ground cardamom

Biscotti: Preheat the oven to 350°F (180°C/gas 4). • Butter two cookie sheets. • Mix the flour, baking powder, cardamom, allspice, and salt in a medium bowl. • Stir in the sugar, candied peel, and lemon and orange zests. • Beat the eggs, egg white, and lemon extract until frothy. • Mix in the dry ingredients. • Form into three 10-inch (25-cm) logs and place 4 inches (10 cm) apart on the prepared cookie sheets. • Glaze: Mix the egg yolk and milk and brush over the logs. Sprinkle with sugar and cardamom. • Bake for 25–30 minutes, or until firm. • Transfer to a cutting board. • Reduce the oven temperature to 300°F (150°C/gas 2). • Cut on the diagonal into 1-inch (2.5-cm) slices. • Bake for 8–10 minutes, or until golden. • Transfer to racks to cool.

Makes: about 35 cookies • Prep: 40 min • Cooking: 35–40 min • Level: 2

ANISEED BISCOTTI

Preheat the oven to 375°F (190°C/gas 5). • Set out a cookie sheet. • Mix the flour, aniseeds, baking powder, and salt in a medium bowl. • Beat the butter and sugar with an electric mixer at medium speed until creamy. • Add the lemon zest and eggs. • Mix in the dry ingredients to form a stiff dough. • Divide the dough in half. Form the dough into two 11-inch (28-cm) logs and place 3 inches (8 cm) apart on the cookie sheet. • Bake for 25–35 minutes, or until firm to the touch. • Transfer to a cutting board to cool for 15 minutes. • Cut on the diagonal into 1-inch (2.5-cm) slices. • Arrange the slices cut-side up on two cookie sheets and bake for 5–7 minutes more, or until golden and toasted. • Transfer to racks to cool.

Makes: about 50 cookies • Prep: 40 min • Cooking: 35–40 min • Level: 2

- 3 cups (450 g) all-purpose (plain) flour
- 2 teaspoons baking powder
- 2 teaspoons ground aniseeds
- ½ teaspoon salt
- ⅔ cup (150 g) butter, softened
- 1 cup (200 g) sugar
- finely grated zest of 2 lemons
- 3 large eggs

Cardamom biscotti

Spice & Nut Cookies

CHOCOLATE GINGER BISCOTTI

- 2½ cups (375 g) all-purpose (plain) flour
- 2 tablespoons unsweetened cocoa powder
- 1 teaspoon baking soda (bicarbonate of soda)
- ½ teaspoon salt
- ¼ teaspoon ground cinnamon
- ¼ teaspoon ground cloves
- 1 cup (200 g) sugar
- 1¼ cups (125 g) finely chopped almonds
- 3 large eggs, lightly beaten
- 2 tablespoons freshly grated fresh ginger
- ½ teaspoon almond extract (essence)

Preheat the oven to 350°F (180°C/gas 4). • Line a cookie sheet with parchment paper. • Mix the flour, cocoa, baking soda, salt, cinnamon, and cloves in a large bowl. • Stir in the sugar and almonds. • Mix in the eggs, ginger, and almond extract to form a stiff dough. • Divide the dough in half. • Form the dough into two 10-inch (25-cm) logs and place 3 inches (8 cm) apart on the prepared cookie sheet, flattening the tops. • Bake for 20–30 minutes, or until lightly browned and firm to the touch. • Transfer to a cutting board to cool for 15 minutes. • Reduce the oven temperature to 300°F (150°C/gas 2). • Cut on the diagonal into 1-inch (2.5-cm) slices. • Arrange the slices cut-side up on two cookie sheets and bake for 10–15 minutes, or until golden and toasted. • Transfer to racks to cool.

Makes: about 40 cookies • Prep: 40 min • Cooking: 30–45 min • Level: 2

FRUIT AND NUT BISCOTTI

Preheat the oven to 325°F (170°C/gas 3). • Spread the blanched almonds on a large baking sheet. Toast for 7 minutes, or until lightly golden. Let cool then cut in half. • Increase the oven temperature to 350°F (180°C/gas 4). • Line two cookie sheets with parchment paper. • Toast the pine nuts in a frying pan over medium heat for 5–7 minutes, or until lightly golden. • Mix the flour, baking powder, and salt in a large bowl. Stir in the sugar, dates, apricots, prunes, halved and whole almonds, pine nuts, and the orange and lemon zests. • Beat the eggs in a medium bowl until frothy. Add to the dry ingredients, reserving 1 tablespoon. • Divide the dough in half. Form into two long logs about 1¼ inches (3 cm) in diameter. • Transfer to the cookie sheets, flattening slightly. • Bake for 15–20 minutes, or firm to the touch. • Transfer to a cutting board to cool for 10 minutes. • Lower oven temperature to 300°F (150°C/gas 2). • Cut on the diagonal into ½ inch (1-cm) slices. • Bake for 7–10 minutes, or until golden. • Transfer to racks to cool.

Makes: about 35 cookies • Prep: 30 min • Cooking: 35–40 min • Level: 1

- ¼ cup (40 g) blanched almonds
- ½ cup (90 g) pine nuts
- 2 cups (300 g) all-purpose (plain) flour
- 1 teaspoon baking powder
- ¼ teaspoon salt
- 1¼ cups (250 g) sugar
- ½ cup (50 g) finely chopped pitted dates
- ¼ cup (25 g) finely chopped dried apricots
- ¼ cup (50 g) finely chopped pitted prunes
- ¼ cup (40 g) whole almonds with skins
- finely grated zest of 1 orange
- 1 teaspoon finely grated lemon zest
- 3 large eggs, lightly beaten

HAZELNUT CLOVE BISCOTTI

- 1¼ cups (175 g) whole hazelnuts
- 1⅔ cups (250 g) all-purpose (plain) flour
- 1 teaspoon ground cinnamon
- ½ teaspoon ground cloves
- ⅛ teaspoon salt
- 2 large eggs + 1 egg yolk
- 1 cup (200 g) sugar
- finely grated zest of 1 lemon
- ½ teaspoon vanilla extract (essence)

Preheat the oven to 325°F (170°C/gas 4). • Spread the hazelnuts on a large baking sheet. Toast for 7 minutes, or until lightly golden. • Transfer to a large cotton kitchen towel. Fold the towel over the nuts and rub them in the towel to remove the thin inner skins. • Discard the skins and coarsely chop the nuts. • Butter a cookie sheet. • Mix the flour, cinnamon, cloves, and salt in a medium bowl. • Beat the eggs and egg yolk and sugar in a large bowl with an electric mixer at high speed until very pale and thick. • Mix in the dry ingredients, hazelnuts, lemon zest, and vanilla to form a smooth dough. • Divide the dough in half. Form the dough into two 12-inch (30-cm) long logs about 1½ inches (4 cm) in diameter and place them 2 inches (5 cm) apart on the prepared sheet. • Bake for 30–40 minutes, or until firm to the touch. • Cool on the cookie sheet for 15 minutes. • Cut on the diagonal into ½-inch (1-cm) slices and transfer to racks to cool completely.

Makes: about 40 cookies • Prep: 30 min • Cooking: 30–40 min • Level: 2

Spice & Nut Cookies

GINGER ROPES

- 1 cup (150 g) all-purpose (plain) flour
- 1/2 cup (75 g) whole-wheat (wholemeal) flour
- 1 tablespoon ground ginger
- 1 teaspoon baking powder
- 1/4 teaspoon salt
- 1/2 cup (125 g) butter, cut up
- 1/3 cup (70 g) firmly packed light brown sugar
- 1/4 cup (25 g) finely chopped walnuts
- 1 large egg, lightly beaten

Mix both flours, ginger, baking powder, and salt in a large bowl. • Use a pastry blender to cut in the butter until the mixture resembles coarse crumbs. • Stir in the brown sugar and walnuts. • Mix in the egg to form a smooth dough. • Cover with plastic wrap (cling film) and refrigerate for 30 minutes. • Preheat the oven to 350°F (180°C/gas 4). • Butter two cookie sheets. • Form tablespoons of the dough into 6-inch (15-cm) ropes and fold the ropes in half. • Twist the dough and place 1½ inches (4 cm) apart on the prepared cookie sheets. • Bake for 12–15 minutes, or until lightly browned and firm to the touch. • Transfer to racks to cool.

Makes: about 36 cookies • Prep: 30 min + 30 min to chill Cooking: 12–15 min • Level: 1

GINGER NUT CRISPS

Preheat the oven to 375°F (190°C/gas 5). • Butter three cookie sheets. • Mix the flour, baking soda, ginger, and salt in a medium bowl. • Beat the brown sugar, corn syrup, water, and egg in a large bowl with an electric mixer at medium speed until well blended. • Stir in the dry ingredients and pecans. • Drop teaspoons of the dough 2 inches (5 cm) apart onto the prepared cookie sheets. • Bake for 10–12 minutes, or until just golden at the edges. • Transfer to racks to cool.

Makes: about 36 cookies • Prep: 20 min • Cooking: 10–12 min • Level: 1

- 2 1/3 cups (250 g) all-purpose (plain) flour
- 2 teaspoons baking soda (bicarbonate of soda)
- 1 tablespoon ground ginger
- 1/4 teaspoon salt
- 1 1/4 cups (250 g) firmly packed light brown sugar
- 3 tablespoons light corn (golden) syrup
- 1/4 cup (60 ml) water
- 1 large egg
- 1 cup (100 g) finely chopped pecans

CORIANDER COOKIES

- 1 cup (150 g) all-purpose (plain) flour
- 1 teaspoon ground coriander
- 1/2 teaspoon ground aniseeds
- 1/8 teaspoon salt
- 2 large eggs
- 3/4 cup (150 g) sugar

Preheat the oven to 350°F (180°C/gas 4). • Butter two cookie sheets. • Mix the flour, coriander, aniseeds, and salt in a large bowl. • Beat the eggs and sugar in a medium bowl with an electric mixer at high speed until pale and thick. • Mix in the dry ingredients until well blended. • Drop teaspoons of the cookie dough 3 inches (8 cm) apart onto the prepared cookie sheets. • Bake for 8–12 minutes, or until faintly tinged with brown on top and slightly darker at the edges. • Use a spatula to turn the cookies over. • Bake for 3–5 minutes more, or until firm to the touch. • Transfer to racks and let cool completely.

Makes: about 25 cookies • Prep: 20 min • Cooking: 12–18 min • Level: 1

GOLDEN GINGER CRISPS

Preheat the oven to 400°F (200°C/gas 6). • Butter two cookie sheets. • Mix the flour, ginger, baking powder, baking soda, allspice, cinnamon, and salt in a large bowl. • Use a pastry blender to cut in the butter until the mixture resembles fine crumbs. • Stir in the sugar and corn syrup until well blended. • Form the dough into balls the size of walnuts and place 2 inches (5 cm) apart on the prepared cookie sheets. • Bake for 10–15 minutes, or until just golden. • Cool on the sheets until the cookies firm slightly. • Transfer to racks and let cool completely.

Makes: about 30 cookies • Prep: 25 min • Cooking: 10–15 min • Level: 1

- 1 1/2 cups (225 g) all-purpose (plain) flour
- 1 tablespoon ground ginger
- 2 teaspoons baking powder
- 2 teaspoons baking soda (bicarbonate of soda)
- 2 teaspoons ground allspice
- 1 teaspoon ground cinnamon
- 1/8 teaspoon salt
- 1/2 cup (125 g) butter, cut up
- 1/2 cup (100 g) sugar
- 1/4 cup (60 ml) light corn (golden) syrup

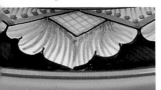

Spice & Nut Cookies

LEMON ZEST CRISPS

- 1⅓ cups (200 g) all-purpose (plain) flour
- ⅛ teaspoon salt
- ⅔ cup (150 g) butter, softened
- ½ cup (100 g) sugar
- 1 large egg
- 1 tablespoon finely grated lemon zest
- 1 teaspoon ice water
- ¾ cup (125 g) almond halves

Mix the flour and salt in a medium bowl. • Beat the butter and sugar in a large bowl until creamy. • Add the egg and lemon zest, beating until just blended. • Mix in the dry ingredients to form a stiff dough. Press the dough into a disk, wrap in plastic wrap (cling film), and refrigerate for 30 minutes. • Preheat the oven to 350°F (180°C/gas 4). • Set out two cookie sheets. • Roll out the dough on a lightly floured surface to ¼ inch (5 mm) thick. • Cut into 2 x 3-inch (4 x 8-cm) rectangles. • Sprinkle the cookies lightly with the water. • Arrange the almond halves on top of the cookies. • Transfer the cookies to the cookie sheets, placing them 1 inch (2.5 cm) apart. • Bake for 20–25 minutes, or until pale gold and firm to the touch. • Cool completely on the sheets.

Makes: about 20 cookies • Prep: 30 min + 30 min to chill
Cooking: 20–25 min • Level: 1

CASHEW SQUARES

Mix the flour and salt in a large bowl. • Use a pastry blender to cut in the butter until the mixture resembles coarse crumbs. • Add the egg yolks, granulated sugar, cashew nuts, lemon zest, and milk to form a stiff dough. • Press the dough into a disk, wrap in plastic wrap (cling film), and refrigerate for 30 minutes. • Preheat the oven to 325°F (170°C/ gas 3). • Butter two cookie sheets. • Roll out the dough on a lightly floured surface to ¼ inch (5 mm) thick. • Cut into 1½-inch (4-cm) wide strips, then cut the strips into 2 1/2-inch (6-cm) rectangles. • Use a spatula to transfer the cookies to the prepared cookie sheets, placing them 1 inch (2.5 cm) apart. • Bake for 12–15 minutes, or until just golden. • Transfer to racks to cool.

Makes: about 30 cookies • Prep: 30 min + 30 min to chill
Cooking: 12–15 min • Level: 1

- 1⅔ cups (250 g) all-purpose (plain) flour
- ⅛ teaspoon salt
- ¼ cup (60 g) butter, cut up
- 3 large egg yolks, lightly beaten
- ¾ cup (150 g) sugar
- ¼ cup (25 g) coarsely chopped cashew nuts
- finely grated zest of ½ lemon
- ⅓ cup (90 ml) milk

FAIRY GLEN COOKIES

- 3 large egg whites
- ⅛ teaspoon salt
- 1¾ cups (350 g) sugar
- 3⅓ cups (330 g) finely ground almonds
- 4 tablespoons orange marmalade
- 18 candied cherries, cut in half

Preheat the oven to 350°F (180°C/gas 4). • Butter three cookie sheets. • Beat the egg whites and salt in a large bowl with an electric mixer until soft peaks form. • With mixer at high speed, gradually add the sugar, beating until stiff, glossy peaks form. Fold in the almonds. • Heat the marmalade in a small saucepan over low heat. Let cool slightly. • Fold the marmalade into the batter. • Fit a pastry bag with a ½-inch (1-cm) star tip. Fill the pastry bag, twist the opening tightly closed. Squeeze out generous 1½-inch (4-cm) stars on the prepared cookie sheets. • Decorate with cherry halves. • Bake for 10–15 minutes, or until just golden. • Transfer to racks to cool.

Makes: about 36 cookies • Prep: 25 min • Cooking: 10–15 min • Level: 2

ANISEED COOKIES

Line two cookie sheets with parchment paper. • Mix the flour, cornstarch, and aniseed in a large bowl. • Beat the eggs, sugar, and salt in a double boiler over barely simmering water with an electric mixer at high speed until pale and thick. Remove from the heat and continue beating until the mixture has cooled. • Use a large rubber spatula to fold the dry ingredients into the batter, followed by the water. • Fit a pastry bag with a ¼-inch (5-mm) plain) tip. Fill the pastry bag and squeeze out ¾ inch (2-cm) round cookies. • Set aside, covered, at room temperature for 12 hours, or until a thin crust has formed. • Preheat the oven to 275°F (140°C/gas 1). • Bake for 25–30 minutes, or until lightly browned. • Transfer to racks to cool.

Makes: about 20 cookies • Prep: 1 hr + 12 hr to rest
Cooking: 25–30 min • Level: 2

- ½ cup (75 g) all-purpose (plain) flour
- 2 tablespoons cornstarch (cornflour)
- 1 tablespoon ground aniseeds
- 2 large eggs
- ½ cup (100 g) sugar
- ¼ teaspoon salt
- 1 teaspoon water

Fresh ginger molasses cookies

FRESH GINGER MOLASSES COOKIES

- ²/₃ cup (150 g) butter, cut up
- ¹/₃ cup (90 ml) light corn (golden) syrup
- ¹/₃ cup (90 ml) dark molasses
- ³/₄ cup (150 g) firmly packed dark brown sugar
- 2 teaspoons finely grated fresh ginger root
- 2²/₃ cups (400 g) all-purpose (plain) flour
- 1¹/₂ teaspoon baking soda (bicarbonate of soda)
- 1 teaspoon ground allspice
- ¹/₈ teaspoon salt
- 2 tablespoons granulated sugar
- 2 large eggs, lightly beaten

Melt the butter, corn syrup, molasses, and brown sugar in a small saucepan over low heat. • Mix in the ginger, remove from the heat, and let cool. • Mix the flour, baking powder, allspice, and salt in a large bowl. • Stir in the granulated sugar. Add the eggs, beating until just blended. • Mix in the corn syrup mixture to form a smooth dough. • Form the dough into four logs, each 8 inches (20 cm) long and 2 inches (5 cm) in diameter. • Wrap in plastic wrap (cling film) and refrigerate for 30 minutes. • Preheat the oven to 325°F (170°C/gas 3). • Line two cookie sheets with parchment paper. • Slice the dough ¹/₂ inch (1 cm) thick and place on the prepared cookie sheets. • Bake for 15–20 minutes, or until the edges are firm. • Cool on the sheets until the cookies firm slightly. • Transfer to racks to cool completely.

Makes: about 60 cookies • Prep: 30 min + 30 min to chill
Cooking: 15–20 min • Level: 2

NUTMEG SPRITZ COOKIES

- 1 cup (150 g) all-purpose (plain) flour
- ¹/₂ teaspoon freshly grated nutmeg
- ¹/₈ teaspoon salt
- ¹/₂ cup (125 g) butter, softened
- 4 tablespoons cream cheese, softened
- ¹/₂ cup (100 g) sugar
- ¹/₂ teaspoon almond extract (essence)
- 1 large egg yolk

Preheat the oven to 350°F (180°C/gas 4). • Set out two cookie sheets. • Mix the flour, ¹/₄ teaspoon nutmeg, and salt in a medium bowl. • Beat the butter, cream cheese, and sugar in a large bowl with an electric mixer on medium speed until creamy. • Add the almond extract and egg yolk, beating until just blended. • Mix in the dry ingredients. • Insert a design plate into a cookie press by sliding it into the head and locking in place. • Press out the cookies, spacing 1well. Dust the cookies with the remaining nutmeg. • Bake for 12–15 minutes, or until just golden, rotating the sheets halfway through for even baking. • Transfer to racks to cool.

Makes: about 30 cookies • Prep: 30 min • Cooking: 12–15 min • Level: 2

GLAZED NUT COOKIES

Cookies: Beat the egg white and salt in a large bowl with an electric mixer at medium speed until frothy. • With mixer at high speed, gradually add the superfine sugar, beating until stiff, glossy peaks form. • Use a large rubber spatula to fold in the hazelnuts, almonds, pistachios, and candied peel to form a stiff dough. Add more ground nuts if the dough is very sticky. • Press the dough into a disk, wrap in plastic wrap (cling film), and refrigerate for 30 minutes. • Preheat the oven to 300°F (150°C/ gas 2). • Line three cookie sheets with parchment paper. • Roll out the dough between sheets of waxed paper dusted with confectioners' sugar to ¹/₄ inch (5 mm) thick. • Cut into 2 x ³/₄-inch (5 x 2-cm) strips. • Use a spatula to transfer the cookies to the prepared cookie sheets, placing them 1 inch (2.5 cm) apart. • Bake for 12–15 minutes, or until golden brown. • Transfer to racks to cool. • Orange Glaze: Mix the confectioners' sugar and orange juice in a small bowl. • Dip the cookies halfway into the glaze and let stand for 30 minutes until set.

Makes: about 35 cookies • Prep: 45 min + 1 hr to chill and set
Cooking: 12–15 min • Level: 2

Cookies
- 1 large egg white
- ¹/₈ teaspoon salt
- ¹/₂ cup (100 g) superfine (caster) sugar
- 1 cup (150 g) finely ground hazelnuts + more as needed
- 1 cup (150 g) finely ground almonds + more as needed
- ¹/₂ cup (50 g) coarsely chopped pistachios
- 2 teaspoon finely chopped candied peel

Orange Glaze
- ¹/₂ cup (75 g) confectioners' (icing) sugar
- 2 tablespoons freshly squeezed orange juice

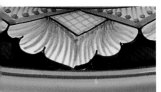

ORANGE SPRITZ COOKIES

- 3 tablespoons all-purpose (plain) flour
- ⅛ teaspoon salt
- 1⅓ cups (200 g) finely ground hazelnuts
- ⅔ cup (100 g) finely ground almonds
- 1 large egg, lightly beaten
- ¼ cup (60 ml) freshly squeezed orange juice
- 1 tablespoon finely grated orange zest
- 1 tablespoon maple or corn (golden) syrup
- 3 tablespoons apricot preserves (jam)
- 2 tablespoons finely chopped pistachios or almonds

Preheat the oven to 300°F (150°C/gas 2). • Line two cookie sheets with parchment paper. • Mix the flour and salt in a small bowl. • Stir the hazelnuts, almonds, and egg in a large bowl. • Mix in the orange juice, orange zest, and 1 tablespoon of maple syrup. • Mix in the dry ingredients, 1 tablespoon at a time, to form a soft, smooth dough. • Fit a pastry bag with a plain 1-inch (2.5-cm) tip. Spoon half the mixture into the pastry bag and squeeze out half moons and wreaths spacing well on the cookie sheets. • Fit a second pastry bag with an 1-inch (2.5-cm) star tip. Spoon the remaining dough into the pastry bag and squeeze out ridged moons and wreaths. • Bake for 12–15 minutes, or until lightly golden. • Transfer to racks to cool. • Warm the preserves in a small saucepan over low heat. • Brush over the warm cookies and sprinkle with the pistachios.

Makes: about 30 cookies • Prep: 30 min • Cooking: 12–15 min • Level: 2

HEARTS OF SPICE

Mix the flour, allspice, baking soda, cinnamon, cloves, ginger, nutmeg, and salt in a medium bowl. • Use a wooden spoon to beat the molasses, brown sugar, and butter in a large bowl until well blended. • Mix in the dry ingredients to form a stiff dough. • Press the dough into a disk, wrap in plastic wrap (cling film), and refrigerate for 30 minutes. • Preheat the oven to 375°F (190°C/gas 5). • Butter two cookie sheets. • Roll out the dough on a lightly floured surface to ¼ inch (5 mm) thick. • Use a 1½-inch (4-cm) heart-shaped cookie cutter to cut out the cookies. Gather the dough scraps, re-roll, and continue cutting out cookies until all the dough is used. • Use a spatula to transfer the cookies to the prepared cookie sheets, placing them 1 inch (2.5 cm) apart. • Bake for 7–10 minutes, or until golden brown. • Transfer to racks to cool.

Makes: about 30 cookies • Prep: 30 min + 30 min to chill Cooking: 7–10 min • Level: 1

- 1¾ cups (275 g) all-purpose (plain) flour
- ¼ teaspoon ground allspice
- ¼ teaspoon baking soda (bicarbonate of soda)
- ¼ teaspoon ground cinnamon
- ¼ teaspoon ground cloves
- ¼ teaspoon ground ginger
- ¼ teaspoon freshly grated nutmeg
- ⅛ teaspoon salt
- ½ cup (125 g) light molasses
- ½ cup (200 g) firmly packed light brown sugar
- ¼ cup (60 g) butter, melted

LEBKUCHEN

Cookies
- 10 cloves
- 1 piece (3-inch/8-cm) cinnamon
- seeds from 5 cardamom pods
- 1 blade mace
- ½ teaspoon freshly grated nutmeg
- 2 cups (300 g) whole almonds
- ½ cup (50 g) finely chopped candied lemon peel
- ½ cup (50 g) finely chopped candied orange peel
- finely grated zest of ½ lemon

Cookies: Preheat the oven to 325°F (170°C/gas 3). • Pound the cloves, cinnamon, cardamom seeds, mace, and nutmeg in a pestle and mortar until finely ground. • Spread the almonds on a large baking sheet. Toast for 7 minutes, or until lightly golden. • Finely chop the almonds. • Increase the oven temperature to 350°F (180°C/gas 4). • Line three cookie sheets with rice paper. • Let the almonds cool completely and transfer to a medium bowl. • Stir in the candied lemon and orange peel, lemon zest, and ground spices. • Mix the flour, baking powder, and salt in a medium bowl. • Beat the eggs and sugar in a large bowl with an electric mixer at high speed until pale and thick. • Beat in the honey and

almond mixture. • Add the kirsch. • Mix in the dry ingredients. • Drop rounded tablespoons of the mixture 2 inches (5 cm) apart onto the prepared cookie sheets. • Bake for 15–20 minutes, or until lightly browned. • Cool on the sheets until the cookies firm slightly. • Transfer the cookies still on the rice paper to racks and let cool completely. • Tear away the excess rice paper from around the cookies. • Glaze: Mix the confectioners' sugar, water, and rum in a small bowl until smooth. • Spread the glaze over the cookies and let stand for 30 minutes until set.

Makes: about 35 cookies • Prep: 50 min + 30 min to chill Cooking: 15–20 min • Level: 2

- 2⅓ cups (350 g) all-purpose (plain) flour
- 1 teaspoon baking powder
- ⅛ teaspoon salt
- 3 large eggs
- 1 cup (200 g) sugar
- 2 tablespoons honey
- 1 teaspoon kirsch

Glaze
- 1 cup (150 g) confectioners' (icing) sugar
- 1 tablespoon warm water
- ½ teaspoon white rum

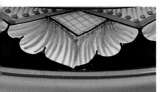

Spice & Nut Cookies

ALMOND WAVES

- 1⅓ cups (200 g) all-purpose (plain) flour
- ⅛ teaspoon salt
- ⅔ cup (150 g) butter, softened
- ⅓ cup (70 g) sugar
- 1 large egg white
- finely grated zest of 1 lemon
- ½ teaspoon vanilla extract (essence)
- 24–26 whole almonds

Preheat the oven to 350°F (180°C/gas 4). • Butter two cookie sheets. • Mix the flour and salt in a medium bowl. • Beat the butter and sugar in a large bowl with an electric mixer at medium speed until creamy. • Add the egg white, lemon zest, and vanilla, beating until just blended. • Mix in the dry ingredients. • Fit a pastry bag with a ½-inch (1-cm) star tip. Fill the pastry bag and twist the opening tightly closed. Squeeze out 1½-inch (4-cm) wide heaps, dragging the cookies forward to finish in a thin point, spacing 2 inches (5 cm) apart on the prepared cookie sheets. • Press an almond onto the thin point of each cookie. • Bake for 15–20 minutes, or until just golden. • Cool on the sheets until the cookies firm slightly. Transfer to racks to finish cooling.

Makes: about 25 cookies • Prep: 25 min • Cooking: 15–20 min • Level: 2

DUTCH SPICE COOKIES

Mix the flour, baking powder, cocoa, ginger, and salt in a large bowl. Use a wooden spoon to mix in the raw sugar, egg, butter, milk, and vanilla to form a soft dough. • Press the dough into a disk, wrap in plastic wrap (cling film), and refrigerate for 30 minutes. • Preheat the oven to 350°F (180°C/gas 4). • Butter two cookie sheets. • Roll out the dough on a lightly floured surface to ¼ inch (5 mm) thick. • Use Christmas cookie cutters to cut out the cookies. Use a spatula to transfer the cookies to the prepared cookie sheets, placing them 1 inch (2.5 cm) apart. Prick all over with a fork. • Bake for 8–10 minutes, or until just golden. • Transfer to racks and let cool completely.

Makes: about 30 cookies • Prep: 30 min + 30 min to chill • Cooking: 8–10 min • Level: 1

- 2⅓ cups (350 g) all-purpose (plain) flour
- 1 teaspoon baking powder
- 1 teaspoon unsweetened cocoa powder
- 1 teaspoon ground ginger
- 1 cup (200 g) raw sugar (Demerara or Barbados)
- 1 large egg
- ½ cup (125 g) butter, melted
- 2 tablespoons milk
- ½ teaspoon vanilla extract (essence)

COCONUT HONEY THINS

- ⅓ cup (50 g) all-purpose (plain) flour
- ¼ teaspoon freshly ground nutmeg
- ⅛ teaspoon salt
- ¼ cup (60 g) butter, softened
- ¼ cup (50 g) firmly packed light brown sugar
- ¾ cup (180 ml) honey
- 1 large egg
- ½ cup (60 g) unsweetened shredded (desiccated) coconut

Preheat the oven to 375°F (190°C/gas 5). • Butter four cookie sheets. • Mix the flour, nutmeg, and salt in a medium bowl. • Beat the butter and brown sugar in a large bowl with an electric mixer at medium speed until creamy. • Beat in the honey and egg. • Mix in the dry ingredients and coconut. • Drop teaspoons of the batter 3 inches (8 cm) apart on the prepared cookie sheets. Do not drop more than eight cookies onto each sheet. Spread the mixture out into thin circles. • Bake for 8–10 minutes, or until faintly tinged with brown on top and slightly darker at the edges. • Working quickly, use a spatula to lift each cookie from the sheet. Transfer to racks to cool.

Makes: about 35 cookies • Prep: 20 min • Cooking: 8–10 min • Level: 2

COFFEE PECAN THINS

Preheat the oven to 350°F (180°C/gas 4). • Butter a cookie sheet. • Beat the butter, sugar, and coffee granules in a large bowl with an electric mixer at medium speed until creamy. • Add the egg, beating until just blended. • Mix in the flour and salt until well blended. • Stir in the pecans and vanilla. • Drop rounded teaspoons of the cookie dough 1 inch (2.5 cm) apart onto the prepared cookie sheets. • Bake for 10–15 minutes, or until just golden. • Cool on the sheet until the cookies firm slightly. Transfer to racks to finish cooling.

Makes: about 12 cookies • Prep: 20 min • Cooking: 10–15 min • Level: 1

- ¼ cup (60 g) butter, softened
- ¼ cup (50 g) sugar
- 1 tablespoon instant coffee granules
- 1 large egg, lightly beaten
- ½ cup (75 g) all-purpose (plain) flour
- ⅛ teaspoon salt
- ¼ cup (25 g) finely chopped pecans
- ½ teaspoon vanilla extract (essence)

Heavenly arches

HEAVENLY ARCHES

- 7 oz (200 g) marzipan, diced and softened
- 2 large eggs
- 2 tablespoons superfine (caster) sugar
- 1 tablespoon vanilla sugar
- ⅓ cup (50 g) cornstarch (cornflour
- ½ teaspoon baking powder
- ¼ teaspoon almond extract (essence)
- ⅛ teaspoon salt
- ½ cup (50 g) slivered almonds, toasted and coarsely chopped

Preheat the oven to 350°F (180°C/gas 4). • Line two cookie sheets with parchment paper. • Beat the marzipan, eggs, superfine and vanilla sugars, cornstarch, baking powder, almond extract, and salt in a large bowl with an electric mixer at low speed until smooth. • Fit a pastry bag with a plain ¼-inch (5-mm) tip. Fill the pastry bag, twist the opening tightly closed, and squeeze about forty small arches spacing them 1 inch (2.5 cm) apart on the prepared cookie sheets. Sprinkle with the almonds, pressing them lightly into the tops. • Bake for 12–15 minutes, or until golden brown. • Cool on the sheet for 5 minutes. • Transfer to racks and let cool completely.

Makes: about 40 cookies • Prep: 50 min • Cooking: 12–15 min • Level: 1

SPICY SQUARES

Mix the flour, ginger, cinnamon, cloves, baking soda, and salt in a medium bowl. • Stir the butter, brown sugar, and molasses in over low heat until the sugar has dissolved. • Remove from the heat and mix in the dry ingredients and lemon zest. • Divide the dough in half. Press into two disks, wrap in plastic wrap (cling film), and refrigerate for 1 hour. • Preheat the oven to 350°F (180°C/gas 4). • Butter two cookie sheets. • Roll the dough out on a lightly floured surface to ¼ inch (5 mm) thick. • Cut into 2-inch (5-cm) squares. • Transfer to the cookie sheets, spacing well. Prick all over with a fork. • Sprinkle with the sugar. • Bake for 5–7 minutes, or until lightly browned. • Transfer to racks and let cool completely.

Makes: about 30 cookies • Prep: 40 min + 1 hr to chill Cooking: 5–7 min • Level: 1

- 1¼ cups (180 g) all-purpose (plain) flour
- 1 teaspoon ground ginger
- 1 teaspoon ground cinnamon
- ¼ teaspoon ground cloves
- ½ teaspoon baking soda (bicarbonate of soda)
- ⅛ teaspoon salt
- ¼ cup (60 g) butter, cut up
- ¼ cup (50 g) firmly packed dark brown sugar
- 2 tablespoons dark molasses (treacle)
- grated zest of 1 lemon
- ¼ cup (50 g) sugar

PECAN MELTING MOMENTS

- 1¼ cups (180 g) all-purpose (plain) flour
- ⅛ teaspoon salt
- ½ cup (125 g) butter, softened
- ⅓ cup (50 g) confectioners' (icing) sugar + extra, to dust
- ½ teaspoon vanilla extract (essence)
- ½ cup (50 g) finely chopped pecans

Preheat the oven to 400°F (200°C/gas 6). • Set out two cookie sheets. • Mix the flour and salt in a medium bowl. • Beat the butter, confectioners' sugar, and vanilla in a large bowl with an electric mixer at medium speed until creamy. • Mix in the dry ingredients and pecans to make a stiff dough. • Press the dough into a disk, wrap in plastic wrap (cling film), and refrigerate for 30 minutes. •• Form the dough into balls the size of walnuts and place 1 inch (2.5 cm) apart on the cookie sheets. • Bake for 10–12 minutes, or until firm to the touch but not browned. • Transfer to racks to cool. • Dust with the remaining confectioners' sugar.

Makes: about 25 cookies • Prep: 25 min + 30 min to chill Cooking: 10–12 min • Level: 1

PEPPER STARS

Melt the butter and molasses in a small saucepan. Set aside. • Mix the flour, baking soda, cinnamon, ginger, peppercorns, cardamom, and salt in a large bowl. • Stir in the sugar, molasses mixture, and egg. • Turn out onto a lightly floured surface and knead until smooth. • Shape into a disk, wrap in plastic wrap (cling film), and refrigerate for 30 minutes. • Preheat the oven to 325°F (170°C/gas 3). • Line two cookie sheets with parchment paper. • Roll out the dough on a lightly floured surface to ¼ inch (5 mm) thick. • Use a star-shaped cutter to cut out the cookies. Transfer to the cookie sheets, spacing well. • Bake for 10–15 minutes, or until firm to the touch. • Cool the cookies on the cookie sheets. Transfer to a rack. • Mix the confectioners' sugar an water in a small bowl. Drizzle over the cookies.

Makes: about 35 cookies • Prep: 40 min + 30 min to chill Cooking: 10–15 min • Level: 1

- ⅓ cup (90 g) butter, cut up
- 2 tablespoons dark molasses (treacle)
- 1½ cups (225 g) all-purpose (plain) flour
- ½ teaspoon baking soda
- ½ teaspoon ground cinnamon
- ½ teaspoon ground ginger
- 3 black peppercorns, crushed
- seeds of 10 cardamom pods, crushed
- ½ teaspoon salt
- ¼ cup (50 g) sugar
- 1 large egg
- 1 cup (150 g) confectioners' (icing) sugar
- 2 tablespoons warm water

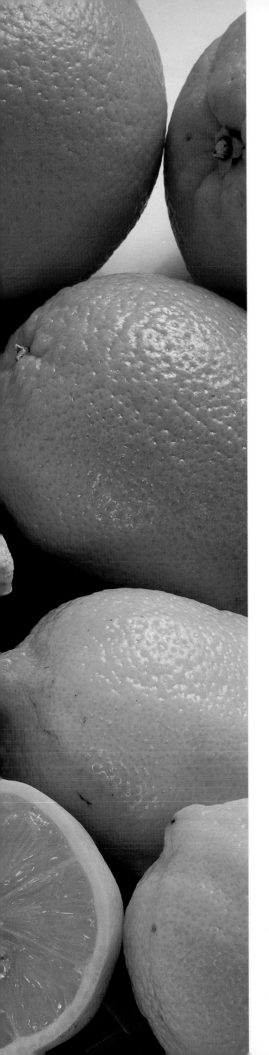

FRESH FRUIT COOKIES

S ome wonderful cookies can be made using fresh fruit as a flavoring or filling. Citrus fruit, such as oranges, lemons, and limes, are the most commonly used fresh-fruit ingredients in cooking baking. Both the juice and the zests are used. To ensure maximum flavor and goodness, always use freshly squeezed fruit juices. Citrus moons, shown left (see recipe page 148), Orange thins (see page 150), and Lemon curd cookies (see page 154) are tasty examples of citrus fruit cookies. But other fruit, such as apples and bananas, can also be used. Try the Green apple cookies (see page 148), the Banana and sunflower seed cookies (see page 152), and the Red delicious cookies (see page 161), among others.

Citrus moons (see page 148)

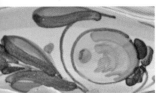

Fresh Fruit Cookies

GREEN APPLE COOKIES

Dough
- 1 cup (250 g) quark or 1⅓ cups (310 g) ricotta cheese
- 2 cups (300 g) all-purpose (plain) flour
- 1 teaspoon baking powder
- ¼ teaspoon salt
- ⅓ cup (90 ml) vegetable oil
- 1–2 tablespoons milk
- ⅓ cup (70 g) sugar
- 1 large egg
- 1 teaspoon finely grated lemon zest
- ¼ teaspoon vanilla extract (essence)
- ⅓ cup (90 g) butter

Filling
- 3 tablespoons golden raisins (sultanas)
- 3 medium apples, peeled, cored, and cubed
- 1 tablespoon butter
- ⅓ cup (70 g) granulated sugar
- Zest of 1 lemon
- 1 teaspoon freshly squeezed lemon juice
- 1 large egg
- ⅓ cup (50 g) confectioners' (icing) sugar, to dust

Dough: Mix all the ingredients for the dough in a large bowl to form a stiff dough. • Filling: Plump the raisins in hot water for 10 minutes. Drain well and pat dry with paper towels. • Preheat the oven to 350°F (180°C/gas 4). • Set out a cookie sheet. • Mix the apples, butter, sugar, and lemon zest and juice in a large saucepan over low heat and simmer for about 5 minutes, or until the apples begin to soften. • Stir in the raisins and let cool completely. • Discard the lemon zest. • Roll out to ¼ inch (5 mm) thick. • Use a round cookie cutter to stamp out 3-inch (8-cm) circles. • Spread with a heaping teaspoonful of the apple filling, leaving a ½-inch (1-cm) border around the edge. • Brush the border with the beaten egg and fold over, pressing down firmly. • Brush the tops with the remaining egg. • Arrange on the cookie sheet about 1 inch (2.5 cm) apart. • Bake for 20–30 minutes, or until golden brown. • Cool on the sheet for 2 minutes. Transfer to racks to cool. • Dust with the confectioners' sugar.

Makes: about 15 cookies • Prep: 1 hr • Cooking: 20–30 min Level: 2

CITRUS MOONS

Cookies: Mix the flour and salt in a medium bowl. • Beat the butter and confectioners' and vanilla sugars in a large bowl until creamy. • Add the whole egg and egg yolk and vanilla, beating until just blended. • Mix in the dry ingredients to form a stiff dough. • Divide the dough in half. Knead the orange zest into one half and lemon zest into the other. • Press into disks, wrap in plastic wrap (cling film), and refrigerate for 30 minutes. • Preheat the oven to 350°F (180°C/gas 4). • Set out three cookie sheets. • Roll out each piece of dough on a lightly floured surface to ¼ inch (5 mm) thick. • Use 2-inch (5-cm) crescent-shaped cookie cutters to cut out cookies. • Transfer to the cookie sheets, spacing well. • Topping: Beat the egg yolk with the water in a small bowl. Brush over the cookies and decorate with almonds. • Bake for 8–10 minutes, or until firm to the touch and the edges are lightly golden. • Transfer to racks to cool.

Makes: about 25 cookies • Prep: 45 min + 30 min to chill Cooking: 8–10 min • Level: 1

Cookies
- 1⅔ cups (250 g) all-purpose (plain) flour
- ⅛ teaspoon salt
- ½ cup (125 g) butter, softened
- ¾ cup (125 g) confectioners' (icing) sugar
- 1 tablespoon vanilla sugar (see page 414)
- 1 large egg + 1 large egg yolk
- ½ teaspoon vanilla extract (essence)
- finely grated zest of 1 orange
- finely grated zest of ½ lemon

Topping
- 1 large egg yolk
- 1 tablespoon water
- 2 tablespoons flaked almonds

ORANGE LADYFINGERS

Preheat the oven to 375°F (190°C/gas 5). • Line two cookie sheets with parchment paper. • Mix the flour and salt in a medium bowl. • Beat the eggs, sugar, and orange zest in a large bowl until pale and very thick. • Gradually fold in the dry ingredients. • Fit a pastry bag with a ½-inch (1-cm) star tip. Fill the pastry bag and squeeze out 2-inch (5-cm) lines, spacing them 3 inches (8 cm) apart on the prepared cookie sheets. • Bake for 5–10 minutes, or until just golden. • Transfer to racks to cool.

Makes: about 20 cookies • Prep: 15 min • Cooking: 5–10 min • Level : 1

- ⅓ cup (50 g) all-purpose (plain) flour
- ⅛ teaspoon salt
- 2 large eggs
- ⅓ cup (70 g) superfine (caster) sugar
- finely grated zest of 1 orange

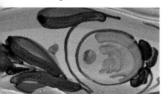

Fresh Fruit Cookies

ORANGE THINS

- 1¼ cups (180 g) all-purpose (plain) flour
- ½ cup (75 g) cornstarch (cornflour)
- ⅛ teaspoon salt
- 3 large eggs, lightly beaten
- 1 cup (200 g) superfine (caster) sugar
- 2 teaspoons finely grated orange zest
- 2 tablespoons sugar crystals

Preheat the oven to 375°F (190°C/gas 5). • Line two baking sheets with parchment paper. • Mix the flour, cornstarch, and salt in a medium bowl. • Use a whisk to beat the eggs, superfine sugar, and orange zest in a double boiler over barely simmering water until pale and very thick. • Transfer to a medium bowl. • Use a large rubber spatula to fold in the dry ingredients. • Fit a pastry bag with a ½-inch (1-cm) plain tip. Fill the pastry bag, twist the opening tightly closed, and squeeze out 3-inch (8-cm) lines, spacing 2 inches (5 cm) apart on the prepared cookie sheets. • Sprinkle with the sugar crystals. • Bake for 8–10 minutes, or until just golden. • Cool the cookies on the cookie sheets for 5 minutes. • Transfer to racks and let cool completely.

Makes: about 30 cookies • Prep: 40 min • Cooking: 8–10 min • Level: 1

CHERRY COOKIES

Mix the flour, baking powder, and salt in a large bowl. • Use a pastry blender to cut in the butter until the mixture resembles fine crumbs. • Add the egg, beating until just blended. • Stir in the sugar, cherries, and vanilla to form a soft dough. • Turn the dough out onto a lightly floured surface and knead until smooth. • Form the dough into a long log 2 inches (5 cm) in diameter, wrap in plastic wrap (cling film), and refrigerate for at least 30 minutes. • Preheat the oven to 375°F (190°C/gas 5). • Butter three cookie sheets. • Slice the dough ½ inch (1 cm) thick and place 1 inch (2.5 cm) apart on the prepared cookie sheets. • Bake for 8–10 minutes, or until just golden. • Transfer to racks to cool.

Makes: about 35 cookies • Prep: 40 min + 30 min to chill Cooking: 8–10 min • Level: 1

- 1⅔ cups (250 g) all-purpose (plain) flour
- 1 teaspoon baking powder
- ⅛ teaspoon salt
- ½ cup (125 g) butter, cut up
- 1 large egg, lightly beaten
- ¾ cup (150 g) sugar
- ½ cup (50 g) finely chopped candied cherries
- 1 teaspoon vanilla extract (essence)

LIME COOKIES

- 3½ cups (535 g) all-purpose (plain) flour
- 1 teaspoon baking soda (bicarbonate of soda)
- ½ teaspoon salt
- ½ cup (50 g) sunflower seeds, toasted
- ½ cup (125 g) butter, softened
- 2¼ cups (450 g) granulated sugar
- 2 tablespoons extra-virgin olive oil
- finely grated zest of 2 limes
- 2 large eggs
- 3 tablespoons freshly squeezed lime juice

Preheat the oven to 350°F (180°C/gas 4). • Line three cookie sheets with parchment paper. • Mix the flour, baking soda, and salt in a medium bowl. • Stir in the sunflower seeds. • Beat the butter, 2 cups (400 g) of sugar, oil, and grated zest of 1 lime in a large bowl with an electric mixer on medium speed until creamy. • Add the eggs, beating until just blended. • Mix in the dry ingredients and lime juice. • Mix the remaining sugar and lime zest in a small bowl. • Form the dough into balls the size of walnuts and roll in the lime sugar. • Place 2 inches (5 cm) apart on the prepared cookie sheets, flattening them slightly. • Bake for 10–12 minutes, or until just golden at the edges. • Transfer to racks and let cool completely.

Makes: about 36 cookies • Prep: 25 min • Cooking: 10–12 min • Level: 1

CRISP ORANGE COOKIES

Preheat the oven to 350°F (180°C/gas 4). • Butter two cookie sheets. • Mix the flour, cornstarch, baking powder, and salt in a large bowl. • Beat the butter and ⅔ cup (100 g) confectioners' sugar in a large bowl with an electric mixer at high speed until creamy. • Mix in the dry ingredients and orange zest. • Drop teaspoons of the mixture 2 inches (5 cm) apart onto the prepared cookie sheets. • Bake for 12–15 minutes, or until golden brown. • Cool completely on the sheets.

Makes: about 25 cookies • Prep: 25 min • Cooking: 12–15 min • Level : 1

- 1½ cups (225 g) all-purpose (plain) flour
- 1 tablespoon cornstarch (cornflour)
- ½ teaspoon baking powder
- ⅛ teaspoon salt
- 1 cup (250 g) butter, softened
- ⅔ cup (100 g) confectioners' (icing) sugar + extra, to dust
- finely grated zest of 2 oranges

Fresh Fruit Cookies

BANANA AND SUNFLOWER SEED COOKIES

- ⅓ cup (30 g) sunflower seeds
- ⅓ cup (50 g) old-fashioned rolled oats
- 2 tablespoons honey
- 1 tablespoon sunflower oil
- ⅓ cup (50 g) all-purpose (plain) flour
- 1 large egg, lightly beaten
- 1 large ripe banana, mashed
- 1 tablespoon sunflower seeds, to decorate

Preheat the oven to 350°F (180°C/gas 4). • Butter a cookie sheet. • Chop the sunflower seeds and oats in a food processor until they resemble flour. • Heat the honey and oil in a small saucepan over low heat. • Mix the honey mixture with the sunflower seed mixture and flour in a medium bowl. • Add the egg, beating until just blended. Stir in the banana. • Drop teaspoons of the mixture 1 inch (2.5 cm) apart onto the prepared cookie sheet. • Bake for 12–15 minutes, or until golden brown. • Cool the cookies completely on the cookie sheets. • Sprinkle with the remaining sunflower seeds.

Makes: about 20 cookies • Prep: 20 min • Cooking: 12–15 min • Level: 1

CARROT AND ORANGE COOKIES

Preheat the oven to 375°F (190°C/gas 5). • Oil four cookie sheets. • Mix the flour, baking soda, cinnamon, allspice, nutmeg, ginger, and salt in a medium bowl. • Beat the butter and brown sugar in a large bowl with an electric mixer on medium speed until creamy. • Add the orange zest and vanilla. • Add the eggs, carrots, raisins, coconut, and oats. • Mix in the dry ingredients. • Drop teaspoons of the dough 2 inches (5 cm) apart on the prepared cookie sheets. • Bake for 8–10 minutes, or until golden brown. • Transfer to racks and let cool completely.

Makes: about 60 cookies • Prep: 20 min • Cooking: 8–10 min • Level: 1

- 1⅓ cups (200 g) all-purpose (plain) flour
- 1 teaspoon baking soda (bicarbonate of soda)
- 1 teaspoon ground cinnamon
- ½ teaspoon ground allspice
- ½ teaspoon freshly grated nutmeg
- ¼ teaspoon ground ginger
- ¼ teaspoon salt
- 1 cup (250 g) butter, softened
- 1 cup (200 g) firmly packed light brown sugar
- 1 teaspoon finely grated orange zest
- 1 teaspoon vanilla extract (essence)
- 2 large eggs
- 1½ cups (185 g) finely shredded carrots
- ½ cup (90 g) raisins
- ½ cup (60 g) unsweetened shredded (desiccated) coconut
- ¼ cup (30 g) old-fashioned rolled oats

Banana and sunflower seed cookies

Apple and walnut cookies

APPLE AND WALNUT COOKIES

- 2 cups (300 g) all-purpose (plain) flour
- ½ teaspoon baking powder
- ½ teaspoon baking soda (bicarbonate of soda)
- ½ teaspoon ground cinnamon
- ¼ teaspoon salt
- ½ cup (125 g) butter
- ½ cup (100 g) sugar
- ¼ cup (50 g) firmly packed dark brown sugar
- 1 large egg
- 1 cup (250 ml) applesauce
- 1 Granny Smith apple, peeled, cored, and finely chopped
- 1 cup (100 g) finely chopped walnuts

Preheat the oven to 375°F (170°C/gas 3). • Butter three cookie sheets. • Mix the flour, baking powder, baking soda, cinnamon, and salt in a medium bowl. • Beat the butter and both sugars in a large bowl with an electric mixer on medium speed until creamy. • Add the egg and applesauce, beating until just blended. • Mix in the dry ingredients, apple, and walnuts. • Drop tablespoons of the dough 2 inches (5 cm) apart onto the prepared cookie sheets. • Bake for 15–20 minutes, or until just golden at the edges. • Transfer to racks to cool.

Makes: about 45 cookies • Prep: 20 min • Cooking: 15–20 min • Level: 1

TROPICAL FRUIT BASKETS

Preheat the oven to 350°F (180°C/gas 4). • Butter a large baking sheet. • Heat the butter, corn syrup, and sugar over low heat in a small saucepan until melted. • Remove from heat and stir in the cream of tartar, flour, and ginger. • Drop tablespoons of the mixture onto the prepared baking sheet. Shape into 2-inch (5-cm) rounds, spacing well apart. • Bake for 8–10 minutes, or until golden brown. • Cool the cookies on the sheet for 5 minutes, or until pliable. • Use a thin metal spatula to remove them from the sheet. • Shape into small baskets, fluting the edges with your fingertips. • Let cool completely, then fill with fresh fruit salad just before serving.

Makes: about 6–8 cookies • Prep: 20 min • Cooking: 8–10 min • Level: 2

- ½ cup (125 g) butter
- ½ cup (125 ml) corn (golden) syrup
- ¼ cup (50 g) sugar
- ½ teaspoon cream of tartar
- ¾ cup (125 g) all-purpose (plain) flour
- 2 teaspoons ground ginger
- fresh fruit salad, made with fruits of the season, sliced and marinated with lemon juice and sugar

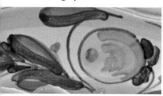

Fresh Fruit Cookies

LEMON CURD COOKIES

- 1½ cups (225 g) all-purpose (plain) flour
- ⅛ teaspoon salt
- ⅔ cup (150 g) butter, cut up
- ⅓ cup (70 g) sugar
- 1 tablespoon finely grated lemon zest
- 2 tablespoons freshly squeezed lemon juice
- 2 large egg yolks
- 1 cup (250 ml) lemon curd (see page 414)

Mix the flour and salt in a medium bowl. • Cut in the butter until the mixture resembles fine crumbs. • Stir in the sugar, lemon zest, juice, and egg yolks to form a stiff dough. • Press into a disk, wrap in plastic wrap (cling film), and refrigerate for 30 minutes. • Preheat the oven to 350°F (180°C/gas 4). • Butter two cookie sheets. • Roll out the dough to ⅛ inch (3 mm) thick. • Use a 3-inch (8-cm) fluted cookie cutter to cut out the cookies. • Use a 1-inch (2.5-cm) crescent-shaped cookie cutter to cut out the centers from half the cookies. Transfer the cookies to the sheets. • Bake for 6–8 minutes, or until golden brown. • Transfer to racks to cool. • Spread the whole cookies with the lemon curd and place the cookies with holes on top.

Makes: about 15 cookies • Prep: 45 min + 30 min to chill Cooking: 6–8 min • Level: 1

LEMON STARS

Preheat the oven to 350°F (180°C/gas 4). • Butter two cookie sheets. • Mix the flour, baking powder, and salt in a large bowl. • Stir in the sugar. • Add the egg, beating until just blended. • Stir in the oil, cream, honey, and lemon zest. • Fit a pastry bag with a ½-inch (1-cm) star tip. Fill the pastry bag, twist the opening tightly closed, and squeeze out generous 1½-inch (4-cm) stars, spacing 1 inch (2.5 cm) apart onto the prepared cookie sheets. • Bake for 10–15 minutes, or until just golden at the edges. • Transfer to racks to cool. • Dot the tops of the cookies with lemon curd and decorate with the candied lemon zest.

Makes: about 25 cookies • Prep: 25 min • Cooking: 10–15 min Level: 2

- 1⅔ cups (250 g) all-purpose (plain) flour
- ½ teaspoon baking powder
- ⅛ teaspoon salt
- ½ cup (100 g) sugar
- 1 large egg
- ⅓ cup (90 ml) sunflower oil
- ¼ cup (60 ml) light (single) cream
- 1 teaspoon honey
- finely grated zest of 1 lemon
- ¼ cup (60 ml) lemon curd (see page 414)
- 2–3 tablespoons candied lemon zest, chopped

Lemon curd cookies

Lemon and carrot cookies

LEMON AND CARROT COOKIES

- 2/3 cup (100 g) all-purpose (plain) flour
- 1 teaspoon baking powder
- 1/8 teaspoon salt
- 1/2 cup (100 g) sugar
- 2 tablespoons finely grated lemon zest
- 1/4 cup (60 g) butter, softened
- 1 cup (125 g) very finely shredded carrots
- 1 tablespoon cold water (optional)

Preheat the oven to 350°F (180°C/gas 4).
• Butter a cookie sheet. • Mix the flour, baking powder, and salt in a medium bowl.
• Reserve 2 teaspoons of the sugar. • Beat the butter and remaining sugar with the lemon zest in a medium bowl with an electric mixer at high speed until creamy.
• Use a wooden spoon to mix in the shredded carrot, followed by the dry ingredients to make a soft dough. • If the dough is stiff, add the water. • Drop tablespoons of the dough 2 inches (5 cm) apart onto the prepared cookie sheet. Sprinkle the tops of the cookies with the reserved sugar. • Bake for 15–20 minutes, or until golden and firm to the touch.
Makes: about 16 cookies • Prep: 40 min • Cooking: 15–20 min • Level: 1

CITRUS CREAM COOKIES

Cookies: Preheat the oven to 350°F (180°C/gas 4). • Butter three cookie sheets.
• Mix the flour and salt in a medium bowl.
• Beat the butter and sugar in a large bowl with an electric mixer at medium speed until creamy. • Add the egg yolks, beating until just blended. • Mix in the dry ingredients, ground almonds, and lemon zest. • Form the dough into balls the size of walnuts and place 1 inch apart on the prepared cookie sheets. Use the back of a fork to flatten each cookie slightly. • Bake for 8–10 minutes, or until pale gold. • Cool on the sheets until the cookies firm slightly. Transfer to racks to finish cooling. • Citrus cream filling: With mixer at high speed, beat the butter and confectioners' sugar in a medium bowl until creamy. • Mix in the lemon and orange zests. • Stick the cookies together in pairs with the filling.
Makes: 16–18 cookies • Prep: 25 min • Cooking: 8–10 min Level: 1

Cookies
- 1 2/3 cups (250 g) all-purpose (plain) flour
- 1/4 teaspoon salt
- 1 cup (250 g) butter, softened
- 3/4 cup (150 g) sugar
- 2 large egg yolks
- 1 1/3 cups finely ground almonds
- 1 tablespoon finely grated lemon zest

Citrus cream filling
- 1/2 cup (125 g) butter, softened
- 3/4 cup (125 g) confectioners' (icing) sugar
- 1 tablespoon finely grated lemon zest
- 1 tablespoon finely grated orange zest

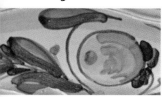

Fresh Fruit Cookies

CRANBERRY HEARTS

Cookies
• 2¼ cups (330 g) all-purpose (plain) flour
• 1½ teaspoons baking powder
• ½ teaspoon ground cinnamon
• ¼ teaspoon salt
• ¾ cup (180 g) butter, softened
• ½ cup (100 g) granulated sugar
• ½ cup (100 g) firmly packed dark brown sugar
• 1 large egg
• ½ teaspoon vanilla extract (essence)
• finely grated zest of 1 lemon

Topping
• 1 cup (250 g) fresh or frozen cranberries
• ¼ cup (50 g) sugar
• ¾ cup (210 g) raspberry preserves

Mix the flour, baking powder, cinnamon, and salt in a medium bowl. • Beat the butter and both sugars in a large bowl until creamy. • Add the egg, vanilla, and lemon zest, beating until just blended. • Mix in the dry ingredients to form a smooth dough. • Press the dough into a disk, wrap in plastic wrap (cling film), and refrigerate for 30 minutes. • Preheat the oven to 350°F (180°C/ gas 4). • Butter two cookie sheets. • Roll out the dough on a lightly floured surface to ¼ inch (5 mm) thick. • Use a 3½-inch (9-cm) heart-shaped cookie cutter to cut out the cookies. • Transfer to the cookie sheets, spacing well. • Bake for 8–10 minutes, or until just golden. • Transfer to racks to cool. • Topping: Process the cranberries, sugar, and preserves in a food processor until puréed. • Transfer to a saucepan and simmer over medium heat until reduced to 1 cup (250 ml). • Let cool for 15 minutes. • Spread the topping over the cookies.

Makes: about 24 cookies • Prep: 1 hr + 30 min to chill Cooking: 8–10 min • Level: 1

PRESSED PINEAPPLE COOKIES

Preheat the oven to 400°F (200°C/gas 6). • Set out two cookie sheets. • Mix the flour, baking powder, and salt in a medium bowl. • Beat the butter and sugar in a large bowl with an electric mixer at high speed until creamy. • Add the egg, beating until just blended. • Mix in the dry ingredients, followed by the pineapple juice. • Insert a star-shaped design plate into a cookie press by sliding it into the head and locking it in place. Press out the cookies, spacing about 1 inch (2.5 cm) apart on the prepared cookie sheets. • Bake for 8–10 minutes, or until just golden at the edges. • Cool on the sheets until the cookies firm slightly. • Transfer to racks and let cool completely.

Makes: about 32 cookies • Prep: 25 min • Cooking: 8–10 min • Level: 2

• 2¼ cups (330 g) all-purpose (plain) flour
• ½ teaspoon baking powder
• ¼ teaspoon salt
• 1 cup (250 g) butter, softened
• ¾ cup (150 g) sugar
• 1 large egg
• 1 tablespoon fresh or canned pineapple juice

CITRUS AND HAZELNUT COOKIES

• ½ cup (125 g) butter, softened
• ¼ cup (50 g) sugar
• 1 large egg, separated
• 1 teaspoon finely grated orange zest
• ½ teaspoon finely grated lemon zest
• ¼ teaspoon salt
• ¾ cup (125 g) all-purpose (plain) flour

Beat the butter and sugar in a large bowl with an electric mixer on medium speed until creamy. • Add the egg yolk, beating until just blended. • Beat in the orange and lemon zests and salt. • Mix in the flour until well blended. • Refrigerate for 30 minutes. • Preheat the oven to 350°F (180°F/gas 4). • Butter two cookie sheets. • Form the dough into balls the size of walnuts. • Beat the egg white lightly in a small bowl. • Dip the balls first in the egg white, then in the hazelnuts until well coated. • Place 1 inch (2.5 cm) apart on the prepared cookie sheets. • Bake for 18–20 minutes, or until firm to the touch. • Transfer to racks and let cool completely.

Makes: about 24 cookies • Prep: 20 min + 30 min to chill Cooking: 18–20 min • Level: 1

• 1 cup (150 g) finely ground hazelnuts

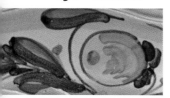

Fresh Fruit Cookies

LIME ESSES

- 3/4 cup (125 g) all-purpose (plain) flour
- 1/8 teaspoon salt
- 1 1/3 cups (200 g) finely ground almonds
- 1 cup (200 g) sugar
- 1 tablespoon finely grated lime zest
- 1/2 cup (125 g) butter, cut up
- 2 large egg whites, lightly beaten

Mix the flour and salt in a large bowl. • Stir in the ground almonds, sugar, and lime zest. • Use a pastry blender to cut in the butter until the mixture resembles fine crumbs. • Mix in the egg whites to form a stiff dough. • Divide the dough in half. Form into two disks, wrap in plastic wrap (cling film), and refrigerate for 30 minutes. • Preheat the oven to 350°F (180°C/gas 4). • Butter three cookie sheets. • Pinch off balls of dough the size of walnuts and shape into rounded S-shape cookies. • Transfer the cookies to the prepared cookie sheets, placing them 1 inch (2.5 cm) apart. • Bake for 12–15 minutes, or until golden brown. • Transfer to racks to cool.

Makes: about 40 cookies • Prep: 25 min + 30 min to chill Cooking: 12–15 min • Level: 1

ORANGE ESSES

Mix the flour and salt in a large bowl. • Stir in the ground almonds, sugar, and orange zest. • Use a pastry blender to cut in the butter until the mixture resembles fine crumbs. • Mix in the egg whites to form a stiff dough. • Divide the dough in half. Form into two disks, wrap in plastic wrap (cling film), and refrigerate for 30 minutes. • Preheat the oven to 350°F (180°C/gas 4). • Butter three cookie sheets. • Pinch off balls of dough the size of walnuts and shape into rounded S-shape cookies. • Transfer the cookies to the prepared cookie sheets, placing them 1 inch (2.5 cm) apart. • Bake, one sheet at a time, for 12–15 minutes, or until golden brown. • Transfer to racks to cool.

Makes: about 40 cookies • Prep: 25 min + 30 min to chill Cooking: 12–25 min • Level: 1

- 3/4 cup (125 g) all-purpose (plain) flour
- 1/8 teaspoon salt
- 1 1/3 cups (200 g) finely ground almonds
- 1 cup (200 g) sugar
- 1 tablespoon finely grated orange zest
- 1/2 cup (125 g) butter, cut up
- 2 large egg whites, lightly beaten

ZESTY LEMON COOKIES

- 1 1/2 cups (225 g) all-purpose (plain) flour
- 1 tablespoon cornstarch (cornflour)
- 1/2 teaspoon baking powder
- 1/4 teaspoon salt
- 1 cup (250 g) butter, softened
- 2/3 cup (100 g) confectioners' sugar + extra, to dust
- finely grated zest of 2 lemons
- confectioners' sugar, to dust

Preheat the oven to 350°F (180°C/gas 4). • Butter two cookie sheets. • Mix the flour, cornstarch, baking powder, and salt in a large bowl. • Beat the butter and confectioners' sugar in a large bowl with an electric mixer at high speed until creamy. • Mix in the dry ingredients and lemon zest. • Drop teaspoons of the mixture 2 inches (5 cm) apart onto the prepared cookie sheets. • Bake for 12–15 minutes, or until golden brown. • Cool completely on the sheets. • Dust with the confectioners' sugar.

Makes about 25 cookies • Prep: 25 min • Cooking: 12–15 min • Level: 1

FRESH LEMON RINGS

Preheat the oven to 350°F (180°C/gas 4). • Line three cookie sheets with parchment paper. • Use a wooden spoon to mix the flour, sugar, eggs, milk, vanilla, butter, lemon zest, and salt in a large bowl to make a smooth dough. • Break off balls of dough the size of walnuts and form into 4-inch (10-cm) ropes. Form the ropes into 1 1/2-inch (4-cm) rings and place 1 inch (2.5 cm) apart on the prepared cookie sheets. • Bake for 15–20 minutes, or until just golden. • Cool completely on the cookie sheets.

Makes: about 35 cookies • Prep: 15 min • Cooking: 15–20 min • Level: 1

- 3 1/3 cups (500 g) all-purpose (plain) flour
- 3/4 cup (150 g) sugar
- 2 large eggs
- 1/2 cup (125 ml) milk
- 1 teaspoon vanilla extract (essence)
- 1/3 cup (90 g) butter, softened
- finely grated zest of 1 lemon
- 1/8 teaspoon salt

RED DELICIOUS COOKIES

- 2 medium Red Delicious apples, peeled, cored, and finely chopped
- ³/₄ cup (150 g) sugar
- 2 cups (300 g) all-purpose (plain) flour
- 1 teaspoon baking powder
- 1 teaspoon ground cinnamon
- ¹/₈ teaspoon salt
- ³/₄ cup (180 g) butter, softened
- 1 large egg
- ³/₄ cup (120 g) raisins
- 1 cup (100 g) corn flakes

Cook the apples with 1 tablespoon of sugar in a small saucepan over low heat, stirring often, until the apples have softened. Remove from the heat and let cool completely. • Preheat the oven to 400°F (200°C/gas 6). • Butter three cookie sheets. • Mix the flour, baking powder, cinnamon, and salt in a medium bowl. • Beat the butter and remaining sugar in a large bowl with an electric mixer on medium speed until creamy. • Add the egg, beating until just blended. • Mix in alternating tablespoons of the dry ingredients and the cooked apples until well blended. • Stir in the raisins and corn flakes. • Drop teaspoons of the dough 1 inch (2.5 cm) apart onto the prepared cookie sheets. • Bake for 10–15 minutes, or until golden brown. • Transfer to racks to cool.

Makes: about 40 cookies • Prep: 30 min • Cooking: 10–15 min • Level: 2

FROSTED PINEAPPLE BITES

Cookies: Preheat the oven to 400°F (200°C/gas 6). • Butter three cookie sheets. • Mix the flour, baking powder, and salt in a medium bowl. • Beat the shortening and brown sugar in a large bowl with an electric mixer on medium speed until creamy. • Add the egg and vanilla, beating until just blended. • Mix in the pineapple, reserving a few pieces for decoration, and the dry ingredients. • Drop teaspoons of the dough 2 inches (5 cm) apart onto the prepared cookie sheets. • Bake for 8–10 minutes, or until just golden at the edges. • Transfer to racks to cool. • Pineapple Glaze: Mix the confectioners' sugar and pineapple juice in a small bowl. • Spread the glaze over the tops of the cookies and top with the reserved pineapple. Let set for 30 minutes.

Makes: about 32 cookies • Prep: 25 min + 30 min to set Cooking: 8–10 min • Level: 1

Cookies
- 2 cups (300 g) all-purpose (plain) flour
- 1¹/₂ teaspoons baking powder
- ¹/₄ teaspoon salt
- ¹/₂ cup (125 g) vegetable shortening
- 1 cup (200 g) firmly packed light brown sugar
- 1 large egg
- ¹/₂ teaspoon vanilla extract (essence)
- 1 can (8 oz/250 g) crushed pineapple, drained (reserve the juice)

Pineapple Glaze
- 3 cups (450 g) confectioners' (icing) sugar
- about ¹/₄ cup (60 ml) pineapple juice (see above)

LEMON CRUNCHIES

- 2¹/₄ cups (330 g) all-purpose (plain) flour
- 1³/₄ cups (350 g) sugar
- 4 large egg whites, lightly beaten
- 1¹/₃ cups (200 g) finely ground almonds
- ²/₃ cup (60 g) finely chopped candied lemon peel
- finely grated zest of 1 lemon
- 1 teaspoon baking soda (bicarbonate of soda)
- ¹/₈ teaspoon salt

Line a cookie sheet with parchment paper. • Mix the flour, sugar, egg whites, almonds, candied lemon peel, lemon zest, baking soda, and salt in a large bowl to form a stiff dough. • Roll out the dough on a lightly floured surface to a 12 x 3-inch (30 x 8-cm) rectangle. • Transfer to the prepared cookie sheet and refrigerate for 30 minutes. • Preheat the oven to 300°F (150°C/gas 2). • Cut the dough in half lengthwise and slice into ¹/₂-inch (1-cm) strips. • Bake for 10–15 minutes, or until just golden. • Transfer to racks to cool.

Makes: about 48 cookies • Prep: 25 min + 30 min to chill Cooking: 10–15 min • Level: 1

GLAZED ORANGE COOKIES

Cookies: Beat the butter and sugar in a large bowl until creamy. • Add the egg yolk and orange zest. • Mix in the flour to form a stiff dough. Refrigerate for 30 minutes. • Preheat the oven to 350°F (180°C/gas 4). • Butter and flour a cookie sheet. • Roll out the dough to ¹/₈ inch (3 mm) thick. • Use a fluted cutter to stamp out small rounds. • Transfer the cookies to the cookie sheet. • Bake for 8–10 minutes, or until golden around the edges. • Cool on the sheet for 5 minutes. Transfer to racks to cool. • Glaze: Mix the confectioners' sugar with the orange juice. • Drizzle over the cookies.

Makes: about 20 cookies • Prep: 40 min + 30 min to chill Cooking: 8–10 min • Level: 1

Cookies
- ¹/₃ cup (90 g) butter, softened
- 5 tablespoons sugar
- 1 large egg yolk
- finely grated zest of 1 orange
- 1¹/₄ cups (180 g) all-purpose (plain) flour

Glaze
- ²/₃ cup (100 g) confectioners' (icing) sugar
- 1 tablespoon fresh orange juice + more as needed

DRIED FRUIT COOKIES

Packed with goodness and energy, dried fruits are the perfect ingredient for a whole range of cookies. In this chapter we have included cookies made with dried cherries, raisins, prunes, dates, apricots, currants, and coconut, among others. Try the Coconut kisses with chocolate cream (see page 166), the Coconut oat cookies (see page 170), or the Raw sugar raisin cookies (see page 184). We have also selected a handful of delicious recipes made with candied fruits—the Candied fruit and ginger cookies (see page 175) and the Walnut and candied cherry cookies (see page 186) are good examples of these.

Coconut crisps (see page 188)

COCONUT COOKIES

- 1¼ cups (180 g) all-purpose (plain) flour
- 2 teaspoons baking soda (bicarbonate of soda)
- ¼ teaspoon salt
- ⅔ cup (40 g) unsweetened shredded (desiccated) coconut
- ½ cup (125 g) butter, softened
- ½ cup (100 g) firmly packed light brown sugar
- 1 teaspoon vanilla extract (essence)
- 1 large egg
- ½ cup (125 g) raspberry or strawberry preserves (jam)

Preheat the oven to 350°F (180°C/gas 4). • Set out two cookie sheets. • Mix the flour, baking soda, and salt in a medium bowl. Stir in the coconut. • Beat the butter, brown sugar, and vanilla in a large bowl with an electric mixer on medium speed until creamy. • Add the egg, beating until just blended. • With mixer at low speed, add the dry ingredients. • Form the dough into balls the size of walnuts and place 1 inch (2.5 cm) apart on the sheets. • Use your thumb to make a slight hollow in the center of each one and fill with a small amount of preserves. • Bake for 12–15 minutes, or until golden brown. • Transfer to racks to cool.

Makes: about 25 cookies • Prep: 20 min • Cooking: 12–15 min • Level : 1

DRIED APRICOT COOKIES

- 1⅓ cups (200 g) all-purpose (plain) flour
- 2 teaspoons baking powder
- ½ teaspoon salt
- ½ cup (125 g) cold butter, cut up
- ¼ cup (50 g) sugar
- 3 tablespoons coarsely chopped dried apricots
- 1 tablespoon coarsely chopped candied pineapple
- 1 tablespoon coarsely chopped candied cherries
- 1 large egg
- 1 tablespoon freshly squeezed orange juice
- 1 teaspoon finely grated orange zest
- 2 tablespoons firmly packed light brown sugar, to sprinkle

Preheat the oven to 400°F (200°C/gas 6). • Line two cookie sheets with parchment paper. • Mix the flour, baking powder, and salt in a large bowl. • Use a pastry blender to cut in the butter until the mixture resembles coarse crumbs. • Stir in the sugar, apricots, pineapple, and cherries. • Beat the egg and orange juice and zest in a small bowl until pale. • Add the egg mixture to the dry ingredients and mix until well blended. • Drop teaspoons of the mixture 2 inches (5 cm) apart onto the cookie sheets. • Sprinkle with the brown sugar. • Bake for 15–20 minutes, or until golden brown. • Cool the cookies on the cookie sheets for 5 minutes. • Transfer to racks to cool completely.

Makes: about 18 cookies • Prep: 20 min • Cooking: 15–20 min • Level : 1

CRISP COCONUT COOKIES

Cookies: Preheat the oven to 325°F (170°C/gas 3). • Line two cookie sheets with parchment paper. • Mix the flour, sugar, baking powder, and salt in a large bowl. • Use a pastry blender to cut in the butter until the mixture resembles fine crumbs. • Stir in the egg yolk mixture and knead into a stiff dough, adding more water if needed. • Wrap in plastic wrap (cling film) and refrigerate for 30 minutes. • Frosting: Beat the egg white with an electric mixer at medium speed until frothy. Add the confectioners' sugar, beating until stiff. • Roll out the dough on a lightly floured surface to ¼ inch (5 mm) thick. Cut into 3 x 8-inch (8 x 20-cm) strips. • Spread with the frosting and sprinkle with coconut. • Cut the strips in half lengthwise and into 1½-inch (4-cm) squares. • Transfer to the prepared cookie sheets, placing them 1 inch (2.5 cm) apart. • Bake for 15–20 minutes, or until lightly golden. • Transfer to racks to cool.

Makes: about 35 cookies • Prep: 40 min + 30 min to chill Cooking: 15–20 min • Level: 1

Cookies
- 1⅓ cups (200 g) all-purpose (plain) flour
- 3 tablespoons sugar
- 1 teaspoon baking powder
- ¼ teaspoon salt
- ½ cup (125 g) butter, cut up
- 1 large egg yolk, lightly beaten with 2 tablespoons cold water

Frosting
- 1 large egg white
- 5 tablespoons confectioners' (icing) sugar, sifted
- 3 tablespoons unsweetened shredded (desiccated) coconut

SOFT COCONUT COOKIES

Preheat the oven to 400°F (200°C/gas 6). • Butter two cookie sheets. • Mix the flour, coconut, baking powder, and salt in a medium bowl. • Beat the butter and sugar in a large bowl with an electric mixer on medium speed until creamy. • Add the egg, beating until just blended. • Mix in the dry ingredients. • Drop tablespoons of the dough 2 inches (5 cm) apart onto the prepared cookie sheets, pressing down lightly with a fork. • Bake for 10–15 minutes, or until golden brown. • Cool on the cookie sheets for 15 minutes. • Transfer to racks to cool completely.

Makes: about 15–20 cookies • Prep: 20 min • Cooking: 10–15 min • Level : 1

- 1 cup (150 g) all-purpose (plain) flour
- 1 cup (125 g) unsweetened shredded (desiccated) coconut
- 1 teaspoon baking powder
- ⅛ teaspoon salt
- ½ cup (125 g) butter, softened
- ½ cup (100 g) sugar
- 1 large egg

Dried Fruit Cookies

COCONUT KISSES WITH CHOCOLATE CREAM

Cookies
- 1⅓ cups (200 g) all-purpose (plain) flour
- 1 teaspoon baking powder
- ⅛ teaspoon salt
- ¾ cup (180 g) butter, softened
- ⅓ cup (70 g) sugar
- ½ teaspoon vanilla extract (essence)
- 1 large egg
- 3 tablespoons unsweetened shredded (desiccated) coconut

Chocolate Cream
- 1 cup (150 g) confectioners' (icing) sugar
- ¼ cup (60 g) butter, melted
- 1 tablespoon unsweetened cocoa powder

Cookies: Preheat the oven to 300°F (150°C/gas 2). • Set out two cookie sheets. • Mix the flour, baking powder, and salt in a medium bowl. • Beat the butter, sugar, and vanilla in a large bowl with an electric mixer at medium speed until creamy. • Add the egg, beating until just blended. • Mix in the dry ingredients. • Place the coconut in a small bowl. • Roll teaspoons of the dough in the coconut and place 1 inch (2.5 cm) apart on the cookie sheets. • Bake for 18–20 minutes, or until lightly browned. • Transfer to racks to cool. • Chocolate Cream: Beat the confectioners' sugar and butter in a small bowl. • Mix in the cocoa powder. • Stick the cookies together in pairs with the chocolate filling.

Makes: about 15 cookies • Prep: 25 min • Cooking: 18–20 min • Level: 1

ZESTY COCONUT COOKIES

Mix the flour and salt into a medium bowl. • Beat the butter and sugar in a large bowl with an electric mixer on medium speed until creamy. • Add the eggs, beating until just blended. • Add the lime zest, lime juice, and vanilla and almond extracts. • Mix in the dry ingredients and ¾ cup (90 g) coconut to form a stiff dough. • Divide the dough in half. Form into two logs 2 inches (5 cm) in diameter, wrap in plastic wrap (cling film), and flatten slightly to form oblongs. • Refrigerate for at least 30 minutes. • Preheat the oven to 375°F (190°C/gas 5). • Butter three cookie sheets. • Slice the dough ¼ inch (5 mm) thick and place 1 inch (2.5 cm) apart on the prepared cookie sheets. • Sprinkle with the remaining coconut. • Bake for 10–12 minutes, or until just golden. • Transfer to racks and let cool completely.

Makes: about 35 cookies • Prep: 40 min + 30 min to chill Cooking: 10–12 min • Level: 1

- 2¼ cups (330 g) all-purpose (plain) flour
- ½ teaspoon salt
- 1 cup (250 g) butter, softened
- 1 cup (200 g) granulated sugar
- 2 large eggs, lightly beaten
- finely grated zest of 1 lime
- 1 tablespoon freshly squeezed lime juice
- ½ teaspoon vanilla extract (essence)
- ¼ teaspoon almond extract (essence)
- 1 cup (125 g) unsweetened shredded (desiccated) coconut

FRUITY RAISIN MOMENTS

- 2 cups (300 g) all-purpose (plain) flour
- 1 teaspoon baking powder
- ¼ teaspoon freshly grated nutmeg
- ⅛ teaspoon salt
- ½ cup (125 g) butter, cut up
- ½ cup (100 g) firmly packed light brown sugar
- ⅔ cup (70 g) finely chopped candied peel
- ⅓ cup (45 g) raisins
- 1 large egg, lightly beaten

Preheat the oven to 400°F (200°C/gas 6). • Butter two cookie sheets. • Mix the flour, baking powder, nutmeg, and salt in a large bowl. • Use a pastry blender to cut in the butter until the mixture resembles coarse crumbs. • Stir in the brown sugar, candied peel, raisins, and egg. • Drop tablespoons of the dough 2 inches (5 cm) apart onto the prepared cookie sheets. • Bake for 20–25 minutes, or until golden brown. • Transfer the cookies to racks to cool.

Makes: about 25 cookies • Prep: 30 min • Cooking: 20–25 min • Level: 1

LEMON, RAISIN, AND OAT COOKIES

Preheat the oven to 375°F (190°C/gas 5). • Butter two cookie sheets. • Mix the flour, baking powder, and salt in a large bowl. • Beat the butter, sugar, and lemon zest in a large bowl with an electric mixer on medium speed speed until creamy. • Add the egg, beating until just blended. • Mix in the dry ingredients, oats, and raisins. • Drop tablespoons of the dough 3 inches (8 cm) apart onto the prepared cookie sheet. • Bake for 10–15 minutes, or until just golden at the edges. • Transfer to racks to cool.

Makes: about 20 cookies • Prep: 20 min • Cooking: 15–20 min • Level: 1

- 1½ cups (225 g) all-purpose (plain) flour
- 1 teaspoon baking powder
- ⅛ teaspoon salt
- ½ cup (125 g) butter, softened
- ½ cup (100 g) sugar
- finely grated zest of 1 lemon
- 1 large egg
- 2 tablespoons old-fashioned rolled oats
- 1 cup (180 g) raisins

Dried Fruit Cookies

AMERICAN COOKIES

- 1 cup (150 g) all-purpose (plain) flour
- ¼ teaspoon baking soda (bicarbonate of soda)
- ⅛ teaspoon salt
- 2 tablespoons butter, softened
- 2 tablespoons vegetable shortening
- ¼ cup (50 g) granulated sugar
- ¼ cup (50 g) firmly packed light brown sugar
- ½ teaspoon vanilla extract (essence)
- 1 large egg
- ½ cup (50 g) coarsely chopped dried cranberries
- ¼ cup (30 g) finely chopped mixed candied peel
- ¼ cup (30 g) finely chopped pecans

Preheat the oven to 375°F (190°C/gas 5).
• Line two cookie sheets with parchment paper. • Mix the flour, baking soda, and salt in a medium bowl. • Beat the butter, shortening, and both sugars in a large bowl with an electric mixer at high speed until creamy. • Add the vanilla and egg, beating until just blended. • Mix in the dry ingredients, cranberries, candied peel, and pecans. • Drop tablespoons of the dough 1½ inches (4 cm) apart onto the prepared cookie sheets. • Bake for 8–10 minutes, or until golden at the edges. • Cool on the sheets until the cookies firm slightly. • Transfer to racks to finish cooling.

Makes: about 25 cookies • Prep: 20 min • Cooking: 8–10 min • Level: 1

CHEWY RAISIN COOKIES

Preheat the oven to 350°F (180°C/gas 4).
• Butter two cookie sheets. • Mix the flour, baking soda, cinnamon, nutmeg, and salt in a medium bowl. • Beat the shortening and sugar in a medium bowl until well blended. • Beat in the egg, followed by the mixed dry ingredients, water, raisins, and walnuts. • Using a tablespoon, drop spoonfuls onto the prepared cookie sheets. • Bake for about 10 minutes, or until golden brown. • Let cool completely.

Makes: about 35 cookies • Prep: 25 min • Cooking: 10–12 min • Level: 1

- 2 cups (300 g) all-purpose (plain) flour
- ½ teaspoon baking soda (bicarbonate of soda)
- ½ teaspoon ground cinnamon
- ½ teaspoon ground nutmeg
- ¼ teaspoon salt
- ½ cup (125 g) vegetable shortening
- ⅔ cup (140 g) firmly packed light brown sugar
- 1 large egg
- 1 cup (180 g) raisins
- ½ cup (125 ml) water
- ½ cup (50 g) chopped walnuts

Chewy raisin cookies

Raisin and white wine drops

RAISIN AND WHITE WINE DROPS

- 1½ cups (225 g) all-purpose (plain) flour
- ½ cup (100 g) sugar
- 1 teaspoon baking powder
- ⅛ teaspoon salt
- ⅓ cup (90 g) butter, cut up
- 1 large egg, lightly beaten
- 3 tablespoons dry white wine
- finely grated zest of 1 lemon
- ½ cup (90 g) golden raisins (sultanas)

Mix the flour, sugar, baking powder, and salt in a large bowl. • Cut in the butter until the mixture resembles coarse crumbs. • Mix in the egg, wine, and lemon zest to form a smooth dough. Knead in the raisins. • Press the dough into a disk, wrap in plastic wrap (cling film), and refrigerate for 30 minutes. • Preheat the oven to 400°F (200°C/gas 6). • Butter two cookie sheets. • Roll out the dough on a lightly floured surface to ¼ inch (5 mm) thick. • Use a 2-inch (5-cm) cookie cutter to cut out the cookies. Continue cutting out cookies until all the dough is used. • Transfer the cookies to the prepared cookie sheets, spacing them 1 inch (2.5 cm) apart. • Bake for 12–15 minutes, or until just golden. • Transfer to racks to cool.

Makes: about 25 cookies • Prep: 30 min + 30 min to chill Cooking: 12–15 min • Level: 1

PEANUT BUTTER AND ORANGE COOKIES

Preheat the oven to 325°F (170°C/gas 3). • Butter two cookie sheets. • Mix the flour, baking powder, and salt in a medium bowl. • Beat the peanut butter, sugar, and orange zest in a large bowl with an electric mixer on medium speed until creamy. • Add the egg, beating until just blended. • Mix in the raisins and dry ingredients. • Form the dough into balls the size of walnuts and place 2 inches (5 cm) apart on the prepared cookie sheets. • Dip a fork in flour and press lines into the tops. • Bake for 12–15 minutes, or until golden brown. • Transfer to racks to cool.

Makes: about 20–25 cookies • Prep: 20 min • Cooking: 12–15 min • Level: 1

- 1 cup (150 g) all-purpose (plain) flour
- 1 teaspoon baking powder
- ⅛ teaspoon salt
- ½ cup (125 ml) smooth peanut butter
- ½ cup (100 g) sugar
- 1 tablespoon finely grated orange zest
- 1 large egg
- ½ cup (90 g) raisins

COCONUT OAT COOKIES

- 3/4 cup (125 g) all-purpose (plain) flour
- 1/8 teaspoon salt
- 1/2 cup (125 g) vegetable shortening
- 1 cup (125 g) unsweetened shredded (desiccated) coconut
- 1 cup (150 g) old-fashioned rolled oats
- 1/2 cup (100 g) sugar
- 2 tablespoons cold water
- 1 tablespoon light molasses (treacle)
- 1 teaspoon baking soda (bicarbonate of soda)

Preheat the oven to 300°F (150°C/gas 2). • Butter two cookie sheets. • Mix the flour and salt in a large bowl. • Use a pastry blender to cut in the shortening until the mixture resembles fine crumbs. • Stir in the coconut, oats, and sugar. • Mix the water, molasses, and baking soda in a small bowl. • Stir the baking soda liquid into the oat mixture to form a stiff dough. Press the dough into a disk, wrap in plastic wrap (cling film), and refrigerate for 30 minutes. • Roll out the dough on a lightly floured surface to 1/4 inch (5 mm) thick. • Use a 3-inch (8-cm) cookie cutter to cut out the cookies. • Transfer to the prepared cookie sheets, placing them 1 inch (2.5 cm) apart. • Bake for 25–30 minutes, or until just golden at the edges. • Transfer to racks and let cool completely.

Makes: about 25 cookies • Prep: 40 min + 30 min to chill Cooking: 25–30 min • Level: 1

COCONUT LIME BITES

Preheat the oven to 350°F (180°C/gas 4). • Line two cookie sheets with parchment paper. • Melt the chocolate in a double boiler over barely simmering water. • Beat the butter and sugar in a medium bowl with an electric mixer on medium speed until creamy. • Add the coconut extract, cream of coconut, melted chocolate, and the lemon and lime zests. • Mix in 1/2 cup (60 g) of shredded coconut and flour. • Turn the dough onto a lightly floured surface and knead until smooth. • Form the dough into balls the size of walnuts. Roll in the remaining coconut and place 2 inches (5 cm) apart on the prepared cookie sheet, flattening them slightly. • Bake for 15–20 minutes, or until just golden. • Transfer to racks to cool.

Makes: about 25–30 cookies • Prep: 30 min • Cooking: 15–20 min • Level: 1

- 2 oz (60 g) semisweet (dark) chocolate, coarsely chopped
- 1/3 cup (90 g) butter, softened
- 1/3 cup (70 g) sugar
- 1 teaspoon coconut extract (essence)
- 2 tablespoons cream of coconut
- 1 teaspoon finely shredded lemon zest
- 1 teaspoon finely shredded lime zest
- 3/4 cup (90 g) unsweetened shredded (desiccated) coconut
- 1 3/4 cups (275 g) all-purpose (plain) flour

PRUNE, RAISIN, AND OAT COOKIES

- 3 cups (540 g) raisins
- 1 cup (250 g) dried cranberries
- 1 cup (250 ml) hot water
- 2 1/2 cups (375 g) all-purpose (plain) flour
- 2 teaspoons ground cinnamon
- 1 1/2 teaspoons baking soda (bicarbonate of soda)
- 1 teaspoon ground ginger
- 1/2 teaspoon baking powder
- 1/2 teaspoon allspice
- 1/2 teaspoon salt

Preheat the oven to 400°F (200°C/gas 6). • Butter four cookie sheets. • Soak the raisins and cranberries in the water in a large bowl for 15 minutes. • Drain well, reserving 1/3 cup (90 ml) of the liquid, and set aside. • Mix the flour, cinnamon, baking soda, ginger, baking powder, allspice, and salt in a medium bowl. • Beat the butter and brown sugar in a large bowl with an electric mixer on medium speed until creamy. • Add the vanilla and eggs, beating until just blended. • Mix in the dry ingredients and reserved liquid. • Stir in the oats, walnuts, prunes, dates, raisins, and cranberries until well blended. • Drop tablespoons of the dough 3 inches (8 cm) apart onto the prepared cookie sheets, flattening them slightly. • Bake for 6–8 minutes, or until just golden at the edges and set. • Let cool on the sheets until the cookies firm slightly. Transfer to racks and let cool completely.

Makes: about 60 cookies • Prep: 20 min + 15 min to soak Cooking: 6–8 min Level: 1

- 3/4 cup (180 g) butter, softened
- 1 1/2 cups (300 g) firmly packed light brown sugar
- 1 1/2 teaspoons vanilla extract (essence)
- 2 large eggs
- 2 cups (300 g) old-fashioned rolled oats
- 2 cups (200 g) coarsely chopped walnuts
- 1 1/4 cups (280 g) coarsely chopped pitted prunes
- 1 1/4 cups (280 g) coarsely chopped pitted dates

Dried Fruit Cookies

FRUIT AND NUT COOKIES

- 1 cup (150 g) all-purpose (plain) flour
- ½ teaspoon ground cinnamon
- ¼ teaspoon baking soda (bicarbonate of soda)
- 2 tablespoons water
- ¾ cup (75 g) finely chopped dates
- ¾ cup (135 g) golden raisins (sultanas)
- ⅓ cup (90 g) butter, softened
- ½ cup (100 g) sugar
- 1 large egg
- ½ cup (50 g) finely chopped walnuts

Preheat the oven to 400°F (200°C/gas 6). • Butter two cookie sheets. • Mix the flour and cinnamon in a medium bowl. • Mix the baking soda and water in a small bowl. Add the dates and raisins. • Beat the butter and sugar in a large bowl with an electric mixer on medium speed until creamy. • Add the egg, beating until just blended. • Stir in the date and raisin mixture. • Mix in the dry ingredients and walnuts. • Drop tablespoons of the dough 1 inch (2.5 cm) apart onto the prepared cookie sheets. • Bake for 8–10 minutes, or until lightly browned. • Cool on the sheets until the cookies firm slightly. • Transfer to racks and let cool completely.

Makes: about 25 cookies • Prep: 20 min • Cooking: 8–10 min • Level: 1

MELTING RAISIN MOMENTS

Plump the raisins in a small bowl of hot water for 10 minutes. Drain well and pat dry with paper towels. • Mix the flour, sugar, baking powder, and salt in a large bowl. • Use a pastry blender to cut in the butter until the mixture resembles coarse crumbs. • Mix in the egg, wine, and lemon zest to form a smooth dough. Knead in the raisins. • Press the dough into a disk, wrap in plastic wrap (cling film), and refrigerate for 30 minutes. • Preheat the oven to 400°F (200°C/gas 6). • Butter two cookie sheets. • Roll out the dough on a lightly floured surface to ¼ inch (5 mm) thick. • Use a 2-inch (5-cm) cookie cutter to cut out the cookies. • Transfer to the prepared cookie sheets, spacing them 1 inch (2.5 cm) apart. • Bake for 12–15 minutes, or until just golden. • Transfer to racks to cool.

Makes: about 25 cookies • Prep: 40 min + 30 min to chill Cooking: 12–15 min • Level: 1

- ½ cup (90 g) golden raisins (sultanas)
- 1½ cups (225 g) all-purpose (plain) flour
- ½ cup (100 g) sugar
- 1 teaspoon baking powder
- ⅛ teaspoon salt
- ⅓ cup (90 g) butter, cut up
- 1 large egg, lightly beaten
- 3 tablespoons dry white wine
- finely grated zest of 1 lemon

ORANGE AND RAISIN COOKIES

- 1⅓ cups (200 g) all-purpose (plain) flour
- ½ teaspoon baking powder
- ½ teaspoon salt
- ½ cup (125 g) butter, softened
- ¾ cup (150 g) sugar
- 1 large egg, lightly beaten
- ½ teaspoon vanilla extract (essence)
- ⅔ cup (120 g) raisins
- 1 tablespoon finely grated orange zest

Preheat the oven to 375°F (190°C/gas 5). • Butter two cookie sheets. • Mix the flour, baking powder, and salt in a medium bowl. • Beat the butter and sugar in a large bowl with an electric mixer on medium speed until creamy. • Add the egg and vanilla, beating until just blended. • Mix in the dry ingredients, followed by the raisins and orange zest. • Drop tablespoons of the dough 2 inches (5 cm) apart onto the prepared cookie sheets. • Bake for 12–15 minutes, or until just golden. • Cool on the sheets until the cookies firm slightly. • Transfer to racks to finish cooling.

Makes: about 25 cookies • Prep: 25 min • Cooking: 12–15 min • Level: 1

CHEWY BROWN COOKIES

Preheat the oven to 325°F (170°C/gas 3). • Butter two cookie sheets. • Chop the dates very finely and place in a large bowl. Add the almonds. • Stir in the egg whites, confectioners' sugar, cocoa, and lemon juice and mix until well blended. • Drop teaspoons of the dough 1 inch (2.5 cm) apart onto the prepared cookie sheets. • Bake for 25–30 minutes, or until just golden at the edges. • Transfer to racks to cool.

Makes: about 30 cookies • Prep: 20 min • Cooking: 25–30 min Level: 1

- 1¾ cups (175 g) finely chopped pitted dates
- 1¾ cups (175 g) finely chopped almonds
- 2 large egg whites
- 1 cup (150 g) confectioners' (icing) sugar
- 1 tablespoon unsweetened cocoa powder
- freshly squeezed juice of 1 lemon

CINNAMON RAISIN COOKIES

- 2⅓ cups (350 g) all-purpose (plain) flour
- 2 teaspoons ground cinnamon
- 1 teaspoon baking powder
- ¼ teaspoon ground cloves
- ½ teaspoon freshly grated nutmeg
- ¼ teaspoon salt
- ½ cup (125 g) butter, softened
- ¾ cup (150 g) firmly packed dark brown sugar
- 2 large eggs
- ½ cup (90 g) raisins
- ½ cup (50 g) flaked almonds

Mix the flour, cinnamon, baking powder, cloves, nutmeg, and salt in a medium bowl. • Beat the butter, brown sugar, and eggs in a large bowl with an electric mixer at medium speed until well combined. • Mix in the dry ingredients, followed by the raisins and almonds. • Cover with plastic wrap (cling film) and refrigerate for 30 minutes. • Preheat the oven to 375°F (190°C/gas 5). • Butter two cookie sheets. • Drop heaped teaspoons of the cookie dough 2 inches (5 cm) apart onto the prepared cookie sheets. • Bake for 8–10 minutes, or until golden brown. • Transfer to racks and let cool.

Makes: about 30 cookies • Prep: 20 min + 30 min to chill Cooking: 8–10 min • Level: 1

BRITISH COOKIES

Mincemeat is a finely chopped mixture of dried fruit, nuts, and spices used to filled pies, tarts, and cookies.
Preheat the oven to 375°F (190°C/gas 5). • Butter three cookie sheets. • Mix the flour, baking soda, and salt in a medium bowl. • Beat the butter and both sugars in a large bowl with an electric mixer at high speed until creamy. • Add the egg, beating until just blended. • Mix in the dry ingredients, mincemeat, and brandy. • Drop heaped teaspoons of the dough 2 inches (5 cm) apart onto the prepared cookie sheets. • Bake, one sheet at a time, for 10–12 minutes, or until golden brown. Transfer to racks to cool

Makes: about 40 cookies • Prep: 40 min • Cooking: 10–12 min • Level: 1

- 1¼ cups (180 g) all-purpose (plain) flour
- ¼ teaspoon baking soda (bicarbonate of soda)
- ⅛ teaspoon salt
- ⅓ cup (90 g) butter, softened
- ¼ cup (50 g) granulated sugar
- ¼ cup (50 g) firmly packed light brown sugar
- 1 large egg
- ¾ cup (180 ml) mincemeat
- 2 teaspoons brandy

CANDIED FRUIT AND GINGER COOKIES

- 1¼ cups (180 g) all-purpose (plain) flour
- 1 teaspoon baking powder
- ⅛ teaspoon salt
- ⅓ cup (90 g) butter, softened
- ⅓ cup (70 g) firmly packed light brown sugar
- 1 large egg, lightly beaten
- ½ teaspoon almond extract (essence)
- seeds of 8 cardamom pods, crushed
- ½ cup (50 g) finely chopped candied cherries
- ½ cup (50 g) finely chopped dried apricots
- ½ cup (50 g) finely chopped crystallized ginger

Preheat the oven to 350°F (180°C/gas 4). • Butter two cookie sheets. • Mix the flour, baking powder, and salt in a medium bowl. • Beat the butter and brown sugar in a large bowl with an electric mixer on medium speed until creamy. • Add the egg, beating until just blended. • Mix in the dry ingredients, almond extract, and crushed cardamom, followed by the cherries, apricots, and ginger. • Drop rounded teaspoons of the dough 1 inch (2.5 cm) apart onto the prepared cookie sheets. • Bake for 20–25 minutes, or until lightly browned. • Transfer to racks and let cool.

Makes: about 24 cookies • Prep: 20 min • Cooking: 20–25 min • Level: 1

RUSTIC COOKIES

Preheat the oven to 425°F (220°C/gas 7). • Butter a cookie sheet. • Mix the flour and salt in a large bowl. Stir in the coconut, sugar, and lemon zest. • Use a pastry blender to cut in the butter until the mixture resembles coarse crumbs. • Add the lemon juice and eggs, mixing until a smooth dough has formed. • Drop heaping tablespoons of the dough 2 inches (5 cm) apart onto the prepared cookie sheet. • Bake for 8–10 minutes, or until lightly browned. • Transfer to racks to cool.

Makes: about 12 cookies • Prep: 20 min • Cooking: 8–10 min • Level: 1

- ¾ cup (125 g) whole-wheat (wholemeal) flour
- ⅛ teaspoon salt
- 1 cup (125 g) unsweetened shredded (desiccated) coconut
- ¼ cup (50 g) sugar
- finely grated zest and juice of ½ lemon
- ¼ cup (60 g) butter, cut up
- 2 large eggs, lightly beaten

Dried Fruit Cookies

CURRANT ROUNDS

- 1²/₃ cups (250 g) all-purpose (plain) flour
- ¹/₈ teaspoon salt
- ¹/₂ cup (125 g) butter, softened
- ¹/₂ cup (100 g) sugar
- 2 large eggs
- ²/₃ cup (120 g) currants

Mix the flour and salt in a medium bowl. • Beat the butter and sugar in a large bowl until creamy. • Add the eggs, beating until just blended. • Mix in the dry ingredients and currants. • Press the dough into a disk, wrap in plastic wrap (cling film), and refrigerate for 30 minutes. • Preheat the oven to 325°F (170°C/gas 3). • Butter two cookie sheets. • Roll the dough out on a lightly floured surface to ¾ inch (2 cm) thick. • Use a 2-inch (5-cm) cookie cutter to cut out the cookies. • Transfer the cookies to the prepared cookie sheets, spacing well. • Bake for 12–15 minutes, or until golden. • Transfer to racks to cool.

Makes: about 20 cookies • Prep: 25 min + 30 min to chill
Cooking: 12–15 min • Level: 1

COCONUT CRESCENTS

Blanch the pistachios in boiling water for 1 minute. Drain well and use a clean cloth to rub off the skins. • Let cool, then transfer to a food processor and process until very finely chopped. • Place the flour on a surface and make a well in the center. • Cut in the butter, coconut, confectioners' sugar, and the egg and egg yolk to make a smooth dough. • Wrap in plastic wrap (cling film) and refrigerate for at least 2 hours. • Divide the dough into balls the size of walnuts. Form into crescent shapes, wrap individually in plastic wrap, and refrigerate for 1 hour more. • Preheat the oven to 350°F (180°C/gas 4). • Butter and flour a large baking sheet. • Sprinkle the cookies with the sugar. Dip in the finely chopped pistachios until well coated. • Arrange on the prepared baking sheet. • Bake for 15–20 minutes, or until firm to the touch. • Cool the cookies completely on the baking sheet.

Makes: about 20 cookies • Prep: 40 min + 3 hr to chill
Cooking: 15–20 min • Level: 2

- 1¹/₄ cups (190 g) pistachios, shelled
- 1¹/₃ cups (200 g) all-purpose (plain) flour
- ¹/₃ cup (90 g) butter, softened
- 2 tablespoons unsweetened shredded (desiccated) coconut
- ¹/₃ cup (50 g) confectioners' (icing) sugar
- 1 large egg + 1 large egg yolk
- ¹/₂ cup (100 g) sugar

Coconut crescents

Pecan balls

PECAN BALLS

- 2 cups (200 g) coarsely chopped pecans
- 1 cup (100 g) coarsely chopped dried apricots
- 1 cup (200 g) firmly packed light brown sugar
- 1 large egg, lightly beaten
- 2¼ cups (280 g) unsweetened shredded (desiccated) coconut

Preheat the oven to 350°F (180°C/gas 4). • Butter two cookie sheets. • Process the pecans, apricots, and brown sugar in a food processor to a finely ground paste. • Add the eggs and process until blended. • Transfer to a large bowl and mix in 1½ cups (185 g) of coconut to form a stiff dough. • Place the remaining coconut in a small bowl. • Form the dough into balls the size of walnuts and roll in the coconut. • Place 1 inch (2.5 cm) apart on the prepared cookie sheets. • Bake for 10–12 minutes, or until golden brown. • Transfer to racks to cool.

Makes: about 35 cookies • Prep: 20 min • Cooking: 10–12 min • Level: 1

SPICY APPLESAUCE COOKIES

Preheat the oven to 350°F (180°C/gas 4). • Butter three cookie sheets. • Mix the flour, cinnamon, ginger, cloves, baking soda, and salt in a medium bowl. • Beat the butter and both sugars in a large bowl with an electric mixer on medium speed until creamy. • Add the vanilla and egg, beating until just blended. • Stir in the applesauce. • Mix in the dry ingredients, followed by the raisins and walnuts. • Drop tablespoons of the dough 2 inches (5 cm) apart onto the prepared cookie sheets. • Bake for 5–7 minutes, or until just golden. • Transfer to racks and let cool.

Makes: about 40 cookies • Prep: 20 min • Cooking: 5–7 min Level: 1

- 2 cups (300 g) all-purpose (plain) flour
- 1 teaspoon ground cinnamon
- 1 teaspoon ground ginger
- ½ teaspoon ground cloves
- ½ teaspoon baking soda (bicarbonate of soda)
- ½ teaspoon salt
- ½ cup (125 g) butter, softened
- ½ cup (100 g) firmly packed light brown sugar
- ⅓ cup (70 g) granulated sugar
- 1 teaspoon vanilla extract (essence)
- 1 large egg
- 1 cup (250 ml) applesauce
- 1 cup (180 g) golden raisins (sultanas
- ¾ cup (75 g) finely chopped walnuts

Allspice cookies

ALLSPICE COOKIES

- 1¼ cups (180 g) all-purpose (plain) flour
- 1 teaspoon baking powder
- ½ teaspoon ground allspice
- ⅛ teaspoon salt
- ⅓ cup (90 g) butter, softened
- ⅓ cup (70 g) + 2 teaspoons sugar
- 1 large egg, separated
- ⅓ cup (45 g) currants
- 1 tablespoon finely chopped mixed candied peel
- ¼ teaspoon brandy
- 2 tablespoons milk + more as needed

Preheat the oven to 375°F (190°C/gas 5). • Butter two cookie sheets. • Mix the flour, baking powder, allspice, and salt in a medium bowl. • Beat the butter and ⅓ cup (70 g) of sugar in a large bowl with an electric mixer on medium speed until creamy. • Add the egg yolk, beating until just blended. • Mix in the dry ingredients, currants, candied peel, and brandy until well blended. • Add enough milk to form a soft, but not sticky, dough. • Cover with plastic wrap (cling film) and refrigerate for 30 minutes. • Roll out the dough to a thickness of ¼ inch (5 mm). • Use a 2-inch (5-cm) cookie cutter to cut out the cookies. Gather the dough scraps, re-roll, and continue cutting out cookies until all the dough is used. Use a spatula to transfer the cookies to a cookie sheet, placing them 1 inch (2.5 cm) apart. Prick all over with a fork. • Bake for 10 minutes. • Beat the egg white lightly in a small bowl. • Remove the cookie sheet from the oven and brush the cookies with the beaten egg white. Sprinkle with the remaining sugar. • Bake for 5–10 minutes more, or until lightly browned. • Cool on the sheets until the cookies firm slightly. Transfer to racks to finish cooling.

Makes: about 24 cookies • Prep: 30 min 30 min to chill Cooking: 15–20 min • Level: 1

CANDIED FRUIT DELIGHTS

Preheat the oven to 350°F (180°C/gas 4). • Line two cookie sheets with parchment paper. • Mix the flour and salt in a medium bowl. • Beat the egg whites in a large bowl with an electric mixer at medium speed until frothy. • With mixer at high speed, gradually add the granulated sugar, beating until stiff, glossy peaks form. • Use a large rubber spatula to fold in the candied peel and dry ingredients. • With mixer at high speed, beat the egg yolks in a small bowl until frothy. • Fold the beaten egg yolks into the batter. • Drop teaspoons of the dough 2 inches (5 cm) apart onto the prepared cookie sheets. • Sprinkle with confectioners' sugar. • Bake for 10–12 minutes, or until pale gold. • Cool on the sheets until the cookies firm slightly. • Transfer to racks to finish cooling.

Makes: about 35 cookies • Prep: 25 min • Cooking: 10–12 min • Level: 1

- 1½ cups (225 g) all-purpose (plain) flour
- ⅛ teaspoon salt
- 3 large eggs, separated
- 1 cup (200 g) sugar
- ½ cup (50 g) very finely chopped mixed candied peel
- 2 tablespoons confectioners' (icing) sugar, to sprinkle

SOFT DATE COOKIES

Preheat the oven to 375°F (190°C/gas 5). • Butter a cookie sheet. • Beat the butter, sugar, and vanilla in a large bowl with an electric mixer at high speed until creamy. • Mix in the flour and dates. • Drop rounded teaspoons of the dough 1 inch (2.5 cm) apart onto the prepared cookie sheet. • Bake for 15–20 minutes, or until just golden. • Cool on the sheets until the cookies firm slightly. • Transfer to racks to finish cooling.

Makes: about 15 cookies • Prep: 10 min • Cooking: 15–20 min • Level: 1

- ½ cup (125 g) butter, softened
- ¼ cup (50 g) sugar
- ½ teaspoon vanilla extract (essence)
- ¼ cup (60 g) finely chopped dates
- ¾ cup (125 g) all-purpose (plain) flour

Dried Fruit Cookies

CHERRY ALMOND BISCOTTI

- ¼ cup (30 g) candied cherries
- 1 tablespoon cherry brandy
- 1½ cups (225 g) all-purpose (plain) flour
- ½ teaspoon baking powder
- ⅛ teaspoon salt
- ¼ cup (60 g) butter, softened
- ½ cup (100 g) granulated sugar
- 2 large eggs
- ½ teaspoon vanilla extract (essence)
- ½ cup (50 g) coarsely chopped almonds

Soak the cherries in the cherry brandy in a small bowl for 15 minutes. Drain and pat dry with paper towels. • Preheat the oven to 375°F (190°C/gas 5). • Butter a cookie sheet. • Mix the flour, baking powder, and salt in a large bowl. • Beat the butter and sugar in a large bowl with an electric mixer at medium speed until creamy. • Add the eggs and vanilla, beating until just blended. • Mix in the dry ingredients, almonds, and cherries to form a stiff dough. • Divide the dough in half. Form into two 12-inch (30-cm) logs and place 2 inches (5-cm) apart on the prepared cookie sheet, flattening them slightly. • Bake for 20–25 minutes, or until firm to the touch. • Transfer to a cutting board to cool for 15 minutes. • Reduce the oven temperature to 325°F (170°C/gas 3). • Cut the partially cooked logs of dough on the diagonal into 1-inch (2.5-cm) slices. • Arrange the slices cut-side up on two cookie sheets and bake for 10–15 minutes, or until golden and toasted. • Transfer to racks to cool.

Makes: about 30 cookies • Prep: 30 min • Cooking: 35–45 min • Level: 2

CANDIED CITRUS COOKIES

Preheat the oven to 325°F (170°C/gas 3). • Spread the whole almonds on a large baking sheet. Toast for 7 minutes, or until lightly golden. Let cool completely and chop coarsely. • Mix the flour, baking powder, cinnamon, cloves, and salt in a medium bowl. • Beat the butter and sugar in a large bowl with an electric mixer at medium speed until creamy. • Add 2 eggs, beating until just blended. • Heat the honey in a small saucepan over low heat until liquid. Stir the warm honey, candied lemon and orange peel, and chopped almonds into the mixture. • Mix in the dry ingredients to form a smooth dough. • Press the dough into a disk, wrap in plastic wrap (cling film), and refrigerate for 1 hour. • Preheat the oven to 350°F (180°C/gas 4). • Line three cookie sheets with parchment paper. • Roll out the dough on a lightly floured surface to ¼ inch (5 mm) thick. • Use a 2½-inch (6-cm) cookie cutter to cut out the cookies. Gather the dough scraps, re-roll, and continue cutting out cookies until all the dough is used. • Use a spatula to transfer the cookies to the prepared cookie sheets, placing them 1 inch (2.5 cm) apart. • Lightly beat the remaining egg and brush over the tops of the cookies. • Decorate with the flaked almonds and candied peel. • Bake for 10–12 minutes, or until just golden and crisp around the edges. • Transfer to racks to cool.

Makes: about 50–60 cookies • Prep: 40 min + 1 hr to chill Cooking: 10–12 min • Level: 2

- 1 cup (150 g) whole almonds
- 3⅓ cups (500 g) all-purpose (plain) flour
- 1½ teaspoons baking powder
- 2 teaspoons ground cinnamon
- ½ teaspoon ground cloves
- ⅛ teaspoon salt
- ½ cup (125 g) butter, softened
- ½ cup (100 g) sugar
- 3 large eggs
- ¾ cup (180 ml) honey
- 1 cup (50 g) chopped candied lemon peel
- 1 cup (100 g) chopped candied orange peel
- 2 tablespoons flaked almonds
- 1–2 tablespoons chopped mixed candied peel

Dried Fruit Cookies

FIJIAN COOKIES

- ½ cup (125 g) butter, softened
- ½ cup (125 g) cream cheese, softened
- 1¼ cups (180 g) confectioners' (icing) sugar
- ¼ teaspoon baking soda (bicarbonate of soda)
- ¼ teaspoon salt
- 1 large egg, lightly beaten
- 1 tablespoon finely grated orange zest
- 1 tablespoon freshly squeezed orange juice
- ½ teaspoon vanilla extract (essence)
- 2¼ cups (330 g) all-purpose (plain) flour
- ½ cup (60 g) unsweetened shredded (desiccated) coconut

Beat the butter and cream cheese in a large bowl with an electric mixer at medium speed for 1 minute. • Beat in the confectioners' sugar, baking soda, and salt. • Add the egg, beating until just blended. • Beat in the orange zest, juice, and vanilla. • Mix in the flour to form a soft dough. • Turn the dough out on a lightly floured surface and knead until smooth. • Divide the dough in half. Form into two 8-inch (20-cm) logs and roll each in the coconut. Wrap in plastic wrap (cling film), and refrigerate for at least 30 minutes. • Preheat the oven to 375°F (190°C/gas 5). • Set out three cookie sheets. • Slice the dough ¼ inch (5 mm) thick and place 1 inch (2.5 cm) apart on the cookie sheets. • Bake for 8–10 minutes, or until just golden. • Cool on the sheet until the cookies firm slightly. • Transfer to racks to finish cooling.

Makes: about 60 cookies • Prep: 40 min + 30 min to chill
Cooking: 8–10 min • Level: 2

POLISH BREAKFAST COOKIES

Preheat the oven to 400°F (200°C/gas 6). • Butter a cookie sheet. • Mix the flour and salt in a large bowl. • Use a pastry blender to cut in the butter until the mixture resembles fine crumbs. • Stir in ⅓ cup (70 g) of sugar and make a well in the center. • Mix in the cream, egg, 2 tablespoons of the wine, and the candied peel to form a smooth dough. • Press the dough into a disk, wrap in plastic wrap (cling film), and refrigerate for 30 minutes. • Roll out the dough on a lightly floured surface to a large rectangle to ¼ inch (5 mm) thick. • Use a rolling pin to transfer the dough to the prepared cookie sheet. • Brush the remaining 1 tablespoon of wine over the dough. Sprinkle with the remaining sugar and almonds. • Bake for 12–15 minutes, or until just golden. • Cut into 2-inch (5-cm) triangles. • Bake for 3–5 minutes more, or until firm to the touch and golden brown. • Cool completely on the cookie sheet.

Makes: about 30 cookies • Prep: 25 min + 30 min to chill
Cooking: 15–18 min • Level: 1

- 1 cup (150 g) all-purpose (plain) flour
- ⅛ teaspoon salt
- ½ cup (125 g) butter, softened
- ⅓ cup (70 g) + 1 tablespoon sugar
- ½ cup (125 ml) heavy (double) cream
- 1 large egg, lightly beaten
- 3 tablespoons sweet white wine, such as Sauternes
- 1 teaspoon finely chopped mixed candied peel
- ⅓ cup (40 g) finely chopped almonds

DIAMOND COOKIES

- 2 cups (300 g) all-purpose (plain) flour
- ½ cup (100 g) granulated sugar
- 1 tablespoon vanilla sugar (see page 414)
- grated zest of ½ lemon
- ¼ teaspoon salt
- ¾ cup (180 g) cold butter, cut up
- 1 large egg, lightly beaten
- 1 tablespoon candied cherries, chopped

Stir the flour, both sugars, lemon zest, and salt in a medium bowl. • Use a pastry blender to cut in the butter until the mixture resembles coarse crumbs. • Make a well in the center and add the egg, mixing until a dough is formed. • Turn out onto a lightly floured surface, working in the candied cherries, candied peel, and nuts. Knead until smooth. • Return to the bowl, cover with plastic wrap (cling film), and refrigerate for 30 minutes. • Preheat the oven to 350°F (180°C/gas 4). • Line two cookie sheets with parchment paper. • Roll

out the dough to ½ inch (1 cm) thick. Use a 2½-inch (6-cm) diamond-shaped cutter to stamp out cookies. • Use a metal spatula to transfer the cookies to the prepared cookie sheets, spacing 1 inch (2.5 cm) apart. • Mix the egg yolk and water in a small bowl. • Brush the cookies with the egg yolk mixture. • Bake for 12–15 minutes, or until lightly browned. • Cool the cookies on the sheets for 10 minutes. Use a metal spatula to transfer to racks to cool.

Makes: about 40 cookies • Prep: 45 min + 30 min to chill
Cooking: 12–15 min • Level: 2

- 2 tablespoons mixed candied peel, chopped
- 2 tablespoons sugared nuts, crushed
- 1 large egg yolk, to brush
- ½ cup (125 ml) water

Dried Fruit Cookies

RAW SUGAR RAISIN COOKIES

- 1 cup (180 g) golden raisins (sultanas)
- 2 cups (300 g) all-purpose (plain) flour
- 1 teaspoon baking powder
- 1 teaspoon ground cinnamon
- ⅛ teaspoon freshly grated nutmeg
- ⅛ teaspoon salt
- ¼ cup (60 ml) milk
- 1 teaspoon fresh lemon juice
- ½ cup (125 g) butter, softened
- 1 cup (200 g) raw sugar (Demerara or Barbados)
- ¼ cup (50 g) granulated sugar
- 2 large eggs

Preheat the oven to 350°F (180°C/gas 4). • Butter two cookie sheets. • Plump the raisins in hot water to cover in a small bowl for 10 minutes. Drain well and pat dry with paper towels. • Mix the flour, baking powder, cinnamon, nutmeg, and salt in a medium bowl. • Mix the milk and lemon juice in a small bowl. • Beat the butter and both sugars in a large bowl with an electric mixer on medium speed until creamy. • Add the eggs, beating until just blended. • Mix in the dry ingredients, milk mixture, and raisins. • Drop teaspoons of the dough 1 inch (2.5 cm) apart onto the prepared cookie sheets. • Bake for 12–15 minutes, or until just golden. • Transfer to racks to cool.

Makes: about 32 cookies • Prep: 25 min • Cooking: 12–15 min • Level: 1

PECAN AND SOUR CREAM COOKIES

Preheat the oven to 375°F (190°C/gas 5). • Butter two cookie sheets. • Mix the flour, baking powder, baking soda, cinnamon, and salt in a medium bowl. • Beat the butter and sugar in a large bowl with an electric mixer on medium speed until creamy. • Add the egg, beating until just blended. • Mix in the sour cream and dry ingredients. • Stir in the pecans. • Drop teaspoons of the dough 1 inch apart onto the prepared cookie sheets. • Bake for 10–15 minutes, or until golden brown. • Transfer to racks to cool.

Makes: about 30 cookies • Prep: 20 min • Cooking: 10–15 min • Level: 1

- 2 cups (300 g) all-purpose (plain) flour
- 2 teaspoons baking powder
- ½ teaspoon baking soda (bicarbonate of soda)
- ½ teaspoon ground cinnamon
- ¼ teaspoon salt
- ½ cup (125 g) butter, softened
- ¾ cup (150 g) sugar
- 1 large egg
- ½ cup (125 ml) sour cream
- ½ (60 g) cup coarsely chopped pecans

WHOLE-WHEAT DATE COOKIES

- 1 cup (150 g) all-purpose (plain) flour
- ⅔ cup (100 g) whole-wheat (wholemeal) flour
- 1 teaspoon baking powder
- ⅛ teaspoon salt
- 1 cup (200 g) finely chopped pitted dates
- ¾ cup (180 g) butter, softened
- ¾ cup (150 g) sugar
- 1 large egg

Preheat the oven to 400°F (200°C/gas 6). • Butter two cookie sheets. • Mix both flours, baking powder, and salt in a large bowl. • Beat the butter and sugar in a large bowl with an electric mixer on medium speed until creamy. • Add the egg, beating until just blended. • Mix in the dry ingredients and dates to make a stiff dough. • Form the dough into balls the size of walnuts and place 2 inches (5 cm) apart on the prepared cookie sheets, flattening them slightly. • Bake for 15–20 minutes, or until lightly browned. • Transfer to racks and let cool.

Makes: about 25 cookies • Prep: 20 min • Cooking: 15–20 min • Level: 1

PECAN DATE COOKIES

Preheat the oven to 400°F (200°C/gas 6). • Butter two cookie sheets. • Mix the flour and cinnamon into a medium bowl. • Mix the baking soda and water in a small bowl. Add the dates and currants. • Beat the butter and sugar in a large bowl with an electric mixer on medium speed until creamy. • Add the egg, beating until just blended. • Stir in the date and currant mixture. • Mix in the dry ingredients and pecans. • Drop tablespoons of the dough 1 inch (2.5 cm) apart onto the prepared cookie sheets. • Bake for 8–10 minutes, or until lightly browned. • Cool on the sheets until the cookies firm slightly. • Transfer to racks and let cool completely.

Makes: about 26 cookies • Prep: 20 min • Cooking: 8–10 min • Level: 1

- 1 cup (150 g) all-purpose (plain) flour
- ½ teaspoon ground cinnamon
- ¼ teaspoon baking soda (bicarbonate of soda)
- 2 tablespoons water
- ¾ cup (75 g) finely chopped dates
- ¾ cup (150 g) currants
- ⅓ cup (90 g) butter, softened
- ½ cup (100 g) sugar
- 1 large egg
- ½ cup (50 g) finely chopped pecans

Dried Fruit Cookies

SUSANNAH SPECIALS

- ½ cup (75 g) all-purpose (plain) flour
- 2 tablespoons cornstarch (cornflour)
- ¼ teaspoon salt
- ⅓ cup (90 g) butter, softened
- ½ cup (100 g) sugar
- 1 tablespoon finely grated lemon zest
- 3 large egg whites
- ½ cup (50 g) finely chopped pitted dates
- 1 tablespoon freshly squeezed lemon juice
- 1 teaspoon rum extract (essence)

Mix the flour, cornstarch, and salt in a medium bowl. • Beat the butter and sugar in a large bowl with an electric mixer on medium speed until creamy. • Add the lemon zest. • With mixer at high speed, beat the egg whites in a large bowl until soft peaks form. • Fold into the butter mixture. • Mix in the dry ingredients, dates, lemon juice, and rum extract. Refrigerate for 30 minutes. • Preheat the oven to 375°F (190°C/gas 5). • Butter two cookie sheets. • Drop teaspoons of the mixture 1½ inches (4 cm) apart onto the prepared cookie sheets. • Bake for 8–10 minutes, or until golden brown. • Transfer to racks to cool.

Makes: about 30 cookies • Prep: 20 min + 30 min to chill Cooking: 8–10 min • Level: 2

MELTING MOMENTS

Preheat the oven to 350°F (180°C/gas 4). • Butter two cookie sheets. • Mix the flour, baking powder, and salt in a large bowl. • Beat the butter and sugar in a large bowl with an electric mixer at high speed until creamy. • Add the egg and vanilla, beating until just blended. • Mix in the dry ingredients and cherries. • Form the dough into balls the size of walnuts and place 1 inch (2.5 cm) apart on the prepared cookie sheets. • Bake for 15–20 minutes, or until just golden. • Cool on the sheets until the cookies firm slightly. • Transfer to racks to finish cooling.

Makes: about 30 cookies • Prep: 20 min • Cooking: 15–20 min • Level: 1

- ¼ cups (180 g) all-purpose (plain) flour
- 1 teaspoon baking powder
- ⅛ teaspoon salt
- ⅓ cup (90 g) butter, softened
- ½ cup (100 g) sugar
- 1 large egg
- 1 teaspoon vanilla extract (essence)
- 1¼ cups finely chopped candied cherries

WALNUT AND CANDIED CHERRY COOKIES

- 2⅓ cups (350 g) all-purpose (plain) flour
- 1 tablespoon baking soda (bicarbonate of soda)
- 1 tablespoon ground ginger
- ¼ teaspoon salt
- 1¼ cups (250 g) firmly packed light brown sugar
- 3 tablespoons light corn (golden) syrup
- ¼ cup (60 ml) water
- 1 large egg
- ½ cup (80 g) finely chopped candied cherries
- ½ cup (60 g) finely chopped walnuts

Preheat the oven to 375°F (190°C/gas 5). • Butter three cookie sheets. • Mix the flour, baking soda, ginger, and salt in a medium bowl. • Beat the brown sugar, corn syrup, water, and egg in a large bowl with an electric mixer at high speed until well blended. • Stir in the dry ingredients, cherries, and walnuts. • Drop teaspoons of the dough 2 inches apart onto the prepared cookie sheets. • Bake, one sheet at a time, for 10–12 minutes, or until just golden at the edges. • Transfer to racks to cool.

Makes: about 36 cookies • Prep: 20 min • Cooking: 10–12 min • Level: 1

BUTTERSCOTCH PECAN COOKIES

Preheat the oven to 350°F (180°C/gas 4). • Butter two cookie sheets. • Mix the flour, baking powder, and salt in a medium bowl. • Beat the butter, brown sugar, and corn syrup in a large bowl with an electric mixer on medium speed for 1 minute. • Mix in the dry ingredients and corn flakes until well blended. • Form the mixture into twenty-four balls the size of walnuts, flattening them slightly. Press the pecan halves into the tops. • Arrange the cookies 1½ inches (4 cm) apart on the prepared cookie sheets. • Bake for 10–15 minutes, or until lightly browned. • Cool the cookies completely on the cookie sheets.

Makes: about 24 cookies • Prep: 20 min • Cooking: 10–15 min • Level: 1

- 1 cup (150 g) all-purpose (plain) flour
- 1½ teaspoons baking powder
- ⅛ teaspoon salt
- ½ cup (125 g) butter, softened
- 1 cup (200 g) firmly packed dark brown sugar
- 1 tablespoon light corn (golden) syrup
- 2 tablespoons corn flakes
- 24 pecan halves, to decorate

Dried Fruit Cookies

COCONUT CRISPS

- 1 cup (150 g) all-purpose (plain) flour
- 1 teaspoon baking powder
- ½ teaspoon salt
- 1 cup (125 g) rolled oats
- ⅓ cup (30 g) unsweetened shredded (desiccated) coconut
- ½ cup (125 g) butter
- 1 cup (200 g) sugar
- 2 tablespoons light molasses (treacle)
- 1 teaspoon baking soda (bicarbonate of soda) dissolved in 1 tablespoon milk

Preheat the oven to 350°F (180°C/gas 4). • Set out two cookie sheets. • Mix the flour, baking powder, and salt in a large bowl. Stir in the oats and coconut. • Melt the butter with the sugar and molasses in a medium saucepan over medium heat. Bring to a boil, stirring constantly. • Remove from the heat and add the baking soda mixture. • Pour the butter mixture into the dry ingredients and mix until well blended. • Let stand for 30 minutes, or until firm. • Form the dough into balls the size of walnuts and place 1½ inches (4 cm) apart on the cookie sheets. • Bake for 10–15 minutes, or until firm to the touch. • Cool the cookies on the cookie sheet for 5 minutes. • Transfer to racks to cool completely.

Makes: about 20 cookies • Prep: 20 min + 30 min to rest
Cooking: 10–15 min • Level: 1

COCONUT CUT OUTS

Preheat the oven to 300°F (150°C/gas 2). • Butter two cookie sheets. • Mix the flour and salt in a large bowl. • Use a pastry blender to cut in the shortening until the mixture resembles fine crumbs. • Stir in the coconut, oats, and sugar. • Mix the water, molasses, and baking soda in a small bowl. • Stir the baking soda liquid into the oat mixture to form a stiff dough. • Shape the dough into a ball, wrap in plastic wrap (cling film), and refrigerate for 30 minutes. • Roll out the dough on a lightly floured surface to ¼ inch (5 mm) thick. • Use a 3-inch (8-cm) cookie cutter to cut out the cookies. Gather the dough scraps, re-roll, and continue cutting out cookies until all the dough is used. • Transfer to the cookie sheet, spacing well. • Bake for about 25 minutes, or until just golden at the edges. • Transfer to racks and let cool completely.

Makes: about 20 cookies • Prep: 30 min + 30 min to chill
Cooking: 25 min • Level: 1

- 1 cup (150 g) all-purpose (plain) flour
- ⅛ teaspoon salt
- ½ cup (125 g) vegetable shortening
- 1 cup (120 g) unsweetened shredded (desiccated) coconut
- 1 cup (150 g) rolled oats
- ½ cup (100 g) sugar
- 2 tablespoons cold water
- 1 tablespoon light molasses (treacle)
- 1 teaspoon baking soda (bicarbonate of soda)

WALNUT CHOCOLATE CHIP COOKIES

- 1⅓ cups (200 g) all-purpose (plain) flour
- 1 teaspoon baking powder
- ⅛ teaspoon salt
- ⅓ cup (90 g) butter, softened
- ½ cup (100 g) granulated sugar
- ½ cup firmly packed light brown sugar
- ½ teaspoon vanilla extract (essence)
- 1 large egg
- ½ cup (90 g) semisweet (dark) chocolate chips
- ⅔ cup (70 g) coarsely chopped walnuts

Preheat the oven to 350°F (180°F/gas 4). • Butter two cookie sheets. • Mix the flour, baking powder, and salt in a large bowl. • Beat the butter, both sugars, and vanilla in a large bowl until creamy. • Add the egg, beating until just blended. • Mix in the dry ingredients, chocolate chips, and walnuts. • Drop tablespoons of the dough 2 inches (5 cm) apart onto the prepared cookie sheets. • Bake for 12–15 minutes, or until just golden. • Cool on the sheets until the cookies firm slightly. • Transfer to racks to finish cooling.

Makes 18–20 cookies • Prep: 20 min • Cooking: 12–15 min
Level: 1

ANZAC COOKIES

Preheat the oven to 300°F (150°F/gas 2). • Set out two cookie sheets. • Mix the oats, coconut, flour, sugar, and salt in a large bowl. • Stir in the butter. • Mix the water, corn syrup, and baking soda in a small bowl. • Stir into the dry ingredients. • Drop teaspoons of the dough 1 inch (2.5 cm) apart on the cookie sheets. • Bake for 12–15 minutes, or until lightly browned. • Transfer to racks to cool.

Makes: about 40 cookies • Prep: 15 min • Cooking: 12–15 min • Level: 1

- ½ cup (75 g) old-fashioned rolled oats
- 1 cup (150 g) unsweetened shredded (desiccated) coconut
- 1 cup (150 g) all-purpose (plain) flour
- ⅓ cup (50 g) superfine (caster) sugar
- ⅛ teaspoon salt
- ⅔ cup (150 g) butter, melted
- 2 tablespoons boiling water
- 1 tablespoon light corn (golden) syrup
- 1 teaspoon baking soda (bicarbonate of soda)

FRUIT AND NUT DIAMONDS

- 1/3 cup (60 g) golden raisins (sultanas)
- 1 1/4 cups (180 g) all-purpose (plain) flour
- 1/2 teaspoon baking powder
- 1/8 teaspoon salt
- 1/2 cup (75 g) rolled oats
- 1/2 cup (50 g) coarsely chopped walnuts
- 2 tablespoons sugar
- 1/3 cup (90 g) butter, melted
- 1/4 cup (60 ml) milk
- 1 large egg, lightly beaten

Plump the raisins in hot water to cover in a small bowl for 10 minutes. • Drain well and pat dry with paper towels. • Mix the flour, baking powder, and salt in a large bowl. • Stir in the raisins, oats, walnuts, and sugar. • Mix in the butter, milk, and egg. • Shape the dough into a disk, wrap in plastic wrap (cling film), and refrigerate for 30 minutes. • Preheat the oven to 425°F (220°C/gas 7). • Line two cookie sheets with parchment paper. • Roll out the dough on a lightly floured work surface to 1/2 inch (1 cm) thick. • Use a sharp knife to cut the dough into 2-inch (5-cm) diamonds. • Transfer the cookies to the prepared cookie sheets, placing them 1 inch (2.5 cm) apart. • Bake for about 15 minutes, or until just golden at the edges. • Transfer to racks to cool.

Makes: about 25 cookies • Prep: 40 min + 30 min to chill
Cooking: 15 min • Level: 1

PEANUT COOKIES

Preheat the oven to 350°F (180°C/gas 4). • Butter three cookie sheets. • Mix the flour, baking soda, and salt in a large bowl. • Beat the butter and both sugars in a large bowl with an electric mixer at high speed until creamy. • Add the vanilla and egg, beating until just blended. • Mix in the dry ingredients, oats, raisins, and peanuts. • Drop heaped teaspoons of the dough 2 inches (5 cm) apart onto the prepared cookie sheets. • Bake for about 15 minutes, or until lightly browned. • Transfer to racks and let cool completely.

Makes: about 45 cookies • Prep: 20 min • Cooking: 15 min
Level: 1

- 1 1/4 cups (180 g) all-purpose (plain)) flour
- 1/2 teaspoon baking soda (bicarbonate of soda)
- 1/2 teaspoon salt
- 1/2 cup (125 g) butter
- 1/2 cup (100 g) sugar
- 1/2 cup (100 g) firmly packed dark brown sugar
- 1/2 teaspoon vanilla extract (essence)
- 1 large egg, lightly beaten
- 1/3 cup (50 g) rolled oats
- 1/2 cup (90 g) raisins
- 1/2 cup (70 g) coarsely chopped peanuts

HAZELNUT STICKS

- 2 1/4 cups (300 g) hazelnuts
- 1 1/4 cups (250 g) sugar
- 1 2/3 cups (250 g) all-purpose (plain) flour
- 1/8 teaspoon salt
- finely grated zest and juice of 1/2 lemon
- 1 cup (250 g) butter, cut up
- 2 large eggs + 1 large egg yolk
- 1 teaspoon milk

Preheat the oven to 325°F (170°C/gas 3). • Sprinkle the nuts on a baking sheet. Toast for 7 minutes, or until lightly golden. • Transfer to a kitchen towel. Fold the towel over and gently rub the nuts to remove the skins. Pick out and discard the skins. • Place 1 2/3 cups of the nuts and 2 tablespoons sugar in a food processor and process until finely ground. Set aside. • Chop the remaining 3/4 cup nuts coarsely and set aside. • Mix the flour and salt in a large bowl. • Stir in the remaining sugar, finely ground hazelnuts, and lemon zest. • Use a pastry blender to cut in the butter until the mixture resembles coarse crumbs. • Use a fork to mix in the lemon juice and whole eggs to form a smooth dough. • Press the dough into a disk, wrap in plastic wrap (cling film), and

refrigerate for 30 minutes. • Set out four cookie sheets. • Roll out the dough on a lightly floured surface to 1/4 inch (3 mm) thick. • Cut into 1 x 2-inch (2.5 x 5-cm) sticks. • Use a spatula to transfer the cookies to the cookie sheets, placing them 1 inch (2.5 cm) apart. • Refrigerate for 20 minutes more. • Preheat the oven to 350°F (180°C/gas 4). • Mix the egg yolk with the milk in a small bowl and brush over the cookies. • Sprinkle with the reserved coarsely chopped hazelnuts. • Bake for 8–10 minutes, or until golden and firm around the edges. • Cool on sheets until the cookies firm slightly. Transfer to racks and let cool.

Makes: about 55 cookies • Prep: 55 min + 50 min to chill
Cooking: 8–10 min • Level: 2

SEED & CEREAL COOKIES

Cookies made with seeds and cereals are usually a healthier alternative to some richer offerings. Try them at breakfast when they can provide much-needed energy for the day ahead, or as a pick-me-up snack during the day. Many of these cookies are deliciously chewy and very satisfying to eat. In this chapter we have included some classics, such as Digestive biscuits (see page 198) and Sesame bars (see page 208), as well as some delicious twists on old favorites, like the Corn flake and sunflower seed cookies, shown left (see recipe on page 194), the Peanut bran cookies (see page 196), and the Coconut oatmeal cookies (see page 211).

Corn flake and sunflower seed cookies (see page 194)

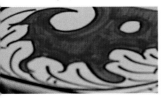

Seed & Cereal Cookies

CHERRY OATIES

- 2 cups (300 g) all-purpose (plain) flour
- 1 tablespoon baking powder
- $1/2$ teaspoon salt
- $3/4$ cup (180 g) butter, softened
- $3/4$ cup (150 g) firmly packed light brown sugar
- 1 teaspoon vanilla extract (essence)
- 1 large egg, lightly beaten
- 2 tablespoons old-fashioned rolled oats
- 10 candied cherries, halved, to decorate

Preheat the oven to 350°F (180°C/gas 4).
• Butter two cookie sheets. • Mix the flour, baking powder, and salt in a medium bowl.
• Beat the butter, brown sugar, and vanilla in a large bowl with an electric mixer at high speed until creamy. • Add the egg, beating until just blended. • Mix in the dry ingredients and oats until well blended.
• Form into balls the size of walnuts and place 2 inches (5 cm) apart on the prepared cookie sheets, flattening them slightly.
• Place half a cherry in the center of each cookie. • Bake for 15–20 minutes, or until lightly browned. • Cool completely on the cookie sheets.

Makes: about 25 cookies • Prep: 15 min • Cooking: 15–20 min • Level : 1

GEORDIE COOKIES

Preheat the oven to 350°F (180°C/gas 4).
• Butter three cookie sheets. • Mix the flour, baking soda, and salt in a large bowl. • Beat the butter and both sugars in a large bowl with an electric mixer at high speed until creamy. • Add the vanilla and egg, beating until just blended. • Mix in the dry ingredients, oats, raisins, and peanuts.
• Drop rounded teaspoons of the dough 2 inches (5 cm) apart onto the prepared cookie sheets. • Bake for 12–15 minutes, or until lightly browned. • Transfer to racks and let cool completely

Makes: about 45 cookies • Prep: 20 min • Cooking: 12–15 min • Level: 1

- $1 1/4$ cups (180 g) all-purpose (plain) flour
- $1/2$ teaspoon baking soda (bicarbonate of soda)
- $1/2$ teaspoon salt
- $1/2$ cup (125 g) butter, softened
- $1/2$ cup (100 g) granulated sugar
- $1/2$ cup (100 g) firmly packed dark brown sugar
- $1/2$ teaspoon vanilla extract (essence)
- 1 large egg
- $1/3$ cup (50 g) old-fashioned rolled oats
- $1/2$ cup (90 g) raisins
- $2/3$ cup (60 g) coarsely chopped walnuts

SCOTTISH COOKIES

- 1 cup (150 g) all-purpose (plain) flour
- $1/2$ teaspoon baking soda (bicarbonate of soda)
- $1/8$ teaspoon salt
- $2/3$ cup (150 g) butter, softened
- $1 1/4$ cups (250 g) firmly packed dark brown sugar
- 1 large egg
- 1 teaspoon vanilla extract (essence)
- 1 cup (150 g) old-fashioned rolled oats
- 1 tablespoon water

Preheat the oven to 350°F (180°C/gas 4).
• Line two cookie sheets with parchment paper. • Mix the flour, baking soda, and salt in a large bowl. • Beat the butter and brown sugar in a large bowl with an electric mixer on medium speed until creamy. • Add the egg, beating until just blended. Add the vanilla. • Mix in the dry ingredients, oats, and water. • Roll teaspoons of the mixture into balls and place on the prepared cookie sheets, about $1 1/2$ inches (4 cm) apart, flattening them slightly. • Bake for 12–15 minutes, or until golden brown. • Transfer to racks to cool.

Makes: about 30 cookies • Prep: 30 min • Cooking: 12–15 min • Level: 1

CORN FLAKE AND SUNFLOWER SEED COOKIES

Preheat the oven to 350°F (180°C/gas 4).
• Butter two cookie sheets. • Mix the flour, baking soda, and salt in a medium bowl.
• Beat the butter and both sugars in a large bowl with an electric mixer on medium speed until creamy. • Add the eggs and vanilla, beating until just blended. • Mix in the dry ingredients, corn flakes, and sunflower seeds. • Drop tablespoons of the dough 2 inches (5 cm) apart onto the prepared cookie sheets. • Bake for 10–15 minutes, or until golden brown. • Cool on the sheets until the cookies firm slightly.
• Transfer to racks to cool.

Makes: about 35 cookies • Prep: 20 min • Cooking: 10–15 min • Level : 1

- $1 1/2$ cups (225 g) all-purpose (plain) flour
- 1 teaspoon baking soda (bicarbonate of soda)
- $1/4$ teaspoon salt
- 1 cup (250 g) butter, softened
- 1 cup (200 g) firmly packed light brown sugar
- 1 cup (200 g) granulated sugar
- 2 large eggs
- $1/2$ teaspoon vanilla extract (essence)
- 2 cups (200 g) corn flakes
- 1 cup (100 g) sunflower seeds

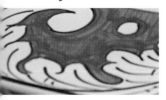

Seed & Cereal Cookies

SUNFLOWER SEED DRIZZLERS

- 2 cups (300 g) all-purpose (plain) flour
- 1 teaspoon ground allspice
- 1 teaspoon baking soda (bicarbonate of soda)
- ¼ teaspoon salt
- 1½ cups (225 g) sunflower seeds
- 1 cup (150 g) old-fashioned rolled oats
- 2 tablespoons sesame seeds
- 1 cup (250 g) butter, cut up
- 2 tablespoons firmly packed dark brown sugar
- 1 tablespoon dark molasses
- 1½ cups (250 g) carob chips

Preheat the oven to 375°F (190°C/gas 5). • Butter two cookie sheets. • Mix the flour, allspice, baking soda, and salt in a large bowl. • Stir in the sunflower seeds, oats, and sesame seeds. • Melt the butter with the brown sugar and molasses in a small saucepan over low heat until the sugar has dissolved completely. • Pour the melted butter mixture into the dry ingredients and mix well. • Drop tablespoons of the mixture 1½ inches (4 cm) apart onto the prepared cookie sheets, flattening with a fork. • Bake for 8–10 minutes, or until just golden. • Transfer to racks to cool. • Melt the carob in a double boiler over barely simmering water. • Drizzle the carob over the cookies and let stand for 30 minutes.

Makes: about 20 cookies • Prep: 25 min + 30 min to set
Cooking: 8–10 min • Level: 1

SUNFLOWER SEED AND GINGER COOKIES

Cookies: Mix the flour, baking powder, cinnamon, and salt in a medium bowl. • Beat the butter and brown sugar in a large bowl with an electric mixer at high speed until creamy. • Add the egg, beating until just blended. • Mix in the raisins, apricots, almonds, and sunflower seeds. • Mix in the dry ingredients to form a soft dough. • Form the dough into a 14-inch (35-cm) log, wrap in plastic wrap (cling film), and refrigerate for at least 30 minutes. • Preheat the oven to 350°F (180°C/gas 4). • Line two cookie sheets with parchment paper. • Slice the dough ½ inch (1 cm) thick and place 1 inch (2.5 cm) apart on the prepared cookie sheets. • Bake for 10–15 minutes, or until just golden. • Transfer to racks and let cool completely. • Glaze: Heat the preserves and butter in a small saucepan over low heat and simmer for 2 minutes. • Drizzle the glaze over the cookies.

Makes: 28 cookies • Prep: 40 min + 30 min to chill
Cooking: 10–15 min • Level: 2

Cookies
- ⅔ cup (100 g) all-purpose (plain) flour
- ½ teaspoon baking powder
- ¼ teaspoon ground cinnamon
- ⅛ teaspoon salt
- ¼ cup (60 g) butter, softened
- ¼ cup (50 g) firmly packed light brown sugar
- 1 large egg
- ½ cup (90 g) finely chopped raisins
- ¼ cup (50 g) finely chopped dried apricots
- ½ cup (50 g) finely chopped almonds
- ¼ cup (50 g) finely chopped sunflower seeds

Glaze
- ½ cup (160 g) ginger preserves
- 2 tablespoons butter

PEANUT AND OAT COOKIES

- 1 cup (150 g) all-purpose (plain) flour
- ½ teaspoon baking powder
- ½ teaspoon baking soda (bicarbonate of soda)
- ½ cup (125 g) butter, softened
- 1 cup (200 g) sugar
- 1 large egg
- ½ cup (50 g) salted peanuts
- 1 cup (150 g) corn flakes
- 2¼ cups (330 g) old-fashioned rolled oats

Preheat the oven to 300°F (150°C/gas 2). • Butter a cookie sheet. • Mix the flour, baking powder, and baking soda in a medium bowl. • Beat the butter and sugar in a large bowl with an electric mixer on medium speed until creamy. • Add the egg, beating until just blended. • Mix in the dry ingredients, peanuts, corn flakes, and oats to make a stiff dough. • Drop teaspoons of the dough 1 inch (2.5 cm) apart onto the prepared cookie sheet. • Bake for 10–15 minutes, or until lightly browned. • Cool on the sheet until the cookies firm slightly. • Transfer to racks and let cool completely.

Makes: about 25 cookies • Prep: 20 min • Cooking: 10–15 min • Level: 1

PEANUT BRAN COOKIES

Preheat the oven to 375°F (190°C/gas 5). • Butter two cookie sheets. • Mix the flour, baking powder, and salt in a medium bowl. • Beat the butter and brown sugar in a large bowl with an electric mixer on medium speed until creamy. • Beat in the peanut butter, egg, and vanilla. • Mix in the dry ingredients and bran. • Form the dough into balls the size of walnuts and place 1½ inches (4 cm) apart on the prepared cookie sheets, flattening them slightly. • Bake for 8–10 minutes, or until just golden. • Transfer to racks to cool.

Makes: about 25 cookies • Prep: 20 min • Cooking: 8–10 min • Level: 1

- 1 cup (150 g) whole-wheat (wholemeal) flour
- ½ teaspoon baking powder
- ⅛ teaspoon salt
- ½ cup (125 g) butter, softened
- ½ cup (100 g) firmly packed dark brown sugar
- 1 cup (250 ml) smooth peanut butter
- 1 large egg
- ½ teaspoon vanilla extract (essence)
- 1 cup (150 g) bran

Seed & Cereal Cookies

DIGESTIVE BISCUITS

- 1 cup (150 g) whole-wheat (wholemeal) flour
- ½ teaspoon baking soda (bicarbonate of soda)
- ¼ teaspoon salt
- ¾ cup (180 g) butter, cut up
- 1 cup (150 g) oat bran
- ½ cup (100 g) sugar
- 1 large egg, lightly beaten

Mix the flour, baking soda, and salt in a medium bowl. • Cut in the butter until the mixture resembles fine crumbs. • Stir in the oat bran and sugar. • Mix in the beaten egg. Press the dough into a disk, wrap in plastic wrap (cling film), and refrigerate for 30 minutes. • Preheat the oven to 375°F (190°C/gas 5). • Butter a cookie sheet. • Roll out the dough on a surface lightly dusted with oat bran to ¼ inch (5 mm) thick. • Use a 2-inch (5-cm) cookie cutter to cut out the cookies. • Transfer the cookies to the prepared cookie sheets, spacing well. • Bake for 10–15 minutes, or until browned. • Transfer to racks and let cool.

Makes: about 20 cookies • Prep: 40 min + 30 min to chill
Cooking: 10–15 min • Level: 1

BREAKFAST COOKIES

Preheat the oven to 350°F (180°C/gas 4). • Line two cookie sheets with parchment paper. • Mix the flour and baking powder in a large bowl. • Beat the butter and brown sugar in a large bowl with an electric mixer at high speed until creamy. • Add the eggs, beating until just blended. • Mix in the dry ingredients, followed by the corn flakes, apricots, and coconut. • Drop rounded teaspoons of the mixture 1½ inches (4 cm) apart onto the prepared cookie sheets. • Bake for 10–12 minutes, or until lightly browned. • Transfer the cookies on the parchment paper to racks to cool.

Makes: about 35 cookies • Prep: 30 min • Cooking: 10–12 min • Level: 1

- ⅔ cup (100 g) all-purpose (plain) flour
- 1 teaspoon baking powder
- ⅓ cup (90 g) butter, softened
- ⅔ cup (140 g) firmly packed light brown sugar
- 2 large eggs
- 2 tablespoons corn flakes
- ½ cup (50 g) finely chopped dried apricots
- 3 tablespoons unsweetened shredded (desiccated) coconut

Breakfast cookies

Date and oat cookies

DATE AND OAT COOKIES

- 1½ cups (225 g) all-purpose (plain) flour
- ½ teaspoon baking powder
- ⅛ teaspoon salt
- ½ cup (125 g) butter, cut up
- 1 large egg, lightly beaten
- 1 cup (200 g) sugar
- ½ cup (75 g) old-fashioned rolled oats
- ½ cup (50 g) coarsely chopped dates

Preheat the oven to 350°F (180°C/gas 4).
• Butter two cookie sheets. • Mix the flour, baking powder, and salt in a large bowl.
• Use a pastry blender to cut in the butter until the mixture resembles fine crumbs.
• Add the egg, beating until just blended.
• Mix in the sugar, oats, and dates. • Drop tablespoons of the dough 2 inches (5 cm) apart onto the prepared cookie sheets.
• Bake for 12–15 minutes, or until lightly browned. • Cool on the sheets until the cookies firm slightly. • Transfer to racks to cool.

Makes: about 20 cookies • Prep: 20 min • Cooking: 12–15 min • Level: 1

DOWNUNDER OAT BARS

Preheat the oven to 325°F (170°C/gas 3).
• Butter a 9-inch (23-cm) square baking pan.
• Melt the butter, sugar, and corn syrup in a small saucepan over medium heat. • Remove from the heat and stir in the flour and oats until well blended. • Spoon the mixture evenly into the prepared pan, pressing down lightly. • Bake for 15–20 minutes, or until golden brown. • Cool completely before cutting into bars.

Makes: about 20 bars • Prep: 15 min • Cooking: 15–20 min Level: 1

- ½ cup (125 g) butter, cut up
- 1 cup (200 g) sugar
- 1 tablespoon light corn syrup (golden) syrup
- ½ cup (75 g) all-purpose (plain) flour
- ½ cup (75 g) old-fashioned rolled oats

Seed & Cereal Cookies

SUNFLOWER SEED DROPS

- 1½ cups (225 g) all-purpose (plain) flour
- 1 teaspoon baking soda (bicarbonate of soda)
- ¼ teaspoon salt
- 1 cup (250 g) butter, softened
- 1 cup (200 g) firmly packed light brown sugar
- 1 cup (200 g) granulated sugar
- 2 large eggs
- ½ teaspoon vanilla extract (essence)
- 2 cups (300 g) old-fashioned rolled oats
- 1 cup (100 g) sunflower seeds

Preheat the oven to 350°F (180°C/gas 4).
• Butter three cookie sheets. • Mix the flour, baking soda, and salt in a medium bowl.
• Beat the butter and both sugars in a large bowl with an electric mixer at high speed until creamy. • Add the eggs and vanilla, beating until just blended. • Mix in the dry ingredients, oats, and sunflower seeds. • Drop tablespoons of the dough 2 inches (5 cm) apart onto the prepared cookie sheets. • Bake for 10–15 minutes, or until golden brown. • Cool on the sheets until the cookies firm slightly. Transfer to racks to finish cooling.

Makes: about 40 cookies • Prep: 20 min • Cooking:10–15 min • Level: 1

OAT AND CHOCOLATE CHIP COOKIES

Preheat the oven to 350°F (180°C/gas 5).
• Set out two cookie sheets. • Mix the oats, both sugars, flour, and salt in a large bowl.
• Make a well in the center and stir in the butter, egg, and vanilla. • Stir in the chocolate chips. • Drop tablespoons of the dough 3 inches (8 cm) apart onto the cookie sheets. • Bake for 5–8 minutes, or until lightly browned and the centers are bubbling. • Transfer to racks and let cool completely.

Makes: about 30 cookies • Prep: 20 min • Cooking: 5–8 min Level: 1

- 2¼ cups (330 g) old-fashioned rolled oats
- 1 cup (200 g) firmly packed light brown sugar
- ½ cup (100 g) granulated sugar
- 2 tablespoons all-purpose (plain) flour
- ¼ teaspoon salt
- 1⅓ cups (330 g) butter, melted
- 1 large egg
- 1 teaspoon vanilla extract (essence)
- ½ cup (90 g) semisweet (dark) chocolate chips

Sunflower seed drops

Corn flake cookies

CORN FLAKE COOKIES

- 1 cup (150 g) all-purpose (plain) flour
- ½ teaspoon baking powder
- ¼ cup (60 g) butter, softened
- ¼ cup (60 g) vegetable shortening
- ½ cup (100 g) sugar
- 1 large egg
- 1 cup (150 g) corn flakes

Preheat the oven to 350°F (180°C/gas 4). • Butter two cookie sheets. • Mix the flour and baking powder in a medium bowl. • Beat the butter, shortening, and sugar in a large bowl with an electric mixer on medium speed until creamy. • Mix in the dry ingredients. • Add the egg, beating until just blended. • Place the corn flakes on a large plate. Drop tablespoons of the batter onto the corn flakes. • Use a spatula to flatten the cookies and turn until completely coated. • Transfer the cookies to the prepared cookie sheets, placing 1 inch (2.5 cm) apart. • Bake for 10–15 minutes, or until just golden. • Transfer to racks to cool.

Makes: about 20 cookies • Prep: 20 min • Cooking: 10–15 min • Level: 1

DATE AND CORN FLAKE COOKIES

Mix the flour, baking soda, and salt in a large bowl. • Beat the shortening and both sugars in a large bowl with an electric mixer on medium speed until creamy. • Add the eggs, beating until just blended. • Mix in the dry ingredients, oats, corn flakes, dates, and chocolate chips to form a stiff dough. • Divide the dough in half. Form into two 8-inch (20-cm) logs, wrap in plastic wrap (cling film), and refrigerate for 30 minutes. • Preheat the oven to 375°F (190°C/gas 5). • Butter two cookie sheets. • Slice the dough ¼ inch (5 mm) thick and place 2 inches (5 cm) apart on the prepared cookie sheets. • Bake for 10–12 minutes, or until lightly golden. • Cool on the sheets until the cookies firm slightly. • Transfer to racks to cool completely.

Makes: about 64 cookies • Prep: 45 min + 30 min to chill Cooking: 10–12 min • Level: 1

- 1 cup (150 g) all-purpose (plain) flour
- ½ teaspoon baking soda (bicarbonate of soda)
- ½ teaspoon salt
- ½ cup (125 g) vegetable shortening
- ½ cup (100 g) firmly packed light brown sugar
- ½ cup (100 g) granulated sugar
- 2 large eggs
- 1 cup (150 g) old-fashioned rolled oats
- ½ cup (50 g) corn flakes
- ½ cup (50 g) finely chopped dates
- ½ cup (90 g) semisweet (dark) chocolate chips

Seed & Cereal Cookies

POPPY SEED ESSES

- 1⅓ cups (200 g) all-purpose (plain) flour
- 1 teaspoon baking powder
- ⅛ teaspoon salt
- ½ cup (125 g) butter, softened
- ½ cup (100 g) sugar
- 1 teaspoon ground aniseeds
- 1 teaspoon finely grated lemon zest
- 1 large egg + 1 large egg yolk + 1 large egg white
- 2 tablespoons + 1 teaspoon milk
- 2 tablespoons poppy seeds

Mix the flour, baking powder, and salt in a medium bowl. • Beat the butter and sugar in a large bowl with an electric mixer at high speed until creamy. • Add the aniseeds and lemon zest. • With mixer at high speed, beat the whole egg and egg yolk and 2 tablespoons of milk until frothy in a large bowl. • Beat the egg mixture into the batter. • Mix in the dry ingredients to form a smooth dough. • Divide the dough in half. • Form into 8-inch (20-cm) logs, wrap in plastic wrap (cling film), and refrigerate for at least 30 minutes. • Preheat the oven to 375°F (190°C/gas 5). • Line two cookie sheets with parchment paper. • Slice the dough ½ inch (1 cm) thick. • Roll each slice into a 6-inch (15-cm) log and form into an S-shape, flattening it slightly. • Place the cookies 1 inch (2.5 cm) apart on the prepared cookie sheets. • Mix the egg white and remaining milk in a small bowl. • Brush over the cookies and sprinkle with poppy seeds. • Bake for 8–10 minutes, or until just golden at the edges. • Transfer to racks to cool.

Makes: about 32 cookies • Prep: 40 min + 30 min to chill
Cooking: 10–12 min Level: 2

ALMOND POPPY SEED COOKIES

Preheat the oven to 350°F (180°C/gas 4). • Line two cookie sheets with parchment paper. • Beat the egg whites in a large bowl with an electric mixer at high speed until soft peaks form. • Use a large rubber spatula to fold in the flour, sugar, almonds, poppy seeds, and almond oil until smooth. • Drop teaspoons of the cookie dough 1 inch (2.5 cm) apart onto the prepared cookie sheets. • Bake for 6–8 minutes, or until golden brown around the edges. • Cool the cookies on the cookie sheet for 1 minute. Transfer to racks to finish cooling.

Makes: about 24 cookies • Prep: 20 min • Cooking: 6–8 min
Level: 1

- 4 large egg whites
- 2 tablespoons all-purpose (plain) flour
- ¼ cup (50 g) superfine (caster) sugar
- 2 cups (300 g) finely ground almonds
- 2 tablespoons poppy seeds
- 1 tablespoon almond oil

POLENTA AND POPPY SEED COOKIES

- 1⅓ cups (200 g) finely ground yellow cornmeal
- 1⅓ cups (200 g) all-purpose (plain) flour
- 2 teaspoons baking powder
- ⅛ teaspoon salt
- ⅔ cup (140 g) granulated sugar
- ⅔ cup (150 g) butter,

Mix the cornmeal, flour, baking powder, and salt in a large bowl. • Stir in the sugar, butter, and 2 eggs. • Add the wine and mix to form a smooth dough. • Press the dough into a disk, wrap in plastic wrap (cling film), and refrigerate for 30 minutes. • Preheat the oven to 400°F (200°C/gas 6). • Butter two cookie sheets. • Roll out the dough on a lightly floured surface to ¼ inch (5 mm) thick. • Cut into 2-inch (5-cm) triangles and

place 1 inch (2.5 cm) apart on the prepared cookie sheets. • Beat the remaining egg with the milk in a small bowl. Brush over the cookies. • Sprinkle with the poppy seeds and confectioners' sugar. • Bake for 15–20 minutes, or until just golden. • Transfer to racks to cool.

Makes: about 36 cookies • Prep: 40 min + 30 min to chill
Cooking: 15–20 min • Level: 2

- softened
- 3 large eggs, lightly beaten
- 2 teaspoons dry white wine
- 1 tablespoon milk
- ⅓ cup (40 g) poppy seeds
- ⅓ cup (50 g) confectioners' (icing) sugar

Seed & Cereal Cookies

ITALIAN RICE COOKIES

- 1²/₃ cups (250 g) rice flour
- ½ teaspoon baking powder
- ⅛ teaspoon baking soda (bicarbonate of soda)
- ⅛ teaspoon salt
- ⅓ cup (70 g) sugar
- ¼ cup (60 ml) best-quality extra-virgin olive oil
- ⅓–²/₃ cup (80–150 ml) water

Preheat the oven to 350°F (180°C/gas 4). • Butter two cookie sheets. • Mix the flour, baking powder, baking soda, and salt in a large bowl. • Stir in the sugar. • Mix in the olive oil and enough water to form a stiff dough. • Form the dough into balls the size of walnuts and place 1 inch (2.5 cm) apart on the prepared cookie sheets, flattening them slightly. • Bake for 20–25 minutes, or until just golden. • Transfer to racks and let cool completely.

Makes: about 25 cookies • Prep: 20 min • Cooking: 20–25 min • Level: 1

WALNUT CRISPS

Preheat the oven to 375°F (190°C/gas 5). • Butter three cookie sheets. • Mix the flour, baking soda, and salt in a large bowl. • Beat the butter and both sugars in a large bowl with an electric mixer on medium speed until creamy. • Add the vanilla and egg, beating until just blended. • Mix in the dry ingredients, followed by the corn flakes and walnuts. • Drop teaspoons of the dough 1 inch (2.5 cm) apart onto the prepared cookie sheets. • Bake for 12–15 minutes, or until lightly browned. • Cool on the sheets until the cookies firm slightly. • Transfer to racks to finish cooling.

Makes: about 36 cookies • Prep: 20 min • Cooking: 12–15 min • Level: 1

- ²/₃ cup (100 g) all-purpose (plain) flour
- ½ teaspoon baking soda (bicarbonate of soda)
- ⅛ teaspoon salt
- ½ cup (125 g) butter, softened
- ¼ cup (50 g) granulated sugar
- ²/₃ cup (70 g) firmly packed light brown sugar
- ½ teaspoon vanilla extract (essence)
- 1 large egg
- ⅓ cup (50 g) corn flakes
- ²/₃ cup (70 g) coarsely chopped walnuts

CORNMEAL COOKIES

- 1½ cups (225 g) all-purpose (plain) flour
- 1 cup (150 g) finely ground yellow cornmeal
- 1 teaspoon baking powder
- ¼ teaspoon salt
- ½ cup (125 g) butter, cut up
- 2 large eggs, lightly beaten
- ²/₃ cup (140 g) firmly packed dark brown sugar

Preheat the oven to 325°F (170°C/gas 3). • Butter two cookie sheets. • Mix the flour, cornmeal, baking powder, and salt in a large bowl. • Use a pastry blender to cut in the butter until the mixture resembles coarse crumbs. • Mix in the eggs and brown sugar to form a soft dough. • Form the dough into balls the size of walnuts and place 1½ inches (4 cm) apart on the prepared cookie sheets. • Bake for 20–25 minutes, or until lightly browned. • Transfer to racks to cool.

Makes: about 35 cookies • Prep: 25 min • Cooking: 20–25 min • Level: 1

CARAWAY MOMENTS

Preheat the oven to 375°F (190°C/gas 5). • Set out two cookie sheets. • Mix the flour, baking powder, and salt in a medium bowl. • Beat the butter and ¼ cup (50 g) of sugar in a large bowl with an electric mixer at high speed until creamy. • Mix in the dry ingredients, followed by the milk to make a soft dough. • Form the dough into balls the size of walnuts and place 2 inches (5 cm) apart on the cookie sheets. • Sprinkle with the caraway seeds and remaining sugar. • Bake for 12–15 minutes, or until lightly browned. • Cool on the sheets until the cookies firm slightly. Transfer to racks to finish cooling.

Makes: about 20 cookies • Prep: 30 min • Cooking: 12–15 min • Level: 1

- 1 cup (150 g) all-purpose (plain) flour
- 1 teaspoon baking powder
- ⅛ teaspoon salt
- 7 tablespoons butter, softened
- ¼ cup (50 g) + 1 tablespoon sugar
- 1 teaspoon milk
- 1 teaspoon caraway seeds

Polenta biscotti

POLENTA BISCOTTI

Biscotti
- 1½ cups (225 g) all-purpose (plain) flour
- 1 teaspoon baking soda (bicarbonate of soda)
- ⅛ teaspoon salt
- 2 large eggs
- 1 cup (200 g) sugar
- 2 tablespoons anisette
- ⅓ cup (50 g) finely ground yellow cornmeal
- finely grated zest of 1 lemon
- 1 teaspoon coriander seeds
- ¼ cup (45 g) almonds

Glaze
- 1 egg yolk
- 2 tablespoons milk
- 2 tablespoons sugar

Biscotti: Preheat the oven to 300°F (150°C/gas 2). • Line two cookie sheets with parchment paper. • Mix the flour, baking soda, and salt in a medium bowl. • Beat the eggs and sugar in a large bowl until thick and creamy. • Beat in the anisette, cornmeal, lemon zest, and coriander seed. • Mix in the dry ingredients and nuts to form a sticky dough. • Form the dough into 3 flat logs, about 2½ inches (6 cm) wide. • Place on the prepared cookie sheets. • Glaze: Mix the egg yolk and milk in a small bowl and brush it over the logs. Sprinkle with sugar. • Bake for 25–30 minutes, or until firm to the touch. • Transfer to a cutting board to cool for 10 minutes. • Cut on the diagonal into ½-inch (1-cm) slices. • Arrange the slices cut-side up on three cookie sheets and bake for 7–10 minutes, or until golden and toasted. • Transfer to racks to cool.

Makes: about 40 biscotti • Prep: 25 min • Cooking: 35–40 min • Level: 2

ANISEED COOKIES

Mix the flour, sugar, and salt in a large bowl. • Gradually mix in the oil and wine. • Add the anisette and aniseeds and knead until smooth. • Refrigerate for 30 minutes. • Preheat the oven to 350°F (180°C/gas 4). • Butter and flour a cookie sheet. • Roll out the dough to ⅛ inch (3 mm) thick. • Use a 2-inch (5-cm) cookie cutter to cut out the cookies. • Continue cutting out cookies until all the dough is used. • Transfer the cookies to the prepared cookie sheet. Prick all over with a fork. • Brush with the beaten egg and sprinkle with the vanilla sugar. • Bake for 12–15 minutes, or until just golden. • Transfer to racks and let cool.

Makes: about 16 cookies • Prep: 40 min + 30 min to chill Cooking: 12–15 min • Level: 1

- 2 cups (300 g) all-purpose (plain) flour
- 1 cup (200 g) sugar
- ⅛ teaspoon salt
- ¼ cup (60 ml) extra-virgin olive oil
- ¼ cup (60 ml) Muscatel wine
- 2 tablespoons anisette
- 1 tablespoon aniseeds
- 1 large egg, lightly beaten
- 1 tablespoon vanilla sugar (see page 414)

WHOLE-WHEAT BRAN COOKIES

- 1 cup (150 g) all-purpose (plain) flour
- 1 cup (150 g) whole-wheat (wholemeal) flour
- 1 cup (150 g) bran flakes or sticks
- 1 teaspoon baking powder
- ⅛ teaspoon salt
- ½ cup (125 g) butter, softened
- ⅓ cup (70 g) sugar
- 1 large egg

Mix both flours, bran, baking powder, and salt in a large bowl. • Beat the butter and sugar in a large bowl with an electric mixer on medium speed until creamy. • Add the egg, beating until just blended. • Mix in the dry ingredients. • Press the dough into a disk, wrap in plastic wrap (cling film), and refrigerate for 30 minutes. • Preheat the oven to 350°F (180°C/gas 4). • Set out two cookie sheets. • Roll out the dough on a lightly floured surface. Use a 2-inch (5-cm) cookie cutter to cut out cookies. Gather the dough scraps, re-roll, and cut out cookies until all the dough is used. • Transfer to the cookie sheets, spacing well. • Bake for 12–15 minutes, or until lightly browned.

Makes: about 35 cookies • Prep: 20 min + 30 min to chill Cooking: 12–15 min • Level: 1

WHEAT GERM CRISPS

Preheat the oven to 350°F (180°C/gas 4). • Butter two cookie sheets. • Stir together the wheat germ, baking soda, cinnamon, nutmeg, and salt in a large bowl. Stir in the oats and sugar. • Melt the butter with the corn syrup and milk in a small saucepan over low heat. • Pour into the dry ingredients and mix until smooth. • Form into balls the size of walnuts and place 2 inches (5 cm) apart on the prepared cookie sheets, flattening slightly. • Bake for 12–15 minutes, or until golden brown. • Cool the cookies completely on the cookie sheets.

Makes: about 25 cookies • Prep: 15 min • Cooking: 12–15 min • Level: 1

- ¾ cup (125 g) wheat germ, toasted
- ½ teaspoon baking soda (bicarbonate of soda)
- 1 teaspoon ground cinnamon
- ½ teaspoon ground nutmeg
- ¼ teaspoon salt
- ½ cup (75 g) old-fashioned rolled oats
- ⅓ cup (70 g) sugar
- ⅓ cup (90 g) butter, cut up
- 1 tablespoon light corn (golden) syrup
- 1 tablespoon milk

Seed & Cereal Cookies

SESAME BARS

- 1⅓ cups (130 g) sesame seeds
- 1 tablespoon tahini (sesame seed paste)
- 1 cup (250 ml) honey
- 1 tablespoon finely grated lemon zest
- ¾ cup (75 g) coarsely chopped walnuts

Place the sesame seeds in a medium frying pan over high heat and stir until nicely roasted. Set aside. • Grease an 8-inch (20-cm) square baking pan with the tahini. • Place the honey in a medium saucepan over low heat and bring to a boil. • Stir in the lemon zest, sesame seeds, and nuts. Simmer for 1–2 minutes. • Spoon the honey mixture into the pan, spreading evenly with the back of the spoon. Set aside to cool then refrigerate until set. • Cut into small squares or bars to serve.

Makes: about 20 bars • Prep: 10 min + 2 hr to chill • Level: 1

SUNFLOWER BUTTER COOKIES

Preheat the oven to 350°F (180°C/gas 4). • Line two cookie sheets with parchment paper. • Mix the flour and salt in a medium bowl. • Beat the butter and both sugars until creamy. • Add the ground sunflower seeds and vanilla. • Mix in the dry ingredients and milk to form a stiff dough. • Divide the dough in half. Form into two 8-inch (20-cm) logs and roll in the finely chopped sunflower seeds. Wrap each in plastic wrap, and refrigerate for 30 minutes. • Slice the dough ½ inch (1 cm) thick and place 1 inch (2.5 cm) apart on the prepared cookie sheets. • Bake for 10–15 minutes, or until golden and the edges are firm. • Cool on the sheet until the cookies firm slightly. • Transfer to racks and let cool completely. Dust with the confectioners' sugar.

Makes: about 32 cookies • Prep: 50 min + 30 min to chill
Cooking: 10–15 min • Level: 2

- 1⅔ cups (250 g) all-purpose (plain) flour
- ⅛ teaspoon salt
- ¾ cup (180 g) butter, softened
- ¼ cup (50 g) granulated sugar
- 2 tablespoons vanilla sugar (see page 414)
- 1 cup (150 g) ground sunflower seeds
- ½ teaspoon vanilla extract (essence)
- 2 tablespoons milk
- 4 tablespoons finely chopped sunflower seeds
- ⅓ cup (50 g) confectioners' (icing) sugar

Sesame bars

Sesame snaps

OPEN SESAME COOKIES

- ⅓ cup (60 g) golden raisins (sultanas)
- ½ cup (125 ml) brandy
- 1 cup (150 g) all-purpose (plain) flour
- 1 cup (150 g) cornstarch (cornflour)
- ⅔ cup (140 g) sugar
- 1 teaspoon baking powder
- ¼ teaspoon ground cinnamon
- ¼ teaspoon salt
- 2 tablespoons extra-virgin olive oil
- ⅔ cup (150 g) butter, softened
- 1¼ cups (125 g) sesame seeds, toasted
- ½ cup (125 ml) water or more as needed

Plump the raisins in the brandy in a small bowl for 15 minutes. Drain and pat dry with paper towels. • Mix the flour, cornstarch, sugar, baking powder, cinnamon, and salt in a large bowl. • Stir in the oil, butter, sesame seeds, and raisins. • Add enough water to form a smooth dough. • Form the dough into a log 1 inch (2.5 cm) in diameter, wrap in plastic wrap (cling film), and refrigerate for 30 minutes. • Preheat the oven to 350°F (180°C/gas 4). • Butter two cookie sheets. • Slice the dough ½ inch (1 cm) thick and place 1 inch (2.5 cm) apart on the prepared cookie sheets. • Bake for 15–20 minutes, or until golden. • Transfer to racks and let cool completely.

Makes: about 35 cookies • Prep: 20 min + 30 min to chill
Cooking: 15–20 min • Level: 1

SESAME SNAPS

Preheat the oven to 400°F (200°C/gas 6). • Butter and flour two cookie sheets. • Beat the butter, sugar, and lemon zest in a large bowl with an electric mixer at high speed until pale and creamy. • With mixer at low speed, gradually beat in the flour. • Place the egg white, honey, and sesame seeds in a small bowl and mix well. The mixture should be dense and dry. • Scoop out rounded tablespoons of dough and shape into balls the size of walnuts. • Place over the sesame mixture and press down with your fingers until 3 inches (8 cm) in diameter. • Place the cookies, sesame seed-side up, on the sheet. • Bake for 10–15 minutes, or until golden brown. • Let cool completely.

Makes: about 30 cookies • Prep: 10 min • Cooking: 10–15 min • Level: 1

- 1 cup (250 g) butter
- 1 cup (200 g) sugar
- 1 tablespoon finely grated lemon zest
- 2 cups (300 g) all-purpose (plain) flour
- 1 large egg white, lightly beaten
- 2 tablespoons honey
- 1⅓ cups (130 g) sesame seeds

Coconut oatmeal cookies

COCONUT OATMEAL COOKIES

- 1 cup (150 g) all-purpose (plain) flour
- ½ teaspoon baking soda (bicarbonate of soda)
- ⅛ teaspoon salt
- 1 cup (125 g) unsweetened shredded (desiccated) coconut
- 1 cup (150 g) old-fashioned rolled oats
- ½ cup (125 g) butter, cut up
- ¾ cup (150 g) sugar
- 2 tablespoons light corn syrup (golden) syrup

Preheat the oven to 350°F (180°C/gas 4). • Butter two cookie sheets. • Mix the flour, baking soda, and salt in a large bowl. Stir in the coconut and oats. • Melt the butter with the sugar and corn syrup in a small saucepan over medium heat. • Mix in the dry ingredients until well blended. • Roll into balls the size of walnuts and place 1 inch (2.5 cm) apart on the prepared cookie sheets, flattening slightly with a fork. • Bake for 15–20 minutes, or until golden brown. • Cool on the sheets until the cookies firm slightly. Transfer to racks to cool.

Makes: about 25 cookies • Prep: 20 min • Cooking: 15–20 min • Level: 1

LEMON CORN FLAKE COOKIES

Mix the flour, baking powder, and salt in a medium bowl. • Beat the butter and sugar in a large bowl with an electric mixer on medium speed until creamy. • Add the egg, beating until just blended. • Stir in the cornflakes and lemon zest. • Mix in the dry ingredients to form a stiff dough. • Form into a 12 x 2-inch (30 x 5-cm) log, wrap in plastic wrap (cling film), and refrigerate for at least 30 minutes. • Preheat the oven to 425°F (220°C/gas 7). • Butter three cookie sheets. • Slice the dough ¼ inch (5 mm) thick and place 1 inch (2.5 cm) apart on the prepared cookie sheets. • Bake for 8–10 minutes, or until just golden. • Transfer to racks and let cool completely.

Makes: about 48 cookies • Prep: 40 min + 30 min to chill Cooking: 8–10 min • Level: 1

- 1½ cups (225 g) all-purpose (plain) flour
- 1 teaspoon baking powder
- ⅛ teaspoon salt
- ½ cup (125 g) butter, softened
- ¾ cup (150 g) sugar
- 1 large egg
- 2 cups (300 g) corn flakes, lightly crushed
- 2 teaspoons finely grated lemon zest

LIGHT GRANOLA COOKIES

- 2 large egg whites
- ⅛ teaspoon salt
- ¾ cup (150 g) granulated sugar
- 1 teaspoon vanilla sugar (see page 414)
- 1 tablespoon all-purpose (plain) flour
- 2 teaspoons cornstarch (cornflour)
- ½ cup (75 g) fine oat flakes or wheat flakes
- finely chopped dates, nuts, and dried fruit (muesli or granola)

Preheat the oven to 275°F (140°C/gas 1). • Line two cookie sheets with parchment or rice paper. • Beat the egg whites and salt in a large bowl with an electric mixer at medium speed until frothy. With mixer at high speed, gradually add both sugars, beating until stiff, glossy peaks form. • Fold in the flour, cornstarch, and oat flakes. • Fit a pastry bag with an 1-inch (2.5-cm) tip. Fill the pastry bag, twist the opening tightly closed, and squeeze out small rounds spacing them 1 inch (2.5 cm) apart on the prepared cookie sheets. • Sprinkle with the dates, nuts, and dried fruit. • Bake for 20–25 minutes, or until lightly golden. • Transfer on the parchment paper to racks and let cool completely.

Makes: about 25 cookies • Prep: 15 min • Cooking: 20–25 min • Level: 1

CORNMEAL AND MAPLE SYRUP BISCOTTI

Preheat the oven to 350°F (180°C/gas 4). • Butter two cookie sheets. • Mix the flour, cornmeal, baking powder, and salt in a medium bowl. • Beat the eggs, egg yolk, and vanilla in a large bowl until frothy. • Mix in the dry ingredients, pecans, and maple syrup. • Form into four logs about 1 inch (2.5 cm) in diameter and place 2 inches (5 cm) apart on the prepared cookie sheets, flattening them slightly. • Bake for 25–30 minutes, or until firm to the touch. • Transfer to a cutting board to cool for 15 minutes. • Reduce the oven temperature to 300°F (150°C/gas 2). • Cut on the diagonal into 1-inch (2.5-cm) slices. • Arrange the slices cut-side down on the cookie sheets and bake for 15–20 minutes, or until golden and toasted. • Transfer to racks to cool.

Makes: about 35 biscotti • Prep: 40 min • Cooking: 40–45 min • Level: 2

- 1⅔ cups (250 g) bread flour
- ⅔ cup (100 g) finely ground cornmeal
- 1 teaspoon baking powder
- ¼ teaspoon salt
- 2 large eggs + 1 large egg yolk
- ½ teaspoon vanilla extract (essence)
- 1 cup (100 g) coarsely chopped pecans
- ½ cup (125 ml) pure maple syrup

BARS & BROWNIES

Bar cookies and brownies are especially quick and easy to make because the batter is mixed and then poured or pressed into a pan and baked in just one batch. Most are cooled in the pan, then sometimes covered with frosting, before being cut into squares or bars. Rich chocolate brownies—some with an almost fudgelike consistency—were invented in America more than one hundred years ago. There are many variations on the basic recipe, and everyone has their own idea on what the perfect brownie should taste like; some are light and cakey, others are rich and velvety. We have included recipes for both kinds. Beyond brownies, bar cookies come in a huge variety of flavors and textures. We have included some classics like Caramel squares (see page 216) as well as some more exotic types, such as Pineapple and ginger squares (see page 240) and Muesli bars (see page 236).

Café squares (see page 214)

Bars & Brownies

CHOCOLATE RASPBERRY SQUARES

Base
- 1 cup (150 g) all-purpose (plain) flour
- 2 tablespoons unsweetened cocoa powder
- 1/4 teaspoon salt
- 1/2 cup (125 g) butter, softened
- 1/2 cup (100 g) sugar
- 1/2 teaspoon vanilla extract (essence)

Filling
- 1/2 cup (160 g) raspberry preserves (jam)
- 1 tablespoon raspberry liqueur
- 1 cup (180 g) semisweet (dark) chocolate chips
- 1 1/2 cups (150 g) finely ground almonds
- 4 large egg whites
- 1 cup (200 g) sugar
- 1/2 teaspoon almond extract (essence)
- 2 tablespoons flaked almonds

Preheat the oven to 325°F (170°C/gas 3). • Line a 13 x 9-inch (33 x 23-cm) baking pan with aluminum foil, letting the edges overhang. • Base: Mix the flour, cocoa, and salt in a medium bowl. • Beat the butter, sugar, and vanilla in a large bowl with an electric mixer on medium speed until creamy. • Mix in the dry ingredients. • Press the mixture into the prepared pan in an even layer. Prick all over with a fork. • Bake until firm to the touch, 15–20 minutes. • Increase the oven temperature to 375°F (190°C/gas 5). • Filling: Mix the preserves and liqueur in a bowl and spread over the base. Sprinkle with the chocolate chips. • Process the finely ground almonds, egg whites, sugar, and almond extract in a food processor until well blended. • Spread over the preserves and sprinkle with the flaked almonds. • Bake until lightly browned, 20–25 minutes. • Using the foil as handles, lift onto a rack and let cool. • Remove the foil and cut into squares.

Makes: about 30 squares • Prep: 25 min • Cooking: 25–35 min • Level : 1

NUTTY COFFEE SQUARES

Preheat the oven to 350°F (180°C/gas 4). • Butter an 8-inch (20-cm) square baking pan. • Place the almonds in a large bowl and pour in enough boiling water to cover completely. Let stand for 5 minutes. • Drain the nuts and place on a kitchen towel. Gently rub to remove the skins. Pick out the skins and discard. • Finely chop the almonds. • Bring the water, the sugar, and the coffee to a boil in a small saucepan until the sugar and coffee have dissolved completely. • Stir in the almonds. • Remove from the heat and set aside. • Beat the egg whites and salt in a large bowl with an electric mixer at high speed until stiff peaks form. • Use a large rubber spatula to fold in the almond mixture. • Pour the batter into the prepared pan. • Bake for 35–40 minutes, or until a toothpick inserted into the center comes out clean. • Cool completely before cutting into squares.

Makes: about 20 squares • Prep: 30 min • Cooking: 35–40 min • Level: 1

- 1 1/3 cups (200 g) whole almonds
- 2 tablespoons water
- 3/4 cup (150 g) sugar
- 2 teaspoons instant coffee granules
- 2 large egg whites
- 1/8 teaspoon salt

CAFÉ SQUARES

- 1 1/2 cups (225 g) all-purpose (plain) flour
- 2 tablespoons unsweetened cocoa powder
- 1 teaspoon baking powder
- 1/8 teaspoon salt
- 2 tablespoons very strong hot coffee
- 1 cup (250 g) butter
- 1 cup (200 g) sugar
- 4 large eggs
- 2 cups (500 ml) rich choco-late frosting, made with milk chocolate (see page 414)

Preheat the oven to 350°F (180°C/gas 4). • Butter a 10-inch (25-cm) baking pan. • Mix the flour, cocoa, baking powder, and salt in a medium bowl. • Beat the butter and sugar in a large bowl with an electric mixer at high speed until creamy. • Beat in the eggs one at a time. • With mixer on low, add the dry ingredients and coffee. • Spoon the batter into the pan. • Bake until almost firm to the touch 25–35 minutes. • Cool completely in the pan. • Spread with the frosting and cut into squares.

Makes: about 30 squares • Prep: 30 minutes Cooking: 25–35 minutes • Level : 1

FROSTED DATE AND NUT SQUARE

Preheat the oven to 350°F (180°C/gas 4). • Butter a jelly-roll pan. • Mix the flour, baking powder, and salt in a medium bowl. • Beat the butter and sugar in a large bowl with an electric mixer on medium speed until creamy. • Add the egg, beating until just blended. • Mix in the dry ingredients, dates, and walnuts. • Spoon the mixture into the prepared pan. • Bake until firm to the touch 25–30 minutes. • Cool completely in the pan. • Melt the chocolate in a double boiler over barely simmering water. • Spread over the top.

Makes: about 30 squares • Prep: 30 min • Cooking: 25–35 min • Level : 1

- 1 cup (150 g) all-purpose (plain) flour
- 1 teaspoon baking powder
- 1/4 teaspoon salt
- 1/2 cup (125 g) butter, softened
- 3/4 cup (150 g) sugar
- 1 large egg
- 2 1/2 cups (250 g) finely chopped pitted dates
- 1 1/3 cups (130 g) finely chopped walnuts
- 8 oz (250 g) semisweet (dark) chocolate, coarsely chopped

Bars & Brownies

CARAMEL SQUARES

Base
- 2 cups (300 g) all-purpose (plain) flour
- ⅛ teaspoon salt
- ⅔ cup (180 g) butter, softened
- ⅓ cup (70 g) sugar
- 2 tablespoons water + more as needed

Topping
- ½ cup (125 g) butter, cut up
- 2 tablespoons light molasses (treacle)
- ⅔ cup (140 g) granulated sugar
- 1 can (14 oz/400 ml) sweetened condensed milk
- 1 quantity rich chocolate frosting (see page 414)

Base: Preheat the oven to 350°F (180°C/ gas 4). • Butter a 10-inch (25-cm) square baking pan. • Mix the flour and salt in a medium bowl. • Beat the butter and sugar in a large bowl with an electric mixer on medium speed until creamy. • Mix in the dry ingredients and enough water to form a soft dough. Transfer to the prepared pan and press into an even layer. Prick all over with a fork. • Bake until just golden, 20–25 minutes. • Cool completely in the pan. • Topping: Melt the butter with the molasses, sugar, and condensed milk in a medium saucepan over low heat. Bring the mixture to a boil, stirring constantly. Simmer until it until darkens and thickens, 10 minutes. • Spread the topping over the base. Let cool completely. • Melt the chocolate in a double boiler over barely simmering water. Spread the chocolate evenly over the topping and let stand until set, 30 minutes. • Cut into squares.

Makes: about 30 squares • Prep: 20 min + 1 hr to set
Cooking: 20–25 min • Level: 2

BITTERSWEET CARAMEL SQUARES

Preheat the oven to 325°F (170°C/gas 3). • Line a 9-inch (23-cm) square baking pan with aluminum foil. • Base: Mix the flour, baking powder, and salt in a large bowl. • Beat the butter and sugar in a large bowl with an electric mixer on medium speed until creamy. • Mix in the dry ingredients. • Spread the mixture evenly in the prepared pan. • Bake for 10–15 minutes, or until golden brown. • Topping: Melt the butter with the sugar, corn syrup, and condensed milk in a medium saucepan over low heat, stirring constantly. Bring to a boil and let boil for 5 minutes. Remove from the heat and let cool slightly. • Spread the caramel topping evenly over the cookie base. • Melt the chocolate in a double boiler over barely simmering water. Pour the chocolate over the caramel topping and let stand for 30 minutes until set. • Cut into squares.

Makes: about 30 squares • Prep: 20 min + 30 min to set
Cooking: 10–15 min • Level: 2

Base
- 1 cup (150 g) all-purpose (plain) flour
- 1 teaspoon baking powder
- ⅛ teaspoon salt
- ½ cup (125 g) butter, softened
- ¼ cup (50 g) sugar

Topping
- ½ cup (125 g) butter
- ½ cup (100 g) sugar
- 2 tablespoons light corn syrup (golden) syrup
- 1 can (14 oz/400 g) sweetened condensed milk
- 8 oz (250 g) semisweet (dark) chocolate, coarsely chopped

WHOLE-WHEAT SODA BARS

- 2 cups (300 g) whole-wheat (wholemeal) flour
- 1 tablespoon ground ginger
- 1½ teaspoons cream of tartar
- ¾ teaspoon baking soda (bicarbonate of soda)
- ⅛ teaspoon salt
- 1¼ cups (310 g) butter, cut up
- ⅓ cup (50 g) old-fashioned rolled oats
- 1½ cups (300 g) firmly packed light brown sugar

Preheat the oven to 325°F (170°C/gas 3). • Butter a 13 x 9-inch (33 x 23-cm) baking pan. • Mix the flour, ginger, cream of tartar, baking soda, and salt in a large bowl. • Use a pastry blender to cut in the butter until the mixture resembles coarse crumbs. • Stir in the oats and brown sugar. • Firmly press the mixture into the prepared pan to form a smooth, even layer. • Bake for 20–30 minutes, or until lightly browned. • Cool completely before cutting into bars.

Makes: about 30 bars • Prep: 20 min • Cooking: 20–30 min
Level: 1

CREAM CHEESE BARS

Preheat the oven to 375°F (190°C (gas 5). • Butter a 9-inch (23-cm) square baking pan. • Base: Mix the graham cracker crumbs and butter in a large bowl until well blended. • Firmly press the mixture into the prepared pan to form a smooth, even layer. • Topping: Beat the cream cheese and sugar in a large bowl with an electric mixer at low speed until smooth. • Beat in the lemon curd, cornstarch, and egg. • Spoon the topping over the cookie base. • Bake for 25–30 minutes, or until firm to the touch. • Cool completely before cutting into bars.

Makes: about 20 bars • Prep: 30 min • Cooking: 25–30 min
Level: 1

Base
- 1¼ cups (150 g) graham cracker crumbs (crushed digestive biscuits)
- ⅓ cup (90 g) butter, melted

Topping
- 1 cup (250 g) cream cheese, softened
- ½ cup (100 g) sugar
- 3 tablespoons lemon curd (see page 414)
- 3 tablespoons cornstarch (cornflour)
- 1 large egg

Bars & Brownies

CHOCOLATE MINT SQUARES

Base
- 2/3 cup (100 g) all-purpose (plain) flour
- 2 tablespoons unsweetened cocoa powder
- 1 teaspoon baking powder
- 1/4 teaspoon salt
- 1/3 cup (70 g) sugar
- 2 tablespoons butter
- 1 large egg, lightly beaten with 1/3 cup (90 ml) water

Filling
- 2 1/4 cups (330 g) confectioners' (icing) sugar
- 1 tablespoon mint liqueur
- 1–2 tablespoons milk

Frosting
- 4 oz (125 g) semisweet (dark) chocolate, coarsely chopped
- 1/3 cup (90 g) butter

Preheat the oven to 350°F (180°C/gas 4). • Butter an 8-inch (20-cm) square baking pan. • Base: Mix the flour, cocoa, baking powder, and salt in a large bowl. Stir in the sugar. • Cut in the butter until the mixture resembles fine crumbs. • Mix in the egg mixture. • Firmly press the mixture into the prepared pan to form a smooth layer. • Bake for 15–20 minutes, or until firm to the touch. • Filling: Mix the confectioners' sugar and mint liqueur until well blended. • Stir in enough milk to achieve a spreadable consistency. • Spread the peppermint mixture over the base. • Frosting: Melt the chocolate and butter over barely simmering water. • Pour the frosting over the peppermint layer. Make a swirling pattern with a fork. • Let stand for 30 minutes until set. • Cut into squares.

Makes: about 20 squares • Prep: 20 min + 30 min to set
Cooking: 15–20 min • Level: 1

IRISH MINT BARS

Preheat the oven to 350°F (180°C/gas 4). • Butter an 8-inch (20-cm) square baking pan. • Base: Mix the flour, coconut, sugar, cocoa, baking powder, and salt in a large bowl. • Use a pastry blender to cut in the butter until the mixture resembles fine crumbs. • Press the mixture evenly into the pan. • Bake for 25–30 minutes, or until lightly browned. • Cool completely in the pan. • Mint Topping: Mix the confectioners' sugar, mint extract, and green food coloring in a small bowl. Add enough water to make a spreadable paste. • Spread the topping over the crispy base. • Cut into bars.

Makes: about 15 bars • Prep: 25 min • Cooking: 25–30 min
Level: 1

Base
- 1 cup (150 g) all-purpose (plain) flour
- 1 cup (125 g) shredded (desiccated) coconut
- 1/4 cup (50 g) granulated sugar
- 1 tablespoon unsweetened cocoa powder
- 1/2 teaspoon baking powder
- 1/8 teaspoon salt
- 1/2 cup (125 g) butter, cut up

Mint Topping
- 1 2/3 cups (250 g) confectioners' (icing) sugar
- 1/2 teaspoon mint extract (essence)
- 1/2 teaspoon green food coloring
- 1/4 cup (60 ml) hot water + more, as needed

Chocolate mint squares

Chocolate squares

CHOCOLATE SQUARES

- 4 large egg whites
- 1¼ cups (250 g) sugar
- 3 cups (300 g) finely ground almonds
- 2 oz (60 g) bittersweet (dark) chocolate, finely grated
- 1 teaspoon vanilla extract (essence)
- 1 quantity rich chocolate frosting, made with milk chocolate (see page 414) (optional)

Preheat the oven to 350°F (180°C/gas 4). • Butter a 13 x 9-inch (33 x 23-cm) baking pan. • Beat 3 of the egg whites in a large bowl with an electric mixer at medium speed until soft peaks form. • With mixer at high speed, gradually add 1 cup (200 g) of sugar, beating until stiff, glossy peaks form. • Use a large rubber spatula to fold in the almonds, chocolate, and vanilla. • Spread the mixture evenly in the prepared pan. • Beat the remaining egg white and remaining sugar until frothy. Brush over the top. • Bake for 20–25 minutes, or until lightly browned. • Cool completely in the pan. If desired, spread with the frosting. Make a swirled pattern with a fork. Cut into squares.

Makes: about 25 squares • Prep: 30 min • Cooking: 20–25 min • Level: 1

MUD BARS

Preheat the oven to 300°F (150°C/gas 2). • Butter and flour a 10-inch (25-cm) springform pan. • Beat the egg whites with an electric mixer at medium speed until frothy. • With mixer at high speed, gradually add the brown sugar, beating until stiff peaks form. • Melt the butter in a medium saucepan over low heat. Remove from the heat and stir in the chocolate until melted. • Use a large rubber spatula to gradually fold the liqueur, vanilla, coffee, and chocolate mixture into the beaten whites. • Spoon the batter into the prepared pan. • Bake until a toothpick inserted into the center comes out clean, about 35 minutes. • Cool completely in the pan on a rack. • Refrigerate until set, about 3 hours. Cut into bars.

Makes: about 24 bars • Prep: 20 min + 3 hours to freeze • Cooking: 35 minutes • Level: 1

- 8 large egg whites
- 1 cup (200 g) firmly packed brown sugar
- 1 cup (250 g) butter
- 8 oz (250 g) bittersweet (dark) chocolate, coarsely chopped
- 3 tablespoons coffee liqueur
- 1 tablespoon vanilla extract (essence)
- 1 tablespoon strong, cold black coffee

Bars & Brownies

RICH CHOCOLATE BROWNIES

- ½ cup (75 g) all-purpose (plain) flour
- ½ teaspoon baking powder
- ⅛ teaspoon salt
- 6 oz (180 g) bittersweet (dark) chocolate, coarsely chopped
- 1½ cups (375 g) butter, cut up
- 5 large eggs
- 2¼ cups (440 g) firmly packed light brown sugar
- 1 teaspoon vanilla extract (essence)

Preheat the oven to 325°F (170°C/gas 3). • Butter and flour a 13 x 9-inch (33 x 23-cm) baking pan. • Mix the flour, baking powder, and salt in a large bowl. • Melt the chocolate and butter in a double boiler over barely simmering water. Remove from the heat and let cool. • Beat the eggs, brown sugar, and vanilla in a large bowl with an electric mixer at high speed until pale and thick. • Use a large rubber spatula to fold in the chocolate mixture, followed by the dry ingredients. • Pour the batter into the prepared pan. • Bake for 35–40 minutes, or until dry on top and almost firm to the touch. Do not overbake. • Cool completely before cutting into squares.

Makes: about 30 brownies • Prep: 35 min • Cooking:35–40 min • Level: 1

PECAN BROWNIES

Preheat the oven to 350°F (180°C/gas 4). • Line a 13 x 9-inch (33 x 23-cm) baking pan with aluminum foil, letting the edges overhang. • Mix the flour, baking powder, and salt in a medium bowl. • Melt the butter and chocolate in a double boiler over barely simmering water. • Remove from the heat and stir in the sugar. • Add the eggs, beating until just blended. • Mix in the dry ingredients, vanilla, and pecans. • Pour the batter into the prepared pan. • Bake for 25–30 minutes, or until dry on top and almost firm to the touch. Do not overbake. • Cool completely in the pan. • Using the foil as handles, lift onto a cutting board. Peel off the foil. Cut into squares.

Makes: about 30 brownies • Prep: 20 min • Cooking: 25–35 min Level: 1

- 3 cups (450 g) all-purpose (plain) flour
- 2 teaspoons baking powder
- ¼ teaspoon salt
- ½ cup (125 g) butter, cut up
- 4 oz (125 g) semisweet (dark) chocolate, coarsely chopped
- 2 cups (400 g) sugar
- 4 large eggs, lightly beaten
- 1 teaspoon vanilla extract (essence)
- ¾ cup (125 g) coarsely chopped pecans

Rich chocolate brownies

Marbled brownies

MARBLED BROWNIES

Base
- 1 cup (250 g) butter
- 5 oz (150 g) semisweet (dark) chocolate, chopped
- 2½ cups (500 g) sugar
- 3 large eggs
- 1 cup (150 g) all-purpose (plain) flour
- 1¼ cups (125 g) coarsely chopped walnuts
- 1 teaspoon vanilla extract (essence)
- ½ teaspoon salt

Topping
- 8 oz (250 g) cream cheese, softened
- ⅔ cup (140 g) sugar
- 1 large egg
- 1 teaspoon vanilla extract (essence)

Preheat the oven to 350°F (180°C/gas 4). • Butter a 13 x 9-inch (33 x 23-cm) baking pan. • Base: Melt the butter and chocolate in a double boiler over barely simmering water. • Remove from the heat and add the sugar and eggs, beating until just blended. • Mix in the flour, walnuts, vanilla, and salt. • Spoon the mixture into the prepared pan. • Topping: Beat the cream cheese, sugar, egg, and vanilla in a large bowl with an electric mixer on medium speed until smooth. • Spoon the mixture over the chocolate base. • Use a knife to swirl the topping. • Bake for 40–45 minutes, or until almost firm to the touch. • Cool completely before cutting into bars.

Makes: about 30 brownies • Prep: 30 min • Cooking: 35–40 min • Level: 2

MARBLED CHOCOLATE SQUARES

Preheat the oven to 350°F (180°C/gas 4). • Butter a 9-inch (23-cm) baking pan. • Cream Cheese Mixture: Beat the cream cheese and sugar in a large bowl until creamy. • Beat in the orange zest and juice and cornstarch. Add the egg. • Chocolate Mixture: Melt the chocolate and butter in a double boiler over barely simmering water. Set aside to cool. • Stir in the sugar and vanilla. • Add the beaten egg mixture, followed by the flour. • Pour the chocolate mixture into the prepared pan. • Drop tablespoons of the cream cheese mixture over the chocolate base. • Swirl the mixtures together to create a marbled effect. • Bake for 25–30 minutes, or until slightly risen around the edges and set in the center. • Cool before cutting into squares.

Makes: about 20 squares • Prep: 25 min • Cooking: 25–30 Level: 2

Cream Cheese Mixture
- 8 oz (250 ml) cream cheese, softened
- ¼ cup (50 g) granulated sugar
- 2 tablespoons finely grated orange zest
- 3 tablespoons freshly squeezed orange juice
- 1 teaspoon cornstarch (cornflour)

Chocolate Mixture
- 8 oz (250 g) semisweet (dark) chocolate, coarsely chopped
- ¼ cup (60 g) butter
- ¾ cup (150 g) sugar
- 2 teaspoon vanilla extract (essence)
- 2 large eggs, lightly beaten with 2 tablespoons cold water
- ½ cup (75 g) all-purpose (plain) flour

Bars & Brownies

CHOCOLATE FRUIT AND NUT SQUARES

- 1½ cups (225 g) self-rising flour
- ½ teaspoon ground cinnamon
- ¼ teaspoon ground cloves
- ¼ teaspoon ground cardamom
- ¼ teaspoon salt
- ½ cup (90 g) raisins
- ½ cup (90 g) golden raisins (sultanas
- ½ cup (125 ml) dark rum mixed with 1 tablespoon cold water
- ¾ cup (75 g) candied cherries, halved
- 1 cup (100 g) chopped walnuts
- 1 cup (100 g) chopped almonds
- 3 oz (90 g) semisweet (dark) chocolate, chopped
- ¾ cup (180 g) butter
- 1 cup (200 g) firmly packed light brown sugar
- finely grated zest of 1 orange
- 3 large eggs, lightly beaten
- 3 tablespoons freshly squeezed orange juice

Preheat the oven to 325°F (170°C/gas 3).
• Butter an 11 x 7-inch (28 x 18-cm) baking pan. Line with parchment paper. • Mix the flour, cinnamon, cloves, cardamom, and salt in a large bowl. • Bring the dark raisins, golden raisins, and rum mixture to a boil in a medium saucepan. Remove from the heat and set aside for 15 minutes. • Mix the raisin mixture, cherries, walnuts, and almonds in a large bowl. Mix in 1 tablespoon of the dry ingredients and stir until well coated. • Melt the chocolate in a double boiler over barely simmering water. • Beat the butter and brown sugar in a large bowl with an electric mixer on medium speed until creamy. • Add the orange zest and melted chocolate. • Add the eggs, beating until just blended, adding 1 tablespoon of the dry ingredients. • Stir in the remaining dry ingredients, followed by the raisin mixture and orange juice. • Spoon the batter into the prepared pan. • Bake until a toothpick inserted into the center comes out clean, 60–70 minutes. • Cool completely then cut into squares.

Makes: about 30 squares • Prep: 30 min • Cooking: 60–70 min Level: 2

CHOCOLATE NUT SQUARES

Preheat the oven to 400°F (200°C/gas 6).
• Butter a 9-inch (23-cm) square baking pan.
• Plump the raisins in a small bowl of hot water for 10 minutes. • Drain well and pat dry with paper towels. • Mix the flour, baking powder, and salt in a medium bowl.
• Beat the eggs and sugar in a large bowl with an electric mixer at high speed until pale and thick. • Add the vanilla and lemon zest. • Mix in the dry ingredients, followed by the milk, rum, raisins, hazelnuts, walnuts, and chocolate. • Pour the mixture into the prepared pan. • Bake for 15–20 minutes, or until a toothpick inserted into the center comes out clean. • Cool completely in the pan. • Spread with the frosting and cut into bars.

Makes: about 20 squares • Prep: 25 min + 10 min to plump the raisins • Cooking: 15–20 min Level: 1

- ½ cup (90 g) golden raisins (sultanas
- 1¼ cups (180 g) whole-wheat (wholemeal) flour
- 1 teaspoon baking powder
- ⅛ teaspoon salt
- 2 large eggs
- ½ cup (100 g) sugar
- ¼ teaspoon vanilla extract (essence)
- finely grated zest of ½ lemon
- 2 tablespoons milk
- 1 tablespoon dark rum
- ¾ cup (75 g) finely chopped hazelnuts
- ½ cup (50 g) chopped walnuts
- 3 oz (90 g) bittersweet (dark) chocolate, finely grated
- 1 quantity chocolate frosting (see page 414)

MERINGUE-TOPPED SQUARES

- ⅔ cup (100 g) all-purpose (plain) flour
- ½ cup (75 g) confectioners' (icing) sugar
- ⅛ teaspoon salt
- ⅓ cup (90 g) butter, softened
- 1 large egg + 2 large egg whites

Preheat the oven to 350°F (190°C/gas 5).
• Butter a 10-inch (25-cm) square baking pan. • Mix the flour, confectioners' sugar, and salt in a large bowl. • Beat in the butter and whole egg until well blended. • Press the mixture into the pan in an even layer.
• Bake for 10 minutes. • Reduce the oven temperature to 300°F (150°C/gas 2). • Warm the preserves in a small saucepan over low heat until liquid. • Spread the preserves over

the base. • Beat the egg whites in a large bowl until soft peaks form. • Gradually add the superfine sugar and cinnamon, beating until stiff, glossy peaks form. • Spread the meringue over the preserves. • Bake until the meringue is lightly browned, 20–25 minutes. • Cool in the pan for 15 minutes.
• Cut into squares and let cool.

Makes: about 25 squares • Prep: 30 min • Cooking: 30–35 min • Level: 1

- ⅔ cup (220 g) raspberry preserves (jam)
- ½ cup (100 g) superfine (caster) sugar
- 1 teaspoon ground cinnamon

Bars & Brownies

HONEY AND WALNUT BROWNIES

- 1 cup (150 g) all-purpose (plain) flour
- ½ teaspoon baking powder
- ⅛ teaspoon salt
- 6 oz (180 g) semisweet (dark) chocolate, coarsely chopped
- ½ cup (125 g) butter, cut up
- ½ cup (100 g) sugar
- ½ cup (125 ml) honey
- 2 large eggs
- 1 cup (100 g) finely chopped walnuts

Preheat the oven to 350°F (180°C/gas 4). • Butter a 9-inch (23-cm) square baking pan. • Mix the flour, baking powder, and salt in a medium bowl. • Melt the chocolate with the butter in a double boiler over barely simmering water. Transfer the chocolate mixture to a large bowl and let cool for 5 minutes. • Beat in the sugar and honey. • Add the eggs, beating until just blended. • Mix in the dry ingredients and walnuts. • Spoon the mixture evenly into the prepared pan. • Bake for 30–35 minutes, or until dry on top and almost firm to the touch. Do not overbake. • Cool completely before cutting into bars.

Makes: about 25 brownies • Prep: 20 min • Cooking: 30–35 min • Level: 1

JAFFA SQUARES

Preheat the oven to 350°F (180°C/gas 4). • Butter an 11 x 7-inch (28 x 18-cm) baking pan. • Mix the flour, cocoa, baking powder, and salt in a medium bowl. • Beat the butter and brown sugar in a large bowl with an electric mixer on medium speed until creamy. • Add the eggs and orange zest, beating until just blended. • Mix in the dry ingredients, orange juice, and dates. • Pour the mixture into the prepared pan. • Bake for 30–35 minutes, or until a toothpick inserted into the center comes out clean. • Cool completely in the pan. • Cut into bars.

Makes: about 20 squares • Prep: 20 min • Cooking: 30–35 min • Level: 1

- 1½ cups (225 g) all-purpose (plain) flour
- 3 tablespoons unsweetened cocoa powder
- 2 teaspoons baking powder
- ¼ teaspoon salt
- ½ cup (125 g) butter, softened
- ¾ cup (150 g) firmly packed light brown sugar
- 3 large eggs
- 1 tablespoon finely grated orange zest
- ¾ cup (180 ml) freshly squeezed orange juice
- 1 cup (100 g) finely chopped pitted dates

CHEWY ROLLED OAT SQUARES

- 1 cup (150 g) all-purpose (plain) flour
- ¼ teaspoon salt
- ½ cup (125 g) butter, softened
- ½ cup (100 g) firmly packed dark brown sugar
- 2½ cups (375 g) old-fashioned rolled oats
- ½ cup (125 ml) store-bought cranberry sauce
- ½ cup (50 g) coarsely chopped walnuts

Preheat the oven to 350°F (180°C/gas 4). • Line an 8-inch (20-cm) baking pan with aluminum foil, letting the edges overhang. • Mix the flour and salt in a medium bowl. • Beat the butter and brown sugar with an electric mixer on medium speed until creamy. • Mix in the dry ingredients and oats. • Firmly press two-thirds of the mixture into the pan in an even layer. • Mix the cranberry sauce and walnuts in a small bowl and spread over the base. • Spoon the remaining oat mixture over the top, pressing down gently. • Bake until lightly browned, 15–20 minutes. • Cool completely in the pan. • Peel off the foil. Cut into squares.

Makes: about 20 squares • Prep: 20 min • Cooking: 15–20 min • Level: 1

WALNUT BROWNIES

Preheat the oven to 325°F (170°C/gas 3). • Butter a 9-inch (23-cm) square baking pan. • Melt the butter and chocolate in a double boiler over barely simmering water, mixing until glossy and smooth. • Remove from the heat and beat in the eggs. • Add the sugar, flour, baking powder, salt, and nuts and beat until well mixed. • Spoon the batter into the prepared pan. • Bake for about 35 minutes, or until a toothpick inserted in the center comes out clean. • Remove from the oven and let cool. • Let cool before cutting into squares.

Makes: 24 brownies • Prep: 15 min • Cooking: 35 min Level: 1

- ½ cup (125 g) butter
- 4 oz (125 g) semisweet (dark) chocolate
- 2 large eggs, lightly beaten
- 1¼ cups (250 g) sugar
- 1 cup (150 g) all-purpose (plain) flour
- 1 teaspoon baking powder
- ⅛ teaspoon salt
- 1 cup (125 g) coarsely chopped walnuts

Coconut almond squares

COCONUT ALMOND SQUARES

Base
- ½ cup (125 g) butter, softened
- ⅔ cup (140 g) firmly packed light brown sugar
- ⅔ cup (100 g) all-purpose (plain) flour
- 2 tablespoons old-fashioned rolled oats
- 2 tablespoons toasted wheat germ
- 1 tablespoon finely grated orange zest
- ⅛ teaspoon salt

Topping
- 2 large eggs, lightly beaten
- ¼ cup (50 g) firmly packed light brown sugar
- ¾ cup (125 g) blanched almonds, halved
- ½ cup (60 g) unsweetened shredded (desiccated) coconut

Preheat the oven to 350°F (180°C/gas 4). • Butter an 8-inch (20-cm) square baking pan. • Base: Beat the butter and brown sugar in a large bowl with an electric mixer on medium speed until creamy. • Mix in the flour, oats, wheat germ, orange juice, and salt until well blended. • Firmly press the mixture into the prepared pan to form a smooth, even layer. • Topping: With mixer at high speed, beat the eggs and brown sugar in a large bowl until pale and thick. • Stir in the almonds and coconut. • Spread the topping evenly over the base. • Bake for 30–35 minutes, or until just golden. • Cool completely before cutting into squares.

Makes: about 16 squares • Prep: 30 min • Cooking: 30–35 min • Level: 1

BUTTER BARS WITH DRIED CURRANTS

Mix the flour, confectioners' sugar, and salt in a large bowl. • Cut in the butter until the mixture resembles fine crumbs. • Add the whole egg to form a stiff dough. • Divide the dough in half. Press each half into a disk, wrap in plastic wrap (cling film), and refrigerate for 30 minutes. • Preheat the oven to 400°F (200°C/gas 6). • Butter four cookie sheets. • Roll out one disk on a lightly floured surface into a 14 x 12-inch (35 x 30-cm) rectangle. Sprinkle with the currants. • Roll out the remaining dough to the same dimensions and place on top of the currants, pressing down lightly. • Cut into bars. • Transfer the cookies to the prepared cookie sheets, placing them 1 inch (2.5 cm) apart. Brush with the remaining beaten egg yolk. • Bake, one sheet at a time, for 10–12 minutes, or until golden brown. • Transfer to racks to cool.

Makes: about 30 bars • Prep: 40 min + 30 min to chill Cooking: 10–12 min • Level: 1

- 2⅓ cups (350 g) all-purpose (plain) flour
- ⅔ cup (100 g) confectioners' (icing) sugar
- ⅛ teaspoon salt
- ¾ cup (180 g) butter, cut up
- 1 large egg + 1 large egg yolk, lightly beaten
- ⅓ cup (45 g) dried currants

COCONUT SQUARES
WITH CANDIED CHERRIES

- 10 oz (300 g) semisweet (dark) chocolate, coarsely chopped
- ½ cup (125 g) butter, softened
- 1¼ cups (250 g) sugar
- 2 large eggs
- ⅔ cup (70 g) candied cherries, coarsely chopped
- 2 cups (250 g) unsweetened shredded (desiccated) coconut

Preheat the oven to 325°F (170°C/gas 3). • Line a 10-inch (25-cm) baking pan with aluminum foil. • Melt the chocolate in a double boiler over barely simmering water. Spread the chocolate over the foil and set aside to cool. • Beat the butter and sugar in a large bowl with an electric mixer on medium speed until creamy. • Add the eggs one at a time, beating until just blended after each addition. • Stir in the cherries and coconut. • Spread over the cooled chocolate. • Bake until a toothpick inserted into the center comes out clean, 15–20 minutes. • Cool completely and cut into squares.

Makes: about 16 squares • Prep: 15 min • Cooking: 15–20 min • Level: 1

DRIED CURRANT
OAT SQUARES

Preheat the oven to 325°F (170°C/gas 3). • Butter a 10-inch (25-cm) square baking pan. • Melt the butter with the corn syrup and brown sugar in a small saucepan until smooth. • Stir together the oats, flour, salt, and currants in a large bowl. • Stir in the butter mixture until well blended. • Spoon the mixture into the prepared pan, pressing down firmly. • Bake for 25–30 minutes, or until lightly browned. • Cool completely in the pan. • Melt the white chocolate in a double boiler over barely simmering water. Use a thin metal spatula to spread the chocolate then cut into squares.

Makes: about 20 squares • Prep: 20 min • Cooking: 25–30 min • Level: 1

- 1 cup (250 g) butter
- ¾ cup (180 g) light corn syrup (golden) syrup
- ½ cup (100 g) firmly packed light brown sugar
- 1 cup (150 g) old-fashioned rolled oats
- ⅔ cup (100 g) all-purpose (plain) flour
- ⅛ teaspoon salt
- ½ cup (90 g) currants
- 3 oz (90 g) white chocolate, coarsely chopped

Bars & Brownies

SIMPLE CHOCOLATE BROWNIES

- 1½ cups (225 g) all-purpose (plain) flour
- ⅛ teaspoon salt
- 7 oz (200 g) semisweet (dark) chocolate, coarsely chopped
- ½ cup (125 g) butter, cut up
- 2 large eggs
- 1 cup (180 g) white chocolate chips
- 1 cup (180 g) milk chocolate chips
- 1 cup (100 g) coarsely chopped pecans

Preheat the oven to 350°F (180°C/gas 4). • Butter an 8-inch (20-cm) square baking pan. • Mix the flour and salt in a medium bowl. • Melt the semisweet chocolate with the butter in a double boiler over barely simmering water. • Transfer the chocolate mixture to a medium bowl and let cool for 5 minutes. • Add the eggs to the batter, beating until just blended. • Mix in the dry ingredients, white and milk chocolate chips, and pecans. • Spoon the batter evenly into the prepared pan. • Bake for 35–40 minutes, or until dry on top and almost firm to the touch. Do not overbake. • Cool completely before cutting into bars.

Makes: about 20 bars • Prep: 20 min • Cooking: 35–40 min Level: 1

CHOCOLATE OAT SQUARES

Preheat the oven to 375°F (190°C/gas 5). • Butter an 8-inch (20-cm) baking pan. • Beat the butter and brown sugar in a large bowl with an electric mixer on medium speed until creamy. • Add the egg yolk, beating until just blended. • Mix in the flour, oats, and salt until well blended. • Firmly press the mixture into the prepared pan to form a smooth, even layer. • Bake for 15–20 minutes, or until just golden. • Topping: Melt the chocolate and butter in a double boiler over barely simmering water. • Spread the melted chocolate over the oat base and sprinkle with the chopped walnuts. • Cut into squares..

Makes: about 16 squares • Prep: 25 min • Cooking: 15–20 min • Level: 1

- ½ cup (125 g) butter, softened
- ⅔ cup (140 g) firmly packed light brown sugar
- 1 large egg yolk
- ⅓ cup (50 g) all-purpose (plain) flour
- 2 tablespoons old-fashioned rolled oats
- ⅛ teaspoon salt

Topping
- 3 oz (90 g) semisweet (dark) chocolate
- 1 tablespoon butter
- ½ cup (50 g) finely chopped walnuts

Simple chocolate brownies

Frosted cocoa squares

FROSTED COCOA SQUARES

- 1½ cups (225 g) all-purpose (plain) flour
- 1 tablespoon unsweetened cocoa powder
- 2 teaspoons baking powder
- ¼ teaspoon salt
- 1 cup (250 g) butter, softened
- 1 cup (200 g) sugar
- 4 large eggs, lightly beaten
- 2 tablespoons milk
- ½ teaspoon vanilla extract (essence)

Frosting
- ¾ cup (125 g) milk chocolate chips
- ¼ cup (60 g) butter
- 2 tablespoons milk
- 1 cup (150 g) confectioners' (icing) sugar

Preheat the oven to 350°F (180°C/gas 4).
• Butter an 11 x 7-inch (28 x 18-cm) baking pan. • Mix the flour, cocoa, baking powder, and salt in a medium bowl. • Beat the butter and sugar in a large bowl with an electric mixer on medium speed until creamy. • Add the eggs, beating until just blended. • Mix in the dry ingredients, milk, and vanilla until well blended. • Spread the mixture evenly in the prepared pan. • Bake for 35–45 minutes, or until firm to the touch and a toothpick inserted into the center comes out clean. • Cool completely in the pan. • Frosting: Melt the chocolate chips and butter with the milk in a double boiler over barely simmering water until well blended. Remove from the heat and beat in the confectioners' sugar until thick and spreadable. • Spread the frosting over the cookie base. Let stand for 30 minutes, or until set. • Cut into squares.

Makes: about 20 squares • Prep: 30 min + 40 min to set
Cooking: 30–40 min • Level: 1

RAISIN SQUARES

Mix the flour, baking powder, and salt in a medium bowl. Stir in the sugar. • Use a pastry blender to cut in the shortening until the mixture resembles fine crumbs. • Stir in the raisins. • Mix in enough water to form a stiff dough. • Press the dough into a disk, wrap in plastic wrap (cling film), and refrigerate for 30 minutes. • Preheat the oven to 400°F (200°C/gas 6). • Butter a cookie sheet. • Roll out the dough on a lightly floured surface to ¼ inch (5 mm) thick. • Use a sharp knife to cut the dough into 2-inch (5-cm) squares. • Use a spatula to transfer the cookies to the prepared cookie sheet, placing them 1 inch (2.5 cm) apart. • Bake for 8–10 minutes, or until golden. • Transfer to racks to cool.

Makes: about 16 squares • Prep: 40 min + 30 min to chill
Cooking: 8–10 min • Level: 1

- ¾ cup (125 g) all-purpose (plain) flour
- ½ teaspoon baking powder
- ⅛ teaspoon salt
- 1 tablespoon sugar
- ⅓ cup (90 g) vegetable shortening or lard
- ½ cup (90 g) raisins
- 2 tablespoons ice water + more as needed

Chewy fruit squares

CHEWY FRUIT SQUARES

- 2 cups (200 g) dried apricots, soaked overnight
- 2 tablespoons sunflower oil
- 1 cup (180 g) raisins
- 2/3 cup (100 g) old-fashioned rolled oats
- finely grated zest of 1 lemon
- 1/2 teaspoon ground cardamom
- 1/8 teaspoon salt

Preheat the oven to 400°F (200°C/gas 6).
• Butter a 9-inch (23-cm) square baking pan.
• Bring the apricots and their soaking liquid to a boil in a small saucepan over low heat and simmer for 5 minutes, or until softened.
• Drain and transfer to a food processor or blender. Process until smooth. • Transfer to a large bowl and add the oil. • Mix in the raisins, oats, lemon zest, cardamom, and salt until well blended. • Spread the mixture evenly in the prepared pan. • Bake for 40–45 minutes, or until firm to the touch. • Cool completely in the pan. • Cut into bars.

Makes: about 30 squares • Prep: 25 min • Cooking: 40–45 min • Level: 1

WALNUT AND APRICOT SQUARES

Preheat the oven to 350°F (180°C/gas 4).
• Butter an 8-inch (20-cm) baking pan.
• Base: Mix the flour and brown sugar in a large bowl. • Use a pastry blender to cut in the butter until the mixture resembles coarse crumbs. • Press the mixture into the pan in a smooth layer. • Bake until lightly browned, 12–15 minutes. • Cool completely in the pan. • Topping: Mix the orange and lemon juices with enough water to make 2/3 cup (150 ml) of liquid. • Simmer the apricots in the liquid until softened, about 15 minutes. • Drain the apricots, reserving the liquid in a small bowl. • Finely chop the apricots and return to the saucepan. Add both zests, the brown sugar, cornstarch, and 1/4 cup (60 ml) apricot liquid. • Bring to a boil and simmer for 1 minute, stirring constantly. Let cool, then spread over the base. Sprinkle with walnuts. • Bake until golden brown, 15–20 minutes. • Cool completely before cutting into bars.

Makes: about 20 bars • Prep: 30 min • Cooking: 30–35 min Level: 2

Base
- 3/4 cup (120 g) all-purpose (plain) flour
- (plain) cup (140 g) firmly packed light brown sugar
- 1/4 cup (60 g) cold butter, cut up

Topping
- finely grated zest and juice of 1 orange
- finely grated zest and juice of 1/2 lemon
- water
- 3/4 cup (75 g) dried apricots
- 1/3 cup (70 g) firmly packed light brown sugar
- 2 teaspoon cornstarch (cornflour)
- 1/2 cup (50 g) finely chopped walnuts

CANDIED CHERRY AND GINGER BARS

- 1 cup (150 g) all-purpose (plain) flour
- 1 teaspoon baking powder
- 1/8 teaspoon salt
- 1 cup (100 g) finely chopped mixed dried fruit
- 1/2 cup (50 g) finely chopped candied (crystallized) ginger
- 1/2 cup (125 g) butter, softened
- 3/4 cup (150 g) sugar
- 1 large egg

Preheat the oven to 300°F (150°C/gas 2).
• Butter an 11 x 7-inch (28 x 18-cm) baking pan. • Mix the flour, baking powder, and salt in a medium bowl. • Stir in the dried fruit and ginger. • Beat the butter and sugar in a large bowl with an electric mixer on medium speed until creamy. • Add the egg.
• Mix in the dry ingredients. • Spoon the mixture into the prepared pan. • Bake for 40–45 minutes, or until golden brown.
• Cool completely before cutting into bars.

Makes: about 20 bars • Prep: 10 min • Cooking: 40–45 min Level: 1

SICILIAN ALMOND AND ORANGE BARS

Soak the orange zest in a bowl of water for 2 days, changing the water twice a day.
• Drain the orange and cut into small thin strips with a sharp knife. • Transfer to a large saucepan. • Add the sugar and almonds. Simmer over low heat for about 30 minutes, stirring constantly, until the mixture is a dark golden brown color. • Turn the mixture out onto a marble cutting board and let cool. • Cut into bars.

Makes: about 45 bars • Prep: 25 min + 2 days to soak Cooking: 30 min • Level: 3

- 1 lb (500 g) orange zest, removed in long strips with a very sharp knife
- 2 1/2 cups (500 g) granulated sugar
- 2/3 cup (100 g) blanched almonds, toasted and coarsely chopped

Bars & Brownies

GLAZED DATE DIAMONDS

- 1²/₃ cups (250 g) all-purpose (plain) flour
- 1 teaspoon ground cinnamon
- 1 teaspoon baking powder
- ¹/₂ teaspoon baking soda (bicarbonate of soda)
- ¹/₂ teaspoon salt
- 1 cup (200 g) firmly packed dark brown sugar
- 2 large eggs, lightly beaten
- 1 cup (250 g) butter, melted
- ¹/₂ cup (125 ml) sour cream
- 1¹/₃ cups (140 g) finely chopped dates
- ³/₄ cup (75 g) finely chopped walnuts or pecans

Lemon Glaze
- 1¹/₃ cups (200 g) confectioners' (icing) sugar
- 3 tablespoons butter, melted
- 1 tablespoon freshly squeezed lemon juice
- 1–2 tablespoons water

Preheat the oven to 350°F (180°C/gas 4). • Butter a 13 x 9-inch (33 x 23-cm) baking pan. • Mix the flour, cinnamon, baking powder, baking soda, and salt in a large bowl. • Stir in the brown sugar. • Add the eggs, beating until just blended. • Beat in the butter and sour cream. • Stir in the dates and walnuts. • Pour the mixture into the prepared pan. • Bake for 20–25 minutes, or until golden brown and a toothpick inserted into the center comes out clean. • Cool completely in the pan. • Lemon Glaze: Mix the confectioners' sugar, butter, and lemon juice in a small bowl. • Add enough water to create a creamy glaze. • Spread the glaze over the cooled cake. • Cut lengthwise into long strips. • Cut the strips into diamonds by running the knife diagonally from one side of the pan to the other.

Makes: about 30 diamond bars • Prep: 25 min • Cooking: 20–25 min • Level: 1

DOUBLE CHOCOLATE MACADAMIA BARS

Preheat the oven to 350°F (180°C/gas 4). • Butter an 8-inch (20-cm) square baking pan. Line with waxed paper. Butter the paper. • Melt both types of chocolate with the butter in a double boiler over barely simmering water. Remove from the heat. • Stir in the brown sugar and honey. • Add the eggs one at a time, beating until just blended after each addition. • Use a large rubber spatula to fold in the flour, baking powder, salt, and nuts. • Spoon the batter into the prepared pan. • Bake for about 30 minutes, or until a toothpick inserted into the center comes out clean. • Cool in the pan for 15 minutes. Cut into bars to serve.

Makes: about 16 bars • Prep: 20 min • Cooking: 30 min Level: 1

- 3 oz (90 g) semisweet (dark) chocolate, coarsely chopped
- 3 oz (90 g) milk chocolate, coarsely chopped
- ¹/₂ cup (125 g) butter
- ¹/₂ cup (100 g) firmly packed dark brown sugar
- 2 tablespoons honey
- 2 large eggs, lightly beaten
- 1 cup (150 g) all-purpose (plain) flour
- 1 teaspoon baking powder
- ¹/₈ teaspoon salt
- ³/₄ cup (100 g) macadamia nuts, finely chopped

ALMOND BANANA CRISP

- 2 tablespoons freshly squeezed lemon juice
- 2 tablespoons honey
- ²/₃ cup (180 ml) water
- 2¹/₄ cups (300 g) coarsely chopped dried apricots
- 2¹/₄ cups (300 g) coarsely chopped dried bananas
- ¹/₂ cup (125 g) butter
- 1 cup (200 g) firmly packed light brown sugar

Bring the lemon juice, honey, and water to a boil with the apricots and bananas in a medium saucepan over medium heat. • Reduce the heat and simmer over low heat for 30 minutes, or until the fruit has softened. • Remove from the heat and let cool for 15 minutes. • Butter an 8-inch (20-cm) baking pan. • Melt the butter with the brown sugar in a medium saucepan over low heat until the sugar has dissolved completely. • Mix in the corn flakes until well coated. • Firmly press half the corn

flake mixture into the prepared pan to form a smooth, even layer. Spoon the apricot and banana mixture evenly over the base and cover with the remaining corn flake mixture. • Cool completely before cutting into squares or bars.

Makes: about 30 bars • Prep: 25 min • Cooking: 20–25 min Level: 1

- 1¹/₄ cups (180 g) corn flakes

Bars & Brownies

MIDDLE EASTERN DATE SQUARES

Date Filling
- 1 lb (500 g) pitted dates
- 1 cup (200 g) firmly packed dark brown sugar
- 1 cup (250 ml) water
- ½ teaspoon vanilla extract (essence)
- ½ teaspoon ground cinnamon

Oat Crust
- 1½ cups (225 g) all-purpose (plain) flour
- 1 cup (200 g) firmly packed dark brown sugar
- 1 teaspoon ground cinnamon
- ½ teaspoon baking soda (bicarbonate of soda)
- ⅛ teaspoon salt
- 1 cup (250 g) butter, cut up
- ⅔ cup (150 g) old-fashioned rolled oats
- ½ cup (50 g) finely chopped walnuts

Preheat the oven to 350°F (180°C/gas 4). • Line a 13 x 9-inch (33 x 23-cm) baking pan with aluminum foil, letting the edges overhang. • Date Filling: Cook the dates with the brown sugar and water in a saucepan over medium heat until the sugar has dissolved completely. • Remove from the heat and add the vanilla and cinnamon. • Transfer to a food processor and process until pureed. • Return to the bowl and let cool completely. • Oat Crust: Mix the flour, brown sugar, cinnamon, baking soda, and salt in a large bowl. • Use a pastry blender to cut in the butter until the mixture resembles coarse crumbs. Stir in the oats and walnuts. • Firmly press half the mixture into the prepared pan to form a smooth, even layer. • Pour the filling over the oat crust and sprinkle with the remaining oat crust mixture. • Bake for 30–35 minutes, or until lightly browned. • Using the foil as handles, lift onto a rack and let cool completely. • Cut into squares.

Makes: about 30 squares • Prep: 40 min • Cooking: 25–30 min • Level: 1

FRUIT SQUARES

Choose firm-ripe, tasty cooking pears for these delicious squares. For a slightly different flavor, substitute the pears with the same quantity of Granny Smith apples.

Preheat the oven to 375°F (190°C/gas 5). • Line an 8-inch (20-cm) baking pan with aluminum foil, letting the edges overhang. • Mix the flour, baking powder, and salt in a medium bowl. • Mix the pears, apricots, honey, and applesauce in a large bowl. • Beat in the oil and eggs until well blended. • Mix in the dry ingredients. • Pour the mixture into the prepared pan. • Sprinkle with the almonds. • Bake for 25–30 minutes, or until just golden and a toothpick inserted into the center comes out clean. • Using the foil as handles, lift onto a rack to cool. • Cut into bars.

Makes: about 20 squares • Prep: 20 min • Cooking: 20–25 min • Level: 1

- 1½ cups (225 g) whole-wheat (wholemeal) flour
- 1½ teaspoons baking powder
- ¼ teaspoon salt
- 3 large firm-ripe pears, peeled, cored, and finely chopped
- 1½ cups (150 g) finely chopped dried apricots
- 2 tablespoons honey
- 1 tablespoon applesauce
- 2 tablespoons vegetable oil
- 2 large eggs, lightly beaten
- ½ cup (50 g) flaked almonds, to decorate

ALMOND TOFFEE SQUARES

Topping
- ⅓ cup (90 g) butter
- ½ cup (100 g) granulated sugar
- 2 tablespoons firmly packed light brown sugar
- 2 tablespoons milk
- 2½ cups (250 g) flaked almonds

Preheat the oven to 350°F (180°C/gas 4). • Butter a 9-inch (23-cm) baking pan. • Topping: Melt the butter with both sugars in a small saucepan over low heat. • Add the milk and bring to a boil, stirring constantly. • Remove from the heat and stir in the almonds. • Base: Mix the flour, baking powder, and salt in a medium bowl. • Beat the butter and sugar in a large bowl with an electric mixer on medium speed until creamy. • Add the egg, beating until just blended. • Mix in the dry ingredients and lemon zest. • Firmly press the mixture into the prepared pan to form a smooth, even layer. • Spread the topping evenly over the cookie base. • Bake for 30–35 minutes, or until just golden. • Cut into squares while the topping is still warm.

Makes: about 15 squares • Prep: 30 min • Cooking: 30–35 min • Level: 1

Base
- 1⅓ cups (200 g) all-purpose (plain) flour
- 1 teaspoon baking powder
- ¼ teaspoon salt
- ½ cup (125 g) butter, softened
- ⅔ cup (140 g) sugar
- 1 large egg
- 1 teaspoon finely grated lemon zest

Bars & Brownies

CHOCOLATE NUT BROWNIES

- 1 cup (150 g) all-purpose (plain) flour
- 1 teaspoon baking powder
- 1/4 teaspoon salt
- 1/2 cup (125 g) butter, cut up
- 1 1/3 cups (270 g) firmly packed light or dark brown sugar
- 1 tablespoon instant coffee granules dissolved in 1 tablespoon hot water
- 1 teaspoon vanilla extract (essence)
- 2 large eggs, lightly beaten
- 5 oz (150 g) semisweet (dark) chocolate, coarsely chopped
- 2 tablespoons coarsely chopped walnuts

Preheat the oven to 350°F (180°C/gas 4).
• Butter a 9-inch (23-cm) square baking pan.
• Mix the flour, baking powder, and salt in a large bowl. • Melt the butter with the brown sugar in a medium saucepan over low heat, stirring constantly. • Stir in the coffee mixture. • Remove from the heat and let cool for 5 minutes. • Add the vanilla and eggs, beating until just blended. • Mix in the dry ingredients, chocolate, and walnuts until well blended. • Pour the mixture into the prepared pan. • Bake for 30–35 minutes, or until dry on the top and almost firm to the touch. Do not overbake. • Cool completely before cutting into bars.

Makes: about 16 brownies • Prep: 15 min • Cooking: 30–35 min • Level: 1

APRICOT BARS

Preheat the oven to 350°F (180°C/gas 4).
• Butter a 10 1/2 x 15 1/2-inch (26 x 36-cm) jelly-roll pan. • Crunchy Topping: Melt the butter in a small saucepan over medium heat. Stir in the brown sugar and oats until well blended. • Cookie Base: Mix the flour, baking powder, and salt in a large bowl and stir in the sugar. Use a pastry blender to cut in the butter until the mixture resembles fine crumbs. • Firmly press the mixture into the prepared pan. • Heat the preserves in a small saucepan over medium heat until liquid. Spread over the cookie base. • Sprinkle with the topping. • Bake for 25–30 minutes, or until lightly browned. • Cool completely before cutting into bars.

Makes: about 30 bars • Prep: 20 min • Cooking: 25–30 min Level: 1

Crunchy Topping
- 1/2 cup (125 g) butter, cut up
- 1 cup (200 g) firmly packed dark brown sugar
- 1/2 cup (75 g) old-fashioned rolled oats

Cookie Base
- 3 2/3 cups (550 g) all-purpose (plain) flour
- 2 teaspoons baking powder
- 1/4 teaspoon salt
- 3/4 cup (150 g) sugar
- 1 cup (250 g) butter, cut up
- 1/2 cup (125 g) apricot preserves (jam)

SUNFLOWER SEED BARS

- 3/4 cup (125 g) cashew nuts, shelled
- 1 teaspoon vegetable or sesame oil
- 4 cups (600 g) sunflower seeds
- 1/3 cup (90 ml) apple juice concentrate or maple syrup
- 1 cup (125 g) shredded (desiccated) coconut
- 1/2 teaspoon vanilla extract (essence)
- 1/4 teaspoon salt

Crisp and healthy, these easy cookies are great for school lunch boxes and afterschool snacks.
Preheat the oven to 350°F (180°C/gas 4).
• Oil an 11 x 7-inch (28 x 18-cm) baking pan. • Process the cashew nuts and oil in a food processor or blender until smooth.
• Stir together the cashew nut mixture, sunflower seeds, apple juice, coconut, vanilla, and salt in a large bowl until well blended. • Press the mixture into the prepared pan, smoothing the top.
• Bake for 25–30 minutes, or until golden brown. • Cool completely before cutting into bars.

Makes: about 30 bars • Prep: 15 min • Cooking: 25–30 min Level: 1

MUESLI BARS

Preheat the oven to 350°F (180°C/gas 4).
• Set out 9-inch (23-cm) square baking pan.
• Mix the butter, peanut butter, and honey in a medium saucepan over low heat until well blended. • Stir in the coconut, muesli, oats, and salt. • Spoon the mixture into the baking pan and level with a spoon. • Bake for 15–20 minutes, or until just golden.
• Cool completely before cutting into bars.

Makes: about 20 bars • Prep: 20 min • Cooking:15–20 min Level: 1

- 1/2 cup (125 g) butter, softened
- 2/3 cup (140 ml) smooth peanut butter
- 1/3 cup (90 ml) honey
- 1/2 cup (60 g) shredded (desiccated) coconut
- 1 cup (150 g) muesli
- 1 1/2 cups (225 g) old-fashioned rolled oats
- 1/8 teaspoon salt

Golden nut squares

GOLDEN NUT SQUARES

- 3/4 cup (125 g) all-purpose (plain) flour
- 1/2 teaspoon baking powder
- 1/4 teaspoon salt
- 1/2 cup (60 g) unsweetened shredded (desiccated) coconut
- 1/2 cup (50 g) finely chopped walnuts
- 2 tablespoons finely ground almonds
- 1/3 cup (50 g) old-fashioned rolled oats
- 3/4 cup (150 g) sugar
- 1/2 cup (125 g) butter, cut up
- 1 tablespoon light corn syrup (golden) syrup
- 1 tablespoon milk
- 1 large egg

Preheat the oven to 350°F (180°C/gas 4).
• Butter an 11 x 7-inch (28 x 18-cm) baking pan. • Mix the flour, baking powder, and salt in a large bowl. • Stir in the coconut, walnuts, almonds, oats, and sugar. • Use a pastry blender to cut in the butter until the mixture resembles fine crumbs. • Dissolve the corn syrup in the milk in a small saucepan over low heat. Add the egg, beating until just blended. • Pour the egg mixture into the dry ingredients and mix well. • Spread the mixture evenly in the baking pan. • Bake for 40–45 minutes, or until golden brown. • Cool completely before cutting into squares.

Makes: about 20 squares • Prep: 15 min • Cooking: 40–45 min • Level: 1

CINNAMON WHOLE-WHEAT BARS

Preheat the oven to 350°F (180°C/gas 4).
• Butter an 8-inch (20-cm) square baking pan. • Heat the milk in a small saucepan over low heat. • Pour the milk into a large bowl, add the dates, and let soak for 15 minutes. • Mix the flour, baking powder, cinnamon, and salt in a medium bowl. • Beat the egg, butter, and orange zest into the date mixture. • Mix in the dry ingredients, followed by the orange flesh. • Spoon the batter into the prepared pan. • Bake for 35–40 minutes, or until a toothpick inserted into the center comes out clean. • Cool completely before cutting into bars.

Makes: about 16 bars • Prep: 20 min + 15 min to soak dates Cooking: 35–40 min • Level: 1

- 2/3 cup (150 ml) milk
- 1/2 cup (100 g) finely chopped dates
- 3/4 cup (125 g) whole-wheat (wholemeal) flour
- 1/2 teaspoon baking powder
- 1/2 teaspoon ground cinnamon
- 1/8 teaspoon salt
- 1 large egg, lightly beaten
- 1/4 cup (60 g) butter, melted
- finely grated zest and chopped flesh of 1 orange

GINGER SQUARES

- 2 cups (300 g) all-purpose (plain) flour
- 2 teaspoons baking powder
- 2 teaspoons ground ginger
- 1/8 teaspoon salt
- 1 cup (250 g) butter, softened
- 1 cup (200 g) sugar

Ginger Frosting
- 1/2 cup (125 g) butter, cut up
- 1 cup (150 g) confectioners' (icing) sugar
- 1 1/2 teaspoons ground ginger
- 1 1/2 tablespoons light corn syrup (golden) syrup

Preheat the oven to 375°F (190°C/gas 5). • Butter a 10½ x 15½-inch (26 x 36-cm) jelly-roll pan. • Mix the flour, baking powder, ginger, and salt in a medium bowl. Beat the butter and sugar in a large bowl with an electric mixer on medium speed until creamy. • Mix in the dry ingredients. • Spoon the mixture evenly into the prepared pan, pressing down lightly. • Bake for 30–35 minutes, or until golden brown. • Cool completely in the pan on a rack. • Ginger Frosting: Melt the butter with the confectioners' sugar, ginger, and corn syrup in a small saucepan over low heat, stirring constantly. • Remove from the heat and stir until smooth. • Pour the frosting evenly over the base and let stand for 15 minutes. • Use a sharp knife to cut into 30 bars.

Makes: about 30 bars • Prep: 20 min • Cooking: 30–35 min Level: 2

TOFFEE PEANUT SQUARES

Preheat the oven to 350°F (180°C/gas 4). • Butter a 10-inch (25-cm) baking pan. • Beat ⅔ cup (150 g) of butter, the egg, ⅓ cup (70 g) brown sugar, and the baking powder in a large bowl until creamy. • Beat in the flour. • Spread the mixture in the prepared pan in an even layer. • Bake until a toothpick inserted into the center comes out clean, 20–25 minutes. • Lower the oven temperature to 300°F (150°C/ gas 2). • Cook the remaining butter, remaining sugar, condensed milk, and salt in a small saucepan over low heat, stirring constantly, until well blended. • Remove from heat and stir in the peanuts. • Pour the peanut mixture over the baked base. • Bake for 15 minutes more. • Turn off the oven and let the squares cool in the oven with the door slightly ajar. • Cut into squares.

Makes: about 30 squares • Prep: 25 min • Cooking: 35–40 min • Level: 2

- 3/4 cup (180 g) butter
- 1 large egg
- 2/3 cup (140 g) firmly packed light brown sugar
- 1/2 teaspoon baking powder
- 1 1/3 cups (200 g) all-purpose (plain) flour
- 1 3/4 cups (430 ml) sweetened condensed milk
- 1/8 teaspoon salt
- 1 cup (100 g) finely chopped peanuts

Toffee peanut squares

Bars & Brownies

PINEAPPLE AND GINGER SQUARES

- 2 cups (300 g) all-purpose (plain) flour
- 1 teaspoon ground ginger
- 1/8 teaspoon salt
- 1 cup (250 g) butter, softened
- 2/3 cup (140 g) firmly packed soft brown sugar
- 1 large egg, lightly beaten
- 1 cup (150 g) chopped candied (crystallized) pineapple
- 1/2 cup (50 g) finely chopped candied (crystallized) ginger

Preheat the oven to 350°F (180°C/gas 4). • Butter a 13 x 9-inch (33 x 23-cm) baking pan. • Mix the flour, ground ginger, and salt in a medium bowl. • Beat the butter and brown sugar in a large bowl with an electric mixer on medium speed until creamy. • Use a wooden spoon to mix in the dry ingredients until the mixture resembles coarse crumbs. Transfer half the mixture to a small bowl and set aside. • Add the egg to the remaining mixture and mix to form a smooth dough. • Firmly press the dough into the prepared pan to form a smooth, even layer. • Sprinkle the candied pineapple and ginger on top. Sprinkle with the reserved crumb mixture. • Bake for 45–50 minutes, or until golden. • Cool in the pan for 15 minutes and cut into squares. • Serve warm.

Makes: about 30 squares • Prep: 25 min • Cooking: 40–45 min • Level: 1

PECAN AND DATE SQUARES

Preheat the oven to 375°F (190°C/gas 5). • Line a 13 x 9-inch (33 x 23-cm) baking pan with aluminum foil, letting the edges overhang. Butter the foil. • Mix the flour, cornstarch, and salt in a large bowl. • Beat the butter, brown sugar, and egg in a large bowl with an electric mixer on medium speed until fluffy. • Mix in the dry ingredients, dates, and pecans to form a stiff dough. • Press the mixture into the prepared pan in an even layer. • Brush with the milk and sprinkle with the granulated sugar. • Bake until just golden, 20–30 minutes. • Cool completely in the pan on a rack. • Using the foil as handles, lift onto a cutting board. Peel off the foil. Cut into squares.

Makes: about 30 squares • Prep: 20 min • Cooking: 20–30 min • Level: 1

- 2/3 cup (100 g) all-purpose (plain) flour
- 2/3 cup (100 g) cornstarch (cornflour)
- 1/8 teaspoon salt
- 1/2 cup (125 g) butter, softened
- 1/2 cup (100 g) firmly packed light brown sugar
- 1 large egg
- 2/3 cup (60 g) finely chopped pitted dates
- 1 cup (100 g) coarsely chopped pecans
- 2 tablespoons milk
- 2 tablespoons granulated sugar

DRIED FRUIT AND SEEDY BARS

- 1/3 cup (90 g) butter, softened
- 1/3 cup (90 g) honey
- 1/2 cup (100 g) raw sugar (Demerara or Barbados)
- 1 1/2 cups (225 g) old-fashioned rolled oats
- 1/2 cup (50 g) coarsely chopped walnuts
- 1/2 cup (90 g) raisins
- 2 tablespoons pumpkin seeds
- 2 tablespoons sunflower seeds
- 2 tablespoons sesame seeds
- 2 tablespoons shredded (desiccated) coconut
- 3/4 teaspoon cinnamon
- 1/8 teaspoon salt

Preheat the oven to 375°F (190°C/gas 5). • Butter an 11 x 7-inch (28 x 18-cm) baking pan. • Melt the butter with the honey and raw sugar in a large saucepan over low heat, stirring constantly. • Bring to a boil and cook until the sugar has dissolved completely. • Stir in the oats, walnuts, raisins, pumpkin seeds, sunflower seeds, sesame seeds, coconut, cinnamon, and salt. • Spoon the mixture evenly into the prepared pan. • Bake for 30–35 minutes, or until just golden. • Cool completely before cutting into bars.

Makes: about 30 bars • Prep: 20 min • Cooking: 30–35 min Level: 1

CORN FLAKE SQUARES

Preheat the oven to 350°F (180°C/gas 4). • Butter an 8-inch (20-cm) square baking pan. • Mix the corn flakes, butter, sugar, cherries, ginger, and salt in a medium bowl . • Firmly press the mixture into the pan. • Bake for 25–30 minutes, or until golden brown. • Let cool before cutting into squares.

Makes: about 16 squares • Prep: 10 min • Cooking: 25–30 min • Level: 1

- 1/2 cup (60 g) corn flakes
- 7 tablespoons butter, melted
- 1/2 cup (100 g) firmly packed dark brown sugar
- 1/2 cup (50 g) candied green cherries
- 1/2 teaspoon ground ginger
- 1/8 teaspoon salt

Bars & Brownies

FROSTED ORANGE SQUARES

Base
- 2²/₃ cups (400 g) all-purpose (plain) flour
- 1 teaspoon baking powder
- ¹/₂ teaspoon salt
- ¹/₂ cup (50 g) finely chopped dried apples
- ³/₄ cup (180 g) butter, cut up
- ¹/₃ cup (70 g) granulated sugar
- 2 tablespoons vanilla sugar (see page 414)
- ¹/₃ cup (90 ml) light corn syrup (golden) syrup
- 1 tablespoon orange-flower water or orange juice
- 1 large egg

Orange Glaze
- 2 cups (300 g) confectioners' (icing) sugar
- 2–3 tablespoons freshly squeezed orange juice
- finely grated zest of 1 orange

Preheat the oven to 350°F (180°C/gas 4).
• Butter an 11 x 7-inch (28 x 18-cm) baking pan. • Base: Mix the flour, baking powder, and salt in a medium bowl. • Process the apples, butter, both sugars, corn syrup, and orange-flower water in a food processor until pureed. • Add the egg, processing until just blended. • Mix in the dry ingredients. • Firmly press the mixture into the baking pan to form a smooth, even layer. • Bake for 15–20 minutes, or until firm to the touch. • Cool completely in the pan. • Orange Glaze: Mix the confectioners' sugar with enough orange juice to make a creamy glaze. • Drizzle over the cake and sprinkle with the orange zest. Cut into squares.

Makes: about 20 squares • Prep: 20 min • Cooking: 10–12 min • Level: 1

PRUNE SQUARES

Cookie Base
- 1²/₃ cups (250 g) all-purpose (plain) flour
- 1 teaspoon baking powder
- ¹/₂ teaspoon salt
- ³/₄ cup (180 g) butter, softened
- 1¹/₂ cups (300 g) firmly packed light brown sugar
- 1 teaspoon vanilla extract (essence)
- 1 large egg, lightly beaten

Prune Filling
- 1¹/₄ cups (310 g) pitted prunes
- 2 cups (500 ml) water
- 4 tablespoons honey
- finely grated zest and juice of ¹/₄ lemon

Preheat the oven to 350°F (180°C/gas 4).
• Butter a 9-inch (23-cm) baking pan. • Cookie Base: Mix the flour, baking powder, and salt in a large bowl. • Beat the butter and brown sugar in a large bowl with an electric mixer on medium speed until creamy. • Add the vanilla and egg, beating until just blended. • Mix in the dry ingredients. • Prune Filling: Bring the prunes and water to a boil in a large saucepan. • Reduce the heat and simmer for 3 minutes. • Drain well and transfer the prunes to a food processor. Add the honey and lemon zest and juice and process until smooth. • Press one-third of the cookie base into the pan in an even layer. Spread with half the prune filling. Sprinkle with half the remaining cookie base and top with the remaining prune filling. Sprinkle with the remaining cookie base. • Bake for 55–65 minutes, or until lightly browned. • Cool completely before cutting into squares.

Makes: about 20 squares • Prep: 30 min • Cooking: 50–55 min • Level: 2

BRAN FLAKE SQUARES

- 1 cup (120 g) bran flake cereal
- ¹/₂ cup (125 g) butter, melted
- ¹/₂ cup (100 g) firmly packed dark brown sugar
- ¹/₂ cup (50 g) coarsely chopped pitted dates
- ¹/₈ teaspoon salt

Preheat the oven to 350°F (180°C/gas 4).
• Butter an 8-inch (20-cm) square baking pan. • Mix the bran flakes, butter, sugar, dates, and salt in a medium bowl . • Firmly press the mixture into the pan. • Bake for 25–30 minutes, or until golden brown. • Cool completely before cutting into squares.

Makes: about 16 squares • Prep: 10 min • Cooking: 25–30 min • Level: 1

APPLE SQUARES

- 1¹/₃ cups (200 g) all-purpose (plain) flour
- 2 teaspoons baking powder
- ¹/₈ teaspoon salt
- 2 large eggs
- 1¹/₄ cups (250 g) + 2 tablespoons sugar
- 2/3 cup (180 ml) light (single) cream
- ¹/₂ cup (125 g) butter
- 3 tart apples, peeled, cored, and thinly sliced

Preheat the oven to 400°F (200°C/gas 6).
• Butter a 13 x 9-inch (33 x 23-cm) baking pan. • Mix the flour, baking powder, and salt in a medium bowl. • Beat the eggs and 1¹/₄ cups (250 g) of sugar until pale and thick. • Bring the cream and butter to a boil in a small saucepan over medium heat. • Stir into the egg mixture. • Mix in the dry ingredients. • Spoon into the prepared pan. Arrange the apple on top and sprinkle with the remaining sugar. • Bake until golden brown, about 20 minutes.

Makes: about 24 squares • Prep: 15 min • Cooking: 25–30 min • Level: 1

MERINGUES & MACAROONS

Light and airy macaroons and meringues are based on a mixture of beaten egg whites and sugar, often with the addition of almonds, cocoa, chocolate, vanilla, nuts, citrus zests or juices, or other flavorings and aromas. Their crisp texture and subtle flavors make them an ideal snack with tea or coffee. But they can also be served with fresh fruit, whipped cream, zabaglione, ice cream, or custard after a meal as dessert. Try the Chocolate meringues (see page 246), for example, as a topping for a rich chocolate ice cream and fresh berryfruit, or serve the Light lemon macaroons (see page 251) with homemade vanilla or lemon ice cream. These cookies are very adaptable, and they also keep well if stored in an airtight container.

Orange pistachio macaroons (see page 260)

Meringues & Macaroons

CHOCOLATE MERINGUES

- ½ cup (100 g) superfine (caster) sugar
- ⅔ cup (100 g) confectioners' (icing) sugar
- 2 tablespoons unsweetened cocoa powder
- 4 large egg whites
- ⅛ teaspoon salt

Preheat the oven to 300°F (150°C/gas 2). • Line two cookie sheets with parchment paper. • Mix the both sugars with the cocoa in a medium bowl. • Beat the egg whites and salt in a large bowl with an electric mixer at medium speed until soft peaks form. • With mixer at high speed, gradually add half the sugar mixture, beating until stiff, glossy peaks form. • Use a large rubber spatula to fold in the remaining sugar mixture. • Fit a pastry bag with a ½-inch (1-cm) star tip. Fill the pastry bag, twist the opening tightly closed, and squeeze out small stars, spacing 1 inch (2.5 cm) apart on the prepared cookie sheets. • Bake for 40–50 minutes, or until the meringues are dry to the touch. • Turn off the oven. Leave in the oven for 30 minutes. • Using the parchment paper as handles, lift the meringues onto a rack. Peel off the paper and let cool completely.

Makes: about 48 meringues • Prep: 25 min + 30 min to cool Cooking: 40–50 min • Level: 2

CHOCOLATE ALMOND MERINGUES

Preheat the oven to 250°F (130°C/gas ½). • Line two cookie sheets with parchment paper. • Beat the egg whites and salt in a large bowl with an electric mixer at medium speed until frothy. • With mixer at high speed, gradually add the superfine sugar, beating until stiff, glossy peaks form. • Fold in the cocoa, cinnamon, and almond extract. • Fit a pastry bag with a 1½-inch (4-cm) star tip. Fill the pastry bag, twist the opening tightly closed, and squeeze out generous rosettes spacing 1 inch (2.5 cm) apart on the prepared cookie sheets. • Bake for 50–60 minutes, or until crisp and dry to the touch. • Cool completely on the sheets.

Makes: about 25 meringues • Prep: 25 min • Cooking: 50–60 min Level: 2

- 2 large egg whites
- ⅛ teaspoon salt
- ¾ cup (150 g) superfine (caster) sugar
- ⅓ cup (50 g) unsweetened cocoa powder
- ½ teaspoon ground cinnamon
- ½ teaspoon almond extract (essence)

BROWN SUGAR MERINGUES

- 4 large egg whites
- 1 cup (200 g) firmly packed light brown sugar
- 3 tablespoons finely chopped almonds

Preheat the oven to 300°F (150°C/gas 2). • Line two cookie sheets with parchment paper. • Mix the egg whites and brown sugar in a large bowl over barely simmering water, stirring until the sugar has dissolved and the mixture is warm to the touch. • Remove the bowl from the heat and whisk with an electric mixer until thick and cool, about 15–20 minutes. • Fold in 1 tablespoon of almonds. • Drop tablespoons of the mixture 2 inches (5 cm) apart onto the prepared cookie sheets. • Sprinkle with the remaining almonds. • Bake until crisp and dry to the touch, 15–20 minutes. • Cool completely in the oven.

Makes: about 16 meringues • Prep: 30 min • Cooking: 15–20 min • Level: 2

HAZELNUT BROWN SUGAR MERINGUES

Preheat the oven to 300°F (150°C/gas 2). • Line two cookie sheets with parchment paper. • Mix the egg whites and brown sugar in a large bowl over barely simmering water, stirring until the sugar has dissolved and the mixture has become warm to the touch. • Remove the bowl from the heat and whisk with an electric mixer until thick and cool, about 15–20 minutes. • Fold in the nuts. • Drop tablespoons of the mixture 2 inches (5 cm) apart onto the prepared cookie sheets. • Bake for 15–20 minutes, or until crisp and dry to the touch. • Cool completely in the oven.

Makes: about 16 meringues • Prep: 30 min • Cooking: 15–20 min • Level: 2

- 4 large egg whites
- 1 cup (200 g) firmly packed dark brown sugar
- 2 tablespoons finely chopped hazelnuts

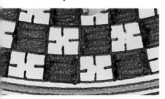

Meringues & Macaroons

MOCHA MERINGUES

- 2 large egg whites
- 1/8 teaspoon salt
- 1 cup (200 g) superfine (caster) sugar
- 1 teaspoon coffee extract (essence)
- 1/2 cup (50 g) coarsely chopped pecans
- 1 tablespoon cornstarch (cornflour)
- 1/2 cup (125 ml) heavy (double) cream, whipped

Preheat the oven to 300°F (150°C/gas 2). • Line a cookie sheet with waxed paper. • Beat the egg whites and salt in a large bowl with an electric mixer at medium speed until frothy. • With mixer at high speed, gradually add the superfine sugar, beating until stiff, glossy peaks form. • Use a large rubber spatula to fold in the coffee extract, pecans, and cornstarch. • Fit a pastry bag with a 1/2-inch (1-cm) star tip. Fill the pastry bag, twist the opening tightly closed, and squeeze out 2-inch (5-cm) stars, spacing 2 inches (5-cm) apart on the prepared cookie sheet. • Bake for 80–90 minutes, or until the meringues are crisp and lightly browned. • Cool the meringues completely in the oven with the door ajar. • Fill with whipped cream just before serving.

Makes: about 15 meringues • Prep: 30 min • Cooking: 80–90 min • Level: 2

COFFEE MERINGUES

Preheat the oven to 250°F (130°C/gas 1/2). • Line two cookie sheets with parchment paper. • Sift 1 tablespoon of confectioners' sugar and the cocoa into a small bowl. Stir in the coffee granules. • Beat the egg whites and salt in a large bowl with an electric mixer at medium speed until soft peaks form. • With mixer at high speed, gradually add the remaining confectioners' sugar, beating until stiff, glossy peaks form. • Fold in the cocoa mixture and vanilla. • Fit a pastry bag with a 1/2-inch (1-cm) star tip. Fill the pastry bag, twist the opening tightly closed, and squeeze out rosettes, spacing 2 inches (5-cm) apart on the prepared cookie sheets. • Bake for 50–60 minutes, or until the meringues are dry to the touch. • Turn the oven off. Carefully lift the meringues off the paper, press in the bottoms slightly, and return to the warm oven for 30 minutes more. • Transfer to racks to cool completely.

Makes: about 20 meringues • Prep: 25 min + 30 min to cool Cooking: 50–60 min • Level: 2

- 1 tablespoon + 1 cup (150 g) confectioners' (icing) sugar
- 1 teaspoon unsweetened cocoa powder
- 1/2 teaspoon instant coffee granules
- 2 large egg whites
- 1/8 teaspoon salt
- 1/2 teaspoon vanilla extract (essence)

HAZELNUT COFFEE MERINGUES

- 2 large egg whites
- 1/8 teaspoon salt
- 1 cup (200 g) superfine (caster) sugar
- 1 teaspoon coffee extract (essence)
- 1/2 cup (50 g) coarsely chopped hazelnuts
- 1 tablespoon cornstarch (cornflour)

Preheat the oven to 300°F (150°C/gas 2). • Line a cookie sheet with waxed paper. • Beat the egg whites and salt in a large bowl with an electric mixer at medium speed until frothy. • Gradually add the superfine sugar, beating until stiff, glossy peaks form. • Use a large rubber spatula to fold in the coffee extract, hazelnuts, and cornstarch. • Fit a pastry bag with a 1/2-inch (1-cm) star tip. Fill the pastry bag, twist the opening tightly closed, and squeeze out 2-inch (5-cm) stars, spacing 2 inches (5 cm) apart on the prepared cookie sheet. • Bake for 80–90 minutes, or until the meringues are crisp. • Cool in the oven with the door ajar.

Makes: about 20 meringues • Prep: 30 min • Cooking: 80–90 min • Level: 2

COCONUT MERINGUES

Preheat the oven to 325°F (170°C/gas 3). Line a cookie sheet with parchment paper. • Beat the egg whites and salt in a large bowl with an electric mixer at medium speed until frothy. With mixer at high speed, gradually add the sugar, beating until stiff, glossy peaks form. • Use a large rubber spatula to fold in the coconut. • Drop teaspoons of the meringue 2 inches (5 cm) apart onto the prepared cookie sheet. • Decorate with the cherries. • Bake for 35–45 minutes, or until dry and crisp. • Turn the oven off and let the meringues cool in the oven with the door ajar.

Makes: about 20 meringues • Prep: 20 min • Cooking: 35–45 min • Level: 1

- 2 large egg whites
- 1/8 teaspoon salt
- 1/2 cup (100 g) superfine (caster) sugar
- 1 cup (125 g) unsweetened shredded (desiccated) coconut
- candied cherries, to decorate

Lemon meringues with almonds

LEMON MERINGUES WITH ALMONDS

- 2 large egg whites
- $\frac{1}{8}$ teaspoon salt
- $\frac{1}{2}$ cup (100 g) superfine (caster) sugar
- 1 teaspoon freshly squeezed lemon juice
- 3 tablespoons finely ground almonds, toasted
- 1 teaspoon cornstarch (cornflour)
- 2 tablespoons flaked almonds, to sprinkle
- 2 tablespoons confectioners' (icing) sugar, to dust

Preheat the oven to 250°F (130°C/gas $\frac{1}{2}$). • Line two cookie sheets with parchment paper. • Beat the egg whites and salt in a large bowl with an electric mixer at medium speed until soft peaks form. Gradually add the sugar and lemon juice, beating until stiff, glossy peaks form. • Fold in the finely ground nuts and cornstarch. • Fit a pastry bag with a $\frac{1}{2}$-inch (1-cm) star tip. Fill the bag, twist the opening tightly closed, and squeeze out small stars and shells, spacing 1 inch (2.5 cm) apart on the cookie sheets. • Sprinkle with the flaked almonds and dust with the confectioners' sugar. • Bake for 50–60 minutes, or until dry to the touch. • Turn off the oven. Leave in the oven for 30 minutes more. • Using the parchment paper as handles, lift onto a rack. Carefully peel off the paper and let cool completely.
Makes: about 25 meringues • Prep: 30 min + 30 min to cool Cooking: 50–60 min • Level: 2

MUDDY MACAROONS

Preheat the oven to 350°F (180°C/gas 4). • Line two cookie sheets with parchment paper. • Melt the chocolate in a double boiler over barely simmering water. • Let cool for 5 minutes. • Mix the almonds, sugar, almond and vanilla extracts, and cocoa in a large bowl. • Make a well in the center and pour in the melted chocolate and three-quarters of the beaten whites. Mix well to make a smooth dough, adding more whites if the dough is too stiff to mold. • Dust your hands with a little confectioners' sugar. • Shape the dough into balls the size of walnuts. • Place 2 inches (5 cm) apart on the prepared cookie sheets. Use a fork to flatten them slightly. Brush with a little water. Dust with confectioners' sugar. • Bake for 10–12 minutes, or until firm to the touch. Cool the macaroons on the sheet for 1 minute. • Transfer to racks and let cool completely.
Makes: about 50 meringues • Prep: 20 min • Cooking: 10–12 min • Level: 2

- 1$\frac{1}{4}$ lb (575 g) bittersweet (plain) chocolate, coarsely chopped
- 1$\frac{1}{3}$ cups (200 g) finely ground almonds
- $\frac{2}{3}$ cup (140 g) sugar
- $\frac{1}{4}$ teaspoon almond extract (essence)
- $\frac{1}{4}$ teaspoon vanilla extract (essence)
- 1 tablespoon unsweetened cocoa powder
- 2 large egg whites, lightly beaten
- 1 teaspoon water
- 2 tablespoons confectioners' (icing) sugar, to dust

LIGHT LEMON MACAROONS

- 2 large egg whites
- 2$\frac{1}{2}$ cups (250 g) finely chopped almonds
- 1$\frac{1}{4}$ cups (250 g) sugar
- 1 tablespoon whole-wheat (wholemeal) flour
- finely grated zest of 1 lemon
- $\frac{1}{2}$ teaspoon vanilla extract (essence)
- $\frac{1}{8}$ teaspoon salt

Preheat the oven to 350°F (150°C/gas 2). • Butter two cookie sheets. • Beat the egg whites in a large bowl with an electric mixer at high speed until stiff peaks form. • Use a large rubber spatula to fold the almonds, sugar, flour, lemon zest, vanilla, and salt into the beaten whites. • Fit a pastry bag with a $\frac{1}{2}$-inch (1-cm) plain tip. Fill the pastry bag, twist the opening tightly closed, and squeeze out dots, spacing 1 inch (2.5 cm) apart on the prepared cookie sheets. • Bake for 20–25 minutes, or until lightly golden. • Cool on the sheets for 5 minutes. • Transfer to racks and let cool completely.
Makes: about 25 macaroon • Prep: 25 min • Cooking: 20–25 min • Level: 2

PEANUT AND ORANGE MACAROONS

Preheat the oven to 300°F (150°C/gas 2). • Line two cookie sheets with parchment paper. • Beat the egg whites, cream of tartar, and salt in a large bowl with an electric mixer at medium speed until frothy. • Add the orange juice. • With mixer at high speed, gradually add the sugar, beating until stiff, glossy peaks form. • Use a large rubber spatula to fold in the peanuts. • Drop teaspoons of the mixture 1 inch (2.5 cm) apart onto the prepared cookie sheets. • Bake for 20–25 minutes, or until the meringues are dry and crisp. • Transfer to racks to cool.
Makes: 25–30 macaroons • Prep: 20 min • Cooking: 20–25 min • Level: 1

- 3 large egg whites
- $\frac{1}{4}$ teaspoon cream of tartar
- $\frac{1}{8}$ teaspoon salt
- 1 teaspoon freshly squeezed orange juice
- $\frac{3}{4}$ cup (150 g) sugar
- $\frac{1}{2}$ cup (50 g) finely chopped peanuts

Meringues & Macaroons

ORANGE AND ALMOND MACAROONS

- 1 cup (150 g) blanched almonds, toasted and finely ground
- ½ cup (100 g) vanilla sugar (see page 414)
- 4 tablespoons orange-flavored sugar
- 2 large egg whites
- ¼ teaspoon almond extract (essence)
- 15 blanched almonds or almond halves
- 1 teaspoon water
- 3 tablespoons confectioners' (icing) sugar, to dust

Preheat the oven to 375°F (190°C/gas 5).
• Line a cookie sheet with parchment paper.
• Mix the almonds with the egg white in a food processor to form a smooth paste.
• Mix the vanilla and orange sugars and gradually work the sugars and almond extract into the almond paste until the mixture is soft. • Form the mixture into balls the size of walnuts. • Place 2 inches (5 cm) apart on the prepared cookie sheet, flattening them slightly. • Lightly press an almond into the top of each cookie. Brush with the water and dust with the confectioners' sugar. • Bake for 15–20 minutes, or until golden and slightly firm to the touch. • Transfer the cookies on their parchment to racks and cool until they firm slightly. • Peel from the paper and let cool completely.

Makes: about 15 macaroons • Prep: 40 min • Cooking: 15–20 min • Level: 1

COCONUT MACAROONS

Preheat the oven to 325°F (170°C/gas 3).
• Line three cookie sheets with parchment paper. • Mix the sugar, coconut, egg whites, lemon zest, and vanilla in a large shallow saucepan. • Cook over low heat, stirring constantly, for about 5 minutes, or until creamy. Do not bring to a boil. Remove from the heat and let cool for 15 minutes, or until thickened for piping. • Fit a pastry bag with a 1/4-inch (5-mm) star tip. Fill the pastry bag, twist the opening tightly closed, and pipe out hazelnut-sized rounds, spacing 1 inch (2.5-cm) apart on the prepared cookie sheets. • Bake, one batch at a time, for 8–10 minutes, or until firm to the touch and golden brown. • Cool the cookies on the cookie sheets for 5 minutes. • Transfer to racks to cool.

Makes: about 50 macaroons • Prep: 40 min • Cooking: 8–10 min • Level: 2

- 2 cups (400 g) sugar
- 1½ cups (185 g) shredded (desiccated) coconut
- 5 large egg whites
- finely grated zest of ½ lemon
- ¼ teaspoon vanilla extract (essence)

NUTTY OAT MACAROONS

- 2 large egg whites
- ½ cup (100 g) raw sugar (Demerara or Barbados)
- 1 tablespoon vanilla sugar (see page 414)
- ½ cup (75 g) old-fashioned rolled oats
- ½ cup (50 g) finely ground hazelnuts
- 1 tablespoon very finely chopped dried figs
- 1 tablespoon freshly squeezed lemon juice
- finely grated zest of 1 lemon
- 2 tablespoons sunflower seeds

Preheat the oven to 350°F (180°C/gas 4).
• Line three cookie sheets with parchment paper. • Beat the egg whites and 1 tablespoon of raw sugar in a large bowl with an electric mixer until soft peaks form. Gradually add the remaining raw sugar, beating until stiff peaks form. • Fold in the vanilla sugar, oats, hazelnuts, figs, lemon juice, and zest. • Drop teaspoons of the mixture 1 inch (2.5 cm) apart onto the prepared cookie sheets. Sprinkle with the sunflower seeds. • Bake for 12–15 minutes, or until lightly browned. • Cool the cookies on the cookie sheet for 15 minutes. Transfer to racks and let cool completely.

Makes: about 45 macaroons • Prep: 20 min • Cooking: 12–15 min • Level: 1

HAZELNUT MACAROONS

Preheat the oven to 300°F (150°C/gas 2).
• Butter a cookie sheet. • Beat the egg whites and salt in a large bowl with an electric mixer at high speed until stiff peaks form.
• Use a large rubber spatula to gradually fold in the confectioners' sugar, followed by the hazelnuts. • Place the bowl over barely simmering water and cook, stirring constantly with a wooden spoon, until the mixture starts to shrink from the sides.
• Drop rounded teaspoons of the mixture ½ inch (1 cm) apart onto the prepared cookie sheet. • Bake for 15–20 minutes, or until just golden. • Transfer to racks and let cool completely.

Makes: about 20 macaroons • Prep: 20 min • Cooking: 15–20 min • Level: 2

- 3 large egg whites
- ⅛ teaspoon salt
- 1 cup (150 g) confectioners' (icing) sugar
- 1 cup (100 g) toasted, finely chopped hazelnuts

Meringues & Macaroons

FROSTED CHOCOLATE MACAROONS

- 2 tablespoons all-purpose (plain) flour
- 1 teaspoon baking powder
- ⅛ teaspoon salt
- 4 large egg whites
- 1½ cups (300 g) superfine (caster) sugar
- 2½ cups (250 g) finely ground almonds
- 3 oz (90 g) semisweet (dark chocolate, coarsely grated
- 1 cup (100 g) mixed candied peel, finely chopped
- Rice paper, cut into 2-inch (5-cm rounds
- 3 oz (90 g) semisweet (dark chocolate, coarsely chopped
- 3 oz (90 g) white chocolate, coarsely chopped

Mix the flour, baking powder, and salt in a large bowl. • Beat the egg whites in a large bowl with an electric mixer at medium speed until frothy. • With mixer at high speed, gradually add the superfine sugar, beating until stiff, glossy peaks form. • Use a large rubber spatula to fold in the almonds, grated chocolate, and candied peel, followed by the dry ingredients until well blended. • Drop spoonfuls of the mixture onto the rice paper circles. Use a thin metal spatula to spread the mixture to ½ inch (1 cm) thick and place on a baking sheet. • Refrigerate for at least 2 hours. • Preheat the oven to 300°F (150°C/gas 2). • Bake for 20–25 minutes, or until firm to the touch. • Transfer to racks to cool. • Tear off any extra paper from around the cookies. • Melt both types of chocolate separately in a double boiler over barely simmering water. • Drizzle over the macaroons, swirling with a knife to create a marbled effect.

Makes: about 25 macaroons • Prep: 50 min + 2 hr to chill Cooking: 20–25 min • Level: 2

GLAZED ALMOND MACAROONS

Preheat the oven to 325°F (170°C/gas 3). • Line two baking sheets with rice paper. • Place the almonds on a baking sheet. Toast for 7 minutes, or until lightly golden. • Chop finely in a food processor. • Mix the flour, cinnamon, and nutmeg in a medium bowl. • Beat the egg whites with an electric mixer at medium speed until frothy. Gradually add the confectioners' sugar and cream of tartar, beating until stiff, glossy peaks form. • Mix the baking soda and water in a small bowl. Fold into the egg whites, followed by the dry ingredients and lemon and orange peels. Fold in the almonds. • Drop heaped spoonfuls 1 inch (2.5 cm) apart onto the paper. Use the back of a wooden spoon to flatten them slightly. Refrigerate for at least 2 hours. • Preheat the oven to 300°F (150°C/gas 2). • Bake for 20–25 minutes, or until golden brown. • Cool the macaroons on the baking sheets for 5 minutes. Transfer to racks to cool. • Tear away excess paper from around the edges. • Lemon Glaze: Mix the confectioners' sugar in a medium bowl. Beat in the lemon juice and hot water, a teaspoon at a time, until thick. • Drizzle with the glaze.

Makes: about 30–35 cookies • Prep: 45 min + 2 hr to chill Cooking: 20–25 min • Level: 2

- 1½ cups (225 g) blanched whole almonds
- ¾ cup (125 g) all-purpose (plain) flour
- 1 teaspoon ground cinnamon
- ⅛ teaspoon freshly grated nutmeg
- 5 large egg whites
- 2 cups (300 g) confectioners' (icing) sugar
- ⅛ teaspoon cream of tartar
- ½ teaspoon baking soda (bicarbonate of soda)
- 1 teaspoon hot water
- ½ cup (50 g) finely chopped candied lemon peel
- ½ cup (50 g) finely chopped candied orange peel

Lemon Glaze
- 1⅓ cups (200 g) confectioners' (icing) sugar
- 2 tablespoons freshly squeezed lemon juice
- 1–2 tablespoons hot water

NUTTY MOMENTS

- 2 large egg whites
- ½ cup (100 g) granulated sugar
- 2 tablespoons vanilla sugar (see page 414)
- ⅛ teaspoon freshly grated nutmeg
- 1 teaspoon fresh lemon juice
- 1 cup (150 g) finely ground shelled hazelnuts, toasted + 25–30 hazelnuts

Preheat the oven to 300°F (150°C/gas 2). • Line two cookie sheets with parchment paper. • Beat the egg whites in a medium bowl with an electric mixer at medium speed in a bowl over barely simmering water. Gradually beat in the granulated and vanilla sugars. • Mix in the nutmeg, and lemon juice and beat until frothy. The mixture should remain just warm to the touch. • Remove from the water and beat with an electric mixer until stiff and glossy. • Fold in the nuts. • Fill a pastry bag fitted with a ½-inch (1-cm) plain tip and squeeze out 1-inch (2.5-cm) rounds onto the cookie sheets. Press a hazelnut into the center of each cookie. • Brush with water and dust with the confectioners' sugar. • Bake for 15–20 minutes, or until just firm to the touch. • Transfer on the parchment to racks and cool until the cookies firm slightly. • Peel from the paper and let cool completely.

Makes: about 30 macaroons • Prep: 50 min • Cooking: 18–20 min • Level: 2

- 1 teaspoon water
- 3 tablespoons confectioners' (icing) sugar, to dust

Meringues & Macaroons

CRISP ALMOND MACAROONS

- 6 cups (900 g) whole almonds
- 2¼ cups (450 g) superfine (caster) sugar
- 6 large egg whites
- ⅛ teaspoon salt
- slivered almonds, to decorate

Preheat the oven to 325°F (170°C/gas 4). • Butter and flour a large cookie sheet. • Spread the almonds out on a separate baking sheet. Toast for 7 minutes, or until lightly golden. Increase the temperature to 350°F (180°C/gas 4). • Use a kitchen towel to rub off the skins. Transfer to a food processor, add 1 cup (200 g) of sugar, and process until finely ground. • Beat the egg whites and salt in a large bowl until soft peaks form. • Fold in the ground almonds and remaining superfine sugar. • Transfer to a large bowl over barely simmering water. Simmer for 20 minutes, or until very thick. • Drop heaped tablespoons 2 inches (5 cm) apart onto the prepared cookie sheet. Top with almonds. • Bake for 40–45 minutes, or until golden brown. • Cool completely on the cookie sheets.

Makes: about 80 cookies • Prep: 40 min • Cooking: 40–45 minutes • Level: 3

CRISP WALNUT MACAROONS

Preheat the oven to 325°F (170°C/gas 3). • Line three cookie sheets first with parchment paper and then rice paper. • Spread the walnuts on a baking sheet. Toast for 7 minutes, or until lightly golden. • Process in a food processor with ⅓ cup (50 g) of sugar until finely ground. • Beat the eggs and remaining sugar in a large bowl with an electric mixer at high speed until pale and thick. • Fold in the lemon zest and juice and ground walnuts. • Drop rounded teaspoons of the mixture onto the prepared cookie sheets, spacing them 1½ inches (4 cm) apart. • Bake for 12–15 minutes, or until lightly browned. • Transfer the cookies still on the parchment paper to racks to cool. • Tear away the excess rice paper from around the cookies.

Makes: 35–40 macaroons • Prep: 20 min • Cooking: 12–15 min • Level: 2

- 2⅓ cups (350 g) walnut halves
- 1⅓ cups (270 g) sugar
- 3 large eggs
- finely grated zest and juice of ½ lemon

Crisp almond macaroons

Mixed macaroons

MIXED MACAROONS

- 1¼ cups (180 g) finely ground almonds
- 1 tablespoon confectioners' (icing) sugar
- 1 teaspoon cornstarch (cornflour)
- 3 large egg whites
- ⅛ teaspoon salt
- ⅔ cup (140 g) superfine (caster) sugar
- 1 tablespoon vanilla sugar (see page 414)
- ½ teaspoon almond extract (essence)
- chopped candied cherries, angelica, and chopped nuts, to decorate

Preheat the oven to 275°F (140°C/gas 1).
• Line three cookie sheets with parchment paper. • Mix the almonds, confectioners' sugar, and cornstarch in a bowl. • Beat the egg whites and salt in a large bowl with an electric mixer at medium speed until frothy. • With mixer at high speed, gradually add the superfine and vanilla sugars until stiff, glossy peaks form. • Fold in the dry ingredients and almond extract. • Fit a pastry bag with a 1½-inch (4-cm) plain tip. Fill the pastry bag, twist the opening tightly closed, and squeeze out small lengths and rings, spacing them 1 inch (2.5 cm) apart on the prepared cookie sheets. • Top with the candied cherries, angelica, and nuts. • Bake for 20–25 minutes, or until golden brown. • Transfer to racks to cool.

Makes: about 45 macaroons • Prep: 30 min • Cooking: 20–25 min • Level: 2

ANGELICA MOMENTS

Preheat the oven to 325°F (170°C/gas 3).
• Line a cookie sheet with parchment paper. • Beat the egg white and salt in a medium bowl with an electric mixer at medium speed until frothy. • With mixer at high speed, gradually add the sugar, beating until stiff, glossy peaks form. • Fold in the ginger, candied cherries, raisins, and almonds. • Drop teaspoons of the batter 2 inches (5 cm) apart onto the prepared cookie sheets. • Bake for 10 minutes. • Remove from the oven and top with angelica. • Bake for 10–15 minutes more, or until firm to the touch. • Transfer to racks to cool.

Makes: about 20 cookies • Prep: 20 min • Cooking: 20–25 minutes • Level: 1

- 1 large egg white
- ⅛ teaspoon salt
- 1 cup (200 g) sugar
- ⅓ cup (30 g) finely chopped candied (crystallized) ginger
- ⅓ cup (30 g) finely chopped candied cherries
- ⅓ cup (30 g) finely chopped seedless raisins
- ⅔ cup (70 g) finely chopped almonds
- ⅓ cup (30 g) finely chopped angelica

Nutty raw sugar macaroons

RAW SUGAR MACAROONS

- ²/₃ cup (100 g) blanched almonds
- ¹/₂ cup (100 g) raw sugar (Barbados or Demerara)
- ¹/₂ teaspoon ground aniseeds
- ¹/₄ teaspoon almond extract (essence)
- 1 large egg white, lightly beaten
- 1 tablespoon finely chopped pine nuts

Preheat the oven to 325°F (170°C/gas 3). • Line a cookie sheet with parchment paper. • Spread the almonds on a large baking sheet. Toast for 7 minutes, or until lightly browned. • Transfer the nuts to a food processor, add the raw sugar, and process until finely ground. • Transfer to a large bowl and stir in the aniseeds. • Beat the egg white and almond extract in a medium bowl until frothy. • Use a large spatula to fold in the nut mixture. • Form the dough into balls the size of walnuts and place 1 inch (2.5 cm) apart on the prepared cookie sheet, flattening them slightly. • Sprinkle the cookies with the pine nuts, pressing them into the dough. • Bake for 20–25 minutes, or until golden and dry to the touch. • Transfer to racks to cool.

Makes: about 16 macaroons • Prep: 30 min • Cooking: 20–25 min • Level: 2

CHOCOLATE ALMOND MACAROONS

Preheat the oven to 325°F (170°C/gas 3). • Line three cookie sheets with rice paper. • Sprinkle the almonds on a baking sheet. Toast for 7 minutes, or until lightly golden. • Set aside to cool. Lower the oven to 275°F (140°C/gas 1). • Beat the egg whites in a large bowl with an electric mixer at medium speed until frothy. • With mixer at high speed, gradually add the sugar, cream of tartar, vanilla, and salt, until stiff, glossy peaks form. • Fold in the chocolate and almonds. • Drop teaspoons of the batter 1½ inches (4 cm) apart onto the rice paper. • Bake for 20–25 minutes, or until lightly browned. • Cool the cookies completely on the cookie sheets. Tear away the excess paper from around the nests.

Makes: about 40 macaroons • Prep: 40 min • Cooking: 20–25 min • Level: 2

- 2 cups (200 g) slivered almonds
- 3 large egg whites
- 1 cup (200 g) superfine (caster) sugar
- ¹/₈ teaspoon cream of tartar
- ¹/₄ teaspoon vanilla extract (essence)
- ¹/₈ teaspoon salt
- 4 oz (125 g) semisweet (dark) chocolate, finely grated

CHOCOLATE AMARETTI COOKIES

- 1 cup (200 g) sugar
- 1¹/₄ cups (180 g) finely ground almonds
- 1 tablespoon cornstarch (cornflour)
- 2 large egg whites
- 1 teaspoon unsweetened cocoa powder
- ¹/₈ teaspoon salt

Preheat the oven to 350°F (180°C/gas 4). • Butter two cookie sheets. • Mix the sugar, almonds, cornstarch, egg whites, cocoa, and salt in a large bowl until well blended. • Drop rounded teaspoons of the dough 1 inch (2.5 cm) apart onto the prepared cookie sheets. • Bake for 10–12 minutes, or until firm to the touch. • Transfer to racks and let cool completely.

Makes: about 30 cookies • Prep: 20 min • Cooking: 10–12 min • Level: 2

MINI ALMOND MACAROONS

Preheat the oven to 300°F (150°C/gas 4). • Line two cookie sheets with aluminum foil. • Process the almonds in a food processor or blender until finely chopped. • Beat the egg whites, confectioners' sugar, and salt in a large bowl placed over barely simmering water with an electric mixer at high speed until stiff peaks form. • Remove the bowl from the water. Stir in the almond extract and chopped almonds. • Drop teaspoons of the mixture 1 inch (2.5 cm) apart onto the prepared cookie sheets. • Bake for 20–30 minutes, or until crisp. • Transfer the meringues on the foil to racks and let cool. .

Makes: about 25 macaroons • Prep: 20 min • Cooking: 20–30 min • Level: 1

- 1¹/₄ cups (175 g) blanched almonds
- 4 large egg whites
- ¹/₈ teaspoon salt
- 2 cups (300 g) confectioners' (icing) sugar
- ¹/₄ teaspoon almond extract (essence)

Meringues & Macaroons

GIANDUIA KISSES

- 2 large egg whites
- ⅛ teaspoon salt
- 2 tablespoons superfine (caster) sugar
- ⅓ cup (50 g) confectioners' (icing) sugar
- 1¼ cups (125 g) finely chopped hazelnuts
- ½ cup (125 g) Nutella (chocolate hazelnut cream)

Gianduia is an Italian word for chocolate hazelnut flavoring. These cookies come from Piedmont.
Preheat the oven to 375°F (190°C/gas 5).
• Line two cookie sheets with parchment paper. • Beat the egg whites and salt in a large bowl with an electric mixer at medium speed until frothy. • With mixer at medium speed, gradually add the superfine sugar, beating until stiff, glossy peaks form. • Use a large rubber spatula to fold in the confectioners' sugar and hazelnuts. • Fit a pastry bag with a 1-inch (2.5-cm) star tip. Fill the pastry bag, twist the opening tightly closed, and squeeze out 1-inch (2.5-cm) stars spacing 1 inch (2.5 cm) apart onto the prepared cookie sheets. • Bake for 8–10 minutes, or until pale gold. • Transfer to racks to cool. • Stick the cookies together in pairs with the chocolate hazelnut cream.
Makes: about 20 cookies • Prep: 30 min • Cooking: 8–10 min • Level: 2

ORANGE PISTACHIO MACAROONS

Preheat the oven to 350°F (180°C/gas 4).
• Line two cookie sheets with parchment paper and grease them with almond oil.
• Mix the flour and salt into a medium bowl. • Process ⅔ cup (100 g) of pistachios in a food processor until finely chopped.
• Transfer to a large bowl and mix in the granulated sugar, candied peel, and orange zest. • Mix in the dry ingredients. • Beat the egg whites in a large bowl with an electric mixer at medium speed until frothy. Gradually add the superfine sugar, beating until stiff, glossy peaks form. • Mix in the pistachios. • Drop teaspoons of the mixture 1½ inches (4 cm) apart onto the prepared cookie sheets. • Sprinkle with the remaining pistachios. • Bake for 10–12 minutes, or until the cookies are lightly golden and the bottoms are firm and just browned. • Dust with the confectioners' sugar and let cool on the parchment. • Transfer to racks to cool completely.
Makes: about 25 macaroons • Prep: 20 min • Cooking: 10–12 min • Level: 2

- ⅓ cup (50 g) all-purpose (plain) flour
- ⅛ teaspoon salt
- ⅔ cup (100 g) + 2 tablespoons pistachios
- ⅔ cup (140 g) sugar
- 3 tablespoons finely chopped orange candied peel
- 1 tablespoon finely grated orange zest
- 3 large egg whites
- ¼ cup (50 g) superfine (caster) sugar
- 2 tablespoons confectioners' (icing) sugar, to dust

CITRUS CRISPS

- 1¾ cups (275 g) whole almonds
- 1 cup (200 g) superfine (caster) sugar
- 1 cup (150 g) confectioners' (icing sugar + extra to dust
- 2 tablespoons chopped candied lemon peel
- ½ teaspoon lime extract (essence)
- 1 large egg white

Preheat the oven to 325°F (170°C/gas 3).
• Line a cookie sheet with rice paper.
• Spread the almonds out on a large baking sheet. Toast in the oven for 7 minutes, or until lightly golden. Transfer to a food processor, add the superfine sugar, and process until finely chopped. • Transfer to a large bowl. Stir in the confectioners' sugar, lemon peel, and lemon extract. • Beat the egg white in a small bowl with an electric mixer at high speed until stiff peaks form. • Fold the beaten white into the almond

mixture. • Spread the mixture into 1-inch (2.5-cm) squares on the prepared cookie sheet. • Cover with a clean kitchen towel and let stand in a cool place overnight. Preheat the oven to 300°F (150°C/gas 2).
• Bake for 55–65 minutes, or until set. Cool completely on the cookie sheet. • Tear off any excess paper and dust with the confectioners' sugar.
Makes: about 15 cookies • Prep: 25 min + 12 hr to rest Cooking: 55–65 min Level: 3

Meringues & Macaroons

CINNAMON CHOCOLATE MACAROONS

- 1 cup (150 g) blanched almonds
- 6 oz (180 g) milk chocolate, coarsely chopped
- ½ cup (100 g) sugar
- 1 tablespoon unsweetened cocoa powder
- ¼ teaspoon ground cinnamon
- 2 large egg whites, lightly beaten
- 1 teaspoon water
- 2 tablespoons confectioners' (icing) sugar

Preheat the oven to 325°F (170°C/gas 3). • Spread the almonds on a large baking sheet. Toast for 7 minutes, or until lightly golden. Let cool. • Transfer to a food processor and chop until finely ground. • Melt 3 oz (90 g) of chocolate in a double boiler over barely simmering water. • Mix the ground almonds, sugar, cocoa, and cinnamon in a large bowl. • Stir in the melted chocolate and enough egg white to form a soft, but not sticky paste. • Refrigerate for 30 minutes. • Line two cookie sheets with parchment paper. • Spoon scant tablespoons of the mixture 1 inch (2.5 cm) apart onto the cookie sheets. • Brush the tops with a little water and sprinkle with the confectioners' sugar. • Bake for 10–12 minutes, or until just firm to the touch. • Transfer to racks to cool. • Melt the remaining chocolate in a double boiler over barely simmering water. • Dip the macaroons halfway into the chocolate. • Let dry on parchment paper for 30 minutes.

Makes: about 25 macaroons • Prep: 35 min + 1 hr to chill and set • Cooking: 10–12 min • Level: 2

COCONUT CREAM MACAROONS

Preheat the oven to 350°F (180°C/gas 4). • Line two cookie sheets with parchment paper. • Melt ⅓ cup (90 g) of butter in a large skillet and toast the oats until lightly golden. • Sift the flour, baking powder, and salt into a large bowl. • Beat the remaining butter and the sugars in a large bowl with an electric mixer at high speed until creamy. • Add the eggs, coconut, cream, and vanilla, beating until just blended. • Mix in the dry ingredients. • Form into balls the size of walnuts and place 2 inches (5 cm) apart on the prepared cookie sheets, flattening them slightly. • Bake for 12–15 minutes, until firm to the touch and golden brown. • Cool on the sheets until the cookies firm slightly. • Transfer to racks and let cool completely.

Makes: about 40 macaroons • Prep: 25 min • Cooking: 12–15 min • Level: 1

- 1¼ cups (310 g) butter, softened
- 2 cups (250 g) old-fashioned rolled oats
- 1⅓ cups (200 g) all-purpose (plain) flour
- 1 teaspoon baking powder
- ¼ teaspoon salt
- ½ cup (100 g) firmly packed light brown sugar
- ½ cup (100 g) raw sugar (Barbados or Demerara)
- 2 large eggs
- 1¼ cups (150 g) shredded (desiccated) coconut
- 3 tablespoons heavy (double) cream
- 1 teaspoon vanilla extract (essence)

NUTTY MACAROONS

- 2 cups (300 g) hazelnuts
- 1 cup (200 g) superfine (caster) sugar
- 4 large egg whites
- ¼ teaspoon salt

Preheat the oven to 325°F (170°C/gas 3). • Line two cookie sheets with parchment paper. • Spread the hazelnuts on a large baking sheet. Toast for 7 minutes, or until lightly golden. • Reduce the oven temperature to 250°F (130°C/gas ½). • Transfer the nuts to a food processor with ½ cup (100 g) of sugar and process until finely ground. • Beat the egg whites and salt in a large bowl with an electric mixer at medium speed until soft peaks form. With mixer at high speed, gradually add the remaining superfine sugar, beating until stiff, glossy peaks form. • Use a large rubber spatula to fold in the hazelnuts. • Drop teaspoons of the mixture 2 inches (5 cm) apart on the prepared cookie sheets. • Bake for 50–60 minutes, or until the macaroons are dry and crisp. • Transfer while still on the parchment paper to a rack to cool.

Makes: 30–35 macaroons • Prep: 20 min • Cooking: 50–60 min • Level: 1

Meringues & Macaroons

POPPY SEED MACAROONS

- ³⁄₄ cup (120 g) blanched almonds
- 1 cup (200 g) sugar
- 2 tablespoons all-purpose (plain) flour
- 2 large egg whites
- ¹⁄₈ teaspoon salt
- ¹⁄₄ teaspoon vanilla extract (essence)
- 1 tablespoon poppy seeds

Preheat the oven to 325°F (170°C/gas 3). • Line a cookie sheet with rice paper. • Spread the nuts on a large baking sheet. Toast for 7 minutes, or until lightly golden. • Increase the oven temperature to 375°F (190°C/gas 5). • Place the almonds and sugar in a food processor and chop until finely ground. • Stir the almond mixture and flour in a medium bowl. • Beat the egg whites and salt with an electric mixer at high speed until stiff peaks form. • Fold in the dry ingredients and vanilla. • Fit a pastry bag with a 1-inch (2.5-cm) star tip. Fill the pastry bag, twist the opening tightly closed, and squeeze out 1-inch (2.5-cm) stars 1 inch (2.5-cm) apart on the prepared cookie sheet. Sprinkle with the poppy seeds. • Bake for 12–15 minutes, or until pale gold. • Cool on the sheets until the cookies firm slightly. • Transfer to racks and let cool completely.

Makes: about 15 macaroons • Prep: 25 min • Cooking: 12–15 min • Level: 2

CANDIED PEEL MACAROONS

Soak the candied peel in the orange liqueur for 1 hour. • Drain, reserving the liqueur. • Preheat the oven to 375°F (190°C/gas 5). • Line two cookie sheets with parchment paper. • Mix the flour, baking powder, and salt in a medium bowl. • Beat the butter and sugar in a large bowl with an electric mixer at high speed until creamy. • Add the lemon extract. • With mixer at high speed, beat in the egg whites and the reserved orange liqueur. • Mix in the dry ingredients. • Fit a pastry bag with a ¹⁄₂-inch (1-cm) plain tip. Fill the pastry bag, twist the opening tightly closed, and squeeze out 1¹⁄₂-inch (4-cm) mounds, spacing 2 inches (5 cm) apart on the prepared cookie sheets. • Lightly press a piece of candied peel into the top of each cookie. • Bake for 8–10 minutes, or until golden brown. • Cool on the sheets until the cookies firm slightly. • Transfer to racks and let cool completely.

Makes: about 30 macaroons • Prep: 40 min + 1 hr to soak Cooking: 8–10 min • Level: 2

- 2 tablespoons finely chopped mixed candied peel
- 2 tablespoons orange liqueur
- 1 cup (150 g) all-purpose (plain) flour
- ¹⁄₄ teaspoon baking powder
- ¹⁄₈ teaspoon salt
- ¹⁄₂ cup (125 g) butter, softened
- ²⁄₃ cup (140 g) sugar
- ¹⁄₂ teaspoon lemon extract (essence)
- 2 egg whites, lightly beaten

PINE NUT CRISPS

- ³⁄₄ cup (150 g) pine nuts
- 1¹⁄₂ cups (150 g) finely chopped almonds
- 1¹⁄₄ cups (250 g) sugar
- ¹⁄₂ teaspoon vanilla extract (essence)
- 2 large egg whites

Line a cookie sheet with parchment paper. • Place small heaps of pine nuts (about 10 pine nuts per heap) on the prepared cookie sheet. • Mix the almonds, sugar, and vanilla in a large bowl. • Beat the egg whites with an electric mixer at high speed until stiff peaks form. • Use a large rubber spatula to fold the beaten whites into the almond mixture. • Drop teaspoons of the mixture on top of the pine nuts to cover them completely. • Refrigerate for 30 minutes. • Preheat the oven to 300°F (150°C/gas 2). • Bake for 18–20 minutes, or until set. • Turn off the oven. Cool completely in the oven with the door ajar.

Makes: about 25 cookies • Prep: 15 min + 30 min to chill Cooking: 18–20 min • Level: 1

MACADAMIA MACAROONS

Preheat the oven to 350°F (180°C/gas 4). • Butter a cookie sheet. • Beat the egg whites and salt in a large bowl with an electric mixer at medium speed until frothy. • With mixer at high speed, gradually add the sugar, beating until stiff, glossy peaks form. • Use a large rubber spatula to fold in the coconut and macadamia nuts. • Drop teaspoons of the mixture 1 inch (2.5 cm) apart onto the prepared cookie sheet. • Bake for 10–15 minutes, or until lightly golden. • Transfer to racks to cool.

Makes: about 20 macaroons • Prep: 15 min • Cooking: 10–15 min • Level: 1

- 2 large egg whites
- ¹⁄₈ teaspoon salt
- ³⁄₄ cup (150 g) sugar
- 1¹⁄₂ cups (185 g) shredded (desiccated) coconut
- 1 cup (100 g) coarsely chopped macadamia nuts

Meringues & Macaroons

HAZELNUT VANILLA MACAROONS

- 4 cups (600 g) hazelnuts + 40 hazelnuts, halved
- 1½ cups (300 g) sugar
- 4 large eggs
- 1 cup (200 g) vanilla sugar (see page 414)

Preheat the oven to 325°F (170°C/gas 3). • Spread the 4 cups of hazelnuts on a large baking sheet. Toast for 7 minutes, or until lightly golden. • Transfer to a large cotton kitchen towel. Fold the towel over the nuts and rub them to remove the thin inner skins. • Discard the skins and process with ½ cup (100 g) of sugar in a food processor or blender until finely ground. • Line three cookie sheets with rice paper. • Beat the eggs and remaining granulated sugar and vanilla sugar in a large bowl with an electric mixer until very pale and thick. • Mix in the ground hazelnuts to form a smooth dough. • Moisten your hands with water and form the dough into balls the size of walnuts. • Place 2 inches (5 cm) apart on the rice paper, flattening each ball slightly and pressing a hazelnut half into the center. • Bake for 10–12 minutes, or until firm to the touch. Transfer on the rice paper to racks to cool. • Tear away the excess rice paper from around the cookies

Makes: about 65 macaroons • Prep: 45 min • Cooking: 10–12 min • Level: 2

GLAZED ORANGE MACAROONS

Preheat the oven to 325°F (170°C/gas 3). • Line three cookie sheets with parchment paper. • Sprinkle the almonds on a large baking sheet. Toast for 7 minutes, or until lightly golden. Lower the oven temperature to 275°F (140°C/gas 1). • Process the almonds in a food processor until finely chopped. • Beat the egg whites, superfine sugar, and vanilla sugar in a double boiler over barely simmering water until stiff peaks form. • Add the orange zest and juice. • Remove from the heat. Use a rubber spatula to fold the almonds and bread crumbs into the batter. • Drop teaspoons of the batter 1 inch (2.5 cm) apart onto the prepared cookie sheets. • Bake for 20–25 minutes, or until pale golden. The macaroons should still be soft but will harden while cooling. • Transfer to racks to cool. • Glaze: Heat the marmalade in a small saucepan and drizzle over the cooled macaroons. Set aside. • Melt the chocolate in a double boiler over barely simmering water. • Drizzle the chocolate over the tops.

Makes: about 50 macaroons • Prep: 50 min • Cooking: 20–25 min • Level: 2

- 1¼ cups (180 g) blanched almonds
- 3 large egg whites
- ¾ cup (150 g) superfine (caster) sugar
- 1 tablespoon vanilla sugar (see page 414)
- finely grated zest of 1 orange
- 1 tablespoon freshly squeezed orange juice
- 1 cup (60 g) fresh bread crumbs

Glaze
- 2 tablespoons orange marmalade
- 2 oz (60 g) semisweet (dark) chocolate, coarsely chopped

APRICOT BRANDY MACAROONS

Macaroons
- ⅓ cup (50 g) all-purpose (plain) flour
- 2 cups (300 g) finely ground walnuts
- 3 large egg whites
- ¼ teaspoon salt
- ¾ cup (150 g) sugar

Preheat the oven to 275°F (140°C/gas 1). • Butter two cookie sheets. • Place the flour in a medium bowl. Stir in the walnuts. • Beat the egg whites and salt in a large bowl until frothy. • Add the sugar, beating until stiff peaks form. • Fold in the dry ingredients. • Fit a pastry bag with a ¾-inch (2-cm) plain tip. Fill the pastry bag, twist the opening tightly closed, and squeeze out mounds the size of walnuts spacing them 1 inch (2.5 cm) apart on the sheets. • Bake for 20–25 minutes, or until the cookies are set and lightly browned. • Transfer the

macaroons to racks and let cool completely. • Filling: Melt the chocolate with the cream in a double boiler over barely simmering water. • Stir in the brandy. • Plunge the pan into a bowl of ice water and stir until the mixture has cooled. • With mixer at high speed, beat until creamy. • Stick the macaroons together in pairs with the filling. Roll in the pistachios.

Makes: about 30 macaroons • Prep: 55 min • Cooking: 20–25 min • Level: 2

Filling
- 8 oz (250 g) white chocolate, coarsely chopped
- ¼ cup (60 ml) light (single) cream
- 2 tablespoons apricot brandy
- 1–2 tablespoons finely chopped pistachios

Meringues & Macaroons

ALMOND STAR MACAROONS

- 3 large egg whites
- 1½ cups (225 g) confectioners' (icing) sugar
- ⅛ teaspoon cream of tartar
- 4 cups (600 g) finely ground almonds
- 2 teaspoons vanilla sugar (see page 414)
- ¼ teaspoon vanilla extract (essence)

Line two cookie sheets with parchment paper. • Beat the egg whites in a large bowl with an electric mixer at medium speed until frothy. With mixer at high speed, gradually add the confectioners' sugar and lemon juice beating until stiff, glossy peaks form. • Spoon 1 cup (250 ml) beaten whites into a small bowl and set aside in the refrigerator as a glaze. • Use a large rubber spatula to fold 3 cups (450 g) almonds, the vanilla sugar, and vanilla into the large bowl of beaten whites. Cover with plastic wrap (cling film) and refrigerate for 30 minutes. • Preheat the oven to 275°F (140°C/gas 1). • Sprinkle a lightly floured surface with the remaining ground almonds. Roll out the dough to ½ inch (1 cm) thick. • Dip a star cutter into cold water and stamp out cookies. Gather the dough scraps, re-roll, and cut out cookies until all the dough is used. • Transfer to the cookie sheets, placing them 1 inch (2.5 cm) apart. Brush a thin layer of reserved chilled egg white over each macaroon. • Bake for 25–30 minutes, or until firm to the touch. • Cool completely on the cookie sheets.

Makes: about 40 macaroons • Prep: 1 hr + 30 min to chill
Cooking: 25–30 min • Level: 2

ALMOND MACAROONS WITH CANDIED CHERRIES

Dust two cookie sheets with rice flour. • Mix the almonds, confectioners' sugar, egg whites, and salt in a large bowl until smooth. • Fit a pastry bag with a ½-inch (1-cm) star tip. Fill the pastry bag, twist the opening tightly closed, and squeeze out rosettes, spacing 1 inch (2.5 cm) apart on the prepared cookie sheets. • Place a piece of candied cherry on top of each cookie. • Refrigerate for 30 minutes. • Preheat the oven to 475°F (250°C/gas 9). • Bake for 3–5 minutes, or until lightly browned at the edges. • Transfer to racks to cool.

Makes: about 25 macaroons • Prep: 25 min + 30 min to chill
Cooking: 3–5 min • Level: 2

- 1¼ cups (125 g) finely ground almonds
- ¾ cup (125 g) confectioners' (icing) sugar
- 2 large egg whites
- ⅛ teaspoon salt
- 6 candied cherries, coarsely chopped

HAZELNUT ORANGE MACAROONS

- 3 large egg whites
- ⅛ teaspoon salt
- 1¾ cups (350 g) sugar
- 3⅓ cups (500 g) finely ground hazelnuts
- 4 tablespoons orange marmalade
- 18 candied cherries, cut in half

Preheat the oven to 350°F (180°C/gas 4). • Butter three cookie sheets. • Beat the egg whites and salt in a large bowl with an electric mixer at medium speed until soft peaks form. • With mixer at high speed, gradually add the sugar, beating until stiff, glossy peaks form. • Fold in the hazelnuts. • Heat the marmalade in a small saucepan over low heat until liquid. Let cool slightly. • Carefully fold the marmalade into the batter. • Fit a pastry bag with a ½-inch (1-cm) star tip. Fill the pastry bag, twist the opening tightly closed. Squeeze out generous 1½-inch (4-cm) stars spacing 2 inches (5 cm) apart on the prepared cookie sheets. • Decorate with cherry halves. • Bake for 10–15 minutes, or until just golden. • Transfer to racks to cool.

Makes: about 36 cookies • Prep: 25 min • Cooking: 10–15 min • Level: 2

Date and pecan delight

DATE AND PECAN DELIGHT

- 1 cup (100 g) finely chopped pitted dates
- 1³/₄ cups (175 g) finely chopped pecans
- 2 large egg whites
- 1 cup (150 g) confectioners' (icing) sugar
- 1 tablespoon unsweetened cocoa powder
- freshly squeezed juice of 1 lemon

Preheat the oven to 325°F (170°C/gas 3). • Butter two cookie sheets. • Chop the dates very finely and place in a large bowl. Add the pecans. • Stir in the egg whites, confectioners' sugar, cocoa, and lemon juice and mix until well blended. • Drop teaspoons of the dough 1 inch (2.5 cm) apart onto the prepared cookie sheets. • Bake for 25–30 minutes, or until just golden at the edges. • Transfer to racks to cool.

Makes: about 40 cookies • Prep: 20 min • Cooking: 25–30 min • Level: 1

ALI BABA BITES

Preheat the oven to 325°F (170°C/gas 3). • Butter two cookie sheets. • Chop the dates very finely and place in a large bowl. Add the walnuts. • Stir in the egg whites, confectioners' sugar, cocoa, and lemon juice and mix until well blended. • Drop teaspoons of the dough 1 inch (2.5 cm) apart onto the prepared cookie sheets. • Bake for 25–30 minutes, or until just golden at the edges. • Transfer to racks and let cool.

Makes: about 40 cookies • Prep: 20 min • Cooking: 25–30 min • Level: 1

- 1³/₄ cups (175 g) finely chopped pitted dates
- 1³/₄ cups (175 g) finely chopped walnuts
- 2 large egg whites
- 1 cup (150 g) confectioners' (icing) sugar
- 1 tablespoon unsweetened cocoa powder
- freshly squeezed juice of 1 lemon

PISTACHIO MACAROONS

- 4 large egg whites
- ³/₄ cup (150 g) superfine (caster) sugar
- 1 tablespoon vanilla sugar (see page 414)
- 2¹/₄ cups coarsely chopped pistachio nuts
- 1 cup (100 g) finely chopped candied orange peel

Preheat the oven to 250°F (130°C/gas ¹/₂). • Line two cookie sheets with parchment paper. • Beat the egg whites and superfine and vanilla sugars in a large bowl with an electric mixer at high speed until stiff peaks form. • Use a large rubber spatula to fold in the pistachios and candied peel. • Drop teaspoons of the batter 2 inches apart onto the prepared cookie sheets. • Bake for 12–15 minutes, or until crisp and dry to the touch, rotating the sheets halfway through for even baking. • Transfer to racks to cool.

Makes: about 40 macaroons • Prep: 30 min • Cooking: 12–15 min • Level: 1

GLAZED ALMOND MACAROONS

Preheat the oven to 350°F (180°C/gas 4). • Line two cookie sheets with rice paper. • Beat the egg whites in a large bowl with an electric mixer at high speed until stiff peaks form. • Use a large rubber spatula to fold in the sugar, almonds, and almond extract. • Fit a pastry bag with a ¹/₂-inch (1-cm) plain tip. Fill the pastry bag, twist the opening tightly closed, and pipe out 3 inch (8-cm) long lines spacing 1¹/₂ inches (4 cm) apart on the prepared cookie sheets. • Bake for 15–20 minutes, or until golden brown. • Cool on the cookie sheets for 1 minute. Transfer to racks to cool. • Tear away the excess rice paper from around the edges. • Melt the chocolate in a double boiler over barely simmering water. • Drizzle the chocolate in a zigzag pattern over the tops.

Makes: about 20 macaroons • Prep: 30 min • Cooking: 15–20 min • Level: 2

- 2 large egg whites
- 1 cup (200 g) superfine (caster) sugar
- 1³/₄ cups (275 g) finely ground almonds
- ¹/₂ teaspoon almond extract (essence)
- 4 oz (125 g) semisweet (dark) chocolate, coarsely chopped

NO-BAKE COOKIES

These are the simplest type of cookies and are usually a firm favorite with children. They are also a good way for children to begin to learn basic baking skills, since there are no hot ovens or burning baking sheets to be dealt with. Most no-bake cookies consist of just a few ingredients, carefully stirred together then pressed into a dish which is chilled in the refrigerator for several hours before being cut into squares or slices to serve. In this chapter, we have included old favorites such as the Chocolate salami, shown left (see recipe on page 274) and Rice krispie squares (see page 282), plus a couple of new takes on this delicious theme, including Chocolate marshmallow slice (see page 274), White chocolate amaretti squares (see page 276), and Marzipan moons (see page 286).

Chocolate salami (see page 274)

No-Bake Cookies

CHOCOLATE MARSHMALLOW SLICE

- ½ cup (125 g) butter, cut up
- 1 tablespoon dark brown sugar
- ⅓ cup (50 g) unsweetened cocoa powder
- 2 tablespoons light corn (golden) syrup
- 8 oz (250 g) semisweet (dark) chocolate, coarsely chopped
- 2 cups (250 g) snipped marshmallows, mixed colors
- 1 cup (180 g) raisins

Set out an 8-inch (20-cm) square of plastic wrap (cling film). • Melt the butter with the brown sugar, cocoa powder, and corn syrup in a small saucepan over low heat until the sugar has dissolved completely. • Melt the chocolate in a double boiler over barely simmering water. Stir the chocolate into the butter mixture. Mix in the marshmallows and raisins. • Spoon the mixture onto the center of the plastic wrap. Roll the mixture to form a cylinder. • Refrigerate for 4 hours, or until firm. • Cut into rounds.

Makes: about 25 slices • Prep: 25 min + 4 hr to chill • Level: 1

CHOCOLATE FRUIT CHEWIES

Set out a 10½ x 15½-inch (26 x 36-cm) jelly-roll pan. • Melt the butter and sugar in a large saucepan over medium heat. • Remove from the heat and stir in the dates, cherries, raisins, and rice krispies until well coated. • Spoon the mixture evenly into the pan, pressing down firmly. • Refrigerate for 2 hours, or until set. • Melt the chocolate in a double boiler over barely simmering water. Pour the chocolate over and let stand for 20 minutes until set. • Use a sharp knife to cut into squares.

Makes: about 16 squares • Prep: 40 min + 2 hr 20 min to chill • Level : 1

- ½ cup (125 g) butter, cut up
- ½ cup (100 g) sugar
- 1¾ cups (175 g) finely chopped pitted dates
- ⅔ cup (70 g) finely chopped candied cherries
- ⅓ cup (45 g) golden raisins (sultanas)
- 2 cups (200 g) rice krispies
- 8 oz (250 g) semisweet (dark) chocolate, coarsely chopped

CHOCOLATE-PEANUT SQUARES

- 4 cups (500 g) plain cookie crumbs
- 1 cup (150 g) coarsely chopped unsalted peanuts
- ½ cup (75 g) confectioners' (icing) sugar
- ¼ cup (60 g) smooth peanut butter
- 12 oz (350 g) semisweet (dark) chocolate, chopped
- 1 cup (250 ml) evaporated milk
- 1 teaspoon vanilla extract (essence)

Butter a 9-inch (23-cm) square baking pan. • Mix the cookie crumbs, peanuts, confectioners' sugar, and peanut butter in a large bowl. • Melt the chocolate and milk over very low heat, stirring constantly until smooth. • Remove from the heat and stir in the vanilla. Pour the chocolate mixture over the cookie crumb mixture in the bowl and stir well to combine. • Spoon into the prepared pan and refrigerate for 2 hours, or until set. • Cut into squares.

Makes: about 24 squares • Prep: 20 min + 2 hr to chill Level: 1

CHOCOLATE SALAMI

Mix the graham cracker crumbs, almonds, apricots, candied cherries, and chocolate chips in a large bowl. • Melt the semisweet chocolate with the butter in a double boiler over barely simmering water. Let cool for 5 minutes. • Pour the chocolate mixture over the graham cracker mixture and mix well. • Turn the mixture onto a sheet of plastic wrap (cling film) and form into a 10-inch (25-cm) log. • Wrap in the plastic wrap and refrigerate for 12 hours. • Slice the log ½ inch (1-cm) thick. • Melt the white chocolate in a double boiler over barely simmering water and drizzle over the sliced cookies.

Makes: about 20 slices • Prep: 20 min + 12 hr to chill Level: 1

- ⅔ cup (80 g) graham cracker crumbs (crushed digestive biscuits)
- ½ cup (50 g) coarsely chopped toasted almonds
- ½ cup (50 g) finely chopped dried apricots
- ½ cup (50 g) coarsely chopped candied cherries
- ⅓ cup (60 g) white chocolate chips
- 5 oz (150 g) semisweet (dark) chocolate, coarsely chopped
- ¼ cup (60 g) butter, cut up
- 2 oz (60 g) white chocolate, coarsely chopped

No-Bake Cookies

WHITE CHOCOLATE AMARETTI SQUARES

- 10 oz (300 g) white chocolate, coarsely chopped
- 2/3 cup (150 g) butter, cut up
- 1/4 cup (60 ml) heavy (double) cream
- 3 oz (90 g) amaretti cookies, crushed
- 2 tablespoons unsweetened shredded (desiccated) coconut
- 1 cup (100 g) coarsely chopped candied cherries
- 1/2 cup (50 g) flaked almonds, toasted

Line an 8-inch (20-cm) square baking pan with parchment paper. • Melt the white chocolate with the butter and cream in a double boiler over barely simmering water. • Mix in the amaretti cookies, coconut, cherries, and almonds until well coated. • Spoon into the prepared pan, spreading evenly. • Refrigerate for 4 hours, or until set. • Use a knife dipped in hot water to cut into squares.

Makes: about 20 squares • Prep: 30 min + 4 hr to chill
Level: 1

COCONUT SQUARES WITH CHOCOLATE

Line an 8-inch (20-cm) pan with aluminum foil. • Beat the butter and confectioners' sugar in a large bowl with an electric mixer at high speed until creamy. • Stir in the coconut, graham cracker crumbs, and vanilla. • Press the mixture into the prepared pan. Refrigerate for 2 hours, or until set. • Melt the chocolate in a double boiler over barely simmering water. Pour over the cookie base in the pan. Refrigerate for 1 hour, or until set. • Cut into squares.

Makes: about 20 squares • Prep: 20 min + 3 hr to chill
Level: 1

- 3/4 cup (180 g) butter, softened
- 1 cup (150 g) confectioners' (icing) sugar
- 1 cup (125 g) unsweetened shredded (desiccated) coconut
- 1 cup (125 g) graham cracker crumbs (crushed digestive biscuits)
- 1 teaspoon vanilla extract (essence)
- 8 oz (250 g) semisweet (dark) chocolate, coarsely chopped

PISTACHIO SQUARES

- 2 cups (400 g) granulated sugar
- 2/3 cup (150 ml) milk
- 2/3 cup (150 g) butter, cut up
- 3 oz (90 g) semisweet (dark) chocolate, coarsely chopped
- 2 tablespoons honey
- 1/3 cup (50 g) pistachios, crushed
- 1 cup (150 g) old-fashioned rolled oats

Butter a 9-inch (23-cm) square baking pan. • Stir the sugar, milk, butter, chocolate, and honey in a large saucepan over low heat until the ingredients have blended. • Wash down the sides of the pan with a pastry brush dipped in cold water to prevent sugar crystals from forming. Cook, without stirring, until the mixture reaches 238°F (114°C), or the soft-ball stage. • Remove from the heat and let cool for 5 minutes. • Stir in the pistachios and oats until creamy. • Pour the mixture into the prepared pan. • Use a sharp knife to score into 20 squares. • Let stand for at least 4 hours, or until firm.

Makes: about 20 squares • Prep: 45 min + 4 hr to set
Level: 2

MINT BALLS

Mix the cookie crumbs, walnuts, 1 cup (150 g) confectioners' sugar, corn syrup, and mint liqueur in a large bowl to form a stiff dough. • Form the dough into balls the size of walnuts and roll in the remaining confectioners' sugar. • Arrange in mini paper liners and serve.

Makes: about 25 cookies • Prep: 20 min • Level: 1

- 1 cup (125 g) plain vanilla cookie crumbs
- 3/4 cup (75 g) finely chopped walnuts
- 1 1/4 cups (180 g) confectioners' (icing) sugar
- 2 tablespoons light corn syrup (golden) syrup
- 1/3 cup (90 ml) mint liqueur

No-Bake Cookies

COFFEE AND PECAN WEDGES

- 1/3 cup (90 g) butter, cut up
- 2 tablespoons sugar
- 1³/₄ cups (200 g) graham cracker crumbs (crushed digestive biscuits)
- 1 cup (100 g) coarsely chopped pecans
- 1 tablespoon instant coffee granules dissolved in 1 tablespoon hot water
- 2 tablespoons plain yogurt

Set out an 8-inch (20-cm) springform pan. • Melt the butter with the sugar in a small saucepan over low heat until the sugar has dissolved completely. • Remove from the heat and mix in the graham cracker crumbs, pecans, coffee, and yogurt. • Firmly press the mixture into the prepared pan to form a smooth, even layer. • Refrigerate for at least 1 hour, or until set. • Loosen and remove the pan sides and cut into wedges.

Makes: 16 cookies • Prep: 20 min + 1 hr to chill • Level: 2

ALMOND BRITTLE

Place the sugar in a large heavy-bottomed saucepan over medium-low heat. Stir in the almonds and vanilla. • Cook, stirring constantly with a wooden spoon, until the sugar begins to stick to the almonds. The mixture should become semi-liquid and the almonds will begin to stick together. • Grease a marble surface with the almond oil. • Pour the mixture onto the surface and let cool to warm. • Use a metal spatula to work the mixture until it is about ½-inch (1-cm) thick. • Leave until almost, but not completely, cool. • Use a long sharp knife to cut the nougat into bars. • Set aside for 12 hours in a cool place before serving.

Makes: 12–16 bars • Prep: 10 min + 12 hr to set • Level: 2

- 1 cup (200 g) sugar
- 2 cups (300 g) almonds
- 1 teaspoon vanilla extract (essence)
- 2 tablespoons almond oil

Coffee and pecan wedges

Peanut butter squares

PEANUT BUTTER SQUARES

- 1¼ cups (310 ml) light corn (golden) syrup
- 1 cup (250 g) smooth peanut butter
- 1 cup (100 g) bran flakes or corn flakes
- 2 cups (200 g) coarsely chopped peanuts
- 8 oz (250 g) semisweet (dark) chocolate, coarsely chopped

Butter an 11 x 7-inch (28 x 18-cm) baking pan. • Bring the corn syrup to a boil with the peanut butter in a medium saucepan over low heat, stirring constantly. • Remove from the heat and mix in the bran flakes and peanuts. • Spoon the mixture into the prepared pan. • Refrigerate for at least 1 hour, or until set. • Melt the chocolate in a double boiler over barely simmering water. • Drizzle the melted chocolate over the peanut base and let stand for 30 minutes until set. • Cut into squares.

Makes: about 25 squares • Prep: 25 min + 90 min to chill and set • Level: 1

CHOCOLATE CORNY SQUARES

Butter an 8-inch (20-cm) round cake pan and line with waxed paper. • Melt the butter and chocolate with the corn syrup in a medium saucepan over low heat. • Stir in the corn flakes and coconut until well blended. • Spoon into the prepared pan, pressing down lightly. • Refrigerate for 3 hours. • Use a sharp knife to cut into wedges.

Makes: about 12 squares • Prep: 15 min + 3 hr to chill Level: 1

- ¼ cup (60 g) butter, cut up
- 4 oz (125 g) semisweet (dark) chocolate, coarsely chopped
- ¼ cup (60 ml) light corn syrup (golden) syrup
- ⅓ cup (40 g) corn flakes
- 2 tablespoons shredded (desiccated) coconut

No-Bake Cookies

BANANA SQUARES

- 2 tablespoons freshly squeezed lemon juice
- 2 tablespoons honey
- $2/3$ cup (150 ml) water
- $2^1/4$ cups (225 g) coarsely chopped dried apricots
- $2^1/4$ cups (225 g) coarsely chopped bananas
- $1/3$ cup (90 g) butter, cut up
- 1 cup (200 g) firmly packed light brown sugar
- $1^1/4$ cups (125 g) corn flakes

Bring the lemon juice, honey, and water to a boil with the apricots and bananas in a medium saucepan over medium heat. • Reduce the heat and simmer over low heat for 25–30 minutes, or until the fruit has softened. • Remove from the heat and let cool for 15 minutes. • Butter an 8-inch (20-cm) baking pan. • Melt the butter with the brown sugar in a medium saucepan over low heat until the sugar has dissolved completely. • Mix in the corn flakes until well coated. • Firmly press half the corn flake mixture into the prepared pan to form a smooth, even layer. Spoon the apricot mixture evenly over the base and cover with the remaining corn flake mixture. • Cool completely before cutting into squares.

Makes: about 20 squares • Prep: 50 min + time to cool Level: 1

CHOCOLATE CHERRY DROPS

Line a cookie sheet with parchment paper. • Melt the chocolate with the butter and rum in a double boiler over barely simmering water. • Mix in the cake crumbs, candied cherries, and golden raisins to form a soft dough. • Drop tablespoons of the mixture onto the prepared cookie sheet. • Refrigerate for at least 1 hour, or until firm to the touch.

Makes: 15–18 cookies • Prep: 20 min + 1 hr to chill • Level: 1

- 3 oz (90 g) semisweet (dark) chocolate, coarsely chopped
- $1/4$ cup (60 g) butter, cut up
- 1 tablespoon dark rum
- $1^1/2$ cups (250 g) cake crumbs
- $3/4$ cup (75 g) coarsely chopped red and green candied cherries
- $1/4$ cup (45 g) golden raisins (sultanas)

CHOCOLATE AND DATE COOKIES

- $2/3$ cup (75 g) graham cracker crumbs (crushed digestive biscuits)
- 1 cup (100 g) finely chopped pitted dates
- $1/2$ cup (50 g) coarsely chopped candied cherries
- 5 oz (150 g) semisweet (dark) chocolate, coarsely chopped
- $1/4$ cup (60 g) butter, cut up
- 2 oz (60 g) white chocolate, coarsely chopped

Mix the graham cracker crumbs, dates, and candied cherries in a large bowl. • Melt the semisweet chocolate with the butter in a double boiler over barely simmering water. Remove from the heat and let cool for 5 minutes. • Pour the chocolate mixture over the graham cracker mixture and mix well. • Turn the mixture onto a sheet of plastic wrap and form into a 10-inch log. • Wrap in the plastic wrap and refrigerate for 12 hours. • Slice the log $1/2$ inch (1 cm) thick. • Melt the white chocolate in a double boiler over barely simmering water and drizzle over the sliced cookies.

Makes: 20 cookies • Prep: 20 min + 12 hr to chill • Level: 1

PISTACHIO MOONS

Lightly dust a work surface with confectioners' sugar. • Roll the marzipan out to about $1/2$ inch (1 cm) thick. • Sprinkle the chopped pistachios and oats evenly over the marzipan and press down lightly with a rolling pin. • Use a 1-inch (2.5-cm) round cutter to stamp out small circles. • Re-roll the leftovers and stamp out more circles until all the marzipan has been used. • Melt the chocolate in a double boiler over barely simmering water. Dip one half of each full moon in the melted chocolate. • Decorate with the almond halves.

Makes: 35–40 cookies • Prep: 50 min • Level: 1

- 14 oz (400 g) marzipan
- $1/3$ cup finely chopped pistachios
- $2/3$ cup (100 g) old-fashioned rolled oats
- 8 oz (250 g) bittersweet (dark) chocolate, coarsely chopped
- 15 pistachio halves, toasted (optional)

No-Bake Cookies

RICE KRISPIE SQUARES

- ½ cup (125 g) butter, cut up
- ½ cup (100 g) sugar
- 1¾ cups (175 g) finely chopped pitted dates
- ⅔ cup (70 g) finely chopped candied cherries
- ⅓ cup (60 g) golden raisins (sultanas
- 2 cups (200 g) rice krispies
- 8 oz (250 g) semisweet (dark) chocolate, coarsely chopped

Set out a 10 x 15-inch (26 x 36-cm) jelly-roll pan. • Melt the butter and sugar in a large saucepan over medium heat. • Remove from the heat and stir in the dates, cherries, raisins, and rice krispies until well coated. • Spoon the mixture evenly into the pan, pressing down firmly. • Refrigerate for 2 hours, or until set. • Melt the chocolate in a double boiler over barely simmering water. Pour the chocolate over and let stand for 20 minutes until set. • Use a sharp knife to cut into squares.

Makes: about 20 squares • Prep: 40 min + 2 hr 20 min to set and chill • Level: 1

ORANGE RICE KRISPIE SQUARES

Butter an 8-inch (20-cm) square baking pan. • Melt the butter with the sugar, honey, peanut butter, and grated chocolate in a large saucepan over low heat until the sugar has dissolved completely. • Remove from the heat and mix in the orange zest and rice krispies until well coated. • Press the mixture lightly into the prepared pan. • Let set for 30 minutes before cutting into squares.

Makes: about 20 squares • Prep: 20 min + 30 min to set • Level: 1

- ¼ cup (60 g) butter, cut up
- ¼ cup (50 g) sugar
- 3 tablespoons honey
- ¼ cup (60 g) smooth peanut butter
- 3 oz (90 g) semisweet (dark) chocolate, grated
- finely grated zest of 1 orange
- 1 cup (100 g) rice krispies

CHOCOLATE RICE KRISPIE SQUARES

- ¾ cup (180 ml) sweetened condensed milk
- 12 oz (350 g) semisweet (dark) chocolate, coarsely grated
- 2 tablespoons butter, softened
- 2 cups (200 g) rice krispies

Grease an 11 x 7-inch (28 x 18-cm) baking pan with sunflower oil. • Heat the condensed milk in a medium saucepan over low heat for 3 minutes, stirring constantly. • Stir in the chocolate and butter and cook until smooth and well blended. • Remove from the heat and stir in the rice krispies until well coated. • Pour the mixture into the pan, smoothing the top. • Let cool for 5 minutes. Use a sharp knife to score the mixture into bars. • When set, cut into squares.

Makes: about 20 squares • Prep: 25 min • Level: 1

LUNCH BOX SQUARES

Butter an 8-inch (20-cm) square baking pan. • Melt the butter in a small saucepan over low heat. Stir in the cocoa, brown sugar, and corn syrup. Bring to a boil and let boil for 1 minute. • Remove from the heat and stir in the crumbs. • Spoon the mixture into the prepared pan, pressing down lightly . • Melt the chocolate in a double boiler over barely simmering water. Pour the melted chocolate over the cookie base. Use a knife to decorate the chocolate in a decorative manner. • Refrigerate for 2 hours. • Cut into squares.

Makes: about 16 squares • Prep: 15 min + 2 hr to chill • Level: 1

- 1 cup (250 g) butter, cut up
- 4 tablespoons unsweetened cocoa powder
- 1 tablespoon firmly packed light brown sugar
- 2 tablespoons light corn syrup (golden) syrup
- 2 cups (250 g) graham cracker crumbs (crushed digestive biscuits)
- 4 oz (125 g) semisweet (dark) chocolate, coarsely chopped

Marshmallow cups

MARSHMALLOW CUPS

- 2 oz (60 g) semisweet (dark) chocolate, coarsely chopped
- 2 oz (60 g) milk chocolate, coarsely chopped
- 2 tablespoons butter, cut up
- 2 tablespoons light corn syrup (golden) syrup
- 1/2 cup (50 g) mini marshmallows
- 1/2 cup (50 g) rice krispies

Set out 15–20 mini paper cases on a cookie sheet. • Melt the semisweet and milk chocolates with the butter and corn syrup in a double boiler over barely simmering water. • Remove from the heat and mix in the marshmallows and rice krispies until well coated. • Spoon evenly into the paper cases. • Refrigerate for 2 hours, or until set.

Makes: 15–20 cookies • Prep: 20 min + 2 hr to set • Level: 1

CHOCOLATE MARSHMALLOW BITES

Line a cookie sheet with waxed paper. • Melt the white chocolate in a double boiler over barely simmering water. • Remove from the heat and mix in the vanilla wafers, pecans, apricots, marshmallows, and candied cherries until well coated. • Drop heaped teaspoons onto the cookie sheet. • Refrigerate for 1 hour, or until set. • Melt the semisweet chocolate in a double boiler over barely simmering water. Remove from the heat and dip the cookies halfway into the semisweet chocolate. • Decorate with the silver balls or sprinkle with sugar strands. • Let stand for 30 minutes until set.

Makes: 18–20 cookies • Prep: 20 min + 90 min to chill and set • Level: 1

- 5 oz (150 g) white chocolate, coarsely chopped
- 2 tablespoons lightly crushed vanilla wafers
- 1/2 cup (50 g) coarsely chopped pecans
- 1/2 cup (50 g) coarsely chopped dried apricots
- 1/2 cup (50 g) mini marshmallows
- 4 candied cherries, coarsely chopped
- 3 oz (90 g) semisweet (dark) chocolate, coarsely chopped
- silver balls or sugar strands, jimmies, sprills, or sprinkles, to decorate

MARSHMALLOW CRUNCHIES

- 7 oz (200 g) milk chocolate, coarsely chopped
- 3 1/2 oz (100 g) semisweet chocolate, coarsely chopped
- 3 tablespoons butter
- 2 oz (60 g) mini marshmallows
- 1/2 cup (60 g) graham cracker (digestive biscuit) crumbs
- 1 cup (100 g) coarsely chopped macadamia nuts
- 1 cup (100 g) coarsely chopped Brazil nuts

Melt the milk and semisweet chocolates with the butter in a double boiler over barely simmering water. • Remove from the heat and let cool for 15 minutes. • Mix in the marshmallows, graham cracker crumbs, and macadamia and Brazil nuts until well mixed. • Set out two large sheets of plastic wrap (cling film) and place a 10-inch (25-cm) square piece of waxed paper on top of each. • Pour half of the mixture onto the center of one piece of waxed paper. • Wrap up tightly in the paper and plastic wrap (cling film), squeezing into a log. • Repeat with the remaining mixture. • Refrigerate for 1 hour, or until firm. • Leave at room temperature for 10 minutes. • Cut the mixture into 1/2-inch (1-cm) thick slices.

Makes: about 40 cookies • Prep: 40 min + 1 hr to chill Level: 1

DOUBLE CHOCOLATE TRUFFLES

Bring the sugar and water to a boil in a large saucepan over low heat. Boil for 2 minutes, or until pale golden. • Transfer to a double boiler and mix in the cream and both types of chocolate. Stir with a wooden spoon until the chocolate has melted completely. • Remove from the heat and let cool completely. • Stir again before putting the mixture in the refrigerator for 30 minutes. • Form the mixture into small balls the size of marbles. Arrange on a sheet of waxed paper and refrigerate for 1 hour. • Mix the candied peel and confectioners' sugar in a small bowl. Roll each truffle in the confectioners' sugar and candied peel and arrange on a serving dish.

Serves: 4 • Prep: 10 min • Cooking: about 1 hr • Level: 2

- 1 tablespoon sugar
- 2 tablespoons water
- 1/2 cup (125 ml) heavy (double) cream
- 5 oz (150 g) white chocolate, chopped
- 4 oz (125 g) semisweet (dark) chocolate, chopped
- 2 tablespoons candied peel, very finely chopped
- 4 tablespoons confectioners' (icing) sugar

No-Bake Cookies

CHOCOLATE ORANGE TRUFFLES

- 2²/₃ cups (400 g) shelled hazelnuts
- 1 cup (200 g) sugar
- 3 tablespoons freshly squeezed mandarin or orange juice
- 2 tablespoons orange or lemon liqueur
- ²/₃ cup (100 g) unsweetened cocoa powder
- sugar strands or sprinkles, to decorate

Place the hazelnuts in a medium bowl. Bring 1 quart (1 liter) of water to a boil and pour over the hazelnuts. Let stand for 5 minutes, then use a slotted spoon to remove and place on a clean kitchen towel. Fold the towel over the hazelnuts and rub gently until the thin inner skins come away. • Place the hazelnuts and sugar in a food processor and chop finely. • Transfer to a large bowl and stir in the mandarin juice and liqueur. • Sift the cocoa into the bowl and mix until well combined. • Use a teaspoon to scoop out the dough and shape into balls the size of large marbles. • Place the sugar strands or sprinkles in a bowl and roll the balls in them so that they are well-coated. • Refrigerate for 4 hours before serving.

Makes about 30 cookies • Prep: 35 min + 4 hr to chill Level: 2

MARZIPAN MOONS

Lightly dust a surface with confectioners' sugar. • Roll the marzipan out to a thickness of about H inch (1 cm). • Sprinkle the chopped pistachios and oats evenly over the marzipan and press down lightly with a rolling pin. • Use a 1-inch (2.5-cm) round cutter to stamp out small circles. • Re-roll the leftovers and stamp out more circles until all the marzipan has been used. • Melt the chocolate in a double boiler over barely simmering water. Dip one half of each full moon in the melted chocolate. • Decorate with the almond halves, if liked.

Makes about 35 cookies • Prep: 30 min • Level: 1

- 14 oz (400 g) marzipan
- ¹/₃ cup (30 g) finely chopped pistachios
- ²/₃ cup (100 g) old-fashioned rolled oats
- 8 oz (250 g) bittersweet (dark) chocolate, coarsely chopped
- 15 almond or pistachios, halved, toasted (optional)

CHOCOLATE MANDARIN SALAMI

- 2²/₃ cups (400 g) shelled hazelnuts
- 1 cup (200 g) sugar
- 3 tablespoons freshly squeezed mandarin juice
- 2 tablespoons orange or lemon liqueur
- ²/₃ cup (100 g) unsweetened cocoa powder
- sugar strands or sprinkles, to decorate

Mix the egg yolks, brandy, and half the sugar in a double boiler over barely simmering water until the mixture lightly coats a wooden spoon or registers 160°F (71°C) on an instant-read thermometer. Plunge the pan into a bowl of ice water and stir until cooled. • Mix in the cookies, cocoa, coffee, and butter. • Stir the egg whites, remaining sugar, and cream of tartar in a double boiler until blended. Cook over low heat, beating constantly with an electric mixer at low speed until the whites register 160°F (71°C) on an instant-read thermometer. Beat at high speed until stiff. • Fold them into the mixture with the hazelnuts. • Transfer the mixture to a sheet of waxed paper. Make a sausage shape with the mixture and wrap in the waxed paper. • Refrigerate for 3 hours. • Cut in slices.

Makes about 30 cookies • Prep: 15 min + 3 hr to chill Level: 1

NO-BAKE CHOCOLATE HAZELNUT TRUFFLES

Process the hazelnuts with the sugar in a food processor until very finely chopped. • Mix in the apple juice, liqueur, and cocoa. • Form the mixture into small balls about ²/₃ inch (1.5 cm) in diameter. • Roll in the sugar sprinkles until well coated. • Arrange on a serving dish and refrigerate for 4 hours. • Serve with coffee.

Makes about 35 cookies • Prep: 40 min + 4 hr to chill Level: 1

- 2²/₃ cups (400 g) hazelnuts
- 1 cup (200 g) sugar
- 3 tablespoons apple juice
- 3 tablespoons apple liqueur
- ¹/₂ cup (75 g) unsweetened cocoa powder
- ¹/₂ cup (75 g) sugar strands or sprinkles

Chocolate hazelnut balls

CHOCOLATE HAZELNUT BALLS

- 2 oz (60 g) semisweet (dark) chocolate, coarsely chopped
- 2½ cups (310 g) vanilla wafer crumbs (plain crushed cookies)
- ½ cup (50 g) finely chopped pecans
- 1 (14 oz/400 g) can sweetened condensed milk
- 10 oz (300 g) white chocolate, coarsely chopped
- 3 oz (90 g) semisweet (dark) chocolate, chopped

Line four cookie sheets with parchment paper. • Melt the semisweet chocolate in a double boiler over barely simmering water. • Mix the vanilla wafer crumbs, pecans, condensed milk, and melted semisweet chocolate in a large bowl until well blended. • Form the mixture into balls the size of walnuts and place 1 inch (2.5 cm) apart on the prepared cookie sheets, flattening them slightly. • Refrigerate for 30 minutes until firm to the touch. • Melt the white chocolate in a double boiler over barely simmering water. • Spread the white chocolate over the tops of the cookies. • Melt the semisweet chocolate in a double boiler over barely simmering water. Spread over the white chocolate. • Let stand for 30 minutes until set.

Makes: about 45 cookies · Prep: 25 min + 1 hr to chill and set Level: 1

CHOCOLATE FRUIT SQUARES

Set out a 9-inch baking pan. • Melt the butter with the corn syrup and cocoa in a small saucepan over medium heat. • Stir in the raisins and cherries until well blended. • Add the broken cookies and stir until well mixed. • Spread the mixture evenly in the pan, pressing down lightly. • Melt the chocolate in a double boiler over barely simmering water. Pour the melted chocolate over the cookie mixture and use a fork to create a swirly decorative effect. • Set aside for 12 hours in a cool place to set completely. • Use a long sharp knife to cut into squares.

Makes: about 10 squares · Prep: 15 min + 12 hr to set · Level: 1

- ½ cup (125 g) butter, cut up
- 3 tablespoons light corn (golden) syrup
- 2 tablespoons unsweetened cocoa powder
- ⅔ cup (90 g) golden raisins (sultanas)
- ⅓ cup (35 g) candied cherries, coarsely chopped
- 10 oz (300 g) plain, fine-textured cookies, broken into small pieces
- 10 oz (300 g) semisweet (dark) chocolate, coarsely chopped

DRIED FRUIT SQUARES

- 1 cup (250 ml) light (single) cream
- ⅓ cup (90 ml) pure maple syrup
- ¾ cup (150 g) firmly packed dark brown sugar
- 1 tablespoon butter
- 1 cup (100 g) corn flakes
- ½ cup (50 g) flaked almonds
- ¼ cup (30 g) unsweetened shredded (desiccated) coconut
- ¾ cup (75 g) finely chopped dried unsweetened banana chips
- ½ cup (90 g) coarsely chopped dried apricots

Butter an 11 x 7-inch baking pan. • Cook the cream, maple syrup, brown sugar, and butter in a medium saucepan over low heat, stirring often, until the sugar has dissolved completely. • Bring to a boil and boil for 10 minutes. • Stir in the corn flakes, almonds, coconut, banana chips, and apricots. • Firmly press the mixture into the prepared pan to form an even layer. • Refrigerate for at least 2 hours. • Cut into squares.

Makes: about 22 squares · Prep: 25 min + 2 hr to chill Level: 1

COFFEE AND WALNUT WEDGIES

Set out an 8-inch springform pan. • Melt the butter with the sugar in a small saucepan over low heat until the sugar has dissolved completely. • Remove from the heat and mix in the graham cracker crumbs, walnuts, coffee, and yogurt. • Firmly press the mixture into the prepared pan to form a smooth, even layer. • Refrigerate for at least 1 hour, or until set. • Loosen and remove the pan sides and cut into wedges.

Makes: about 16 cookies · Prep: 20 min + 1 hr to chill Level: 1

- ⅓ cup (90 g) butter, cut up
- 2 tablespoons sugar
- 1¾ cups graham cracker crumbs (crushed digestive biscuits)
- 1 cup (120 g) coarsely chopped walnuts
- 1 tablespoon instant coffee granules dissolved in 1 tablespoon hot water
- 2 tablespoons plain yogurt

No-Bake Cookies

PRALINE SQUARES

- 3/4 cup (150 g) sugar
- 1 tablespoon) vanilla sugar (see page 414)
- 1/3 cup (90 g) butter
- 1 tablespoon honey
- 2 oz (60 g) marzipan, grated
- 3/4 cup (125 g) toasted hazelnuts, finely chopped
- 1 cup (150 g) toasted almonds, coarsely chopped
- 2/3 cup (70 g) candied cherries, finely chopped
- 3 tablespoons candied lemon peel, finely chopped
- 1 tablespoon pistachios, crushed
- 1/8 teaspoon salt
- 3 oz (90 g) semisweet (dark) chocolate, coarsely chopped

Line a large baking sheet with aluminum foil. Oil the foil. • Melt both sugars in a medium saucepan over low heat. Stir in the butter, honey, and marzipan. • Add the hazelnuts, almonds, candied cherries, lemon peel, pistachios, and salt. Cook, stirring constantly, for 3–5 minutes until well mixed. • Pour the mixture onto the foil. • Flatten the mixture and spread it out to 1/2 inch (1-cm) thick. • Set aside to cool. • Melt the chocolate in a double boiler over barely simmering water. • Spread over the cookie. • Use a sharp knife to cut into squares.

Makes: about 35 squares • Prep: 20 min + time to set
Level: 1

MILK CHOCOLATE MACADAMIA SLICE

Melt the milk and semisweet chocolates and butter in a double boiler over barely simmering water. • Remove from the heat and let cool for 15 minutes. • Mix in the marshmallows, graham cracker crumbs, and macadamia and Brazil nuts until well coated. • Set out two large sheets of plastic wrap and place a 10-inch square piece of parchment paper on top of each. • Pour half of the mixture onto the center of one piece of parchment paper. • Wrap up tightly in the paper and plastic wrap, squeezing it into a log. • Repeat with the remaining mixture. • Refrigerate for 1 hour, or until firm. • Leave at room temperature for 10 minutes. • Cut the mixture into 1/2-inch (1-cm) thick slices.

Makes: 40 cookies • Prep: 40 min + 1 hr to chill • Level: 1

- 8 oz (250 g) milk chocolate, coarsely chopped
- 3 1/2 oz (100 g) semisweet (dark) chocolate, coarsely chopped
- 3 tablespoons butter, cut up
- 2 1/2 oz (75 g) mini marshmallows
- 1/2 cup graham cracker crumbs (crushed digestive biscuits)
- 1 cup (120 g) coarsely chopped macadamia nuts
- 1/2 cup (60 g) coarsely chopped Brazil nuts

FROSTED CHOCOLATE COOKIE BARS

- 1/2 cup (125 g) butter, cut up
- 1 1/2 tablespoons light corn syrup (golden) syrup
- 2 tablespoons unsweetened cocoa powder
- 1 cup (180 g) golden raisins (sultanas)
- 2 cups (250 g) graham cracker crumbs (crushed digestive biscuits
- 6 oz (180 g) semisweet (dark) chocolate, coarsely chopped

Set out a 10 1/2 x 15 1/2-inch (26 x 36-cm) jelly-roll pan. • Melt the butter with the corn syrup and cocoa in a medium saucepan over low heat. • Remove from the heat and stir in the raisins and graham cracker crumbs. • Firmly press the mixture onto the baking pan. • Melt the chocolate in a double boiler over barely simmering water. • Pour the melted chocolate evenly over the cookie base. • Let stand until set and cut into small bars.

Makes: about 25 bars • Prep: 20 min + time to set • Level: 1

CHOCOLATE WALNUT SQUARES

Line an 8-inch (20-cm) baking pan with waxed paper. • Melt the butter and chocolate with the corn syrup in a double boiler over barely simmering water. • Stir in the graham cracker crumbs and walnuts and mix until well blended. • Firmly press the mixture into the prepared pan. • Refrigerate for 3 hours. • Use a sharp knife to cut into squares, peeling off the paper.

Makes: about 20 squares • Prep: 15 min + 3 hr to chill
Level: 1

- 1/4 cup (60 g) butter, cut up
- 8 oz (250 g) semisweet (dark) chocolate, coarsely chopped
- 3 tablespoons light corn syrup (golden) syrup
- 2 cups (250 g) graham cracker crumbs (crushed digestive biscuits)
- 1 cup (100 g) coarsely chopped walnuts

TEA CAKES, TARTLETS, & MUFFINS

T he recipes in this chapter include a mouth-watering array of small cakes, pastries, madeleines, and tartlets, as well as some delicious ideas for scrumptious muffins and cupcakes. Not really cookies, but tiny cakes that can be served alongside a platter of cookies at coffee mornings or afternoon teas or as after-school snacks. Make an eye-catching impression with the Petits fours, shown left (see recipe on page 302), the Butterfly cakes (see page 313), or the Chocolate chile muffins (see page 326). Many of the muffins and madeleines are also perfect at breakfast time.

Petits fours (see page 302)

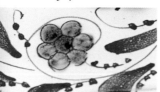

Tea Cakes, Tartlets, & Muffins

DUSTED HONEY MADELEINES

- ⅓ cup (50 g) all-purpose (plain) flour
- ⅛ teaspoon salt
- 3 large eggs
- finely grated zest of 1 lemon
- 2 tablespoons lavender honey
- ½ cup (125 g) butter, melted
- 3 tablespoons confectioners' (icing) sugar, to dust

French Madeleine pans are available from specialist baking stores.
Preheat the oven to 425°F (220°C/gas 7). • Butter two madeleine pans (for 20–24 madeleines). • Mix the flour and salt in a large bowl. • Beat the eggs and lemon zest in a large bowl with an electric mixer at high speed until pale and thick. Add the honey and beat until creamy. • Fold in the dry ingredients, followed by the butter. • Spoon the batter into the prepared pans. • Bake for 15–20 minutes, or until a toothpick inserted into one comes out clean. • Cool the madeleines in the pans for 15 minutes. Transfer to racks to cool completely. • Dust with the confectioners' sugar.
Makes: about 20 madeleines • Prep: 20 min • Cooking: 15–20 min • Level : 1

LEMON MADELEINES

Madeleines: Preheat the oven to 350°F (180°C/gas 4). • Butter a madeleine pan (for 12 madeleines). • Mix the flour, baking powder, and salt in a medium bowl. • Beat the butter and vanilla sugar in a large bowl with an electric mixer at medium speed until creamy. • Add the egg yolk and lemon zest and juice. • Mix in the dry ingredients. • Beat the egg white in a medium bowl until stiff peaks form. Fold into the batter. • Spoon the batter evenly into prepared pan, filling each cup three-quarters full. • Bake for 10–12 minutes, or until springy to the touch. • Cool the madeleines in the pan for 15 minutes. • Transfer to racks and let cool completely. • Lemon Glaze: Melt the butter with the lemon juice in a small saucepan over low heat. • Remove from the heat and beat in the confectioners' sugar. • Drizzle over the madeleines and let stand for 30 minutes until set.
Makes: about 12 madeleines • Prep: 20 min + 30 min to set Cooking: 10–12 min • Level: 1

Madeleines
- ½ cup (75 g) all-purpose (plain) flour
- 1 teaspoon baking powder
- ⅛ teaspoon salt
- ⅓ cup (90 g) butter, softened
- ⅓ cup (70 g) vanilla sugar (see page 414)
- 1 large egg, separated
- finely grated zest and juice of 1 lemon

Lemon Glaze
- 1 teaspoon butter
- 2–3 tablespoons freshly squeezed lemon juice
- 1 cup (150 g) confectioners' (icing) sugar

ALMOND MADELEINES

- ½ cup (75 g) all-purpose (plain) flour
- ½ teaspoon baking powder
- ⅛ teaspoon salt
- 2 large eggs
- ½ cup (100 g) sugar
- ½ cup (125 g) butter, melted
- ½ teaspoon finely grated lemon zest
- 1 tablespoon freshly squeezed lemon juice
- ½ teaspoon vanilla extract (essence)
- ¼ cup (30 g) finely chopped almonds

Preheat the oven to 375°F (190°C/gas 5). • Butter a madeleine pan (for 12 madeleines). • Mix the flour, baking powder, and salt in a medium bowl. • Beat the eggs and sugar in a large bowl with an electric mixer at medium speed until blended. • Mix in the dry ingredients, followed by the butter, lemon zest and juice, and vanilla. • Stir in the almonds. • Spoon the batter into the prepared pans, filling each one about three-quarters full. • Bake for 10–12 minutes, or until springy to the touch. • Cool the madeleines in the pans for 15 minutes. • Transfer to racks and let cool completely.
Makes: about 12 madeleines • Prep: 25 min • Cooking: 10–12 min • Level : 1

PISTACHIO-ALMOND MADELEINES

Preheat the oven to 375°F (190°C/gas 5). • Butter two madeleine pans (for 20–24 madeleines). • Mix the flour, confectioners' sugar, and salt in a medium bowl. • Stir in the pistachios. • Beat the egg whites in a large bowl with an electric mixer at high speed until stiff peaks form. • Fold in the dry ingredients, followed by the butter, honey, and almond extract. • Spoon the batter evenly into the prepared pans. • Bake for 12–15 minutes, or until a toothpick inserted into one comes out clean. • Cool the madeleines in the pans for 15 minutes. • Transfer to a rack and let cool completely.
Makes: 20–24 madeleines • Prep: 20 min • Cooking: 12–15 min • Level : 1

- ⅔ cup (100 g) all-purpose (plain) flour
- 1⅔ cups (250 g) confectioners' (icing) sugar
- ⅛ teaspoon salt
- ½ cup (75 g) finely ground pistachios
- 4 large egg whites
- ¾ cup (180 g) butter, melted
- 1 tablespoon honey
- ½ teaspoon almond extract (essence)

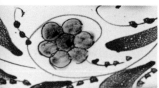

Tea Cakes, Tartlets, & Muffins

COFFEE MADELEINES

- ½ cup (75 g) all-purpose (plain) flour
- 2 tablespoons unsweetened cocoa powder
- ⅛ teaspoon baking soda (bicarbonate of soda)
- ⅛ teaspoon salt
- 2 large eggs
- 1 teaspoon instant coffee granules
- ½ teaspoon vanilla extract (essence)
- 1 cup (150 g) confectioners' (icing) sugar
- ½ cup (125 g) butter, melted
- 1 quantity chocolate frosting (see page 414)

Preheat the oven to 375°F (190°C/gas 5). • Butter two madeleine pans (for 20–24 madeleines). • Mix the flour, cocoa, baking soda, and salt in a medium bowl. • Beat the eggs, coffee, and vanilla in a large bowl with an electric mixer at high speed until blended. • Beat in the confectioners' sugar and continue beating until thick. • Mix in the dry ingredients and butter. • Spoon the batter into the prepared cups, filling each three-quarters full. • Bake for 10–12 minutes, or until springy to the touch. • Cool the madeleines in the pans for 15 minutes. • Transfer to racks and let cool completely. Spread with the frosting.

Makes: about 20 madeleines • Prep: 25 min • Cooking: 10–12 min • Level: 1

SPICY MADELEINES

Mix the flour, cinnamon, baking powder, nutmeg, and salt in a medium bowl. • Beat the eggs and vanilla in a large bowl with an electric mixer at high speed for 3 minutes. • Gradually add the sugar, beating until the batter falls off the beater in ribbons. • Fold in the dry ingredients and butter. • Refrigerate for 30 minutes. • Let rest at room temperature for 15 minutes. • Preheat the oven to 375°F (190°C/gas 5). • Butter two madeleine pans (for 20–24 madeleines). • Spoon the batter into the prepared pans. • Bake for 10–12 minutes, or until brown and springy to the touch. • Cool the madeleines in the pans for 15 minutes. • Transfer to racks and let cool. • Dust with the confectioners' sugar.

Makes: about 24 madeleines • Prep: 30 min + 45 min to chill Cooking: 10 min • Level: 2

- 1 cup (150 g) all-purpose (plain) flour
- 1 teaspoon ground cinnamon
- ½ teaspoon baking powder
- ¼ teaspoon ground nutmeg
- ⅛ teaspoon salt
- 3 large eggs
- 1 teaspoon vanilla extract (essence)
- ⅔ cup (170 g) sugar
- ½ cup (125 g) butter, melted
- ⅓ cup (50 g) confectioners' (icing) sugar

LEMON HONEY MADELEINES

- 1 cup (150 g) all-purpose (plain) flour
- 1 teaspoon baking powder
- ⅛ teaspoon salt
- 2 large eggs
- ½ cup (125 ml) honey
- ¼ cup (50 g) sugar
- finely grated zest of 1 lemon
- 1 tablespoon freshly squeezed lemon juice
- ½ teaspoon vanilla extract (essence)
- ⅓ cup (90 g) butter, melted
- ⅓ cup (50 g) confectioners' (icing) sugar

Mix the flour, baking powder, and salt in a medium bowl. • Beat the eggs, honey, and granulated sugar in a large bowl with an electric mixer at high speed until pale and thick. • Use a large rubber spatula to fold in the dry ingredients, lemon zest and juice, and vanilla, followed by the butter. • Refrigerate for 30 minutes. • Let rest at room temperature for 15 minutes. • Preheat the oven to 375°F (190°C/gas 5). • Butter a madeleine pan (for 12 madeleines). • Spoon the batter into the prepared pan. • Bake for 10–12 minutes, or until golden brown and springy to the touch. • Cool the madeleines in the pan for 15 minutes. • Transfer to racks and let cool completely. • Dust with confectioners' sugar just before serving

Makes: about 12 madeleines • Prep: 40 min + 45 min to chill Cooking: 10–12 min • Level: 1

ORANGE MADELEINES

Mix the flour and salt in a medium bowl. • Beat the eggs in a large bowl with an electric mixer at medium speed for 3 minutes. • Gradually add the sugar, beating until the batter falls off the beater in ribbons. • Fold in the dry ingredients, followed by the butter, orange-flower water, and lemon zest. • Refrigerate for 30 minutes. • Let rest at room temperature for 15 minutes. • Preheat the oven to 375°F (190°C/gas 5). • Butter two madeleine pans (for 20–24 madeleines). • Spoon the batter into the prepared pans. • Bake for 10–12 minutes, or until golden brown and springy to the touch. • Cool in the pans for 15 minutes. • Transfer to racks and let cool completely. • Dust with confectioners' sugar.

Makes 20–24 madeleines · Prep: 30 min. + 45 min. to chill and rest · Cooking: 10–12 min. · Level: 1

- ⅔ cup (100 g) all-purpose (plain) flour
- ⅛ teaspoon salt
- 2 large eggs
- ½ cup (100 g) sugar
- ⅓ cup (90 g) butter, melted
- 1 teaspoon orange-flower water
- ½ teaspoon finely grated lemon zest
- ⅓ cup (50 g) confectioners' sugar

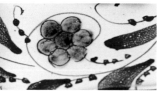

Tea Cakes, Tartlets, & Muffins

CHOCOLATE MADELEINES

- 1 cup (150 g) all-purpose (plain) flour
- $\frac{1}{2}$ teaspoon baking powder
- $\frac{1}{8}$ teaspoon salt
- 3 large eggs
- $\frac{1}{2}$ cup (100 g) sugar
- 2 tablespoons vanilla sugar (see page 414)
- 4 oz (125 g) bittersweet (dark) chocolate, coarsely chopped
- $\frac{1}{2}$ cup (125 g) butter, cut up
- $\frac{1}{3}$ cup (50 g) confectioners' (icing) sugar

Mix the flour, baking powder, and salt in a medium bowl. • Beat the eggs in a large bowl with an electric mixer at high speed for 3 minutes. • Gradually add the granulated and vanilla sugars, beating until the batter falls off the beaters in ribbons. • Fold in the dry ingredients. • Melt the chocolate with the butter in a double boiler over barely simmering water. • Gently fold in the chocolate mixture. • Refrigerate for 30 minutes. • Let rest at room temperature for 15 minutes. • Preheat the oven to 375°F (190°C/gas 5). • Butter two madeleine pans (for 20–24 madeleines). • Spoon the batter into the prepared pans. • Bake, one pan at a time, for 10–12 minutes, or until brown and springy to the touch. • Cool the madeleines in the pans for 15 minutes. • Transfer to racks to cool. • Dust with confectioners' sugar.

Makes: about 24 madeleines • Prep: 30 min + 45 min to chill and rest • Cooking: 10–12 min • Level: 2

WALNUT MADELEINES

Preheat the oven to 375°F (190°C/gas 5). • Butter two madeleine pans (for 24 madeleines). • Mix the flour, baking powder, cardamom, baking soda, and salt in a medium bowl. • Beat the eggs and sugar in a large bowl with an electric mixer at high speed until blended. • Mix in the dry ingredients, followed by the butter, orange zest and juice, and vanilla. • Stir in the walnuts. • Spoon the batter into the prepared cups, filling each cup about three-quarters full. • Bake for 10–12 minutes, or until springy to the touch, rotating the pans halfway through for even baking. • Cool the madeleines in the pans for 15 minutes. • Transfer to racks and let cool completely.

Makes: about 24 madeleines • Prep: 25 min • Cooking: 10–12 min • Level: 1

- $\frac{1}{2}$ cup (75 g) all-purpose (plain) flour
- $\frac{1}{2}$ teaspoon baking powder
- $\frac{1}{4}$ teaspoon ground cardamom
- $\frac{1}{8}$ teaspoon baking soda (bicarbonate of soda)
- $\frac{1}{8}$ teaspoon salt
- 2 large eggs
- $\frac{1}{2}$ cup (100 g) sugar
- $\frac{1}{2}$ cup (125 g) butter, melted
- 1 teaspoon finely grated orange zest
- 1 tablespoon freshly squeezed orange juice
- $\frac{1}{2}$ teaspoon vanilla extract (essence)
- $\frac{1}{4}$ cup finely chopped walnuts

Chocolate madeleines

Hazelnut madeleines

SCALLOP MADELEINES

- 1 cup (150 g) all-purpose (plain) flour
- 1 teaspoon baking powder
- 1/8 teaspoon salt
- 1/2 cup (125 g) butter, softened
- 1/2 cup (100 g) sugar
- 2 large eggs

Preheat the oven to 375°F (190°C/gas 5). • Scrub eight medium scallop shells well, dry thoroughly, and butter them. Arrange on a cookie sheet. • Mix the flour, baking powder, and salt in a medium bowl. • Beat the butter and sugar in a large bowl with an electric mixer at high speed until creamy. • Add the eggs, beating until just blended. • Mix in the dry ingredients to form a soft dough. • Divide the mixture evenly among the shells. • Bake for 12–15 minutes, or until golden brown and firm to the touch. • Transfer to racks to cool.

Makes: about 8 madeleines • Prep: 20 min • Cooking: 12–15 min • Level: 1

HAZELNUT MADELEINES

Preheat the oven to 375°F (190°C/gas 5). • Butter two madeleine pans (for 20–24 madeleines). • Mix the flour, confectioners' sugar, and salt in a large bowl. • Stir in the hazelnuts. • Beat the egg whites in a large bowl with an electric mixer at high speed until stiff peaks form. • Fold in the dry ingredients, followed by the butter and chocolate hazelnut spread. • Spoon the batter evenly into the prepared pan. • Bake for 12–15 minutes, or until a toothpick inserted into one comes out clean. • Cool the madeleines in the pans for 15 minutes. Transfer to racks and let cool completely.

Makes: about 24 madeleines • Prep: 20 min • Cooking: 35 min • Level: 1

- 1/2 cup (75 g) all-purpose (plain) flour
- 1²/₃ cups (250 g) confectioners' (icing) sugar
- 1/8 teaspoon salt
- 1/2 cup (75 g) finely ground hazelnuts
- 4 large egg whites
- 3/4 cup (180 g) butter, melted
- 8 oz (250 ml) chocolate hazelnut spread (Nutella), softened

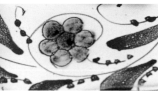

BLUEBERRY FRIANDS

- ½ cup (75 g) all-purpose (plain) flour
- ⅛ teaspoon salt
- 1¼ cups (180 g) finely ground almonds
- ¾ cup (180 g) butter, softened
- 1⅔ cups (250 g) confectioners' (icing) sugar
- 6 large egg whites
- ½ cup (125 g) blueberries

Preheat the oven to 350°F (180°C/gas 4). • Butter two 12-cup mini muffin pans. • Mix the flour and salt in a medium bowl. Stir in the almonds. • Beat the butter and confectioners' sugar in a large bowl with an electric mixer at high speed until creamy. • Mix in the dry ingredients and egg whites. • Pour the batter evenly into the prepared cups and place some blueberries on top of each. • Bake for 25–30 minutes, or until a toothpick inserted into one comes out clean. • Transfer to racks to cool.

Makes: about 24 friands • Prep: 25 min • Cooking:25–30 min • Level: 1

PLUM FRIANDS

Preheat the oven to 350°F (180°C/gas 4). • Butter two 12-cup mini muffin pans. • Cut each half-plum into three. • Mix the flour, nutmeg, cinnamon, and salt in a medium bowl. Stir in the almonds. • Beat the butter and confectioners' sugar in a large bowl with an electric mixer at high speed until creamy. • Mix in the dry ingredients and egg whites. • Pour the batter evenly into the prepared cups and place a piece of plum on top of each. • Bake for 25–30 minutes, or until a toothpick inserted into the centers comes out clean. • Transfer to racks to cool.

Makes: about 24 friands • Prep: 25 min • Cooking: 25–30 min Level: 1

- 8 oz (250 g) firm-ripe plums, halved and pitted
- ½ cup (75 g) all-purpose (plain) flour
- 1 teaspoon finely grated nutmeg
- ¼ teaspoon ground cinnamon
- ⅛ teaspoon salt
- 1¼ cups (180 g) finely ground almonds
- ¾ cup (180 g) butter, softened
- 1⅔ cups (250 g) confectioners' (icing) sugar
- 6 large egg whites

Blueberry friands

Strawberry friands

RASPBERRY FRIANDS

- ½ cup (75 g) all-purpose (plain) flour
- ⅛ teaspoon salt
- 1¼ cups (180 g) finely ground almonds
- ¾ cup (180 g) butter, softened
- 1⅔ cups (250 g) confectioners' (icing) sugar
- 6 large egg whites
- ½ cup (125 g) raspberries

Preheat the oven to 350°F (180°C/gas 4). • Butter two 12-cup mini muffin pans. • Mix the flour and salt in a large bowl. Stir in the almonds. • Beat the butter and confectioners' sugar in a large bowl with an electric mixer on medium speed until creamy. • Mix in the dry ingredients and egg whites. • Pour the batter evenly into the prepared cups and place a raspberry on top of each. • Bake for 25–30 minutes, or until a toothpick inserted into the centers comes out clean. • Transfer to racks to cool.

Makes: about 24 friands • Prep: 25 min • Cooking: 25–30 min • Level: 1

STRAWBERRY FRIANDS

Preheat the oven to 350°F (180°C/gas 4). • Butter two 12-cup mini muffin pans. • Mix the flour and salt in a medium bowl. Stir in the almonds. • Beat the butter, confectioners' sugar, and vanilla in a large bowl with an electric mixer on medium speed until creamy. • Mix in the dry ingredients and egg whites. • Pour the batter evenly into the prepared cups and place a half strawberry on top of each. • Bake for 25–30 minutes, or until a toothpick inserted into one comes out clean. • Transfer to racks to cool.

Makes: about 24 friands • Prep: 25 min • Cooking: 25–30 • Level: 1

- ⅔ cup (100 g) all-purpose (plain) flour
- ⅛ teaspoon salt
- 1 cup (150 g) finely ground almonds
- ¾ cup (180 g) butter, softened
- 1⅔ cups (250 g) confectioners' (icing) sugar
- ½ teaspoon vanilla extract (essence)
- 6 large egg whites
- 10 strawberries, cut in half

Tea Cakes, Tartlets, & Muffins

PALMIERS

- ⅓ cup (70 g) superfine (caster) sugar
- ½ teaspoon ground cardamom
- 8 oz (250 g) frozen puff pastry, thawed

Preheat the oven to 350°F (180°C/gas 4). • Butter a cookie sheet. • Stir together the sugar and cardamom in a small bowl. Lightly sprinkle a surface with 1 tablespoon of the sugar mixture. • Unfold or unroll the pastry to an 10-inch (25-cm) square. • Sprinkle with 1 tablespoon of the sugar mixture. • Fold the long sides of the pastry over to meet in the center. Sprinkle with 1 tablespoon sugar mixture and fold in half lengthways. • Slice the pastry into 12 portions. • Place the cookies cut-side down 2 inches apart on the prepared cookie sheets. • Sprinkle with the remaining sugar mixture. • Bake for 10–12 minutes, or until just golden. • Transfer to racks to cool.

Makes: about 12 palmiers • Prep: 15 min • Cooking: 20–25 min • Level: 2

LEMON ROCK CAKES

Preheat the oven to 375°F (190°C/gas 5). • Butter a baking sheet. • Beat the flour, butter, lemon zest, and baking powder in a large bowl with an electric mixer at medium speed until well blended. • Add the egg, sugar, lemon juice, and raisins. • Drop heaping tablespoons of the batter onto the prepared sheet, spacing them 2 inches (5 cm) apart. Sprinkle with the sugar. • Bake for 15–20 minutes, or until golden brown. • Cool the cakes on racks.

Makes: about 12–15 cakes • Prep: 10 min • Cooking: 15–20 min • Level: 1

- 1½ cups (225 g) all-purpose (plain) flour
- ⅓ cup (90 g) butter, melted
- 1 tablespoon finely grated lemon zest
- 2 teaspoons baking powder
- 1 large egg, lightly beaten
- ⅓ cup (70 g) sugar
- 2 tablespoons freshly squeezed lemon juice
- ⅔ cup (120 g) raisins
- 2 tablespoons raw sugar

PETITS FOURS

- 1 cup (150 g) all-purpose (plain) flour
- 1 cup (150 g) cornstarch (cornflour)
- 1 teaspoon baking powder
- ⅛ teaspoon salt
- 6 large eggs, separated
- ¾ cup (150 g) sugar
- 2 tablespoons vanilla sugar (see page 414)
- 2 tablespoons unsweetened cocoa powder
- 1–2 tablespoons dark rum

Preheat the oven to 375°F (190°C/gas 5). • Line two 13 x 9-inch (33 x 23-cm) baking pans with parchment paper. • Mix the flour, cornstarch, baking powder, and salt in a large bowl. • Beat the egg yolks and granulated and vanilla sugars in a large bowl with an electric mixer at high speed until pale and thick. • Mix in the dry ingredients. • With mixer at high speed, beat the egg whites in a large bowl until stiff peaks form. • Use a large rubber spatula to fold the beaten whites into the batter. • Spoon half the mixture into a separate bowl. Mix in the cocoa powder and rum. • Mix the orange and lemon zest into the remaining mixture. • Spoon one mixture evenly into each of the prepared pans. • Bake for 12–15 minutes, or until golden brown and springy to the touch. • Cool in the pans for 15 minutes. • Turn out onto a sheet of waxed paper dusted with confectioners' sugar. • Use 1-inch (2.5-cm) cookie cutters to cut out pairs of shapes from each cake. • Stick the cake shapes together in pairs with the preserves. • Mix the confectioners' sugar and lemon juice in a small bowl to make a spreadable icing. • Spoon the icing over the shapes, letting it run down the sides. • Decorate with a combination of the nuts, candies, and marzipan fruits.

Makes: about 35–40 cookies • Prep: 50 min • Cooking: 12–15 min Level: 3

- 2 teaspoons finely grated orange zest
- 2 teaspoons finely grated lemon zest
- ⅔–¾ cup (220–240 g) apricot preserves (jam)
- 3⅓ cups (500 g) confectioners' (icing) sugar
- 3–4 tablespoons freshly squeezed lemon juice
- chopped nuts, sweets, sugar flowers and petals, chocolate flakes, candied fruits and peel, colored sugar crystals, silver balls

Neapolitan rum cakes

NEAPOLITAN RUM CAKES

- 1 oz (30 g) fresh yeast or 2 (¼ oz/7 g) packages active dry yeast
- ¼ cup (60 ml) warm water
- 5 large eggs
- 3 tablespoons sugar
- ½ cup (125 ml) extra-virgin olive oil
- 2 tablespoons butter, melted and cooled
- 3 cups (450 g) all-purpose (plain) flour
- ⅛ teaspoon salt
- 1⅓ cups (240 g) sugar
- 2 cups (500 ml) water
- 1 lemon, sliced
- ½ cup (125 ml) rum

Place the yeast in a small bowl with ½ cup (125 ml) warm water. Stir until dissolved then set aside for 10 minutes. • Beat the eggs and 3 tablespoons of sugar until pale and creamy. • Gradually beat in the oil, butter, and yeast mixture. • Mix in the flour and salt. • Knead the dough until soft and elastic. • Fill 12 babà molds just under half full, cover, and leave in a warm place until the dough has risen to just below the rim of each mold. • Preheat the oven to 350°F (180°C/gas 4). Bake for 15–20 minutes. • Boil the 1⅓ cups (330 ml) sugar and water for 10 minutes, or until syrupy. • Add the lemon and rum and leave to cool. • When the rum cakes are cooked, set aside to cool before soaking them in the rum syrup. Leave on a wire rack to drain.

Makes: about 12 large rum cakes • Prep: 30 min + 1 hr to rise
Cooking: 15–20 min • Level: 2

EGG CUSTARD TARTLETS

Preheat the oven to 300°F (150°C/gas 2). • Mix the egg yolks and whole eggs in a jug or bowl. Beat slowly with the whisk. Add the sugar and beat until it is dissolved. • Pour in the milk and cream, and beat well until foamy. • Roll out the pastry and cut it into circles large enough to line the inside of the tartlet pans. Press the pastry pieces into the pans. Fill each tart case with the egg mixture. • Place the tartlets on a baking sheet and bake for 45 minutes, or until golden brown. • Let cool for 10 minutes. • Remove from the pans and place them on a rack to cool completely.

Makes: about 20 tartlets • Prep: 30 min • Cooking: 45 min
Level: 2

- 2 large eggs + 3 large egg yolks
- 1 cup (250 ml) milk
- 2 tablespoons single (light) cream
- 10 oz (300 g) frozen pastry (flaky or shortcrust)

JELLY TARTLETS

- 4 oz (125 g) cream cheese, softened
- ½ cup (125 g) butter, softened
- ¾ cup (125 g) all-purpose (plain) flour
- 1 cup (250 g) raspberry preserves (jam)
- ⅓ cup (50 g) confectioners' sugar, to dust

Preheat the oven to 350°F (180°C/gas 4). • Butter twenty-four mini-muffin cups. • Beat the cream cheese and butter in a large bowl with an electric mixer at high speed until creamy. • Mix in the flour to form a smooth dough. • Roll out the dough on a lightly floured surface to ⅛ inch (3 mm) thick. • Use a 2-inch fluted cookie cutter to cut out twenty-four dough rounds. • Line the muffin cups with the dough. • Drop teaspoons of the raspberry preserves into the cups. • Bake for 15–20 minutes, or until the preserves are bubbling. • Transfer to racks and let cool completely. • Dust with the confectioners' sugar.

Makes: about 24 cookies • Prep: 30 min • Cooking: 15–20 min • Level: 1

MINI MARSHMALLOW TARTS

Mix the flour and salt in a large bowl. • Use a pastry blender to cut in the butter until the mixture resembles fine crumbs. Add enough water to form a smooth dough. • Press the dough into a disk, wrap in plastic wrap (cling film), and refrigerate for 30 minutes. • Preheat the oven to 400°F (200°C/gas 6). • Set out a mini muffin pan (12 cups). • Roll out the pastry on a lightly floured surface to ⅛ inch (3 mm) thick. Use a 2-inch (5-cm) cookie cutter to cut out rounds and use them to line the pans. Drop teaspoons of preserves into the bases. • Bake for 12–15 minutes, or until just golden. • Place the marshmallows on top of the preserves and bake until the marshmallows have melted. Top each tart with an almond half. • Transfer to racks to cool.

Makes: 12 tarts • Prep: 40 min + 30 min to chill
Cooking: 14–17 min • Level: 2

- ¾ cup (125 g) all-purpose (plain) flour
- ⅛ teaspoon salt
- ¼ cup (60 g) butter, cut up
- 1 tablespoon water, + more as needed
- ¼ cup (60 g) raspberry or strawberry preserves (jam)
- 12 pink or white marshmallows, to decorate
- 12 almond halves, to decorate

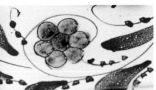

Tea Cakes, Tartlets, & Muffins

REDCURRANT TARTLETS

Pastry
- 1²/₃ cups (250 g) all-purpose (plain) flour
- 2 tablespoons confectioners' (icing) sugar
- ⅛ teaspoon salt
- ²/₃ cup (150 g) butter, cut up
- 1 large egg
- 1–2 tablespoons water

Redcurrant Filling
- 2 cups (500 g) redcurrants
- 1½ cups (300 g) sugar
- 1⅓ cups (330 ml) water
- ²/₃ cup (100 g) custard powder
- 2–4 tablespoons water

Pastry: Mix the flour, confectioners' sugar, and salt in a medium bowl. • Use a pastry blender to cut in the butter until the mixture resembles coarse crumbs. • Add the egg and enough water to form a stiff dough. • Divide the dough in half. Press the dough into disks, wrap each in plastic wrap (cling film), and refrigerate for 30 minutes. • Preheat the oven to 375°F (190°C/gas 5). • Set out three 12-cup mini-muffin pans. • Roll out the dough on a lightly floured surface to ⅛ inch (3 mm) thick. • Use a 2-inch (5-cm) round cookie cutter to cut out rounds. Gather the dough scraps, re-roll, and continue cutting out until all the dough is used. • Press the rounds into the prepared cups and prick all over with a fork. • Bake for 8–10 minutes, or until the pastry is pale gold. • Cool completely in the pans. • Redcurrant Filling: Bring the redcurrants, sugar, and water to a boil in a medium saucepan over medium heat. • Simmer for 5–7 minutes, or until tender. • Transfer to a food processor or blender and process until pureed. • Mix the custard powder with enough water to form a smooth paste and stir into the puree. • Return the mixture to the saucepan and bring to a boil over low heat, stirring constantly. • Spoon the filling into the pastry bases and refrigerate for 1 hour

Makes: about 36 tartlets • Prep: 45 min + 90 min to chill
Cooking: 8–10 min • Level: 1

COCONUT TARTLETS

Pastry: Mix the flour and salt in a large bowl. • Use a pastry blender to cut in the butter and lard until the mixture resembles fine crumbs. • Mix in enough ice water to form a smooth dough. • Shape into a ball, wrap in plastic wrap (cling film), and refrigerate for at least 30 minutes. • Preheat the oven to 350°F (180°C/gas 4). • Butter twelve 2 x ¾-inch (5 x 2-cm) tartlet pans. • Roll out the pastry on a lightly floured surface to ¼ inch (5 mm) thick. Use a pastry cutter to stamp out twelve rounds to slightly larger than the tartlet pans. Press the pastry rounds into the prepared pans. • Filling: Heat the raspberry jelly in a small saucepan until liquid. Brush some jelly over each pastry base. • Beat the egg white in a medium bowl with an electric mixer at high speed until stiff peaks form. Use a rubber spatula to fold in the sugar, coconut, and almonds. • Spoon the coconut mixture evenly into the pastry bases. • Bake for 20–25 minutes, or until golden brown. • Cool the tarts completely in the pans.

Makes: about 12 tartlets • Prep: 40 min + 30 min to chill
Cooking: 20–25 min • Level: 2

Pastry
- 1¼ cups (180 g) all-purpose (plain) flour
- ⅛ teaspoon salt
- ¼ cup (60 g) butter, cut up
- ¼ cup (60 g) lard or vegetable shortening, cut up
- 1–2 tablespoons ice water

Filling
- ½ cup (120 g) tablespoons raspberry jelly
- 1 large egg white
- ⅓ cup (70 g) superfine (caster) sugar
- 2 tablespoons unsweetened shredded (desiccated) coconut
- 2 tablespoons finely ground almonds

Coconut almond squares

ALMOND RUM TARTLETS

Pastry
- 1⅓ cups (200 g) all-purpose (plain) flour
- ⅛ teaspoon salt
- ⅓ cup (90 g) butter, cut up
- ⅓ cup (50 g) finely ground hazelnuts
- ⅓ cup (70 g) granulated sugar
- 1 tablespoon vanilla sugar (see page 414)
- 2–3 tablespoons water

Almond Rum Filling
- 3 tablespoons butter, softened
- ¼ cup (50 g) firmly packed light brown sugar
- 1 large egg + 1 egg yolk
- ¼ teaspoon almond extract (essence)
- ⅓ cup (50 g) all-purpose (plain) flour
- ⅔ cup (100 g) finely ground almonds
- 3 tablespoons milk
- 1 tablespoon rum
- ¼ cup (90 g) apricot preserves (jam)

Pastry: Mix the flour and salt in a medium bowl. • Use a pastry blender to cut in the butter until the mixture resembles coarse crumbs. • Mix in the hazelnuts and both sugars. • Mix in enough water to form a soft, but not sticky, dough. • Press the dough into a disk, wrap in plastic wrap (cling film), and refrigerate for 30 minutes. • Preheat the oven to 375°F (190°C/gas 5). • Set out two 12-cup mini-muffin pans. • Almond Rum Filling: Beat the butter and brown sugar in a large bowl with an electric mixer at medium speed until creamy. • Add the whole egg and almond extract, beating until just blended. • Mix in the flour, almonds, 2 tablespoons milk, and rum. • Roll out the dough on a lightly floured surface to ⅛ inch (3 mm) thick. • Use a 2½-inch (6-cm) fluted cookie cutter to cut out twenty-four rounds. Press the dough circles into the prepared cups. • Gather the dough scraps and re-roll. Use a 1-inch (2.5-cm) star-shaped cookie cutter to cut out twenty-four small stars. • Drop ½ teaspoon of the apricot preserves into each pastry base and spoon in the filling. • Place the pastry stars lightly on top of the filling. • Beat the remaining egg yolk with the remaining milk and brush over the stars. • Bake for 15–20 minutes, or until the pastry is pale golden and the filling has set. • Cool completely before removing from the pans.

Makes: about 24 tartlets • Prep: 1 hr + 30 min to chill • Cooking: 15–20 min • Level: 2

NUT TARTLETS

Pastry: Mix the flour and salt in a medium bowl. Stir in the sugar and orange zest. • Use a pastry blender to cut in the butter until the mixture resembles coarse crumbs. • Mix in the egg yolk to form a smooth dough. • Press the dough into a disk, wrap in plastic wrap (cling film), and refrigerate for 30 minutes. • Preheat the oven to 350°F (180°C/gas 4). • Butter twenty-four mini-muffin cups. • Roll out the dough on a lightly floured surface to ⅛ inch (3 mm) thick. • Use a fluted 2-inch (5-cm) cookie cutter to cut out twenty-four dough rounds. • Press the dough rounds into the prepared cups and prick all over with a fork. • Bake for 10–15 minutes, or until the pastry is just golden. • Transfer to racks to cool. • Filling: Mix the sugar with the water in a small saucepan. Wash down the sides of the pan with a pastry brush dipped in cold water to prevent sugar crystals from forming. Simmer over low heat until the syrup is golden, about 10 minutes. • Mix in the pecans, pine nuts, honey, and cream until well blended. • Spoon the filling into the cups and let cool completely.

Makes: about 24 tartlets • Prep: 45 min • Cooking: 10–15 min • Level: 2

Pastry
- 1¼ cups (180 g) all-purpose (plain) flour
- ⅛ teaspoon salt
- ¼ cup (50 g) sugar
- finely grated zest of 1 orange
- ¼ cup (60 g) butter, cut up
- 1 large egg yolk, lightly beaten

Filling
- ¼ cup (50 g) sugar
- 1 tablespoon water
- ¾ cup (75 g) finely chopped pecans
- ¼ cup (30 g) pine nuts
- 2 tablespoons honey
- 1 tablespoon light (single) cream

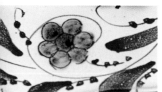

Tea Cakes, Tartlets, & Muffins

WHITE CHOCOLATE TARTLETS

- 1³/₄ cups (275 g) all-purpose (plain) flour
- ¹/₈ teaspoon salt
- ¹/₂ cup (125 g) butter, softened
- ¹/₂ cup (100 g) sugar
- 1 large egg yolk
- 5 oz (150 g) white chocolate, coarsely chopped

Mix the flour and salt in a medium bowl. • Beat the butter and sugar in a large bowl with an electric mixer at medium speed until creamy. • Add the egg yolk, beating until just blended. • Mix in the dry ingredients. • Cover with plastic wrap (cling film) and refrigerate for 30 minutes. • Preheat the oven to 350°F (180°C/gas 4). • Set out two 12-cup mini muffin pans. • Form the dough into balls the size of walnuts and press into the cups. • Prick all over with a fork. • Bake for 12–15 minutes, or until just golden. • Transfer to racks to cool. • Melt the white chocolate in a double boiler over barely simmering water. Fill each tartlet with the melted chocolate.

Makes: about 24 tartlets • Prep: 30 min + 30 min to chill Cooking: 12–15 min • Level: 2

RASPBERRY TARTLETS

- 12 store-bought tartlet shells
- 1 cup (250 g) raspberries + about 24 extra
- ²/₃ cup (100 g) confectioners' (icing) sugar
- ¹/₂ cup (125 ml) raspberry liqueur
- finely grated zest and juice of 1 lemon
- ²/₃ cup (150 g) ricotta cheese, drained
- 1 cup (250 ml) plain yogurt
- 1¹/₂ tablespoons unflavored gelatin
- ¹/₄ cup (60 ml) cold water
- 1¹/₂ cups (375 ml) heavy (double) cream

Set out the tartlet shells. • Process 1 cup (250 g) raspberries in a food processor until puréed. • Transfer to a large bowl and stir in the confectioners' sugar, liqueur, lemon zest and juice, ricotta, and yogurt. • Sprinkle the gelatin over the water in a saucepan. Let stand 1 minute. Stir over low heat until the gelatin has completely dissolved. • Stir the gelatin into the raspberry mixture and refrigerate until thickened. • Beat the cream in a medium bowl until stiff. Fold the cream into the raspberry mixture. • Spoon the raspberry mixture into a pastry bag with a ¹/₄-inch (5-mm) plain tip. Pipe into the tartlets. Decorate with the raspberries. • Refrigerate for 1 hour before serving.

Makes: 12 tartlets • Prep: 50 min + 1 hr to chill • Level: 1

LEMON TARTLETS

Pastry: Mix the flour, confectioners' sugar, and salt in a medium bowl. • Use a pastry blender to cut in the butter until the mixture resembles coarse crumbs. • Add the egg and enough water to form a stiff dough. • Divide the dough in half. Press the dough into disks, wrap each in plastic wrap (cling film), and refrigerate for 30 minutes. • Preheat the oven to 325°F (170°C/gas 3). • Spread the hazelnuts on a large baking sheet. Toast for 7 minutes, or until lightly golden. • Transfer to a large cotton kitchen towel. Fold the towel over the nuts and rub with the towel to remove the thin inner skins. Pick out the nuts and coarsely chop. • Increase the oven temperature to 375°F (190°C/ gas 5). • Set out four 12-cup mini-muffin pans. • Roll out the dough on a lightly floured surface to ¹/₈ inch (3 mm) thick. • Use a 2-inch (5-cm) round cookie cutter to cut out rounds. • Gather the dough scraps, re-roll, and continue cutting out rounds until all the dough is used. • Press the rounds into the muffin cups and prick all over with a fork. • Bake for 8–10 minutes, or until the pastry is pale gold. • Cool completely in the pans. • Lemon Filling: Mix the lemon curd and cream in a small bowl. Spoon the filling into the pastry bases. • Decorate with the chopped hazelnuts and lemon zest.

Makes: about 48 mini tartlets • Prep: 40 min + 30 min to chill • Cooking: 8–10 min • Level: 2

Pastry
- 1²/₃ cups (250 g) all-purpose (plain) flour
- 2 tablespoons confectioners' (icing) sugar
- ¹/₈ teaspoon salt
- ²/₃ cup (150 g) butter, cut up
- 1 large egg
- 1–2 tablespoons water

Lemon Filling
- ¹/₂ cup (125 ml) lemon curd (see page 414)
- ¹/₄ cup (60 ml) heavy (double) cream
- 1¹/₂ cups (225 g) hazelnuts
- curls of lemon zest, to decorate

COFFEE ECLAIRS

- 1 recipe choux pastry (see page 417)
- 1 large egg mixed with 1 teaspoon water

Coffee Filling
- 1 cups (250 ml) heavy (double) cream
- ⅓ cup (70 g) sugar
- 1 tablespoon instant coffee granules

Frosting
- 1½ cups (225 g) confectioners' (icing) sugar
- 1 tablespoon instant coffee granules, dissolved in 1 tablespoon boiling water
- chocolate-covered coffee beans, to decorate

Preheat the oven to 425°F (220°C/gas 7). • Line a baking sheet with parchment paper. • Place the pastry in a pastry bag fitted with a ¾-inch (2-cm) tip and pipe sixteen 4-inch (10-cm) strips onto the sheet. Brush with the egg. • Bake for 15 minutes. Reduce the oven temperature to 400°F (200°C/gas 6) and bake for 15 minutes more. • Transfer to racks to cool. • Using a sharp knife, carefully cut each éclair in half lengthwise. • Coffee Filling: Beat the cream, sugar, and coffee in a large bowl until stiff. • Frosting: Mix the confectioners' sugar and coffee in a small bowl. • Place the filling in a pastry bag with a ¼-inch (5-mm) tip and fill the bottom half of each éclair with filling. Cover with the top half of the éclair. • Spread each éclair with the frosting. Refrigerate for 15 minutes. Decorate with the coffee beans.

Makes: about 16 eclairs • Prep: 45 min + 15 min to chill Cooking: 30 min • Level: 3

PASTRY CREAM KISSES

Preheat the oven to 325°F (170°C/gas 3). • Butter 2–3 baking sheets. • Beat the eggs and sugar in a large bowl until pale and thick. • Fold in the lemon zest and flour, alternating with the Sambuca and milk. Make a fairly soft dough and shape into balls the size of walnuts. • Place on the prepared sheets 1 inch (2 cm) apart. • Bake for 8–10 minutes, or until lightly browned. • Cool on a rack. • Vanilla Pastry Cream: Beat the egg yolks and sugar until pale and creamy. Stir in the flour, then gradually add the milk and vanilla. Cook over medium heat until thick. Let cool. • Poke a hole in the flat bottom of each one to make room for the filling. Let cool completely. • Brush with a little milk and fill with the cream, sticking them together in pairs. • Dip in the liqueur to color. Roll in the sugar.

Makes: about 50 pastries • Prep: 30 min • Cooking: 8–10 min • Level: 2

- 6 large eggs
- 4 cups (800 g) sugar
- 2 cups (500 ml) milk
- finely grated zest of 1 lemon
- 1 cup (250 ml) Sambuca
- 3 lb (1.5 kg) all-purpose (plain) flour, or more as needed
- 1 cup (250 ml) Alchermes liqueur
- raw sugar, to roll

Vanilla Pastry Cream
- 8 large egg yolks
- ½ cup (125 g) sugar
- ¾ cup (125 g) all-purpose (plain) flour
- 1 quart (1 liter) boiling milk
- 1 teaspoon vanilla extract (essence)

Coffee eclairs

Butterfly cakes

CREAM CAKES

- 1 oz (25 g) fresh yeast or 2 packages (¼-oz/7-g) active dry yeast
- 2⅔ cups (650 ml) warm water
- 6 cups (900 g) all-purpose (plain) flour
- ⅓ cup (90 ml) extra-virgin olive oil
- 6 large eggs + 4 large egg yolks, lightly beaten
- 1 cup (200 g) sugar
- finely grated zest of 1 lemon
- ½ teaspoon vanilla extract (essence)
- 1 large egg, lightly beaten, to brush
- 2 cups (500 ml) light (single) cream
- 4 tablespoons confectioners' (icing) sugar

Dissolve the yeast in 1 cup (250 ml) of water. Let stand until foamy. • Place 2 cups (300 g) of flour in a large bowl. Pour in the yeast mixture and enough warm water to form a dough. • Place the dough in a bowl. Cover with a cloth and let rise in a warm place until doubled in bulk. • Place the remaining flour on a work surface. Knead in the oil, eggs, egg yolks, sugar, lemon zest, and vanilla. Add the remaining water to form a dough. • Knead in the dough that has doubled in bulk. • Shape into small oval loaves. Arrange on baking sheets and let rest until doubled in bulk. • Preheat the oven to 350°F (180°C/gas 4). • Brush the loaves with the egg. • Bake for 15–20 minutes, or until golden. • Beat the cream in a medium bowl until stiff. • Slice the loaves and fill with the cream. Sprinkle with the confectioners' sugar.

Makes: about 40 cream cakes • Prep: 50 min + 90 min to rise • Cooking: 15–20 min • Level: 2

BUTTERFLY CAKES

Preheat the oven to 350°F (180°C/gas 4). • Arrange 20–24 paper baking cups on baking sheets. • Mix the flour, baking powder, and salt in a medium bowl. • Beat the butter, sugar, and vanilla in a large bowl with an electric mixer at medium speed until creamy. • Add the eggs, one at a time, until just blended after each addition. • With mixer at low speed, gradually beat in the dry ingredients, alternating with the milk and lemon juice. • Spoon the batter into the baking cups, filling them half full. • Bake for 10–15 minutes, or until golden brown. • Cool the cakes on racks. • With mixer at high speed, beat the cream in a medium bowl until stiff. • Cut a small circle about ½-inch (1-cm) deep from the top of each cake. Fill with ½ teaspoon of jam and 1 teaspoon of whipped cream. Cut the tops in half and arrange like butterfly wings.

Makes: 20–24 butterfly cakes • Prep: 15 min • Cooking: 10–15 min Level: 1

- 2 cups (300 g) all-purpose (plain) flour
- 2 teaspoons baking powder
- ¼ teaspoon salt
- ⅔ cup (150 g) butter, softened
- ¾ cup (150 g) granulated sugar
- 1 teaspoon vanilla extract (essence)
- 2 large eggs
- ½ cup (125 ml) milk
- 1 tablespoon freshly squeezed lemon juice
- ½ cup (160 g) strawberry preserves (jam)
- 1 cup (250 ml) heavy (double) cream

Orange tartlets with meringue

ORANGE TARTLETS WITH MERINGUE

Pastry
- 1²/₃ cups (250 g) all-purpose (plain) flour
- 2 tablespoons confectioners' (icing) sugar
- ⅛ teaspoon salt
- ⅔ cup (150 g) butter, cut up
- 1 large egg
- 1–2 tablespoons water
- ½ cup (125 ml) orange curd

Meringue Topping
- 2 large egg whites
- 2 teaspoons water
- ⅛ teaspoon cream of tartar
- ⅛ teaspoon salt
- ½ cup (100 g) superfine (caster) sugar
- 1 teaspoon finely grated orange zest

Pastry: Mix the flour, confectioners' sugar, and salt in a medium bowl. • Cut in the butter until the mixture resembles coarse crumbs. • Add the egg and enough water to form a dough. • Divide the dough in half. Wrap in plastic wrap (cling film), and refrigerate for 30 minutes. • Preheat the oven to 400°F (200°C/gas 6). • Set out four 12-cup mini-muffin pans. • Roll out the dough on a lightly floured surface to ⅛ inch (3 mm) thick. • Use a 2-inch (5-cm) round cookie cutter to cut out rounds. • Gather the dough scraps, re-roll, and continue cutting out rounds until there are at least 48 rounds. • Press the rounds into the prepared cups and prick all over with a fork. • Bake for 8–10 minutes, or until the pastry is pale gold. • Cool completely in the pans. • Drop ½ teaspoon of the orange curd into each pastry base. • Meringue Topping: Stir the egg whites, water, cream of tartar, and salt in a double boiler until blended. Cook over low heat, beating constantly with a hand-held electric mixer at low speed until the mixture registers 160°F (71°C) on an instant-read thermometer. Transfer to a bowl and beat at high speed, gradually adding the superfine sugar until stiff peaks form. • Fit a pastry bag with a ½-inch (1-cm) star tip. Fill the pastry bag with the meringue and squeeze over the tarts in a decorative manner. • Bake for 6–8 minutes, or until lightly browned. • Cool completely in the pans.

Makes: about 48 tartlets • Prep: 40 min + 30 min to chill Cooking: 15–20 min • Level: 2

ALMOND TARTLETS

Preheat the oven to 350°F (180°C/gas 4). • Set out a 12-cup mini muffin pan. • Roll out the pastry to ¼ inch (5 mm) thick. Use a 2-inch (5-cm) cookie cutter to stamp out twelve rounds. • Line the cups with the pastry rounds. • Brush with 1 teaspoon of cherry jelly. • Mix the cake crumbs, almonds, and flour in a medium bowl. • Melt the butter in a small saucepan. • Stir in the sugar and remove from the heat. • Add the egg. • Fold in the dry ingredients and vanilla. • Spoon the mixture into the prepared cups. • Bake for 25–30 minutes, or until golden brown and a toothpick inserted into a center comes out clean. • Turn out of the cups and let cool. • Brush with the apricot jam. • Mix the confectioners' sugar with the water. • Spread with the frosting.

Makes: about 12 tartlets • Prep: 30 min • Cooking: 25–30 min • Level: 1

- 4 oz (125 g) frozen flaky pie pastry, thawed
- ¼ cup (90 g) cherry jelly or cherry jam
- ¼ cup (30 g) plain cake crumbs
- ½ cup (75 g) finely ground almonds
- 1 teaspoon all-purpose (plain) flour
- ½ cup (125 g) butter
- ½ cup (100 g) sugar
- 1 large egg, lightly beaten
- ½ teaspoon vanilla extract (essence)
- 3 tablespoons apricot preserves (jam)
- ¾ cup (125 g) confectioners' (icing) sugar
- 1 teaspoon warm water or more as needed

MINI COCONUT TARTLETS

Preheat the oven to 425°F (210°/gas 7). • Set out 24 paper baking cups. • Stir together the coconut and sugar in a large bowl. • Add the eggs, beating until just blended. • Stir in the orange zest, flour, baking powder, and salt. • Drop heaped teaspoons of the mixture into the paper cups. • Bake for 10–12 minutes, or until golden brown and firm to the touch. • Cool the cookies for 10 minutes in the pan. • These are best still warm from the oven.

Makes: about 24 tartlets • Prep: 20 min • Cooking: 10–12 min • Level: 2

- 2 cups (120 g) unsweetened shredded (desiccated) coconut
- 1¼ cups (250 g) sugar
- 3 large eggs, lightly beaten
- 2 tablespoons finely grated orange zest
- 2 tablespoons all-purpose (plain) flour
- ½ teaspoon baking powder
- ⅛ teaspoon salt

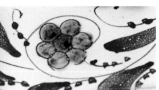

Tea Cakes, Tartlets, & Muffins

BUCKWHEAT MUFFINS

- ²/₃ cup (100 g) all-purpose (plain) flour
- ²/₃ cup (100 g) buckwheat flour
- 1 tablespoon unsweetened cocoa powder
- 1 tablespoon ground almonds
- 1 teaspoon baking powder
- ¹/₈ teaspoon salt
- ¹/₃ cup (90 g) butter, softened
- ¹/₂ cup (100 g) firmly packed soft brown sugar
- 3 large eggs
- 2 tablespoons milk
- ¹/₂ teaspoon vanilla or rum extract (essence)
- 2 oz (60 g) semisweet (dark) chocolate, finely grated
- 2 oz (60 g) white chocolate, coarsely chopped

Preheat the oven to 350°F (180°C/gas 4).
• Line two 12-cup mini muffin pans with paper cups. • Mix both flours, cocoa, almonds, baking powder, and salt in a medium bowl. • Beat the butter and brown sugar in a large bowl with an electric mixer on medium speed until creamy. • Add the eggs, milk, and vanilla, beating until just blended. • Mix in the dry ingredients and semisweet chocolate. • Fit a pastry bag with a plain ¹/₂-inch (1-cm) tip. Fill the pastry bag, twist the opening tightly closed, and squeeze out small rounds into each prepared cup. • Bake for about 15 minutes, or until lightly browned and a toothpick inserted in the centers comes out clean. • Cool in the pans for 3 minutes. Transfer to racks and let cool completely. • Melt the white chocolate in a double boiler over barely simmering water. Spoon the chocolate into a small freezer bag and cut off a tiny corner. Pipe chocolate lines over the muffins in a decorative manner. Let set for 30 minutes. Transfer to racks to finish cooling.

Makes: about 24 mini muffins • Prep: 25 min + 30 min to set • Cooking: 15 min • Level: 2

PISTACHIO MUFFINS

Preheat the oven to 325°F (170°C/gas 3).
• Butter and flour a 12-cup muffin pan, or line with foil or paper baking cups. • Mix the ground pistachios and sugar in a large bowl. • Beat the egg whites in a large bowl with an electric mixer at high speed until stiff peaks form. • Stir the egg yolks and orange zest into the pistachio mixture. • Use a large rubber spatula to gradually fold the pistachio mixture into the beaten whites, alternating with the cornstarch. • Spoon the batter into the prepared molds, filling each two-thirds full. • Bake for 15–20 minutes, or until a toothpick inserted into the center comes out clean. • Cool the cakes on racks.

Makes: about 12 muffins • Prep: 20 min • Cooking: 15–20 min • Level: 1

- 1¹/₄ cups (180 g) pistachio nuts, blanched and finely ground
- 1 cup (200 g) sugar
- 4 large eggs, separated
- 2 tablespoons grated orange zest
- ¹/₂ cup (75 g) cornstarch (cornflour)

DRIED APRICOT MUFFINS

- 2 cups (300 g) all-purpose (plain) flour
- 1 tablespoon baking powder
- ¹/₄ teaspoon salt
- ²/₃ cup (70 g) chopped dried apricots
- ³/₄ cup (180 ml) cold water
- ¹/₂ cup (125 g) butter, cut up
- ³/₄ cup (150 g) firmly packed brown sugar
- ¹/₂ cup (125 ml) milk

Preheat the oven to 350°F (180°C/gas 4).
• Butter and flour a 12-cup muffin pan, or line with foil or paper baking cups. • Mix the flour, baking powder, and salt in a large bowl. • Bring the apricots and water in a saucepan over medium heat to a boil. Reduce the heat and simmer for 5 minutes. Remove from the heat and beat in the butter and sugar until the sugar has dissolved. Stir in the milk, eggs, and vanilla. Stir the apricot mixture into the dry ingredients. • Spoon the batter into the prepared cups, filling each two-thirds full.
• Bake for 15–20 minutes, or until a toothpick inserted into the center comes out clean. • Cool the muffins on racks.

Makes: about 12 muffins • Prep: 10 min • Cooking: 15–20 min • Level: 1

- 1 large egg, lightly beaten
- 2 teaspoons vanilla extract (essence)

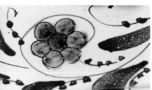

Tea Cakes, Tartlets, & Muffins

LIME MUFFINS WITH YOGURT

- 5 limes
- ½ cup (125 g) fresh ricotta cheese, drained
- ¾ cup (150 g) sugar
- 1⅔ cups (250 g) all-purpose (plain) flour
- 2 teaspoons baking powder
- ¼ teaspoon salt
- 2 large eggs
- ½ cup (100 g) firmly packed light brown sugar
- ¾ cup (200 g) plain yogurt
- ⅓ cup (90 ml) sunflower oil
- ¼ cup (30 g) confectioners' (icing) sugar

Preheat the oven to 350°F (180°C/gas 4). • Butter a 12-cup muffin pan. • Grate the zest of 2 limes. Squeeze the juice from 4 limes and thinly slice the remaining lime. • Beat the ricotta, 1 tablespoon of sugar, and 2 tablespoons of the lime juice in a bowl. • Mix the flour, baking powder, and salt in a medium bowl. • Beat the eggs, remaining sugar, brown sugar, yogurt, oil, lime zest, and ⅓ cup (90 ml) lime juice in a large bowl with an electric mixer on medium speed until smooth. • With mixer at low speed, gradually beat in the dry ingredients. • Spoon half the batter into the cups. Spoon some of the ricotta mixture into each cup. Cover with the remaining batter. • Bake until well risen and springy to the touch, 15–20 minutes. • While the muffins are baking, heat the remaining lime juice with the confectioners' sugar in a small saucepan over low heat. Bring to a boil and add the sliced lime. Simmer until the syrup is slightly thickened and the lime slices are transparent, about 10 minutes. Remove from the heat. • Drizzle the hot muffins with the syrup. • Let cool slightly before turning out onto a wire rack. Top with the slices of lime cooked in the syrup.

Makes: about 12 muffins • Prep: 20 min • Cooking: 15–20 min • Level: 2

FRESH APRICOT MUFFINS

Preheat the oven to 350°F (180°C/gas 4). • Butter a 12-cup muffin pan. • Mix the flour, baking powder, and salt in a medium bowl. • Beat the eggs, sugar, vanilla, milk, and butter in a large bowl with an electric mixer on medium speed until smooth. • With mixer at low speed, gradually add the dry ingredients, beating until the mixture is smooth and creamy. • Spoon the batter into the prepared pan. Arrange a few slices of apricot on top of each muffin and dust with confectioners' sugar. • Bake until well risen and springy to the touch, 15–20 minutes. • Let cool slightly before turning out onto a wire rack. • Dust with the extra confectioners' sugar before serving.

Makes: about 12 muffins • Prep: 20 min • Cooking: 15–20 min • Level: 1

- 1⅔ cups (250 g) all-purpose (plain) flour
- 2 teaspoons baking powder
- ¼ teaspoon salt
- 2 large eggs
- ½ cup (100 g) sugar
- ½ teaspoon vanilla extract (essence)
- 1 cup (250 ml) skimmed milk
- ½ cup (125 g) butter, melted
- 4 ripe apricots, pitted and sliced
- 4 tablespoons confectioners' (icing) sugar + extra, to dust

PRUNE AND WALNUT MUFFINS

- 2 cups (300 g) all-purpose (plain) flour
- 2 teaspoons baking powder
- 1 teaspoon ground cinnamon
- ¼ teaspoon salt
- 2 large eggs
- 1 cup (250 g) plain yogurt

Preheat the oven to 350°F (180°C/gas 4). • Butter three 6-cup muffin pans. • Mix the flour, baking powder, cinnamon, and salt in a medium bowl. • Beat the eggs, yogurt, sugar, and oil in a large bowl with an electric mixer on medium speed until smooth. • With mixer at low speed, gradually beat in the dry ingredients. Stir in the coarsely chopped walnuts and prunes.

• Spoon the batter into the prepared pans and top each muffin with half a walnut. • Bake until well risen and springy to the touch, 15–20 minutes. • Let cool slightly before turning out onto a wire rack.

Makes: about 18 muffins • Prep: 20 min • Cooking: 15–20 min • Level: 1

- ½ cup (100 g) dark brown sugar
- ⅓ cup (90 ml) sunflower oil
- 1¼ cups (125 g) coarsely chopped walnuts
- 8 oz (200 g) prunes, pitted and coarsely chopped
- 18 walnut halves

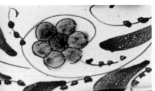

Tea Cakes, Tartlets, & Muffins

CHOCOLATE MUFFINS WITH CHERRY TOPPING

Muffins
- 5 oz (150 g) semisweet (dark) chocolate, coarsely chopped
- ½ cup (125 g) butter
- 1⅔ cups (250 g) all-purpose (plain) flour
- 2 teaspoons baking powder
- ¼ teaspoon salt
- ¾ cup (150 g) sugar
- 2 large eggs
- 1 teaspoon vanilla extract (essence)
- 24 fresh cherries, pitted and coarsely chopped

Cherry Topping
- 1 teaspoon cornstarch (cornflour)
- ½ cup (125 ml) white port
- 8 oz (250 g) fresh cherries, with stalks
- ½ cup (100 g) sugar

Muffins: Preheat the oven to 375°F (190°C/gas 5). • Butter a 12-cup muffin pan. • Melt the chocolate and butter in a double boiler over barely simmering water. Remove from the heat and let cool. • Mix the flour, baking powder, and salt in a medium bowl. • Beat the eggs, sugar, and vanilla in a large bowl with an electric mixer on medium speed until pale and creamy. • With mixer on low, gradually beat in the dry ingredients and the melted chocolate mixture. • Spoon half the batter into the prepared pan. Place two chopped cherries in each muffin and top with the remaining batter. • Bake until well risen and springy to the touch, 15–20 minutes. • Let cool slightly before turning out onto a wire rack. • Cherry Topping: Place the cornstarch in a small bowl and stir in the port until smooth. • Place the cherries and sugar in a medium saucepan over low heat. Stir in the port mixture and simmer for 10 minutes. • Decorate the cooled muffins with the cherry topping just before serving.

Makes: about 12 muffins • Prep: 20 min • Cooking: 15–20 min • Level: 2

ORANGE MUFFINS WITH STICKY ORANGE SAUCE

Preheat the oven to 350°F (180°C/gas 4). • Grease a 12-cup muffin pan. • Mix the flour, baking powder, and salt in a medium bowl. Add the almonds and the orange zest and mix well. • Beat the butter, eggs, milk, and half the sugar in a large bowl with an electric mixer on medium speed until smooth. • With mixer at low speed, gradually add the dry ingredients, beating until the mixture is smooth and creamy. • Spoon the batter into the prepared pan. • Bake until well risen and springy to the touch, 15–20 minutes. • While the muffins are baking, heat the orange juice and remaining sugar in a small saucepan over low heat. Bring to a boil and simmer until the syrup is reduced by half, about 15 minutes. Remove from the heat and add the liqueur. • Drizzle the hot muffins with the orange syrup. • Let cool slightly before turning out onto a wire rack. • Decorate with orange zest.

Makes: about 12 muffins • Prep: 20 min • Cooking: 15–20 min • Level: 2

- 2 cups (300 g) all-purpose (plain) flour
- 2 teaspoons baking powder
- ⅔ cup (60 g) finely ground almonds
- grated zest of 2 large unwaxed oranges
- ½ cup (125 g) butter, melted
- 2 large eggs
- 1 cup (250 ml) milk
- 1 cup (200 g) sugar
- 1 cup (250 ml) freshly squeezed orange juice
- ¼ cup (60 ml) Cointreau or other orange liqueur
- zest of 1 large unwaxed orange, cut into julienne strips

MAPLE SYRUP TARTLETS

Pastry
- 1¼ cups (180 g) all-purpose (plain) flour
- ⅛ teaspoon salt
- ½ cup (125 g) butter, cut up
- 1–2 tablespoons milk

Syrup Filling
- ½ cup (125 ml) pure maple syrup
- ⅔ cup (100 g) all-

Pastry: Mix the flour and salt in a medium bowl. • Use a pastry blender to cut in the butter until the mixture resembles coarse crumbs. • Add enough milk to form a stiff dough. • Press the dough into a disk, wrap in plastic wrap (cling film), and refrigerate for 30 minutes. • Preheat the oven to 375°F (190°C/gas 5). • Set out two 12-cup mini-muffin pans. • Roll out the dough on a lightly floured surface to ⅛ inch (3 mm) thick. • Use a 2-inch (5-cm) fluted cookie cutter to cut out rounds. • Gather the dough scraps, re-roll, and continue cutting out rounds until all the dough is used. Press the

dough rounds into the prepared cups. • Syrup Filling: Drop teaspoons of the maple syrup into each pastry base. • Mix the flour and baking powder in a medium bowl. • Beat the butter and brown sugar in a medium bowl with an electric mixer at high speed until creamy. • Add the egg and vanilla, beating until just blended. • Mix in the dry ingredients and milk. • Spoon the mixture evenly into the prepared cups. • Bake for 15–20 minutes, or until golden brown. • Transfer to racks to cool.

Makes: about 24 tartlets • Prep: 45 min + 30 min to chill • Cooking: 15–20 min • Level: 2

purpose (plain) flour
- ½ teaspoon baking powder
- ¼ cup (60 g) butter, softened
- ¼ cup (50 g) firmly packed light brown sugar
- 1 large egg, lightly beaten
- ½ teaspoon vanilla extract (essence)
- 1 tablespoon milk

Mandarin and chocolate muffins

MANDARIN AND CHOCOLATE MUFFINS

- 12 oz (350 g) mandarins, peeled and divided into segments
- 2 cups (300 g) all-purpose (plain) flour
- 2 teaspoons baking powder
- ¼ teaspoon salt
- 5 oz (150 g) yogurt-flavored chocolate, coarsely chopped
- 2 large eggs
- 1 cup (250 ml) milk
- ¾ cup (150 g) sugar
- ⅓ cup (90 ml) vegetable oil

Set aside 24 mandarin segments for decoration and then chop the rest. • Preheat the oven to 350°F (180°C/gas 4). • Butter a 12-cup muffin pan. • Mix the flour, baking powder, and salt in a medium bowl. • Add the chopped mandarins and chocolate. • Beat the eggs, milk, sugar, and oil in a large bowl with an electric mixer at medium speed until smooth. • With mixer at low speed, gradually beat in the dry ingredients. • Spoon the batter into the prepared pan and then top each muffin with two of the reserved mandarin segments. • Bake until well risen and springy to the touch, 15–20 minutes. • Let cool slightly before turning out onto a wire rack.

Makes: about 12 muffins • Prep: 15 min • Cooking: 15–20 min • Level: 1

SHELL COOKIES

Preheat the oven to 400°F (200°C/gas 6). • Butter and flour a madeleine pan. • Mix the flour and salt in a medium bowl. • Beat the eggs and sugar in a large bowl with an electric mixer at high speed until pale and thick. • Mix in the dry ingredients and lemon zest until well blended. • Stir in the melted butter. • Spoon the batter into the prepared pan, filling each cup three-quarters full. • Bake for 6–8 minutes, or until golden brown. • Transfer to racks to cool.

Makes: about 12 cookies · Prep: 20 min · Cooking: 6–8 min Level: 1

- ½ cup (75 g) all-purpose (plain) flour
- ⅛ teaspoon salt
- 2 large eggs
- ½ cup (100 g) sugar
- 1 teaspoon finely grated lemon zest
- ¼ cup (60 g) butter, melted

FRUIT AND YOGURT MUFFINS

- 2 cups (300 g) all-purpose (plain) flour
- 2 teaspoons baking powder
- 1/4 teaspoon salt
- 3 ripe apples, peeled, cored, and grated
- 2/3 cup (200 g) orange marmalade
- 2 large eggs
- generous 3/4 cup (200 g) plain yogurt
- 1/2 cup (100 g) sugar
- 1/3 cup (90 ml) vegetable oil
- 1 large ripe banana, mashed
- 2 tablespoons sugar crystals

Preheat the oven to 350°F (180°C/gas 4). • Butter three 6-cup muffin pans. • Mix the flour, baking powder, and salt in a medium bowl. • Combine the apples and marmalade in another bowl. • Beat the eggs, yogurt, sugar, and oil in a large bowl with an electric mixer at medium speed. • With mixer at low speed, gradually beat in the dry ingredients until smooth. Stir in the banana. • Half fill the muffin cups with batter. Add a spoonful of the apple and marmalade mixture. Cover with the remaining batter. Sprinkle with sugar crystals. • Bake until well risen and springy to the touch, 15–20 minutes. • Let cool slightly before turning out onto a wire rack.

Makes: about 16 muffins • Prep: 15 min • Cooking: 15–20 min • Level: 1

FROSTED JAFFA MUFFINS

Preheat the oven to 400°F (200°C/gas 6). • Butter three 6-cup muffin pans. • Melt the chocolate and butter in a double boiler over barely simmering water. • Mix the flour, cocoa, baking powder, and salt in a large bowl. • Stir in the sugar. • Add the eggs, milk, and orange zest, beating with an electric mixer on low speed until well blended. • Beat in the melted chocolate mixture. • Spoon the batter into the prepared pan. • Bake until well risen and springy to the touch, 20–25 minutes. • Let cool slightly before turning out onto a wire rack. Let cool completely. • Frosting: Melt the chocolate and butter in a double boiler over barely simmering water. • Remove from the heat and stir in the Cointreau. • Spread the muffins with the frosting. Top with the orange zest and let stand until the frosting has set.

Makes: about 15 muffins • Prep: 15 min • Cooking: 20–25 min • Level: 1

Muffins
- 5 oz (150 g) semisweet (dark) chocolate, coarsely chopped
- 1/3 cup (90 g) butter
- 2 1/2 cups (375 g) all-purpose (plain) flour
- 4 tablespoons unsweetened cocoa powder
- 2 teaspoons baking powder
- 1/4 teaspoon salt
- 3 tablespoons sugar
- 2 large eggs
- 1 cup (250 ml) milk
- 1 tablespoon finely grated orange zest

Frosting
- 8 oz (250 g) semisweet (dark) chocolate, chopped
- 1/4 cup (60 g) butter
- 1 tablespoon Cointreau or other orange liqueur
- finely grated orange zest

Fruit and yogurt muffins

Tea Cakes, Tartlets, & Muffins

PEAR AND GINGER MUFFINS

- 2 large ripe pears, peeled, cored, and cut into small cubes
- 2 oz (60 g) stem ginger preserved in syrup, with syrup
- 1²/₃ cups (250 g) all-purpose (plain) flour
- 2¹/₂ teaspoons baking powder
- ¹/₄ teaspoon salt
- ³/₄ cup (75 g) chopped walnuts
- 2 tablespoons unsweetened cocoa powder
- 2 large eggs
- ¹/₂ cup (100 g) sugar
- ¹/₂ cup (100 g) butter, softened
- 1 cup (250 ml) milk
- 4 oz (125 g) white chocolate
- 12 walnut halves, to decorate

Place the pears in a bowl with 1 tablespoon of the syrup from the ginger and mix well. Drain the ginger and chop very finely. • Preheat the oven to 350°F (180°C/gas 4). • Butter a 12-cup muffin pan. • Mix the flour, baking powder, salt, walnuts, and cocoa in a medium bowl. • Beat the eggs and sugar in a large bowl with an electric mixer on medium speed until creamy. • Gradually add the butter and milk, alternating with the dry ingredients. • Stir in the ginger and pears by hand. • Spoon the batter into the prepared pan. • Bake until well risen and springy to the touch, 15–20 minutes. • Let cool slightly before turning out onto a wire rack. Let cool completely. • Melt the white chocolate in a double boiler over barely simmering water. Drizzle over the muffins. Top each muffin with a walnut half. Let cool completely before serving.

Makes: about 12 muffins • Prep: 20 min • Cooking: 15–20 min • Level: 2

BRAN MUFFINS

Preheat the oven to 350°F (180°C/gas 4). • Butter a 12-cup muffin pan. • Mix the flour, bran, baking powder, baking soda, and salt in a medium bowl. • Beat the butter and brown sugar in a large bowl with an electric mixer on medium speed until cream. • Beat in the egg, followed by the mixed the dry ingredients, milk, and raisins. • Spoon the batter into the prepared pans. • Bake until well risen and springy to the touch, about 15–20 minutes. • Let cool slightly before turning out onto a wire rack.

Makes: about 12 muffins • Prep: 15 min • Cooking: 15–20 min • Level: 1

- 1¹/₂ cups (225 g) all-purpose (plain) flour
- 1 cup (150 g) wheat bran
- 2 teaspoons baking powder
- 1 teaspoon baking soda (bicarbonate of soda)
- ¹/₂ teaspoon salt
- ¹/₄ cup (60 g) butter, softened
- ³/₄ cup (150 g) firmly packed light brown sugar
- 1 large egg
- ³/₄ cup (200 ml) milk
- ¹/₂ cup (75 g) raisins

COCONUT CRANBERRY MUFFINS

- 4 oz (125 g) white chocolate, chopped
- 1 cup (250 ml) milk
- 1²/₃ cups (250 g) all-purpose (plain) flour
- 2 teaspoons baking powder
- ¹/₄ teaspoon salt
- 5 oz (150 g) dried cranberries
- ¹/₂ cup (50 g) unsweetened shredded (desiccated) coconut
- 2 large eggs
- ¹/₂ cup (100 g) sugar
- ¹/₃ cup (90 ml) sunflower oil

Preheat the oven to 350°F (180°C/gas 4). • Butter a 12-cup muffin pan. • Melt the chocolate with the milk in a double boiler over barely simmering water. Remove from the heat and let cool. • Mix the flour, baking powder, and salt in a medium bowl. Stir in the cranberries and coconut. • Beat the eggs, sugar, and oil in a large bowl with an electric mixer on medium speed until smooth. • With mixer on low, gradually beat in the dry ingredients and chocolate mixture. • Spoon the batter into the prepared pan. • Bake until springy to the touch, about 20 minutes. • Let cool slightly before turning out onto a wire rack.

Makes: about 12 muffins • Prep: 20 min • Cooking: 20 min Level: 1

ALMOND SHELL COOKIES

Preheat the oven to 400°F (200°C/gas 6). • Butter and flour a madeleine pan (for 12 madeleines). • Mix the flour and salt in a medium bowl. • Beat the eggs and sugar in a large bowl with an electric mixer at high speed until pale and thick. • Mix in the dry ingredients, almonds, and almond extract until well blended. • Stir in the melted butter. • Spoon the batter into the prepared pan, filling each cup three-quarters full. • Bake for 6–8 minutes, or until golden brown. • Transfer to racks to cool.

Makes: about 12 cookies • Prep: 20 min • Cooking: 6–8 min Level: 1

- ¹/₂ cup (75 g) all-purpose (plain) flour
- ¹/₈ teaspoon salt
- 2 large eggs
- ¹/₂ cup (100 g) sugar
- ¹/₃ cup (50 g) finely ground almonds
- ¹/₄ teaspoon almond extract (essence)
- ¹/₄ cup (60 g) butter, melted

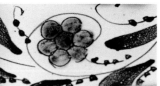

Tea Cakes, Tartlets, & Muffins

CHOCOLATE CHILE MUFFINS

- 4 oz (125 g) bittersweet (dark) chocolate, broken into pieces
- 1/2 cup (125 g) butter
- 1 cup (150 g) all-purpose (plain) flour
- 2 tablespoons unsweetened cocoa powder
- 2 teaspoons baking powder
- 1 teaspoon chile powder
- 1/4 teaspoon salt
- 1 1/4 cups (125 g) finely ground almonds
- 2 large eggs
- 1/2 cup (100 g) sugar
- 1 cup (250 ml) milk
- 1 cup (250 ml) whipped cream
- 1/2 teaspoon chile powder

Preheat the oven to 350°F (180°C/gas 4). • Butter a 12-cup muffin pan. • Melt the chocolate and butter in a double boiler over barely simmering water. Set aside to cool. • Mix the flour, cocoa, baking powder, chile, and salt in a medium bowl. Stir in the almonds. • Beat the eggs, sugar, and milk in a large bowl with an electric mixer on medium speed until smooth. • With mixer on low speed, gradually beat in the dry ingredients, alternating with the chocolate and butter mixture. • Spoon the batter into the prepared pan. • Bake until well risen and springy to the touch, 15–20 minutes. • Let cool slightly before turning out onto a wire rack. Let cool completely. • Decorate each muffin with a little whipped cream and a pinch of chile powder.

Makes: about 12 muffins • Prep: 20 min • Cooking: 15–20 min • Level: 1

CHOCOLATE COCONUT MUFFINS

Preheat the oven to 350°F (180°C/gas 4). • Butter a 12-cup muffin pan. • Beat the coconut and 1/2 cup (125 ml) of the rum in a small bowl. • Mix the flour, cocoa, baking powder, and salt in a medium bowl. • Place the butter and milk in a saucepan over low heat and stir until the butter has melted. Remove from the heat. • Beat the eggs and sugar in a large bowl with an electric mixer at high speed until pale and creamy. • Gradually beat in the butter, milk, and coconut mixture, alternating with the dry ingredients. Spoon the batter into the prepared pan. • Bake until well risen and springy to the touch, 15–20 minutes. • Let cool slightly before turning out onto a wire rack. Let cool completely. • Melt the chocolate with the remaining rum in a double boiler over barely simmering water. Spread each muffin with the frosting.

Makes: about 12 muffins • Prep: 15 min • Cooking: 20 min Level: 1

- scant 2/3 cup (75 g) shredded (desiccated) coconut
- 2/3 cup (150 ml) rum
- 1 cup (150 g) all-purpose (plain) flour
- 1/3 cup (50 g) unsweetened cocoa powder
- 2 teaspoons baking powder
- 1/4 teaspoon salt
- 1/2 cup (125 g) butter, melted
- 1 cup (250 ml) milk
- 2 large eggs
- 3/4 cup (150 g) sugar
- 6 oz (180 g) milk chocolate, broken into pieces

NUTTY MUFFINS WITH YOGURT

- 1 cup (150 g) all-purpose (plain) flour
- 2 1/2 teaspoons baking powder
- 1 teaspoon cinnamon
- 1 teaspoon ginger
- 1/4 teaspoon salt
- 1/2 cup (75 g) raisins
- 1 cup (120 g) finely ground hazelnuts
- 1/2 cup (75 g) candied lemon peel, chopped
- 2 large eggs
- 1 cup (250 ml) yogurt
- 1/2 cup (100 g) sugar
- 1/2 cup (125 g) butter, melted
- 36 blanched almonds

Preheat the oven to 350°F (180°C/gas 4). • Butter a 12-cup muffin pan. • Mix the flour, baking powder, cinnamon, ginger, and salt in a medium bowl. Stir in the raisins, hazelnuts, and candied lemon peel. • Beat the eggs, yogurt, and sugar in a large bowl with an electric mixer on medium speed until smooth. • With mixer on low speed, gradually beat in the dry ingredients and butter. • Spoon the mixture into the prepared pan. Top each muffin with 3 almonds. • Bake until well risen and springy to the touch, 15–20 minutes. • Let cool slightly before turning out onto a wire rack.

Makes: about 12 muffins • Prep: 20 min • Cooking: 15–20 min • Level: 1

MUFFINS WITH CARAMEL SAUCE

Preheat the oven to 350°F (180°C/gas 4). • Butter a 12-cup muffin pan. • Mix the flour, baking powder, and salt in a medium bowl. • Beat the eggs, butter, sugar, caramel flavoring, and milk in a large bowl with an electric mixer on medium speed until smooth. • With mixer on low, gradually beat in the dry ingredients. • Spoon the batter into the prepared pan. • Bake until well risen and springy to the touch, 15–20 minutes. • Let cool slightly before turning out onto a wire rack. Top with the caramel sauce before serving.

Makes: about 12 muffins • Prep: 20 min • Cooking: 15–20 min • Level: 1

- 2 cups (300 g) all-purpose (plain) flour
- 2 teaspoons baking powder
- 1/4 teaspoon salt
- 2 large eggs
- 1/2 cup (100 g) butter, melted
- 3/4 cup (150 g) sugar
- 2 tablespoons caramel flavoring
- 1 cup (250 ml) milk
- 1/3 cup (90 ml) ready-made caramel sauce

Tea Cakes, Tartlets, & Muffins

FRUITY ALMOND MUFFINS

- 1²/₃ cups (250 g) all-purpose (plain) flour
- 2¹/₂ teaspoons baking powder
- ¹/₄ teaspoon salt
- ¹/₂ cup (50 g) finely ground almonds
- generous ¹/₂ cup (100 g) chopped dried apricots
- 4 oz (125 g) marzipan, cut into small cubes
- generous ¹/₃ cup (100 ml) freshly squeezed orange juice
- 2 large eggs
- ¹/₂ cup (100 g) sugar
- finely grated zest of 1 large orange
- 1 cup (250 ml) milk
- ¹/₃ cup (90 ml) vegetable oil

Preheat the oven to 350°F (180°C/gas 4). • Butter a 12-cup muffin pan. • Mix the flour, baking powder, and salt in a medium bowl. • Place the almonds, apricots, marzipan, and orange juice in a blender and chop to make a smooth paste. • Beat the eggs, sugar, orange zest, milk, and oil, in a large bowl with an electric mixer on medium speed until smooth. • With mixer on low speed, gradually add the dry ingredients, beating until smooth. • Spoon half the batter into the prepared pan. Spoon some of the orange and almond mixture into each cup. Cover with the remaining batter. • Bake until well risen and springy to the touch, about 20 minutes. • Let cool slightly before turning out onto a wire rack.

Makes: about 12 muffins • Prep: 20 min • Cooking: 20–25 min • Level: 1

PEAR AND PECAN MUFFINS

- 3 cups (450 g) all-purpose (plain) flour
- 2 teaspoons baking powder
- 1 teaspoon cinnamon
- ¹/₂ teaspoon freshly grated nutmeg
- ¹/₄ teaspoon salt
- ¹/₂ cup (100 g) firmly packed brown sugar
- 1 cup (100 g) chopped pecans, toasted
- 14 oz (400 g) firm-ripe pears, peeled, cored, and thinly sliced
- 2 large eggs
- 1¹/₂ cups (375 ml) milk
- 1 teaspoon vanilla extract (essence)
- ¹/₂ cup (125 g) butter
- 10 pecan nuts, cut in half
- confectioners' (icing) sugar, to dust

Preheat the oven to 350°F (180°C/gas 4). • Butter two 12-cup muffin pans. • Mix the flour, baking powder, cinnamon, nutmeg, and salt in a large bowl. • Stir in the brown sugar, chopped pecans, and pears. • Add the eggs, milk, and vanilla and beat with an electric mixer on medium speed until well blended. • Stir in the butter. • Spoon the batter into the prepared cups. Top each muffin with half a pecan. • Bake until well risen and springy to the touch, about 20 minutes. • Let cool slightly before turning out onto a wire rack. • Dust with the confectioners' sugar just before serving.

Makes: about 20 muffins • Prep: 15 min • Cooking: 20–25 min • Level: 1

DESSERT MUFFINS

Preheat the oven to 350°F (180°C/gas 4). • Butter a 12-cup muffin pan. • Mix the flour, potato starch, and baking powder in a large bowl. • Beat the butter and ²/₃ cup (100 g) of confectioners' sugar in a large bowl with an electric mixer on medium speed until pale and creamy. • Add the ginger, egg, and egg yolks, beating until just blended. • With mixer on low speed, gradually add the chocolate and dry ingredients to make a smooth batter. • Spoon the batter into the prepared cups. • Bake until well risen and springy to the touch, 15–20 minutes. • Let cool slightly before turning out onto a wire rack. Let cool completely. • Chocolate Sauce: Melt the chocolate and cream in a double boiler over barely simmering water. • Tropical Coulis: Place the mango, papaya, passionfruit, sugar, and rum in a food processor or blender and chop until smooth. • Place the warm muffins on serving dishes. • Spoon a little of each sauce onto the dishes around the base of the muffins. Dust with the confectioners' sugar and sprinkle with the almonds. Garnish with the whipped cream and serve.

Makes: about 12 muffins • Prep: 30 min • Cooking: 15–20 min • Level: 2

- ¹/₃ cup (50 g) all-purpose (plain) flour
- 2 tablespoons cornstarch (cornflour)
- 1 teaspoon baking powder
- ¹/₃ cup (90 g) butter
- 1 cup (150 g) confectioners' (icing) sugar
- 1 tablespoon fresh minced ginger
- 1 large egg + 3 large egg yolks
- 2 oz (60 g) semisweet (dark) chocolate, melted

Chocolate Sauce
- 4 oz (125 g) bittersweet (dark) chocolate, coarsely chopped
- ¹/₂ cup (125 ml) heavy (double) cream

Tropical Coulis
- 4 oz (125 g) mango, peeled and coarsely chopped
- 4 oz (125 g) papaya, peeled and seeded
- 1 passionfruit, pulped and strained
- ¹/₃ cup (75 g) sugar
- 2 tablespoons dark rum

- confectioners' (icing) sugar, to dust
- flaked almonds, to decorate
- whipped cream, to serve

Cashew and pear muffins

CASHEW AND PEAR MUFFINS

- 3 large ripe pears, peeled, cored and chopped
- 2 tablespoons freshly squeezed lemon juice
- 1²/₃ cups (250 g) all-purpose (plain) flour
- 2¹/₂ teaspoons baking powder
- ¹/₄ teaspoon salt
- 1 cup (100 g) finely chopped cashew nuts
- 2 large eggs
- ¹/₂ cup (100 g) sugar
- ¹/₃ cup (90 ml) sunflower oil
- 1 cup (250 ml) milk
- 4 tablespoons confectioners' (icing) sugar, to dust

Place the chopped pears in a medium bowl with the lemon juice and mix well. • Preheat the oven to 350°F (180°C/gas 4). • Butter a 12-cup muffin pan. • Mix the flour, baking powder, and salt in a medium bowl. Stir in the cashews. • Beat the eggs, sugar, oil, and milk in a large bowl with an electric mixer on medium speed until smooth. • With mixer on low speed, gradually beat in the dry ingredients and pear mixture. • Spoon the batter into the prepared pan. • Bake until well risen and springy to the touch, 15–20 minutes. • Let cool slightly before turning out onto a wire rack. • Dust with confectioners' sugar just before serving.

Makes: about 12 muffins • Prep: 15 min • Cooking: 15–20 min • Level: 1

MARBLED MUFFINS

Preheat the oven to 350°F (180°C/gas 4). • Butter a 12-cup muffin pan. • Mix the flour, almonds, baking powder, and salt in a small bowl. • Melt the chocolate with half the cream in a double boiler over barely simmering water. • Beat the cocoa, orange zest, and remaining cream in a small bowl. • Beat the eggs, yogurt, butter, and sugar in a large bowl with an electric mixer on medium speed until smooth. • With mixer on low, beat in the dry ingredients. • Divide the mixture between two bowls. Add the melted chocolate to one bowl and the cocoa mixture to the other. Place alternate spoonfuls of the light and dark batters in the prepared pan. • Bake until springy to the touch, 15–20 minutes. • Let cool slightly before turning out onto a wire rack.

Makes: about 12 muffins • Prep: 20 min • Cooking: 15–20 min • Level: 1

- 1 cup (150 g) all-purpose (plain) flour
- 1 cup (100 g) finely ground almonds
- 2¹/₂ teaspoons baking powder
- ¹/₄ teaspoon salt
- 3 oz (90 g) white chocolate, broken into pieces
- ¹/₃ cup (90 ml) heavy (double) cream
- 2 tablespoons unsweetened cocoa powder
- grated zest of ¹/₂ orange
- 2 large eggs
- ³/₄ cup (200 g) plain yogurt
- ¹/₃ cup (90 g) butter, softened
- ¹/₂ cup (100 g) sugar

BLUEBERRY MUFFINS WITH WHITE CHOCOLATE FROSTING

- 1²/₃ cups (250 g) all-purpose (plain) flour
- 2 teaspoons baking powder
- ¹/₄ teaspoon salt
- 8 oz (250 g) white chocolate, broken into pieces
- ³/₄ cup (200 ml) milk
- 2 large eggs
- ¹/₂ cup (100 g) sugar
- ¹/₂ teaspoon vanilla extract (essence)
- ¹/₃ cup (90 g) butter, softened
- 8 oz (250 g) frozen blueberries, thawed

Preheat the oven to 350°F (180°C/gas 4). • Butter a 12-cup muffin pan. • Mix the flour, baking powder, and salt in a medium bowl. • Melt 5 oz (150 g) of the chocolate with the milk in a double boiler over barely simmering water. • Beat the eggs, sugar, vanilla, butter, and melted chocolate mixture in a large bowl with an electric mixer at medium speed until smooth. • With mixer on low, beat in the dry ingredients. • Stir the blueberries in by hand. • Spoon the batter into the prepared pan. • Bake until springy to the touch, 15–20 minutes. • Let cool slightly before turning out onto a wire rack. Let cool completely. • Melt the remaining chocolate in a double boiler over barely simmering water. • Drizzle the melted chocolate over the muffins.

Makes: about 12 muffins • Prep: 20 min • Cooking: 15–20 min • Level: 1

ANISEED MUFFINS

Preheat the oven to 350°F (180°C/gas 4). • Butter a 12-cup muffin pan. • Mix the flour, baking powder, and salt in a medium bowl. Stir in the pine nuts and 2 teaspoons of aniseed. • Beat the eggs, sugar, oil, and milk in a large bowl with an electric mixer on medium speed until smooth. • With mixer on low speed, gradually beat in the dry ingredients. • Spoon the batter into the prepared pan. • Bake until well risen and springy to the touch, 15–20 minutes. • Let cool slightly before turning out onto a wire rack. Let cool completely. • Beat the confectioners' sugar, lemon juice, and remaining aniseed in a small bowl. • Spread the muffins with this mixture.

Makes: about 12 muffins • Prep: 20 min • Cooking: 15–20 min • Level: 1

- 1²/₃ cups (250 g) all-purpose (plain) flour
- 2¹/₂ teaspoons baking powder
- ¹/₄ teaspoon salt
- generous ¹/₂ cup (100 g) pine nuts
- 3 teaspoons ground aniseed
- 2 large eggs
- ¹/₂ cup (100 g) sugar
- ¹/₃ cup (90 ml) vegetable oil
- 1 cup (250 ml) milk
- 1 cup (150 g) confectioners' (icing) sugar
- 2 tablespoons freshly squeezed lemon juice

Tea Cakes, Tartlets, & Muffins

APPLE AND RAISIN MUFFINS

- 3 large ripe apples, peeled, cored, and grated
- finely grated zest and juice of 1 lemon
- 1²/₃ cups (250 g) all-purpose (plain) flour
- 2¹/₂ teaspoons baking powder
- ¹/₄ teaspoon salt
- generous ¹/₂ cup (100 g) raisins
- 1 cup (250 g) ricotta cheese, drained
- ²/₃ cup (150 ml) milk
- ¹/₂ cup (100 g) sugar
- 2 large eggs
- ¹/₂ cup (125 g) butter, melted
- 4 tablespoons confectioners' (icing) sugar, to dust

Place the apples in a medium bowl with the lemon zest and juice. Mix well. • Preheat the oven to 350°F (180°C/gas 4). • Butter a 12-cup muffin pan. • Mix the flour, baking powder, and salt in a medium bowl. Stir in the raisins. • Beat the ricotta, milk, sugar, eggs, and butter in a large bowl with an electric mixer at medium speed until smooth. • With mixer on low speed, gradually beat in the dry ingredients and apple mixture. • Spoon the batter into the prepared pan. • Bake until well risen and springy to the touch, 20–25 minutes. • Let cool slightly before turning out onto a wire rack. • Dust with the confectioners' sugar just before serving.

Makes: about 12 muffins • Prep: 15 min • Cooking: 20–25 min • Level: 1

RICE MUFFINS

Preheat the oven to 350°F (180°C/gas 4). • Butter a 12-cup muffin pan. • Mix the flour, baking powder, and salt in a large bowl. • Add the eggs one at a time, beating with an electric mixer on medium speed until just blended after each addition. • With mixer on low, add the milk, butter, sugar, rum, and salt, beating until smooth. • Stir in the rice. • Spoon the batter into the prepared pan. • Bake until well risen and springy to the touch, 15–20 minutes. • Let cool slightly before turning out onto a wire rack. • Dust with the confectioners' sugar just before serving.

Makes: about 12 muffins • Prep: 15 min • Cooking: 15–20 min • Level: 1

- 1 cup (150 g) all-purpose (plain) flour
- 1 teaspoon baking powder
- ¹/₄ teaspoon salt
- 3 large eggs
- 1 cup (250 ml) milk
- ¹/₄ cup (60 g) butter, melted
- ¹/₂ cup (100 g) sugar
- 1 tablespoon rum
- ¹/₂ teaspoon salt
- 1 cup (100 g) boiled rice, well cooked
- ¹/₃ cup (50 g) confectioners' (icing) sugar, to dust

Apple and raisin muffins

Carrot and pine nut muffins

CARROT AND PINE NUT MUFFINS

- 8 oz (250 g) finely grated carrots
- 1²/₃ cups (250 g) all-purpose (plain) flour
- 1¹/₂ teaspoons baking powder
- ¹/₄ teaspoon salt
- ¹/₂ cup (100 g) finely chopped pine nuts
- ²/₃ cup (100 g) confectioners' (icing) sugar + extra, to dust
- ³/₄ cup (180 g) butter
- 4 large eggs + 1 large egg yolk

Preheat the oven to 375°F (190°C/gas 5). • Butter a 12-cup muffin pan. • Mix the flour, baking powder, and salt in a medium bowl. Stir in the pine nuts. • Beat the confectioners' sugar and butter in a large bowl with an electric mixer at medium speed until pale and creamy. • Add the egg yolks one at a time, beating until just combined after each addition. • With mixer on low speed, gradually add the dry ingredients and carrots, beating until smooth. • Beat the egg whites in a large bowl with mixer at high speed until stiff peaks form. Fold the whites into the batter. • Spoon the batter into the prepared pan. • Bake until well risen and springy to the touch, 15–20 minutes. • Let cool slightly before turning out onto a wire rack. • Dust with the confectioners' sugar just before serving.

Makes: about 12 muffins • Prep: 15 min • Cooking: 15–20 min • Level: 1

ROSE MUFFINS

Preheat the oven to 350°F (180°C/gas 4). • Butter a 12-cup muffin pan. • Mix the flour, baking powder, and salt in a medium bowl. Stir in the almonds. • Beat the eggs, yogurt, half the sugar, and the oil in a large bowl with an electric mixer at medium speed until smooth. • With mixer on low speed, gradually beat in the dry ingredients. • Spoon the batter into the prepared pan. • Bake until well risen and springy to the touch, 15–20 minutes. • Let cool slightly before turning out onto a wire rack. • Place the remaining sugar and the water in a small saucepan over low heat and bring to a boil. Simmer until the syrup is slightly reduced, 3–4 minutes. Remove from the heat and let cool. Add the rose water and lemon juice and mix well. • Drizzle the muffins with the rose syrup and then let cool completely. • Dissolve the confectioners' sugar in 1–2 teaspoons of boiling water in a small bowl. Drizzle this mixture over the muffins and then decorate with rose petals.

Makes: about 12 muffins • Prep: 15 min • Cooking: 15–20 min • Level: 1

- 2 cups (300 g) all-purpose (plain) flour
- 2 teaspoons baking powder
- ¹/₄ teaspoon salt
- ¹/₂ cup (50 g) finely ground almonds
- 2 large eggs
- scant 1¹/₄ cups (300 g) plain yogurt
- 1 cup (200 g) sugar
- ¹/₃ cup (90 ml) vegetable oil
- ¹/₃ cup (90 ml) water
- ¹/₄ cup (60 ml) rose water
- ¹/₄ cup (60 ml) freshly squeezed lemon juice
- ¹/₃ cup (50 g) confectioners' (icing) sugar
- crystallized rose petals, to decorate

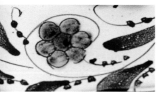

Tea Cakes, Tartlets, & Muffins

GINGER MUFFINS WITH ORANGE PRESERVES

- 1⅔ cups (250 g) all-purpose (plain) flour
- 2½ teaspoons baking powder
- ¼ teaspoon salt
- finely grated zest of 1 lemon
- 2 large eggs,
- ½ cup (100 g) sugar
- ½ cup (125 ml) heavy (double) cream
- ½ cup (125 ml) milk
- freshly squeezed juice of 1 lemon
- ⅔ cup (150 g) butter, melted
- 3 oz (90 g) stem ginger preserved in syrup, drained and chopped
- 4 tablespoons orange preserves (marmalade)

Preheat the oven to 350°F (180°C/gas 4). • Butter a 12-cup muffin pan. • Mix the flour, baking powder, and salt in a medium bowl. Stir in the lemon zest. • Beat the eggs, sugar, cream, milk, lemon juice, and butter in a large bowl with an electric mixer on medium speed until smooth. • With mixer on low speed, gradually beat in the dry ingredients. • Spoon the batter into the prepared pan. • Bake until well risen and springy to the touch, 15–20 minutes. • Let cool slightly before turning out onto a wire rack. • Melt the preserves in a small saucepan over low heat. Brush the muffins with the marmalade just before serving.

Makes: about 12 muffins • Prep: 15 min • Cooking: 15–20 min • Level: 1

CHERRY ALMOND MUFFINS

Preheat the oven to 350°F (180°C/gas 4). • Butter three 6-cup muffin pans. • Mix the flour, baking powder, and salt in a large bowl. • Beat the butter, 1 cup (200 g) of sugar, and almond extract in a large bowl with an electric mixer at medium speed until creamy. • Add the eggs one at a time, beating until just blended after each addition. • With mixer at low speed, gradually beat in the dry ingredients, alternating with the milk. • Stir in the cherries and almonds. • Spoon the batter into the prepared pans. Sprinkle with the remaining sugar • Bake until well risen and springy to the touch, about 20 minutes. • Let cool slightly before turning out onto a wire rack.

Makes: about 18 muffins • Prep: 20 min • Cooking: 20 min Level: 1

- 2 cups (300 g) all-purpose (plain) flour
- 2 teaspoons baking powder
- ¼ teaspoon salt
- ½ cup (125 g) butter
- 1¼ cups (250 g) sugar
- ½ teaspoon almond extract (essence)
- 2 large eggs
- ½ cup (125 ml) milk
- 1 cup (200 g) canned cherries, drained, pitted, and coarsely chopped
- 1 cup (75 g) coarsely chopped almonds, lightly toasted

FROSTED ZUCCHINI MUFFINS

Muffins

- 2 cups (300 g) all-purpose (plain) flour
- 2 teaspoons baking powder
- 1 teaspoon baking soda (bicarbonate of soda)
- ¼ teaspoon salt
- ½ cup (100 g) firmly packed brown sugar
- 1 tablespoon finely grated lemon zest
- 1 cup (75 g) chopped walnuts
- ½ cup (180 g) raisins
- 2 large eggs

Preheat the oven to 350°F (180°C/gas 4). • Butter three 6-cup muffin pans. • Mix the flour, baking powder, baking soda, and salt in a large bowl. Stir in the brown sugar, lemon zest, walnuts, and raisins. • Beat the eggs, oil, lime juice, and milk in a large bowl with an electric mixer on medium speed until smooth. Stir the egg mixture into the dry ingredients. Fold in the zucchini. • Spoon the batter into the prepared cups. • Bake until well risen and springy to the touch, about 20 minutes. • Let cool slightly before turning out onto a wire rack. Let cool completely. • Lime

Frosting: Beat the cream cheese and confectioners' sugar in a bowl with an electric mixer at medium speed until creamy. Beat in the lime zest and enough juice to make a thick, spreadable frosting. • Spread the frosting over the cooled muffins.

Makes: about 18 muffins • Prep: 15 min • Cooking: 15–20 min • Level: 1

- ⅓ cup (90 ml) vegetable oil
- ¼ cup (60 ml) freshly squeezed lime juice
- ¼ cup (60 ml) milk
- 1 cup (200 g) firmly packed shredded zucchini (courgettes)

Lime Frosting

- 3 oz (90 g) cream cheese
- 1 cup (150 g) confectioners' (icing) sugar
- 1 tablespoon finely grated lime zest
- 1 tablespoon freshly squeezed lime juice

HONEY AND THYME MUFFINS

- 1 cup (150 g) all-purpose (plain) flour
- 1½ teaspoons baking powder
- ¼ teaspoon salt
- 1 tablespoon finely chopped thyme
- 1 cup (100 g) finely ground almonds
- 2 large eggs
- ½ cup (125 g) clear honey
- ⅓ cup (70 g) demerara or raw sugar
- ⅓ cup (90 g) butter, softened
- 1 cup (250 ml) milk

Preheat the oven to 350°F (180°C/gas 4). • Butter a 12-cup muffin pan. • Mix the flour, baking powder, and salt in a medium bowl. Stir in the almonds and thyme. • Beat the eggs, honey, 3 tablespoons of the demerara sugar, butter, and milk in a large bowl with an electric mixer at medium speed until smooth. • With mixer on low, gradually beat in the dry ingredients. • Spoon the batter into the prepared pan and sprinkle with the remaining sugar. • Bake until well risen and springy to the touch, 15–20 minutes. • Let cool slightly before turning out onto a wire rack.
Makes: about 12 muffins • Prep: 15 min • Cooking: 15–20 min • Level: 1

BANANA CHOCOLATE CHIP MUFFINS

Preheat the oven to 350°F (180°C/gas 4). • Butter three 6-cup muffin pans. • Mix both flours, baking powder, baking soda, and salt in a large bowl. • Beat the butter and sugar in a large bowl with an electric mixer at medium speed until creamy. • Add the eggs one at a time, beating until just blended after each addition. • With mixer on low, beat in the bananas, followed by the dry ingredients, alternating with the milk. • Stir in the chocolate chips and walnuts by hand. • Spoon the batter into the prepared pans. • Bake until well risen and springy to the touch, 15–20 minutes. • Let cool slightly before turning out onto a wire rack.
Makes: about 12 muffins • Prep: 15 min • Cooking: 15–20 min • Level: 1

- 1 cup (150 g) whole-wheat (wholemeal) flour
- 1 cup (150 g) all-purpose (plain) flour
- 2 teaspoons baking powder
- ½ teaspoon baking soda (bicarbonate of soda)
- ¼ teaspoon salt
- ½ cup (125 g) butter
- 1 cup (200 g) sugar
- 3 large eggs
- 2 large bananas, mashed
- ¼ cup (60 ml) milk
- 1 cup (180 g) semisweet (dark) chocolate chips
- 1 cup (100 g) walnuts, chopped

PASSIONFRUIT MUFFINS

- 2 cups (300 g) all-purpose (plain) flour
- 2 teaspoons baking powder
- ½ teaspoon baking soda (bicarbonate of soda)
- ¼ teaspoon salt
- ½ cup (125 g) butter, softened
- ¾ cup (150 g) sugar
- 2 large eggs
- ½ cup (125 ml) heavy (double) cream
- ½ cup (60 g) finely chopped candied mango
- 4 tablespoons fresh passionfruit pulp

Yogurt Cream
- ½ cup (125 ml) heavy (double) cream
- ½ cup (125 ml) yogurt
- 2 teaspoons finely grated lemon zest
- 1 tablespoon fresh passionfruit pulp

Preheat the oven to 350°F (180°C/gas 4). • Butter a 12-cup muffin pan. • Mix the flour, baking powder, baking soda, and salt in a large bowl. • Beat the butter and sugar in a large bowl with an electric mixer at medium speed until creamy. • Add the eggs, one at a time, beating until just blended after each addition. • With mixer at low speed, gradually beat in the dry ingredients, alternating with the cream. • Stir in the mango and passionfruit pulp. • Spoon the batter into the prepared cups. • Bake until well risen and springy to the touch, about 20 minutes. • Let cool slightly before turning out onto a wire rack. Let cool completely. • Yogurt Cream: With mixer at high speed, beat the cream and yogurt in a medium bowl until stiff. Fold in the lemon zest and passion fruit pulp. • Cut a small "hat" from the top of each muffin. Fill with the cream and top with the "hat."
Makes: about 12 muffins • Prep: 30 min • Cooking: 20–25 min • Level: 2

MUFFINS WITH STRAWBERRY SAUCE

Preheat the oven to 350°F (180°C/gas 4). • Butter three 6-cup muffin pans. • Mix both flours, the baking powder, and salt in a medium bowl. • Beat the butter and sugar in a large bowl with an electric mixer at medium speed until creamy. • Add the eggs, one at a time, beating until just blended after each addition. • With mixer at low speed, gradually beat in the dry ingredients, alternating with the milk. • Spoon the batter into the prepared cups. • Bake until well risen and springy to the touch, 15–20 minutes. • Let cool slightly before turning out onto a wire rack. • Strawberry Sauce: Melt the butter in a medium saucepan over low heat. Add the strawberries and sugar and simmer until the strawberries have broken down, about 15 minutes. • Spoon over the muffins and serve warm.
Makes: about 12 muffins • Prep: 25 min • Cooking: 15–20 min • Level: 1

Muffins
- 1 cup (150 g) all-purpose (plain) flour
- 1 cup (150 g) whole-wheat (wholemeal) flour
- 2 teaspoons baking powder
- ¼ teaspoon salt
- ⅓ cup (90 g) butter
- ½ cup (100 g) sugar
- 1 cup (250 ml) milk
- 2 large eggs

Strawberry Sauce
- 3 tablespoons butter
- 1 lb (500 g) strawberries
- ⅓ cup (75 g) superfine (caster) sugar

FRITTERS

Deep-fried or pan-fried, fritters are always a special treat. Many fritter recipes originated in the farmhouse kitchens of various European countries over the centuries. Ingredients are wholesome and strongly linked to the seasons, with apple and pumpkin fritters prevalent in the late summer and fall. Every region of Italy, for example, has a host of fritter recipes to offer family and guests. Many of these recipes are tied to special occasions, such as Carnival time—the joyous period of feasting that precedes the forty days of Lent before Easter. Italian fritters often mimic classic savory dishes in shape or form, such as the ravioli-shaped Cardamom fritters, shown left, (see recipe on page 340) or Sweet ravioli (see page 342), a classic recipe from Liguria, in northwestern Italy. Delicious churros are a favorite fritter of Spanish origin that have become popular the world over (see our recipe on page 365), while donuts are the all-time classic fritter in North America.

Cardamom fritters (see page 340)

Fritters

RAISIN FRITTERS

- 1½ cups (225 g) all-purpose (plain) flour
- ½ teaspoon baking powder
- ⅛ teaspoon salt
- ¼ cup (60 ml) vegetable shortening
- ⅓ cup (70 g) sugar + extra to sprinkle
- ½ cup (90 g) dried currants
- 2 tablespoon water + more as needed
- vegetable oil, for frying

Mix the flour, baking powder, and salt in a large bowl. • Use a pastry blender to cut in the shortening until the mixture resembles fine crumbs. • Stir in the sugar and currants. • Mix in enough water to form a smooth dough. • Press the dough into a disk, wrap in plastic wrap (cling film), and refrigerate for 30 minutes. • Roll out the dough on a lightly floured surface to ½ inch (1 cm) thick. • Use a 2-inch (5-cm) cookie cutter to cut out the cookies. • Heat the oil in a large deep frying pan until very hot. • Fry the cookies in small batches for 5–7 minutes, or until golden brown. • Drain well on paper towels. • Sprinkle with the remaining sugar and serve hot.

Makes: about 15 fritters • Prep: 40 min + 30 min to chill
Cooking: about 20 min • Level : 1

CARDAMOM FRITTERS

Mix the flour and salt in a large bowl. • Beat the egg yolks and egg white, rose water, milk, and cardamom in a large bowl with an electric mixer at medium speed until well blended. • Mix in the dry ingredients to form a smooth dough. • Turn the dough out onto a lightly floured surface and knead until smooth. • Cover with a clean kitchen towel and let stand for 2 hours. • Form into balls the size of walnuts. • Roll the balls out to ⅛ inch (3 mm) thick and 3 inches (8 cm) in diameter. • Carefully fold the dough over, using a fork to press down the edges. • Cover with a kitchen towel and let stand for 5 minutes. • Heat the in a deep fryer or large deep frying pan to very hot. • Fry the cookies in batches until lightly browned all over, about 5–7 minutes per batch. • Drain well on paper towels. • Dust with the confectioners' sugar.

Makes: about 25–30 fritters • Prep: 30 min + 2 hr to stand
Cooking: 30 min • Level: 2

- 2⅔ cups (400 g) all-purpose (plain) flour
- ⅛ teaspoon salt
- 3 large egg yolks + 1 large egg white
- ¼ cup (60 ml) rose water
- ½ cup (125 ml) milk
- ½ teaspoon ground cardamom
- vegetable oil, for frying
- ⅓ cup (50 g) confectioners' (icing) sugar, to dust

BANANA FRITTERS

- 6 firm-ripe bananas, peeled
- 1 tablespoon sugar
- 1 tablespoon all-purpose (plain) flour
- 1 teaspoon ground ginger
- ½ teaspoon ground cinnamon
- vegetable oil, for frying

Mash the bananas in a medium bowl. • Stir in the sugar, flour, ginger, and cinnamon, mixing well. • Heat the oil in a deep fryer or frying pan until very hot. • Drop tablespoons of the batter into the oil and fry the fritters in batches for 5–7 minutes, or until crisp and golden brown all over. • Drain well on paper towels. • Serve hot.

Makes: about 16–20 fritters • Prep: 30 min • Cooking: 25 min • Level : 1

SWEET RICOTTA FRITTERS

Place the ricotta into a large bowl. Add the eggs, sugar, orange zest, salt, baking soda, and drained raisins. Lastly, stir in the sifted flour. Mix until smooth. Leave to rest for 1 hour. • Heat the oil to very hot in a large frying pan. Scoop out tablespoonfuls of the batter and fry in batches of 6–8 until golden brown. • Drain on paper towels. • Sprinkle with the confectioners' sugar and serve hot.

Makes: about 15 fritters • Prep: 15 min + 1 hr to rest
Cooking: 20 min • Level : 1

- 1⅔ cups (400 g) ricotta cheese, drained
- 3 eggs
- ⅓ cup (70 g) sugar
- finely grated zest of 1 orange
- ⅛ teaspoon salt
- ⅛ teaspoon baking soda (bicarbonate of soda)
- ¼ cup (40 g) raisins, soaked in rum overnight
- 1½ cups (225 g) all-purpose (plain) flour
- vegetable oil, for frying
- ¾ cup (120 g) confectioners' (icing) sugar

Fritters

SWEET RAVIOLI

- zest of 1 large orange
- scant cup (150 g) chopped candied fruit
- 1/2 cup (50 g) chopped candied peel
- scant 1/2 cup (100 g) butter
- 4 large egg yolks
- 3 cups (450 g) all-purpose (plain) flour
- 1/2 teaspoon salt
- 1 cup (250 g) butter, melted
- vegetable oil, for frying
- 1/4 cup (50 g) sugar, to sprinkle

Put the orange zest, candied pumpkin, candied peel, and butter in a food processor and blend until smooth. • Add 2 egg yolks, one at a time, mixing well after each addition. • Mix the flour and salt in a large bowl. • Add the remaining egg yolks and enough water to make a very stiff dough. Knead for 10–15 minutes, until smooth and elastic. • Roll out the dough on a lightly floured surface to 1/2 inch (1 cm) thick. • Drizzle half the melted butter over half the surface of the dough. Fold the dough over the butter and roll it out again to 1/2 inch (1 cm) thick. • Drizzle the remaining butter over half the surface of the dough. Fold the dough over the butter and roll it out again to 1/2 inch (1 cm) thick. • Fold the dough and re-roll it 4 or 5 times, until the butter is well incorporated and the dough is smooth and elastic. Roll out the dough on a lightly floured surface to a thickness of 1/4 inch (5 mm). • Place hazelnut-sized dots of the fruit mixture 1 inch (2.5 cm) apart over half the surface of the dough. Fold the remaining dough over this and press it down around the dots of fruit mixture to seal them in. • Use a small round pastry cutter to cut out the ravioli and arrange them on a lightly floured plate. • Heat the oil in a deep fryer until very hot. Fry the ravioli in small batches until golden brown all over, 5–7 minutes per batch. • Remove with a slotted spoon and drain on paper towels. • Transfer to a serving dish and dust with sugar. Serve hot.

Makes: about 20–25 fritters • Prep: 20 min + 1 hr to set Cooking: 30 min • Level: 3

SWEET POTATO FRITTERS

Cook the potatoes in a large pot of salted boiling water for 20 minutes, or until tender. Drain and peel the potatoes. • Mash with a potato ricer until smooth. • Add the butter, sugar, egg yolks, rum, cinnamon, and candied peel. • Mix well to make a soft dough. Make the mixture into hazelnut-sized balls. • Dip each ball in the egg white and then in the bread crumbs. • Arrange them on a plate sprinkled with some of the bread crumbs. • Heat the oil in a large frying pan or deep fryer to very hot. Fry the fritters in small batches for 2–3 minutes, or until golden brown and crispy. • Remove with a slotted spoon and drain on paper towels. • Transfer to a serving dish and dust with the confectioners' sugar. • Serve hot.

Makes: about 20–25 fritters • Prep: 20 min + 30 min to set Cooking: 10 min • Level: 2

- 1 lb (500 g) floury (baking) potatoes
- 3/4 cup (180 g) butter
- 1 cup (200 g) sugar
- 5 large egg yolks
- 1/4 cup (60 ml) rum
- pinch of ground cinnamon
- 1/3 cup (30 g) finely chopped candied peel
- 2 large egg whites, lightly beaten
- 3/4 cup (90 g) fine dry bread crumbs
- vegetable oil, for frying
- 4 tablespoons confectioners' (icing) sugar, to dust

FRIED EGG CREAM

Place the egg yolks and sugar in a heavy, medium saucepan and beat well until pale and frothy. • Stir in the flour a little at a time and mix well. Keep stirring as you add the tepid milk and the lemon zest. • Place the saucepan over very low heat and simmer, stirring slowly and continuously with a wooden spoon, until very thick. • Turn out onto a lightly oiled marble slab or into a shallow container and let cool. • Cut diagonally into diamond shapes. • Lightly whisk the egg whites. Dip the custard into the egg whites and coat with bread crumbs. • Heat the oil in a deep fryer until very hot. Fry in small batches until golden brown all over, 5–7 minutes per batch. • Remove with a slotted spoon and drain on paper towels.

Makes: about 30 fritters • Prep: 30 min • Cooking: 25–30 min • Level: 1

- 5 eggs, separated
- 3/4 cup (150 g) sugar
- 1 1/3 cups (200 g) all-purpose (plain) flour
- 1 quart (1 liter) milk, warmed
- finely grated zest of 1 lemon
- 1 3/4 cups (100 g) fresh bread crumbs
- vegetable oil, for frying

Fritters

RICE AND APPLE FRITTERS

- 1 cup (200 g) short-grain rice
- ²⁄₃ cup (150 ml) milk
- ½ cup (100 g) sugar
- 1 lb (500 g) apples, peeled, cored, and coarsely grated
- 2 large eggs, lightly beaten
- 2 tablespoons rum
- 1 tablespoon golden raisins (sultanas), soaked in warm water for 15 minutes and drained
- ½ teaspoon vanilla extract (essence)
- finely grated zest of 1 lemon
- ⅓ cup (50 g) all-purpose (plain) flour
- vegetable oil, for frying
- ⅓ cup (50 g) confectioners' (icing) sugar, to dust

Cook the rice in the milk in a large saucepan over low heat for 20–25 minutes, or until very tender. If the rice begins to stick to the pan, add a little boiling water. • Remove the saucepan from the heat. Stir in the sugar, apples, eggs, rum, raisins, vanilla, and lemon zest. Add the flour and mix well. • Heat the oil in a large frying pan or deep fryer until very hot. Fry spoonfuls of the mixture in small batches for 3–4 minutes until browned all over. • Remove the fritters with a slotted spoon and drain on paper towels. • Dust with confectioners' sugar and serve hot.

Makes: about 22–25 fritters • Prep: 20 min • Cooking: 15–20 min • Level: 1

SLICED APPLE FRITTERS

Beat the egg yolks in a large bowl with an electric mixer at high speed until pale. • With mixer at medium speed, beat in the flour, wine, extra-virgin oil, and salt. • Cover with a clean cloth and let stand for 1 hour. • Core the apples and slice crosswise. Drizzle with the lemon juice to prevent them from turning brown. • With mixer at high speed, beat the egg whites in a large bowl until stiff peaks form. Use a large rubber spatula to fold them into the batter. • Dip the apple slices in the batter, turning to coat well. • Heat the oil in a deep fryer or frying pan until very hot. • Fry the apple slices in batches for 5–7 minutes, or until lightly browned all over. • Drain well on paper towels. • Dust with the confectioners' sugar and serve hot.

Makes: about 16–20 fritters • Prep: 25 min + 1 hr to rest batter • Cooking: 25–30 min • Level: 2

- 2 large eggs, separated
- ¾ cup (125 g) all-purpose (plain) flour
- ½ cup (125 ml) dry white wine
- 2 tablespoons extra-virgin olive oil
- ⅛ teaspoon salt
- 6 tart apples, peeled and cored
- freshly squeezed juice of 1 lemon
- vegetable oil, for frying
- ⅓ cup (50 g) confectioners' (icing) sugar, to dust

Rice and apple fritters

Golden raisin fritters

GOLDEN RAISIN FRITTERS

- 1 oz (30 g) fresh yeast or 2 (¼-oz/7-g) packets active dry yeast
- 2 cups (500 ml) warm water
- 3⅓ cups (500 g) all-purpose (plain) flour
- 1 cup (250 ml) milk
- finely grated zest of 1 lemon
- ¼ teaspoon salt
- 2 large eggs
- ¾ cup (150 g) sugar
- generous ½ cup (100 g) golden raisins (sultanas)
- vegetable oil, for frying
- 2 tablespoons confectioners' (icing sugar, to dust

Mix the yeast and a little of the water in a cup. • Add enough flour to make a firm dough. • Cover and let rise for 2 hours. • Mix the remaining water, milk, lemon zest, salt, remaining flour, and the risen dough in a large bowl until smooth. Add the eggs and mix well. • Cover and let rise for about 2 hours. Add the sugar and the raisins and mix well. • Heat the oil in a deep fryer or large frying pan until very hot. Fry spoonfuls of the mixture in small batches until golden brown all over, about 5 minutes each batch. • Remove with a slotted spoon and drain on paper towels. • Dust with the confectioners' sugar and serve hot.

Makes: 30–35 fritters • Prep: 20 min + 4 hr to rise
Cooking: 20–25 min • Level: 2

ORANGE RICE FRITTERS

Mix the milk and water in a large saucepan. Add the rice and salt. • Bring to a boil over medium heat then simmer over low heat until all the liquid has been absorbed, about 40 minutes. • Remove from heat and stir in the egg yolks, ½ cup (100 g) of sugar, the flour, orange, vanilla, and orange liqueur until well blended. • Let stand for 30 minutes. • Heat the oil in a deep fryer or frying pan until very hot. • Drop scant tablespoons of the batter into the oil and fry in batches for 5–7 minutes, or until crisp and golden brown all over. • Drain well on paper towels. • Dust with the remaining sugar and serve.

Makes: about 20 fritters • Prep: 20 min + 30 min to stand
Cooking: 25 min • Level: 1

- 2 cups (500 ml) milk
- 1¼ cups (300 ml) water
- 1 cup (200 g) short-grain rice
- ⅛ teaspoon salt
- 3 egg yolks
- ¾ cup (150 g) sugar
- ¾ cup (125 g) all-purpose (plain) flour
- 6 oz (180 g) oranges, cut into small pieces
- 1 teaspoon vanilla extract (essence)
- 1 tablespoon orange liqueur
- vegetable oil, for frying

Fritters

FRITTERS WITH CITRUS SYRUP

Fritters

- ¹/₄ cup (60 ml) milk
- ¹/₄ cup (60 g) butter, cut up
- 2 tablespoons sugar
- 1 oz (30 g) fresh compressed yeast or 2 (¹/₄-oz/7-g) packages active dry yeast
- ¹/₈ teaspoon salt
- 1 cup (150 g) all-purpose (plain) flour
- 1 large egg
- vegetable oil, for frying

Citrus Syrup

- ¹/₂ cup (100 g) sugar
- 1 cup (250 ml) water
- zest of 1 lemon and 1 orange, in 1 long piece
- 1 vanilla pod
- 1 clove

Fritters: Heat the milk, butter, and sugar in a small saucepan. Let cool then stir in the yeast. • Place the flour and salt in a small bowl. Add the egg and the yeast mixture, stirring until smooth. If the dough is too dry, add a little tepid water. • Knead on a floured work surface until smooth and elastic, about 20 minutes. • Divide the dough into pieces the size of walnuts. Place on a large plate or baking sheet in a warm place and let rise for 30 minutes.
• Citrus Syrup: Place the sugar, water, lemon and orange zest, vanilla pod, and clove in a medium saucepan over low heat. Simmer until the sugar is completely dissolved. • Heat the oil in a deep-fryer and fry the fritters in batches until golden brown all over. Drain on paper towels. • Dip the fritters in the hot syrup and serve.

Makes: about 30 fritters • Prep: 35 min • Cooking:30 min Level: 1

APPLE FRITTERS

Sift the flour, baking powder, and salt into a large bowl. Beat in the sugar, lemon zest, orange juice, rum, and eggs. Add the milk gradually and stir until smooth. • Stir in the raisins and apples. • Heat the oil in a deep fryer or frying pan until very hot. • Drop scant tablespoons of the batter into the oil and fry in batches for 5–7 minutes, or until crisp and golden brown all over. • Drain well on paper towels. • Dust with the confectioners' sugar and serve hot.

Makes: about 20 fritters • Prep: 20 min • Cooking: 25–35 min • Level: 1

- 2²/₃ cups (400 g) all-purpose (plain) flour
- 1 teaspoon baking powder
- ¹/₈ teaspoon salt
- ²/₃ cup (140 g) superfine (caster) sugar
- finely grated zest of 1 lemon
- freshly squeezed juice of ¹/₂ orange
- 2 teaspoons dark rum
- 2 eggs
- ²/₃ cup (150 ml) milk
- ¹/₂ cup (90 g) golden raisins (sultanas
- 1¹/₂ lb (750 g) apples, peeled, cored, and cut into small sticks
- vegetable oil, for frying
- ¹/₃ cup (50 g) confectioners' (icing) sugar

Fritters with citrus syrup

Amaretti rice fritters

AMARETTI RICE FRITTERS

- 2 cups (500 ml) milk
- ½ teaspoon vanilla extract (essence)
- ¼ teaspoon salt
- 2 tablespoons all-purpose (plain) flour
- 1 cup (200 g) sticky rice
- 2 tablespoons butter
- ⅓ cup (70 g) sugar + extra, to sprinkle
- 2 small eggs
- ½ cup (60 g) crushed amaretti cookies
- ½ cup (60 g) fine dry bread crumbs
- vegetable oil, for frying

Place the milk in a large saucepan with the vanilla and salt. Stir in the flour and rice.
• Bring to a boil over medium heat. Simmer, stirring often, until the mixture is thick and creamy and the rice is very tender, 30–35 minutes. Add a little water to the pan if the mixture becomes too thick. Remove from the heat. • Stir in the butter, half the sugar, 1 egg, and the amaretti cookies. • Turn the mixture out onto a greased surface sprinkled with bread crumbs. Spread to ½ inch (1 cm) thick. Let cool. • Cut the mixture into disks using a 3-inch (8-cm) cookie cutter. • Beat the remaining egg in a small bowl. • Put the remaining bread crumbs on a plate. Dip the disks in the beaten egg and then in the bread crumbs, coating well. • Fry in small batches until golden brown all over. Remove with a slotted spoon and drain on paper towels.
• Sprinkle with the sugar and serve hot.

Makes: about 30 brownies • Prep: 30 min • Cooking: 35–40 min • Level: 1

LEMON AND EGG FRITTERS

Place the water, salt, butter, sugar, and lemon zest in a saucepan and bring to a boil. • Add the flour and stir with a wooden spoon. Continue cooking, stirring continuously, until the dough is thick and comes away from the sides of the saucepan. Remove from the heat and set aside to cool. • When cool, stir in the eggs one at a time. The dough should be soft, but not runny. • Set aside to rest for at least 1 hour. • Heat the oil in a deep-sided frying pan until very hot, but not smoking. • Use a teaspoon to scoop up the dough and drop it into the hot oil. Fry the fritters, a few at a time, until they are plump and golden brown. • Remove the fritters from the oil with a slotted spoon and drain on paper towels. Keep warm. Repeat until all the dough has been used up. • Sprinkle with confectioners' sugar and serve hot.

Makes: about 20 fritters • Prep: 25 min + 1 hr to rest • Cooking: 25–30 • Level: 2

- 1 cup (250 ml) water
- ⅛ teaspoon salt
- ½ cup (125 g) butter
- ¼ cup (50 g) superfine (caster) sugar
- finely grated zest of 1 lemon
- 1⅔ cups (250 g) all-purpose (plain) flour
- 8 eggs
- vegetable oil, for frying
- confectioners' (icing) sugar, to dust

Fritters

CARNIVAL FRITTERS

- 1²/₃ cups (250 g) all-purpose (plain) flour + ¹/₃ cup (50 g) extra
- 2 tablespoons butter, softened
- 2 large eggs
- ¹/₄ cup (50 g) superfine (caster) sugar
- 1¹/₂ tablespoons Vin Santo or other good quality sweet dessert wine
- ¹/₄ teaspoon salt
- 1¹/₂ tablespoons finely grated orange zest
- vegetable oil, for frying
- ¹/₃ cup (50 g) confectioners' (icing) sugar, sifted

Mix the flour onto a work surface and make a well in the center. Add the butter, eggs, sugar, dessert wine, salt, and orange zest. Gradually combine with the flour and knead well. The dough should be soft but hold its shape well. • Cover with a clean cloth and leave to rest for 30 minutes. • Roll out into a thin sheet using a lightly floured rolling pin. • Cut into diamonds, rectangles, and into broad rectangular strips that can be tied loosely into a knot if wished. • Heat the oil to very hot and fry a few at a time until pale golden brown all over. • Remove with a slotted spoon and drain on paper towels. • Serve at once, sprinkled with the confectioners' sugar.

Makes: about 20–25 fritters • Prep: 20 min + 20 min to stand
Cooking: 20–25 min • Level: 2

GOOD FRIDAY FRITTERS

Bring the milk, 3 tablespoons of sugar, and anise to a boil in a medium saucepan. • Sift the flour into a large bowl. • Stir in the lemon zest, cinnamon, and vanilla and make a well in the center. • Pour in the boiling milk mixture and stir until smooth. • Add the eggs, one at a time, until just blended after each addition. • Add the apples. • Heat the oil in a large frying pan to very hot. • Scoop out tablespoonfuls of the batter and fry in batches for 5–7 minutes, or until golden brown all over. • Drain well on paper towels. • Dust with the remaining sugar.

Makes: about 20 fritters • Prep: 20 min • Cooking: 15–20 min • Level: 1

- 1³/₄ cups (430 ml) milk
- ¹/₂ cup (100 g) sugar
- 1 teaspoon anise
- 1¹/₂ cups (225 g) all-purpose (plain) flour
- grated zest of 1 lemon
- ¹/₂ teaspoon ground cinnamon
- ¹/₂ teaspoon vanilla extract (essence)
- 4 large eggs
- 4 apples, peeled, cored, and finely chopped
- vegetable oil, for frying

CANNOLI

Cannoli
- 1¹/₃ cups (200 g) all-purpose (plain) flour
- 1 tablespoon unsweetened cocoa powder
- 2 tablespoons sugar
- generous 1 tablespoon lard, softened
- 2 large eggs, lightly beaten
- 2 tablespoons marsala
- vegetable oil, for frying

These fritters are filled with fresh ricotta cheese sweetened with candied fruits and chocolate. They are a traditional dessert in Sicily. You will need cannoli molds to prepare them.
Cannoli: Mix the flour and cocoa in a medium bowl. • Stir in the sugar, lard, eggs, and marsala to make a smooth dough. • Roll the dough out on a lightly floured surface to ¹/₈ inch (3 mm) thick and cut into twelve 4-inch (10-cm) disks. • Heat the oil in a deep-fryer over medium heat. • Wrap a pastry disk around each cannoli molds, pressing the overlapping edges together to seal. • Fry the cannoli, still on the mold, in small batches, for about 5 minutes, or until bubbly and golden brown. • Remove with a slotted spoon and drain on paper towels. Let cool slightly before carefully removing the mold. • Filling: Beat the ricotta with the sugar and vanilla with a wooden spoon in a large bowl. Add the chocolate and candied fruit. • Just before serving, fill the pastry tubes with the filling and arrange on a serving dish. • Dust with the confectioners' sugar and serve.

Makes: 12 cannoli • Prep: 30 min • Cooking: 30–35 min Level: 3

Filling
- 2 cups (500 g) ricotta cheese
- 1¹/₂ cups (300 g) sugar
- 1 teaspoon vanilla extract (essence)
- 4 oz (125 g) semisweet (dark) chocolate, chopped
- ¹/₂ cup (100 g) chopped candied fruit or peel

Fritters

ST. JOSEPH'S DAY FRITTERS

- 1 cup (250 ml) water
- 1/2 cup (125 g) butter, cut up
- 1/4 cup (50 g) sugar
- 1/4 teaspoon salt
- finely grated zest of 1 lemon
- 2 cups (300 g) all-purpose (plain) flour
- 8 large eggs
- vegetable oil, for frying
- 1 cup (150 g) confectioners' (icing) sugar, to dust

Bring the water, butter, sugar, salt, and lemon zest to a boil in a medium saucepan. • Add the flour all at once and stir with a wooden spoon. Continue cooking, stirring constantly, until the dough is thick and starts to come away from the sides of the saucepan. Remove from the heat and set aside to cool. • When cool, add the eggs, one at a time, beating until just blended. The dough should be soft, but not runny. • Set aside to rest for 1 hour. • Heat the oil in a deep-fryer or large frying pan. • Fry teaspoons of the dough in small batches for 5–7 minutes, or until golden brown. • Drain well on paper towels. • Dust with the confectioners' sugar just before serving.

Makes: about 50 fritters • Prep: 25 min + 1 hr to rest
Cooking: 30–35 min • Level: 1

BRANDY FRITTERS

Mix the flour, sugar, and salt in a large bowl. • Turn out onto a pastry board and shape into a mound. Make a well in the center and add the butter, eggs, and brandy. Combine all the ingredients, gradually working in the flour to form a smooth, well-blended dough. • Cover with a clean cloth and leave to rest in a warm place for 2 hours. • Roll out the dough to make a very thin sheet about 1/8 inch (3 mm) thick. • Use a fluted pastry wheel to cut the pastry into strips 1 1/4 inch (3 cm) wide and 8 inch (20 cm) long. • Tie each strip loosely into a knot and deep fry a few at a time in very hot oil until pale golden brown. • Drain on paper towels. • Dust with the confectioners' sugar before serving.

Makes: about 40 fritters • Prep: 20 min + 2 hr to rest
Cooking: 30 min • Level: 2

- 3 1/3 cups (500 g) all-purpose (plain) flour
- 2 tablespoons superfine (caster) sugar
- 1/8 teaspoon salt
- 2 tablespoons butter, cut into small pieces
- 4 large eggs
- 3 tablespoons Cognac (or other grape brandy)
- vegetable oil, for frying
- confectioners' (icing) sugar, to dust

NEAPOLITAN CHRISTMAS FRITTERS

- 3 1/2 cups (375 g) all-purpose (plain) flour
- 1/4 teaspoon salt
- 4 large eggs, lightly beaten
- 1/2 cup (125 ml) anisette
- 2 tablespoons superfine (caster) sugar
- vegetable oil, for frying
- 3/4 cup (200 ml) honey
- 1 cup finely chopped candied orange
- 1 cup finely chopped candied lemon peel
- 1/2 cup (100 g) sugar confetti

Mix the flour and salt in a large bowl. • Mix in the eggs, anisette, and superfine sugar until well blended. Set aside to rest for 2 hours. • Form tablespoonfuls of the dough into sticks about the thickness of a pencil. Cut into 1/2-inch (1-cm) pieces. • Heat the oil in a large deep fryer or frying pan until very hot. • Fry the cookies in batches for 5–7 minutes, or until just golden all over. • Drain well on paper towels. • Heat the honey in a large saucepan over low heat until liquid. Add the cookies and candied peel and stir until well coated. • Transfer to a serving plate and decorate with the sugar confetti.

Makes: about 90 fritters • Prep: 30 min + 2 hr to rest
Cooking: 30 min • Level: 3

KENTISH FRITTERS

Mix the flour, baking powder, and salt in a large bowl. • Use a pastry blender to cut in the shortening until the mixture resembles fine crumbs. • Stir in the 1/4 cup (50 g) of sugar and the currants. • Add 2 tablespoons water to form a smooth dough, adding more water as needed. • Press the dough into a disk, wrap in plastic wrap, and refrigerate for 30 minutes. • Roll out the dough on a lightly floured surface to 1/2 inch (5 mm) thick. • Use a 2-inch (5-cm) cookie cutter to cut out the cookies. • Heat the oil in a large deep skillet until very hot. • Fry the cookies in small batches for 5–7 minutes, or until golden brown. • Drain well on paper towels. • Sprinkle with the remaining 2 tablespoons sugar and serve hot.

Makes: about 12–15 fritters • Prep: 40 min + 30 min to chill
Cooking: 30 min • Level: 3

- 1 1/2 cups (225 g) all-purpose (plain) flour
- 1/2 teaspoon baking powder
- 1/8 teaspoon salt
- 1/4 cup (60 ml) vegetable shortening
- 1/3 cup (70 g) sugar
- 1/2 cup dried currants
- 2 tablespoons water, + more as needed
- vegetable oil, for frying

PINEAPPLE FRITTERS

- 1 large ripe pineapple, peeled, sliced, and cored
- freshly squeezed juice of 2 lemons
- 1²/₃ cups (250 g) all-purpose (plain) flour
- pinch of salt
- 2 large eggs, separated
- 2 tablespoons butter, melted
- ¼ cup (50 g) sugar
- ¾ cup (200 ml) milk
- vegetable oil, for frying
- 4 tablespoons confectioners' (icing) sugar

Place the pineapple in a bowl and drizzle with the lemon juice. Cover and set aside while you prepare the batter. • Mix the flour and salt in a large bowl. Make well in the centre and add the egg yolks, butter, and sugar. Mix well. • Gradually stir in the milk. Cover and let rest for 2 hours. • Beat the egg whites until stiff and fold them into the batter. • Heat the oil in a deep fryer or small, deep frying pan to very hot. • Drain the pineapple slices well then dip them in the batter. • Fry in small batches until golden brown all over, 5–10 minutes per batch. • Remove with a slotted spoon and drain on paper towels. • Dust with confectioners' sugar and serve hot.

Makes: about 16 fritters • Prep: 30 min + 2 hr to rest batter
Cooking: 30–35 min • Level: 1

BATTERED FRESH FRUIT

Beat the eggs in a large bowl with an electric mixer at high speed until pale. • With mixer at medium speed, beat in 2 tablespoons of flour and the milk. • Cover with a clean cloth and let stand in a warm place for 1 hour. • Peel the pineapple and cut the flesh into ½-inch (1-cm) thick slices. Cut each slice in 4. • Peel the bananas and cut in 4. • Stir the baking powder and vanilla into the batter. • Dip the pineapple, bananas, and apples in the batter, turning to coat well. • Heat the oil in a deep fryer or frying pan until very hot. • Fry the fruit in batches for 5–7 minutes, or until crisp golden brown all over. • Drain well on paper towels. • Dust with the confectioners' sugar and serve hot.

Makes: about 16–20 fritters • Prep: 30 min + 1 hr to rest batter • Cooking: 30 min • Level: 1

- 3 large eggs
- 4 tablespoons all-purpose (plain) flour
- 1 quart (1 liter) milk
- 1 small pineapple
- 2 firm-ripe bananas
- 2 tart apples, cut into wedges
- ½ teaspoon baking powder
- 1 teaspoon vanilla extract (essence)
- vegetable oil, for frying
- ⅓ cup (50 g) confectioners' (icing) sugar, to dust

FRIED COOKIE ROSETTES

- 3 cups (450 g) all-purpose (plain) flour
- ½ teaspoon salt
- 1 tablespoon vegetable shortening
- 3 large eggs, lightly beaten
- ¼ cup (60 ml) Champagne
- ¼ cup (50 g) sugar
- vegetable oil, for frying
- sugar strands, jimmies, sprills, or sprinkles, to decorate

Mix the flour and salt in a large bowl. • Use a pastry blender to cut in the shortening until the mixture resembles fine crumbs. • Make a well in the center and mix in the eggs, Champagne, and sugar to form a stiff dough. • Press the dough into a disk, wrap in plastic wrap, and refrigerate for 30 minutes. • Heat the oil in a deep fryer or large frying pan until very hot. • Roll out the dough on a lightly floured surface to ¼ inch (3 mm) thick. • Use a fluted pastry cutter to cut the dough into 15 x ½-inch (40 x 1-cm) strips. • Fold the strips in half lengthways and roll up, pinching the bottom together to open the top into a ruffled flower shape. • Fry the cookies in small batches, turning them with a slotted spoon, for 3–5 minutes, or until golden and crisp. • Drain well on paper towels. • Sprinkle with the sugar strands.

Makes: about 30 fritters • Prep: 30 min + 30 min to chill Cooking: 30 min • Level: 3

Fritters

PEAR FRITTERS

- 1 lb (500 g) firm ripe pears, peeled, cored, and cut in cubes
- ⅓ cup (75 g) sugar
- 3 tablespoons water
- 12 oz (300 g) frozen puff pastry, thawed
- 1 large egg, lightly beaten
- vegetable oil, for frying
- ½ cup (125 g) apple preserves (jam)
- 1 tablespoon white rum
- 2 tablespoons confectioners' (icing) sugar, to dust

Place the pears, sugar, and water in a medium saucepan over low heat. Simmer for 25 minutes, stirring often. • Roll out the pastry on a floured surface to ¼-inch (3-mm) thick. • Use a 3-inch (8-cm) cookie cutter to cut out disks. • Brush the edges of half the pastry disks with the beaten egg. Place a little of the pear mixture into the center of each of these disks. Cover with the plain disk, pressing down on the edges to seal. • Heat the oil in a deep fryer and fry the fritters in batches until golden brown. • Remove with a slotted spoon and drain on paper towels. • Heat the apple preserves in a small saucepan. Remove from the heat and stir in the rum. • Dust the fritters with confectioners' sugar and serve hot with the apple sauce.

Makes: about 20 fritters • Prep: 30 min

Cooking: 30 min • Level: 2

FILLED JELLY FRITTERS

Mix the flour, baking powder, and salt in a large bowl. • Use a pastry blender to cut in the butter until the mixture resembles coarse crumbs. • Stir in the sugar. Add the eggs and rum to form a smooth dough. • Press the dough into a disk, wrap in plastic wrap (cling film), and refrigerate for 30 minutes. • Roll out the dough on a floured surface to ¼ inch (3-mm) thick. • Use a 2-inch (5-cm) cookie cutter to cut out fritters. • Place a little jelly on one half of each cookie, then fold the other half over. Seal the edges. • Heat the oil in a deep fryer or large frying pan. • Fry the cookies in small batches for 5–7 minutes, or until golden brown. • Drain well on paper towels. • Dust with confectioners' sugar.

Makes 30 cookies • Prep: 40 min + 30 min to chill

Cooking: 30 min • Level: 3

- 3⅓ cups (500 g) all-purpose (plain) flour
- 1 tablespoon baking powder
- ⅛ teaspoon salt
- ¼ cup (60 g) butter, cut up
- 1 cup (200 g) sugar
- 3 large eggs, lightly beaten
- 3 tablespoons dark rum
- ½ cup (150 g) black cherry or sweet cherry jelly
- vegetable oil, for frying
- ⅓ cup (50 g) confectioners' (icing) sugar, to dust

Pear fritters

Fig fritters

CRISP PETAL FRITTERS

- 2 cups (300 g) all-purpose (plain) flour
- ¼ teaspoon salt
- 2 large eggs
- 2 tablespoons sugar
- ⅓ cup (90 ml) light (single) cream
- ⅓ cup (90 ml) dry white wine
- vegetable oil, for frying
- ⅓ cup (50 g) confectioners' (icing) sugar, to dust

Sift the flour and salt into a medium bowl. • Use a wooden spoon to mix the eggs and sugar in a large bowl. • Stir in the cream and white wine until well blended. • Mix in the dry ingredients to form a smooth dough. • Press the dough into a disk, wrap in plastic wrap (cling film), and refrigerate for 30 minutes. • Roll out the dough on a lightly floured surface until paper-thin. • Use a 3-inch (8-cm) fluted round cookie cutter to cut out fritters. Gather the dough scraps, re-roll, and continue cutting out cookies until all the dough is used. • Pinch the center of the cookies to crinkle them slightly. • Heat the oil in a large frying pan or deep fryer until very hot. • Fry the cookies in small batches for about 3 minutes, or until crisp and golden brown. • Drain well on paper towels. • Dust with the confectioners' sugar just before serving.

Makes: 25–30 fritters • Prep: 40 min + 30 min to chill
Cooking: 25 min • Level: 3

FIG FRITTERS

Mix the flour, baking powder, and half the salt in a medium bowl. • Add the egg yolks, butter, and 1 tablespoon of confectioners' sugar. Stir with a wooden spoon, gradually incorporating the milk and mixed dry ingredients, until smooth. Let rest for 1 hour. • Peel the figs and cut in quarters. • Beat the egg whites and remaining salt with an electric mixer on high speed until stiff peaks form. Fold into the batter. • Heat the oil in a deep-fryer. Dip the figs in the batter and fry in batches in the hot oil until golden brown all over. • Remove with a slotted spoon and drain on paper towels. • Dust with the remaining confectioners' sugar and serve hot.

Makes: about 30 fritters • Prep: 30 min + 1 hr to rest the batter • Cooking: 30 min • Level: 2

- 1⅓ cups (200 g) all-purpose (plain) flour
- 1 teaspoon baking powder
- ¼ teaspoon salt
- 2 large eggs, separated
- ¼ cup (60 g) melted butter
- 5 tablespoons confectioners' (icing) sugar
- ¾ cup (200 ml) milk
- 12 oz (350 g) firm ripe figs
- vegetable oil, for frying

Pumpkin fritters

PUMPKIN FRITTERS

- 2 lb (1 kg pumpkin
- 1 cup (180 g) seedless white raisins (sultanas, soaked
- ¼ cup (50 g) sugar
- ⅔ cup (100 g) all-purpose (plain) flour
- 1 tablespoon baking powder
- finely grated zest of 1 lemon
- ⅛ teaspoon salt
- vegetable oil, for frying
- sugar, to sprinkle

Peel the pumpkin and remove the seeds and fibrous matter. Slice the flesh and place in a saucepan with sufficient cold water to cover. • Cook until the flesh is just tender (not too long, about 20 minutes). Drain well and press in a cloth to absorb any excess moisture. • Place in a bowl, add the drained raisins, the sugar, the flour and baking powder sifted together, the lemon zest, and salt. Mix thoroughly with a spoon and then shape into little balls about the size of a walnut. • Fry in batches in plenty of very hot oil, removing with a slotted spoon when golden brown all over. Drain on paper towels. • Sprinkle with sugar and serve hot.

Makes: about 30 fritters • Prep: 30 min • Cooking: 35 min Level: 2

ORANGE FLOWER FRITTERS

Sift the flour onto a clean work surface and make a well in the center. • Add the eggs, orange flower water, baking powder, lemon zest, sugar, and salt. Mix to make a smooth dough. • Roll out the dough on a lightly floured work surface to ¼ (5 mm) thick. • Cut the dough into strips 1½ x 6 inches (4 x 15 cm) using a pastry wheel. • Heat the oil in a large frying pan or deep fryer to very hot. • Fry the strips for 3–4 minutes until golden brown. • Remove with a slotted spoon and transfer to a layer of paper towels. • Arrange on a serving dish and dust with the confectioners' sugar. • Serve hot.

Makes: about 30 fritters • Prep: 25 min • Cooking: 30 min Level: 2

- 2⅔ cups (400 g) all-purpose (plain) flour
- 2 large eggs, lightly beaten
- 1 tablespoon orange flower water
- 1½ teaspoons baking powder
- finely grated zest of 1 lemon
- ¾ cup (150 g) sugar
- ⅛ teaspoon salt
- vegetable oil, for frying
- ⅓ cup (50 g) confectioners' (icing) sugar, to dust

HONEY AND ANISE FRITTERS

- 3⅓ cups (500 g) all-purpose (plain flour
- ½ teaspoon salt
- generous ⅓ cup (100 g) butter, cut into pieces
- 3 large eggs, lightly beaten
- ¼ cup (60 ml) anisette (aniseed liqueur)
- vegetable oil, for frying
- ¾ cup (200 ml) clear honey
- ¾ cup (150 g) sugar
- 1 tablespoon cocoa
- finely grated zest of 1 orange

Mix the flour and salt in a large bowl. • Rub in the butter using your fingertips until the mixture resembles bread crumbs. • Make a well in the center and pour in the eggs. • Mix with your fingertips beginning from the center. • Add the anisette and mix to make a smooth dough. Make the dough into balls about the size of hazelnuts and arrange on a floured plate. • Heat the oil in a deep fryer until very hot. Fry the dough balls in small batches for until golden brown, about 5 minutes each batch. • Remove with a slotted spoon and drain on a layer of paper towels. • Continue until all the dough is cooked. • Cook the honey and sugar in a large

saucepan over medium heat. Add the cocoa and the orange and lemon zests. Lower the heat and simmer for 15–20 minutes, or until a slightly cooled drop of the syrup will make a thread between your fingers. • Add the dough balls and mix gently to coat all the balls with the syrup. • Lightly oil a serving dish and transfer the mixture onto the serving dish. Use your hands to mold it into a dome shape. • Decorate with the candied peel and serve warm.

Makes: about 35 fritters • Prep: 30 min • Cooking: 40–45 min • Level: 3

- finely grated zest of 1 lemon
- 2 tablespoons chopped candied peel

Fritters

FRUIT AND NUT FRITTERS

- 1²/₃ cups (250 g) all-purpose (plain) flour
- ³/₄ cup (180 ml) milk
- ¹/₃ cup (70 g) sugar
- 3 tablespoons butter, melted
- 3 egg yolks
- 1 teaspoon baking powder
- 1 tablespoon Marsala wine
- 1 teaspoon ground cinnamon
- ¹/₈ teaspoon salt
- 10 oz (300 g) dried fruit and nuts, such as prunes, pineapple, papaya, pear, apricots, peanuts, hazelnuts, pecans, walnuts, or figs
- vegetable oil, for frying
- ¹/₃ cup (50 g) confectioners' (icing) sugar, to dust

Beat the flour, milk, sugar, butter, egg yolks, baking powder, Marsala, cinnamon, and salt in a large bowl with an electric mixer at medium speed until smooth. • Cover with a clean cloth and let stand in a warm place for 1 hour. • Chop the dried fruit and nuts in a food processor or until very finely chopped. • Shape the fruit and nut mixture into balls the size of walnuts. • Dip the balls into the batter, turning to coat well. • Heat the oil in a deep fryer or frying pan until very hot. • Fry the gnocchi in batches for 5–7 minutes, or until crisp and golden brown all over. • Drain well on paper towels. • Dust with the confectioners' sugar and serve hot.

Makes: about 20 fritters • Prep: 15 min + 1 hr to rest batter

Cooking: 30 min • Level: 2

FRIED AMARETTI COOKIES

Mix the flour and salt in a large bowl. • Stir together the milk, egg yolks, butter, and sugar. • Mix into the dry ingredients, beating gently to ensure no lumps form. • Set aside in a warm place for 2 hours. • Stick the cookies together in pairs with the preserves. • Brush the cookies with the rum. • Beat the egg whites in a large bowl with an electric mixer at high speed until stiff peaks form. • Use a large rubber spatula to fold the beaten whites into the rested batter. • Heat the oil in a a deep fryer or frying pan until very hot. • Dip the cookies in the batter and fry in small batches for 5–7 minutes, or until golden brown all over. • Drain well on paper towels. • Dust with the confectioners' sugar just before serving.

Makes: about 24 cookies • Prep: 25 min + 2 hr to rest

Cooking: 30 min • Level: 3

- 1¹/₃ cups (200 g) all-purpose (plain) flour
- ¹/₄ teaspoon salt
- ³/₄ cup (200 ml) milk
- 2 large eggs, separated
- 2 tablespoons butter, melted
- 2 tablespoons sugar
- 48 small Italian amaretti cookies (store-bought)
- 2 tablespoons raspberry preserves (jam)
- ¹/₄ cup (60 ml) light rum
- vegetable oil, for frying
- ¹/₃ cup (50 g) confectioners' (icing) sugar

FRIED BOW TIES

- 1¹/₂ cups (225 g) all-purpose (plain) flour
- ¹/₄ teaspoon baking powder
- ¹/₄ teaspoon salt
- 5 large egg yolks
- 2 tablespoons sugar
- 2 tablespoons sour cream
- 1¹/₂ teaspoons dark rum
- ¹/₂ teaspoon vanilla extract (essence)
- vegetable oil, for frying•

Sift the flour, baking powder, and salt into a medium bowl. • Beat the egg yolks and granulated sugar in a large bowl with an electric mixer at high speed until pale and thick. • Beat in the sour cream, rum, and vanilla. • Mix in the dry ingredients to form a stiff dough. • Turn the dough out onto a lightly floured surface and knead until smooth. • Press the dough into a disk, wrap in plastic wrap (cling film), and refrigerate for 30 minutes. • Roll out the dough to ¹/₈ inch (3 mm). Cut into 4 x 1¹/₂-inch (10 x 4-cm) strips. • Gather the dough scraps, reroll, and continue cutting out strips until all the dough is used. • Make a slit at one end of the strip and thread the other end of the strip through it to make a bow. • Heat the oil in a deep fryer or frying pan until very hot. • Fry the cookies in small batches for 5–7 minutes, or until just golden all over. • Drain well on paper towels. • Dust with the confectioners' sugar just before serving.

Makes: about 30 fritters • Prep: 40 min + 30 min to chill

Cooking: 30 min • Level: 3

¹/₂ cup (75 g) confectioners' (icing) sugar, to dust

Sweet almond ravioli

SWEET ALMOND RAVIOLI

Filling
- 1 lb (500 g) almonds
- 3/4 cup (150 g) sugar
- 1 large egg
- 2 tablespoons orange flower water
- vegetable oil, for frying
- 6 tablespoons confectioners' (icing) sugar, to dust

Pastry
- 2 cups (300 g) all-purpose (plain) flour
- 2 cups (300 g) fine ground semolina
- 1/4 teaspoon salt
- 1 cup (250 ml) warm water
- 3 oz (90 g) lard, softened

Filling: Chop the almonds in a food processor until smooth, gradually adding the sugar as you work. Add the egg and orange flower water. • Pastry: Mix both flours and salt in a large bowl. Stir in enough of the water to obtain a firm dough. • Knead the dough on a floured surface, gradually working in the lard as you knead. • Roll out the dough on a lightly floured surface to 1/4 inch (3-mm) thick. • Use a 3-inch (8-cm) cookie cutter to cut out disks. • Place some almond filling at the center of each disk. Fold the pastry over the filling in half-moon shapes and seal the edges with a fork. • Heat the oil in a deep fryer or frying pan until very hot. Fry the fritters until golden brown on both sides. • Dust with the confectioners' sugar and serve hot.

Makes: about 35 fritters • Prep: 45 min • Cooking: 30 min Level: 3

DANISH AEBLESKIVER FRITTERS

Sift the flour, baking powder, baking soda, and salt into a large bowl. • Beat in the sugar, butter, and buttermilk until smooth. • Beat the egg white in a large bowl with an electric mixer at high speed until stiff peaks form. • Use a large rubber spatula to fold the beaten white into the batter. • Heat a 7-hole aebleskiver pan over medium heat and spoon 1 tablespoon of the oil into each hole. • Spoon 2 tablespoons of the batter into each hole and fry for about 3 minutes, or until the oil begins to bubble at the edges. • Use a long-handled fork to turn the cookies and fry for about 3 minutes, or until golden brown. • Use the fork to remove the cookies from the pan. Drain well on paper towels. • Repeat with the remaining oil and batter until all the batter has been used.

Makes: about 14 cookies • Prep: 25 min • Cooking: 30 min • Level: 3

- 1 cup (150 g) all-purpose (plain) flour
- 1 teaspoon baking powder
- 1/4 teaspoon baking soda (bicarbonate of soda)
- 1/4 teaspoon salt
- 1 tablespoon sugar
- 2 tablespoons butter, melted
- 1 cup (250 ml) buttermilk
- 1 large egg white
- vegetable oil, for frying

ORANGE FRITTERS

- 1 oz (30 g) fresh compressed yeast or 2 ($\frac{1}{4}$-oz/7-g) packages active dry yeast
- 1 cup (250 ml) milk, lukewarm
- 3$\frac{1}{3}$ cups (500 g) all-purpose (plain) flour
- Pinch of salt
- $\frac{3}{4}$ cup (150 g) sugar
- 2 tablespoons Cointreau
- $\frac{1}{4}$ cup (60 g) butter, melted
- 2 large eggs
- finely grated zest of 2 oranges
- vegetable oil, for frying

Place the yeast a small bowl and dissolve with 4 tablespoons of the milk. Set aside for 15 minutes. • Sift the flour and salt into a large bowl. Stir in half the sugar, the Cointreau, and butter. Add the eggs one at a time and mix well. • Add the yeast mixture, orange zest, and remaining milk. Mix well. Cover and let rise in a warm place for 1 hour. • Heat the oil in a deep fryer or small, deep frying pan to very hot. • Drop spoonfuls of the batter into the oil and cook until golden brown all over, 3–5 minutes.Remove with a slotted spoon and drain on paper towels. • Sprinkle with the remaining sugar and serve hot.

Makes: about 35 fritters • Prep: 20 min • Cooking: 30–35 min • Level: 2

POLISH FRITTERS

Mix the flour and salt in a large bowl. • Make a well in the center and mix in the egg yolks and whole egg, sugar, rum, and vanilla to form a stiff dough. • Press the dough into a disk, wrap in plastic wrap (cling film), and refrigerate for 30 minutes. • Heat the oil in a large deep skillet until very hot. • Roll out the dough on a lightly floured surface until paper thin. • Use a fluted pastry cutter to cut the dough into 2-inch (5-cm) diamonds. Gather the dough scraps, re-roll, and continue cutting out cookies. Make a slit in the center of each cookie and pull one point of the diamond through the slit. • Fry the cookies in small batches, turning halfway through with a slotted spoon, for 2–3 minutes, or until crisp. • Drain well on paper towels. • Dust with the confectioners' sugar.

Makes: 20–25 fritters • Prep: 40 min + 30 min to chill Cooking: 20 min • Level: 3

- 1$\frac{1}{3}$ cups (200 g) all-purpose (plain) flour
- $\frac{1}{8}$ teaspoon salt
- 6 large egg yolks + 1 small egg, lightly beaten
- 1 tablespoon sugar
- 2 teaspoons dark rum
- $\frac{1}{4}$ teaspoon vanilla extract (essence)
- vegetable oil, for frying
- $\frac{1}{3}$ cup (50 g) confectioners' (icing) sugar, to dust

Orange fritters

LEMON RICE FRITTERS

- 1 cup (200 g) short-grain, pudding rice (or sticky rice)
- 2 cups (500 ml) whole (full) cream milk
- 1 tablespoon butter
- 3 tablespoons sugar
- finely grated zest of 1/2 lemon
- 2 large eggs
- 1/4 teaspoon salt
- 1/3 cup (50 g) all-purpose (plain) flour
- 1/3 cup (50 g) golden raisins (sultanas), soaked in warm water for 15 minutes, drained and squeezed
- 3 tablespoons rum
- vegetable oil, for frying
- 2/3 cup (100 g) confectioners' (icing) sugar

Simmer the rice in the milk for 1 hour, or until the grains have almost disintegrated. • Stir the butter into this very thick mixture and remove from the heat. • Add the sugar and lemon zest. • Stir in the eggs one at a time, then add the salt, flour, raisins, and rum. Stir thoroughly and chill for about 1 hour in the refrigerator. • Heat the oil in a large frying pan or deep fryer until very hot. To test, drop a tiny piece of fritter into the oil. If bubbles form around it immediately, it is hot enough. • Drop tablespoons of the fritter mixture into the hot oil. Fry 5–6 fritters together until they are golden brown all over. This should take about 4 minutes for each fritter. • Drain on paper towels. Dust with the confectioners' sugar and serve hot.

Makes: about 30 fritters • Prep: 25 min • Cooking: 40–45 min • Level: 1

NORWEGIAN CHRISTMAS FRITTERS

Mix the flour, cardamom, and salt in a medium bowl. • Beat the egg yolks and sugar in a large bowl with an electric mixer at high speed until pale and thick. • Beat in the cream, butter, and brandy until well blended. • Mix in the dry ingredients and lemon zest to form a stiff dough. Divide the dough into four. Press each into a disk, wrap in plastic wrap (cling film), and refrigerate for 30 minutes. • Heat the oil in a large deep skillet until very hot. • Take one-quarter of the dough. Keep the remainder chilled. Roll out on a lightly floured surface to 1/8 inch (3 mm). Cut the dough into 3-inch (8-cm) diamonds. • Cut a 1-inch (2.5-cm) slit in the center of each fritter. Gently pull one corner through the slit to form a "knot." • Fry the cookies in small batches for 2–3 minutes, turning halfway through with a slotted spoon, until golden brown. • Drain well on paper towels. Repeat with the remaining dough. • Dust with the confectioners' sugar just before serving.

Makes: about 24 fritters • Prep: 20 min • Cooking: 20–30 min • Level: 3

- 1 cup (150 g) all-purpose (plain) flour
- 1/2 teaspoon ground cardamom
- 1/8 teaspoon salt
- 3 large egg yolks
- 4 tablespoons sugar
- 2 tablespoons light (single) cream
- 2 teaspoons butter, melted
- 2 teaspoons brandy
- 2 teaspoons finely grated lemon zest
- vegetable oil, for frying
- 1/3 cup (50 g) confectioners' (icing) sugar, to dust

NORWEGIAN CARDAMOM FRITTERS

- 1 large egg + 3 large egg yolks
- 1 tablespoon sugar
- 1/4 cup (60 ml) heavy (double) cream
- 1 tablespoon butter, melted
- 1/4 teaspoon ground cardamom
- 1 1/2 cups (225 g) all-purpose (plain) flour
- 1/8 teaspoon salt
- vegetable oil, for frying

Beat the egg and egg yolks and sugar in a large bowl with an electric mixer at high speed until pale and thick. • Beat in the cream, butter, and cardamom. • Mix in the flour and salt to form a stiff dough. • Press the dough into a disk, wrap in plastic wrap, and refrigerate for 30 minutes. • Roll out the dough on a lightly floured surface to 1/8 inch (3 mm) thick. • Cut into 2-inch diamonds. • Gather the dough scraps, reroll, and continue cutting out diamonds until all the dough is used. • Heat the oil in a large frying pan or deep fryer until very hot. • Fry the cookies in small batches for 5–7 minutes, or until golden brown all over. • Drain well on paper towels.

Makes: about 40 fritters • Prep: 40 min + 30 min to chill Cooking: 30 min • Level: 1

Fritters

CINNAMON FRITTERS

- 2 cups (300 g) all-purpose (plain) flour
- 1/3 cup (70 g) sugar
- 2 teaspoons ground cinnamon
- 1 teaspoon baking powder
- 1/4 teaspoon salt
- finely grated zest of 1 lemon
- 3 large eggs, lightly beaten
- 1/4 cup (60 g) butter, melted
- vegetable oil, for frying
- confectioners' (icing) sugar, to dust

Mix the flour, sugar, cinnamon, baking powder, salt, and lemon zest in a large bowl. • Add the eggs and beat until smooth. Stir in the butter. • Knead the dough on a lightly floured work surface for 2–3 minutes. • Roll out the dough to about ½ inch (1 cm) thick. Cut into small shapes—diamonds, triangles, squares, etc. • Heat the oil in a large frying pan or deep fryer to very hot. • Fry the dough in small batches until golden brown on both sides. • Drain on paper towels. • Dust with confectioners' sugar and serve hot.

Makes: about 25–30 fritters • Prep: 20 min • Cooking: 20 min • Level: 1

BROWN SUGAR FRITTERS

Mix the flour, baking powder, allspice, and salt in a large bowl. • Use a pastry blender to cut in the butter until the mixture resembles coarse crumbs. • Mix in the brown sugar, currants, and mixed peel. • Add the egg and enough milk to form a smooth dough. • Press the dough into a disk, wrap in plastic wrap (cling film), and refrigerate for 30 minutes. • Roll out the dough on a lightly floured surface to ¼ inch (5 mm) thick. • Use a 2-inch cookie cutter to cut out the cookies. • Gather the dough scraps, re-roll, and continue cutting out cookies until all the dough is used. • Preheat a griddle or cast-iron skillet and grease lightly with butter. • Fry the cookies for 4 minutes. • Use a spatula to turn the cookies over and cook for 3–4 minutes on the other side, or until golden brown on both sides. • Sprinkle with sugar and serve hot.

Makes: 18–20 fritters • Prep: 20 min + 30 min to chill Cooking: 10 min • Level: 2

- 1²/₃ cups (250 g) all-purpose (plain) flour
- 1 teaspoon baking powder
- 1/4 teaspoon ground allspice
- 1/8 teaspoon salt
- 1/2 cup (125 g) butter, cut up
- 1/3 cup (70 g) firmly packed light brown sugar
- 1/2 cup (60 g) dried currants
- 1½ tablespoons finely chopped mixed peel
- 1 large egg, lightly beaten
- 1–3 tablespoons milk
- 1–2 tablespoons superfine (caster) sugar, to sprinkle

Cinnamon fritters

Potato fritters

POTATO FRITTERS

CHURROS

- 1½ lb (750 g) floury (baking) potatoes
- ½ cup (125 g) butter
- 1 cup (200 g) sugar
- 5 large egg yolks
- ¼ cup (60 ml) rum
- 1 cup (150 g) all-purpose (plain) flour
- 1 teaspoon vanilla extract (essence)
- ⅓ cup (30 g) finely chopped candied peel
- 2 large egg whites, lightly beaten
- ¾ cup (90 g) fine dry bread crumbs
- vegetable oil, for frying
- 2 tablespoons confectioners' (icing) sugar, to dust

Cook the potatoes in a large pot of salted boiling water for 20 minutes until tender. Drain and peel the potatoes. • Mash them with a potato ricer until smooth. • Add the butter, sugar, egg yolks, rum, flour, vanilla, and candied peel. • Mix well to make a soft dough. Make the mixture into hazelnut-sized balls. • Dip each ball in the egg white and then in the bread crumbs. • Arrange them on a plate sprinkled with some of the bread crumbs. • Heat the oil in a large frying pan over medium heat. Fry the mixture in small batches for 2–3 minutes, or until they are golden brown and crispy. • Remove with a slotted spoon and drain them on a layer of paper towels. • Transfer to a serving dish and dust with the confectioners' sugar. • Serve hot.

Makes: about 20 fritters • Prep: 45 min • Cooking: 30 min Level: 2

Heat the sugar, water, and butter in a large saucepan over medium heat and bring to a boil. Stir in the flour and salt using a wooden spoon and simmer until the dough comes away from the sides of the pan, about 2 minutes. Remove from the heat and beat in the eggs, stirring continuously until incorporated. • Heat the oil in a deep fryer over medium-high heat until it is hot enough to fry a small piece of bread golden when tested. • Place the dough in a pastry bag fitted with a ½-inch (1-cm) star tip nozzle. Pipe 4-inch (10-cm) lengths into the hot oil and fry until golden. Remove from the oil using tongs or a slotted spoon and drain on kitchen towel. Continue this process until all the dough is finished. • Sprinkle generously with extra sugar and dust with the cinnamon.

Makes: about 30 fritters • Prep: 20 min • Cooking: 30 min Level: 2

- 3 tablespoons sugar extra, to sprinkle
- 2 cups (500 ml) water
- 3 tablespoons butter
- 2½ cups (375 g) all-purpose (plain) flour
- ¼ teaspoon salt
- 2 large eggs, lightly beaten
- vegetable oil, for frying
- 1 teaspoon cinnamon, to dust

PARTY COOKIES

P arties and holidays should be celebrated in style—and what better way than with a platter of freshly baked cookies! Children love cookies and in this chapter we have included a good selection of recipes that are suitable for birthday parties and various celebrations for the younger set. Try the Gingerbread people, shown left (see recipe on page 384), the Trick or treaters (see page 370), or the Chocolate mice (see page 386), among others. But there are plenty of recipes for the rest of the family too, and for a host of different occasions, from Christmas to Mother's Day, and from Halloween to Valentine's Day.

Gingerbread people (see page 384)

Halloween spookies

HALLOWEEN SPOOKIES

Cookies
- 1¾ cups (215 g) graham cracker crumbs (crushed digestive biscuits)
- ¾ cup (150 g) sugar
- 2 tablespoons unsweetened cocoa powder
- ½ cup (75 g) finely ground almonds
- ⅓ cup (90 g) butter, melted
- 2 tablespoons milk + more as needed

Colored Butter Icing
- ½ cup (125 g) butter, softened
- 1⅔ cups (250 g) confectioners'(icing) sugar
- ½ teaspoon vanilla extract (essence)
- few drops blue, yellow, or red food coloring
- small candies, licorice whips, and candied cherries, to decorate

Cookies: Mix the graham cracker crumbs, sugar, cocoa, and almonds in a large bowl. • Stir in the melted butter and enough milk to form a stiff dough. • Divide the mixture into about 20 pieces and form into balls the size of walnuts. • Flatten into 1-inch (2.5-cm) thick rounds. • Colored Butter Icing: Beat the butter, confectioners' sugar, and vanilla in a large bowl with an electric mixer at high speed until creamy. • Divide into three small bowls. Add the food coloring to each bowl. Mix pale colors for smiley faces and deep blue and red icing for a spooky design. • Spread the icing over the tops of the cookies. • Decorate with candies or candied cherries to resemble eyes and noses. • Cut up the licorice whips into short lengths to resemble smiley mouths, hair, and other decorative details.

Makes: about 20 cookies • Prep: 30 min • Level : 1

PIZZELLE COOKIES

- 1⅓ cups (200 g) all-purpose (plain) flour
- 1 teaspoon baking powder
- ⅛ teaspoon salt
- 2 large eggs
- 1¾ cups (150 g) sugar
- 1 teaspoon vanilla extract (essence)
- ⅓ cup (90 g) butter, melted

Preheat a pizzelle iron. • Mix the flour, baking powder, and salt in a medium bowl. • Beat the eggs and ¾ cup (150 g) sugar in a large bowl with an electric mixer at high speed until pale and thick. • Add the vanilla and butter. • Mix in the dry ingredients. • Drop tablespoons of the batter onto the center of the iron. Lower the top so that the batter spreads. • Cook for 1 minute, or until browned at the edges. Remove the cookie from the iron. • Repeat, stacking the cookies between sheets of waxed paper. • Let cool completely. • If you are using an electric pizzelle iron, follow the manufacturer's directions for preheating and baking.

Makes: about 22 cookies • Prep: 20 min • Cooking: 20 min Level: 3

HALLOWEEN COOKIES

Cookies: Mix the flour, confectioners' sugar, baking powder, ginger, and salt in a large bowl. • Use a pastry blender to cut in the butter until the mixture resembles coarse crumbs. • Stir in the pecans, almonds, egg yolk, and corn syrup to form a smooth dough. • Press the dough into a disk, wrap in plastic wrap, and refrigerate for 30 minutes. • Preheat the oven to 350°F (180°C/gas 4). • Line three cookie sheets with parchment paper. • Roll out the dough on a lightly floured surface to ¼ inch (5 mm) thick. • Use ghost-shaped, bat-shaped, and round cookie cutters to cut out the cookies. Gather the dough scraps, re-roll, and continue cutting out cookies until all the dough is used. • Use a spatula to transfer the cookies to the prepared cookie sheets, placing them 1 inch (2.5 cm) apart. • Bake for 10–12 minutes, or until just golden at the edges. • Cool on the sheets until the cookies firm slightly. • Transfer to racks and let cool completely. • Glaze: Mix 1⅓ cups (200 g) of confectioners' sugar with the lemon juice. • Divide the glaze in three and tint with the food colorings. • Keep white for ghosts, use black for bats, and mix red and yellow food coloring to make orange "pumpkin-cookies." • Spread the glaze over the cookies. • Mix the remaining confectioners' sugar with the water and cocoa to make a spreading consistency. • Spoon the frosting into a small freezer bag and cut off a tiny corner. • Pipe over the cookies in a decorative manner .

Makes: about 20 cookies • Prep: 1 hr + 30 min to chill Cooking: 10–12 min • Level: 2

Cookies
- 1⅓ cups (200 g) all-purpose (plain) flour
- ⅓ cup (50 g) confectioners' (icing) sugar
- ¼ teaspoon teaspoon baking powder
- ¼ teaspoon teaspoon ground ginger
- ⅛ teaspoon salt
- ½ cup (125 g) butter
- 1 cup (120 g) finely ground pecans
- 1 tablespoon finely ground almonds
- 1 large egg yolk, lightly beaten
- 2 tablespoons light corn (golden) syrup
- 2 tablespoons milk + more as needed

Glaze
- 1⅔ cups (250 g) confectioners' (icing) sugar
- 1–2 tablespoons freshly squeezed lemon juice
- 1–2 drops red and yellow food coloring
- few drops black food coloring gel
- 1 teaspoon warm water
- ½ teaspoon unsweetened cocoa powder

Party Cookies

TRICK OR TREATERS

- 1½ cups (225 g) all-purpose (plain) flour
- ¼ teaspoon baking soda (bicarbonate of soda)
- ¼ teaspoon salt
- ½ cup (125 g) butter, softened
- ½ cup (100 g) firmly packed light brown sugar
- 1 large egg
- 2 oz (60 g) semisweet (dark) chocolate, coarsely chopped
- 7 oz (200 g) store-bought ready-to-roll white fondant
- 2 drops orange food coloring (or red and yellow)

Mix the flour, baking soda, and salt in a medium bowl. • Beat the butter and brown sugar in a large bowl until creamy. • Add the egg, beating until just blended. • Melt the chocolate in a double boiler over barely simmering water. • Stir the melted chocolate into the butter mixture. • Mix in the dry ingredients to form a stiff dough. • Press the dough into a disk, wrap in plastic wrap, and refrigerate for 30 minutes. • Preheat the oven to 350°F (180°C/gas 4). • Butter two cookie sheets. • Roll out the dough on a lightly floured surface to ¼ inch (5 mm) thick. • Use a 3-inch (8-cm) cookie cutter to cut out the cookies. Continue cutting out cookies until all the dough is used. • Transfer the cookies to the prepared cookie sheets, placing them 1 inch (2.5 cm) apart. • Bake for 10–15 minutes, or until just golden. • Transfer to racks and let cool completely. • Knead the white fondant frosting until malleable. • Divide the fondant into two portions. • Place one portion in a bowl and mix in the orange food coloring until no white streaks remain. • Roll out the plain fondant on a surface lightly dusted with confectioners' sugar to ⅛ inch (3 mm) thick. • Use the cookie cutter to cut out enough fondant rounds to cover half the cookies. Cut each round in half and brush with water. • Place wet-side down on half of each cookie. • Repeat with the orange fondant and place on the other half of each cookie. • Use an edible black candy writer to draw spooky designs.

Makes: about 15 cookies • Prep: 25 min + 30 min to chill Cooking: 10–15 min • Level: 2

HALLOWEEN CHOCOLATE CHIP COOKIES

Preheat the oven to 375°F (190°C/gas 5). • Set out two cookie sheets. • Mix the flour, baking powder, baking soda, cinnamon, and salt in a large bowl. • Use a pastry blender to cut in the butter until the mixture resembles fine crumbs. • Stir in the sugar, pumpkin, and orange zest. • Stir in the chocolate chips. • Drop teaspoons of the dough 2 inches (5 cm) apart onto the cookie sheets. • Bake for 8–10 minutes, or until golden. • Transfer to racks to cool.

Makes: about 20 cookies • Prep: 20 min • Cooking: 8–10 min • Level: 1

- 1 cup (150 g) all-purpose (plain) flour
- ½ teaspoon baking powder
- ½ teaspoon baking soda (bicarbonate of soda)
- ½ teaspoon cinnamon
- ⅛ teaspoon salt
- ¼ cup (60 g) butter
- ½ cup (100 g) sugar
- ½ cup (125 ml) canned pumpkin purée
- ½ tablespoon finely grated orange zest
- ½ cup (90 g) semisweet (dark) chocolate chips

BELGIAN KRUMKAKE COOKIES

Beat the butter and brown sugar in a large bowl with an electric mixer at medium speed until creamy. • Add the eggs, vanilla, and salt, beating until just blended. • Gradually mix in the flour to form a smooth dough. • Refrigerate for 12 hours. • Lightly butter a krumkake iron and place over medium heat. The iron is ready to use when a drop of water holds its shape on the surface of the iron. • Stir the batter well and drop a tablespoon (or enough batter to fit your iron) of the batter onto the center of the hot iron. Lower the top so that the batter spreads. • Cook for 1 minute, or until browned at the edges. • Lift up the top and, working quickly, remove the cookie from the iron with a krumkake roller. The cookie should be cone-shaped. • Repeat with the remaining cookie dough. • Let cool completely. • If you are using an electric krumkake iron, follow the manufacturer's directions for preheating and baking.

Makes: 12 cookies • Prep: 20 min + 12 hr to chill • Cooking: 15 min • Level: 3

- ½ cup (125 g) butter, softened
- 1 cup (200 g) firmly packed light brown sugar
- 3 large eggs
- ¼ teaspoon vanilla extract (essence)
- ¼ teaspoon salt
- 4 cups (600 g) all-purpose (plain) flour

Party Cookies

ANGELICA CHRISTMAS COOKIES

- 2 cups (300 g) all-purpose (plain) flour
- ¼ teaspoon salt
- 2 oz (60 g) semisweet (dark) chocolate, coarsely chopped
- ½ cup (125 g) butter, softened
- 1 cup (200 g) sugar
- 1 teaspoon vanilla extract (essence)
- 2 tablespoons milk
- 1 large egg, lightly beaten
- 2 tablespoons chopped angelica

Preheat the oven to 350°F (180°C/gas 4). • Butter four cookie sheets. • Mix the flour and salt in a medium bowl. • Melt the chocolate in a double boiler over barely simmering water. • Beat the butter and sugar in a large bowl with an electric mixer at high speed until creamy. • Add the vanilla, milk, and egg, beating until just blended. • Mix in the dry ingredients and chocolate. • Insert a Christmas tree design plate into the press by sliding it into the head and locking in place. Press out the cookies, spacing about 1½ inches (4 cm) apart on the prepared cookie sheets. • Place a piece of angelica across each cookie. • Bake for 8–10 minutes, or until just colored and crisp. • Transfer to racks to cool.

Makes: about 48 cookies • Prep: 30 min • Cooking: 8–10 min • Level: 2

VANILLA CHRISTMAS COOKIES

Mix the flour, baking powder, and salt in a medium bowl. • Beat the butter and sugar in a large bowl with an electric mixer at medium speed until creamy. • Add the egg and vanilla, beating until just blended. • Mix in the dry ingredients. • Divide the dough in half. Form into two 6-inch (15-cm) logs, wrap each in plastic wrap (cling film), and refrigerate for 30 minutes. • Preheat the oven to 375°F (190°C/gas 5). • Butter three cookie sheets. • Slice the dough ¼ inch (5 mm) thick and place 1 inch (2.5 cm) apart on the cookie sheets. Reserve three slices. • Work the red food coloring into the reserved dough until there are no white streaks. • Roll out the red dough on a lightly floured surface and cut off small hat shapes. Gather the dough scraps and force through a garlic press to form hair. • Arrange the hats and hair on top of the cookies. • Bake for 6–8 minutes, or until just golden at the edges. • Transfer to racks to cool. • Mix the confectioners' sugar and water in a small bowl to form a stiff paste. • Stick the candy on top of the cookies with the icing to form eyes, mouths, and noses.

Makes: about 45 cookies • Prep: 40 min • Cooking: 6–8 min Level: 2

- 2½ cups (375 g) all-purpose (plain) flour
- ½ teaspoon baking powder
- ⅛ teaspoon salt
- ¾ cup (200 g) butter, softened
- 1 cup (200 g) sugar
- 1 large egg, lightly beaten
- ½ teaspoon vanilla extract (essence)
- few drops red food coloring
- 2 tablespoons confectioners' (icing) sugar
- 2 teaspoons water, + more as needed
- colored candies, to decorate

DUTCH CHRISTMAS COOKIES

- 3 cups all-purpose (plain) flour
- 1¼ cups (250 g) sugar
- 1 cup (100 g) finely ground almonds
- ½ cup (50 g) coarsely chopped almonds
- 1 teaspoon ground cinnamon
- ½ teaspoon ground nutmeg
- ¼ teaspoon ground cardamom
- ⅛ teaspoon salt

Mix the flour, sugar, finely ground and chopped almonds, cinnamon, nutmeg, cardamom, and salt in a large bowl. • Cut in the butter until the mixture resembles coarse crumbs. • Beat the egg, milk, and almond extract in a small bowl until frothy. • Mix the beaten egg mixture into the dry ingredients to form a smooth dough. • Refrigerate for 30 minutes. • Preheat the oven to 350°F (180°C/gas 4). • Butter two cookie sheets and sprinkle with flaked almonds. • Form the dough into balls the size of walnuts. Roll out on a lightly floured

surface to ⅛ inch (3 mm) thick. • Dust a spekulatius mold with flour and press a dough disk into it. Cut off any surplus and tap the cookie out onto the prepared cookie sheet. • If you do not have a mold, roll the dough out to ¼ inch (5 mm) thick. Use a cookie cutter to cut out cookies and use a toothpick to draw lines across the dough. • Bake for 8–10 minutes, or until just golden at the edges. • Transfer to racks to cool.

Makes: 50 cookies • Prep: 50 min + 30 min to chill Cooking: 8–10 min • Level: 3

- ⅓ cup (90 g) butter, cut up
- 1 large egg, lightly beaten
- ¼ cup (60 ml) milk
- ½ teaspoon almond extract (essence)
- flaked almonds, to sprinkle

Party Cookies

JAM STARS

- 3 cups (450 g) all-purpose (plain) flour
- ⅛ teaspoon salt
- 1 cup (200 g) granulated sugar
- ¼ cup (50 g) vanilla sugar (see page 414)
- ½ cup (125 g) butter, cut up
- 1 large egg + 3 large egg yolks
- 1 teaspoon vanilla extract (essence)
- 3 tablespoons damson plum or raspberry preserves
- ½ cup (75 g) confectioners' (icing) sugar

Mix the flour and salt into a large bowl. Stir in both sugars. • Cut in the butter until the mixture resembles coarse crumbs. • Mix in the egg and egg yolks and vanilla. • Divide the dough in half. Wrap in plastic wrap (cling film) and refrigerate for 30 minutes. • Preheat the oven to 350°F (180°C/gas 4). • Roll out the dough to ⅛ inch (3 mm) thick. • Use differently sized (1–2-inch (2.5–5-cm) star cutters to cut out the cookies. • Transfer the cookies to cookie sheets, placing them 1 inch (2.5 cm) apart. • Refrigerate for 10 minutes. • Bake for 8–12 minutes, or until just golden. • Transfer to racks and let cool completely. • Stick the differently sized cookies together with the preserves—the largest at the bottom, the smallest on top. • Dust with the confectioners' sugar.

Makes: about 30 cookies • Prep: 50 min + 30 min to chill
Cooking: 8–10 min • Level: 2

CHRISTMAS BAUBLES

Preheat the oven to 300°F (150°C/gas 3). • Line three cookie sheets with parchment paper. • Beat the egg whites in a large bowl until frothy. • Gradually add the confectioners' sugar until stiff, glossy peaks form. Set aside two heaped tablespoons of the meringue in a small bowl. • Fold the almonds, flour, cinnamon, almond extract, and salt into the remaining mixture. • Form into small balls and place 1 inch (2.5 cm) apart on the cookie sheet. • Top with the reserved meringue. • Bake for 30–40 minutes, or until just golden. • Cool on the sheets until the cookies firm slightly. Transfer to racks and let cool completely. • Frosting: Mix the confectioners' sugar and water in two separate bowls. Add drops of each food coloring to each bowl. Drizzle over the cookies.

Makes: 35–45 cookies • Prep: 50 min • Cooking: 30–40 min
Level: 2

- 3 large egg whites
- 1⅔ cups (250 g) confectioners' (icing) sugar
- 1½ cups (225 g) finely ground almonds
- 2 tablespoons all-purpose (plain) flour
- 2 teaspoons ground cinnamon
- ¼ teaspoon almond extract (essence)
- ⅛ teaspoon salt

Frosting
- 1 cup (150 g) confectioners' (icing) sugar
- 1–2 tablespoons hot water
- 2–3 drops red and green food coloring

Christmas baubles

Christmas twists

CHRISTMAS TWISTS

- 1½ cups (225 g) all-purpose (plain) flour
- ¼ teaspoon salt
- ⅔ cup (100 g) confectioners' (icing) sugar
- ⅔ cup (150 g) butter, softened
- 1 large egg
- 1 teaspoon peppermint extract (essence)
- ½ teaspoon vanilla extract (essence)
- ¼ cup (50 g) crushed red-and-white candy canes
- few drops red food coloring

Preheat the oven to 350°F (180°C/gas 4).
• Set out two cookie sheets. • Mix the flour and salt in a large bowl. • Beat the confectioners' sugar and butter in a large bowl with an electric mixer on medium speed until creamy. • Add the egg and peppermint and vanilla extracts. • Mix in the dry ingredients.
• Divide the dough between two bowls. • Mix the candy into one and the food coloring into the other. • Form tablespoons of the candy dough into 4-inch (10-cm) ropes. Repeat with the colored dough. • Twist one candy dough rope and one colored dough rope together to form a striped rope. • Shape one end of the rope into a curve to resemble a candy cane and place 2 inches (5 cm) apart on the cookie sheets. • Bake for 10–12 minutes, or until firm to the touch. • Transfer to racks to cool.

Makes: 20–25 cookies • Prep: 30 min • Cooking: 10–12 min
Level: 1

CHURCH WINDOW COOKIES

Mix the confectioners' sugar, flour, salt, butter, cream, and vanilla in a large bowl to form a smooth dough. • Press into a disk, cover with plastic wrap (cling film) and refrigerate for 30 minutes. • Preheat the oven to 400°F (200°C/gas 6). • Line two cookie sheets with parchment paper. • Roll out the dough on a lightly floured surface to ⅛ inch (3 mm) thick. • Use Christmas-shaped cookie cutters, such as holly, stars, and snowmen, to cut out the cookies. Transfer the cookies to the prepared cookie sheets, placing them 1 inch (2.5 cm) apart.
• Use a sharp knife to cut a small hole in each cookie. Place a candy piece in each hole. • Bake for 5–7 minutes, or until the cookies are lightly browned and the candies have melted. • Let cool completely.

Makes: about 25 cookies • Prep: 40 min + 30 min to chill
Cooking: 5–7 min • Level: 2

- 1¼ cups (180 g) all-purpose (plain flour
- ⅓ cup (50 g) confectioners' (icing) sugar
- ⅛ teaspoon salt
- ½ cup (125 g) butter, softened
- 1 tablespoon heavy (double) cream
- ½ teaspoon vanilla extract (essence)
- 25 lightly crushed hard candies, mixed colors

Party Cookies

CHRISTMAS STARS

- 1¼ cups (175 g) all-purpose (plain) flour
- ⅛ teaspoon salt
- ½ cup (125 g) butter, softened
- ⅓ cup (70 g) confectioners' (icing) sugar
- 1 tablespoon milk
- ½ teaspoon vanilla extract (essence)
- 5 oz (150 g) assorted clear, hard, colored candies, such as lollipops

Mix the flour, salt, butter, confectioners' sugar, milk, and vanilla in a large bowl. • Place on a lightly floured surface and knead until smooth. • Return to the bowl, cover with plastic wrap (cling film), and refrigerate for 30 minutes. • Preheat the oven to 400°F (200°C/gas 6). • Line two cookie sheets with parchment paper. • Roll out the dough on a lightly floured surface to ⅛ inch (3 mm) thick. • Use a 2-inch (5-cm) star-shaped cookie cutter to cut out the cookies. Use a 1-inch (1-5-cm) star-shaped cutter to cut out the centers. • Transfer the cookies to the prepared sheets, placing ½ inch (1 cm) apart. • Bake for 8–10 minutes, or until just golden. • Lightly crush the candy and arrange the candy into the cookie centers. • Bake for 3–5 minutes, or until the candy has melted. • Cool on the sheets for 10 minutes. • Transfer to racks and let cool completely.

Makes: 16–20 cookies • Prep: 50 min + 30 min to chill
Cooking: 11–15 min • Level: 3

CHRISTMAS RINGS

Preheat the oven to 400°F (200°C/gas 6). • Butter two cookie sheets. • Mix the flour and salt in a medium bowl. • Beat the butter and ¼ cup (50 g) sugar in a large bowl with an electric mixer at high speed until creamy. • Add the egg yolk, beating until just blended. • Mix in the dry ingredients and orange zest. • Form tablespoons of the dough into 6-inch (15-cm) ropes. • Shape into circles with slightly overlapping ends and place 1 inch (2.5 cm) apart on the sheets. • Brush with the egg white and sprinkle with the remaining sugar. • Decorate with the cherries. • Bake for 10–12 minutes, or until lightly browned. • Cool on the sheets until the cookies firm slightly. Transfer to racks.

Makes: about 24 cookies • Prep: 30 min • Cooking: 10–12 min • Level: 1

- 1⅓ cups (200 g) all-purpose (plain) flour
- ⅛ teaspoon salt
- ½ cup (125 g) butter, softened
- ½ cup (100 g) sugar
- 1 large egg, separated
- 1 teaspoon finely grated orange zest
- 3 green candied cherries and 3 red candied cherries, finely chopped, to decorate

Christmas rings

Christmas cookies

CHRISTMAS COOKIES

- 1¼ cup (60 g) butter
- 1 tablespoon honey
- ⅓ cup (70 g) firmly packed light brown sugar
- 1½ cups (225 g) all-purpose (plain) flour
- 2 teaspoons ground cinnamon
- 1 teaspoon ground ginger
- ½ teaspoon baking soda (bicarbonate of soda)
- ⅛ teaspoon salt
- 3 tablespoons milk
- 1 large egg, separated
- 2 tablespoons very finely chopped candied red and green cherries

Melt the butter with the honey and brown sugar in a small saucepan. Let cool slightly. • Mix the flour, cinnamon, ginger, baking soda, and salt in a medium bowl. Mix in the butter mixture, milk, and egg yolk until stiff. Refrigerate for 1 hour. • Preheat the oven to 350°F (180°C/gas 4). • Butter two cookie sheets. • Roll out the dough to of ¼ inch (5 mm) thick. • Use a 2-inch (5-cm) star-shaped cookie cutter to cut out the cookies. • Place 1 inch (2.5 cm) apart on the sheets. • Lightly beat the egg white and brush over the tops of the cookies. Sprinkle with the cherries. • Make a hole in one point of each cookie. • Bake for 10–15 minutes, or until golden. • Let cool completely. • Thread ribbons through the holes and hang on the Christmas tree.

Makes: about 25 cookies • Prep: 30 min + 1 hr to chill
Cooking: 10–15 min • Level: 1

NORWEGIAN CHRISTMAS COOKIES

Mix the flour, cardamom, and salt in a medium bowl. • Beat the eggs and sugar in a large bowl with an electric mixer at high speed until pale and thick. • With mixer at high speed, beat the cream in a medium bowl until stiff. • Mix the dry ingredients into the egg batter, followed by folding in the cream, until well blended. • Lightly butter a krumkake iron and place over medium heat. • The iron is ready to use when a drop of water holds its shape on the surface of the iron. • Drop a tablespoon (or enough dough to fit your iron) of the cookie dough onto the center of the iron. • Lower the top so that the cookie dough spreads. • Cook for 1 minute, or until browned at the edges. • Lift up the top and, working quickly, remove the cookie from the iron with a krumkake roller. The cookie should be cone-shaped. • Repeat with the remaining cookie batter. • Let cool completely.

Makes: about 12 cookies • Prep: 20 min • Cooking: 15 min
Level: 3

- 1¼ cups (175 g) all-purpose (plain) flour
- ½ teaspoon ground cardamom
- ⅛ teaspoon salt
- 2 large eggs
- ¾ cup (150 g) sugar
- ¾ cup (200 ml) heavy (double) cream

CINNAMON CHRISTMAS COOKIES

- 2 large egg whites
- 1¼ cups (250 g) superfine (caster) sugar
- 1 tablespoon vanilla sugar (see page 414)
- 1½ tablespoons dark rum
- 1 tablespoon butter, melted
- 2 teaspoons unsweetened cocoa powder
- 1½ teaspoons cinnamon
- ½ teaspoon cloves
- 2½ cups (375 g) finely ground almonds + more as needed for rolling
- ½ teaspoon baking powder
- 1 quantity vanilla frosting (see page 417)

Beat the egg whites and both sugars in a large bowl with an electric mixer at high speed until thick and glossy. • Mix in the rum, butter, cocoa, cinnamon, cloves, ground almonds, and baking powder to form a stiff dough. • Press into a disk, wrap in plastic wrap (cling film), and refrigerate for 30 minutes. • Preheat the oven to 350°F (180°C/gas 4). • Line four cookie sheets with parchment paper. • Roll out the dough between sheets of waxed paper ¼ inch (5 mm) thick. • Use a 1½-inch (4-cm) heart-shaped cookie cutter to cut out the cookies. • Bake for 8–10 minutes, or until pale gold and firm at the edges. • Transfer to racks to cool. • Spread the cookies with frosting.

Makes: about 40 cookies • Prep: 45 min + 30 min to chill • Cooking: 8–10 min • Level: 1

ALMOND LACE COOKIES

- ¼ cup (60 g) butter, cut up
- ½ cup vanilla sugar (see page 414)
- ½ cup (75 g) finely ground almonds
- 3 tablespoons all-purpose (plain) flour
- ⅛ teaspoon salt
- 2 tablespoons heavy cream

Preheat the oven to 375°F (190°C/gas 5). • Line two cookie sheets with parchment paper. • Melt the butter in a saucepan over low heat. • Stir in the vanilla sugar, almonds, flour, salt, and cream. • Drop teaspoons of the mixture 2 inches (5 cm) apart onto the cookie sheets. Use a thin spatula to spread them thinly. Do not place more than four cookies on each sheet. • Bake for 5–7 minutes, or until golden brown. • Cool on the sheet for 1 minute. Transfer the cookies to a cool surface to crispen. • If you are making baskets, cool for 1 minute on the cookie sheet before lifting them off with a thin metal spatula. • Working quickly, drape over an upturned cup. Press the cookie down gently and pleat with your fingers to form a cup.

Makes: about 18 cookies • Prep: 15 min • Cooking: 5–7 min • Level: 3

CHRISTMAS STOCKING COOKIES

Preheat the oven to 425°F (210°C/gas 7). • Butter four cookie sheets. • Mix the flour and salt in a large bowl. • Use a pastry blender to cut in the butter until the mixture resembles fine crumbs. • Stir in the sugar and semolina flour. • Divide the mixture into four separate bowls. • Mix the currants into one bowl, the almond extract into the second bowl, the cinnamon into the third, and the lemon zest into the remaining bowl. • Add enough of the egg yolk mixture to the bowls to form each into a stiff dough. • Christmas Wreaths: Roll out the currant mixture on a lightly floured surface ¼ inch (5 mm) thick. • Use a fluted cookie cutter to cut out ring-shaped cookies. • Star Cookies: Roll out the almond extract mixture to the same thickness. Use a star-shaped cookie cutter to cut out the cookies. • Bell Cookies: Roll out the cinnamon mixture to the same thickness. Use a bell-shaped cookie cutter to cut out cookies. • Christmas Tree Cookies: Roll out the lemon zest mixture to the same thickness. Use a tree cookie cutter to cut out the cookies. • Gather the dough scraps separately, re-roll, and continue cutting out cookies until all the dough is used. • Transfer all the cookies to the prepared cookie sheets, placing 1 inch (2.5 cm) apart. • Bake for 10–15 minutes, or until lightly browned. • Cool on the sheets until the cookies firm slightly. Transfer to racks to finish cooling. • Mix the confectioners' sugar with enough water to make creamy glaze. Stir in the green food coloring. Spread the star cookies with the frosting and decorate with a half cherry. • Stick the bell cookies together in pairs with the chocolate frosting and decorate the edges with silver balls. • Warm the raspberry preserves in a small saucepan over low heat until liquid. • Stick the Christmas tree cookies together in pairs with the preserves.

Makes: about 40 cookies • Prep: 1 hr • Cooking: 10–15 min • Level: 2

- 1⅔ cups (250 g) all-purpose (plain) flour
- ¼ teaspoon salt
- ¾ cup (200 g) butter
- ¾ cup (150 g) sugar
- ⅓ cup (50 g) semolina flour
- 2 tablespoons currants
- ½ teaspoon almond extract (essence)
- 1 teaspoon ground cinnamon
- finely gated zest of ½ lemon
- 1 large egg yolk mixed with 2–3 tablespoons water
- ⅓ cup (50 g) confectioners' (icing) sugar
- 1 tablespoon water, or more as needed
- ¼ teaspoon green food coloring
- candied cherries, cut in half
- ½ cup (125 g) chocolate butter frosting (see page 416)
- silver balls, to decorate
- ½ cup (150 g) raspberry preserves (jam)

Party Cookies

CHRISTMAS CHERRY COOKIES

- 1½ cups (225 g) all-purpose (plain) flour
- ½ teaspoon baking soda (bicarbonate of soda)
- ⅛ teaspoon salt
- ½ cup (125 g) butter, softened
- ¾ cup (150 g) firmly packed light brown sugar
- 2 large eggs
- 1½ cups (150 g) coarsely chopped pitted dates
- 1½ cups (150 g) coarsely chopped walnuts
- ½ cup (90 g) golden raisins (sultanas)
- ¼ cup (60 ml) whiskey
- 18 maraschino cherries, drained and cut in half

Preheat the oven to 350°F (180°C/gas 4). • Butter two cookie sheets. • Mix the flour, baking soda, and salt in a large bowl. • Beat the butter and brown sugar in a large bowl with an electric mixer until creamy. • Add the eggs, beating until just blended. • Mix in the dry ingredients. • Stir in the dates, walnuts, raisins, and whiskey to form a stiff dough. • Drop teaspoons of the dough 2 inches (5 cm) apart onto the prepared cookie sheets. Top each cookie with a half cherry. • Bake for 8–10 minutes, or until lightly browned. • Transfer the cookies to racks to cool.

Makes: about 35 cookies • Prep: 20 min • Cooking: 8–10 min • Level: 1

CHRISTMAS BUTTER COOKIES

Preheat the oven to 325°F (170°C/gas 3). • Set out two cookie sheets. • Mix the flour, cinnamon, and salt in a large bowl. • Use a pastry blender to cut in the butter until the mixture resembles coarse crumbs. • Stir in ⅔ cup (140 g) sugar and the coffee. • Press the dough into a disk and knead it lightly. • Place the hazelnuts on a large plate. • Form the dough into balls the size of walnuts and roll in the hazelnuts until well coated. • Place the cookies 1 inch (2.5 cm) apart on the cookie sheets, flattening them slightly. Sprinkle with the remaining sugar. • Bake for 20–25 minutes, or until faintly tinged with brown on top and slightly darker at the edges. • Cool on the sheets until the cookies firm slightly. • Transfer to racks to finish cooling.

Makes: about 35 cookies • Prep: 25 min • Cooking: 20–25 min • Level: 1

- 1½ cups (225 g) all-purpose (plain) flour
- ½ teaspoon ground cinnamon
- ⅛ teaspoon salt
- ⅔ cup (140 g) + 2 tablespoons sugar
- 2 teaspoons instant coffee granules, dissolved in 1 tablespoon hot water
- 1 cup (250 g) butter, cut up
- 2 cups (200 g) coarsely chopped toasted hazelnuts

CHRISTMAS CARD COOKIES

- 1½ cups (225 g) all-purpose (plain) flour
- ⅓ cup (50 g) unsweetened cocoa powder
- ½ teaspoon baking powder
- ½ teaspoon baking soda (bicarbonate of soda)
- ¼ teaspoon salt
- ½ cup (125 g) butter, softened
- ¾ cup (150 g) sugar
- ½ teaspoon vanilla extract (essence)
- 1 large egg

Mix the flour, cocoa, baking powder, baking soda, and salt in a medium bowl. • Beat the butter and sugar in a large bowl with an electric mixer on medium speed until creamy. • Add the vanilla and egg, beating until just blended. • Mix in the dry ingredients to form a stiff dough. • Press the dough into a disk, wrap in plastic wrap (cling film), and refrigerate for 30 minutes. • Preheat the oven to 350°F (180°C/gas 4). • Butter four cookie sheets. • Roll out half the dough on a lightly floured surface to ¼ inch (5 mm) thick. • Cut out 2 x 4-inch (5 x 10-cm) rectangles. • Repeat with the remaining dough. • Use a spatula to transfer the cookies to the prepared cookie sheets, placing them ½ inch (1 cm) apart. • Bake for

8–10 minutes, or until lightly browned. • Cool on racks until the cookies firm slightly. • Transfer to racks to finish cooling. • Use a sharp knife to trim the edges if the cookies have lost their shape during the baking. • Colored Frosting: Beat the confectioners' sugar and butter in a medium bowl until well blended. • Gradually add the milk to form a thick paste. • Stir in the food coloring of your choice until no white streaks remain. • Spoon the frosting into a small freezer bag and cut off a tiny corner. • Pipe your greeting message over the cookies and pipe decorative lines around the edge of the cookies.

Makes: 10–12 cookies • Prep: 40 min. • Cooking: 8–10 min. per batch • Level: 2

Colored Frosting
- 3 cups (450 g) confectioners' (icing) sugar
- ⅓ cup (90 g) butter, softened
- ¼ cup (60 ml) milk
- few drops food coloring

Party Cookies

Almond garlands

ALMOND GARLANDS

- 1½ cups (225 g) all-purpose (plain) flour
- ½ teaspoon baking powder
- ⅛ teaspoon salt
- 1 cup (250 g) butter, softened
- ½ cup (100 g) sugar
- 1 large egg yolk
- ½ teaspoon almond extract (essence)
- ⅓ cup (50 g) finely ground almonds

Preheat the oven to 350°F (180°C/gas 4). • Set out three cookie sheets. • Mix the flour, baking powder, and salt in a medium bowl. • Beat the butter and sugar in a large bowl with an electric mixer at high speed until creamy. • Add the egg yolk and almond extract, beating until just blended. • Mix in the dry ingredients and almonds until well blended. • Fit a pastry bag with a ½-inch (1-cm) star tip. Fill the pastry bag, twist the opening tightly closed, and squeeze out 2-inch rings onto the cookie sheets, spacing them 1 inch (2.5 cm) apart. • Bake for 8–10 minutes, or until golden brown. • Cool on the sheets until the cookies firm slightly. Transfer to racks and let cool completely.

Makes: about 40 cookies • Prep: 25 min • Cooking: 8–10 min • Level: 1

GINGERBREAD SQUARES

Preheat the oven to 325°F. • Line a 13 x 9-inch (32 x 23-cm) baking pan with aluminum foil, letting the edges overhang. Butter the foil. • Mix the flour, ginger, baking powder, cinnamon, and salt in a medium bowl. • Heat the corn syrup and butter in a small saucepan over low heat. Cook, stirring constantly, until the butter has melted. • Mix into the dry ingredients. • Stir in the marmalade, egg, and enough hot water to form a soft dough. • Spread the mixture in the prepared pan. • Bake for 45–55 minutes, or until a toothpick inserted into the center comes out clean. • Cool completely in the pan on a rack. • Using the foil as handles, lift onto a cutting board. Peel off the foil. • Cut into squares.

Makes: about 30 squares • Prep: 20 min • Cooking: 45–55 min • Level: 1

- 1½ cups (225 g) all-purpose (plain) flour
- 2 teaspoons ground ginger
- 1 teaspoon baking powder
- 1 teaspoon ground cinnamon
- ⅛ teaspoon salt
- 1 cup (250 g) light corn (golden) syrup
- ¼ cup (60 g) butter
- 1 cup (250 g) orange marmalade
- 1 large egg, lightly beaten
- 2 tablespoons hot water

SWISS CHRISTMAS COOKIES

- 1½ cups (225 g) confectioners' (icing) sugar
- 1½ cups (225 g) all-purpose (plain) flour
- ¼ teaspoon baking powder
- ⅛ teaspoon salt
- 2 large eggs
- 2 tablespoons butter, softened
- 1 tablespoon ground aniseeds

Butter two cookie sheets. • Place the confectioners' sugar in a medium bowl. • Mix the flour, baking powder, and salt in a separate medium bowl. • Beat the eggs in a large bowl with an electric mixer at medium speed until frothy. • Gradually beat in the confectioners' sugar, butter, and aniseeds until pale and thick. • Mix in the dry ingredients to form a stiff dough. • Knead the dough on a lightly floured surface until smooth. Roll out the dough on a lightly floured surface to ¼ inch (5 mm) thick. • Dust a springerle pin with flour and firmly roll over the dough to imprint the patterns. Cut off any surplus dough and separate the printed squares with a knife. • Transfer the cookies to the prepared cookie sheets, placing them 2 inches (5 cm) apart. • Let stand in a cool place for 24 hours. • Preheat the oven to 300°F (150°C/gas 2). • Bake, one sheet at a time, for 15–25 minutes, or until just golden. • Transfer to racks and let cool completely.

Makes: about 25 cookies • Prep: 40 min + 24 hr to rest
Cooking: 15–25 min • Level: 2

CHRISTMAS TREE COOKIES

Mix the flour and salt in a medium bowl. • Beat the butter in a large bowl until creamy. • Mix in the dry ingredients and milk to form a smooth dough. • Refrigerate for 30 minutes. • Preheat the oven to 375°F (190°C/gas 5). • Set out three cookie sheets. • Roll out the dough to ¼ inch (5 mm) thick. • Use a 2-inch (5-cm) tree-shaped cookie cutter to cut out the cookies. • Dip the cookies in the sugar and place 1 inch (2.5 cm) apart on the cookie sheets. • Bake for 8–10 minutes, or until just golden at the edges. • Let cool completely. • Filling: Beat the butter and vanilla in a medium bowl until creamy. • Beat in the confectioners' sugar and milk. • Add the green food coloring. • Stick the cookies together with the filling.

Makes: about 24 cookies • Prep: 45 min + 30 min to chill
Cooking: 8–10 min Level: 1

- 2 cups (300 g) all-purpose (plain) flour
- ¼ teaspoon salt
- 1 cup (250 g) butter, softened
- ⅓ cup (90 ml) milk
- ¾ cup (150 g) sugar

Filling
- ½ cup (125 g) butter, softened
- ½ teaspoon vanilla extract (essence)
- 2 cups (300 g) confectioners' (icing) sugar
- 1½ tablespoons milk
- few drops green food coloring

Christmas tree cookies

PARTY PECAN TORTOISES

- ½ cup (75 g) all-purpose (plain) flour
- 1 tablespoon instant coffee granules
- ½ teaspoon baking powder
- ⅛ teaspoon salt
- 14 oz (400 g) semisweet (dark) chocolate, coarsely chopped
- ¼ cup (60 g) butter
- 1½ cups (300 g) sugar
- 1 teaspoon vanilla extract (essence)
- 4 large eggs
- 2 cups (200 g) finely chopped pecans + 1 cup (100 g) pecan halves
- 1 cup (180 g) semisweet (dark) chocolate chips

Preheat the oven to 350°F (180°C/gas 4). • Line two cookie sheets with parchment paper. • Mix the flour, coffee baking powder, and salt in a large bowl. • Melt the chocolate and butter in a double boiler over barely simmering water. • Stir in the sugar until completely dissolved. • Remove from the heat and mix in the vanilla and eggs. • Mix in the dry ingredients, finely chopped pecans, and chocolate chips. • Drop tablespoons of the dough 3 inches (8 cm) apart onto the prepared cookie sheets. • Press four pecan halves into each corner of the cookies to resemble the legs of a turtle and an additional one to resemble a head. • Bake for 8–10 minutes, or until just set. • Let cool completely.

Makes: about 24 cookies • Prep: 20 min • Cooking: 8–10 min • Level: 1

GINGERBREAD PEOPLE

Mix the flour, baking powder, and salt in a medium bowl. • Beat the butter and sugar in a large bowl with an electric mixer at medium speed until creamy. • Add the milk, ginger, and egg. • Mix in the dry ingredients. • Press the dough into a disk, wrap in plastic wrap (cling film), and refrigerate for 30 minutes. • Preheat the oven to 350°F (180°C/gas 4). • Butter two cookie sheets. • Roll out the dough on a lightly floured surface to ¼ inch (5 mm) thick. • Use large gingerbread people cookie cutters to cut out the figures. • Gather the dough scraps, re-roll, and continue cutting out cookies until all the dough is used. • Use a spatula to transfer to the prepared cookie sheets, placing them ½ inch (1 cm) apart. • Bake for 10–12 minutes, or until just golden at the edges. • Transfer to racks to cool. • Use the candy writers to decorate the cookies.

Makes: about 8–10 cookies • Prep: 40 min + 30 min to chill Cooking: 10–12 min • Level: 2

- 2 cups (300 g) all-purpose (plain) flour
- 1 teaspoon baking powder
- ¼ teaspoon salt
- ½ cup (125 g) butter, softened
- ½ cup (100 g) sugar
- 1 tablespoon milk
- 1 tablespoon ground ginger
- 1 large egg
- colored candy writers, to decorate

SAINT CATHERINE'S COILS

- 2½ cups (375 g) all-purpose (plain) flour
- ½ teaspoon baking soda (bicarbonate of soda)
- 1 teaspoon ground cinnamon
- ⅛ teaspoon salt
- 1 cup (250 g) butter, softened
- ½ cup (100 g) sugar
- ⅔ cup (100 g) finely ground almonds

Mix the flour, baking soda, cinnamon, and salt in a large bowl. • Use a pastry blender to cut in the butter until the mixture resembles fine crumbs. • Stir in the sugar, almonds, currants, caraway seeds, if using. • Add the egg and mix to make a firm dough. • Press the dough into a disk, wrap in plastic wrap (cling film), and refrigerate for 30 minutes. • Preheat the oven to 400°F (200°C/gas 6). • Butter two cookie sheets. • Roll out the dough on a lightly floured surface to an 8 x 6-inch (20 x 15-cm) rectangle. • Use a pastry brush to brush

lightly with water. Sprinkle with the remaining 2 tablespoons sugar. • Cut the dough into ½ x 6-inch (1 x 15-cm) long strips and shape into rounded ropes. Form each rope into a tight circular coil. Use a spatula to transfer the cookies to the prepared cookie sheets, flattening them slightly. • Bake for 10–12 minutes, or until golden brown, rotating the sheets halfway through for even baking. • Transfer to racks to cool.

Makes: about 24 cookies • Prep: 40 min + 30 min to chill Cooking: 10–12 min • Level: 1

- ½ cup (70 g) dried currants
- 2 teaspoons caraway seeds (optional)
- 1 large egg, lightly beaten
- 2 teaspoons water

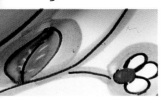

Chocolate mice

CHOCOLATE MICE

- 5 oz (150 g) semisweet (dark) chocolate, coarsely chopped
- 1/3 cup (90 ml) heavy (double) cream
- 1 cup (125 g) chocolate wafer crumbs (crushed plain chocolate biscuits)
- 1/3 cup (50 g) confectioners' (icing) sugar
- 24 silver balls, to decorate
- 24 flaked almonds, to decorate
- red licorice whips, to decorate

Melt the chocolate with the cream in a double boiler over barely simmering water. • Mix in the chocolate wafer crumbs until well blended. • Cover with plastic wrap and refrigerate for 1 hour, or until firm. • Form the dough into balls the size of tangerines, tapering one end to resemble the nose. • Roll half the balls in the confectioners' sugar until well coated. • Decorate all with the silver balls to resemble the eyes, almonds for ears, and a small length of licorice for the tail. • Refrigerate for 2 hours.

Makes: about 12 cookies • Prep: 20 min + 3 hr to chill
Level: 1

ICE CREAM BASKETS

- 4 large egg whites
- 1/8 teaspoon salt
- 2 tablespoons poppy seeds
- 1/4 cup superfine (caster) sugar
- 1 tablespoon vanilla sugar (see page 414)
- 2 tablespoons all-purpose (plain) flour
- 2 1/4 cups (300 g) finely ground almonds
- vanilla ice cream, to serve
- fresh fruit coulis, to serve

Preheat the oven to 350°F (180°C/gas 4). • Line three cookie sheets with parchment paper. • Beat the egg whites and salt in a large bowl with an electric mixer at high speed until soft peaks form. • Use a large rubber spatula to fold in the poppy seeds, superfine sugar, vanilla sugar, flour, and almonds. • Drop tablespoons of the mixture 2 inches apart onto the cookie sheets. Use a spatula to spread them thinly. Do not place more than four cookies on each sheet. • Bake for 5–7 minutes, or until golden brown. • Cool the cookies for 1 minute on the cookie sheet. • Use a thin metal spatula to lift up each cookie. • Working quickly, drape over an upturned glass or cup. Press the cookie down gently and pleat with your fingers to form a cup. • Cool the cookies completely. To serve, fill each basket with a scoop of ice cream. Top with a spoonful of coulis.

Makes 12–15 cookie baskets • Prep: 15 min • Cooking: 5–7
min • Level: 3

MOTHER'S DAY COOKIES

Mix the flour, baking powder, and salt in a medium bowl. • Beat the cream cheese and butter in a large bowl with an electric mixer at high speed until creamy. • Process the egg, cocoa, and nougat in a food processor until well blended. • Mix the nougat mixture into batter. • Mix in the dry ingredients to form a smooth, and not sticky, dough. • Press the dough into a disk, wrap in plastic wrap (cling film), and refrigerate for 30 minutes. • Preheat the oven to 375°F (190°C/gas 5). • Line two cookie sheets with parchment paper. • Roll out the dough on a lightly floured surface to 1/2 inch (5 mm) thick. • Use a 3-inch (8-cm) heart-shaped cookie cutter to cut out the cookies. Gather the dough scraps, re-roll, and continue cutting out cookies until all the dough is used. • Use a spatula to transfer the cookies to the prepared cookie sheets, placing them 1 inch (2.5 cm) apart. • Bake for 12–15 minutes, or until lightly browned and the edges are firm, rotating the sheets halfway through for even baking. • Cool on the sheets until the cookies firm slightly. Transfer to racks to finish cooling. • Frosting: Mix the confectioners' sugar, vanilla, and enough milk to form a thick paste. • Divide into three bowls. Leave one mixture plain and tint the remaining mixtures with the red and green food coloring. • Spread each cookie top with the frosting, making some pink, some green, and others white. • Use a contrasting colored candy writer to pipe a special message or design on top of the cookies. • Decorate with the sugar flowers.

Makes 12–16 cookies • Prep: 40 min + 30 min to chill
Cooking: 12–15 min • Level: 2

- 2 cups (300 g) all-purpose (plain) flour
- 1 teaspoon baking powder
- 1/8 teaspoon salt
- 2/3 cup (180 g) cream cheese or quark, softened
- 1/3 cup (90 g) butter, softened
- 1 large egg
- 1/4 cup (25 g) unsweetened cocoa powder
- 3 1/2 oz (100 g) nougat, cut into small pieces

Frosting

- 1 cup confectioners' sugar
- 1/4 teaspoon vanilla extract (essence)
- 1 tablespoon milk, + more as needed
- 2–3 drops each red and green food coloring
- colored candy writers, to decorate
- sugar flowers, to decorate

Valentine cookies

VALENTINE COOKIES

- 2⅓ cups (350 g) all-purpose (plain) flour
- 2 teaspoons ground cinnamon
- 1 teaspoon baking soda (bicarbonate of soda)
- ¼ teaspoon ground cloves
- ⅛ teaspoon salt
- ½ cup (125 g) butter, cut up
- ⅔ cup (140 g) granulated sugar
- ¼ cup (60 ml) light molasses (treacle)
- 1 tablespoon finely grated lemon zest
- 1 large egg, lightly beaten
- colored candy writers, to decorate

Mix the flour, cinnamon, baking soda, cloves, and salt in a medium bowl. • Cut in the butter until the mixture resembles fine crumbs. • Stir in the sugar, molasses, lemon zest, and egg to form a stiff dough. • Press the dough into a disk, wrap in plastic wrap (cling film), and refrigerate for 30 minutes. • Preheat the oven to 375°F (190°C/gas 5). • Butter a cookie sheet. • Roll out the dough on a lightly floured surface to ¼ inch (5 mm) thick. • Use a 4-inch (10-cm) heart-shaped cookie cutter to cut out the cookies. • Use a spatula to transfer the cookies to the prepared cookie sheet, placing them 1 inch (2.5 cm) apart. • Bake for 10–15 minutes, or until lightly browned. • Transfer to racks to cool. • Use various colored candy writers to pipe a message onto each cookie.

Makes: about 8–10 cookies • Prep: 45 min + 30 min to chill Cooking: 30–35 min • Level: 1

SNOWMEN

- ½ cup (125 g) butter, cut up
- 3 cups mini marshmallow pieces
- 6 cups (300 g) rice krispies cereal
- 8 oz (250 g) white chocolate, coarsely chopped
- ¼ cup snowflake sprinkles (optional)
- black and red licorice, to decorate

Line a 10½ x 15½-inch (26 x 34-cm) jelly-roll pan with aluminum foil. • Melt the butter with the marshmallows in a small saucepan over low heat. • Remove from the heat and stir in the rice krispies. • Lightly press the mixture into the prepared pan. • Refrigerate for 30 minutes, or until firmly set. • Use a snowman-shaped cookie cutter or 3-inch (8-cm) cookie cutters to cut out the cookies. • Press craft sticks into the base of the cookies to form handles. • Melt the white chocolate in a double boiler over barely simmering water. • Spread the chocolate over the tops of the cookies and decorate with the snowflakes, if using, and licorice to form eyes and mouths. • Let stand for 30 minutes until set.

Makes: 10–12 cookies · Prep: 25 min. + 60 min. to chill and stand · Level: 3

TRAFFIC LIGHT COOKIES

Mix the flour and salt in a large bowl. • Beat the butter and sugar in a large bowl with an electric mixer at medium speed until creamy. • Add the egg, beating until just blended. • Mix in the dry ingredients to form a stiff dough. • Press the dough into a disk, wrap in plastic wrap (cling film), and refrigerate for 30 minutes. • Preheat the oven to 400°F (200°C/gas 6). • Butter two cookie sheets. • Roll out the dough on a lightly floured surface to ¼ inch (5 mm) thick. • Use a sharp knife to cut out forty 1 x 3-inch (2.5 x 8-cm) rectangles. • Use an apple corer to make three circular holes in half of the rectangles. • Use a spatula to transfer the cookies to the prepared cookie sheets, placing them ½ inch (5 mm) apart. • Bake for 15–20 minutes, or until just golden. • Transfer to racks to cool. • Mix the confectioners' sugar with the water in a small bowl to achieve a thick, spreading consistency. • Divide the icing into three bowls. • Use a wooden spoon to mix the red, green, and orange (or red and yellow) food colors alternately into the icings until no white streaks remain. • Warm the preserves in a small saucepan over low heat until liquid. • Use a thin metal spatula to spread the plain rectangles with the preserves. Place the rectangles with holes on top of the preserves. • Use a teaspoon to fill the three holes in each cookie with the red, orange, and green icing.

Makes: about 20 cookies • Prep: 40 min + 30 min to chill Cooking: 15–20 min • Level: 2

- 2⅓ cups (350 g) all-purpose (plain) flour
- ⅛ teaspoon salt
- ¾ cup (200 g) butter, softened
- ⅔ cup (140 g) sugar
- 1 large egg, lightly beaten
- ¾ cup (125 g) confectioners' (icing) sugar
- 1 tablespoon warm water
- few drops each red, green, and orange (red and yellow) food colorings
- 2 tablespoons raspberry preserves (jam)

Peppermint lollipops

PEPPERMINT LOLLIPOPS

- 2 cups (300 g) all-purpose (plain) flour
- 1 1/2 teaspoons baking powder
- 1/4 teaspoon salt
- 1/3 cup (90 g) butter, softened
- 1/3 cup (90 g) vegetable shortening
- 3/4 cup (150 g) sugar
- 1 large egg, lightly beaten
- 1 tablespoon milk
- 1/2 teaspoon vanilla extract (essence)
- 1/2 cup (50 g) crushed peppermint candies

Mix the flour, baking powder, and salt in a medium bowl. • Beat the butter, shortening, and sugar in a large bowl with an electric mixer on medium speed until creamy. • Add the egg, milk, and vanilla. • Mix in the dry ingredients to form a smooth dough. • Divide the dough in half. Press into two disks, wrap in plastic wrap (cling film), and refrigerate for 30 minutes. • Preheat the oven to 350°F (180°C/gas 4). • Set out four cookie sheets. • Roll the dough on a lightly floured surface into a 12 x 9-inch (30 x 23-cm) rectangle. • Use a fluted pastry wheel to cut into twelve 3-inch (8-cm) squares. • Transfer to the cookie sheets. Do not place more than six cookies on each sheet. • Sprinkle with the candies, pressing into the dough. • Cut 1-inch (2.5-cm) slits in each corner toward the center. Fold every other corner into the center to make a windmill. • Press craft sticks into the base of the squares, pressing the dough around so they are firmly held. • Bake for 6–8 minutes, or until just golden at the edges. • Cool on the sheets until the cookies firm slightly. • Transfer to racks to cool.

Makes: about 12 cookies • Prep: 30 min + 30 min to chill Cooking: 6–8 min • Level: 2

NOVEMBER 5 COOKIES

Preheat the oven to 400°F (200°C/gas 6). • Butter two cookie sheets. • Mix the all-purpose and whole-wheat flours, confectioners' sugar, cinnamon, cloves, and salt in a large bowl. • Use a pastry blender to cut in the butter until the mixture resembles coarse crumbs. • Add the egg yolk and vanilla and mix to form a smooth dough. • Press the dough into a disk, wrap in plastic wrap, and refrigerate for 30 minutes. • Roll out the dough on a lightly floured surface to 1/8 inch (3 mm) thick. • Use a 3-inch (8-cm) cookie cutter to cut out the cookies. Gather the dough scraps, re-roll, and continue cutting out cookies until all the dough is used. • Use a spatula to transfer the cookies to the prepared cookie sheets, placing them 1 inch (2.5 cm) apart. • Sprinkle with the raw sugar. • Bake for 12–15 minutes, or until golden. • Transfer to racks to cool.

Makes: 30–35 cookies • Prep: 40 min • Cooking: 12–15 min Level: 1

- 3/4 cup (125 g) all-purpose (plain) flour
- 3/4 cup (125 g) whole-wheat (wholemeal) flour
- 3/4 cup (125 g) confectioners' (icing) sugar
- 1 teaspoon ground cinnamon
- 1/8 teaspoon ground cloves
- 1/8 teaspoon salt
- 1/3 cup (90 g) butter, cut up
- 1 large egg yolk, lightly beaten
- 1/4 teaspoon vanilla extract (essence)
- 1 tablespoon raw sugar (Barbados or Demerara)

BIRTHDAY LOLLIPOPS

- 3 cups (450 g) all-purpose (plain) flour
- 1 teaspoon baking powder
- 1/2 teaspoon baking soda (bicarbonate of soda)
- 1/4 teaspoon salt
- 1 cup (250 g) butter, softened
- 1 1/2 cups (300 g) sugar
- 1/2 teaspoon vanilla extract (essence)

Mix the flour, baking powder, baking soda, and salt in a medium bowl. • Beat the butter and sugar in a large bowl with an electric mixer on medium speed until creamy. • Add the vanilla and eggs, beating until just blended. • Mix in the dry ingredients and 1 cup M&Ms. • Press the dough into a disk, wrap in plastic wrap (cling film), and refrigerate for 30 minutes. • Preheat the oven to 375°F (190°C/gas 5). • Line two cookie sheets with parchment paper. • Roll 2 tablespoons of dough into a ball and insert a wooden craft stick into the dough. Flatten

completely with the base of a glass. • Repeat with the remaining dough. • Place the cookies 2 inches apart on the cookie sheets. • Bake for 10–12 minutes, or until just golden at the edges. • Cool on racks until the cookies firm slightly. • Transfer to racks to finish cooling. • Spoon the frosting into a small freezer bag and cut off a tiny corner. • Pipe lines of frosting over the cookies and press the remaining M&Ms on top.

Makes: 25–30 cookies · Prep: 30 min. · Cooking: 10–12 min. · Level: 2

- 2 large eggs
- 2 cups (250 g) M&Ms
- 1 quantity vanilla frosting (see page 417)

Party Cookies

EASTER CURRANT COOKIES

- 1¼ cups (180 g) all-purpose (plain) flour
- 1 teaspoon baking powder
- ⅛ teaspoon salt
- ⅓ cup (90 g) butter, softened
- 1 cup (200 g) sugar
- 1 large egg, lightly beaten
- 1 tablespoon dried currants

Preheat the oven to 325°F (170°C/gas 3). • Butter a cookie sheet. • Mix the flour, baking powder, and salt in a medium bowl. • Beat the butter and sugar in a large bowl with an electric mixer at high speed until creamy. • Add the egg, beating until just blended. • Mix in the flour to form a smooth dough. • Knead in the currants. • Transfer the dough to a lightly floured surface and roll out to ¼ inch (5 mm) thick. • Use a 3-inch (8-cm) cookie cutter to cut out the cookies. • Gather the dough scraps, re-roll, and continue cutting out the cookies until all the dough is used. • Arrange on the prepared cookie sheets, placing them 1 inch (2.5 cm) apart. • Bake for 10–15 minutes, or until lightly browned. • Transfer to racks to cool.

Makes: about 16 cookies • Prep: 40 min • Cooking: 10–15 min • Level: 1

CRUNCHY FRUIT SQUARES

- 1 cup (250 ml) light (single) cream
- ⅓ cup (90 ml) pure maple syrup
- ⅔ cup (140 g) firmly packed dark brown sugar
- 1 tablespoon butter
- 1 cup (100 g) corn flakes
- ½ cup (50 g) flaked almonds
- ¼ cup (30 g) unsweetened shredded (desiccated) coconut
- ¾ cup finely chopped dried unsweetened banana chips
- ½ cup coarsely chopped dried apricots

Butter an 11 x 7-inch (28 x 18-cm) baking pan. • Cook the cream, maple syrup, brown sugar, and butter in a medium saucepan over low heat, stirring often, until the sugar has dissolved completely. • Bring to a boil and boil for 10 minutes. • Stir in the corn flakes, almonds, coconut, banana chips, and apricots. • Firmly press the mixture into the prepared pan to form an even layer. • Refrigerate for at least 2 hours. • Cut into squares.

Makes: 22 squares • Prep: 25 min + 2 hr to chill • Level: 1

DOMINOES

Preheat the oven to 375°F (190°C/gas 5). • Butter a cookie sheet. • Mix the flour, cocoa, and salt in a medium bowl. • Use a pastry blender to cut in the butter until the mixture resembles fine crumbs. • Stir in the sugar. • Add the egg to form a stiff dough. Press into a disk, cover with plastic wrap, and refrigerate for 30 minutes. • Roll out the dough on a lightly floured surface to ¼ inch (5 mm) thick. • Use a sharp knife to cut the dough into 2½ x 1½-inch (7 x 4-cm) rectangles. • Use a spatula to transfer the cookies to the prepared cookie sheet, placing them ½ inch (1 cm) apart. • Bake for 12–15 minutes, or until just colored at the edges. • Transfer to racks to cool. • Vanilla Filling: Beat the butter, confectioners' sugar, and vanilla in a small bowl with an electric mixer at high speed until creamy. • Chocolate Frosting: Melt the chocolate with the milk and water in a double boiler over barely simmering water, stirring often, until well blended. • Remove from the heat and beat in ¾ cup confectioners' sugar. • Stick the cookies together in pairs with the filling. • Use a thin metal spatula to spread the tops of the cookies with the chocolate frosting. Let stand for 30 minutes until set. • Decorating Frosting: Beat ⅓ cup (50 g) confectioners' sugar with the water to make a thick frosting. • Spoon the frosting into a small freezer bag and cut off a tiny corner. • Pipe a horizontal line across the center of each cookie and domino dots in each half square.

Makes: 8–10 cookies • Prep: 40 min + 1 hr to chill and set Cooking: 12–15 min • Level: 2

- ¾ cup (125 g) all-purpose (plain) flour
- 2 teaspoons unsweetened cocoa powder
- ⅛ teaspoon salt
- ¼ cup (60 g) butter, cut up
- ⅓ cup (70 g) sugar
- 1 large egg, lightly beaten

Vanilla Filling
- ¼ cup (60 g) butter, softened
- ½ cup (75 g) confectioners' (icing) sugar
- ½ teaspoon vanilla extract (essence)

Chocolate Frosting
- 2 oz (60 g) bittersweet (dark) chocolate, coarsely chopped
- 1 tablespoon milk
- 1 tablespoon water
- ¾ cup (125 g) confectioners' (icing) sugar

Decorating Frosting
- ⅓ cup (50 g) confectioners' (icing) sugar
- 1 tablespoon lukewarm water

MINTY HEARTS

- 1 cup (150 g) all-purpose (plain) flour
- 1/8 teaspoon salt
- 1/2 cup (125 g) butter, softened
- 1/3 cup (70 g) sugar
- 1/2 large egg, lightly beaten
- 1/2 teaspoon vanilla extract (essence)
- 1/2 teaspoon mint extract (essence)
- few drops green food coloring
- 30 Hershey kisses

Preheat the oven to 400°F (200°C/gas 6). • Butter two cookie sheets. • Mix the flour and salt in a medium bowl. • Beat the butter, sugar, egg, and vanilla and mint extracts in a large bowl with an electric mixer at high speed. • Mix in the dry ingredients, followed by the food coloring. • Refrigerate for 30 minutes. • Insert a star-shaped design plate into a cookie press by sliding it into the head and locking in place. Press out the cookies, spacing about 1 inch (2.5 cm) apart on the prepared cookie sheet. • Bake for 8–10 minutes, or until just golden at the edges. • Working quickly, press a chocolate into the center of each cookie. • Cool on the sheets until the cookies firm slightly. • Transfer to racks and let cool.

Makes: about 30 cookies • Prep: 25 min + 30 min to chill
Cooking: 8–10 min • Level: 2

DRIZZLED CHOCOLATE ALMOND COOKIES

Mix the flour, cinnamon, baking powder, and salt in a medium bowl. • Melt the butter in a medium saucepan over low heat. • Remove from the heat and stir in the milk and brandy. • Mix in the dry ingredients, finely ground almonds, and brown sugar. • Form the dough into a log 2 inches in diameter, wrap in plastic wrap, and refrigerate for 15 minutes. • Unwrap and roll in the finely chopped almonds. • Rewrap the log and refrigerate for 30 minutes. • Preheat the oven to 375°F (190°C/gas 5). • Butter three cookie sheets. • Slice the dough 1/4 inch (5 mm) thick and place 1 inch apart on the prepared cookie sheets. • Bake for 8–10 minutes, or until just golden. • Transfer to racks and let cool completely. • Melt the chocolate in a double boiler over barely simmering water. • Spoon the chocolate into a small freezer bag and cut off a tiny corner. • Drizzle over the cookies.

Makes: about 36 cookies • Prep: 40 min + 45 min to chill
Cooking: 8–10 min • Level: 1

- 2 cups (300 g) all-purpose (plain) flour
- 3/4 teaspoon ground cinnamon
- 1/2 teaspoon baking powder
- 1/4 teaspoon salt
- 3 tablespoons butter
- 1/4 cup (60 ml) milk
- 2 tablespoons brandy
- 1 cup finely ground almonds + 1 cup finely chopped almonds
- 1/2 cup (100 g) firmly packed light brown sugar
- 6 oz (180 g) semisweet (dark) chocolate, coarsely chopped

FORTUNE COOKIES

- 3 large egg whites
- 3/4 cup (150 g) sugar
- 1 cup (150 g) all-purpose (plain) flour
- 1/2 cup (125 g) butter, melted
- 1/2 teaspoon vanilla extract (essence)
- 1/2 teaspoon almond extract (essence)
- 2 tablespoons cold water

These are great party cookies! Write aphorisms, quotes, or poems onto pieces of paper ready to pop into the cookies during baking.

Preheat the oven to 375°F. • Butter four cookie sheets. • Beat the egg whites and sugar in a large bowl with an electric mixer at high speed until frothy. • With mixer at low speed, beat in the flour, butter, vanilla and almond extracts, and water. • Drop teaspoons of the mixture onto the prepared cookie sheets, spreading it out to 3-inch circles. • Bake for 5–7 minutes, or until just golden at the edges. • Use a spatula to

remove the cookies, placing a message in the center. Fold the cookies in half, enclosing your message, to form a semicircle. Hold the rounded edges of the semicircle between your thumb and index finger. Place your other index finger at the center of the folded edge and push in. • Let cool completely.

Makes: 40–50 cookies • Prep: 25 min • Cooking: 5–7 min
Level: 3

Party Cookies

ALL SAINTS COOKIES

- ³/₄ cup (125 g) all-purpose (plain) flour
- ¹/₂ teaspoon ground cinnamon
- ¹/₄ teaspoon ground cloves
- ¹/₈ teaspoon salt
- ¹/₃ cup (90 g) butter, softened
- ¹/₃ cup (70 g) sugar
- 1 large egg yolk
- 2 tablespoons milk + more as needed

Mix the flour, cinnamon, cloves, and salt in a medium bowl. • Beat the butter and sugar in a large bowl until creamy. • Add the egg yolk, beating until just blended. • Mix in the dry ingredients and enough milk to form a soft dough. • Press the dough into a disk, wrap in plastic wrap (cling film), and refrigerate for 30 minutes. • Preheat the oven to 350°F (180°C/gas 4). • Butter a cookie sheet. • Roll out the dough on a lightly floured surface to thickness of ½ inch (1-cm). • Use a 2-inch (5-cm) cookie cutter to cut out the cookies. Gather the dough scraps, re-roll, and continue cutting out cookies until all the dough is used. • Use a sharp knife to mark a cross on top of each cookie. • Use a spatula to transfer the cookies to the prepared cookie sheet. • Bake for 10–15 minutes, or until deep golden. • Transfer to racks to cool.

Makes: about 15 cookies • Prep: 40 min + 30 min to chill Cooking: 10–15 min • Level: 1

ALMOND TUILES

Preheat the oven to 425°F (210°C/gas 7). • Line three cookie sheets with parchment paper. Set out two rolling pins. • Mix the flour and cocoa in a small bowl. • Beat the egg whites and salt in a large bowl with an electric mixer at medium speed until frothy. With mixer at high speed, gradually add the superfine sugar, beating until stiff, glossy peaks form. • Fold in the dry ingredients. • Fold in the cream and butter. • Drop tablespoons of the dough onto the cookie sheet, placing them 3 inches (8 cm) apart. Do not drop more than six cookies onto each sheet. Sprinkle with the almonds. • Bake for 4–6 minutes, or until the cookies are faintly tinged with gold. • Working quickly, use a spatula to lift the cookies off the sheet and drape over a rolling pin. Slide off the pin and onto racks to finish cooling.

Makes: 12–15 cookies • Prep: 20 min • Cooking: 4–6 min Level: 3

- 1 tablespoon all-purpose (plain) flour
- 1 tablespoon unsweetened cocoa powder
- 2 large egg whites
- ¹/₈ teaspoon salt
- ¹/₄ cup (50 g) superfine (caster) sugar
- 1 tablespoon heavy (double) cream
- 1 tablespoon butter, melted
- 2 tablespoons flaked almonds

BERRY CRISPS

- ¹/₄ cup (60 g) butter
- ¹/₄ cup (50 g) sugar
- 2 teaspoons honey
- ¹/₃ cup (40 g) finely ground pecans
- ¹/₃ cup (40 g) silvered almonds
- ¹/₄ cup (30 g) dried cranberries or cherries
- ¹/₄ cup (25 g) all-purpose (plain) flour

Preheat the oven to 350°F (180°C/gas 4). • Line two cookie sheets with parchment paper. • Melt the butter with the sugar and honey in a medium saucepan over low heat, stirring constantly, until the sugar has dissolved completely. • Remove from the heat and mix in the almonds, cranberries, and pecans. • Stir in the flour and mix well. • Drop teaspoons of the mixture 3 inches (8 cm) apart onto the prepared cookie sheets, spreading them out as thinly as possible. • Bake, one sheet at the time, for 8–10 minutes, or until they are golden brown at the edges. • Cool on the sheets until the cookies firm slightly. Transfer to racks and let cool completely.

Makes: about 20 cookies • Prep: 15 min • Cooking: 8–10 min • Level: 2

GINGER CURLS

Preheat the oven to 350°F (180°C/gas 4). • Butter four cookie sheets. • Butter a rolling pin. • Mix the flour, ginger, and salt in a medium bowl. • Heat the molasses, butter, and brown sugar in a small saucepan over low heat until the sugar has dissolved completely. • Mix the molasses mixture into the dry ingredients. • Stir in the lemon juice. • Drop teaspoons of the dough 3 inches (8 cm) apart onto the prepared cookie sheets. Do not bake more than five cookies on one sheet. • Bake, one sheet at a time, for 8–10 minutes, or until golden brown. • Cool on the sheets until the cookies firm slightly. • Working quickly, use a spatula to lift each cookie off the sheet and drape it over the rolling pin. • Let cool completely.

Makes: 16–20 cookies • Prep: 40 min • Cooking: 8–10 min Level: 3

- ²/₃ cup (100 g) all-purpose (plain) flour
- 1 teaspoon ground ginger
- ¹/₈ teaspoon salt
- ¹/₃ cup (90 ml) dark molasses (treacle)
- ¹/₂ cup (125 g) butter
- ¹/₂ cup (100 g) firmly packed dark brown sugar
- 1 tablespoon freshly squeezed lemon juice

KITTY CAT COOKIES

- 2 tablespoons butter, softened
- ¼ cup (50 g) sugar
- 1 tablespoon honey
- 3 tablespoons all-purpose (plain) flour
- 1 tablespoon unsweetened cocoa powder
- 1 large egg white
- ¼ teaspoon rum extract (essence)
- ¼ teaspoon lemon or vanilla extract (essence)
- ¼ cup (45 g) semisweet (dark) chocolate chips

Beat the butter and sugar in a large bowl with an electric mixer at high speed until creamy. • Beat in the honey, flour, cocoa, and egg white. Add the rum and lemon extracts. • Refrigerate for 1–2 hours. • Draw the outline of a cat's face and ears (about 3¼ x 3 inches (8.5 x 8 cm) on a acetate square or plastic lid. Cut along the outline to make a stencil. • Preheat the oven to 325°F (170°C/gas 3). • Line three cookie sheets with parchment paper. • Place the stencil on the parchment at the top corner of the cookie sheet. • Hold the stencil in position and spread a thin layer of the mixture across it with a rubber spatula, making sure the ears are filled in! • Carefully lift the stencil and place on the parchment next to the cat face you just made, spacing 2 inches (5 cm) apart. • Do not place more than eight cookies on one sheet. • Bake, one sheet at a time, for 6–8 minutes, or until the edges are firm. • Cool on the sheets until the cookies firm slightly. • Transfer to racks to cool. • Decorate with the chocolate chips to resemble eyes and noses.

Makes: about 24 cookies • Prep: 30 min + 2 hr to chill Cooking: 6–8 min • Level: 2

ORANGE CONES WITH COFFEE CREAM

Coffee Cream: Melt the chocolate with the cream in a double boiler over barely simmering water. • Stir in the coffee and liqueur. • Let cool completely. • Cover with plastic wrap (cling film) and refrigerate for 2 hours. • Orange Cookies: Preheat the oven to 300°F (150°C/gas 2). • Butter two cookie sheets. • Butter two rolling pins. • Mix the flour and salt in a medium bowl. • Beat the sugar, butter, and orange zest and juice in a large bowl until well blended. • Mix in the dry ingredients. • Drop teaspoons of the mixture 3 inches (8 cm) apart onto the cookie sheets. Do not drop more than five cookies on one sheet. • Bake for 10–12 minutes, or until just golden at the edges. • Working quickly, use a spatula to lift each cookie from the sheet and drape it over a rolling pin. Remove from the rolling pin and overlap the edges to form a cone. Let cool completely. • Fit a pastry bag with a ¼-inch (5-mm) star tip. Fill with the coffee cream, twist the opening tightly closed, and fill the cookies.

Makes: 10 cookies • Prep: 40 min + 2 hr to chill • Cooking: 10–12 min • Level: 3

Coffee Cream
- 3 oz (90 g) bittersweet (dark) chocolate, coarsely chopped
- ½ cup (125 ml) heavy (double) cream
- 1 tablespoon instant coffee granules
- 1 teaspoon coffee liqueur

Orange Cookies
- ⅓ cup (50 g) all-purpose (plain) flour
- ⅛ teaspoon salt
- ¼ cup (50 g) sugar
- 1 tablespoon butter, softened
- ½ teaspoon finely grated orange zest
- 1½ tablespoons freshly squeezed orange juice

HAZELNUT CREAM CONES

- ⅔ cup (100 g) all-purpose (plain) flour
- ⅛ teaspoon salt
- ⅓ cup (90 g) butter, softened
- ⅔ cup (100 g) confectioners' (icing) sugar
- ½ teaspoon vanilla extract (essence)
- 4 large egg whites, lightly beaten

Preheat the oven to 400°F (200°C/gas 6). • Butter four cookie sheets. • Butter two rolling pins. • Mix the flour and salt in a medium bowl. • Beat the butter and confectioners' sugar in a large bowl with an electric mixer at medium speed until creamy. • Mix in the dry ingredients and vanilla. • Stir in the egg whites. • Fit a pastry bag with a ½-inch (1-cm) plain tip. Fill the pastry bag, twist the opening tightly closed, and squeeze out small ovals, spacing them 3 inches (8 cm) apart on the cookie sheets. • Do not pipe more than 5 cookies on one sheet. • Bake for 5–8 minutes, or until just golden at the edges. • Working quickly, use a spatula to lift each cookie from the sheet and drape it over a rolling pin. Remove from the rolling pin and overlap the edges to form a cone. Let cool completely. • Hazelnut Cream: Melt the chocolate hazelnut cream in a double boiler over barely simmering water. • Beat the cream until thick. • Fold the cream into the chocolate mixture. • Fit a pastry bag with a ¼-inch (5-mm) star tip. Fill the pastry bag and pipe the cream into the cones.

Makes: about 36 cookies • Prep: 40 min • Cooking: 5–8 min Level: 3

Hazelnut Cream
- ⅔ cup (180 g) chocolate hazelnut cream (Nutella)
- 1 cup (250 ml) heavy (double) cream

Party Cookies

MARSHMALLOW KISSES

- 1½ cups (225 g) all-purpose (plain) flour
- 2 tablespoons unsweetened cocoa powder
- 1 teaspoon baking powder
- ⅛ teaspoon salt
- ½ cup (125 g) butter, cut up
- ½ cup (100 g) sugar
- 1 large egg yolk, lightly beaten
- 20–24 white marshmallows

Preheat the oven to 375°F (190°C/gas 5). • Butter three cookie sheets. • Mix the flour, cocoa, baking powder, and salt in a medium bowl. • Use a pastry blender to cut in the butter until the mixture resembles fine crumbs. Stir in the sugar. • Mix in the egg yolk. Press the dough into a disk, wrap in plastic wrap, and refrigerate for 30 minutes. • Roll out the dough out on a lightly floured surface to a thickness of ¼ inch (5 mm). • Use a 2-inch (5-cm) cookie cutter to cut out the cookies. Cut out the centers from half of the cookies with a 1-inch (2.5-cm) cookie cutter. Gather the dough scraps, re-roll, and continue cutting out cookies until all the dough is used. • Bake, one sheet at a time, for 10–15 minutes, or until golden brown. Transfer the cookies with holes to racks. • Place a marshmallow on the top of each whole cookie and bake for 3 minutes, or until the marshmallow has melted. Immediately stick a ring cookie on top of each marshmallow base. • Transfer to racks to cool.

Makes: about 16 cookies • Prep: 30 min + 30 min to chill Cooking: 10–15 min • Level: 1

DECORATED COOKIES

Cookie Base: Mix the flour, baking soda, and salt in a medium bowl. • Use a pastry blender to cut in the butter until the mixture resembles fine crumbs. • Stir in the brown sugar. • Add the honey and enough egg to form a stiff dough. • Press the dough into a disk, wrap in plastic wrap, and refrigerate for 30 minutes. • Preheat the oven to 375°F (190°C/gas 5). • Butter two cookie sheets. • Roll out the dough on a lightly floured surface to a thickness of ¼ inch (5 mm). • Use various shaped cookie cutters to cut out the cookies. • Gather the dough scraps, re-roll, and continue cutting out cookies until all the dough is used. • Use a spatula to transfer the cookies to the prepared cookie sheets, placing them 1 inch (2.5 cm) apart. • Bake for 7–10 minutes, or until pale gold. • Transfer to racks to cool. • Spread the tops of the cookies with the preserves. • Roll out the fondant on a surface lightly dusted with confectioners' sugar to ¼ inch (5 mm) thick. • Cut out the same shapes to top the cookies with the fondant. Place the matching shape of icing on top of each cookie. • Use a paint brush to decorate the tops of the cookies with the food colorings.

Makes: about 15 cookies • Prep: 30 min • Cooking: 50–55 min • Level: 1

Cookie Base
- 1⅔ cups/250 g) all-purpose (plain) flour
- 1 teaspoon baking powder
- ½ teaspoon salt
- ¾ cup (180 g) butter, softened
- 1½ cups (300 g) firmly packed light brown sugar
- 1 teaspoon vanilla extract (essence)
- 1 large egg, lightly beaten

Prune Filling
- 1¼ cups (300 g) pitted prunes
- 2 cups (500 ml) water
- ¼ cup (60 g) honey
- finely grated zest and juice of ¼ lemon

PECAN WEDDING CAKES

- 1 cup (250 g) butter, softened
- 1¾ cups (275 g) confectioners' (icing) sugar
- 2½ cups (425 g) all-purpose (plain) flour
- 1 teaspoon vanilla extract (essence)

Beat the butter and ¾ cup (125 g) confectioners' sugar in a large bowl with an electric mixer at high speed until creamy. • Mix in the flour, vanilla and almond extracts, and pecans. • Refrigerate for 30 minutes. • Preheat the oven to 350°F (180°C/gas 4). • Butter three cookie sheets. • Form the dough into balls the size of walnuts and place 2 inches (5 cm) apart on the prepared cookie sheets. • Use the bottom of a glass to flatten them slightly. • Bake, one sheet at a time, for 12–15 minutes, or until lightly browned. • Transfer to racks and let cool completely. • Roll in the remaining confectioners' sugar until well coated.

Makes: about 35 cookies • Prep: 35 min + 30 min to chill Cooking: 12–15 min • Level: 1

- 1 teaspoon almond extract (essence)
- 1 cup (100 g) finely chopped pecans

Pink drizzlers

PINK DRIZZLERS

- 1 cup (150 g) all-purpose (plain) flour
- 3/4 cup (125 g) cornstarch (cornflour)
- 2 teaspoons unsweetened cocoa powder
- 1 teaspoon ground cinnamon
- 1/2 teaspoon allspice
- 1/2 teaspoon baking soda (bicarbonate of soda)
- 1/4 teaspoon ground ginger
- 1/4 teaspoon freshly grated nutmeg
- 1/4 teaspoon salt
- 1/2 cup (125 g) butter
- 3/4 cup (140 g) sugar
- 1 tablespoon light corn (golden) syrup
- 2 large eggs
- 2–3 tablespoons raspberry preserves
- 3–4 tablespoons confectioners' (icing) sugar
- 3–4 teaspoons warm water
- 2 drops red food coloring

Mix the flour, cornstarch, cocoa, cinnamon, allspice, baking soda, ginger, nutmeg, and salt in a medium bowl. • Beat the butter, sugar, and corn syrup in a large bowl with an electric mixer at medium speed until creamy. • Add the eggs, beating until just blended. • Mix in the dry ingredients to form a smooth dough. Press the dough into a disk, wrap in plastic wrap, and refrigerate for 30 minutes. • Preheat the oven to 350°F (180°C/gas 4). • Butter two cookie sheets. • Roll out the dough on a lightly floured surface to 1/2 inch (1 cm) thick. • Use a 2-inch (5-cm) cutter to cut into rounds. • Transfer the cookies to the prepared cookie sheets, placing them 1 inch (2.5 cm) apart. • Bake for 8–10 minutes, or until firm. • Cool completely on the cookie sheets. • Stick the cookies together in pairs with the preserves. • Mix the confectioners' sugar, water, and food coloring to make a soft frosting. Spread the frosting over the tops.

Makes: about 20 cookies • Prep: 30 min + 30 min to chill Cooking: 8–10 min • Level: 1

HANUKKAH COOKIES

Beat the butter and cream cheese in a large bowl with an electric mixer at high speed until creamy. • Mix in the flour to form a smooth dough. Divide the dough in half and press each half into a disk. Wrap in plastic wrap and refrigerate for 30 minutes. • Preheat the oven to 375°F (190°C/gas 5). • Set out two cookie sheets. • Combine the raisins, sugar, and cinnamon in a small bowl. • Roll out one piece of the dough on a lightly floured surface to 1/4-inch (5-mm) thick circle. • Cut the circle into sixteen wedges. • Sprinkle half the raisin mixture over the entire surface, leaving a 1/4-inch (5-mm) border. • Roll up each wedge from the wide end to the point, tucking the point under. Repeat with the remaining dough and filling. • Transfer the cookies to the cookie sheets. • Bake for 10–15 minutes, or until the bottoms are lightly browned, rotating the sheets halfway through for even baking. • Transfer to racks and let cool completely. • Dust with the confectioners' sugar.

Makes: 32 cookies • Prep: 30 min • Cooking: 10–15 min Level: 2

- 2 cups (500 g) butter, softened
- 1 lb (500 g) cream cheese, softened
- 2 cups (300 g) all-purpose (plain) flour
- 1/2 cup (70 g) golden raisins (sultanas)
- 2 tablespoons granulated sugar
- 1 tablespoon ground cinnamon
- 4 tablespoons confectioners' (icing) sugar, to dust

FLORENTINES

- 1/2 cup (125 ml) heavy (double) cream
- 1/2 vanilla pod
- 1 cup (200 g) sugar
- 1/4 cup (60 g) butter
- 1 1/3 cups flaked almonds
- 1 1/3 cups hazelnuts, coarsely chopped
- 1 1/2 cups mixed candied peel, coarsely chopped

Preheat the oven to 350°F. • Butter two cookie sheets. Bring the cream, vanilla pod, sugar, and butter to a boil in a medium saucepan over low heat, stirring constantly. • Remove from the heat. • Let cool completely and remove the vanilla pod. • Stir together the almonds, hazelnuts, candied peel, cherries, and flour in a medium bowl. Mix the dry ingredients into the cream mixture. • Use a tablespoon to drop 2-inch heaps of batter onto the prepared cookie sheets, spacing 2 inches

apart. • Bake for 10–15 minutes, or until golden brown. • Cool the cookies on the cookie sheets for 3 minutes. • Use a thin metal spatula to transfer to racks and let cool completely. • Melt the chocolates separately in double boilers over barely simmering water. • Use the metal spatula to spread a thin layer of both chocolates on the smooth side of the cookies. • Use a fork to make wavy lines across the chocolate.

Makes: about 30 cookies • Prep: 50 min • Cooking: 10–15 min • Level: 3

- 1/4 cup (30 g) candied cherries, finely chopped
- 1/3 cup (50 g) all-purpose (plain) flour
- 3 oz (90 g) semisweet (dark) chocolate, coarsely chopped
- 3 oz (90 g) white chocolate, coarsely chopped

Party Cookies

HONEY BEE COOKIES

- 1¼ cups (180 g) whole-wheat (wholemeal) flour
- ½ teaspoon baking powder
- ⅛ teaspoon salt
- 2 tablespoons honey
- ⅓ cup (90 ml) extra-virgin olive oil
- ½ teaspoon vanilla extract (essence)
- 1 large egg
- 1–2 tablespoons milk (optional)
- ⅓ cup (50 g) confectioners' (icing) sugar

Preheat the oven to 350°F (180°C/gas 4). • Butter two cookie sheets. • Mix the flour, baking powder, and salt in a medium bowl. • Mix the honey and olive oil in a large bowl until well blended. • Add the vanilla and egg, beating until just blended. • Mix in the dry ingredients to form a soft dough. • If the dough is stiff, add the milk. • Fit a pastry bag with ½-inch (1-cm) star tip. Fill the pastry bag, twist the opening tightly closed, and squeeze out small heaps, spacing 2 inches (5 cm) apart on the prepared cookie sheet. • Bake for 15–20 minutes, or until lightly browned. • Transfer to racks to cool. • Dust with the confectioners' sugar.

Makes: about 28 cookies • Prep: 25 min • Cooking: 15–20 min • Level: 2

PASSOVER COOKIES

- 5 large eggs
- 2½ cups (500 g) sugar
- 1¼ cups (300 ml) vegetable oil
- 1¼ cups (180 g) matzo meal
- 1½ cups (225 g) unsweetened cocoa powder
- 1¼ cups (125 g) finely chopped pecans

Preheat the oven to 325°F (170°C/gas 3). • Oil a 13 x 9-inch (33 x 23-cm) baking pan. • Beat the eggs and sugar in a large bowl with an electric mixer at high speed until pale and thick. • Beat in the oil until well blended. • Mix in the matzo meal and cocoa. • Pour the batter into the prepared pan and sprinkle with the pecans. • Bake for 30–35 minutes, or until dry on top and almost firm to the touch. Do not overbake. • Cool completely before cutting into bars.

Makes: about 35 cookies • Prep: 25 min • Cooking: 30–35 min • Level: 1

HAMANTASCHEN

- 1½ cups (375 g) vegetable shortening
- 1 cup (200 g) sugar
- 3 large eggs
- 3 tablespoons honey
- 2 tablespoons freshly squeezed lemon juice
- ⅓ cup (90 ml) cold water
- ½ teaspoon vanilla extract (essence)
- 4 cups (600 g) all-purpose (plain) flour
- 1 lb (500 g) dried pitted prunes, soaked overnight and drained
- 1¼ cups (125 g) coarsely chopped walnuts
- 2 teaspoons ground cinnamon

Beat the shortening and ½ cup (100 g) sugar in a large bowl with an electric mixer at high speed until creamy. • Add 2 eggs, beating until just blended. • Stir in the honey, 1 tablespoon lemon juice, water, and vanilla. • Mix in the flour to form a smooth dough. Press into a disk, cover with plastic wrap, and refrigerate for 30 minutes. • Preheat the oven to 375°F (190°C/gas 5). • Butter three cookie sheets. • Chop the prunes coarsely. • Mix the prunes, walnuts, remaining 1 tablespoon lemon juice, 1 teaspoon cinnamon, and 1 tablespoon sugar in a small bowl. • Roll out the dough on a lightly floured surface to ¼ inch (5 mm) thick. • Use a 3-inch (8-cm) cookie cutter to cut out the cookies. Gather the dough scraps, re-roll, and continue cutting out cookies until all the dough is used. • Drop teaspoons of the prune mixture into the center of the cookies. • Lift up three sides of each circle to form a triangular shape, pinching the edges of the dough together to seal. • Beat the remaining egg and brush over the cookies. Mix the remaining sugar and 1 teaspoon cinnamon and sprinkle over the cookies. • Use a spatula to transfer the cookies to the cookie sheets, placing them 2 inches (5 cm) apart. • Bake, one sheet at a time, for 12–15 minutes, or until just golden at the edges. • Transfer to racks and let cool completely.

Makes: about 45 cookies • Prep: 30 min + 30 min to chill Cooking: 12–15 min • Level: 2

Party Cookies

PINWHEEL COOKIES

- 2½ cups (425 g) all-purpose (plain) flour
- ½ teaspoon baking soda (bicarbonate of soda)
- 1 teaspoon ground cinnamon
- ⅛ teaspoon salt
- 1 cup (250 g) butter, softened
- ½ cup (100 g) sugar
- ⅔ cup (100 g) finely ground almonds
- ½ cup (90 g) dried currants
- 2 teaspoons caraway seeds (optional)
- 1 large egg, lightly beaten
- 2 teaspoons water

Mix the flour, baking soda, cinnamon, and salt in a large bowl. • Cut in the butter until the mixture resembles fine crumbs. • Stir in the sugar, almonds, currants, caraway seeds, if using. • Add the egg and mix until firm. • Refrigerate for 30 minutes. • Preheat the oven to 400°F (200°C/gas 6). • Butter two cookie sheets. • Roll out the dough to an 8 x 6-inch (20 x 15-cm) rectangle. • Brush lightly with water. Sprinkle with the remaining sugar. • Cut the dough into ½ x 6-inch (1 x 15-cm) long strips and shape into rounded ropes. Form each rope into a tight circular coil. Transfer the cookies to the prepared cookie sheets, flattening them slightly. • Bake for 10–12 minutes, or until golden brown. • Transfer to racks to cool.

Makes: about 25 cookies • Prep: 35 min + 30 min to chill
Cooking: 10–12 min • Level: 1

SPICED CRISPIES

Mix the flour, cinnamon, cloves, ginger, and baking powder in a large bowl. • Melt the butter with the sugar and corn syrup in a medium saucepan. • Let cool for 10 minutes. • Stir in the almonds, lemon zest, and candied peel. • Mix in the dry ingredients. • Refrigerate for 1 hour, or until firm. • Preheat the oven to 375°F (190°C/gas 5). • Butter two cookie sheets. • Roll out the dough to ¼ inch (5 mm) thick. • Use a 2-inch (5-cm) cookie cutter to cut out the cookies. Continue cutting out cookies until all the dough is used. • Transfer the cookies to the prepared cookie sheets, placing them 1 inch (2.5 cm) apart. • Place a flaked almond piece on top of each cookie. • Bake for 8–10 minutes, or until just golden. • Transfer to racks to cool.

Makes: about 30 cookies • Prep: 30 min + 1 hr to chill
Cooking: 8–10 min • Level: 1

- 2 cups (300 g) all-purpose (plain flour
- 2 tablespoons ground cinnamon
- 2 teaspoons ground cloves
- 1½ teaspoons ground ginger
- 1 teaspoon baking powder
- ¼ teaspoon salt
- ⅔ cup (150 g) butter, cut up
- ⅔ cup (140 g) sugar
- ½ cup (125 ml) light corn (golden) syrup
- ⅓ cup (30 g) coarsely chopped almonds
- 1 tablespoon finely grated lemon zest
- 1 tablespoon finely chopped mixed candied peel
- 1 tablespoon flaked almonds

Pinwheel cookies

Pecan and cranberry bars

GERMAN SPICE COOKIES

- ³/₄ cup (125 g) all-purpose (plain) flour
- 1 teaspoon ground cinnamon
- ¹/₄ teaspoon ground cloves
- ¹/₂ teaspoon ground mace
- ¹/₈ teaspoon salt
- ¹/₂ teaspoon finely grated lemon zest
- ¹/₈ teaspoon ground aniseeds
- ¹/₈ teaspoon ground black pepper
- ¹/₃ cup (90 ml) honey
- ¹/₃ cup (90 ml) light molasses (treacle)
- ¹/₄ cup (50 g) sugar
- 2 tablespoons butter
- 1 large egg, lightly beaten

Preheat the oven to 375°F (190°C/gas 5).
• Butter two cookie sheets. • Mix the flour, cinnamon, cloves, mace, and salt in a large bowl. • Stir in the lemon zest, aniseeds, and black pepper. • Mix the honey, molasses, and granulated sugar in a medium saucepan over low heat. • Cook, stirring constantly, until the sugar has dissolved completely.
• Add the butter and remove from the heat.
• Add the egg, beating until just blended.
• Mix in the dry ingredients to form a stiff dough. • Drop teaspoons of the dough 2 inches (5 cm) apart onto the prepared sheets. • Bake for 12–15 minutes, or until firm and golden brown. • Cool on the sheets until the cookies firm slightly. • Transfer to racks and let cool completely.

Makes: about 30 cookies • Prep: 40 min • Cooking: 12–15 min • Level: 1

PECAN AND CRANBERRY BARS

Preheat the oven to 350°F (180°C/gas 4).
• Butter a 9-inch (23-cm) square baking pan.
• Mix the flour, cinnamon, and salt into a medium bowl. • Mix the butter and sugar in a medium bowl. • Add the egg, beating until just blended. • Mix in the dry ingredients, pecans, and cranberries until well blended.
• Spread the mixture in the prepared pan.
• Bake for 30–35 minutes, or until just golden and a toothpick inserted into the center comes out clean. • Cool completely in the pan. • Dust with the confectioners' sugar and cut into squares.

Makes: about 16 bars • Prep: 20 min • Cooking: 30–35 min Level: 1

- 1 cup (150 g) all-purpose (plain) flour
- ¹/₂ teaspoon ground cinnamon
- ¹/₈ teaspoon salt
- ¹/₄ cup (60 g) butter, melted
- ³/₄ cup (150 g) sugar
- 1 large egg, lightly beaten
- ²/₃ cup (70 g) finely chopped pecans
- ¹/₂ cup (125 g) fresh or frozen cranberries
- 2 tablespoons confectioners' (icing) sugar, to dust

Party Cookies

SPIDERS' WEB COOKIES

• 18 Dusted Sugar Cookies (see page 54)

Fondant
• 2 cups (400 g) granulated sugar
• 3/4 cup (180 ml) cold water
• 1/4 teaspoon cream of tartar
• 2 tablespoons confectioners' (icing) sugar, to dust
• 1/2 cup (160 g) apricot preserves
• 4 oz (125 g) bittersweet (dark) chocolate, coarsely chopped

Prepare the cookies and let cool completely. • Fondant: Bring the sugar, water, and cream of tartar to a boil in a medium saucepan. Wash down the sides of the pan with a pastry brush dipped in cold water to prevent sugar crystals from forming. Cook, without stirring, until the mixture reaches 238°F (114°C), or the soft-ball stage. • Sprinkle a lightly oiled baking sheet with cold water. Pour the fondant syrup onto the sheet and let cool until warm, 10–15 minutes. When ready, the fondant should hold an indentation made with a fingertip. • Work the fondant, lifting from the edges toward the center, folding it until it begins to thicken, lose its gloss, and turn pure white. • Dust your hands with confectioners' sugar and knead the fondant until smooth. Place in a bowl and cover with a clean cloth. Let stand overnight. • Knead the fondant until malleable. Roll out on a surface lightly dusted with confectioners' sugar to 1/4 inch (5 mm) thick. • Drape the fondant over the cookies and cut out the fondant to fit the tops of the cookies. • Warm the preserves in a small saucepan over low heat until liquid. • Spread the preserves over the cookies and place the fondant layers on top. • Melt the chocolate in a double boiler over barely simmering water. • Spoon the chocolate into a freezer bag and cut off a tiny corner. • Pipe over the cookies in concentric circles. • Let stand for 5 minutes until set. • Draw through the lines from the center outward to create a spider's web effect.

Makes: about 18 cookies • Prep: 1 hr • Cooking: 8–10 min Level: 3

BOWTIE COOKIE

Preheat the oven to 400°F (200°C/gas 6). • Butter a cookie sheet. • Use a pencil and ruler to draw a 12 x 8-inch (30 x 20-cm) rectangle on a sheet of parchment paper. Draw triangles, points facing inward, at each end of the rectangle to resemble a double-edged bowtie. Cut out the template. • Place the template on the prepared cookie sheet. • Beat the butter and confectioners' sugar in a large bowl with an electric mixer at high speed until creamy. • Stir in the egg whites, followed by the flour and salt. • If the mixture separates, place over barely simmering water and mix. • Set aside 2 tablespoons of the mixture. Stir the cocoa into the remaining batter. • Use a thin metal spatula to spread a small amount of plain cookie batter around the inside edge of the template to form a border. • Spread the remaining plain batter in the center of the template. • Spoon the cocoa batter into a small plastic freezer bag. Cut off the corner and pipe over the edges. • Bake for 8–10 minutes, or until just golden. • Use a spatula to loosen the edges and transfer to a rack to cool completely.

Makes: 1 large cookie • Prep: 30 min • Cooking: 8–10 min Level: 2

• 1/3 cup (90 g) butter, softened
• 3/4 cup (125 g) confectioners' (icing) sugar
• 4 large egg whites, lightly beaten
• 1/2 cup (75 g) all-purpose (plain) flour
• 1/8 teaspoon salt
• 1 tablespoon unsweetened cocoa powder

Party Cookies

FESTIVE WALNUT CRANBERRY BARS

- 1¼ cups (180 g) all-purpose (plain) flour
- ⅛ teaspoon salt
- ½ cup (125 g) butter, melted
- ¾ cup (150 g) sugar
- 1 large egg, lightly beaten
- ⅔ cup (70 g) finely chopped walnuts
- ½ cup (125 g) fresh or frozen cranberries
- 1 cup (150 g) confectioners' (icing) sugar
- 2–3 tablespoons hot water
- 2–3 drops red food coloring

Preheat the oven to 350°F (180°C/gas 4).
• Butter a 9-inch (23-cm) baking pan. • Mix the flour and salt in a medium bowl. • Mix the butter and sugar in a medium bowl.
• Add the egg, beating until just blended.
• Mix in the dry ingredients, walnuts, and cranberries. • Spread the mixture in the prepared pan. • Bake for 30–35 minutes, or until golden and a toothpick inserted into the center comes out clean. • Cool completely in the pan. • Cut into squares.
• Mix the confectioners' sugar and water in a small bowl. Add the food coloring until well blended. Drizzle the glaze over the tops of the cookies.

Makes: about 20 bars • Prep: 20 min • Cooking: 30–35 min Level: 1

SPICY COOKIE SANDWICHES

Mix the flour, cocoa, allspice, cinnamon, ginger, and salt in a medium bowl. • Beat the butter and sugar in a large bowl with an electric mixer at medium speed until creamy. • Add the egg yolk and lemon zest and juice, beating until just blended. • Mix in the dry ingredients and almonds to form a stiff dough. • Press the dough into a disk, wrap in plastic wrap (cling film), and refrigerate for 30 minutes. • Preheat the oven to 350°F (180°C/gas 4). • Set out three cookie sheets. • Roll out the dough on a lightly floured surface to ¼ inch (5 mm) thick. • Use a 2-inch (5-cm) cookie cutter to cut out the cookies. • Transfer the cookies to the cookie sheets, placing them 1 inch (2.5 cm) apart. • Bake for 25–35 minutes, or until lightly browned and firm to the touch.
• Transfer to racks to cool. • Stick the cookies together in pairs with the preserves.

Makes: about 15 cookies • Prep: 25 min + 30 min to chill Cooking: 25–35 min Level: 1

- ⅔ cup (100 g) all-purpose (plain) flour
- 2 teaspoons unsweetened cocoa powder
- ½ teaspoon ground allspice
- ½ teaspoon ground cinnamon
- ½ teaspoon ground ginger
- ⅛ teaspoon salt
- ¾ cup (180 g) butter, softened
- ½ cup (100 g) sugar
- 1 large egg yolk
- 1 tablespoon finely grated lemon zest
- 2 tablespoons freshly squeezed lemon juice
- 2 cups (300 g) finely ground almonds
- ⅓ cup (60 g) raspberry preserves (jam)

BUTTER DIAMONDS

- 2 cups (500 g) all-purpose (plain) flour
- 1 teaspoon ground cinnamon
- 1 teaspoon ground ginger
- ⅛ teaspoon salt
- 1 cup (250 g) butter, softened
- 1 cup (200 g) sugar
- 1 teaspoon almond extract (essence)
- 1 large egg, separated
- 1 tablespoon cold water
- 1 cup (100 g) finely chopped walnuts

Preheat the oven to 350°F (180°C/gas 4).
• Butter a 10½ x 15½-inch (26 x 36-cm) jelly-roll pan. • Mix the flour, cinnamon, ginger, and salt in a medium bowl. • Beat the butter and sugar in a large bowl with an electric mixer at medium speed until creamy. • Add the almond extract and egg yolk, beating until just blended. • Mix in the dry ingredients to form a smooth dough. • Firmly press the dough into the pan in an even layer. • Beat the egg white and water in a small bowl and brush it over the dough. Sprinkle with walnuts. • Bake for 15–20 minutes, or until lightly browned. • Cool completely in the pan. • Cut into diamonds.

Makes: about 18 cookies • Prep: 20 min • Cooking: 15–20 min • Level: 1

ZESTY COOKIES

Preheat the oven to 375°F (190°C/gas 5).
• Butter two cookie sheets. • Mix the all-purpose and rice flours, baking powder, and salt in a medium bowl. • Beat the butter and sugar in a large bowl with an electric mixer until creamy. • Add the egg and lemon zest, beating until just blended. • Mix in the dry ingredients. • Drop tablespoons of the dough 1 inch (2.5 cm) apart onto the prepared cookie sheets. • Bake for 8–10 minutes, or until pale golden. • Transfer to racks to cool.

Makes: about 20 cookies • Prep: 25 min • Cooking: 8–10 min • Level: 1

- 1¾ cups (275 g) all-purpose (plain) flour
- ⅓ cup (50 g) rice flour
- 1¼ teaspoons baking powder
- ⅛ teaspoon salt
- ¼ cup (60 g) butter, softened
- ¾ cup (150 g) sugar
- 1 large egg
- 1 tablespoon finely grated lemon zest

BASIC RECIPES

The cookies in this book were all tested using large (2-oz/60-g) eggs. Remember to take the eggs out of the refrigerator an hour or two before you begin baking. Butter should also stay an hour or so at room temperature to soften a little before use. Modern flour is all pre-sifted so there is no need to sift it before adding to the batter. Always use shiny, light-colored (silver) baking sheets for baking cookies; they spread the heat more evenly than darker ones and will brown the bottoms of your cookies without burning them. Most cookies are quick and easy to make, although some taste better with frosting and others can be stuck together in pairs with lemon curd or buttercream. In this chapter we have selected just eight basic recipes that can be used with many of the recipes in this book.

Rolled cookie dough

Basic Recipes

RICH CHOCOLATE FROSTING

- 2 cups (400 g) sugar
- 1 cup (250 mld) heavy (double) cream + 1–2 tablespoons as needed
- 8 oz (250 g) bittersweet (dark) chocolate, coarsely chopped
- 2 tablespoons butter
- 1 teaspoon vanilla extract (essence)

Replace the bittersweet chocolate in this recipe with the same amount of milk or white chocolate, as required.
Bring the sugar and 1 cup cream to a boil in a saucepan over medium heat. Boil for 1 minute, then remove from the heat. • Stir in the chocolate. • Return the saucepan to medium heat and cook, without stirring, until the mixture reaches 238°F (115°C), or the soft-ball stage. Remove from the heat. • Add the butter and vanilla, without stirring, and place the saucepan in a larger pan of cold water for 5 minutes before stirring. • Beat with a wooden spoon until the frosting begins to lose its sheen, 5–10 minutes. Immediately stir in 1 tablespoon cream. Do not let the frosting harden too much before adding the cream. • Let stand for 3–4 minutes, then stir until it has a spreadable consistency. Add more cream, 1 teaspoon at a time, if it is too stiff.
Makes about 2 cups (500 g) • Prep: 15 min • Cooking: 10 min • Level: 1

CHOCOLATE FROSTING

Stir together the confectioners' sugar and cocoa in a double boiler. Add the butter, vanilla, and enough of the water to make a firm paste. • Stir over simmering water until the frosting has a spreadable consistency, about 3 minutes.
Makes: about 1 cup (250 g) • Prep: 5 min • Level: 1

- 2 cups (300 g) confectioners' (icing) sugar
- 1/4 cup (30 g) unsweetened cocoa powder
- 2 tablespoons butter, softened
- 1 teaspoon vanilla extract (essence)
- about 2 tablespoons boiling water

LEMON CURD

- 3 large eggs
- 1/2 cup (100 g) sugar
- 3 tablespoons finely grated lemon zest
- 1/3 cup (90 mld) freshly squeezed lemon juice
- 1/2 cup (125 g) butter, cut up

Replace the lemon zest and juice with lime zest and juice for a delicious homemade lime curd.
Beat the eggs, sugar, and lemon zest and juice in a saucepan until well blended. Cook over low heat, stirring constantly with a wooden spoon, until the mixture lightly coats a wooden spoon or registers 160°F (80°C) on an instant-read thermometer. • Add the butter, stirring until it has melted before adding more. Immediately plunge the pan into a bowl of ice water and stir until the mixture has cooled. • Transfer to a bowl, cover with plastic wrap, and refrigerate.
Makes about 1 1/2 cups (350 g) • Prep: 25 min • Level: 1

VANILLA SUGAR

Fill a glass jar with the sugar. • Add the vanilla pods, seal tightly, and set aside for 7–10 days. When you open the jar, the sugar will be flavored with vanilla. • As the pods have a long aromatic life, just add more sugar as needed.
Makes: about 2 cup (400 g) • Prep: 7–10 days • Level: 1

- 2 cups (400 g) sugar
- 2 vanilla pods, cut into 2 or 3 pieces

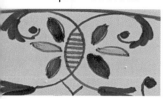

COFFEE BUTTERCREAM

- 2 tablespoons very strong black coffee, lukewarm
- 3/4 cup (150 g) sugar
- 3 large egg yolks
- 1 cup (250 g) butter, softened

Stir the coffee and sugar in a saucepan over medium heat. • Cook, without stirring, until the mixture reaches 238°F (114°C), or the soft-ball stage. • Beat the egg yolks in a double boiler with an electric mixer at high speed until pale. • Gradually beat the syrup into the beaten yolks. • Place over barely simmering water, stirring constantly with a wooden spoon, until the mixture lightly coats a metal spoon. • Immediately plunge the pan into a bowl of ice water and stir until cooled. • Beat the butter in a large bowl until creamy. Beat into the egg mixture.

Makes: about 2 cups (500 g) • Prep: 25 min • Level: 1

CHOCOLATE BUTTER FROSTING

Beat the butter in a medium bowl with an electric mixer at high speed until creamy. • Beat in the confectioners' sugar and cocoa until well blended.

Makes: about 1 cup (250 g) • Prep: 5 min • Level: 1

- 1/2 cup (125 g) butter, softened
- 1 cup (150 g) confectioners' (icing) sugar
- 1/3 cup (50 g) unsweetened cocoa powder

Coffee buttercream

Vanilla frosting

VANILLA FROSTING

- 1½ cups (300 g) sugar
- 2 large egg whites
- ⅓ cup (90 mld) water
- ¼ teaspoon salt
- ¼ teaspoon cream of tartar
- 1 teaspoon vanilla extract (essence)

Stir the sugar, egg whites, water, salt, and cream of tartar in a saucepan until blended. Cook over low heat, beating constantly with an electric mixer at low speed until the whites register 160°F (80°C) on an instant-read thermometer. Transfer to a bowl and beat at high speed until the egg whites form stiff peaks. • Remove from the heat and stir in the vanilla. • Beat until smooth and spreadable.

Makes about 2 cups (500 mld) • Prep: 10 min • Level: 1

CHOUX PASTRY

Place the water, butter, sugar, and salt in a large pan over medium-low heat. When the mixture boils, remove from the heat and add the flour all at once. • Use a wooden spoon to stir vigorously until a smooth paste forms. Return to medium heat and stir constantly until the mixture pulls away from the pan sides. Remove from the heat and let cool for 5 minutes. • Add the eggs, beating until just blended after each addition. • Use as required.

Makes: about 14 oz (400 g) • Prep: 25 min • Level: 3

- 2 cups (500 mld) water
- ⅔ cup (180 g) butter, cut up
- 1 tablespoon sugar
- ¼ teaspoon salt
- 1⅔ cups (250 g) all-purpose (plain) flour

INDEX

A

Ali baba bites, 271
All saints cookies, 396
Allspice biscotti, 130
Allspice cookies, 179
Almond banana crisp, 232
Almond brittle, 278
Almond butter wedges, 27
Almond chocolate chip cookies, 90
Almond crisps, 46
Almond fingers, 123
Almond garlands, 382
Almond lace cookies, 378
Almond macaroons with candied cherries, 268
Almond madeleines, 294
Almond poppy seed cookies, 202
Almond rose water balls, 121
Almond rum tartlets, 309
Almond shell cookies, 324
Almond squares, 124
Almond star macaroons, 268
Almond tartlets, 315
Almond toffee squares, 234
Almond tuiles, 396
Almond waves, 142
Almond wedgies, 43
Amaretti rice fritters, 347
American cookies, 168
Angelica christmas cookies, 372
Angelica moments, 257

Aniseed and olive oil cookies, 207
Aniseed biscotti, 131
Aniseed cookies, 136
Aniseed muffins, 331
Anzac cookies, 188
Apple and raisin muffins, 332
Apple and walnut cookies, 153
Apple fritters, 346
Apple squares, 242
Apricot bars, 236
Apricot brandy macaroons, 266

B

Banana and sunflower seed cookies, 152
Banana chocolate chip cookies, 75
Banana chocolate chip muffins, 336
Banana fritters, 340
Banana squares, 280
Barbados cream kisses, 105
Battered fresh fruit, 353
Belgian krumkake cookies, 370
Berry crisps, 396
Birthday lollipops, 391
Bittersweet caramel squares, 216
Black pepper and spice cookies, 113
Blueberry friands, 300
Blueberry muffins with white chocolate frosting, 331

Bowtie cookie, 408
Bran flake squares, 242
Bran muffins, 324
Brandy fritters, 350
Brandy wedges, 27
Breakfast cookies, 198
British cookies, 175
Brown pecan shortbread, 38
Brown sugar drops, 36
Brown sugar fritters, 364
Brown sugar kisses, 52
Brown sugar meringues, 246
Brown sugar pecan snaps, 57
Buckwheat muffins, 316
Butter bars with dried currants, 227
Butter cookies with chocolate, 20
Butter diamonds, 410
Butter esses, 31
Butter rings, 29
Butter wreaths, 20
Buttercream kisses, 96
Butterfly cakes, 313
Buttermilk cookies, 48
Butterscotch pecan cookies, 186

C

Café kisses, 96
Café squares, 214
Candied cherry and ginger bars, 231
Candied citrus cookies, 180
Candied fruit and ginger cookies, 175

Candied fruit delights, 179
Candied peel macaroons, 264
Cannoli, 348
Caramel squares, 216
Caraway crisps, 46
Caraway diamonds, 120
Caraway moments, 204
Caraway rose cookies, 46
Cardamom biscotti, 131
Cardamom cookies, 119
Cardamom fritters, 340
Carnival fritters, 348
Carrot and orange cookies, 152
Carrot and pine nut muffins, 333
Cashew and pear muffins, 331
Cashew squares, 136
Cavour biscotti, 102
Cherry almond biscotti, 180
Cherry almond muffins, 334
Cherry and white chocolate cookies, 75
Cherry cookies, 150
Cherry oaties, 194
Cherry shortbread, 20
Cherry-topped shortbread, 20
Cherry-topped whirls, 40
Chewy brown cookies, 172
Chewy fruit squares, 231
Chewy raisin cookies, 168
Chewy rolled oat squares, 224

Choc-top drops, 69
Chocolate almond bites, 66
Chocolate almond macaroons, 259
Chocolate almond meringues, 246
Chocolate amaretti cookies, 259
Chocolate and date cookies, 280
Chocolate and vanilla piped cookies, 32
Chocolate apricot pretzels, 80
Chocolate butter frosting, 416
Chocolate cherry drops, 280
Chocolate chile muffins, 326
Chocolate chip and candied cherry cookies, 62
Chocolate chip cookie cakes, 76
Chocolate chip wedgies, 22
Chocolate chip wedges, 75
Chocolate citrus twists, 84
Chocolate coconut muffins, 326
Chocolate corny squares, 279
Chocolate cream kisses, 62
Chocolate diamonds, 120
Chocolate died fruit wafers, 80
Chocolate fleck cookies, 88
Chocolate frosting, 414
Chocolate fruit and nut squares, 222
Chocolate fruit chewies, 274

Chocolate fruit squares, 289
Chocolate ginger biscotti, 132
Chocolate hazelnut balls, 289
Chocolate hazelnut cookies, 70
Chocolate hazelnut hearts, 79
Chocolate hazelnut truffles, 72
Chocolate madeleines, 298
Chocolate mandarin salami, 286
Chocolate marshmallow bites, 285
Chocolate marshmallow slice, 274
Chocolate meringues, 246
Chocolate mice, 386
Chocolate mint squares, 218
Chocolate muffins with cherry topping, 320
Chocolate cinnamon munchies, 77
Chocolate munchies, 65
Chocolate nut biscotti, 84
Chocolate nut brownies, 236
Chocolate nut squares, 222
Chocolate oat squares, 228
Chocolate orange cookies, 86
Chocolate orange truffles, 286
Chocolate paprika cookies, 84
Chocolate peanut bites, 72
Chocolate-peanut squares, 274

Chocolate pecan wedges, 88
Chocolate pretzels, 92
Chocolate raspberry squares, 214
Chocolate rice krispie squares, 282
Chocolate salami, 274
Chocolate sandwiches, 64
Chocolate spice cookies, 88
Chocolate squares, 219
Chocolate tipped arches, 65
Chocolate vanilla cookies, 66
Chocolate vanilla drop cookies, 76
Chocolate wafers, 88
Chocolate walnut squares, 290
Chocolate wheel cookies, 69
Choux pastry, 417
Christmas baubles, 374
Christmas butter cookies, 380
Christmas card cookies, 380
Christmas cherry cookies, 380
Christmas cookies, 377
Christmas rings, 376
Christmas stars, 376
Christmas stocking cookies, 378
Christmas tree cookies, 383
Christmas twists, 375
Church window cookies, 375
Churros, 365
Cinnamon chocolate macaroons, 262
Cinnamon christmas cookies, 378

Cinnamon crisps with strawberry, 54
Cinnamon fritters, 364
Cinnamon hazelnut cookies, 108
Cinnamon pecan cookies, 116
Cinnamon raisin cookies, 175
Cinnamon whole-wheat bars, 238
Citrus and hazelnut cookies, 156
Citrus cream cookies, 155
Citrus crisps, 260
Citrus moons, 148
Citrus shortbread, 19
Cocoa balls, 77
Cocoa corn flake cookies, 80
Coconut almond squares, 227
Coconut and walnut shortbread, 24
Coconut biscotti, 130
Coconut cookies, 164
Coconut cranberry muffins, 324
Coconut cream macaroons, 262
Coconut crescents, 176
Coconut crisps, 188
Coconut cut outs, 188
Coconut honey thins, 142
Coconut kisses with chocolate cream, 166
Coconut lime bites, 170
Coconut macaroons, 252
Coconut meringues, 248
Coconut oat cookies, 170
Coconut oatmeal cookies, 211
Coconut squares with candied cherries, 227
Coconut squares with chocolate, 276

Coconut tartlets, 306
Coffee and pecan wedges, 278
Coffee and walnut wedgies, 289
Coffee butterball cookies, 98
Coffee buttercream, 416
Coffee drops, 101
Coffee eclairs, 312
Coffee madeleines, 296
Coffee meringues, 248
Coffee pecan thins, 142
Coffee pinwheels, 96
Coffee-glazed hazelnut cookies, 100
Coriander cookies, 134
Corn flake and sunflower seed cookies, 194
Corn flake cookies, 201
Corn flake squares, 240
Cornmeal and maple syrup biscotti, 211
Cornmeal cookies, 204
Cranberry hearts, 156
Cream cakes, 313
Cream cheese bars, 216
Crisp almond macaroons, 256
Crisp butter cookies, 23
Crisp coconut cookies, 164
Crisp orange cookies, 150
Crisp petal fritters, 355
Crisp walnut macaroons, 256
Crunchy coffee cookies, 100
Crunchy fruit squares, 392
Currant rounds, 176

D
Danish aebleskiver fritters, 360
Date and corn flake cookies, 201

Date and oat cookies, 199
Date and pecan delight, 271
Decorated cookies, 400
Dessert muffins, 328
Diamond cookies, 182
Digestive biscuits, 198
Dominoes, 392
Double chocolate cherry cookies, 79
Double chocolate cookies, 72
Double chocolate macadamia bars, 232
Double chocolate nut biscotti, 87
Double chocolate nut cookies, 92
Double chocolate truffles, 285
Downunder oat bars, 199
Dried apricot cookies, 164
Dried apricot muffins, 316
Dried currant oat squares, 227
Dried fruit and seedy bars, 240
Dried fruit squares, 289
Drizzled chocolate almond cookies, 394
Drizzled chocolate fingers, 70
Dusky chocolate cookies, 90
Dusted cookies, 80
Dusted honey madeleines, 294
Dusted sugar cookies, 54
Dutch christmas cookies, 372
Dutch shortbread, 24
Dutch spice cookies, 142

E
Easter Currant cookies, 392

Egg custard tartlets, 305
Espresso cookies, 101

F
Fairy glen cookies, 136
Festive walnut cranberry bars, 410
Fig fritters, 355
Fijian cookies, 182
Filled jelly fritters, 354
Filled marzipan cookies, 70
Florentines, 403
Fortune cookies, 394
Fresh apricot muffins, 318
Fresh ginger molasses cookies, 139
Fresh lemon rings, 158
Fried amaretti cookies, 358
Fried bow ties, 358
Fried cookie rosettes, 353
Fried egg cream, 342
Fritters with citrus syrup, 346
Frosted chocolate cookie bars, 290
Frosted chocolate hearts, 98
Frosted chocolate logs, 92
Frosted chocolate macaroons, 254
Frosted cocoa squares, 229
Frosted date and nut square, 214
Frosted jaffa muffins, 323
Frosted mace cookies, 51
Frosted nut and raisin cookies, 110
Frosted orange squares, 242
Frosted pineapple bites, 161
Frosted zucchini muffins, 334

Fruit and nut biscotti, 132
Fruit and nut cookies, 172
Fruit and nut diamonds, 190
Fruit and nut fritters, 358
Fruit and yogurt muffins, 323
Fruit squares, 234
Fruity almond muffins, 328
Fruity raisin moments, 166

G
Geordie cookies, 194
German spice cookies, 407
Gianduia kisses, 260
Ginger and brandy shortbread, 36
Ginger and candied peel cookies, 114
Ginger curls, 396
Ginger molasses cookies, 54
Ginger muffins with orange preserves, 334
Ginger nut crisps, 134
Ginger pecan cookies, 113
Ginger ropes, 134
Ginger shortbread, 18
Ginger squares, 239
Gingerbread people, 384
Gingerbread squares, 382
Gingernuts, 116
Glazed almond cookies, 124
Glazed almond crisps, 126
Glazed almond macaroons, 254
Glazed almond macaroons, 271
Glazed almond specials, 123
Glazed butter esses, 34

Glazed chocolate coffee cookies, 72
Glazed crimson cookies, 58
Glazed date diamonds, 232
Glazed nut cookies, 139
Glazed nutty cookies, 114
Glazed orange cookies, 161
Glazed orange macaroons, 266
Glazed raspberry kisses, 38
Glazed sugar kisses 46
Gold dust butter cookies, 29
Golden crisps, 54
Golden ginger crisps, 134
Golden nut squares, 238
Golden raisin fritters, 345
Good Friday fritters, 348
Green apple cookies, 148

H
Halloween chocolate chip cookies, 370
Halloween cookies, 369
Halloween spookies, 369
Hamantaschen, 404
Hanukkah cookies, 403
Hazelnut brown sugar meringues, 246
Hazelnut clove biscotti, 132
Hazelnut coffee cookies, 98
Hazelnut coffee meringues, 248
Hazelnut cookies, 110
Hazelnut cream cones, 398
Hazelnut florentines, 82
Hazelnut horseshoes, 126
Hazelnut kisses, 123
Hazelnut macaroons, 252

Hazelnut madeleines, 299
Hazelnut orange macaroons, 268
Hazelnut shortbread, 28
Hazelnut sticks, 190
Hazelnut vanilla macaroons, 266
Hearts of spice, 140
Heavenly arches, 145
Honey and anise fritters, 357
Honey and nut shortbread, 43
Honey and spice cookies, 119
Honey and thyme muffins, 336
Honey and walnut brownies, 224
Honey bee cookies, 404
Honey cookies, 57

I
Ice cream baskets, 386
Irish mint bars, 218
Italian rice cookies, 204

J
Jaffa squares, 224
Jam stars, 374
Jelly tartlets, 305

K
Kentish fritters, 350
Kitty cat cookies, 398

K
Lavender hearts, 52
Lebkuchen, 140
Lemon almond cookies, 124
Lemon and carrot cookies, 155
Lemon and egg fritters, 347
Lemon butter cookies, 18
Lemon corn flake cookies, 211

Lemon cornmeal cookies, 16
Lemon crunchies, 161
Lemon curd, 414
Lemon curd cookies, 154
Lemon drops, 43
Lemon honey madeleines, 296
Lemon madeleines, 294
Lemon meringues with almonds, 251
Lemon rice fritters, 362
Lemon rock cakes, 302
Lemon snackers, 116
Lemon stars, 154
Lemon tartlets, 310
Lemon zest crisps, 136
Lemon, raisin, and oat cookies, 166
Light granola cookies, 211
Light lemon macaroons, 251
Lime cookies, 150
Lime esses, 158
Lime muffins with yogurt, 318
Lombardy cookies, 119
Lunch box squares, 282

M
Macadamia macaroons, 264
Mandarin and chocolate muffins, 322
Mantecados, 40
Maple syrup tartlets, 320
Marbled brownies, 221
Marbled chocolate squares, 221
Marbled muffins, 331
Marshmallow crunchies, 285
Marshmallow cups, 285
Marshmallow kisses, 400
Marzipan cookies, 108
Marzipan cutout cookies, 14

Marzipan moons, 286
Melting moments, 186
Melting raisin moments, 172
Meringue-topped squares, 222
Middle eastern date squares, 234
Milk chocolate macadamia slice, 290
Mini almond macaroons, 259
Mini coconut tartlets, 315
Mini marshmallow tarts, 305
Mint balls, 276
Mint chocolate kisses, 62
Mint frosted butter cookies, 16
Minty hearts, 394
Mixed macaroons, 257
Mocha meringues, 248
Mocha nut cookies, 105
Mocha spirals, 98
Mother's day cookies, 386
Mud bars, 219
Muddy macaroons, 251
Muesli bars, 236
Muffins with caramel sauce, 326
Muffins with strawberry sauce, 336

N
Neapolitan christmas fritters, 350
Neapolitan rum cakes, 305
No-bake chocolate hazelnut truffles, 286
Northern lights cookies, 58
Norwegian cardamom fritters, 362
Norwegian christmas cookies, 377